Historical Dictionary of the French Fourth and Fifth Republics, 1946–1991

Historical Dictionaries of French History

This series covers French history from the Revolution through the Fifth Republic. It provides comprehensive coverage of each era, including not only political and military history but also social, economic, and art history.

Historical Dictionary of the French Revolution, 1789–1799
Samuel F. Scott and Barry Rothaus, editors

Historical Dictionary of Napoleonic France, 1799–1815
Owen Connelly, editor

Historical Dictionary of France from the 1815 Restoration to the Second Empire
Edgar Leon Newman, editor

Historical Dictionary of the French Second Empire, 1852–1870
William E. Echard, editor

Historical Dictionary of the Third French Republic, 1870–1940
Patrick H. Hutton, editor-in-chief

Historical Dictionary of the French Fourth and
Fifth Republics, 1946–1991
Wayne Northcutt, editor-in-chief

Historical Dictionary of the French Fourth and Fifth Republics, 1946–1991

WAYNE NORTHCUTT,
Editor-in-Chief

Greenwood Press
New York • Westport, Connecticut • London

Library of Congress Cataloging-in-Publication Data

Historical dictionary of the French Fourth and Fifth Republics,
1946–1991 / Wayne Northcutt, editor-in-chief.
p. cm.
Includes bibliographical references and index.
ISBN 0-313-26356-6 (alk. paper)
1. France—History—1945- —Dictionaries. I. Northcutt, Wayne.
DC401.H57 1992
944.082—dc20 91-17387

British Library Cataloguing in Publication Data is available.

Library of Congress Catalog Card Number: 91-17387
ISBN: 0-313-26356-6

First published in 1992

Greenwood Press, 88 Post Road West, Westport, CT 06881
An imprint of Greenwood Publishing Group, Inc.

Printed in the United States of America

The paper used in this book complies with the Permanent Paper Standard issued by the National Information Standards Organization (Z39.48-1984).

10 9 8 7 6 5 4 3 2 1

For M. J. Johnson

Contents

Contributors

Pierre Aubery, Oakland, California
David S. Bell, University of Leeds (Great Britain)
Jeff Bridgford, Heriot-Watt University (Great Britain)
Janet Bryant, Portsmouth Polytechnic (Great Britain)
Jean Carduner, University of Michigan
Tony Chafer, Portsmouth Polytechnic (Great Britain)
Jean-René Chotard, Université de Sherbrooke (Canada)
Thomas R. Christofferson, Drew University
James J. Cooke, University of Mississippi
Margaret H. Darrow, Dartmouth College
H. D. Dauncey, University of Bath (Great Britain)
Leslie Derfler, Florida Atlantic University
Allen Douglas, University of Texas at Austin
Irene Earls, University of Central Florida
Chiarella Esposito, University of Mississippi
Jeffra J. Flaitz, State University of New York at Buffalo
Julius W. Friend, Foreign Service Institute
Robert L. Frost, State University of New York at Albany
John Gaffney, Aston University (Great Britain)
Paul J. Godt, The American University of Paris (France)
Lydie J. Haenlin, Wells College
W. Scott Haine, The American University
Robert A. Harmsen, Université de Montréal (Canada)
Steven C. Hause, University of Missouri-St. Louis
Charles Hauss, Colby College
John S. Hill, Ohio State University
Jolyon Howorth, University of Bath (Great Britain)
Patrick H. Hutton, University of Vermont
Raymond A. Jonas, University of Washington
William R. Keylor, Boston University
Mohammed Khane, University of Bradford (Great Britain)
John Kirkland, Bucknell University

Kay L. Lawson, San Francisco State University
Philippe Le Prestre, Université du Québec à Montréal (Canada)
David L. Looseley, University of Bradford (Great Britain)
Mairi Maclean, University of London (Great Britain)
Susan Milner, Aston University (Great Britain)
Rita D. Moore, Portland State University
Bernard H. Moss, University of Auckland (New Zealand)
J. Kim Munholland, University of Minnesota
Francis J. Murphy, Boston College
Wayne Northcutt, Niagara University
Peggy Anne Phillips, University of Miami
Jesse R. Pitts, University of Virginia
André J. M. Prévos, Penn State Worthington Scranton Campus
Charles Rearick, University of Massachusetts
Jack E. Reece, University of Pennsylvania
Paul F. Rogers, University of Bradford (Great Britain)
Ivan C. Scott, University of Toledo
Michael Seidman, Rutgers University
Martin Siegel, Kean College of New Jersey
Michael S. Smith, University of South Carolina
Charles L. Stinger, State University of New York at Buffalo
Alec Stone, Middlebury College
Judith F. Stone, Western Michigan University
Homer B. Sutton, Davidson College
Dominique S. Thévenin, University of Wisconsin-Eau Claire
John N. Tuppen, Ecole supérieure de commerce de Lyon (France)
K. Steven Vincent, North Carolina State University
René Viton, Cassis, France
Irwin M. Wall, University of California, Riverside
Margaret Collins Weitz, Suffolk University
James A. Winders, Appalachian State University

Preface

The *Historical Dictionary of the French Fourth and Fifth Republics, 1946–1991* is a comprehensive reference work that includes 269 entries on a variety of subjects ranging from politics to economics to foreign and defense policy to society and culture. Sixty-three scholars in five different countries—the United States, Canada, France, Great Britain, and New Zealand—have contributed to this volume. The contributors represent a number of fields, including history, political science, literature, and language. This interdisciplinary work is intended to serve as a handy reference tool for students as well as for advanced scholars in a variety of disciplines seeking in-depth information on contemporary France.

While historians in the United States have been relatively slow to stake out post–World War II France as a field of study (outpaced largely by political scientists), interest in the Fourth and Fifth Republics is slowly developing among historians in this country. In this regard, the journal *French Historical Studies* recently published a special issue (spring 1991) edited by Kim Munholland of the University of Minnesota that featured a variety of articles on France since the war. Various events in the recent past have helped to generate interest in the history of contemporary France, such as the election of socialist president François Mitterrand in 1981 and his re-election in 1988, the emergence of a centrist Republic in France under Mitterrand, the elaborate festivities surrounding the bicentennial of the French Revolution of 1789, and scholarly conferences on postwar France. This last includes conferences in this country and in France, in 1990, marking the centennial of Charles de Gaulle's birth. International events, too, have given an impetus to a growing interest in France since 1945, events such as the fall of the Berlin Wall in 1989 and the unification of Germany, the historic changes in Eastern Europe and the dissolution of the Soviet Union (now known as a Commonwealth of Independent States), the planned economic integration of the European Economic Community scheduled for the end of 1992, the new Europe that is now emerging, and the close Franco-American cooperation at various points in the 1980s and the 1990s (including the Persian Gulf War of 1991). These events encourage scholars and others interested in France to ponder the nation's future role on the European continent and on the world's stage. Perhaps the recent changes in Europe, coupled with the waning of the Cold War, will encourage historians to view the era from the end of the Second World War to roughly 1989 as a closed chapter in European history and international relations and will stimulate more scholarly interest in the history of the French Fourth and Fifth Republics, especially with the opening of archives in both France and the United States.

A number of scholars, including Munholland in his introduction to the 1991 special issue of *French Historical Studies*, have suggested that the history of twentieth-century France is divided into two periods. The first four-and-one-half decades of the century can be viewed as a period of decline, an era in which France experienced the harsh consequences of the First World War, the paralysis of the interwar years, and the humiliating defeat at the outset of World War II. Since the end of the war, however, the nation has met many of the challenges of modernization, and these years can been seen as a period of renewal, at least in political, economic, and institutional terms. Politically, postwar France has made a transition from a regime of parties under the Fourth Republic and a bipolar political system (especially under the Fifth Republic) to a more consensual pluralistic system in which alternating left- and right-wing governments are now possible. In this regard, France is no longer the political exception in Western Europe. A consensus has also developed in France over the years around one of Charles de Gaulle's legacies, the nation's *force de frappe*. Economically, France has become a major power on the continent and has provided impressive leadership in recent years in helping to promote the economic integration of the European Economic Community and the rise of what many expect to be a powerful trading colossus. Institutionally, the constitution of the Fifth Republic has been more flexible and durable than once thought and is now widely accepted in France, which was not the case at the beginning of the new republic in 1958.

While the history of postwar France can be viewed as the story of renewal, a comparative study of the Fourth and Fifth Republics reveals that they are different in significant ways. One of the most obvious and important differences is that while political and institutional feebleness characterized the Fourth Republic, this has not been the case during the Fifth. The Fourth Republic, too, experienced a growing inability to implement a noteworthy foreign policy, while under the Fifth Republic de Gaulle and his successors have been able to pursue ambitious foreign and defense policies. Also, while the Fourth Republic was characterized by a regime of parties, as mentioned earlier, the Fifth has seen the emergence of strong presidents, such as de Gaulle and François Mitterrand, who possess enormous powers under the constitution adopted in 1958. Moreover, although the Fourth Republic experienced a long string of unstable governments, the Fifth has witnessed political stability and even the emergence of a centrist republic under Mitterrand that is characterized by a large degree of political consensus. Another important difference has been the rapid emergence of women in the workplace and their increasing entry on the political stage, highlighted, of course, by Mitterrand's May 15, 1991 appointment of Edith Cresson as the nation's first woman prime minister. Still another difference between the two republics is that the Fifth in the 1980s and early years of the 1990s has witnessed a strong and relatively persistent wave of racism and anti-Semitism, a phenomenon that indicates that in some areas renewal has not occurred. Under the Fourth Republic, too, the *Parti communiste français* (PCF) was the leading party of the French left; yet, under the Fifth Republic Mitterrand and the socialists have marginalized the PCF, and the *Parti socialiste* (PS) is now the dominant party of the French left and the dominant party in France. The political landscape of the nation has changed drastically under the Fifth Republic. While the Fourth Republic was riddled by Cold War tensions, the Fifth, at least since roughly 1989, is now responding to a post–Cold War world that has seen the demise of the Soviet Union. Finally, the economic impotence of France at the end of the Second World War has been replaced by a relatively strong economic power that is a leader in the EEC, as noted earlier, as member states prepare for their rendezvous with integration and, following the December 1991 Maastricht summit, aim not only for economic integration but for monetary and political union as well as a common foreign and defense policy. Although some of the differences/changes discussed here began under the Fourth Republic, they are often closely identified with the Fifth and distinguish it from the earlier republic. Thus, while the history of postwar France in many ways is the story of a new France, it is also the story of a new Europe.

As the reader will quickly observe, the topics contained in this volume are listed alphabetically. (In Appendix II the reader will find a complete list of the entries according to categories.) Each entry begins with a defining phrase or sentence that helps the reader to identify the relevance of the subject, and most entries include a summary statement that stresses the significance of the topic. Following the individual entry, the reader will find a select bibliography for future reference, the contributor's name, and a list of related topics. Included in the list of topics are broad thematic entries, covering political, economic, social, and intellectual trends, which help to provide an overview of the postwar period and help to place individual entries in a specific context.

The reader may be interested in learning more about the methodology utilized in preparing the *Dictionary* for publication. As editor-in-chief, I first drew up a list of provisional entries after consulting many of the standard works in French and English on postwar France. Next, this provisional list was circulated among thirty-five scholars in history, political science, and the general field of French studies who were informed of the project and invited to add or delete topics. Included among those who offered suggestions on the provisional list were Stanley Hoffmann at Harvard University, Mark Kesselman at Columbia University, John Merriman at Yale University, Karen Offen at Stanford University, David Pinkney at the University of Washington, Thomas Schaeper at St. Bonaventure University, David Schalk at Vassar College, Eugen Weber at the University of California at Los Angeles, and Gordon Wright at Stanford University. In addition to these scholars, a number of contributors also made valuable recommendations on the topics to be included.

Following the completion of the final list of entries, a set number of words was assigned to each entry. The Greenwood Publishing Group recommended that the total number of manuscript pages for the *Dictionary* be approximately 800 manuscript pages. Consequently, page lengths were established according to the relative importance of each topic. A standard entry was assigned 250 words, a major entry 500–700 words, an entry of exceptional importance 750–1,250 words, and large thematic entries 1,250–1,750 words. For the most part, contributors stayed within the recommended guidelines for the length of each entry.

Locating qualified contributors involved a huge amount of domestic and international correspondence. In order to find potential contributors, I reviewed the past programs of annual meetings of a number of professional organizations and specialized conferences held on contemporary France. I also attempted to develop a list of historians working on modern France by consulting the American Historical Association's *Guide to Departments of History*. Several scholars in this country and Great Britain associated with major professional journals recommended a number of contributors. Among those who helped in this regard were David S. Bell (*Contemporary European Affairs*), Bernard Petit (*Contemporary French Civilization*), and Vincent Wright (*West European Politics*).

This work clearly demonstrates the value of teamwork in scholarly endeavors. For the most part, historians and other scholars in the humanities and social sciences work alone as they research and write articles or books, yet this volume has necessitated a large amount of cooperation with a sizable group of scholars in various countries. The contact with other scholars of contemporary France has been most gratifying and rewarding. I hope that this *Dictionary* will show others the value of scholarly teams working together in the humanities and the social sciences, an approach that seems to be more prevalent in Europe than in the United States.

As this *Dictionary* is a cooperative venture, I am indebted to numerous colleagues who made this volume possible. An enormous debt of thanks is owed to Patrick Hutton, editor in chief of the two-volume *Historical Dictionary of the Third French Republic, 1870–1940*. Not only did he share with me the lessons of his experience in editing an historical dictionary, but he also wrote a large number of entries for this volume. I also would like to convey my deep gratitude to all contributors for their cooperation and assistance in preparing this manuscript. Thanks, too, should be paid to those mentioned above who took time away from their busy schedules to help me build a list of entries or identify contributors. Cynthia Harris, Susan Baker, and Sally Scott of the Greenwood Publishing Group were understanding and supportive during this project. I am indebted to Ms. Harris for offering me the opportunity to undertake what was for me a new, unique, and exciting scholarly endeavor. Thanks also must be paid to Brenda Hanning who did a masterful job of copyediting this manuscript.

A number of colleagues at Niagara University facilitated the completion of this work. In this regard, I would like to thank John B. Stranges, academic vice-president at Niagara University, for a reduced teaching load that permitted large blocks of time to be devoted to this manuscript. Thanks must also be extended to colleagues in the History Department, especially the chair, Gerald Carpenter, who were supportive of my editing chores. I am also thankful for an Academic Year Research Grant from Niagara University that helped to defray expenses for technical support for this project. Last but not least, I would like to thank Anita Phelps for her secretarial assistance.

Wayne Northcutt

The Dictionary

A

ACADEMIE FRANCAISE, learned society founded in 1634 by Cardinal Richelieu to safeguard the purity of the French language. The *Académie*'s forty members were charged with the task of preparing a dictionary and definitive texts on French grammar, rhetoric, and poetry. The first edition of the *Dictionnaire de l'Académie* appeared in 1694. While eight editions of the dictionary have been published to date, only one grammar text has been produced; it appeared in 1933. The objective to prepare texts on rhetoric and poetry has never been realized.

Membership in the *Académie* has traditionally been a coveted honor. Even prominent writers such as Hugo, Dumas, and Racine were not automatically offered seats in the *Académie*, but were forced to make repeated and sometimes humiliating attempts to gain entry. Such devices produced an invitation for some, but many other noteworthy French poets and writers such as Descartes, Balzac, Flaubert, Zola, Proust, Camus, Sartre, and Rousseau were spurned. In 1980 Marguerite Yourcenar became the first woman to be inducted.

While the members of the *Académie française*, known as the "Immortals," have prided themselves on the importance of their mission, they have not been successful in fixing the French language. Modern French contains over 2,200 English words in regular use as well as thousands of other words that continue a pattern of infiltration, but foreign borrowings and neologisms of any kind rarely meet with official acceptance. However, the *Académie*, under pressure from the Rocard government and authors of an increasingly large number of books criticizing the perceived illogic of French spelling, in May of 1990 approved a series of orthographic changes that included the elimination of the circumflex in certain words like *huître* (oyster) and *août* (August), and the dropping of the hyphen in a select group of words such as *pique-nique* (picnic). Attempting to prevent the reforms from being carried out, some members of the *Académie* charged that its illustrious group never voted on the spelling changes and were not fully informed of the government's proposed reform of the language. Backed by the conservative newspaper *Le Figaro* and several center-right politicians, some members of the *Académie* pressed for a reevaluation of its original recommendation supporting the spelling changes, arguing that the "purity" of the language was at stake. On January 17, 1991 the *Académie* reversed itself and adopted a proposal by the anthropologist Claude Lévi-Strauss, who recommended that the traditional spelling be retained but that the new forms be tolerated. In time, suggested Lévi-Strauss, usage would determine which form would prevail. Following the *Académie's* reversal, the government is not expected to make the reforms mandatory. Aside from occasionally sanctioning reforms initiated for the most part from without and exercising moral authority over the French language, the *Académie française* has wielded scant influence over the development of French.

S. de Gramont, *The French: Portrait of a People* (New York, 1969); J. Flaitz, *The Ideology of English: French Perceptions of English as an International Language* (Berlin, 1988); *The New York Times*, January 27, 1991.

J. J. Flaitz

Related entries: CULTURAL POLICY; *LA FRANCOPHONIE*; *FRANGLAIS;* POPULAR CULTURE; ROMILLY, JACQUELINE DE; YOURCENAR, MARGUERITE.

AGRICULTURE, a significant sector of the French economy. France is the most important agricultural producer in Europe. It has 24.3 percent of the surface of the twelve countries that make up the European Economic Community (EEC), 24.3 percent of the arable land, 24.6 percent of the pastures, and 27.3 percent of the forests. It also has the richest lands in the EEC with the exception of certain areas of Belgian Flanders. Until 1945 the land was cultivated by about 25 percent of the French labor force, and about 45 percent of the French population lived in agglomerations of less than two thousand inhabitants, where the peasant style of life predominated: continuous hard work on small family farms oriented to self-sufficiency, traditional methods with little recourse to machinery or chemical fertilizers, high prices protected by tariffs, and a rural proletariat paid essentially by room and board. Today the rural population is down to 26.4 percent.

A good idea of typical pre–World War II village life can be obtained from movies such as *Regain, Farrebique* (1946), *Biquefarre* (1983), or more recently *Jean de Florette* and *Manon des sources.*

Forty-five years later the observer can see that a revolution has taken place. The agricultural labor force in 1989 was down to 1,562,000, 6.5 percent of the work force, many of them part-time. Even though France's competitors have not stood still, France has caught up with Germany as far as productivity is concerned, and in the process the countryside has changed substantially. In 1929 there were four million farms, the median holding being about 4.5 hectares (ha.) (eleven acres). By 1961 the number of farms had fallen to two million. By 1987 the number of farms was down to one million, the median size farm being eighteen ha. (45 acres) but the average being twenty-eight ha. (70 acres). Holdings of more than fifty ha. (125 acres) were 15 percent of the total number of farms but accounted for 46.6 percent of French cultivated land, a higher percentage than in Germany.

Agricultural productivity per unit of labor and acreage had increased by a factor of ten. Tractors, which numbered only about forty thousand in 1939, numbered a million and a half in 1984–85.

Today the model of the self-sufficient family farm has been broken. Farmers now have debts on which they must pay principal and interest every month. They must produce for the market and must subordinate their traditions to its fluctuating demands. Still, there are many who love the ownership and cultivation of the land, even when the holdings are too small to support their families. Attachment to the land is so important a facet of the French value system that it has slowed the departure of "excess farmers." Many of them have hung on and even prospered. In one out of every two farms someone works outside the home and contributes his or her salary to the family budget. There is an underground economy (barter, exchange of services, etc.) that escapes the tax collector but permits small landowners to survive and even thrive. Farms left by departing owners have also been bought by middle-class urbanites intent on having their *maison de campagne*. Others have been transformed into hotels or artisanal workshops.

The interpenetration of city and country is much more apparent today. There is no longer a peasant civilization living practically by itself, with a few notables acting as intermediaries with government authorities. The peasants, who were very difficult to organize for long-term complex goals, have now become farmers—masters of all sorts of cooperatives for the sale of their products and for the purchase of tools, fertilizers, and machinery. They are virtuosos in demonstrating for their demands.

The mounting productivity of French farms led some to believe that agriculture could be the "green oil" of the French economy instead of remaining a heavy drain on the public purse (H. Mendras says that French consumers pay for two-thirds of their food at the store and one-third at the tax collector's office) and on the EC's purse. It was only in 1979 that the agricultural balance of payment turned lastingly positive. In 1988 food exports (including agricultural industries and processed foods) exceeded food imports by 39 billion francs, but it could not overcome the trade deficit (which excludes armaments and services) of some 90 billion francs. Furthermore, France's high performance is in areas of international saturation: cereals, sugar, milk and milk products, and meat. There could be renewed friction with the United States in the competition for markets after 1992.

Annuaire statistique 1987; H. Mendras, *La Fin des paysans* (Avignon, Fr., 1984), *La Seconde Révolution française* (Paris, 1988).

J. R. Pitts

Related entries: PEASANTRY; PISANI, EDGARD; POPULATION TRENDS; SOCIAL STRATIFICATION.

AHRWEILER, HELENE (GLYCATSI) (1926–), professor, scholar, and academic administrator. Born in Athens on August 29, 1926, she received the *licence* in letters and philosophy from the University of Athens in 1950; seven years later she received the diploma of the *Ecole pratique des hautes études* in Paris. In 1960 she received a doctorate in history and, in 1966, the *Doctorat ès-lettres*. Her professional career started with her appointment as researcher in the *Centre national pour la recherche scientifique* (1955–67), where she was made *maître de recherche* in 1964. Then she was elected professor of the Sorbonne and director of the *Centre de recherche d'histoire et civilisation byzantines et du Proche-Orient chrétien* in 1967. Subsequently she was named director of the Department of History and president of the Research Commission of the Faculty of Letters and Human Sciences of Paris (1969–70). The following year she was elected vice-president of the University of Paris I (Panthéon-Sorbonne) and in 1976, president of that university, the first woman to be elected president of a French university, a post she held until 1981. Since that time she has been honorary president of the university.

On December 8, 1982, Ahrweiler was named Rector of the Academy and Chancellor of the Universities of Paris, the first woman to hold that important office. The chancellor supervises all the public scholarly institutions of the city: over six hundred elementary and nursery schools, three hundred *lycées*, eight universities, and many other institutions of higher education totaling close to a million-and-a-half students as well as some thirty thousand instructors. Ahrweiler has served on the boards of academic councils and associations, international as well as national—vice-president then president (1985) of the *Maison des sciences de l'homme*, vice-president of the *Conseil d'orientation* of the Pompidou Center (Beaubourg), and director of the Pompidou Center beginning in 1989 following the completion of her rectorship—and received many honors and recognitions. She is a member of the Academy of Athens, the Academy of Berlin, the British Academy, the Polish Academy of Sciences, and the Royal Academy of Belgium. In 1973–1974 she was invited to the Harvard Byzantine Center at Dumbarton Oaks.

Her many publications focus on the Byzantine world: the state, political ideology, administration, society and historical geography, and, more generally, on the Mediterranean world during the Middle Ages. Her thesis, *Byzance et la mer: La Marine de guerre, la politique et les institutions maritimes de Byzance aux VIIe-XVe siècles*, was published in Paris in 1966. Additional publications include *Etudes sur les structures administratives et sociales de Byzance* (Paris, 1971); *L'Idéologie politique de l'Empire byzantin* (Paris, 1975); *Byzance: Pays et territoires* (Paris, 1976); and *Byzantium, Crossroad of the World* (in Greek; Athens, 1984), as well as many articles and reviews.

Who's Who in France, 1990–1991 (Paris, 1990).

M. C. Weitz

Related entries: ANNALES SCHOOL; EDUCATIONAL REFORM; MUSEUMS.

ALGERIA, RELATIONS WITH. France conquered Algeria in 1830. After 1848, Algeria together with its three departments was considered an integral part of France; in 1962, after nearly eight years of war, Algeria became an independent sovereign nation.

Maintenance of the French Empire was among the arguments justifying Vichy France's accommodation with Germany after the fall of France in 1940. Marshal Pétain shielded mainland France, or part of it, against occupation, but he also sought to prevent the disaggregation of the empire by preserving at least a semblance of French authority. Such considerations also lay behind Charles de Gaulle's suggestion, dismissed in favor of the Pétainist solution, that the government continue the fight against Germany after the fall of France from headquarters in Algeria.

As the end of the war approached, colonial independence, including independence for Algeria, seemed to be on the agenda. In January 1944 de Gaulle spoke at Brazzaville of self-administration for "colonial peoples" and of the possibility of eventual self-government, an ambiguous proposal that did not prevent colonial peoples from concluding that the Liberation would be followed by steps toward liberation from colonial domination. That such remarks were not intended to include Algeria was clear by October 1947 when de Gaulle spoke in Algiers against policies that would lead "French Moslems [to] believe that it could be allowable for them to separate their fate from that of France." Even so, talk of armed resistance and struggle for liberation during the war years had raised hopes that proved difficult to restrict to European populations.

Such expectations, combined with the clear sense that France had emerged weakened and vulnerable from the years of war and occupation, inspired the demonstration on May 8, 1945 (VE-Day) in the Algerian market town of Sétif. An attempt to control the demonstration led to brutal fighting, followed by mutual reprisals, leading to the death of over one hundred Europeans and at least one thousand dead among the Moslems. Even though there would be no immediate follow-up to Sétif, there can be little doubt but that this was the opening salvo in the struggle for Algerian independence.

The war proper began nine years later, on All Saints' Day (November 1) 1954, when the National Liberation Front (FLN) announced its formation through several simultaneous actions in Algeria. By the time the peace agreement was signed at Evian on March 18, 1962, 17,456 French soldiers had died. Estimates of the number of deaths on the Moslem side are sketchier, but conservative (French) estimates put the figure at 141,000 combatants. To these figures must be added civilian casualties. European civilian casualties, including deaths at the hands of the *Organisation de l'armée secrète* (OAS), exceeded ten thousand persons. Such deaths among Moslems were no fewer than 82,300, though estimates of total civilian and combatant deaths among Moslems range from 300,000 to the round figure of one million cited by the Algerian government. In any event, the count of civilian dead among Europeans and Moslems rivaled that of military dead.

The Algerian problem in post–1945 France had proved intractable. The post–1945 status quo provided for two electoral colleges—one European, one Moslem—with equal representation in the National Assembly even though the two populations were far from equal in size. The favored solution among many politicians of mainland France was full equality and a single electoral college for Algerian Europeans and Moslems. Since Moslem Algerians outnumbered the *pieds-noirs* by a ratio of nine to one, most *pieds-noirs* would countenance equal representation for Moslem Algerians only on condition of the full integration of Algeria with France—a move that would safely reduce the Moslem population to a minority of ten million in a "Eurafrican" France with a population of some fifty million. Such proposals were rejected by the radical left, which favored independence for Algeria on moral grounds, but also by pragmatists such as Raymond Aron who pointed out that the Moslem fertility rate would erode much of the European margin within a generation and would precipitate a political crisis.

It was the very insistence upon Algeria's coidentity with France that made the Algerian War such a bitter and protracted affair. Immigration and political exile had given Algeria a large population of European settlers, the so-called *pieds-noirs* who, in 1954, made up perhaps one-tenth of the population of ten million in Algeria. Since they owned one-third of the cultivable land and held many of the better jobs, the *pieds-noirs* had a large stake in Algeria, but resisted reforms leading to equal representation, which would have given the more numerous Moslem Algerians an overwhelming majority in Algerian affairs. The imminent investiture of Pierre Pflimlin as prime minister, and the conviction that he would negotiate with the FLN, prompted the *pieds-noirs* and the Army to seize power in Algiers on May 13, 1958 and form a Committee of Public Safety. They made it amply clear that only de Gaulle commanded their respect and thus only he could save the situation. De Gaulle's Republic was overwhelmingly approved by the Algerian electorate, European and Moslem, and including Moslem women for the first time, on September 28, 1958. Even though the FLN urged abstention, 80 percent of the electorate turned out to vote and 97 percent of those voting approved the constitution of the Fifth Republic. Once in power, de Gaulle immediately began to make overtures to the FLN. The concluding round of talks between France and the FLN took place at Evian and resulted in a signed agreement on March 18, 1962.

Relations between France and Algeria in the postindependence era have been variable. In most cases the French evacuated bases and installations ahead of the dates guaranteed in the Evian Accords. President Valéry Giscard d'Estaing made the first visit by a French head of state in the postindependence era in 1975. In the 1980s the decline in oil and gas revenues hurt Algeria—economic growth slipped below 1 percent per year while the population of Algeria continued to increase at a rate of nearly 3 percent per year. With nearly 300,000 new workers reaching employable age each year, many young workers sought employment in France. Where there were 100,000 Moslem Algerian workers in France in 1940, there are perhaps as many as 800,000 today.

French trade with Algeria has fallen off considerably since 1962. During the peak year of 1958, nearly 20 percent of French exports went to Algeria and throughout the post–1945 period up to Evian that share remained in double digits. The importance of the Algerian market fell after Evian, ranging between 2 percent and 3 percent of French exports in the 1970s and 1980s. Even so, France remained Algeria's most important supplier with 23 percent of imports to Algeria, down from 84 percent in 1958.

Misery and government-mandated austerity programs in Algeria sparked demonstrations followed by the eruption of political violence on October 4, 1988. President Chadli Benjedid proclaimed a state of siege and brought in tanks to restore order in Algiers and elsewhere. By the time fighting was over, there were at least one thousand dead, thousands wounded, and nearly ten thousand arrested. The French left, rendered mute initially by its anti-imperialist reflexes, joined in condemning the brutal repression.

A more telling condemnation of the FLN came from Algerian voters in the municipal elections of 1990. Nearly 40 percent of voters abstained; many others voted for the fundamentalist *Front islamique du salut* (FIS). The FIS won control in 853 of 1,539 new municipal councils, including major urban centers such as Alger and Constantine. The victory prompted fears in France that a new wave of Algerian immigrants—political refugees from Islamic fundamentalism—would soon demand asylum.

R. Aron, *L'Algérie et la République* (Paris, 1958); A. Horne, *A Savage War of Peace, Algeria 1954–1962* (New York, 1987); T. Smith, *The French Stake in Algeria, 1945–1962* (Ithaca, N.Y., 1978); J. Soustelle, *Aimée et souffrante Algérie* (Paris, 1956); J. Talbott, *The War without a Name* (New York, 1980); "La Victoire des islamistes en Algérie," *Le Monde*, June 16, 1990.

R. A. Jonas

Related entries: BEN BELLA, AHMED; DECOLONIZATION; DE GAULLE, CHARLES; IMMIGRANTS; PFLIMLIN, PIERRE; REFERENDA; SOUSTELLE, JACQUES.

ALTHUSSER, LOUIS (1918–1990), philosopher and Marxist theorist. Althusser was born in Algeria and, in 1939, entered the *Ecole normale supérieure*. As a young man, he was a devout Roman Catholic. After World War II, however, influenced by his wife, Hélène, and several friends, he became a Marxist and joined the *Parti communiste français* (PCF). Althusser remained a member of the party during the stormy period of the early Cold War, the crushing of the Hungarian rebellion, de-Stalinization, the Sino-Soviet conflict, the Chinese Cultural Revolution, 1968 in Prague, and beyond. While such celebrated intellectuals as Maurice Merleau-Ponty and Jean-Paul Sartre renounced the party, Althusser maintained his loyalty, preserving an ominous silence regarding even the most embarrassing and distasteful episodes in the recent history of the PCF, even while his theoretical work implied some significant departures from party orthodoxy.

Althusser's chief sphere of activity throughout his career was the *Ecole normale supérieure*, where his teaching influenced many of his students to criticize the PCF in his name. For example, Althusser's students saw in his vigorous reassertion of Leninism an implied endorsement of Cultural Revolution–era

Maoism, while of course the PCF toed the Soviet line. Yet, in one of the most glaring examples of the contradiction between Althusser's philosophy and party policy, Althusser remained staunchly silent when the party launched its strong criticism of the radical students of 1968, so many of whom had imbibed his very teachings. During the 1970s Althusser's influence declined in France while it gained abroad, particularly in Great Britain, where the Althusserian focus on ideology shaped a whole generation of radical interdisciplinary culture critics (not, characteristically, political activists). England was also the source of some of the most strident critiques of Althusser, and most of the writings of the last stage of his career were devoted to responses to these and other critiques, and to idiosyncratic self-criticisms.

Althusser's break with the PCF came finally in 1978. By this point he was largely isolated in French cultural life and suffered repeated bouts of severe depression. In 1979 Nicos Poulantzas, Althusser's most celebrated follower and an important political theorist in his own right, committed suicide. Althusser's own shocking exit came in September 1980, when he strangled his wife, Hélène, immediately turned himself in to the police, and was found not guilty by reason of insanity and committed permanently to Sainte-Catherine's Hospital in Paris. Many were outraged by the leniency of this sentence, particularly a number of feminists who saw in it the excuse routinely made for violence against women, here accorded a tragically unbalanced, great philosopher.

The Althusserian moment in French Marxist thought thus came to an end, but, from at least the mid–1960s to the early 1970s, it dominated the theoretical climate of Gallic Marxism and came to eclipse the existential Marxism of the immediate postwar era. Like other examples of what Merleau-Ponty called "Western Marxism," beginning with the rediscovery by Georg Lukács of the Hegelian sources of Marxist thought and the publication for the first time (1932) of the more thoroughly "humanist" 1844 manuscripts of the "Young Marx," Sartre's Marxism embraced humanism. Sartre's theoretical explorations unfolded outside the PCF, but the party's chief theoretician of the 1950s, Roger Garaudy, was a thoroughgoing Marxist humanist.

Althusserianism positioned itself squarely against this humanist tradition. In *Pour Marx* (1965, For Marx), Althusser stated his clear preference for Marx's "mature" writings, especially *Capital*, and argued that a profound rupture or "epistemological break" (*coupure épistemologique*, a phrase Althusser borrowed from Gaston Bachelard) separated the neo-Hegelian early writings of Marx from those texts that establish Marxism as a "science," that is, the science of historical materialism. Thus, for Althusser, the Marxist humanist enthusiasm for the "Young Marx" was regressive. Within France specifically, his rejection of Sartre's existentialist Marxism was in keeping with the structuralist interrogation of the autonomous subject in language and culture in favor of the prior social construction of human beings in language.

Althusser, generally known for drawing upon non-Marxist philosophical traditions even while proclaiming a return to "scientific" Marxism, was deeply influenced by structuralism in general and by the work of Jacques Lacan in particular. His "return to Marx," that is, to Marx's text, resembled the Lacanian *retour à Freud*. Thus, whether or not he ought to be called a structuralist, Althusser's method certainly falls within the overall structuralist project of re-reading texts. This was exemplified by his collaborative (with Etienne Balibar) critical reading of *Das Kapital* in *Lire le Capital* (1965, Reading Capital). Lacan's psychoanalytic concept of the "imaginary" also influenced Althusser's discussion of "ideology." Refinement of the Marxist concept of ideology was one of Althusser's most significant contributions to Marxist theory. He died of heart failure on October 22, 1990.

L. Althusser, *Pour Marx* (Paris, 1965); L. Althusser, Etienne Balibar, *Lire le Capital* (Paris, 1965); T. Benton, *The Rise and Fall of Structural Marxism* (New York, 1984); S. B. Smith, *Reading Althusser: An Essay on Structural Marxism* (Ithaca, N.Y., 1984).

J. A. Winders

Related entries: FRENCH COMMUNIST PARTY; GARAUDY, ROGER; LACAN, JACQUES; LEVI-STRAUSS, CLAUDE; MARXISM; NEW PHILOSOPHERS; SARTRE, JEAN-PAUL; STRUCTURALISM; STUDENT REVOLTS.

***ANNALES* SCHOOL,** specifically, historical writing identified with the journal *Les Annales d'histoire économique et sociale*, founded by Lucien Febvre and Marc Bloch in 1929, renamed *Les Annales: Economies, sociétés, civilisations* in 1946, and published continuously into our own time. More broadly, the term refers to the historiography practiced by these scholars, their students, and admirers. As such, it has been a leading influence upon French historical writing in the mid- and late-twentieth century.

Annales scholarship carried forward and perfected the techniques of modern historical writing developed in the nineteenth century, particularly in Germany. This positivist school of historiography, identified with Charles-Victor Langlois and Charles Seignobos in France at the turn of the twentieth century, insisted upon assiduous research and scrupulous analysis of documentary evidence. *Annales* scholars vastly expanded the task, however, and diversified the methodological repertoire with which it was to be accomplished. Researching beyond the public archives on which their predecessors had relied, Bloch and Febvre urged their colleagues to attempt a "total history" that would encompass cultural geography, material realities, demographic trends, social traditions, and collective psychology. Borrowing methods from economists, geographers, social psychologists, and anthropologists, Bloch and Febvre made the University of Strasbourg the center for their pioneering scholarship during the 1930s.

After World War II the center of *Annales* scholarship shifted to Paris, where it became identified with graduate training in the Sixth Section of the *Ecole pratique des hautes études*. While *Annales* historiography thenceforth took on a more academic cast, it was nonetheless viewed as a rebellious force within the academy by historians at the Sorbonne and the *Ecole des Chartes* who clung to more traditional methods. The intellectual stature of *Annales* scholars nonetheless grew steadily over the following decades, thanks in part to their masterful use of new techniques of quantification and computer-assisted research.

The prestige of the *Annales*' approach may also have reflected a disillusionment with the nineteenth-century historians' faith in progress through political solutions. Rejecting politics as the backbone of history, *Annales* historians also rejected the narrative form in which history had traditionally been written. In terms of deep sources, they owed a long-standing debt to Karl Marx's analysis of economic processes, and a more recent one to Emile Durkheim's studies of collective behavior. From a theoretical perspective, however, their major ties were with structuralism. *Annales* historians were committed to a search for deeper patterns in the past, which they perceived to be complex and often incongruent structures. They believed that historical research would uncover not a single record of events, but synchronous layers of series of events, each proceeding at its own tempo—from the rapid changes of political history on the surface of the past to the deepest patterns of environmental history in which time virtually stood still (*l'histoire immobile*). The *Annales*' search for alternative models with which to interpret the past was based upon a new awareness of the relativity of historical time. Social history required a different temporal framework from political history, for it moved at a slower pace. *Annales* historians therefore became famous for their consideration of history *à la longue durée*. But their major achievement was to show that social, economic, and cultural realms of the past may be considered autonomously, not as background for events of political significance.

The quintessential model for the *Annales* school was devised by Fernand Braudel, editor of *Les Annales* from 1956 to 1972. Braudel set forth his structuralist method in his monumental *La Méditerranée et le monde méditerranéen à l'époque de Philippe II* (1949). He reversed the historians' traditional ordering of topics by beginning with environmental factors, then proceeding to social customs before examining political events. In this way, he showed how the significance of political episodes diminishes when juxtaposed to the more stable frameworks of social and geological time. The age of Philip II, he explained, was best grasped as a conjuncture of temporal patterns, each operating according to a different dynamic. Because Braudel's work was encyclopedic in its erudition and scope, it served as a model of aspiration rather than practice for most *Annales* historians, who tended to reaffirm a larger historiographical trend toward specialization.

Annales historiography in the 1940s and 1950s focused on economic and demographic issues. But by the 1960s and 1970s, interest shifted toward cultural topics. Robert Mandrou's *Introduction à la France moderne* (1961), resurrecting Febvre's early interest in collective psychology (and based in part on notes he bequeathed), signaled the transition. By the late 1960s, the history of collective mentalities, with its focus on the attitudes of ordinary people toward everyday life, was a thriving field. The most popular work of this genre was Emmanuel Le Roy Ladurie's *Montaillou, village occitan de 1294 à 1324* (1975), a case history of everyday life in a medieval village in the Languedoc. This and similar studies examined judicial records for the insights they provided into religious beliefs, social interactions, and popular mores. Somewhat apart but taking its inspiration from the *Annales* school were historical studies of the rhetorical uses of language. Michel Foucault's histories of discourse about asylums, sexuality, and the self are the best known, but the approach has influenced recent historical writing about the French Revolution (François Furet) and the national memory (Pierre Nora).

By the 1980s, *Annales* scholarship had become too varied to be considered a coherent school of historiography. But the *Annales* temper—a respect for the blending of innovative methodologies and exacting research—continues to pervade contemporary French historiography and accounts for its enduring international prestige.

A. Burguière, ''Annales (Ecole des),'' in *Dictionnaire des sciences historiques*, ed. A. Burguière (Paris, 1986); J. Glénisson, ''L'Historiographie française contemporaine,'' in *Recherche historique en France de 1940 à 1965*, ed. J. Schneider (Paris, 1965); G. Iggers, *New Directions in European Historiography*, rev. ed. (Middletown, Conn., 1984); J. Revel, ''Histoire et sciences sociales: Les Paradigmes des *Annales*,'' *Annales: ESC* 34 (1979); T. Stoianovich, *French Historical Method: The Annales Paradigm* (Ithaca, N.Y., 1976).

P. H. Hutton

Related entries: ARIES, PHILIPPE; BRAUDEL, FERNAND; FOUCAULT, MICHEL; LE ROY LADURIE, EMMANUEL; STRUCTURALISM.

ANTI-SEMITISM, far weaker than before World War II, has remained an often-elusive element in French culture and politics. Anti-Semitism (the doctrine that Jews are a dangerous foreign minority) has been shaped in France, since World War II, by: (1) the discrediting of political anti-Semitism by its association with Nazism and the holocaust (reinforced by the outlawing of anti-Semitic or other racist propaganda in 1972), and (2) the creation of the state of Israel with its own interests but with the passionate support of most of the diaspora. Thus, political anti-Semitism has been either marginal or disguised (or both), and opposition to the state of Israel and its supporters, dubbed anti-Zionism, could be confused with, or serve as a cover for, an anti-Semitism now politically damning.

The fascistic radical right, with its attendant anti-Semitism and denial of Nazi crimes, reappeared almost immediately, but as a lunatic fringe, whose most distinguished spokesperson has remained Maurice Bardèche. Though primarily anticommunist, ''nationalist revolutionary'' organizations like *Occident* (in the 1960s) and to a degree *Ordre nouveau* (in the 1970s), with Fredericksen's *Fédération d'action nationale et européenne* (FANE) closest to Nazi formulations, continued to see Jews (sometimes dubbed Zionists) as leaders in a conspiracy stretching from Moscow to Wall Street. (A minority among neofascists admiringly considers Israel a populist, militarist, racially conscious state.) Similar groups were apparently behind the wave of anti-Semitic terrorism in the late 1970s, which culminated in the bombing outside the synagogue on the rue Copernic in 1980.

More traditional anti-Semitic echoes surfaced in the career of the radical-right populist Pierre Poujade (1956). The persistence, on a nonpoliticized level, of an anti-Semitic substratum appeared in 1969 in the famous ''rumors'' of Orléans and other provincial cities that Jewish merchants were using their boutiques for the white-slave trade, an apparent updating of the blood libel.

The anti-Israeli turn of the French Communist party in the early 1950s was associated with an anti-Zionist campaign that slipped into anti-Semitism in its rhetoric and anti-Jewish discrimination in party affairs. With the 1967 war and the rise of the Palestinian movement, the rest of the French radical left became increasingly anti-Israeli; but, unless one considers forceful opposition to the Zionist settlement of Palestine to be anti-Semitism, anti-Jewish racism has remained essentially an appanage of the radical right. De Gaulle's shift to a pro-Arab foreign policy in 1967 was accompanied by his famous characterization of the Jews as an ''elite people, sure of themselves and domineering,'' in which traditional anti-Semitism seemed to have attached itself to foreign policy concerns explicable in other terms.

The renewal of radical right thought in the 1970s was accompanied by a new development from earlier anti-Semitic theorizing. The ideological movement led by Alain de Benoist and the organization *Groupement de recherche et d'études pour la civilisation européenne* (GRECE) denies, even excoriates, racism, blaming it on the same forces that produced Marxism, liberalism, and Christianity. All these ''totalitarianisms'' are the product of the fundamentally intolerant impulse of biblical monotheism, original to Judaism but continued by Christianity. Exploiting Renan's distinction between Indo-European and Semitic cultures (partly updated with materials from Dumézil), Benoist and his followers see an original pagan Indo-European culture terrorized and infected by an alien, domineering monotheism of Near Eastern origin, itself responsible for evils from cosmopolitan capitalism and imperialism to communism and fascism.

The breakthrough of the National Front of Jean-Marie Le Pen (around 11 percent in elections since 1983) has brought the shadow of anti-Semitism closer to mainstream politics. Le Pen disclaims anti-Semitism, and his demagoguery is usually directed against the largely Maghrebian ''immigrants.'' Major lieutenants, like Bernard Antony, continue to espouse a reactionary Catholic anti-Semitism with strong Maurrassian echoes. Le Pen's own brushes with anti-Semitic rhetoric and positions can be seen as revealing slips or coded messages to anti-Semitic followers. Finally, France has its ''revisionists'' who, on absurd evidence, dispute the reality of Nazi genocide.

J. Algazy, *L'Extrême-droite en France de 1965 à 1984* (Paris, 1989); A. Douglas, '' 'La Nouvelle Droite': G.R.E.C.E. and the Revival of Radical Rightist Thought in Contemporary France,'' *The Tocqueville Review* 6 (1984); E. Morin et al., *La Rumeur d'Orleans* (Paris, 1969); B. Philippe, *Etre juif dans la société française* (Paris, 1979).

A. Douglas

Related entries: LE PEN, JEAN-MARIE; MIDDLE EAST, RELATIONS WITH; MINORITIES, PROBLEMS OF; POLITICAL TRENDS; POUJADISTS.

ARAGON, LOUIS (1897–1982), poet and novelist who went from being a writer of surrealism to being one of the French Communist party's (PCF) leading and most faithful intellectuals. After completing medical training, he served in World War I hospitals where he met André Breton in 1917. The two went on to become the leaders of the French dada movement and then surrealism. As the surrealists strengthened their opposition to bourgeois culture into an opposition to bourgeois society, and in reaction to the Moroccan Rif war, Aragon joined the PCF in 1927 along with Breton. For several years, as the surrealists sought to maintain their independent service to the proletarian revolution, the PCF avoided formalizing Aragon's membership.

In 1928 Aragon met the Russian Jewish writer Elsa Triolet who became his lifelong companion. She encouraged his novelistic tendencies (seen as culpable by the surrealists) and introduced him to Soviet letters and society.

The 1930 Kharkov conference (after which Aragon was obliged to sign a statement critical of surrealism) and the flap over a political poem, *Front rouge* (1931), led to his final break with surrealism and acceptance by the PCF. During the period of Popular Front coalition building, Aragon became a journalist first for *L'Humanité* and then editor of the new daily *Ce soir*, as well as the vigorous proponent of socialist realism. His novel *Les Cloches de Bâle* (1933) began a series that he entitled *Le Monde réel*.

After the fall of France to Germany at the beginning of World War II, Aragon and Elsa were among those who began resistance activity almost immediately, eventually going underground. Poet of the Resistance, Aragon used chivalric codes to evoke French nationalism, the Resistance, and his own "lady" Elsa, as in *La Diane française* (1945).

The Liberation projected Aragon into political and literary leadership. As secretary-general of the *Comité national d'écrivains*, editor of *Les Lettres françaises* (till 1972), and member of the PCF Central Committee, he steered intellectuals toward PCF positions. Author of a pro-Jdanovite campaign for socialist realism, Aragon illustrated his theses with the three-volume novel *Les Communistes* (1949–50), which defended the actions of the party during the difficult period from the Hitler-Stalin Pact through the defeat.

In later years, Aragon's writing again became more experimental (*Le Roman inachevé*, 1956; *Le Fou d'Elsa*, 1963; *Théâtre/roman*, 1974), and his support for aesthetic modernism led to conflicts with party conservatives, like his public humiliation in 1953 over Picasso's sketch of Stalin.

Through his trips to the Soviet Union, Aragon became increasingly aware both of Stalin's crimes and of the halting politics of de-Stalinization in that country. Remaining loyal to the PCF, he struggled for a genuine liberalization, (excoriating the "normalization" in Czechoslovakia) to the point of earning a Soviet rebuke in 1969.

P. Daix, *Aragon, une vie à changer* (Paris, 1975); D. Desanti, *Les Clés d'Elsa* (Paris, 1983).

A. Douglas

Related entries: FRENCH COMMUNIST PARTY; LITERATURE; PRESS.

ARIES, PHILIPPE (1914–1984), pioneering historian of popular culture. His *L'Enfant et la vie familiale sous l'ancien régime* (1960), a study of long-range changes in attitudes toward children, stimulated research on this and other topics of everyday life. His historical writings contributed to the historiographical definition of the history of collective mentalities.

He was born in Blois, the scion of a family deeply immersed in the lure of its royalist heritage. His sentimental attachment to his family's traditions inspired his interest in both politics and history. As a young man, he wrote for the newspapers of the neoroyalist *Action française*, and after the war he continued to contribute to conservative magazines of commentary. History, however, was his abiding passion. An able but undisciplined student, he studied at the *Lycée Janson-de-Sailly* (Paris), the University of Grenoble, and the Sorbonne, where he earned his *diplôme d'études supérieures*. Refusing to take his exam for the *agrégation* seriously, he failed it twice and so was ineligible to teach in the national system of higher education.

During World War II he taught briefly in a Vichy-sponsored academy and frequented the National Library, where he read widely in social and cultural history. He also published his first scholarly study, *Les Traditions sociales dans les pays de France* (1943), which presaged his later work on the mores of traditional society. Toward the end of the war, he accepted a position as an archivist for a governmental institute monitoring commerce in tropical fruit and worked there for thirty-seven years.

All the while, he pursued his historical research as an avocation and published important studies along the way, among them: *Les Populations françaises et leurs attitudes devant la vie depuis le xviii*ᵉ *siècle* (1948), a demographic study that evinces his skill with quantitative methods; *Le Temps de l'histoire* (1954), a personalized history of French historiography (essential for understanding his purpose and method); the aforementioned *L'Enfant et la vie familiale*, for which he won international recognition; and *L'Homme devant la mort* (1981), a like study of long-range changes in attitudes toward death and dying in Western society. Although French historians were slow to acknowledge the significance of his studies, they elicited much interest among American scholars. In 1976 he was awarded a fellowship at the Woodrow Wilson Center in Washington, D.C., and during the 1970s he lectured frequently in the United States. In 1978 he received a teaching appointment at the *Ecole des hautes études sociales*. During his last years, he joined French colleagues in editorial ventures dealing with the history of private life, sexuality, and historiography.

Grand in scope, Ariès's scholarship reveals his profound respect for traditional French society. He showed the postwar generation aspects of the cultural and social life of the old regime that had been layered over by the political preoccupations of modern historical scholarship. In some measure, he succeeded in rehabilitating the ideal of traditionalism that his political counterparts had so conspicuously tarnished during the Vichy years.

P. Ariès, *Un Historien du dimanche* (Paris, 1980); A. Burguière, "Philippe Ariès," in *Dictionnaire des sciences historiques*, ed. A. Burguière (Paris, 1986); J. Friguglietti,

''Philippe Ariès,'' *French Historical Studies* 13 (1984); P. Hutton, ''Philippe Ariès: Traditionalism as a Vision of History,'' *Proceedings of the Western Society for French History* 15 (1988); F. Léger, ''Philippe Ariès: L'Histoire d'un historien,'' *La Revue universelle des faits et des idées* 65 (1986).

P. H. Hutton

Related entries: ANNALES SCHOOL; BRAUDEL, FERNAND; FOUCAULT, MICHEL; POPULAR CULTURE.

ARMS SALES, an essential part of French security policy, allowing economies of scale in weapons production for the French armed forces. French policy on arms exports is conditioned by three factors. The first factor is the persistent political determination to maintain a vigorous and largely independent national arms industry, producing the full range of military equipment. This has necessitated a major export sector, as domestic markets are not large enough to support a comprehensive armaments industry. The second factor is the broad public and state support for arms sales, generally much more supportive than in other major Western European countries. The final factor is that French arms sales have been concentrated to an unusually large extent in the Third World, and several Third World regions that traditionally have been strong markets for French arms sales have declined in significance in recent years. As a result, French arms sales exports actually declined in the latter part of the 1980s.

For most of the 1980s France was the world's third-largest arms exporter, with a share of total arms exports of around 10 percent to 13 percent. This meant that France followed the United States and the Soviet Union, each with about a one-third share of the market. Over the period 1982–86, 86.1 percent of French arms exports went to Third World countries. This compares with 51.6 percent for the United States, 76.1 percent for the Soviet Union, and 66.5 percent for the United Kingdom.

France has traditionally had three main areas of arms sales concentration, francophone Africa, India, and the Middle East, especially Iraq. France was particularly successful in maintaining high levels of arms exports to Iraq during the Iran-Iraq War from 1979 to 1988, but its arms exports as a whole appear to have peaked in 1986, with a decline in the two following years. The ending of the Iran-Iraq War and the Persian Gulf War may exacerbate this trend.

In terms of dollar amounts of arms exports (U.S. dollars at constant 1985 prices, in millions of dollars), in 1984 France exported $3,853 worth of armaments, $4,046 in 1985, $4,122 in 1986, $3,073 in 1987, and $2,881 in 1988. France's traditional strength in arms exports has been with low-cost, high-performance weapons, especially aircraft, usually simplified export versions of weapons developed for the French armed forces. The trend toward high-technology weapons requirements in the Third World, especially the Middle East, has aided competitor countries such as the United States and the United Kingdom. Furthermore, the debt problem facing much of francophone Africa, coupled with relatively low oil prices affecting many Middle East countries, has meant that traditional recipient states for French arms exports have been less able to afford new weapons systems.

While France continues to succeed in exporting some categories of weapons such as helicopters and antiship missiles, it seems likely to face much stiffer competition in the 1990s as the defense budgets of many industrialized countries are cut back sharply and defense industries consequently seek to compete more vigorously in Third World markets.

I. Anthony, "The Trade in Major Conventional Weapons," in *SIPRI Yearbook 1989: World Armaments and Disarmament* (Oxford, 1989).

P. F. Rogers

Related entries: DEFENSE POLICY; ECONOMIC POLICY; ECONOMIC TRENDS; MIDDLE EAST, RELATIONS WITH; THIRD WORLD, RELATIONS WITH.

ARON, RAYMOND (1905–1983), sociologist and political analyst, who, as teacher and writer, warned successive generations of the political dangers of romantic revolutionism and of the importance of liberal values. Born in Paris to an assimilated and unreligious Jewish family in 1905, Aron attended the *Lycée Condorcet* and the *Lycée Hoche* (Versailles) before entering the *Ecole normale supérieure* (1924–28), where he befriended classmates Jean-Paul Sartre and Paul Nizan. He placed first in the *agrégation* examination of 1928 and, following eighteen months of military service, he spent several years in Germany, first at the University of Cologne and then at the French Institute in Berlin. He witnessed the rise of Nazism and worked on two books about German sociologists and historians, the first writings of an immensely productive career. Aron wrote nearly forty books, more than six hundred articles, and approximately four thousand newspaper and magazine editorials.

During the early 1930s Aron concluded that his abilities were more critical than creative and that he would be more successful studying the history and nature of social and political knowledge than writing philosophy. His political sympathies shifted at about the same time; as a student he had sympathized with socialism, but during the 1930s his reflections on the fascist and communist regimes of Germany, Italy, and Russia made him suspicious of regimes that substituted ideology for liberal freedoms. By the mid–1930s, his pragmatism made him critical of the economic policy of the Popular Front.

In 1938 he published his thesis, *Introduction à la philosophie de l'histoire*, which like his earlier books emphasized the dangers of deterministic fatalism and naive optimism. His focus on the relationship between thought and action, and especially social theory and political practice, remained sensitive to complexities: the weight of historical traditions and accidents, the partial nature of even the most sophisticated knowledge of politics and history, the limits of possible change, the unintended consequences of actions. It was a liberal and pluralistic orientation that would inform many of his later analyses of industrial society (e.g., *Dix-huit leçons sur la société industrielle*, 1962), and his studies of international relations and sociopolitical thinkers (e.g., *Paix et guerre entre les nations*, 1962, and *Les Grandes Doctrines de sociologie historiques*, 2 vols., 1960–62).

During World War II Aron went to London to work with Charles de Gaulle's Free French and to edit the paper *France libre*. When he returned to Paris after the Liberation, he taught classes at the *Institut d'études politiques* and at the *Ecole nationale d'administration* (ENA), and he wrote for *Combat* (1946–47). His attachment to a dual career of journalism and teaching seems to date from these years. When he failed to get elected to the Sorbonne in 1948, he decided to remain in Paris as a journalist rather than teach in the provinces. He was subsequently elected professor of sociology at the Sorbonne in 1955, and five years later he became a director of studies at the *Ecole pratique des hautes études*. In 1963 he was named to the *Académie des sciences morales et politiques*; in 1970 he became professor at the Collège de France.

After the war Aron came to believe that the left was exhibiting the most dangerous form of political romanticism. He carried on a running critique of Marxism, the French Communist party (PCF), and the Soviet Union that led to bitter public disputes with left-leaning intellectuals like Sartre. The most famous publication on this theme was *L'Opium des intellectuels* (1955), but he also published essays that were critical of the Marxism of both Louis Althusser and Sartre (see *D'une sainte famille à l'autre*, 1969) and dismissive of the romanticism and ideological frenzy of students (see *La Révolution introuvable*, 1968, about the 1968 student revolt).

These stances placed Aron on the right of the French political spectrum during the 1940s, 1950s, and 1960s, though he often took independent positions. Between 1947 and 1977 he wrote for the conservative newspaper *Le Figaro*, but broke ranks with the right by arguing that Algerian independence was inevitable. He joined de Gaulle's *Rassemblement du peuple français* (RPF) in 1947, but was often critical of de Gaulle's specific policies, such as the general's excessively punitive policy toward Germany. Aron also favored an "Atlanticist" foreign policy that would coordinate French policy with that of the United States, rather than the strident independence advocated by de Gaulle.

Aron's popularity remained marginal until the mid–1970s, when left-wing disillusionment with the Gulag and, more generally, with Marxism led many to reconsider the importance of France's liberal heritage. To many disenchanted leftists, Aron's liberal agenda, and his long-running battle for pragmatic moderate change, began to look prophetic.

Aron suffered a heart attack in April 1977, but resumed a rigorous schedule of writing editorials (now for *L'Express*) and teaching via radio and television interviews. In September 1983, he published his *Mémoires: 50 ans de réflexion politique*, which became an immediate national best-seller. He had just finished testifying on behalf of Bertrand de Jouvenel in the libel trial against Zeev Sternhell when he suffered heart failure, on October 17, 1983.

R. Colquhoun, *Raymond Aron*, 2 vols. (Beverly Hills, Calif., 1986); G. Fessard, *La*

Philosophie historique de Raymond Aron (Paris, 1980); S. Hoffmann, "Raymond Aron (1905–1983)," *New York Review of Books*, December 8, 1983.

K. S. Vincent

Related entry: INTELLECTUAL TRENDS.

ART AND ARCHITECTURE, includes painting, sculpture, and architecture in France from 1946 to 1991. Until 1940 Paris was the center of the artistic world and also many important artistic movements, such as German expressionism, Russian constructivism, Italian futurism, and Dutch De Stijl. After World War II the United States, Japan, and South America became the major forces. Even though the long-established French academies of art and architecture, devoted to the traditions of ancient and Renaissance ideals, have always opposed new radical artists and architects, they are still in existence and have, in most cases, been an impediment to new ideas and artistic materials. It was the intolerance of these academies that drove the most experimental artists to seek other options for training, causing Paris to lose its grip on most future influences not only in painting and sculpture, but also architecture as well. Opposition to the unbending curriculum of the *Ecole des beaux-arts*, for example, led major painters to frequent the *Académie suisse*, a free school in which there were no lessons. Architects, having different sorts of patrons, were, with few exceptions, forced to follow academic traditions. The result was that engineers trained at the *Ecole polytechnique* and *Ecole centrale*, which were innovative with materials such as iron, led the way to the skyscraper, which developed in the United States with the help of French-trained engineers. And so, with the exception of the outstanding work of Le Corbusier (Charles Edouard Jeanneret, 1887–1965) and the earlier projects by Auguste Perret (1874–1954), important French architectural contributions to the twentieth century have been few.

Perret's reconstruction of Le Havre in 1947 may be considered an example of modern classicism, although most historians would agree it is rather uninspired. Nevertheless Perret, known for his bold experiments with reinforced concrete, is considered one of the most important French architects of his generation. (The revolutionary experiments in Paris today under President François Mitterrand are, with few exceptions, the designs of foreign architects.) A few French buildings are noteworthy, although many of them have designs created by non-French architects and engineers. For example, the civil engineer Pier Luigi Nervi and the architects Marcel Breuer and Bernard Zehrfuss were responsible for the design and construction of an ambitious postwar structure, the UNESCO building (United Nations Educational Scientific and Cultural Organization) erected in Paris in the place de Fontenoy. Also, the Y-shaped eight-story Secretariat building is adjoined to a conference hall, designed principally by Nervi, called the most brilliant concrete designer of the age. The total complex is well-adapted to a rather difficult site and is adorned by a number of paintings, sculptures, and murals. Breuer developed the plans and ideas for the UNESCO building further in his work on a research center for IBM France at La Guade Var between 1960 and

1962. This complex has a comparable Y-plan with windows set within deep concrete frames, and the entire building is on concrete *pilotis* (stilts).

One of the most influential French architects of the twentieth century was Le Corbusier. Although he designed buildings all over the globe, his work in France is some of his most revolutionary. His pilgrimage Chapel of Ronchamp, 1950–54, is no doubt one of the great religious structures of the twentieth century. Molded of white concrete, it is topped by a contrasting dark, seemingly floating concrete roof, and is accented by towers. The actual surface of the concrete is left rough, just as it came out of the timber shuttering, a startling effect that has since become commonplace. The interior is lit by irregular windows of different shapes and sizes that open up from small apertures to create large and small focused tunnels of light. It was in the sculptural quality of his concrete that Le Corbusier ranked among the best. Another example of his concrete can be seen at the monastery at La Tourette at Evreux, 1957–60. A thick square of undressed concrete with austere cells for the monks, it is arranged in a large U around a central courtyard. Toward the realization of how individuals dwell in cities and his earlier plan for a "vertical city," Le Corbusier designed a number of *unité d'habitation* complexes. The unit in Marseille (1947–52) is a seventeen-story building with its own restaurant, rooftop *crèche* (day nursery for infants), gymnasium, and shops. The arrangement of duplex apartments is ingenious: two stories, with double-height living rooms. Fifteen-foot windows look out either to the mountains or the Mediterranean.

In Paris, the Georges Pompidou National Center of Art and Culture, known as *Beaubourg*, 1971–77, designed by Renzo Piano (1937–) and Richard Rogers (1933–) is a six-level building known for its unusual design. Its functions are fully exposed and the pipes, tubes, ducts, and corridors are color-coded according to use (blue for air-conditioning, green for water, yellow for electricity, red for the movement of people). Over four thousand visitors a day see the galleries, center for industrial design, library, science, and music centers.

More recently, President Mitterrand has undertaken the most stupendous building program since the Second Empire (1852–70), when Paris was completely rebuilt by Napoleon III. Mitterrand's nine-part program, originally known as the *grands projets*, is now being called the *grands travaux* as the projects reach completion. Within months of his election, Mitterrand announced his $3 billion building projects. His first target was the renovation and expansion of the Louvre. He chose the Chinese-born American architect Ieoh Ming Pei (1917–) to design the 71-foot-high glass pyramid that forms the new entrance to the museum. It is 108 feet wide at the base and carries 105 tons of glass. Pei also put 650,000 square feet of new exhibition space underground beneath the Cour Napoléon. To complement the pyramid a new plaza, created between the outstretched wings of the museum, faces the Tuileries gardens. The entire project will be finished in 1993, in time for the museum's two-hundredth anniversary. Mitterrand has also had a gigantic new finance ministry built on the Seine in the eastern Paris district of Bercy. The architects are Paul Chemetov and Borja Huidobro. The

Seine is also the site of two more of the *grands projets*. Across from the Louvre on the Left Bank is the Musée d'Orsay by architect Gae Aulenti and A.C.T. Architecture. Near the Musée d'Orsay and to the east is the *Institut du monde arabe* by Jean Nouvel, probably France's most gifted architect since Le Corbusier. The other projects include the *Grande arche de la défense*, in the shape of an open-ended cube, the new Opéra at the Bastille, designed by the Canadian architect Carlos Ott, and a science and technology center known as La Villette.

While architecture held its own during the Fourth Republic and made news during the Fifth Republic, painting found a larger audience. The most important French painter to emerge after World War II, Jean Dubuffet (1901–1985), was forty-three years old when he held his first one-man show in 1944 at the Galerie René in Paris. His works, called *Pâtes*, are made of sand, glass, tar, and other materials. This "pigment" has been scratched and manipulated into shapes resembling the human figure. Always with a preference for the unexamined and amateur spontaneity, he began his own collection in 1945 which includes *l'art brut* (raw art), thousands of works in all media produced by children and the mentally ill. Dubuffet can be categorized as one of the most prolific painters in history. His figures are sometimes sinister and drawn in the naive manner of a child. His space, an important consideration after the dismantling of traditional Renaissance one-point perspective, is composed as in a primitive painting. The depth, shown by stratification, has the lowest level nearest the viewer. In the late 1950s he made a number of paintings of doors developed out of assemblages. Between 1962 and 1966 he was working on a project he referred to as the "Twenty-Third Period of My Works," for which he coined the name *L'Hourloupe*. These drawings, inspired by doodling with a red ballpoint pen while telephoning, are free-form, abstract shapes that flow and change like amoebas. He covered various surfaces (some gigantic—one is 27 feet long) with countless little figures, producing an effect similar to a jigsaw puzzle.

Another gifted artist of the Paris school after World War II was Nicolas De Staël (1914–1955), who painted with a palette knife and used masses of pigment. He achieved considerable feeling of deep recession into depth with a juxtaposition of color tones. He committed suicide in a mood of despair when he felt his work had reached an impasse.

Also in the Paris school was Yves Klein (1928–1962), who experimented with nearly every sort of material and was the first artist to exhibit as his own creative work the bare walls of an art gallery. Using his favorite color, ultramarine blue, he impregnated everything from sponges to plaster casts of his friends' nude bodies; Klein covered his nude models with blue pigment and told them to roll on the canvas, leaving prints of their entire anatomies. He was thus the inventor of body art. He is best known, however, for his "fire paintings," made by applying flame to painted asbestos.

Sculpture has been noteworthy in the eyes of only a few historians. French sculptress Germaine Richier (1904–1959) is known for her engravings, book illustrations, and ceramics. Having been an assistant to Rodin, Richier inherited the main line of modern figurative sculpture. Between 1950 and 1951 she produced a large bronze piece called *Don Quixote of the Forest*. In 1953 she produced *The Horse with Six Heads,* a miracle of bronze casting, so thin as to be nearly transparent, with the surface torn everywhere like flesh that has been picked by vultures. She produced *The Tree* in 1956. While Richier passed the limits of bronze casting, César (César Baldaccini, 1921–   ) created the same effects with iron scraps and fragments of machines. Although he has worked with abstraction, he inevitably returns to the figure. His *Nude*, a study in bronze, is a lower torso with a pair of legs. In the 1960s he crushed automobile bodies under pressure and produced massive, varicolored blocks. His 1959 *The Yellow Buick* is known best. Another artist, Daniel Buren, exhibited—inside the *Salon de Mai* of 1968, on two hundred billboards all over Paris, and on the back of a sandwich-man walking around outside the gallery—pieces of green-and-white striped cloth that looked like awning canvas. There was no content to the work.

Art and architecture of the 1970s and 1980s have been called postmodern. Artists and architects have moved away from the revolution that successfully overthrew all Renaissance tradition. Today one sees an attempt to destroy modernism. At the same time there is no firm evidence of a new style to replace it.

H. Arnason, *History of Modern Art* (Englewood Cliffs, N.J., 1977); L. Benevolo, *History of Modern Architecture,* 2 vols. (Cambridge, Mass., 1977); G. Hamilton, *Painting and Sculpture in Europe* (New York, 1983); S. Hunter, J. Jacobus, *Modern Art* (New York, 1985).

I. Earls

Related entries: CULTURAL POLICY; MITTERRAND, FRANCOIS; POMPIDOU, GEORGES.

ASTERIX LE GAULOIS, possibly the most famous cartoon character in France today, was born of René Goscinny's quill and Albert Uderzo's brush in 1951 for the weekly magazine *Pilote*. Nearly thirty adventures of the feisty Gaul have been published in single volumes, by Dargault from 1961 to 1979 and by Albert-René since then. As of January 1989, two-hundred-million copies in forty languages had been sold.

When the Roman legions threaten to take over his village, the last independent territory in Gaul, Astérix and his friends set out to keep the invaders at bay, aided by their wise druid Panoramix, whose magic brew gives them extraordinary strength. Successful in every encounter, they soon travel all over the Roman Empire helping local warriors and their chiefs rebel against Caesar.

Humor stems mostly from the use of frequent anachronistic references, puns, and other wordplay. For example, using the name of the Gallic general Vercingétorix for a model, character names are made of words in which the ending is changed to *-ix*, regardless of the original meaning, for example, Obélix, Idéfix, Analgésix.

Each adventure satirizes aspects of contemporary French society that the creators found unhealthy: stereotypes, prejudices, xenophobia, snobbery, lack of civic sense, and so on. Since Goscinny's death in 1977, Uderzo has written as well as illustrated new Astérix adventures, carefully maintaining Goscinny's style, wit, and inspiration.

Astérix's fame is spilling outside of the cartoon world: An animated film, *Les Douze travaux d'Astérix*, in 1979, a children's show performed in Paris for the 1988–89 holiday season, and the Village d'Astérix theme park under construction in Marne-la-Vallée, testify to the influence of this remarkable character on French popular culture.

Astérix (Paris, 1961–).

L. J. Haenlin

Related entries: POPULAR CULTURE; SOCIAL TRENDS.

ATTALI, JACQUES (1943–), a leading economist and adviser to President François Mitterrand. Attali was born in Algiers on November 1, 1943. His father was a merchant, and his family was Jewish. He began his education in Algiers and then continued it in Paris where he graduated from the *Lycée Janson-de-Sailly*. He then received a diploma from the *Institut d'études politiques*, graduated from both the *Ecole nationale d'administration* (ENA) and the *Ecole polytechnique*, and ultimately earned a *doctorat d'état* in economics.

He began his career as an *ingénieur des mines* in 1968 but switched to the *Conseil d'Etat* in 1970. During the 1970s he also taught at the ENA and the *Ecole polytechnique* and directed a research laboratory at the University of Paris-IX.

In the 1970s, Attali became one of France's leading left-wing economists and intellectuals. In all, he has published ten books, mostly analyzing the economy, but also essays on music and a biography of Sir Sigmund Warburg.

His works were among the more influential in leading the Socialist party (PS) to attempt both to modernize the French economy and to provide more purchasing power and a better standard of living for the population. During the 1970s he was one of the most popular and articulate critics of the capitalism of the Western democracies and the socialism of the Soviet bloc. In their place he offered *autogestion*, a decentralized form of socialism in which workers would own and manage businesses as part of a society in which people took control of the decisions that shaped their lives.

In 1981 he headed the team of advisers that ran François Mitterrand's presidential campaign. Since then he has served as a special counselor to President Mitterrand. Mitterrand is known to use him as a sounding board for his ideas, and Attali is generally considered to be the third most important person on the president's staff. During the debates within the government in 1983 on how to react to the difficulties its economic reforms were facing, Attali apparently advocated maintaining them, losing, however, when Prime Ministers Pierre Mauroy and then Laurent Fabius embarked on a policy of austerity.

He claims always to have three books in progress. His twin brother, Bernard, is also a noted economist who has had a distinguished career in both the public and private sectors and is currently head of Air France. In 1990 Jacques Attali was appointed head of a newly created European reconstruction and development bank to aid Eastern European nations.

J. Attali, *La Nouvelle Economie française* (Paris, 1978); B. Brown, *Socialism of a Different Kind* (Westport, Conn., 1982); G. Ross, S. Hoffmann, S. Melzacher, eds., *The Mitterrand Experiment* (New York, 1987); D. Singer, *Is Socialism Doomed?* (New York, 1988).

C. Hauss

Related entries: AUROUX LAWS; *AUTOGESTION*; CHEVENEMENT, JEAN-PIERRE; *COHABITATION*; COMMON PROGRAM; DEBRAY, REGIS; DECENTRALIZATION; DELORS, JACQUES; ECONOMIC POLICY; ECONOMIC TRENDS; FABIUS, LAURENT; INDUSTRIAL POLICY; MARXISM; MAUROY, PIERRE; MITTERRAND, FRANCOIS; ROCARD, MICHEL; SOCIALIST PARTY (PS); TECHNOLOGY; UNIFIED SOCIALIST PARTY.

AURIOL, VINCENT (1884–1966), veteran socialist politician in the parliament of the Third Republic who served with distinction as the first president of the Fourth Republic (1947–53). Auriol was born in Revel (Haute-Garonne), a small town in southwestern France where his ancestors had been farmers. He pursued his studies at the University of Toulouse, earning a doctorate in law and a *licence* in philosophy. For a time he practiced law in that city. While a student, he had become active in left-wing politics. He joined the Socialist party (SFIO) in 1905, wrote for the socialist newspaper *La Cité*, and in 1909 was a founding editor of *Le Midi socialiste*. In 1914 he was elected to the Chamber of Deputies to represent his home district of Muret, a post he held until the fall of the Republic in 1940. He was appreciated by his colleagues for his eloquence and the warmth of his personality. He sided with Léon Blum in the schism of the Socialist party in 1920 and served in the Chamber as secretary-general of the Socialist delegation for eleven years (1928–39). During his tenure he acquired a reputation as an expert in finance and served on a number of parliamentary and governmental committees dealing with international monetary issues. Blum named him minister of finance in his popular front government of 1936 and minister of state in that of 1938. He was also minister of justice in the cabinet of Camille Chautemps in 1937.

Reluctant to accede to the armistice dictated by Nazi Germany in June 1940, Auriol was one of eighty deputies who voted against granting executive power to Philippe Pétain under the new Vichy regime. Considered an obstructionist by Vichy leaders, he was briefly imprisoned, then placed under house arrest. In 1942 he escaped, joined the Resistance, and by October 1943 made his way to London to join Free French forces under Charles de Gaulle. During the last years of the war he held a variety of positions in de Gaulle's provisional government in Algiers and France. As a mediator among the diverse forces working to reestablish the Republic, Auriol acquired the respect that led to his election as president of both the first (1945) and second (1946) constituent assemblies.

Inspiring confidence among nearly all republican politicians, he was easily elected president of the Republic in January 1947 by that regime's first parliament (452 votes to 242 for his nearest competitor).

Like most of his socialist colleagues, Auriol had earlier favored a regime in which political power would be vested primarily in the National Assembly. Like his predecessor Jules Grévy (1879–86), he had once advocated the abolition of the office of the presidency altogether. However, faced with the challenge of filling the role, he was determined that his role would be more than ceremonial. As president, he made the fullest possible use of his moral authority. The constitution of the Fourth Republic set sharp limits on his official powers. But fractious conditions within the National Assembly enabled him to play a leadership role beyond that anticipated by the framers of the constitution. He was obliged to deal with twelve ministerial crises during his seven-year term, for which he solicited fifty-nine potential premiers. Only a president with such long experience in parliament and such widespread support among its members could have led the government through such crises so ably.

Auriol was simple and unassuming, and most of his colleagues appreciated his informality and his capacity for jest. At the same time, he conceived of his task as a high calling. He endeavored to put the national interest over party interests, and he was suspicious of the parties of the extreme left (communist) and right (Gaullist) as threats to the constitutional settlement. He used his presidential authority to hold the parliament accountable to what he characterized in 1951 as "the profound and permanent will of the country." To this end, he gave advice to premiers on major issues of public policy; he influenced the choice of cabinet leaders, and in some instances forestalled their resignations; he remanded for reconsideration legislation that he believed violated the best interests of the nation.

In contrast with his predecessors of the Third Republic, Auriol traveled widely and spoke vigorously on public issues, particularly those affecting foreign affairs. An ardent opponent of Soviet expansionism, he backed collective security through the North Atlantic Treaty Organization (NATO). At the same time, he wished to insure France's independence of action in international affairs, and he remained inveterately suspicious of a remilitarized Germany. Auriol also took seriously his role as president of the French Union. While favoring an enlightened colonial policy, he was reluctant to consider the dissolution of the overseas empire. He used his power as presiding officer of the High Judicial Council to insure the independence of that sphere of government from parliamentary influence. A compassionate man, he invoked his power of pardon frequently, particularly in cases of capital punishment.

In 1953 Auriol decided not to seek re-election. At the end of the decade, he served on the Constitutional Council of the Fifth Republic, but resigned in 1960 because of his reservations about the authoritarian direction the new regime might take under de Gaulle. Resolute in his commitment to parliamentary democracy, he opposed a constitutional amendment of 1962 for the direct election of the president of the Republic.

Historical judgments of Auriol's presidency have generally been highly favorable. His experience, personal qualities, and shrewd use of his opportunities enabled him to lead a regime troubled by divisiveness and tenuous loyalties. He brought dignity to an office that in the past had often been ridiculed. A humanist socialist in the tradition of Jean Jaurès, he is remembered for his generosity of spirit and his high political ideals.

A. Dansette, *Histoire des présidents de la république* (Paris, 1960); L. Derfler, *President and Parliament* (Boca Raton, Fla., 1983); J. Jolly, ed., *Dictionnaire des parlementaires français* (Paris, 1960); J. Raymond, "Auriol," in *Dictionnaire biographique du mouvement ouvrier français, 1914–1939* (Paris, 1982); A. Richie, "Vincent Auriol," in *Biographical Dictionary of French Political Leaders since 1870*, ed. D. Bell et al. (New York, 1990).

P. H. Hutton

Related entries: BIDAULT, GEORGES; BLUM, LEON; CONSTITUTION OF THE FIFTH REPUBLIC; CONSTITUTION OF THE FOURTH REPUBLIC; CONSTITUTIONAL COUNCIL; COTY, RENE; DE GAULLE, CHARLES; MOLLET, GUY; POLITICAL TRENDS; SOCIALIST PARTY (SFIO).

AUROUX LAWS, a series of four labor laws named after the minister of labor, Jean Auroux, which were implemented by the socialist government in 1982 as part of its program of *autogestion*. Conceived as early as 1970 in the main principles of the CFDT (*Confédération française démocratique du travail*) Charter and advocated in the 1975 Sudreau report, the Auroux laws increased working-class citizenship by extending freedom of speech over working conditions in the workplace; expanded the rights of unions to organize, proselytize, collect dues, and represent workers in an enterprise; extended collective bargaining through required annual negotiations at both individual firm and industry levels; and established procedures for workers to monitor health and safety conditions in the workplace. Although the *patronat* opposed the laws because they granted unions excessive powers to represent workers, extended democratic control over private property, and imposed national standards for collective bargaining in place of local negotiations, they quickly concluded that the laws could be used to provide continuity and stability in the workplace, with only minimal increase in union or worker control. Union opposition to the laws was not as great: The *Confédération générale du travail* (CGT) and the CFDT thought the laws did not go far enough in extending worker control, while the *Force ouvrière* (FO) opposed them for implementing *autogestion* and reinforcing the power of the state. The net effect of the laws was not the implementation of *autogestion* in industrial relations, but rather the modernization of those relations, much as Jean Auroux himself had argued in his 1981 report.

J. Auroux, *Les Droits des travailleurs, rapport au Président de la République et au Premier ministre* (Paris, 1981); B. H. Moss, "After the Auroux Laws: Employees, Industrial Relations and the Right in France," *West European Politics* 1 (1988); P. Ortscheidt, *L'Entreprise face au nouveau droit de travail* (Paris, 1985); W. R. Smith,

"Towards *Autogestion* in Socialist France: The Impact of Industrial Relations Reform," *West European Politics* 1 (1987).

T. R. Christofferson

Related entry: AUTOGESTION.

AUTOGESTION, democratic control of organizations at the local level, first appeared in French dictionaries in 1960, was used to describe worker management of factories in Yugoslavia and Algeria, and became widely known in May 1968 when anarchist students established action committees and other means of local democratic decision making to replace bureaucratic statist structures. To the anarchists, the triumph of *autogestion* meant the end of political parties and the state, the abolition of work, the elimination of productivist values, and the restoration of the *carnavalesque* spirit. These utopian ideals derived from Pierre-Joseph Proudhon, the young Marx, Michael Bakunin, the Paris Commune, and the Soviet workers' councils. They all had in common the rejection of communist authoritarianism and capitalism.

During and after 1968, *autogestion* influenced virtually every group on the political left. Edmond Maire, the head of the *Confédération française démocratique du travail* (CFDT), came out in favor of *autogestion* in 1968, along with Michel Rocard, the head of the Unified Socialist Party (PSU). The CFDT's concept of *autogestion* emphasized workers' control and management of the factory within the context of a socialist society in which democratic planning prevailed at all levels. In contrast, Rocard's form of *autogestion* was strongly anticommunist and tended toward libertarianism, emphasizing self-development, cultural diversity, regional autonomy, and other "second left" themes. These were reiterated in the mid–1970s by Pierre Rosanvallon and Jacques Julliard, who believed that *autogestion* was primarily an open-ended process of pragmatic experimentation within civil society.

In the Socialist party, *autogestion* did not make inroads until after the Epinay Congress of 1971. The CERES faction (Center of Socialist Study and Research) of the party, led by Jean-Pierre Chevènement, was the first to adopt it, emphasizing the role of class struggle and the need to break with the capitalist system, while arguing that the party and the state must play roles equal to the local level in forging *autogestion*. Chevènement rejected totally the Rocardian, *gauche américaine* approach. In 1974, however, Rocard and Edmond Maire joined the Socialist party (PS), and in 1975 the party adopted "Fifteen Theses on Autogestion," which combined ideas from all camps. In 1977, the Communist party adopted *autogestion*, emphasizing the primary role of the party in the development of working-class democracy.

By 1981, when the left came to power, *autogestion* was a prominent but ill-defined part of its program. Such leftist reforms as decentralization of government, the Auroux laws regarding the workplace, and the democratization of the Plan all tended toward *autogestion*, but fell far short of the objective of total democracy as the foundation of a socialist society. In the 1986 electoral campaign, *autogestion* was hardly mentioned by the Socialist party. Only a handful of far-left groups kept the concept alive.

B. Brown, *Socialism of a Different Kind* (Westport, Conn., 1982); M. Charzat, J.-P. Chevènement, G. Toutain, *Le Ceres, un combat pour le socialisme* (Paris, 1975); H. Hamon, P. Rotman, *La Deuxième Gauche. Histoire intellectuelle du CFDT* (Paris, 1984); P. Rosanvallon, *L'Age de l'autogestion* (Paris, 1976).

T. R. Christofferson

Related entries: AUROUX LAWS; CHEVENEMENT, JEAN-PIERRE; COHN-BENDIT, DANIEL; *CONFEDERATION FRANCAISE DEMOCRATIQUE DU TRAVAIL*; DECENTRALIZATION; FRENCH COMMUNIST PARTY; MAIRE, EDMOND; PLAN; ROCARD, MICHEL; SOCIALIST PARTY (PS); UNIFIED SOCIALIST PARTY.

B

BADINTER, ROBERT (1928–   ), lawyer, minister of justice, president of the Constitutional Council. The son of an immigrant Jewish furrier, Badinter's adolescence was spent fleeing from town to town, escaping the fate of his father, who never returned from deportation. After a brilliant university career, which included a Masters degree at Columbia in American civil law, and later the *agrégation de droit* from the Sorbonne, Badinter became a barrister at the Paris Court of Appeal in 1951. Although specializing in commercial dossiers (his legal practice is one of the most successful in Paris), Badinter eventually emerged as one of the most brilliant criminal defense lawyers in France. At the same time, he was a dedicated teacher, holding chairs at the Universities of Dijon, Besançon, Amiens, and Paris. His second marriage, to Elisabeth Bleustein-Blanchet in 1966, consolidated his position as a man of wealth and social influence.

He is best known to the public for his passionate campaign against the death penalty. In 1972 he failed to save the life of Roger Bontemps, guillotined as the accomplice of murderer Claude Buffet. But in 1977 his pleas in favor of Patrick Henry overwhelmed the courthouse in Troyes and marked a turning point in French legal history. Henry was sentenced to life imprisonment for murder, and from that date, all those sentenced to death in France chose Badinter as their appeal lawyer. None was guillotined.

He entered politics via François Mitterrand's *Convention des institutions républicaines* and joined the Socialist party (PS) on its foundation in 1971. In 1976 he submitted to Mitterrand a "Charter of Freedoms," which was to become the basis for the socialists' legal program in the 1980s. Increasingly critical of the erosion of the judicial process that marked the final years of Valéry Giscard d'Estaing's presidency, Badinter was the obvious candidate for minister of justice under Mitterrand. His appointment, in June 1981, was greeted with vibrant enthusiasm by the legal profession. He embarked on his ministerial career intent on revolutionizing French judicial institutions. Within five years, while having achieved less than he wished, he had nevertheless laid the foundations for a new legal order.

His greatest achievement was the abolition of the death penalty (October 1981) and his successful resistance to repeated attempts by the right wing to reinstate it. He also abolished a series of repressive "exceptional" laws or institutions: discrimination against homosexuals, the *Cour de sûreté de l'Etat*, and the *loi anticasseurs*, which had made the organizers of demonstrations financially responsible for any damage caused by them. Certain special military tribunals were also abolished, as was the previous administration's law on "security and liberty," which had accelerated the process of sentencing at the same time as it gave the police greater powers of arrest and detention. Badinter was less successful in removing the powers of patronage and influence over young lawyers, which had traditionally been exercised by the *Conseil supérieur de la magistrature*, whose nine members are appointed by the president of the Republic. Nor was he able, largely for budgetary reasons, to achieve his own ambition of a drastic reduction in the prison population and a major improvement in prison conditions. But Badinter presided over a dramatic restructuring of France's legal institutions as well as modernizing and humanizing the essence of the laws. His spirit informs every page of the new Penal Code, which passed through parliament in 1989–90, but which he had set in motion as early as 1982.

Arguably, Badinter was the most "revolutionary" of all Mitterrand's ministers. The butt of vituperative personal attacks from the right, often tinged with anti-Semitism, he was undoubtedly the most controversial minister. As the inevitability of *cohabitation* approached, Mitterrand was prescient enough in February 1986 to appoint Badinter president of the Constitutional Council, where he has overseen the legality of France's democratic process and initiated major reforms in the procedures governing the Council's activities.

R. Badinter, *L'Exécution* (Paris 1973), *Liberté, libertés* (Paris, 1973); R. Badinter, E. Badinter, *Condorcet, un intellectuel en politique* (Paris, 1988).

J. Howorth

Related entries: COHABITATION; CONSTITUTIONAL COUNCIL; MITTERRAND, FRANCOIS; SOCIALIST PARTY (PS).

BALLADUR, EDOUARD (1929–), lawyer, adviser to government, and one of a new breed of businessmen-turned-politician, who, as minister of the economy, of finance and privatization, masterminded the privatization program implemented under the Chirac government (1986–88). Balladur was a student of law first at the *Institut des sciences politiques* in Paris, then at the prestigious *Ecole nationale d'administration* (1952–57). On graduating, he joined the *Conseil d'Etat* as a junior official, a position he held until 1962, when he became adviser to the director of French radio and television, *Office de radio-télévision française* (ORTF). Five years later Balladur was invited to join the ORTF board of directors.

Balladur's ten-year association with Georges Pompidou began in 1964. From 1966 to 1968, he was officially attached to Prime Minister Pompidou's staff as economic adviser. When Pompidou was replaced by Maurice Couve de Murville, Balladur became chairman of the *Société française pour la construction et l'exploitation du tunnel routier sous le Mont-Blanc* (1968–81). Having served as assistant secretary-general of Pompidou's Elysée staff since 1969, he became, for a brief period in 1974, secretary-general. Following the death of Pompidou in 1974, Balladur then exchanged the world of political administration for that of business, becoming chairman first of the *Générale de services informatiques* in 1974, then of the *Compagnie européenne d'accumulateurs* in 1980, both subsidiaries of the French giant *Compagnie générale d'électricité.*

Balladur did not formally enter politics until March 16, 1986, when he was elected deputy from Paris on the Gaullist RPR (*Rassemblement pour la République*) ticket. His apprenticeship in politics could not have been shorter: Four days later he joined the cabinet of the newly appointed Gaullist Prime Minister Jacques Chirac as minister of state in charge of the economy, finance and privatization. The privatization bill became law on August 6, 1986, despite President François Mitterrand's opposition, and a For Sale notice was attached to the state's share of sixty-five of France's top companies, with an overall estimated value of 275 billion francs.

As finance minister, Balladur went a long way toward achieving his avowed objective, the creation of a national *actionnariat populaire*. When, in March 1988, only sixteen months after the first sell-off, he presented to the Council of Ministers the results of that part of the privatization program that had been effected, he was able to describe a nation where popular share ownership was growing. By 1988, one in eight French citizens was a shareholder. Balladur's greatest mistake—which he has since recognized—was to appoint personally the members of the "hard core" of investors, designed to give an element of stability to newly privatized firms following their change of status.

As Chirac's closest adviser, Balladur had been tapped to become prime minister had Chirac succeeded in his May 1988 bid for the presidency. Today, Balladur is a deputy in the National Assembly.

E. Balladur, *Je crois en l'homme plus qu'en l'Etat* (Paris, 1987), *Passion et longueur de temps* (Paris, 1989); A. Hamdouch, *L'Etat d'influence* (Paris, 1989); A. Routier, *La République des loups* (Paris, 1989).

M. Maclean

Related entries: CHIRAC, JACQUES; *COHABITATION*; GAULLIST PARTY; POMPIDOU, GEORGES; PRIVATIZATION.

BARBIE, KLAUS (1913–), SS officer, sentenced in 1987 for war crimes. Recruited by the Nazi secret police (the Gestapo) in 1935, he remained a midlevel figure in the state police till 1942 when he was assigned to Lyon. In this city he was in charge of antiguerilla warfare and intelligence gathering. At the Montluc prison, he became known for his direct involvement in torture. Some fifteen thousand persons were imprisoned at the Montluc prison; up to nine hundred among them were shot to death and many more were tortured. Specifically, Barbie was charged with having tortured and killed Jean Moulin, a leader in the Resistance movement. Along with the killing of Resistance figures, he ordered the deportation of Jews, including children, to the Auschwitz death camp. In January 1945 he left Lyon for a new assignment in the Ruhr area of Germany.

After Germany's unconditional surrender, Barbie's name was on the Allied list of wanted war criminals. Twice arrested, he twice escaped. In April 1947 he was introduced to the American intelligence services; in May the U.S. Army Counter Intelligence Corps, CIC, hired him. At that time according to a CIC officer, Barbie was characterized as "strongly anticommunist and a Nazi idealist." Barbie's American handlers did not ignore the fact that he was the so-called Butcher of Lyon, but they considered he knew too much about U.S. intelligence operations to be delivered to the French authorities, who demanded his extradition. Early in 1951 the CIC spirited him away to South America. Via Genoa, and under the new identity of Herr Altmann, he left aboard an Italian vessel bound for Buenos Aires. Barbie and his family settled in La Paz, and he became a naturalized Bolivian in 1957.

He remained in South America for thirty-two years as a businessman. Identified in 1971, he was finally extradited in 1983, and a trial was held in the spring of 1987 in Lyon. At the trial seven hundred journalists gathered to cover both a story and a scandal that many thought would deeply divide France. The seventy-four-year-old man, who claimed to be innocent, was defended by the well-known lawyer Jacques Verges. Found guilty, he was sentenced in July 1987 to a life term in prison. Throughout the trial the French press carried stories on the proceedings as the nation began to confront a painful dimension of its wartime history.

H. Footit, J. Simmonds, *France 1943–1945* (New York, 1988); C. Simpson, *Blowback: America's Recruitment of Nazis and Its Effects on the Cold War* (New York, 1988).

J.-R. Chotard

Related entry: UNITED STATES, RELATIONS WITH.

BARRAULT, JEAN-LOUIS (1910–), actor, director, writer, and theater manager, who, along with his actress-wife Madeleine Renaud, brought French theatrical arts to international acclaim with a concept of "total theater." Initiated into experimental theater at the *Atelier* in 1931, Barrault began his career as a director with an adaptation of William Faulkner's novel *As I Lay Dying* in 1935, when he also made his debut as a film star in *Les Beaux Jours*. By 1940 he became a member of the prestigious state-sponsored *Comédie française*, hoping to reform this company's repertory and style. After introducing works by Paul Claudel and attempting new interpretations of classic plays, he left this tradition-bound company in 1945 with Renaud, one of its leading members.

During the next decade Barrault staged stunning performances with a talented troupe at the Marigny theater. Modern and classical plays were brought to francophile audiences throughout the world, with yearly tours providing much-needed prestige to postwar France. In 1958 Barrault was rewarded with a reappointment to the *Comédie française* as codirector, first at the *Théâtre du Palais Royal*, and finally for the next decade as director of the left-bank *Théâtre national de l'Odéon*, where he electrified the repertory with daring mixtures of works by new authors, including Eugène Ionesco, Marguerite Duras, and Claudel, six of whose literary plays he helped to revise in a close collaboration with the master.

Barrault's film successes brought him popular support outside Paris, particularly in his role as mine in Marcel Carne's *Les Enfants du paradis*, which dated from 1945 but which did not receive the critical attention it deserved until the next decade. But just as Barrault was perfecting the techniques of experimental French theater at home and abroad, he became embroiled in the student upheaval of 1968 by allowing the demonstrators to use the Odéon theater as the center of their protests. Dismissed by an indignant André Malraux, the minister of culture, Barrault suddenly emerged a hero of the left, flaunting his vision of a revolutionary theater in defiance of the government. Plays such as *Rabelais*, critical of the establishment inspired by Alfred Jarry, Antonin Artaud, and Voltaire, were presented at unconventional sites in the 1970s including a wrestling hall, the Orsay railroad station, and in 1981 at a former skating rink near the Champs-Elysées.

A power in the French cultural scene of the Fourth and Fifth Republics, made into a popular figure by television and film, in regional theater, and at innumerable international festivals, Barrault can be compared to his contemporary, the late Laurence Olivier, in England but to no other French theatrical figure in this period. His ideas and experiences are preserved in his autobiographies and interviews with scholars and journalists, which remain invaluable sources for French social and cultural history since the war.

J.-L. Barrault, *Souvenirs pour demain* (Paris, 1972) [trans. as *The Memoirs of Jean-Louis Barrault* (New York, 1974)]; *Cahiers Renaud-Barrault* (1953–); R. C. Lamont, "Entretien avec Jean-Louis Barrault," *French Review* 45, no. 1 (October 1971).

M. Siegel

Related entries: CULTURAL POLICY; MALRAUX, ANDRE; STUDENT REVOLTS.

BARRE, RAYMOND (1924–), statesman and former prime minister. The early years of his life were spent on the island of Réunion where he was born on April 12, 1924 at Saint-Denis. In 1946 he came to mainland France to study at the *Institut d'études politiques* in Paris, having shown himself to be an extremely able and intelligent pupil while at the *Lycée Leconte-de-Lisle* in Saint-Denis. Awarded the *agrégation* (law and political economy) and having completed his doctoral thesis, he took up a post at the University of Caen (1950), only to leave immediately to teach for three years at the *Institut des hautes études* at Tunis. In 1954 he returned to Caen where he remained as a professor until 1959; the previous year, 1958, he had also accepted the post of director of research in economic affairs at the *Fondation nationale des sciences politiques* in Paris. It was during this period that Barre wrote his celebrated textbook (subsequently updated) on political economy (*Economie politique* vols. 1 and 2, 1955), which was to become a standard work of reference in this field. In 1959 Raymond Barre was offered his first opportunity to enter politics, when invited by Jean-Marcel Jeanneney, minister for industry and commerce, to become the director of his ministerial cabinet. However, in 1962 he returned to his preferred domain of education, becoming professor at the *Institut d'études politiques* at Paris.

From 1967, however, a new stage began in Raymond Barre's political career when he was invited by Charles de Gaulle to take up the post of French vice-president responsible for economic affairs at the European Economic Community (EEC) Commission in Brussels. He remained there until 1973, when he returned to Paris and reverted once more to his favored activity of lecturing. By now, though, in view of his wide experience and reputation for competence, he was increasingly solicited to participate in government commissions or undertake special studies. Such was the case, for example, with the Barre report published in 1976 dealing with new forms of housing subsidy (*Rapport de la commission d'étude d'une réforme du logement*, La Documentation française, 1976).

In January 1976 Barre was appointed to his first ministerial post, becoming minister for foreign trade and commerce, following a reshuffle of the Chirac government. Then, in August of the same year, following Jacques Chirac's resignation, he was asked by Valéry Giscard d'Estaing to become prime minister, also taking over the post of economic and finance minister. Unlike his predecessor, Barre worked closely with the president, although his government faced opposition from Chirac and the *Rassemblement pour la République* (RPR). During his five years as prime minister, one of the main tasks facing Barre was the need to improve the country's economic performance, notably in the wake of the 1973 oil crisis. He became notorious for the *Plan Barre*, a package of measures designed to restore France's economic health, but adjudged by many as too austere. This was claimed to be a major factor leading to Barre's reputation as one of France's most unpopular modern prime ministers. During this period he was also elected to the National Assembly in the general elections of 1978, becoming *député* in the department of Rhône. He was subsequently reelected in this constituency in the general elections of 1981, 1986, and 1988.

With the defeat of Giscard by François Mitterrand in the 1981 presidential elections, Raymond Barre resigned as prime minister and returned to academic life. In the same year he was author of a book (*Une Politique pour l'avenir*) reflecting on his experience during his years as head of the government and outlining the challenges still facing the French economy. He also launched a monthly newsletter (*Faits et arguments*), setting out his views on a series of key issues influencing French society. During the early 1980s he withdrew from the forefront of French politics. However, after 1982, with the socialist government increasingly forced to introduce a range of austerity measures in an effort to redress the country's ailing economy (adopting in effect the same policies that Barre had advocated in the late 1970s), he experienced a resurgence of public opinion in his favor. Barre had always refused to align himself with any of the major French political parties, preferring an independent stance, although agreeing to be affiliated with the *Union pour la démocratie française* (UDF) parliamentary group. During the 1980s an unofficial grouping of "Barrist" supporters developed, largely among "centrist" politicians. The ideas that he defended were reflected in a book published in 1984, *Réflexions pour demain*.

Prior to the 1986 general elections Barre strongly opposed the idea of *coha-*

bitation between a socialist president (Mitterrand) and a right-wing government. He argued that such a situation was in direct contradiction with the spirit of the French constitution, which envisaged a partnership at the head of the state between the president and prime minister. However, when this enforced coexistence arose, despite his continued opposition to the principle, he remained loyal to the Chirac government. During the two years of *cohabitation* he appeared as an increasingly strong potential challenger to Mitterrand in the forthcoming presidential contest. He also published two further books outlining his views (*Au tournant du siècle* and *Questions de confiance*). Yet, in the first round of the elections (April 1988) he was placed a distant third behind Mitterrand and Chirac. One of the factors advanced to explain this defeat was Barre's reluctance to be tied to a major political formation (in this case the UDF) and therefore benefit from its networks and resources. Following the elections he once again withdrew from the center stage of French politics, although nevertheless launching a *Convention libérale, européenne et sociale* (CLES) as a forum for reflection and debate among centrist politicians.

Throughout his career Barre has enjoyed a reputation as one of France's leading economists. He is also renowned for his integrity and loyalty and for his respect for the country's institutions. As a politician he is known for his liberal approach to the running of the economy, for his natural conservatism, and for his strong support for European integration. He is one of only a few academics who has demonstrated his ability not only to formulate but also to implement policies. By his opponents he is seen to remain too detached from his electorate, too inflexible in his attitudes, and too professorial in his approach. He is also reproached for his independent stance, although for Barre, his ability to express freely his ideas, without party constraints, represents a considerable strength.

H. Amouroux, *Monsieur Barre* (Paris, 1986); R. Barre, *Au tournant du siècle* (Paris, 1987), *Questions de confiance* (Paris, 1988), *Réflexions pour demain* (Paris, 1984); A. Duhamel, *Le V président* (Paris, 1987).

J. N. Tuppen

Related entries: CHIRAC, JACQUES; ELECTIONS; GISCARD D'ESTAING, VALERY; POLITICAL TRENDS; UNION FOR FRENCH DEMOCRACY.

BARTHES, ROLAND (1915–1980), structuralist, semiologist, and a master of French prose. He is best known, perhaps, as a literary critic; but few have enjoyed the fame and notoriety experienced in the late 1960s and 1970s by Barthes, whose somewhat idiosyncratic works, characterized by their penetrating analyses of French culture, have been widely read, translated, and have even joined best-seller lists. Embracing a systematic, scientific approach to language and to literature, Barthes is nevertheless equally concerned with the pleasure that may be gleaned from a text. He therefore favors literature that accords the reader an active role, where he can "write" as he reads, displacing in this way the author from the central position he has traditionally occupied. Indeed, like Michel Foucault, Barthes believed in the "death" of the author.

Barthes was born on November 12, 1915 in Cherbourg, although he spent the greater part of his childhood in the town of Bayonne in southwest France. Barthes's background was Protestant and middle-class; but the death of his father, a naval officer, in 1916, meant that life was never easy. At the age of nine, Barthes moved to Paris with his mother, who took work as a bookbinder. Here he attended the *Lycée Montaigne*, then the more prestigious *Lycée Louis-le-Grand*, where he hoped to prepare for the entrance exam to the *Ecole normale supérieure*. But this was not to be: Two months after the completion of his *baccalauréat* in philosophy in 1934, Barthes experienced his first attack of tuberculosis and was sent to Bedous in the Pyrenees to recuperate. Tuberculosis continued to interrupt his career for the greater part of his life, condemning Barthes to short-term professional appointments: He worked briefly as a teacher in Biarritz in 1939, later as a *pion* at *Lycées Voltaire* and *Carnot*, later still in publishing. It was not until 1962 that Barthes obtained secure employment as a teacher at the *Ecole pratique des hautes études*. But the monastic way of life of the sanatorium, which he had come to know—and which he experienced for the entirety of World War II—gave him the opportunity to read a great deal. Anatole France, Marcel Proust, André Gide, Paul Valéry, and the novels of the interwar years were the raw materials for his subsequent writings.

Barthes's earliest articles, published in *Combat* in 1947, were primarily inspired by his reading of *L'Etranger* by Albert Camus, whose "*écriture blanche*" seemed to him to challenge the presumptions of meaning and order characteristic of traditional literature; he called it "zero-degree writing." All of his subsequent works were commissioned: The articles on Camus grew into *Le Degré zéro de l'écriture* (1953); *Mythologies* (1957) offered an irreverent critique of mass culture; *Critique et vérité* (1966), which propelled Barthes to fame, proffered a structuralist science of literature and led in 1970 to *S/Z*, his most extensive literary analysis. But Barthes's theories and formulas, no sooner constructed, were purposefully undermined by his own self-mockery: *Roland Barthes par Roland Barthes* (1975) set out precisely to demystify his previous projects.

The pinnacle of Barthes's career came with his appointment, on the recommendation of Michel Foucault, to a chair of literary semiology at the illustrious Collège de France in 1976. Yet, it was typical of Roland Barthes, and his modesty, that he should speak in his inaugural address not of finding but of seeking, even of forgetting and unlearning, and that he should describe wisdom not in conventional academic terms but rather as the ability to savor life to the full. In February 1980 Barthes was struck by a vehicle while crossing the road outside the Collège de France; he died four weeks later.

J. Culler, *Barthes* (London, 1983); S. Heath, *Vertige du déplacement* (Paris, 1974); A. Lavers, *Roland Barthes* (London, 1982).

M. Maclean

Related entries: CAMUS, ALBERT; FOUCAULT, MICHEL; INTELLECTUAL TRENDS; LEVI-STRAUSS, CLAUDE; STRUCTURALISM.

BARZACH, MICHELE (1943–), doctor, gynecologist, politician, and minister of health and the family under the Chirac government (1986–88), who led the French government's attack on the killer disease AIDS (Acquired Immune Deficiency Syndrome). Born in Casablanca of French parents, Barzach moved to France to study medicine at the *Faculté de médecine de Paris*, and in 1970 she began practising in Paris as a fully qualified gynecologist. It was not until the 1980s, however, that she entered politics. In 1983 she was elected assistant mayor for social affairs in the fifteenth *arrondissement*; one year later, she became the Gaullist party's national representative for social affairs. When Jacques Chirac was appointed prime minister, following the victory of the French right-wing parties in the legislative elections of March 1986, Barzach joined the Ministry of Social Affairs as minister of health and of the family. The two years she spent there might have been unmarked were it not for the fact that the beginning of her tenure in office coincided with an appeal to the nation launched by biologist Luc Montagnier of the *Institut Pasteur*, who urged the expeditious construction of a foundation for AIDS research. The war against AIDS has been waged unseen in France since the earliest cases were announced there in 1982, in spite of the country's record as the European nation with the highest number of registered AIDS patients. Barzach took up the gauntlet and was responsible for the promotion of the disease to a *grande cause nationale* in 1987, for the creation of a foundation for research into the disease, and for the government's first anti-AIDS campaign (which brought her into conflict with National Front leader Jean-Marie Le Pen). Criticizing both the structure and the evolution of the RPR, in December 1990 Barzach announced her resignation from the Gaullist party and from her position as a deputy in the National Assembly. However, it will be for her part in the ongoing struggle against AIDS, for which she earned the respect and support of President Mitterrand, that Barzach will be remembered.

M. Maclean, "The AIDS Crisis," in *Contemporary France* 2, ed. J. Howorth and G. Ross (London, 1988); M. Szafran, *Chirac ou les passions du pouvoir* (Paris, 1986).

M. Maclean

Related entries: CHIRAC, JACQUES; *COHABITATION*; GAULLIST PARTY.

BASQUE QUESTION, at the heart of which lie efforts of Basque nationalists in France to preserve their ancient language and customs against the encroachments of a more powerful French civilization. It also involves their attempts to wrest from Paris some measure of local home rule for the historic Basque provinces of Labourde, Basse-Navarre, and Soule, which were combined during the French Revolution into the large southwestern department of Basse-Pyrénées. Unlike Spain, however, where the Basque question has leavened national politics since the end of the eighteenth century, the issue is of recent vintage in France and has not played a prominent role in French political life. Nor has the Basque question struck a responsive chord among more than a few inhabitants of the French Basque country or been able to mobilize large numbers of voters there behind nationalist candidates for public office.

The French government has accordingly paid scant attention to the Basque question, deeming it politically unimportant and the Basque region itself as remote, insignificant, and backward. This attitude is easy enough to understand. Compared even to the Basque country in Spain, the Basque region in France is small and thinly populated. The French region is only one-sixth as large as the Basque area in Spain and numbers approximately 130,000 inhabitants, compared to 850,000 Spanish Basques. Moreover, unlike the Spanish Basques who inhabit one of the most heavily industrialized, prosperous, and urbanized regions in the entire country, the French Basques live in an overwhelmingly rural and agrarian department that contributes little to the global French economy. The gross domestic product of France's isolated and mountainous Basque region is in fact but one-eighth that of its counterpart in Spain. A dynamic economy vitally important to the material well-being of France at large has therefore not developed in the Basse-Pyrénées that might have propelled the Basque question into an issue of national political significance.

Historically, the Basque question was first raised during the French Revolution when deputies from the the three Basque provinces sought unsuccessfully to defend their traditional laws (*fors*), devout Catholic beliefs, village commons, and single-heir inheritance system against triumphant Jacobin centralization. The defeat of Basque particularism during the Revolution was so thorough and far-reaching that powerful secular forces were set in motion that eroded the strength of Basque culture and language usage until well into the twentieth century. Not until the foundation in 1934 of the small monthly periodical *Aintzina* did a public forum exist for the discussion of the Basque question. More conservative and Catholic than nationalist in orientation, *Aintzina* ceased publication in 1937. Encouraged, however, by the avowed interest of Vichy in the administrative reorganization of France on a regional basis, the editors of *Aintzina* resumed its publication in 1942–43. At the same time young Basque nationalists in Paris aligned themselves with Nazi occupation officials who expressed sympathy for federalism and ethnic autonomy, though it seems the chief German interest was in a weak or dismembered France. The Basque question consequently became tainted with collaboration and at war's end was generally discredited.

A nationalist movement based on the Basque question did not reappear until 1960, with the foundation of the periodical *Enbata* on the conservative remnants of *Aintzina*. Two years later a similarly named Basque political party was organized, and one of its leaders, Michel Labéguerie, was elected to parliament. This was a fluke, however, owing to the absence of a viable Gaullist candidate and the massive electoral support of local Catholics. Moreover, Labéguerie eschewed Basque nationalist themes in his campaign, soon quit *Enbata*, and joined the *Centre démocrate*. The dissolution of *Enbata* by Paris on January 30, 1974 in the wake of the assassination of Spanish prime minister Carrero Blanco by Basque terrorists several weeks earlier dealt the Basque nationalist movement in France a crippling blow. Its candidates in recent parliamentary elections have not been able to capture even 5 percent of the votes cast in a single constituency.

The failure of Basque nationalism on the terrain of electoral politics has confined the Basque question today almost exclusively to the plane of cultural action. Most local Basque enthusiasts thus focus their attention on the promotion of Basque language instruction or on the formation of folklore groups devoted to the preservation of Basque dance, theater, and song.

J. E. Jacob, "The Basques of France," *Political Anthropology* 1 (1975); P. Letamendia, *Nationalismes au pays basque* (Bordeaux, Fr., 1987).

J. E. Reece

Related entry: MINORITIES, PROBLEMS OF.

BAUDIS, DOMINIQUE (1947–), mayor of Toulouse and former media journalist. Baudis graduated from the *Institut d'études politiques* in Paris in 1968. He first gained public notoriety as a television anchorman (1976–80). His direct involvement with French political life dates back to 1983 when he succeeded his father, Pierre Baudis, as mayor of Toulouse (France's fourth largest city). Taking over such a political inheritance was not easy in a city that had been traditionally socialist before the election of his father to city hall. Consequently, he adopted his father's above-politics approach, claiming that the only card he carried was that of a journalist.

From 1983 to 1986 Baudis held the position of regional counsel for the Midi-Pyrénées region, the area surrounding Toulouse. In 1986 he became president of the regional council. In addition to those two important posts, Baudis was a member of the European Parliament from 1984 to 1988 and has been general counsel of the Haute-Garonne department since 1985. In 1986 he successfully ran for a seat in the National Assembly. However, since he already held four different posts, he relinquished his seat.

In 1989, prior to the European Parliament elections, Baudis and other reform-minded conservatives asked former French president Valéry Giscard d'Estaing to renounce his candidacy as the head of the conservative *Union pour la démocratie française/Rassemblement pour la République* (UDF-RPR) slate. Baudis chose to join the *rénovateurs*, a group of twelve conservative politicians whose ambition was to improve the unification of the right in order to oppose better the ruling socialists. Giscard nonetheless remained at the head of the UDF-RPR slate and scored an impressive victory in the European Parliament elections.

Experts regard Baudis as a master of the media and foresee an impressive future for him in national politics.

J.-F. Doumic, H. Lacharmoise, eds., *Le Guide du pouvoir* (Paris, 1989).

D. S. Thévenin

Related entries: GISCARD D'ESTAING, VALERY; NOIR, MICHEL; REGIONS.

BEAUVOIR, SIMONE DE (1908–1986), author and feminist, born in Paris into an upper-middle-class family. Given a conventional, conservative upbringing with an emphasis on Catholic morals, she lost her faith during adolescence.

From 1913 to 1925 she studied at the *Cours Désir* in Paris, then at several Catholic institutions until 1927 when she enrolled in the Sorbonne. Two years later she received the *licence* and the *agrégation*, where she placed second behind Jean-Paul Sartre, whom she had recently met at the *Ecole normale supérieure* where they were both preparing for these rigorous exams. The ''Castor'' (beaver), so nicknamed because of her assiduity, was to be Sartre's companion until his death in 1980.

Beginning in 1931 she took a series of teaching positions: at the *Lycée Montgrand* in Marseille; two years later at the *Lycée Jeanne d'Arc* in Rouen; in 1938 at the *Lycée Molière Passy*; and then at the *Lycée Camille-Sée* in Paris. She gave up teaching assignments in 1943 to devote herself exclusively to writing, with the publication of *L'Invitée* (1943, She came to stay), a novel based upon Sartre and his circle written between 1939 and 1941. She joined Sartre in 1945 in editing the monthly review, *Les Temps modernes*. Her *Pour une morale de l'ambiguité* (1947; *The Ethics of Ambiguity,* 1949) offers a humanistic, positive view that contrasts with Sartre's darker vision of the human condition. Her observations and notes of a four-month lecture tour of the United States in 1947 appear in *L'Amérique au jour le jour* (1948, America day by day).

The publication of *The Second Sex* in 1949 brought her world renown. This lengthy, extensively documented essay contends that society is responsible for women's secondary status: ''*On ne naît pas femme, on le devient*'' (One is not born a woman, rather one becomes a woman.) Discrimination is pervasive, traceable to the earliest periods of recorded history. Women's subjugation is due to social and cultural factors, reinforced by education. This pioneering work had a pervasive influence on women everywhere (it was translated into many languages). By her own admission, Beauvoir was not initially a militant in the feminist struggle. With the emergence of the French feminist movement of the 1970s she became actively engaged in feminist activities. Yet, even before this, for feminists—including Americans like Betty Friedan and Kate Millett—*The Second Sex* quickly became a bible. The book represented the work of a pioneering woman who had crossed many borders through her powerful ideas and with the courage and determination of her convictions. Her involvement and presence, including signing the ''Manifesto of the 343,'' a public declaration by 343 women who admitted to having had illegal abortions, contributed immensely to a new generation of French feminists. In 1974 she became president of the League for Women's Rights.

Beauvoir's considerable output includes novels, essays, memoirs, sociological studies, and travel accounts. She herself considered the Goncourt prizewinner, *Les Mandarins* (1954, The mandarins), to be her favorite novel. The work portrays the profound postwar confusion in the political views of the former *résistants*. Generally acknowledged as a *roman à clef*, *Les Mandarins* has been viewed as closer to political reality than are her memoirs. It details the political and intellectual activities of Sartre, Albert Camus, and others from the Liberation to the end of the 1940s and discusses their hopes and deceptions.

At Beauvoir's death the world press paid tribute to a remarkable woman who had been "wedded to her century." *Le Deuxième Sexe* (1949) was judged one of the most influential works of the twentieth century; she had a major impact upon the attitudes of contemporaries, who were nevertheless not necessarily aware of her existence. She was the last survivor of a great generation of French writers. Extensive details about her life are to be found in fictionalized depictions in her novels as well as in her autobiographical works: *Mémoires d'une jeune fille rangée* (1958, Memoirs of a dutiful daughter); *La Force de l'âge* (1960, The prime of life); *La Force des choses* (1963, The force of circumstances); *Une Mort très douce* (1964, A very easy death); and *Tout compte fait* (1972, All said and done).

M. Evans, *Simone de Beauvoir: A Feminist Mandarin* (London, 1985); E. Fallaize, *The Novels of Simone de Beauvoir* (London, 1988); J. Heath, *Simone de Beauvoir* (Hempstead, Eng., 1989); T. Moi, *Feminist Theory and Simone de Beauvoir* (Oxford, 1989).

M. C. Weitz

Related entries: EXISTENTIALISM; FEMINISM; LITERATURE; SARTRE, JEAN-PAUL; SOCIAL TRENDS; WOMEN, CONDITION OF.

BECKETT, SAMUEL (1906–1989), Irish-born playwright and novelist. Beckett was educated at Trinity College in Dublin (B.A. and M.A.) and then served as a *lecteur d'anglais* at the *École normale supérieure*. He briefly taught French at Trinity College before leaving academic life in 1932. After traveling and then settling for a time in London, he moved to France in 1937, where he remained. There, shortly before World War II, he was associated with the literary circle around James Joyce. His earliest writings very much resemble those of Joyce. Remaining in occupied France during the war, Beckett occasionally served with the Resistance, but, as with most details of his life, he was hesitant to speak of those years. During the years immediately following the war, Beckett made a decisive move in his literary career, that of adopting the French language. He wrote some of his most highly regarded fiction during the late 1940s and early 1950s: *Mercier et Camier, Molloy, Malone meurt*, and *L'Innommable*. Many critics have observed that Beckett's choice of French purged his literary language of its Joycean extravagance, paving the way for an increasingly spare, visceral style.

It was as a dramatist that Beckett first made his mark. *En attendant Godot* (1953, *Waiting for Godot*), Beckett's first and most famous play (as well as one of the most controversial and widely discussed plays of this century), debuted in January 1953. It was greeted with the kind of explosive and tumultuous response the French have reserved for only a few plays, such as Victor Hugo's *Hernani* (1830) or Alfred Jarry's *Ubu Roi* (1896). The play features few props, an almost completely bare stage, and two incessantly talkative tramps who while away the time *en attendant Godot*, whose identity remains a mystery. They encounter only three other human beings. Most of the play's "action" involves their diversions "while waiting." This play has been subjected to an avalanche of interpretations, running the gamut from Christian to existentialist to bleakly nihilistic to joyously slapstick. Beckett's next play, *Fin de partie* (1957, Endgame), solidified his reputation as a playwright, as did such subsequent plays as *Krapp's Last Tape* (1958), which, unlike Beckett's stories and novels, were written more often in English. Such later works of fiction as *Comment c'est* (1961, *How it is*) and *Imagination morte imaginez* (1965, Imagination dead imagine) showed him to have embarked upon a seemingly impossible quest to wring the most poignant human expression out of an increasingly stripped-down prose purged of the usual niceties of description and elaborated plot or character development. For his bold explorations in writing, Beckett received the Nobel Prize for Literature in 1969, for which honor the notoriously reclusive author expressed seeming annoyance and vexation.

He continued to publish dramatic works and short fiction regularly, and the pieces, such as the fictions collected in *Pour finir encore et autres foirades* (1976, *Fizzles*), have become radically brief, as if the writer wished to paint himself into an ever-smaller corner. The more this trend continued, the more the burgeoning industry of Beckett criticism proclaimed his genius, devoting numerous publications and conferences to his work, especially during 1986 in honor of his eightieth birthday. Beckett died in December of 1989.

D. Bair, *Samuel Beckett: A Biography* (New York, 1978); S. Beckett, *Choix de textes* (Paris, 1975), *Théâtre 1* (Paris, 1971); S.E. Gontarski, ed., *On Beckett: Essays and Criticism* (New York, 1986).

J. A. Winders

Related entries: INTELLECTUAL TRENDS; LITERATURE.

BEN BELLA, AHMED (1918–), a leader of the Algerian Revolution and first president of the Algerian Republic. Born of a poor Muslim family in the small town of Marnia, Ben Bella first encountered discrimination in secondary school in Tiemcen. Drafted in 1937, he fought in the Battle of France and, after a stint in Algeria as a soccer star, joined Free French troops in the Italian campaign in 1943–44. He finished his military service as a highly decorated sergeant.

After the war Ben Bella joined the nationalist *Mouvement du triomphe des libertés démocratiques* (MTLD) and took part in municipal administration. In a typical response to pro-independence views, hoodlums backed by local authorities forced the young nationalist politician into outlawry. In 1947 he joined with a small group of other young MTLD members to found the secret *Organisation spéciale* dedicated to armed struggle against the French. The group was dismantled by the French police by 1950, and Ben Bella was arrested only to escape in 1952, eventually making his way to Cairo.

In late 1954, Ben Bella was one of the nine ''historic leaders'' who founded the National Liberation Front (FLN), which began the insurrection against France on November 1. While the war raged in Algeria, Ben Bella served as FLN representative in Cairo negotiating with Gamal Nasser's government for military supplies and diplomatic support. In 1956 the Moroccan plane carrying Ben Bella and another FLN diplomat to Tunis was skyjacked by its French flight crew to Algeria, and Ben Bella was imprisoned in France. After the 1962 Evian accords granting Algerian independence, Ben Bella, with the support of Houari Boumedienne and forces of the Algerian National Liberation Army, became the first president of the Algerian Republic.

Ben Bella pushed policies of Arabization, nonalignment, and workers' control. He was deposed in 1965 in a military coup led by Boumedienne, and held in secret until his release in 1980. From exile, Ben Bella has been trying to organize an opposition movement based on Islamic revivalist principles.

B. Droz, E. Lever, *Histoire de la guerre d'Algérie* (Paris, 1984); R. Merle, *Ahmed Ben Bella* (New York, 1967).

A. Douglas

Related entries: ALGERIA, RELATIONS WITH; DECOLONIZATION; THIRD WORLD, RELATIONS WITH.

BEREGOVOY, PIERRE (1925–), socialist politician, minister of social affairs, and minister of finance and economy under Mitterrand. He was born December 23, 1925 in Déville-les-Rouen (Seine-Maritime). Beginning work at sixteen as a machine operator, Bérégovoy later worked as a railroad man and then for many years as an employee of *Gaz de France*. Active at a young age in socialist youth organizations, he left the Socialist party (SFIO) for the *Parti socialiste autonome* (PSA) in 1958 and remained active in its successor group, the *Parti socialiste unifié* (PSU), until 1967. Rejoining the renewed Socialist party (PS) in 1969, he was named to its directing committee and executive bureau in the same year.

Bérégovoy became closely associated in 1971 with François Mitterrand, the new PS first secretary. He was a PS national secretary from 1973 to 1975, an unsuccessful National Assembly candidate in 1978, and was named secretary-general of the Elysée when Mitterrand became president in 1981. In 1982 he became minister for social affairs. He was elected mayor of Nevers in 1983.

As a minister, Bérégovoy introduced small fees for hospital expenses to cut the social security deficit, but he sided in March 1983 with those left-oriented Mitterrand advisers who wanted France to leave the European Monetary System. Once a decision to remain had been taken, he followed the president toward more moderate economic views. Appointed minister of finance and the economy in July 1984, he gained the confidence of the financial community and introduced a financial futures market. He also was influential in the decision to issue blocks of nonvoting stock in subsidiaries of nationalized industries in order to raise capital.

Bérégovoy was elected a National Assembly deputy from the Nièvre department in 1986, when the PS lost its parliamentary majority. In 1988 he was reelected when Mitterrand won a second term and dissolved the Assembly. He again became minister of finance and economy in the Rocard government formed in 1988, a position he retained in the government of Edith Cresson (1991–).

However, at the outset of the Cresson cabinet his portfolio was greatly expanded to include finance, trade, and industry in an effort to enhance French competitiveness as the government prepared for the economic integration of the Common Market at the beginning of 1993. One of the few leading French socialists to come from a working-class background, Bérégovoy was a prominent exponent of those Mitterrand followers who assumed a more moderate stance after experiencing the problems of power.

P. Bauchard, *La Guerre des deux roses* (Paris, 1986); J. W. Friend, *Seven Years in France* (Boulder, Colo., 1989); G. Ross, S. Hoffmann, S. Malzacher, eds., *The Mitterrand Experiment* (New York, 1987).

J. W. Friend

Related entries: FABIUS, LAURENT; MITTERRAND, FRANCOIS; SOCIALIST PARTY (PS).

BERGERON, ANDRE (1922–), from 1963 to 1989 was the general secretary of the nation's third largest union, *Force ouvrière* (FO). Born in Suarce (Territoire de Belfort) the son of a devout Protestant and prosocialist railroad employee, he attended school in Belfort where he was greatly influenced by a pacifist, socialist teacher. At fourteen, he left school, became an apprentice printer, joined the *Confédération générale du travail* (CGT), and participated in the 1936 strikes. During World War II he spent thirty months in a German labor camp before being liberated by the Soviets in 1945. After the war he was elected secretary of the Belfort *Syndicat du livre* and helped organize a local noncommunist section of the CGT. In December 1947, in the wake of the disastrous communist-led strikes of that year, he met with other noncommunist CGT leaders to form an independent CGT–*Force ouvrière*. Although he played an active role in the union, he remained relatively unknown until he was elected to the national *Bureau confédéral* in 1956, a position that he has held ever since.

André Bergeron is an anticommunist reformist, opposed to *dirigisme* and the involvement of unions in politics, in favor of collective bargaining and the economic improvement of the working class. He is the product of the Third Republic's primary school system: anti-clerical, pragmatic, nationalist, and republican-socialist in outlook, with no time for Marxist or *autogestionnaire* ideas. In 1968, when asked what he thought the future of French society looked like, he answered in typical fashion: "I have enough to do with society today."

Eschewing ideas and professions of faith, Bergeron has consistently adhered to a syndicalist, corporatist position. In the 1950s he played a major role in negotiating both the retirement and unemployment insurance plans for workers. In 1968 he condemned the revolutionary utopianism of the students and unions, outlining instead a detailed program of piecemeal reforms. When the *autogestionnaire* head of the chemical workers challenged him for control of the union at the 1968 congress, the members solidly backed Bergeron, as they did again in 1971 when the union went on record against *autogestion* and in support of liberal, pluralist democracy as the best political system. In 1969, for the first and last time, Bergeron counseled FO members on how to vote in an election, advocating a "no" vote on Charles de Gaulle's referendum because it would undermine union power and freedom.

During the 1970s Bergeron cooperated with rightist governments and expressed skepticism about the Union of the Left to the degree that Jean-Pierre Chevènement advocated expelling him from the Socialist party (PS). Bergeron and the FO thought that a contractual policy and international cooperation were necessary to solve the post–1973 economic crisis. With the 1981 socialist victory, Bergeron and the FO found themselves opposed to everything that the new goverment did: the inclusion of communists in it, the massive nationalization of industry, the rapid increase in the minimum wage, the decentralization laws, the Auroux laws, the Savary law, the *relance* of the economy, the plans for rigor, and so forth. As a result, the FO was the only major union to increase its membership in the 1980s, going from 700,000 to one million, and becoming one of the largest unions in France. From 1989 he has been president of the *Union nationale pour l'emploi dans l'industrie et le commerce* (UNEDIC).

A. Bergeron, *Ma Route et mes combats* (Paris, 1976), *1500 jours, 1980–1984* (Paris, 1984); A. Bergougnioux, *Force ouvrière* (Paris, 1982), "The Trade Union Strategy of the CGT-FO," in *The French Workers' Movement: Economic Crisis and Political Change*, ed. M. Kesselman (London, 1984); J.-L. Validire, *André Bergeron, une force ouvrière* (Paris, 1984).

T. R. Christofferson

Related entries: CONFEDERATION FRANCAISE DEMOCRATIQUE DU TRAVAIL; CONFEDERATION GENERALE DU TRAVAIL; FORCE OUVRIERE; KRASUCKI, HENRI; MAIRE, EDMOND; SEGUY, GEORGES; TRADE UNION MOVEMENT.

BICENTENNIAL CELEBRATION (1989), the extravaganza celebrating the French Revolution of 1789, which became an important symbol for François Mitterrand's new centrist Republic. The year-long festivities were not just a French event but part of a worldwide celebration. Besides having important political significance, the event also generated record revenues for the tourist industry in France in 1989, over $5 billion according to French government estimates.

The original celebration was announced by Mitterrand's socialist government in the early 1980s and was referred to as "Expo '89," an event that would combine a world's fair with the celebration of the Revolution of 1789. Seeing the tremendous symbolic value in such an event for the socialists, the Gaullist mayor of Paris, Jacques Chirac, placed obstacles before the Mitterrand government. On July 5, 1983, President Mitterrand announced that the $2 billion event would not take place as planned because of Chirac's opposition. The socialist president then decided to link his *grands projets* scheme (vast architectural monuments for the capital) to a bicentennial celebration. Consequently, the celebration in 1989 featured several shiny new monuments in Paris, such as the modern Opera at the Bastille, the spectacular pyramid at the Louvre, and the huge arch at La Défense.

The year-long celebration culminated on July 14, 1989, Bastille Day (French independence day). The responsibility for organizing the celebration was given to Jack Lang, minister of culture (1981–86 and 1988–), who in 1988 was given the title Minister of Culture, Communication, *Grands Travaux*, and the Bicentennial. A Bicentennial Commission was also established to assist with planning. The events comprising the bicentennial stressed the image of a united nation with an agreed-upon heritage and France's republicanism, an image that ignored the subversive nature of the Revolution. Mitterrand even told the press on Bastille Day of 1989 that Danton deserved to be in the Panthéon, but not Robespierre. He also told the press on the same day that King Louis XVI was a brave man and that he (Mitterrand) would not have voted for the execution of the king!

The Bastille Day celebration in 1989 included several unique features. First, Mitterrand had scheduled a summit of the seven leaders of the industrialized nations of the Western world during France's most patriotic holiday. This, of course, guaranteed that world attention would be focused on France and its celebration, not to mention its president. Second, Mitterrand invited representatives from the poorest nations to attend the summit, suggesting that the government was still committed to promoting "Third Worldism" after some setbacks in the early and mid–1980s. Third, an evening parade called the *Marseillaise* followed the traditional morning military parade down the Champs-Elysées. This evening *spectacle* featured six thousand participants from various cultures from around the world and the American opera star Jessye Norman who sang the French national anthem. This evening affair was produced by the French advertising whiz Jean-Paul Goude. The spectacular bicentennial celebration, especially the Bastille Day events, which were capped by a late-night fireworks display at the Etoile and Concorde, dazzled many.

Le Monde praised Mitterrand for the largest *fête* that the capital had seen in a long time. This newspaper also noted that, in terms of political stakes won and lost, Chirac was the loser because he had failed to take part in the memorable July 14 occasion. In essence, the celebration helped to reinforce the image of a centrist Republic as Mitterrand sought to strengthen his opening to the center, which had begun only a year earlier with the appointment of the right-wing socialist Michel Rocard as prime minister.

F. Chaslin, *Les Paris de François Mitterrand* (Paris, 1985); W. Northcutt, *Mitterrand: A Political Biography* (New York, 1992), "François Mitterrand and the Political Use of Symbols: The Construction of a Centrist Republic," *French Historical Studies* 17 (1991).

W. Northcutt

Related entries: CHIRAC, JACQUES; ELECTIONS; LANG, JACK; MITTERRAND, FRANCOIS; POLITICAL TRENDS; SOCIALIST PARTY (PS).

BIDAULT, GEORGES (1899–1983), active in Catholic-Democratic circles before the war, played a prominent role in the Resistance, and was an organizer and founder of the *Conseil national de la Résistance*, which grouped together the different political tendencies. Bidault succeeded Jean Moulin as its head after the latter arranged the rallying of the internal Resistance to General Charles de Gaulle. Bidault participated in the insurrection in Paris and was at the *Hôtel de ville* on August 25, 1944 in order to greet de Gaulle, whom he accompanied on the famous victory march down the Champs Elysées. This merited Bidault the position of minister of foreign affairs in the Provisional government, a position he was to hold for five years during the Fourth Republic, from 1944 to 1948, and again in 1953–54. He was also twice premier, from July to December 1946, and again from October 1949 to June 1950. He was one of the leaders of the *Mouvement republicain populaire (MRP)*, the only genuinely Christian-Democratic party France has ever had, which he helped to found after the war.

Bidault's stewardship of French foreign policy was full of initiatives, and he did much to determine the French position in international affairs during the early Cold War. He presided over a government including communist ministers, with whom he initially collaborated in a straightforward manner; this, plus his advocacy of a punitive peace with Germany, won him the hostility and suspicion of the Americans, who never held him in high regard. Nevertheless, when Moscow failed to support French aims in Germany at the Moscow conference of March-April 1947, Bidault declared France's loyalty to the western camp, to U.S. Secretary of State Marshall, and the communists were expelled from the French government immediately thereafter. With Ernest Bevin, Bidault coordinated the European response to the Marshall Plan, eventually convening a conference of sixteen recipient nations in Paris, which became the Organization for European Economic Cooperation. Bidault was also instrumental in seeing to it that the Soviet Union would play no role in the Marshall Plan, insisting on American terms of inspection of the European economies in late June 1947, which he knew the Russians could not accept.

Bidault became increasingly concerned with the alleged Soviet threat to Western Europe during 1947, initiating military talks with the Americans in the hope of contracting an alliance. These at first led nowhere, but Bidault softened French opposition to the reconstruction of Germany, which he recognized was the price of Marshall Plan assistance, and joined in Bevin's call for a military alliance to complete the structure of economic cooperation in January 1948. Marshall told the Europeans to take the initiative first themselves; Bevin and Bidault responded by negotiating the Brussels treaty with the Benelux countries, concluded in March 1948. In the meantime, panicked by the Czech coup, Bidault wrote to Marshall in the strongest possible terms, insisting that the United States join a military alliance of the West in the face of a Soviet block of enslaved nations taking shape in the East. The NATO talks were under way by the time Bidault left office in July 1948, and he should certainly be considered a founding figure in the alliance and a principal actor in the European effort to get the Americans permanently involved in the affairs of the old continent.

Bidault was also important in the effort to achieve European integration. It was during his period as premier in 1959 that Jean Monnet proposed the Coal and Steel Pool, which became known as the Schuman Plan, the ancestor of the European Economic Community. Bidault joined Schuman in championing the plan. It is sometimes said that Bidault's foreign policy was more nationalistic and Schuman's (from 1948 to 1953) more European, but both were leaders of the MRP, and it is difficult to distinguish between the actual policies they followed. Bidault succeeded Schuman as foreign affairs minister again in January 1953, but this time achieved little glory. He was a strident colonialist, sharing the conviction of many of the French that without the empire the nation was destined to suffer a fate of decadence and decline. He deposed the nationalist Sultan of Morocco, inflaming further the situation in French North Africa, and negotiated increasing American involvement in the war in Indochina. He also temporized under American pressure to achieve ratification of the European Defense Community (EDC), allowing the EDC treaty to become bound up with the Indochina conflict. Bidault did, however, force Washington to agree to the convening of the Geneva conference in 1954, and after the French defeat at Dien Bien Phu, he appears to have made a good-faith effort to negotiate French withdrawal, when it became clear that the Americans would not put their own forces into the conflict. But the Laniel government fell in June 1954 under the stain of Dien Bien Phu, and it fell to Pierre Mendès-France to negotiate peace in Indochina and bury the EDC.

Bidault had close ties to circles of French *colons* in Algeria and opposed any talk of withdrawal during that conflict. He eventually came into conflict with de Gaulle, supported the attempted putsch of the generals in Algeria, and was linked to the terrorism of the *Organisation de l'armée secrète* (OAS). As a consequence, his parliamentary immunity was lifted in 1962, and he fled into exile in Spain. De Gaulle amnestied him following the May 1968 events, and he returned to France.

A. Grosser, *La Quatrième République et sa politique extérieure* (Paris, 1961); R. Poidevin, *Robert Schuman, homme d'état* (Paris, 1987); G. Bidault, *Resistance: The Political Autobiography of Georges Bidault*, trans. M. Sinclair (New York, 1967).

I. M. Wall

Related entries: ALGERIA, RELATIONS WITH; CHRISTIAN DEMOCRATS; DEFENSE POLICY; FOREIGN POLICY; INDOCHINA, RELATIONS WITH; MARSHALL PLAN; MONNET, JEAN; SCHUMAN PLAN; UNITED STATES, RELATIONS WITH.

BLUM, LEON (1872–1950), jurist, man of letters, socialist leader, and prime minister. Of Alsatian-Jewish roots, Blum was born in Paris into a successful though modest trading family. After dabbling in literature and philosophy at the *Ecole normale supérieure*, he devoted himself to the study of law and in 1895 embarked on a successful career as *auditeur* at the *Conseil d'Etat*. At the same time, he commanded attention as a literary and theater critic.

Although he joined Jean Jaurès's *Parti socialiste français* in 1902, his political activity was minimal prior to 1914. It was the war that changed the dilettante and aesthete into a militant and politician. Blum was appointed *chef de cabinet* in his friend Marcel Sembat's Ministry of Public Works, but more important, the death of Jaurès and the impact of war and revolution devastated the old Socialist party and thrust him into a leading role. By 1919, it was Blum who, in an effort to revive the Jaurèsian flame and to keep at bay the Bolshevik sirens, was charged with drafting the party's program. At the Congress of Tours in 1920, it was he who made the crucial speech vindicating the democratic, republican traditions of French socialism (a speech that is still compulsory reading for the current generations of would-be French socialist activists). Despite the temporary victory of the pro-Bolshevik wing of the Socialist party (SFIO), which was to siphon off three-quarters of the party members to form the French Communist party (PCF), the intellectual and political rigor of Blum's speech at Tours transformed him into the natural leader of the rump of the SFIO.

Throughout the 1920s and early 1930s, Blum gave national and (above all) parliamentary leadership to the struggling party. His daily editorial in *Le Populaire* demonstrated the range of his interests, the subtlety of his analysis, and the measured, statesmanlike quality of his approach. But one urgent political problem required a solution. The "party of opposition," which Blum himself accepted as having a "revolutionary" objective, could no longer avoid facing up to the responsibilities of power. Blum's celebrated distinction between the "conquest" and the "exercise" of power (1924) hinged on the difference between an outright socialist electoral victory, which would be interpreted as a mandate for a revolutionary break with existing institutions, and, on the other hand, an electoral outcome in which the socialists would be the strongest party in a parliamentary majority including the radicals. This second scenario implied that the SFIO would assume governmental responsibility, but would eschew any revolutionary changes, contenting itself with the management of existing institutions—as far as possible in the interests of the working class.

When, in June 1936, Blum came to power as the first socialist prime minister of France, he was faced with the brimming-over impatience of the workers, suffused with a century and a half of revolutionary rhetoric, with the rock-solid hostility of the bourgeoisie, prepared to stop at nothing, including physical violence, to reverse the verdict of the ballot box, and with an international situation scarred by civil war in Spain and careering rapidly out of control. Not surprising, his attempt to exercise power according to the above formula was a failure. Although the mass strikes of June 1936 stampeded a panic-stricken bourgeoisie into accepting the major package of social reforms known as the Matignon Agreements (which consecrated official recognition of collective bargaining, paid vacations, the forty-hour work week, trade union rights, etc.), Blum found himself powerless to deal with the two most crucial issues confronting his government: the economy and foreign affairs.

Faced with a massive flight abroad of French capital, strenuous opposition to his economic policies from the monied classes, and a hostile Senate, Blum resigned after only thirteen months in office. His second premiership (March-

April 1938) was even shorter and less successful. In foreign affairs, while totally lucid about the seriousness of European developments, and while launching a major rearmament bid, Blum's vacillation over support for the Spanish republicans alienated both the vituperative Catholic right and the increasingly disillusioned communist and socialist left.

Blum was one of the thirty-six socialist deputies who refused to vote for Pétain on July 10, 1940. Arrested by the Vichy authorities, he turned his trial at Riom in 1941 into a major political triumph, an intellectual and historical defense of the Republic that remains a landmark in the story of the Resistance. He was deported to Buchenwald in April 1943 and liberated by the Americans two years later.

The last five years of his life offered him a triple role: first, as leader of the SFIO, whose ideology he attempted to shift progressively away from Marxism toward a form of humanism that found little favor either with the traditional or with the new generation of activists; second, as national leader and (briefly) prime minister, playing a crucial role in ensuring that the institutions of the new Republic remained parliamentary rather than becoming presidential. He also attempted to find a peaceful settlement to the growing Indochinese crisis and helped to prepare the Treaty of Brussels, later to engender the Western European Union. Finally, he played an important role as roving international statesman, securing favorable conditions for the liquidation of French war debts (the Blum-Byrnes Agreements, August 1946) and as French representative to the founding meeting of UNESCO.

He died suddenly during a party meeting on March 30, 1950. He remains revered by many as a model of democratic, humanist socialism.

L. Blum, *L'Oeuvre de Léon Blum*, 7 vols. (Paris, 1954–65), *Léon Blum, chef de gouvernement* (Paris, 1967); J. Colton, *Léon Blum, Humanist in Politics*, (New York, 1966); G. Ziebura, *Léon Blum et le Parti socialiste* (Paris, 1967).

J. Howorth

Related entry: SOCIALIST PARTY (SFIO).

BOKASSA AFFAIR (1979), allegations that President Valéry Giscard d'Estaing had received gifts of diamonds from Bokassa, emperor of what was then called the Central African Empire, allegations that Giscard failed to explain and that may have contributed to his defeat in the presidential elections of 1981. Jean-Bedel Bokassa was born February 22, 1917 in Bobangui, attended school in Brazzaville, and rose to the rank of chief sergeant in the French army. He fought in Indochina and in the Central African Republic, which his uncle had founded in 1958. Bokassa rose to the rank of general by 1971. He held various government posts, including that of minister of national defense, before proclaiming himself emperor of France's client state. However, as news of atrocities and barbarism gained notoriety, the government, at the promptings of the Elysée, had reversed itself in its dealings with Bokassa. Allegations in the fall of 1979 that President Giscard had accepted gifts of diamonds from Bokassa affected at the very least the dignity of the French presidency, particularly when Giscard refused to explain, although such explanations are considered normal in other democracies. This tarnishing of his personal reputation, reinforced by other behavior, presented an image of an overbearing and authoritarian president contemptuous of criticism and contributed to Giscard's loss in the presidential election of 1981 to François Mitterrand.

L. Derfler, *President and Parliament: A Short History of the French Presidency* (Boca Raton, Fla., 1983); *Who's Who in France, 1975–1976* (Paris, 1975).

L. Derfler

Related entry: GISCARD D'ESTAING, VALERY.

BOUCHARDEAU, HUGUETTE (BRIAUT) (1935–), professor, politician, writer. Bouchardeau received the *agrégation* in philosophy from the University of Lyon and completed the thesis for the *doctorat de troisième cycle* in education. Initially she was a teacher at the *Lycée Honoré d'Urfé*, then in 1970 became *maître de conférence en sciences de l'éducation* at the University of Lyon. Active in the French family-planning group of the *Mouvement pour la liberté de l'avortement et de la contraception* (MLAC), she assumed responsibility for women's issues in the *Parti socialiste unifié* (PSU) and in 1979 served as secretary-general of the party. Two years later she was a candidate for the French presidency. During the years 1983–84 she was designated secretary of state attached to the minister in charge of the environment and the quality of life; she was minister of the environment from 1984 to 1986. In 1986 she was elected a socialist deputy from Doubs. Bouchardeau's writings reveal her concerns: women, politics, and the environment. In 1977 she published *Pas d'histoire les femmes: 50 ans d'histoire des femmes, 1918–1968*, which details French women's efforts to ameliorate their condition, including the women's pacifist movement (1915–40) and the birth control campaign (1918–71). Her more recent publications are *Hélène Brion* (1978), *Un Cri dans leur monde* (1980), and *Ministère du possible* (1986). She became director of the collection ''Mémoire des Femmes'' at Editions Syros in 1978.

H. Bouchardeau, *Ministère du possible* (Paris, 1986); J.-F. Doumic, H. Lacharmoise, eds., *Le Guide du pouvoir* (Paris, 1989).

M. C. Weitz

Related entries: ECOLOGY MOVEMENT; ELECTIONS; FEMINISM; MITTERRAND, FRANCOIS; POLITICAL TRENDS; UNIFIED SOCIALIST PARTY.

BOULEZ, PIERRE (1925–), composer, orchestra conductor, and author of works on musical theory. Boulez has been a leader of the musical avant-garde since 1970 and continues to write music that explores the new tonal systems with the collaboration of acoustical scientists at the *Institut de recherche et coordination acoustique/musique* in Paris, where he is the director. He remains the principal publicist for his highly complex musical opus from that center, only occasionally performing with orchestras elsewhere.

While a student at the Paris Conservatory from 1942 to 1945, Boulez studied classical theory under Olivier Messiaen. But private studies in counterpoint and the serialism techniques of Schoenberg with René Leibowitz became crucial for his musical career, which began in 1946 when he became the musical director of Jean-Louis Barrault's acting company in Paris. In such works as his cantata *Le Soleil des eaux*, Boulez experimented for the first time in France with the forces of serial composition in the manner of such composers as Webern. By the mid–1950s Boulez proclaimed his creation of a "total serial style" of pitch, duration, loudness, and attack in his *Le Marteau sans maître*, made up of an elaborate polyphonic structure for contralto and six instruments based on three short poems by René Char.

However, during the next decade Boulez radically changed the direction of the serial style with works like his Third Piano Sonata and especially with *Pli selon pli*, an orchestral piece that was greatly influenced by Mallarmé's poetry. These works expanded serialism by the extensive use of tonal percussion in unexpected relation with the full harmonics of the orchestra.

Beginning in 1954, Boulez combined composition with conducting. His direction of the "*domaine musical*" concerts in Paris, which offered rich programs in Renaissance and baroque music as well as avant-garde works, brought him invitations to conduct major orchestras outside of France. In 1969 he became the chief conductor of the BBC Symphony Orchestra in London, which led that same year to the launching of his brilliant decade as director of the New York Philharmonic Orchestra. By 1977, however, he felt a need to return to writing and composition and to escape from the controversies related to his championing of the cause of contemporary music. He returned to Paris and rededicated himself to writing and composition. While Boulez's models of the total serial music have failed to dominate contemporary musical works, his impact upon French and world musicology continues to challenge all aspects of the musical culture of our time.

P. Griffiths, *Boulez* (London, 1978); P. Heyworth, "Profiles: Taking Leave of Predecessors, Pierre Boulez," *The New Yorker*, March 24 and 31, 1973; *The New Grove Dictionary of American Music* (New York, 1986).

M. Siegel

Related entries: CULTURAL POLICY; LITERATURE.

BOURGES-MAUNOURY, MAURICE (1914–), industrialist, radical deputy, and twenty-second prime minister of the Fourth Republic. Born on August 19, 1914 in Luisant (Eure-et-Loire), he attended the Collège Stanislas in Paris and the *Ecole libre des sciences politiques*, earned a law degree from the *Université de Paris*, and graduated from the *Ecole polytechnique* as an artillery officer.

Bourgès-Maunoury joined the Resistance in 1941 after a year of internment as a prisoner of war. After serving as military delegate of the National Council of the Resistance in 1943–44, he was appointed assistant chief of staff of the French army and later regional commissioner of the Republic at Bordeaux. For his distinguished service Bourgès-Maunoury received numerous decorations, including the *Croix de guerre*, Legion of Honor, and the *Croix de la Libération*, as well as foreign decorations.

Upon his discharge from the army, Bourgès-Maunoury joined the Radical-Socialist party, was elected to the second Constituent Assembly, then to the National Assembly representing Haute-Garonne, a seat he held continuously from 1946 to 1958. He had a rapid political ascent, achieving his first cabinet rank at the age of thirty-three. By the time he formed his own cabinet in 1957—at age forty-two, the youngest prime minister in the Fourth Republic—he had participated in eleven governments, holding a variety of portfolios including the Ministries of Finance, Interior, and National Defense.

Bourgès-Maunoury specialized in foreign affairs and defense policy. A strong advocate of European economic and military unification, he resigned from the Mendès-France government in September 1954 to protest the National Assembly's rejection of the European Defense Community. As minister of defense under Guy Mollet (February 1956–May 1957), he presided over the Suez invasion. But Algeria dominated his career. He held key positions for Algerian policy from 1955 to 1958, advocating a compromise solution linking continued French sovereignty and a military presence with economic reforms to raise the standard of living in Algeria, and gradual decentralization of power to semiautonomous, ethnically defined regions within a federalist system.

Bourgès-Maunoury's minority government (June–September 1957) was supported only by the Socialist party (SFIO), largely because he continued Mollet's policy agenda and retained most of the previous cabinet. All other parties, including the *Mendésiste* group within his own Radical party, opposed him. His government finally fell after only three months over a key vote on his Algeria policy.

After 1958 Bourgès-Maunoury withdrew from national politics, although he continued to serve on the bureau of the Radical party until 1970. He retained local positions as mayor (until 1971) and municipal councillor of Bessières (Haute-Garonne), and general councillor of the canton of Montastruc-la-Conseillère, a post that he held continuously from 1949 to 1973. He presently resides in Paris, administers the newspaper *La Dépêche du Midi*, and sits on the boards of several industrial and financial enterprises.

C. Bourdache, *Les Années cinquante* (Paris, 1980); M. D. Candee, ed., *Current Biography* (New York, 1957); *Who's Who in France, 1988–89* (Paris, 1988).

R. D. Moore

Related entries: ALGERIA, RELATIONS WITH; DECOLONIZATION; EUROPEAN DEFENSE COMMUNITY; FRENCH UNION; MENDES-FRANCE, PIERRE; MOLLET, GUY; PRESS; RADICAL PARTY; SOCIALIST PARTY (SFIO); SUEZ CRISIS.

BRAUDEL, FERNAND (1902–1985), one of the twentieth century's most acclaimed historians, famed for his classic *La Méditerranée et le monde méditerranéen à l'époque de Philippe II*, headed the *Annales* school of historiography during the 1950s and 1960s and guided it to a position of international prominence. Born in a village in Lorraine, Braudel grew up there and in Paris. He began historical studies in a traditional way, at the Sorbonne in 1920, where he embarked upon a conventional thesis, the Mediterranean policy of King Philip II (1556–98) of Spain. A prolonged stint as a *lycée* teacher in Algeria, lasting with but short interruptions from 1923 to 1932, provided a different vantage point on the Mediterranean, seen "upside down" from the opposite shore of Europe, and encouraged a broader conception of the sea's history. During this period he also made contact with Lucien Febvre (1878–1956), cofounder with Marc Bloch of the journal *Annales*. It was Febvre, persistent critic of the limitations of traditional diplomatic history and incessant advocate of a history linked to geography, economics, anthropology, and the other social sciences, who suggested to Braudel that between the two, the Mediterranean and Philip II, the former was the greater historical protagonist and the more significant subject. Braudel came increasingly under Febvre's tutelage during the 1930s, but it was only during confinement as a prisoner of war in Germany between 1940 and 1945 that he was able at length to compose his great study, working from memory without notes.

La Méditerranée . . . (1949; rev. 2d ed., 1966; English trans. 1972) was intended as a *histoire totale* of the Mediterranean world as it existed in the sixteenth century. Braudel organized his book according to three registers or dimensions of time: the *longue durée*, or centuries-long, nearly immobile "structures," in which the patterns of human habitation were shaped by the forces of geography and climate; the cyclical *conjonctures*, principally governed by economic trends, of the "long" sixteenth century lasting from 1450 to 1650; and finally, the short-term political and military events of Philip II's regime. Of the three divisions of time, Braudel held the *longue durée* to be the most fundamental, with the consequence that the latitude for individual choice and decision, even that of a Philip II, was severely constrained.

During the postwar period, Braudel assumed increasingly prominent positions in French academic and intellectual life: chair at the Collège de France (1949), successor to Febvre as editor of *Annales* (1956–68) and as president of the *VIème Section* of the *Ecole pratique des hautes études* (1956–72), and first director of the *Maison des sciences de l'homme* (1962). During the 1960s Braudel exercised a major influence on the younger generation of *Annales* historians, encouraging particularly the use of quantitative methods of analysis to investigate the material, biological, and economic bases of life.

During the 1960s and 1970s Braudel worked on a second huge study, the three-volume *Civilisation matérielle, économie et capitalisme, XVᵉ-XVIIIᵉ siècle* (1967–79; English trans., 1981). Here his concern was to trace the economic life of Europe as seen in global perspective during the period from the voyages of discovery to the industrial revolution. These centuries saw the gradual emergence of capitalism and of Europe's domination of the world economy. Yet, Braudel underscores the limitations on human agency imposed by the long-lasting "structures of everyday life" (the title of the first volume of the work). These included the "biological *ancien régime*" of frequent epidemics, famines, short life expectancies, very high infant and childhood mortality, and chronic malnutrition; the low yields of agriculture; the inevitable energy shortages resulting from the inadequacies of wood as the basic fuel; the disincentives to technological innovation; and the obstacles to economic growth created by the majority of the goods that society produced remaining within a barter economy.

Braudel devoted the last five years of his life to a proposed four-volume history of France, of which he completed only the first two. The first volume, *L'Identité de la France*: *Espace et histoire* (1986; English trans., 1988), is devoted to history and the environment. In it Braudel reiterates his objections to what he regarded as the superficiality of narrative history, arguing instead for a "structural" history that would deal with the regional diversity of France, the integrative function exercised by networks of trade and communication, and the key role played by French cities in the nation's development. His second volume, entitled *L'Identité de la France: Les Hommes et les choses* (English trans., 1990), examined long-term population trends and production. To the end, Braudel consistently viewed the foundation level of history as that of the *longue durée* of human geography. In Braudel's view of history, even more than for Febvre, Bloch, and many of the younger *Annales* historians, there is little room for the role of culture or human consciousness in history (e.g., for religion, law, political commitments, philosophical ideas, literature, or the arts). Instead it is the material and ecological conditions of human existence that determine the limits of human possibility.

F. Braudel, "Personal Testimony," *Journal of Modern History* 44 (1972); J.H. Hexter, "Fernand Braudel and the *Monde Braudellien* . . . ," *Journal of Modern History* 44 (1972); O. Hufton, "Fernand Braudel," *Past & Present* 112 (1986); S. Kinser, "Annaliste Paradigm? The Geohistorical Structure of Fernand Braudel," *American Historical Review* 86 (1981).

C. L. Stinger

Related entry: ANNALES SCHOOL.

BROADCAST MEDIA, radio and television. The evolution of radio and television broadcasting in France is largely the story of how monopolistic state control gradually loosened and then disintegrated altogether. The notion that broadcasting constitutes an essential "public service" that justifies the maintenance of state monopoly long functioned as political orthodoxy in France. On the right, from Charles de Gaulle's liberation government onward, radio and television were viewed as necessary instruments of nation building in a divided society; the left, for its part, feared that privatization of the airwaves would inevitably lead to their domination by big capital. In the mid–1980s, the clear emergence and rapid development of telecommunications as a central strategic and international industry of the future, increasing demands from the private sector to participate in this development, and the triumph of new political ideas emphasizing decentralization of the state (on the left) and deregulation of industry (on the right) contributed to events leading to the abandonment of the state's monopoly. As a result, the broad contours of the French audiovisual landscape have been redrawn and are today virtually unrecognizable from a vantage point of even a decade ago.

The French press and broadcast media have traditionally operated under radically different legal regimes. Whereas the private sector provided print information and services, the public sector exercised tight control over all other communications networks. As new technologies appeared, state authority to regulate their uses was simply grafted on to existing administrative arrangements. Thus, in 1923 the state's monopoly on telegraph communication was extended to radio broadcasts (radio emissions had begun in 1921, from atop the Eiffel Tower); and, later, television (which broadcast regularly starting in 1948) was coupled with radio to form a single industry under unified, bureaucratic management. During the 1930s, some private radio broadcasting was allowed, upon licensing by the government, and on the condition that license holders registered as nonprofit organizations and pledged not to take advertising money. These rights were soon rescinded, however, as stations became dominated by newspaper and corporate concerns, functioned as forums for reactionary political activity, and persistently violated the prohibition on advertising.

From 1945 to 1981, all private broadcasting was formally prohibited by law, on the theory that the interests of the state and of the regime transcended any countervailing rights. In the 1945–64 period, the media was regulated by the RTF (*Radiodiffusion-télévision française*), an agency under the direct control of the Ministry of Communications. The RTF possessed virtually no political autonomy: not only was its top management appointed by the government, but also the minister of communications actively—and on a daily basis—participated in broadcast decisions. In the Fourth Republic, governments consciously used the airwaves as a means of shaping public opinion in favor of government policy, but also of defending the regime against its enemies, namely Gaullists and communists (who were virtually denied access). In the first decade of the Fifth Republic, the media was used to consolidate executive power and to counter what the government considered to be "the negative press." In both cases, broadcasting in the "public interest" was scarcely distinguishable from broadcasting in the "government's interest."

It is important to note, however, that the political meaning and impact of centralized control of the broadcast media on French political life was very different from one Republic to the next. In the Fourth Republic, certain negative effects of this control—the potential for demagoguery, low morale or even alienation of journalists, widespread cynicism toward the media on the part of the public—were somewhat mitigated, but not eliminated, by the fact that unstable, coalition governments were the norm and that within these governments parties rotated control of the ministry. The founding of the Gaullist Republic, however, polarized politics between right and left, and between Gaullists and their opponents. Although after 1958, broadcasting in the public interest continued to mean shameless advocacy of the government's position, such uses proved to be increasingly controversial and divisive.

This was all the more true in the case of television. In the 1958–68 period, the number of television sets jumped tenfold, from one million to over ten million. At the same time, politicians, and especially General de Gaulle, perfected the medium as a means of direct appeal. A popular equation of the period—''Gaullism equals personal power plus the monopoly over television broadcasting''—is perhaps not an exaggeration. Indeed, the general's use of television broadcasts to rally the electorate to his side at crucial moments (in referendum campaigns on the Algerian question and on the direct election of the president, for example) is today part and parcel of the Gaullist myth. But it is also further evidence of a general phenomenon: the extraordinary power of television, in all polities, to personalize political leadership and to penalize those with limited or no access.

Since 1964 the state monopoly has been reorganized on several occasions, the overall effect of which has been gradually to wean the government from day-to-day management. In 1964 the RTF was replaced by the ORTF (*Office de radio-télévision française*), but with no loss of government control (indeed the ORTF's chairman, director, and board of directors were named by the government). Gaullist loss of the presidency proved to be a watershed event. In 1974 Valéry Giscard d'Estaing purged the office of Gaullists and broke it up into four autonomous companies: one radio group, *Radio-France*, and three television channels, TF1 (*Télévision française* 1), A2 (*Antenne* 2), and FR3 (*France-Régions* 3). In 1981 the socialists passed legislation to allow nonprofit radio broadcasting, if under close supervision; and in 1982 government-sponsored legislation granted significant autonomy to the four state companies and created a regulatory agency, the *Haute autorité de la communication audiovisuelle*, to monitor broadcast policy, fix rules for advertising and campaign time, and so on.

By 1984 both left and right, if for different reasons, largely favored the expansion of private radio broadcasting and the creation of private television channels. In 1984–85 three such channels were authorized: *Canal Plus*, TV5, and TV6. In 1986 the new Chirac government, in line with its neoliberal agenda, had parliament adopt legislation that replaced the *Haute autorité* with the CNCL (*Commission nationale de la communication et des libertés*), giving it a mandate to allocate frequencies to literally hundreds of new radio stations, to privatize TF1, and to reallocate (by selling) the broadcasting rights for TV5 and TV6. The legislation was referred by the socialists to the Constitutional Council, which approved it but only on condition that the government strengthen the antitrust provisions governing the purchases. As a result, no person or group was allowed to own more than 25 percent of any television channel, and provisions were made to prohibit excessive concentration in the new radio industry.

As a result of these reforms, the broadcast media is today organized as follows. Public radio transmissions are directed by *Radio-France* (*Société nationale de radiodiffusion*), which manages the following major, national stations: *France-Culture*, featuring information, criticism, and debate on the arts, philosophy, and so on; *France-Inter*, providing general news coverage, popular music, and entertainment; and *France-Musique*, devoted primarily to classical music. *Radio-France* is also the umbrella organization for more than fifty regional radio stations and provides an international service that broadcasts to the rest of Europe, as well as Africa and Asia. In addition to *Radio-France*, French listeners have long been able to tune in to three other major commercial networks: RTL (*Radio-Télévision Luxembourg*), *Radio-Monte-Carlo*, and *Europe 1*. Private-sector radio broadcasting has exploded since the recent reforms were enacted: there are today more than fifteen hundred private radio stations operating in metropolitan France, one hundred of which are located in Paris.

Television broadcasting, too, is organized into public and private services, and can be further divided by technology used. There remain two traditional public channels: A2, an all-purpose station whose ratings are second only to those of the recently privatized TF1; and FR3, which broadcasts regional news and cultural programs. The private sector is composed of *Canal Plus*, a pay-for-view network principally owned by the Havas press group (25%) and featuring uncut movies and sports events, and three national channels affected by the 1986 reforms. One of these is TF1, France's most-watched channel. Shares in TF1 were purchased by the builder, Francis Bouygues (25%), the Robert Maxwell media group (10%), various French companies (15%), private shareholders (40%), and TF1 employees (10%). *La Cinq* (formerly the francophone cultural channel, TV5), is a channel dominated by American programming. *La Cinq* is largely controlled by its president, Robert Hersant, who owns 25 percent of the stock but dominates the consortium that controls the majority of shares. M6 (formerly the music television channel, TV6) is also dominated by American programming. M6 was purchased by the Metropole group, and principal participants include RTL (25%), *Lyonnaise des Eaux* (25%), investment institutions (37%), and the Amaury press group (2.5%).

The development of satellite technology and of European cable networks will provide further opportunities for expansion in the near future. Since the mid–1980s the French government, working with its European Community partners and with European consortia, has allocated a number of satellite broadcast frequencies. Satellite channels now, or soon to be in operation include: TV5, a European, francophone, cultural station; *La Sept*, a state-run Franco-German cultural channel; and the TDF satellite networks, a Franco-Luxembourgeois multichannel venture. Finally, the country is gradually being covered by a national cable network, linked to a greater European cable system, with a capacity for several dozen channels.

Although a substantial private sector now exists, it is crucial to note that the state, in the form of the CNCL, obliges private television channels to operate within certain broad parameters. They must produce a minimum number of original programs, devote a certain number of hours to the arts and to children's programs, and they are forbidden from surpassing fixed advertising limits. Since the return of the socialists in 1988, the government has tightened enforcement of these restrictions and has begun to fine private stations for not complying with French content rules.

The public has undoubtedly benefited from these changes. It now enjoys a range of choice roughly equivalent to that of its European neighbors, and the quality of broadcast journalism has also generally risen with the decline of government control. In the pre–1980 period, news programs and documentaries were shamelessly slanted toward government positions, and regular, overt manipulation of programming by the government could be considered a general perquisite of executive power. Journalists who refused to toe the line saw their stories killed or lost their jobs altogether; and changes of government resulted in wholesale purging of editorial and news staffs. Today a healthy pluralism is evident, at least for public affairs programs. On the other hand, French television offerings are today much more dominated by foreign productions: A recent analysis of programming, for example, showed that American productions accounted for over 60 percent of entertainment programming, followed by French productions (29%), British (7%), and others.

J. Cluzel, *La Télévision après six réformes* (Paris, 1988); P. Grivet, P. Herreng, *La Télévision* (Paris, 11th ed., 1982); R. Kuhn, "France and the New Media," *West European Politics* 8, no. 1 (1985); Special Issue, "La Nouvelle Réforme de l'audiovisuel," *Revue française de droit administratif* 3, no. 3 (1987); A. de Tarle, "France: The Monopoly that Won't Divide," in *Television and Political Life,* ed. A. Smith (New York, 1979).

A. Stone

Related entries: DE GAULLE, CHARLES; GISCARD D'ESTAING, VALERY; MITTERRAND, FRANCOIS; POLITICAL TRENDS; POMPIDOU, GEORGES.

C

CAFES, while not as ubiquitous as under the Third Republic, remain vital institutions of informal social life. From an all-time high of virtually 508,000 at the end of the Popular Front (1938), the number of cafés plummeted to 314,515 in 1946 due to the privations of war and the restrictions of the Vichy regime. The numbers continued to decline during the 1950s—262,523 at the start of the Fifth Republic (1959)—and through the 1960s and early 1970s, until they reached a plateau of 228,000 under Georges Pompidou (1973). Their number has remained roughly the same ever since.

The declining numbers are largely the product of government regulation. In 1955 the Mendès-France government, as part of a comprehensive antialcohol program, codified previous measures of Vichy and the Liberation regimes. The 1955 drinking establishment code created a fourfold licensing and taxation system based upon the type of drink: first, shops selling only nonalcoholic drinks; second, those also serving fermented drinks; third, those offering wine; and fourth, all drinks available. Along with limiting the type of drink sold, government regulations also reconfirmed previous spatial restrictions. No new cafés could be placed within specified distances, varying according to local ordinance, of schools, cemeteries, churches, and hospitals. The health code promulgated in the same year continued an earlier ordinance restricting cafés to one per three thousand inhabitants in new housing developments and cities. As a result, new towns throughout France have had few cafés. For example, in the Paris region, Massy, with a population of thirty thousand, still had only three cafés in 1969, one-third of its legal ration. La Courneuve, called a bistro desert, had only one shop for 9,700 residents. Paris, despite a drop in its number of cafés, from thirty thousand during the *belle époque* to twelve thousand during the 1980s, still has one bar for every four hundred Parisians. Local studies have shown, especially one on Le Havre's dock workers, that limiting or eradicating cafés does not necessarily end alcohol abuse. Often it is merely converted from a public vice to a private one.

But the decline in cafés cannot be simply attributed to government regulation. The vast social and economic changes of the past forty years have diminished the social functions of cafés. The rise of a fully developed consumer culture and an improvement in the housing stock have fundamentally altered the way the French spend their time and money. By the 1970s a galaxy of consumer durables had flooded French stores, and improvements in housing had made the home a center of leisure. The share of café going in the average leisure budget has dropped from 40 percent to 26 percent over the past generation. Increasingly, potential café customers save their money for consumer durable items, such as cars, televisions, refrigerators, and, more recently, computers and video machines, rather than spend it freely and rapidly on café sociability. As modern media and transportation expand people's horizons, the local bar on the corner has gone into decline. Laurence Wylie, in the two villages he studied intensively, Chanzeau in Anjou and Peyrane in the Vaucluse, noted the decline of the café as the center of town life. Like others who have studied contemporary rural France, Wylie found that the television and the automobile had destroyed café sociability and thus much of the vitality of village life.

Despite this diminution in functions, the café still has the potential to remain an important social institution in the life of any community. After achieving power in 1981, the socialists attempted to reinvigorate café life. Many socialist mayors had become convinced that grass-roots political action required architecture on a human scale in order to facilitate community life. This idea also accorded well with the socialists' attempt to decentralize power. In 1983 Prime Minister Pierre Mauroy, the mayor of Lille, drafted a mission statement on this matter. In February 1984 President François Mitterrand presented seventy-five architectural projects as a part of a new project, *Banlieues 89* (Suburbs 89). This ambitious plan to reanimate life in Parisian suburbs was drawn up by two young "agitator-architects," Roland Castro and Michel Cantal-Dupart. Cafés were at the center of their designs. They felt suburbs suffered from a poverty of convivial places. They wished to create a different type of bistro, one that would be a place of culture rather than simply a drink shop. To initiate the project, Paul Quilès, the minister of urbanism and housing, broke with previous regulations and authorized the creation of bistros in all the government housing projects (*habitation à loyer modéré*, or HLM). It is still too soon to tell how successful this government-sponsored attempt to restore a "necessary conviviality" will ultimately be.

Yet, amidst the doomsday predictions of the café's demise and the socialist government's attempts at resuscitation, the café remains a living institution. Although it may not be as universally enjoyed as at one time, drinking and socializing remain a central ritual in the lives of millions. This vitality has been found in small working-class towns in the Paris area as well as amidst that gaudy tourist mecca, Montmartre. What seems to unite café *habitués* today more than in the past is a strong gregarious instinct. At least in Paris, this sociability seems to cross class lines more than in the nineteenth century. At the counter or on a terrace, the French can retrieve some of the face-to-face contact that an increasingly automated and computerized society denies them. Surprise, chance, and synchronicity are all possible in the café to a degree not found in most other places. Some recent books detail the continued vitality of café slang and ritual. They provide eloquent testimony to the stubbornness and persistence of café sociability and show it will not soon be superseded.

M. Bozon, "La Fréquentation des cafés dans une petite ville ouvrière," *Ethnologie française* (1982); J.-P. Castelain, *Manières de vivre, manières de boire* (Paris, 1989); M. Chatelain-Courtois, *Les Mots du vin et de l'ivresse* (Paris, 1984); R. Giraud, *L'Argot du bistro* (Paris, 1989).

W. S. Haine

Related entries: LEISURE; SOCIAL TRENDS; WINE PRODUCTION AND CONSUMPTION.

CAMUS, ALBERT (1913–1960), novelist, Nobel Prize winner, playwright, and journalist. Like Jean-Paul Sartre and André Malraux, Camus was born into a war-stricken world where God, together with humanism, had "died," and where progress, democracy, and reason had failed. The writer's struggle was therefore to find meaning and value (or not, as the case may be) in a meaningless world. Camus rejected the stark pessimism of existentialism and proffered another, measurably more hopeful vision of life, in which the moral indifference aroused by an awareness of absurdity gives way to a more positive confirmation of individual human worth, fraternity, and solidarity. For Camus, recognition of "the absurd" thus becomes a point of departure for "revolt" in favor of justice and moderation.

Camus was born a *pied-noir*, of French and Spanish extraction, in the village of Mondovi in the Constantine department of Algeria on November 7, 1913. His father was killed at the battle of the Marne soon after the outbreak of World War I, and the family moved to Belcourt, one of the poorer suburbs of Algiers. From 1918 to 1923 he attended a local primary school, where he was noticed by one of his teachers, Louis Germain, who helped him win a scholarship to grammar school at Bab-el-Oued. It was here that Camus met the writer and schoolteacher Jean Grenier, who introduced him to such authors as André Gide, André Malraux, and Henry de Montherlant. Images of childhood pervade much of Camus's writing: the Mediterranean at Bab-el-Oued, the barren Algerian desert, and above all his mother. But his depiction of French Algeria as a world of laughter and sunshine, beauty and innocence ignores its darker side: Camus's family was poverty-stricken, and he himself was found in 1930 to be tubercular. Ill health cut short his university career (preventing him from taking the *agrégation* at the University of Algiers following his *licence* and subsequent *diplôme d'études supérieures* in philosophy) and forced him to give up sports, which he relished. Moreover, his first marriage to a drug addict ended in failure.

It was failure of a different kind—the failure to find employment in North Africa when war broke out in 1939—that forced Camus to abandon Algeria for Paris in March 1940. A variety of jobs had kept body and soul together during his twenties, but his career was now in journalism: He had served as an apprentice with *Alger-Républicain* from 1937 to 1939, and now joined *Paris-Soir*. Again his career was interrupted when the German army invaded Paris in June 1940. He left France for Oran, where he began to write *La Peste* (1947). The plague that is the subject of the novel symbolized the occupation of France by the Nazis, and the values it extolled—courage and fraternity—were those required to combat Nazism. Despite Camus's activities in the Resistance (which he joined on his return to France in 1942), including the editorship of the clandestine journal *Combat*, the war proved to be a particularly productive period for Camus as a writer and novelist. *Le Mythe de Sisyphe* (1942) introduced his concept of the absurd, the drudgery of a meaningless task. Sisyphus, condemned to push his stone up a hill, sees it continually roll down, experiencing, however, a brief moment of freedom each time the boulder is released. This served as a symbol of the absurdity of existence for Camus. *L'Etranger* (1942) tells the story of Meursault, a young French-Algerian clerk who is condemned to death ostensibly for murdering an Arab; more accurately, his fault in society's eyes is his failure to display those emotions that are required of him. His own intellectual freedom and lucidity in the face of imminent death nevertheless allow him to rise above the society that has condemned him. These novels and those that followed—*L'Homme révolté* (1951), which explained his concept of revolt, and *La Chute* (1956)—revealed Camus's love of life and at the same time showed his despair. They refused, however, to offer any false hope, any inauthentic peace of mind; and always they sought to undermine the complacency of the reader. It was as a novelist, rather than a dramatist, that Camus was awarded the Nobel Prize for literature in 1957. Despite his passion for theater, his plays, *Caligula* (1939) and *Les Justes* (1949), enjoyed only moderate success.

In early January 1960, Camus was killed in a car accident near Villeblevin. Camus may have lost the dialectic battle with Sartre over support for the Soviet Union, but the moral victory was his. He was hailed as the moral conscience of his generation. The next generation, however, was more concerned with writing as writing than with writing as commitment or revolt. Camus's refusal to take sides during the Algerian War was judged, and condemned. And with the birth of the "new novel," which Camus himself had anticipated, his work was largely eclipsed. He continues nevertheless to enjoy a high reputation as a moral thinker.

J. Cruikshank, *Albert Camus and the Literature of Revolt* (New York, 1960); J. Grenier, *Albert Camus* (Paris, 1968); H. Lottman, *Albert Camus* (New York, 1979); P. McCarthy, *Camus* (New York, 1982).

M. Maclean

Related entries: BEAUVOIR, SIMONE DE; EXISTENTIALISM; INTELLECTUAL TRENDS; SARTRE, JEAN-PAUL.

CAPITANT, RENE (1901–1969), left-wing Gaullist deputy and minister during the provisional government and under the Fifth Republic. Born in La Tronche (Isère) on August 19, 1901 and educated in Paris, he followed his father, the distinguished jurist Henri Capitant, into a career in the law. Appointed to professorships at Strasbourg, Algiers, and Paris, he was a leading advocate of constitutional revision during the Third and Fourth Republics. Capitant favored strong executive leadership and recognized in Charles de Gaulle a man prepared to provide it. He rallied to the general's Free French movement in North Africa and later was one of the founders of the resistance movement there, including the *Combat* movement in Algiers. Named a delegate to the *Assemblée consultative* in November 1943, he resigned from this body upon his nomination as minister of education in de Gaulle's new provisional government, retaining this post until 1945. His advanced political views and influence on de Gaulle were both in evidence in 1945 when, on Capitant's suggestion, the provisional government published an ordinance requiring firms to set up consultative workers' committees, a harbinger of the participationist reforms that would come in the wake of the events of May–June 1968.

Capitant was elected deputy to the constituent assembly in 1945, a seat that he held during the first legislature of the Fourth Republic as well. In mid–1946 he founded the short-lived *Union gaulliste pour la quatrième république* and later became, despite its pronounced conservative orientation, national president of the far more successful *Rassemblement du peuple français*. A vigorous critic of the government's Indochina policy in the late 1940s, Capitant put his academic career at risk in 1957 when he denounced the use of torture by French forces in Algeria. He spent the next three years as director of the *Maison franco-japonaise* in Tokyo. Thus missing the upheaval of May 1958 that ended the Fourth Republic, he returned to Paris in 1960 and founded the left-wing Gaullist *Union démocratique du travail* (UDT). After 1962 he sat in parliament as a UDT deputy for the Latin Quarter.

Throughout the 1960s Capitant was a vocal Gaullist champion of the interests of French workers. He also promoted what he called "social Gaullism" in the pages of his UDT weekly *Notre République*. Personally hostile to Prime Minister Georges Pompidou, in May 1968 he accused him of regime-threatening incompetence. He then resigned his parliamentary seat rather than support the government on an opposition motion of censure against the prime minister that failed by only eleven votes. Capitant continued to enjoy the confidence of de Gaulle, however, and was imposed on the beleaguered Pompidou as minister of justice the following month. He retained this post when Maurice Couve de Murville succeeded to the prime ministership in July, but abruptly resigned it upon de Gaulle's resignation as president on April 27, 1969. Less than a month later he died suddenly, in a Paris hospital.

R. Capitant, *Ecrits politiques, 1960–1970* (Paris, 1971).

J. E. Reece

Related entries: DE GAULLE, CHARLES; GAULLISM; GAULLIST PARTY.

***CARREFOUR DU DEVELOPPEMENT* AFFAIR,** a financial and political scandal affecting both left and right that first came to public notice in April of 1986. The association *Carrefour du développement* was contracted by the Ministry of Cooperation to provide facilities and services for the 1984 Franco-African summit in Bujumbura. It subsequently emerged that the summit meeting had cost 67 million francs, of which only 17 million were officially accounted for, the remainder having been paid to the association *Carrefour du développement* or to pay false bills. Yves Chalier, who was socialist cooperation minister Christian Nucci's head of cabinet and also the treasurer of *Carrefour du développement*, was initially implicated, since it appeared that some of the missing money had been used for his own personal expenses. He subsequently disappeared, to Brazil as it later transpired, and only returned to France when both his former wife and girlfriend were taken into custody. After his return he alleged in an interview that the misappropriation of funds had taken place with the knowledge of the minister, Nucci, and that some of the money had been used by the latter for his election campaign in Isère. He further alleged that the false papers he had used to return to France had been obtained from the head of the *Direction de la surveillance du territoire* (DST), France's counterespionage service. It was later also claimed that the issuing of these papers had been authorized by the then right-wing interior minister, Charles Pasqua, who apparently wanted Chalier back in France as he was thought to have information that could be used to embarrass the Socialist party in the 1988 elections. Both left and right were now implicated, and there was thus no longer anything that either side could hope to gain politically from the affair. At the time of writing, neither Nucci nor Pasqua had yet appeared before the Supreme Court, despite the seriousness of the allegations made against them: Socialist deputies in the National Assembly have helped to prevent Nucci from appearing before the Court, and Pasqua can probably rely upon his supporters in the Senate to do the same for him.

Le Monde, dossiers et documents: Bilan du septennat, 1981–1988 (Paris, 1988).

T. Chafer

Related entries: ELECTIONS; PASQUA, CHARLES; SOCIALIST PARTY (PS).

CATHOLICISM, the religious affiliation claimed by 81 percent of the French population. However, the influence of the church in France since 1940 is uneven. If it has earned the allegiance of four out of five French people, contributed to the downfall of a government (Pierre Mauroy in 1984, over the issue of Catholic schools), or drawn millions to its shrines (4.5 million pilgrims to Lourdes in 1987, more than Mecca), the church has also been challenged by schism, by declining religious practice, and by its apparent irrelevance to many of the French in matters of faith and morals.

One measure of religious devotion among Catholics is attendance at mass. A study of one thousand rural cantons in France in the late 1950s showed that on average 43 percent of adult Catholic women and 24 percent of adult Catholic men attended mass regularly, at least once per month. There are other measures of devotion, however. Participation in the sacrament of communion is an important part of Catholic piety, and in this same sample 15 percent of adult Catholic women and 3 percent of adult Catholic men received communion at least once per month—Catholic men may accompany Catholic women to mass but rarely to communion.

Religious practice has its regional dimension too. Regular attendance at mass was most common in the rural areas of the west (Brittany and lower Normandy, also the western Pyrenees), parts of the east (Alsace, Jura, and Savoie), and the southeastern edge of the Massif Central (from Lyon through the Auvergne). In these areas the number of *pascalisants*—those fulfilling their Easter obligation, a threshold measurement of Catholic practice—numbered upward from 80 percent in the early 1960s. In these same devout regions perhaps only 30 to 40 percent of the Catholic population received communion regularly. These figures were lower for urban areas in these regions.

A *Sofres* poll conducted in 1986 showed that many of these figures had fallen since the 1950s. The French still turned to the church at the great moments in life: birth (97% of French were baptized), marriage (87% of those married did so in church), and death (72% desire a Catholic funeral). However, the church seemed oddly irrelevant to most French outside of these great moments: only 16 percent attended mass at least once per month; only 31 percent fulfilled their Easter obligation of confession and communion. Birthrates among practicing Catholics no longer differ markedly from the rest of the population.

Catholicism relies heavily on sacramental ritual; the Catholic faithful, by extension, rely heavily on their clergy to perform these rituals. Religious vocations are thus a matter of deep concern. For the early twentieth century, the number of Catholic vocations, and thus the number of priests and nuns, remained in roughly proportional relationship to the size of the population; the ''*années creuses*'' of French fertility were also *années creuses* for eventual religious vocations. This relationship changed with those classes coming of age in the post–1945 period. There were far fewer vocations among those reaching adulthood in the 1950s than among those reaching adulthood in the 1930s. The decline in vocations was even more abrupt among those coming of age in the 1970s, so that whereas there were just over one thousand priests ordained in 1950, there were fewer than two hundred in 1975—at a time when the number of men of ordainable age was higher than ever.

Practicing Catholics have tended to be more conservative than other French voters; a map representing the vote for Valéry Giscard d'Estaing in the second round of the presidential election of 1974 bears a striking resemblance to the map of regular churchgoers. In fact, religious practice remains the most reliable single predictor of political behavior in France. While practicing Catholics tend to be more conservative than other voters, they are not seduced by reactionary politics. A *Sofres* poll conducted in 1986 showed that only 2 percent of practicing Catholics believed that Jean-Marie Le Pen was the best candidate for Catholics, and when asked which candidate a Catholic must never support, practicing Catholics named the extreme right-wing Le Pen more often than any other candidate, more often even than the candidate of the Communist party. The left has not benefited, however, from Catholic resistance to the radical right. Devout Catholics may be found among militants of parties of the left and even among party luminaries—one thinks of Jacques Delors—but only 11 percent of practicing Catholics, versus 33 percent of the electorate at large, would identify with the left or extreme left. The Catholic voter tends to be a center-right voter.

For all of that, efforts to date to create a durable political formation ''of Catholic inspiration'' have failed. For a time in the immediate postwar period, progressive Catholic political and social ideals were closely associated with the *Mouvement républicain populaire* (MRP) of Georges Bidault, leader of the National Resistance Council. The ideological origins of the MRP extended beyond the Resistance, back to various efforts of the early and late Third Republic to reconcile Catholicism with the Republic and the modern world. These connections made many more traditionally minded Catholics uncomfortable with the MRP; more to the point, the MRP benefited from certain short-lived historical factors. Thus, even though the MRP emerged in the elections of June 1946 as France's most popular party, this was not so much because of broad commitment to the MRP's program of social engagement as because of the lack of alternatives for supporters of the traditional right, in disarray after Vichy, who perceived the MRP to be the best vehicle for the expression of Gaullist and anticommunist sentiments. Support for the MRP slipped by more than half between 1946 and 1951, the first election after the creation of the Gaullist *Rassemblement du peuple français* (RPF). The onset of the Algerian War plainly revealed profound left-right differences among Catholics that could no longer be accommodated within the MRP. By 1956 MRP support had largely withdrawn to the bastions of traditional Catholic piety: the west, Alsace, and the Alps.

Certain issues do transcend left-right differences among Catholics; Catholic education is one of them. A series of demonstrations in provincial capitals against Alain Savary's plan to integrate lay and Catholic schools led to the largest demonstration in the history of France: one million demonstrators swamped Paris on June 24, 1984. Within a month Minister Savary, his reforms, and the Mauroy government were gone. Such incidents demonstrate the enduring power of the church in French life. Some would even claim that a Catholic revival is under way in France and point, in support, to plans to build a new cathedral in the diocese of Evry—the first new cathedral in France in over a century. At the very least, socialist minister of culture Jack Lang's decision to donate five million francs to the project heralded a new era in church-state relations.

Ultratraditionalists among French Catholics, the so-called *intégristes* who numbered perhaps 200,000, were increasingly active in the 1980s in their attack on the post–Vatican II developments within the church. They discovered the limits of Catholic dissent when their leader, Monseignor Marcel Lefebvre, whose positions echo the antimodernism of Pope Pius IX's 1867 Syllabus of Errors, was excommunicated after consecrating four bishops without papal permission in June 1988—the first schism in the Catholic church since 1870.

W. Bosworth, *Catholicism and Crisis in Modern France* (Princeton, 1962); G. Cholvy, Y.-M. Hilaire, *Histoire religieuse de la France contemporaine*, vol. 3 (Paris, 1988);

F.-A. Isambert, J.-P. Terrenoire, *Atlas de la pratique religieuse des catholiques en France* (Paris, 1980); A. Latreille, *De Gaulle, la Libération, et al. Eglise catholique* (Paris, 1978); F. Lebrun, ed., *Histoire des catholiques en France du XVe siècle à nos jours* (Toulouse, 1980); ''Un Sondage sur les Français et la religion,'' *Le Monde*, October 1, 1986.

R. A. Jonas

Related entries: BIDAULT, GEORGES; CHRISTIAN DEMOCRATS; *CONFEDERATION FRANCAISE DES TRAVAILLEURS CHRETIENS*; DELORS, JACQUES; EDUCATIONAL REFORM; SAVARY, ALAIN.

CENTRIST PARTIES reflect more than any other political force the changes that have occurred in France since 1945. Widely blamed for France's political problems under the Third Republic and the defeat in 1940, the centrist parties and politicians emerged from World War II in disfavor. With the collapse of the tripartite coalition of the Liberation government (1944–46) and the onset of the Cold War, the centrists rapidly regained their position and dominated Fourth Republic (1946–58) politics. Under the Fifth Republic the focus of political competition shifted toward contests between left and right, and the centrists saw their influence ebb until they were no longer a serious force by the mid–1970s.

Before World War II the centrist parties were little more than loose groupings of politicians whose primary loyalties were to their constituents and their own careers. Their one common denominator was a resistance to change. The overwhelming majority of centrist politicians also voted to end the Third Republic and give full power to Marshal Pétain and what came to be the Vichy government. Many collaborated with the Germans. Few participated in the Resistance.

Consequently, the centrists were excluded from the Council of the Resistance and then from the provisional government headed by General Charles de Gaulle. Composed of Gaullists, communists, socialists, and Christian democrats (who would become one of the centrist parties under the Fourth Republic), the provisional government enacted sweeping social and economic reform. That coalition foundered, however, in 1946. De Gaulle resigned as prime minister that year when his coalition partners opted for a constitution that concentrated power in the hands of parliament, not the executive as the general had preferred.

Meanwhile, the old centrist parties had begun to regain support. The radicals and their allies won nearly 12 percent of the vote, and the loose grouping of conservatives nearly thirteen. The new Christian democratic *Mouvement républicain populaire* (MRP) won almost as many votes as the two traditional centrist parties combined.

The following year the pressures of the Cold War finally undermined the leftist coalition when communist ministers left the government of socialist Paul Ramadier. France then turned to what was called the ''third force'' of the socialists (SFIO) plus the four main centrist parties: the Radical-Socialist party, the MRP, a loose grouping of conservatives, and the Democratic and Socialist Union of the Resistance (UDSR). The Radical-Socialist party, it was often quipped, was neither radical nor socialist, but a conservative group of small-town politicians committed to a republican form of government, anticlericalism, and the socioeconomic status quo. During the 1950s it was also home to Pierre Mendès-France and other technocratic modernizers. The MRP started as a socially progressive party committed to European integration and the modernization of France. As the Fourth Republic wore on, it gradually moved to the right, especially on social and foreign policy. Of the four groups, only the MRP had any degree of party discipline. The third "party" was a loose grouping of conservatives who went by various names, including moderates, independents, and peasants, though these labels did not necessarily correspond to a deputy's social origins or political views. Ideologically, the conservatives were a diverse lot, with some willing to cooperate with the socialists and others with strong ties to the antidemocratic far right. The smallest of the four was the UDSR, the only party with its roots exclusively in the resistance efforts against the Germans. Its leaders had links with all the other parties that had been involved in the Resistance, which made it a logical alliance partner for them all. On the other hand, that also meant that UDSR deputies took a wide variety of positions as reflected in its two most prominent leaders, the conservative René Pleven and François Mitterrand, who by the end of the Fourth Republic was seen as one of France's most progressive, noncommunist politicians. Nineteen of the subsequent twenty prime ministers were drawn from the ranks of these four parties. They also dominated the other key ministries, except for the interior and industry, both of which were frequently headed by socialists.

The centrist politicians presided over governments that were no more successful than their predecessors under the Third Republic. Ideological divisions and the conflicting ambitions of the politicians themselves broke governing coalitions apart on the average of once every nine months, after which the parties would have to rebuild their majority. That pattern of "crisis and compromise" left France ill-prepared to cope with the growing burden of domestic and international issues, and the Fourth Republic finally succumbed to the revolt in Algeria in May 1958. Again, the centrist parties bore the brunt of the blame for the collapse of a republic. This time, however, they were not to recover.

Most centrist politicians reluctantly supported de Gaulle, and many ran in the 1958 legislative elections as part of the very loose Gaullist coalition. By 1962, almost all had gone into the opposition. Some left because they opposed Algerian independence, others because they could not stand the new presidential regime. For most, the last straw came in 1962. That April, de Gaulle asked Michel Debré to resign as prime minister and replaced him with Georges Pompidou, a relative unknown who had never run for office, let alone served in the parliament before.

Then, following an assassination attempt that nearly claimed his life that August, de Gaulle announced a referendum on the direct election of the president. The Constitutional Council declared the referendum illegal. De Gaulle decided to proceed with it anyway. The centrists and the rest of the opposition then overthrew the Pompidou government, the first and only time the National Assembly has done so since 1958. De Gaulle responded by dissolving the National Assembly, the first time that had been done since the 1870s.

The French had to go to the polls twice that fall, and each time the centrist parties lost badly. The referendum passed handily, winning 62 percent of the votes cast. In the legislative elections the centrist parties won the same 37 percent of the vote they had four years before. This time, however, because a small faction of the *indépendants* headed by Valéry Giscard d'Estaing split from the rest of the party and supported the Gaullists, the government emerged with enough seats for a firm majority it could count on for the next five years. The centrists, in other words, were eliminated from power.

Over the next twelve years the centrists fared worse and worse. In the 1965 presidential election, the centrist and relatively youthful Jean Lecanuet projected a Kennedy-like image in the first election in which television played a significant role, but won only 15.8 percent of the first ballot vote, not even half what François Mitterrand won as the single candidate of the left.

In 1967, 1968, and 1973 the centrist parties formed electoral alliances in an attempt to rebuild their support, but each time their vote, and especially their representation in parliament, continued to decline. The centrist Alain Poher did make it to the second round of the presidential elections, not so much out of his own popularity, but because the left was so divided in the aftermath of the events of May 1968. The centrists disappeared as a significant organized force in 1974, when the *réformateurs,* as the leaders of the 1973 coalition were called, supported Giscard at the first ballot rather than presenting a candidate of their own.

There could be a future for centrist parties in France. Public opinion remains clustered around the center, and after the 1988 legislative elections, Pierre Méhaignerie organized the Christian democrats as a separate party group in the National Assembly. Nonetheless, given the bipolar nature of the legislative and presidential elections, a substantial recovery by the centrists seems unlikely.

N. Leites, *On the Game of Politics in France* (Stanford, Calif., 1959); D. MacRae, *Parliament, Politics, and Society in France* (New York, 1967); P. M. Williams, *Crisis and Compromise* (London, 1964); F. L. Wilson, *French Political Parties Under the Fifth Republic* (Boulder, Colo., 1982).

C. Hauss

Related entries: BOURGES-MANOURY, MAURICE; CHRISTIAN DEMOCRATS; CONSTITUTION OF THE FIFTH REPUBLIC; CONSTITUTION OF THE FOURTH REPUBLIC; CONSTITUTIONAL COUNCIL; DEBRE, MICHEL; DE GAULLE, CHARLES; DEMOCRATIC AND SOCIALIST UNION OF THE RESISTANCE; ELECTIONS; ELECTORAL SYSTEM; FAURE, EDGAR; GAULLIST PARTY; GISCARD D'ESTAING, VALERY; LECANUET, JEAN; MEHAIGNERIE, PIERRE; MENDES-FRANCE, PIERRE; MITTERRAND, FRANCOIS; MOLLET, GUY; NATIONAL CENTER OF INDEPENDENTS AND PEASANTS; PFLIMLIN, PIERRE; PINAY, ANTOINE; PLEVEN, RENE; POHER, ALAIN; RADICAL PARTY; RAMADIER, PAUL; REFERENDA; SCHUMANN, MAURICE; SERVAN-SCHREIBER, JEAN-JACQUES; SOCIALIST PARTY (PS, SFIO); STALEMATE SOCIETY; TRIPARTITISM; UNION FOR FRENCH DEMOCRACY.

CHABAN-DELMAS, JACQUES (1915–), sportsman, Resistance leader, liberal Gaullist statesman, and long-time mayor of Bordeaux, has played an important role at crucial moments of the Fourth and Fifth Republics. He entered political life through his wartime activities in the Resistance. Mobilized as a reserve officer, he saw action against Italian forces along the Riviera in 1940. Shortly after demobilization he joined the Resistance, adopted "Chaban" as a *nom de guerre*, and in 1942 he contacted the Free French Movement in London. His position with the Finance Inspectorate enabled him to travel throughout France, establishing contact with diverse Resistance groups. In 1944 he became the National Military Representative for Charles de Gaulle's government of National Liberation with the rank of brigadier general.

In August 1944 Chaban went to London to persuade Allied commanders not to bypass Paris, where the Resistance planned to rise. Upon his return to Paris he urged the Resistance to accept an armistice that would permit evacuation of German troops. He then left the city to join General Leclerc's forces and accompanied their triumphal entry on August 24. In his capacity as National Military Delegate, Chaban helped established Gaullist control of City Hall in Paris, averting a possible communist bid for power. Subsequently he became minister of information in de Gaulle's provisional government.

On November 10, 1946 he won election as deputy from the Gironde with support from the Gaullists and the Radical party. The following year he became mayor of Bordeaux, a post that he has held ever since. Throughout the Fourth Republic, Chaban-Delmas maintained ties with the radicals and with the Gaullists. With de Gaulle's approval he joined the Radical party in 1946. In 1951 he left the radicals to join the executive committee of the Gaullist Rally of the French People (RPF). With the dissolution of the RPF in 1953 Chaban joined with other Gaullist deputies to form the Social Republicans (URAS) in the National Assembly, serving as president of that group.

In 1954 Chaban joined the government of Pierre Mendès-France as minister of public works, transportation, and tourism. He opposed formation of the European Defense Community (EDC) and briefly left the government, returning to the cabinet after defeat of the EDC and the resignations of the ministers who had favored it. Chaban's participation in the Mendès-France government gained him the suspicion of right-wing Gaullists, who accused him of excessive flexibility. In the political campaign before the elections of January 2, 1956, Chaban-Delmas led the Social Republicans into cooperation with other parties of the center and noncommunist left to form a Republican Front against the appeal of the extreme right-wing, antiparliamentary movement of Pierre Poujade. In the aftermath of that election, which revealed strength at either extreme—Poujadist and communist—of the electoral spectrum, a government headed by the socialist Guy Mollet included Chaban as minister of state with responsibility for veterans' affairs.

Although the intractable problem of Algeria plagued the Mollet government, this ministry proved to be the longest-lived of the Fourth Republic. When it fell in May 1957, Chaban-Delmas lost his ministerial post, but he returned to office in November under Félix Gaillard as minister of national defense, a position that strengthened his ties with veterans' organizations working to preserve French Algeria. As defense minister he accepted responsibility for the bombing of the Tunisian border town of Sakiet, an event that brought international criticism upon France and precipitated the final crisis of the Fourth Republic. After the return of de Gaulle in June 1958, Chaban became one of the founding members of the Gaullist party, the UNR. He won election to the National Assembly from the Gironde, and his colleagues elected him the Assembly's president, a position that he held throughout de Gaulle's presidency (December 1958–June 1969) and on two other occasions (April 1978–May 1981 and April 1986–June 1988).

When Georges Pompidou succeeded de Gaulle as president of the Fifth Republic, he selected Chaban-Delmas to be his prime minister. Chaban combined his long-standing Gaullism with an ability to appeal to centrist elements, and his cabinet included members of the MRP such as Maurice Schumann and the independent, Valéry Giscard d'Estaing. In the aftermath of the events of May 1968, Chaban embarked upon a policy of opening up a "stalemated" French society. He gave greater independence to state-owned enterprises, liberalized the ORTF, the state-run radio and television service, pressed for decentralization, and settled a series of labor disputes on generous terms. Yet these moderate, liberal reforms, embodied in a "new society" program, failed to satisfy Chaban's critics to the left and right.

Opposition from left of center came from Jean-Jacques Servan-Schreiber, then leader of the Radical party, who decided to challenge Chaban in a by-election at Bordeaux. Chaban crushed his would-be rival by winning over 63 percent of the vote to Servan-Schreiber's 16 percent. The challenge on the right came from orthodox Gaullists who were increasingly upset over the "new society." They received Chaban coolly at national conferences, and an inner circle of conservative Gaullists on the presidential staff persuaded Pompidou that Chaban-Delmas had become too powerful after the prime minister received an overwhelming vote of confidence on his handling of the ORTF reform. In July 1972 Pompidou abruptly dismissed him, despite Chaban's popularity in parliament.

After Pompidou's death in 1974 Chaban-Delmas ran for the presidency, ostensibly as standard-bearer of the Gaullists, but he came in third on the first ballot behind the socialist candidate, François Mitterrand, and the independent, Giscard, who received conservative Gaullist support from Jacques Chirac's faction. Chaban continued to play a role in both national and regional politics as president of the National Assembly and as president of the Aquitaine Regional Council (1974–79, 1985–88). Moderate Gaullists favored him as a possible candidate for the presidency in place of the more abrasive Chirac in 1988, but he declined a nomination. In 1961 Chaban-Delmas won the French national tennis championship in the seniors' division.

J. Bunel, P. Meunier, *Chaban-Delmas* (Paris, 1972); J. Chastenet, *Chaban-Delmas* (Paris, 1989); M. Larkin, *France since the Popular Front* (Oxford, 1988); J.-P. Rioux,

The Fourth Republic 1944–1958 (Cambridge, 1987); V. Wright, *The Government and Politics of France* (New York, 1983).

J. K. Munholland

Related entries: CHIRAC, JACQUES; DECENTRALIZATION; DE GAULLE, CHARLES; GAULLIST PARTY; GISCARD D'ESTAING, VALERY; POMPIDOU, GEORGES; RADICAL PARTY; SERVAN-SCHREIBER, JEAN-JACQUES; STALEMATE SOCIETY.

CHAD CRISIS, a crisis that precipitated French intervention and produced an important victory for the foreign policy of President François Mitterrand in Africa. Chad, a former French colony, was the scene of intermittent French military intervention between 1978 and 1987 and was the largest action France has undertaken (prior to the Gulf crisis) since the end of the Algerian War. Resentment of the Moslem northerners against southern Presidents Tombalbaye and Malloum led to rebellion, the principal leaders being the rivals Hissène Habré and Oueddeï Goukouni.

French interest in this former colony was almost entirely strategic: Goukouni had allied himself with Libya, and if Libyan intervention succeeded in dominating Chad, the sub-Saharan states might stand open to Qaddafi's persuasion and subversion. France first intervened in April 1978, supporting Malloum against the northern rebels. Malloum was later reconciled with Habré, and in 1980, after civil war had erupted between Habré's and Goukouni's forces, the French withdrew.

After Goukouni's Libyan allies occupied the capital, N'Djamena, in January 1981, Goukouni announced the "fusion" of Chad and Libya, alarming the African chiefs of state. The French then negotiated Libyan evacuation of N'Djamena, and an inter-African force moved in. In June 1982, however, Habré's forces took control of the capital, and Goukouni fled. Although some French officials opposed cooperating with Habré, whose men had kidnapped a French ethnologist in the 1970s and murdered an officer sent to negotiate her release, President Mitterrand concluded that Habré was in control of the country.

In June 1983, after Goukouni's men, with Libyan aid, scored some successes and Qaddafi had committed his air force and more troops, the French government reluctantly concluded that serious consequences in French Africa would follow Chad's absorption into the Libyan sphere of influence. France dispatched several hundred military instructors and deployed three thousand French troops on the fifteenth parallel. This Operation Manta was meant to mark French determination to defend Chad south of the fifteenth parallel, including N'Djamena, and to reassure Habré and the African presidents. No French ground troops went into action against the Libyans.

An abortive diplomatic solution in September 1984 saw French, but not Libyan, withdrawal. Mitterrand looked foolish, as the Libyans remained in Chad while the French withdrew. But in February 1986 when Goukouni's men and the Libyans attacked across the sixteenth parallel, the French introduced a new force, code-named *Epervier*, with a large contingent of airplanes and some twelve hundred troops. Their goal was to guarantee Chad south of the sixteenth parallel (and allow Habré's men to operate north of it).

Goukouni then quarreled with Qaddafi and his forces rallied to Habré, leaving the Libyans few pro-Libyan Chadians to legitimate his expedition. Between January and April 1987 the Chadian forces defeated the Libyans in several battles, capturing a large number of weapons and forcing a Libyan retreat up to the Aouzou strip along the Libyan frontier. French aid had of course been decisive in these Chadian victories, but Paris had avoided direct and overt involvement. Little French blood had been shed and French policy had triumphed, without France having to make more than a carefully limited military commitment.

S. Cohen, *La Monarchie nucléaire* (Paris, 1986); T. de Montbrial et al., *RAMSES-Rapport annuel mondial sur le système écononomique et les stratégies* (Paris, 1987).

J. W. Friend

Related entries: FOREIGN POLICY; THIRD WORLD, RELATIONS WITH.

CHALANDON, ALBIN (1920–), civil servant, Gaullist politician, and industrial administrator. Chalandon, the son of an industrialist, was born on June 11, 1920 at Reyrieux in the Ain. He attended three *lycées*—Ampère at Lyon, Michelet at Vanves, and Condorcet in Paris. He also holds a *licence* in letters from the University of Paris.

He began his career as an *inspecteur des finances* and held a number of important administrative posts mostly dealing with industrial reconstruction and finance in the late 1940s and early 1950s. During those years, he was also responsible for professional and social action for the first Gaullist party (RPF). In 1952, he joined the *Banque commerciale de Paris*, where he remained in a number of capacities until 1968 when he was administrator and director general.

In the meantime, he continued his political career. In 1959 he became general secretary of the new Gaullist party, the UNR, and has remained an important Gaullist leader to this day. He was elected to parliament on four occasions (1967, 1968, 1973, and 1986). He is best known politically for his years as minister of industry in Georges Pompidou's last cabinet and then as minister of housing and equipment under Maurice Couve de Murville and Jacques Chaban-Delmas. Chalandon is often credited with and criticized for the rapid urban renewal of Paris and other cities that saw the construction of massive office and apartment complexes and the gentrification of many city centers.

In 1977 Chalandon left active political life and was named president of the national energy firms ERAP (*Entreprise de recherches et d'actions pétrolières*), and ELF-Aquitaine, where he remained until 1983. During those six years, his firms began an aggressive campaign to find new sources of energy in France and abroad that would give the country a more secure and inexpensive source of energy.

In 1986 he was once again elected to parliament. He then served as minister of justice in the *cohabitation* government of Gaullist Jacques Chirac until the left regained control of the Matignon in 1988.

Chalandon was, in short, an archetypical businessman-bureaucrat-politician who was responsible, in part, for France's dramatic economic and political revival in the thirty years after the end of World War II.

W. Adams, C. Stoffaës, *French Industrial Policy* (Washington, 1986); J. Charlot, *The Gaullist Phenomenon* (London, 1971); J. Fourastié, *Les Trentes Glorieuses* (Paris, 1978); G. Martinet, *L'Etat UDR* (Paris, 1973).

C. Hauss

Related entries: CHABAN-DELMAS, JACQUES; CHIRAC, JACQUES; *COHABITATION*; COUVE DE MURVILLE, MAURICE; DEBRE, MICHEL; DE GAULLE, CHARLES; ECONOMIC POLICY; ECONOMIC TRENDS; ELECTIONS; GAULLIST PARTY; GISCARD D'ESTAING, VALERY; INDUSTRIAL POLICY; MESSMER, PIERRE; MIDDLE EAST, RELATIONS WITH; NATIONALIZATIONS; POMPIDOU, GEORGES; STALEMATE SOCIETY; TECHNOLOGY; UNION FOR FRENCH DEMOCRACY.

CHEVENEMENT, JEAN-PIERRE (1939–), economist, politician and minister, and leader of the pseudo-Marxist left wing of the French Socialist party. Born into a family of *instituteurs* in the territory of Belfort, Chevènement's political career has been deeply influenced by his origins. His socialism derives from the fervent social republicanism of his parents and the manufacturing industrial base of Belfort. His strong sense of national identity recalls the heroic defense that the citizens of Belfort mounted against the Germans in 1870–71, a resistance that spared them the fate of Alsace, of which they had previously been considered a part.

After graduating from the University of Besançon and the *Institut d'études politiques* in Paris, Chevènement studied at the *Ecole nationale d'administration* (1963–65) and began a brief career as a commercial civil servant, holding posts both in the finance ministry and overseas.

His main passion was politics, however. After joining the Socialist party (SFIO) in 1964, he rapidly emerged as the political and intellectual leader of a small group of ideological renovators seeking to rejuvenate the somewhat moribund party of Guy Mollet. This group, which established itself in 1965 under the title of *Centre d'études, de recherches et d'éducation socialistes* (CERES), urged three main changes on the SFIO: First, the adoption of a politically more sensitive approach to relations with the Communist party (PCF), involving acceptance of the principle of left unity and a common program of government; second, a more rigorous theoretical base for a socialist economic and industrial policy, forged around large-scale nationalization, protectionism, and "reconquest of the internal market"; and third (although, for obvious reasons, this element was downplayed in public pronouncements) a less critical attitude toward de Gaulle's foreign, nuclear, and defense policy.

Chevènement played a crucial role in the tumultuous events separating the collapse of the old SFIO in 1968–69 and the revival of the *Parti socioliste* (PS) under François Mitterrand in 1971–72. As political secretary of the Paris socialist federation from 1969 to 1970 and as a national secretary, a member of the executive bureau and of the *comité directeur* of the party after 1971, it was, in effect, Chevènement's tactical alliance with Mitterrand, at the new party's founding conference (Suresnes, 1971), that allowed the current president of the Republic to emerge as the *de facto* leader of the Socialist party.

Chevènement was entrusted by Mitterrand with the drafting of the new party's two most important policy documents: *Changer la Vie* (1972), the party's contribution to the PS-PCF common program of government, and *Projet socialiste* (1979–80), the document that served as a basis for Mitterrand's successful presidential bid in 1981. Elected as deputy for Belfort in 1973, Chevènement has been reelected at each subsequent election. He has also played a major part in local politics as mayor of Belfort (since 1983) and as vice-president and then president (1982) of the regional council of Franche-Comté.

After Mitterrand's election to the presidency in 1981, Chevènement was appointed as a minister of state to the key department of research and technology, to which was added, in 1982, the portfolio of industry. He was closely associated with the first period of the Mitterrand presidency, which was characterized by massive state expenditure (on nationalizations and social programs), economic nationalism (through commercial tariffs and restrictions on capital transfer), and popular consumerism of French products. When, in 1984, the constraints of international economic interdependence proved these policies to be potentially ruinous and the "socialist experiment" moved, under Prime Minister Laurent Fabius, into a second phase marked by liberalism and obeisance to market forces, Chevènement was discreetly kicked sideways to become Minister of Education.

In that post he brought to French schools and colleges, which had for over a decade been subjected to increasingly internationalist and vocationalist orientations, a return to the most traditional educational virtues of the Third Republic: a stress on national history, civic instruction, and hard work. He was on the point of becoming the most controversial education minister since Jules Ferry when his ministerial career was cut short by the right-wing victory in the 1986 legislative elections.

During the period of *cohabitation*, Chevènement fought hard to promote, within the PS, the fortunes of his statist, pseudo-Marxist program. In 1983 he had attempted to inject a more populist image into his group by renaming CERES the *Club République moderne* and by launching a new review with the telling title, *République*. But the ideological tide in France was still flooding toward the market, and when Mitterrand was reelected in 1988 it was Chevènement's archrival within the PS, Michel Rocard, who was offered the prime ministership.

In 1988, Chevènement was, hardly surprisingly, given the defense portfolio. In this task, he commanded the absolute respect of the officer corps and succeeded in maintaining intact the Gaullist priorities (primarily nuclear) within a shrinking defense budget constantly under pressure from the less military-minded Rocard. When the Gulf crisis erupted in August 1990, Chevènement gradually parted company with Mitterrand's position. Dedicated to the preservation of peace, fiercely anti-American, and increasingly ill-at-ease with the wave of anti-Iraqi feeling that swept through France (Chevènement, whose wife is Egyptian, was a founding member of the France-Iraq Friendship Society), the minister of defense was unable to live with his conscience once the war began. He resigned on January 29, 1991, at the height of the fighting, a move that was acclaimed by friends as courageous and by adversaries as treacherous. In a hard-fought by-election for his parliamentary seat in Belfort, he was reelected in June 1991 with the narrowest of margins.

Prior to his resignation as defense minister, Chevènement was seen as a potential president of the republic, although his style of leadership and his ideological principles always made him as many adversaries as they did allies within the left.

J.-P. Chevènement, *Les Socialistes, les Communistes et les Autres* (Paris, 1977); *Apprendre pour entreprendre* (Paris, 1985); J-P. Chevènement; P. Messmer, *Le Service militaire* (Paris, 1977); D. Hanley, *Keeping Left? CERES and the French Socialist Party* (Manchester, 1986).

J. Howorth

Related entries: DEFENSE POLICY; EDUCATIONAL REFORM; INDUSTRIAL POLICY; MIDDLE EAST, RELATIONS WITH; MITTERRAND FRANCOIS; SOCIALIST PARTY (PS).

CHIRAC, JACQUES (1932–), former prime minister and leading French politician who is currently mayor of Paris and leader of the *Rassemblement pour la République* (RPR). Chirac was born in Paris on November 29, 1932, although most of his childhood was spent in the rural surroundings of Limousin, not far from Brive, the area from which his parents originated. Despite these rural origins, the majority of Chirac's education was completed in the capital, where in 1951 he moved to study at the *Institut d'études politiques*. Here his friends included a number of his current political rivals, notably Michel Rocard. Subsequently, he passed the entrance examination for the *Ecole nationale d'administration* from where he graduated in 1959.

Following a short period of service in Algeria, Jacques Chirac then took up a post in 1960 as auditor at the *Cours des comptes* in Paris. Soon, however, he moved on to join the General Secretariat of the government, where he worked until 1967. In this year, at the still youthful age of thirty-four, he was offered his first ministerial post, becoming secretary of state for employment (only a short time after having been elected *député* for the department of Corrèze). Then, after a period working under Valéry Giscard d'Estaing as minister responsible for the budget, he was appointed in 1971 to the post of minister responsible for relations with Parliament. The following year he moved on to become minister of agriculture and in 1974 he was offered the post of minister of the interior. This rapid advance in Chirac's career owed much to his personal qualities, for he was noted as an able and efficient worker, but it also reflected the patronage of the then-president, Georges Pompidou, who had great respect for his minister's energy and ambition.

With Giscard elected president following Pompidou's unexpected death in April 1974, Chirac was offered the post of prime minister in the new government. He accepted and took office in May of that year. With their combination of youthfulness, energy, and undoubted ability, the Giscard-Chirac tandem appeared an ideal duo to conduct the nation's affairs. However, the partnership was not to last, and in August 1976 Chirac resigned, claiming that Giscard had restricted his freedom of movement to an excessive degree. The gulf between the two men widened, and in 1981 Chirac entered the presidential election of that year as a challenger to Giscard. He was eliminated in the first round, scoring only 18 percent of the vote, but he had split the vote of the right, a factor that undoubtedly contributed to the narrow defeat of Giscard by the socialist François Mitterrand in the second round of the election.

The socialists' victory in the general election of 1981 imposed a period of enforced exclusion from government office on Chirac. However, with the victory of the right in the 1986 election the situation changed. As leader of the largest party of the new majority, RPR, Chirac was invited by Mitterrand to become prime minister. He accepted the challenge, so giving rise to two years of *cohabitation* with a left-wing president. Despite the expectation that this arrangement (unprecedented in the life of the Fifth Republic) would not last and despite major disagreements (notably over Chirac's privatization plans), the two leaders continued their period of coexistence until the presidential election of 1988.

Chirac had hoped that his two years in government would provide the necessary springboard to presidential victory, but this was not to be the case. In the election of June 1988 he was beaten by Mitterrand in the second round of the contest, scoring only a lowly 46 percent of the total vote. Once again the right had been split, not just by the candidate of the *Union pour la démocratie française* (UDF), Raymond Barre, but also by the National Front and Jean-Marie Le Pen. Moreover, in Mitterrand, Chirac had been faced with an astute challenger who had succeeded in unifying the vote of the left wing.

Apart from his posts in government, Chirac has held a number of other important offices. In 1976 he took control of the Gaullist party, launching the RPR to replace the *Union des démocrates pour la République*. This successful bid for leadership of the Gaullist movement had been partly inspired by the recognition of the importance that the support of a strong party machine could play in any subsequent bid for high office. Since this period Chirac has remained president of the movement.

In 1977 Chirac took on a further important role—he was elected mayor of Paris. He was reelected in both 1983 and 1989, and, in the latter election the RPR scored a landslide victory, taking control of all twenty electoral districts in the city. As mayor he was given his first experience of the difficulties of cohabiting with a socialist president after Mitterrand's victory in 1981. He also found himself in conflict with the socialist government, notably over its legislation to dilute the mayor's powers by decentralizing certain responsibilities to the councils of the city's *arrondissements* (1983). Conversely, control of the

Paris *Mairie* enabled Chirac to build up a staff of experienced collaborators (who subsequently followed him when he was prime minister) and to experiment with ideas such as privatization (various municipal services were privatized), later applied at a national level.

Until the defeat in 1988, Chirac's career had been extremely successful. His rise to high office had been rapid, amply demonstrating his immense energy and determination, and the strength of his ambition. His success might also be attributed to his capacity for hard work and his incessant activity. However, the reverse suffered in the presidential elections led to greater emphasis being accorded to certain negative qualities of his character: his excessive haste and impetuosity, his abrasiveness and abrupt manner, his dependence on others for guidance, and his opportunism. Since 1988, therefore, Chirac's position as "natural" leader of the opposition and undisputed head of the RPR has been increasingly challenged, notably by those anxious to see the movement embrace new policies and a new direction.

M. Ambroise-Rendu, *Paris-Chirac* (Paris, 1987); T. Desjardins, *Un Inconnu nommé Chirac* (Paris, 1983); F.-O. Giesbert, *Jacques Chirac* (Paris, 1987); M. Szafran, *Chirac ou les passions du pouvoir* (Paris, 1986).

J. N. Tuppen

Related entries: COHABITATION; ELECTIONS; GAULLIST PARTY; GAULLISM; GISCARD D'ESTAING, VALERY; MITTERRAND, FRANCOIS; PARIS REGION; POLITICAL TRENDS.

CHRISTIAN DEMOCRATS (MRP), a pillar of tripartitism and a key governmental party under the Fourth Republic, which has largely ceased to exist as a distinct political entity under the Fifth Republic. Originally called the *Mouvement républicain de libération* and stemming directly from the Catholic Resistance, the *Mouvement républicain populaire* (MRP) was founded at a convention in Paris on November 25–26, 1944. The new political party descended from a long line of movements that had sought to effect a historic reconciliation between Catholics and the republican regime. Most notably, the MRP appears as the heir of Marc Sangnier's *Le Sillon* and *Jeune République*, as well as the interwar *Parti démocrate populaire*. Ideologically, drawing from a substantial body of social Catholic thought, the MRP advocated a "third way" between the flawed materialist paths of both liberalism and communism.

The MRP rapidly emerged as the most successful Christian democratic party in French history. Receiving 23.9 percent of the votes cast in the October 1945 constituent assembly election, it was outpolled only by the communists. The party's precipitous rise may be explained in part by the post-Liberation ethos of renewal. It must, however, also be attributed to the discredit of traditional conservative parties and the perception of the MRP as the "party of fidelity" to General Charles de Gaulle.

Despite its tactical commitment to tripartitism, the MRP provisionally broke with its communist and socialist partners over the constitutional question. It led the successful "No" campaign in the May 1946 referendum. In the ensuing constituent assembly election, the MRP won 28.2 percent of the vote and briefly became "the first party of France." Nevertheless, accepting a markedly similar constitutional text soon thereafter, it failed to carry a significant portion of its electorate in the October 1946 referendum. A warning had been served, though the party rebounded to capture 25.9 percent of the vote in the first Fourth Republic legislative election.

The year 1947 was a turning point for the MRP. The formation of the Gaullist *Rassemblement du peuple français* in April and the breakup of tripartitism in May led to MRP participation in a series of "third force" governments. These centrist ministries were united by little beyond support for the regime itself; both religious/secular and socioeconomic divisions ran deep.

Frustrated in government, the party also suffered a severe electoral decline. The MRP won only 12.6 percent of the vote in the 1951 parliamentary election and 11.1 percent in that of 1956. Moreover, it increasingly became a regional party concentrated in the northeast and northwest, as well as the department of Nord and a broken string of departments from Savoy to the Pyrenees. Whereas the party had participated in every government but one (Blum) from the Liberation until 1951, it was officially absent from three governments in the period 1951–58 (Mendès-France, Mollet, Bourgès-Maunoury). Similarly, while two premiers had been drawn from the party's ranks in the first legislature of the Fourth Republic (Robert Schuman and Georges Bidault), it was to provide only one more (Pierre Pflimlin) during the final two.

In 1958 the MRP overwhelmingly supported de Gaulle's return to power and weathered the first election of the Fifth Republic surprisingly well. Together with Bidault's newly formed *Démocratie chrétienne de France*, it tallied the same 11.1 percent of the vote as it had two years earlier. The desire for a liberal solution to the Algerian problem kept the mainstream of the MRP in the general's camp until 1962. After Algerian independence the party's fervent support of European integration, as well as de Gaulle's presidentialization of the regime, quickly pushed it into opposition. From this position it managed to poll only 8.9 percent of the vote in the November 1962 legislative election.

Having clearly lost its place in the Fifth Republic, the MRP national convention at La Baule in May 1963 voted to merge into a broader political movement. In 1966, it joined Jean Lecanuet's *Centre démocrate*. Largely spent as a partisan force, Christian democracy in France, like liberalism in Britain, nonetheless remains an important strand in the basic fabric of the nation's political life.

F.-G. Dreyfus, *Histoire de la démocratie chrétienne en France* (Paris, 1988); M. Einaudi, F. Goguel, *Christian Democracy in Italy and France* (Notre Dame, Ind., 1951); R. E. M. Irving, *Christian Democracy in France* (London, 1973); P. Letamendia, *Le MRP* (thesis, Bordeaux, 1975).

R. A. Harmsen

Related entries: BARRE, RAYMOND; BIDAULT, GEORGES; CATHOLICISM; CENTRIST PARTIES; *CONFEDERATION FRANCAISE DES TRA-*

VAILLEURS CHRETIENS; LECANUET, JEAN; MEHAIGNERIE, PIERRE; PFLIMLIN, PIERRE; POHER, ALAIN; SCHUMAN, ROBERT; SCHUMANN, MAURICE; TRIPARTITISM; UNION FOR FRENCH DEMOCRACY.

CINEMA, as everywhere, has lost its position as the most popular mass medium in France. French movie audiences peaked in 1957 with approximately 412 million spectators; in 1982 they stood at 200 million. This decline has been accompanied by fewer movie houses, one in three closing between 1957 and 1971. Competition from television shows no signs of abating, and recent end of the state monopoly as well as increasing access to cable stations and videocasette players should further intensify competition. However, of all national film industries, the French and the American ones have most successfully responded to the challenge of the "small screen." Throughout the 1970s French film production did not slump, maintaining an average output of approximately two hundred features a year. In 1978, a dismal year for attendance and profits, forty-seven French directors produced their first feature.

Of all twentieth-century art, film is particularly sensitive to the conflicting requirements of mass entertainment, profitability, and creativity. In addition, French cinema has had a unique commercial and artistic relation with its principal model and rival, Hollywood. Since World War II, if not before, American movies have been a permanent commercial threat to the French film industry; simultaneously, they have inspired and revitalized French directors. Within the larger context of the transformation of all mass media, French *cinéastes* in a complex dialectic with Hollywood have been especially creative and innovative.

Immediately after the war French filmmakers rapidly returned to the traditions of the late 1930s. Some changes did occur: Training for careers in the movie industry was given greater professional status with the creation of the *Institut des hautes études du cinéma* (IHEC); a government office of film, the *Centre national du cinéma français* was established; the first Cannes festival, heavily subsidized by the Fourth Republic, opened in 1946; and Nazi collaborators were purged from the industry. But even these changes were less innovative than they appeared. The Cannes festival had been scheduled to open in September 1939. Much more important in the training of future French filmmakers than the IHEC was the *Cinémathèque*, which had already been established in 1937. Rather than technique, the *Cinémathèque* communicated a passion for movies and an acute sense of film tradition to young Parisians. The purge of collaborators was fraught with ambiguity and uncertainty. Several important directors who had continued or begun their career during the German Occupation and Vichy had few problems in continuing their work after 1945.

Censorship also remained in force in France until 1972. During the Fourth and Fifth Republics film distributors were required to apply for a *visa d'exploitation*. From 1917 to 1960 this application was made to the *Commission de contrôle*, attached to the prime minister's office. In the Fifth Republic the *Commission* was shifted first to the Ministry of Information and then, after 1968, to the Ministry of Cultural Affairs. Through all these moves the *Commission* retained the right to refuse the *visa* on the grounds of "immorality or danger to public peace." Between 1961 and 1972 thirty films were banned, some, such as Godard's *Le Petit Soldat* (1960) and Pontecorvo's *The Battle of Algiers* (1967), for political reasons. In the late 1980s mayors still retained the power to ban films in their municipalities.

While institutions, including the continuing presence of French studios, provided links between the post–1945 years and the prewar years, the most important source of continuity was the commitment of French directors to a particular style characterized as *cinéma de qualité*. Many of the films of the late 1940s and early 1950s shared this carefully planned and controlled approach, which relied on the dialogue and plot of a detailed script, often adapted from a literary source. These films excelled in high technical quality with meticulously constructed and lit studio sets. They often analyzed personal relations from a cool and distanced perspective. Several directors who had already established international reputations before the war created and refined this style. Marcel Carné, who collaborated closely with the writer Jacques Prévert, created *Les Enfants du paradis* under difficult conditions during the Occupation, but it was only released in 1945. This film, which his later work never matched, embodied the importance of a highly literary script and the centrality of nineteenth-century narrative. Max Ophuls, who had spent the war in Hollywood, returned to France and directed *La Ronde* (1950), a Schnitzler play, and *Lola Montès* (1955), his last film.

The most important source of continuity between the 1930s and the postwar period was the great genius of Jean Renoir. He too had spent the war in Hollywood. His first completely French postwar production was *French Cancan* (1954), an exuberant, joyous, color musical paying homage to *la belle époque*. The nostalgia was heightened by casting Jean Gabin in the role of an aging impresario. *French Cancan* incorporated Renoir's distinctive humanism and *joie de vivre*, the studio crafting, and the influence of Hollywood's best musicals. Still none of Renoir's films of the postwar period approached the brilliance or social and political relevance of his works of the late 1930s. Younger directors also promoted and continued the prewar French traditions. René Clement's *Les Jeux interdits* (1952) had a strong script based on a novel and poignantly portrayed the impact of war on two children. Rejected at Cannes, it won Hollywood's Academy Award for Best Foreign Film. Henri-Georges Clouzot excelled in the *policier* genre and *film noir*: most noteworthy was *Les Diaboliques* (1955).

While the major direction of French film in the late 1940s and early 1950s was continuity with the past and the domination of studio films with strong scripts, there was room for unique talents. Henri Bresson's extraordinarily crafted films focused on spiritually intense subjects and powerful images. His output remained small, eight films in twenty-five years; among the most important was *Journal d'un curé de campagne* (1951). Jacques Tati in *Jour de fête* (1949) and *Les Vacances de M. Hulot* (1953) revived comedy with a return to the grand moments of silent film with worldwide success, but few French followers.

By the late 1950s there was no question that the reputation of French cinema had been restored and that the industry had at least recovered from the austerity and control of the Occupation/Vichy period. However, filmmakers were obsessed with the *défi américain*. Immediately after the war the French industry was especially concerned that Hollywood would dump five years of wartime production in France. When the Fourth Republic negotiated loans and trade agreements with Washington in 1946, the final Blum-Byrnes accord included clauses protecting the French film industry. They stipulated that French films must be shown for a minimum of sixteen weeks per year in all French theaters (extended in 1948 to twenty weeks, these restrictions ended in 1961). In addition the eight major American distributors agreed to limit their exports to 124 dubbed features in 1946–47. The intent was to forestall further French restrictions and protect what was already a high number of exports. The French government responded with further regulations. After 1947 the *visa d'importation* could only be granted if no more than two years had elapsed between the original release and the dubbed version of the film.

In addition to protectionist policies, the Fourth Republic and then, with greater resources, the Fifth Republic supported filmmakers and encouraged independent directors. A tax on movie-theater tickets generated funds that were dispensed by the *Centre national du cinéma français*. In most cases directors and producers received advances on future profits and tax breaks. Often these advances were awarded to projects that had special artistic and innovative qualities (Bresson's films for example). During the 1970s approximately 300 million francs were spent annually on these advances. The French governments also have supported special theaters, *circuits d'art et d'essai*, to promote innovative and high-quality film.

Despite these government policies, American competition continued to loom large. One commercial response was to attempt to match Hollywood style, production, and distribution, which of course the French have had extreme difficulty duplicating. Beginning in the 1960s, international coproductions became more frequent, especially between French and Italian studios. A few very large coproductions occurred between French and American companies, such as *Paris brûle-t-il?/Is Paris Burning* (1966) directed by René Clement. The major French studio Gaumont became less financially conservative in the 1960s under the pressure of American competition. In the 1970s it aimed to recapture portions of the French and European markets.

Neither government controls nor corporate strategies have successfully eliminated *le défi américain*. But during the late 1950s and into the 1960s a most extraordinary dynamic occurred between a new generation of French directors and American movies. Coming of age in the *Cinémathèque* and the Paris *ciné-clubs*, this new generation viewed Hollywood films not as commercial competitors but as inspirations. In turn this disparate group of young directors established a new kind of cinema, transforming bits and pieces of some Hollywood genres and creating a new pace, style, and sensibility in film that would eventually, albeit indirectly, influence even Hollywood production. Journalists of *L'Express* in the early 1960s labeled this phenomenon *la nouvelle vague*. Between 1958 and 1963 there was an enormous output of new films by first-time directors: 170 first features. Most of these broke with the traditions of the *cinéma de qualité* and studio production. The new directors were aided by the availability of state support, flexible union regulations in the film industry, and the underdevelopment of production and distribution organizations, which enabled independents to enter more easily. Technological innovations in film stock and cameras made independent, individualistic experiments more feasible. In addition, as the first group of directors to have grown up with movies, they had a strong sense of film history. Finally, the period was one of both dynamic economic expansion and deep, often unspoken, political tensions around Gaullism and the Algerian War.

There were at least two main groups within what was called *la nouvelle vague*. The first and most prominent included those not-quite-so-young men who had first gained notoriety as film critics in the important journal *Les Cahiers du cinéma*. Established in 1951 by André Bazin and Jacques Doniol-Valcroze, it analyzed all film as a serious art form. An educator and intellectual, Bazin stressed the role of individual creativity in film, a view strongly marked by the Christian existentialism of the immediate post-Liberation years. He promoted a group of younger men on the journal's staff, François Truffaut, Claude Chabrol, Jean-Luc Godard, and Eric Rohmer. All of them, Truffaut most forcefully, damned the finely crafted literary French films of the late 1940s and 1950s, especially those of Carné and Prévert.

By the late 1950s the *Cahiers* group moved from writing about movies to making them. In 1959 Truffaut won the Cannes prize for best direction for his first feature *Les 400 Coups*. He followed this humanistic autobiography with *Tirez sur le pianiste* (1960), in part an homage to Hollywood *film noir*, and then in 1961 the lyrical *Jules et Jim* suffused with the presence of Jeanne Moreau. All were independent productions; *Les 400 Coups* and *Jules et Jim* were produced by Truffaut's own company. In 1959 another member of the *Cahiers* group, Jean-Luc Godard, tried his hand at directing. His first feature, *A bout de souffle*, was shot in one month on a budget of $90,000. Godard followed this with an extraordinary period of productivity, creating thirteen features between 1960 and 1967 and breaking all the rules of cinema. By 1964 Godard had also formed his own independent company. Throughout the 1960s other members of the *Cahiers* editorial staff took up directing and became associated with *la nouvelle vague*: Claude Chabrol, Eric Rohmer, and Jacques Rivette.

The second major group included under the loose rubric *nouvelle vague* consisted of directors who emerged from documentary production and who often had close ties with the literary movement of the "new novel." The dominant presence in this group was Alain Resnais, who had already established himself as an innovative director of documentaries with the powerful and brilliantly edited contemplation of the Nazi concentration camps, *Nuit et brouillard* (1955). In 1959, supported by a state grant, he made his first feature, *Hiroshima, mon amour*, introducing entirely new concepts of filmmaking. *Hiroshima* used a script by one of the practitioners of the new novel, Marguerite Duras, and two years later Resnais collaborated with Alain Robbe-Grillet, another new novelist, in *L'Année dernière à Marienbad*. Both Duras and Robbe-Grillet would, by the mid–1960s, themselves shift from writing to filmmaking; by the 1970s directing had become Marguerite Duras's principal creative activity. In the same circle was Agnès Varda, whose early training had been in still photography. Her first feature, *La Pointe courte* (1955), predates the *nouvelle vague*, and despite the success of her second film, *Cléo de 5 à 7* (1962), she had considerable difficulty finding producers in the 1960s. Through the 1970s she maintained her interest in women's issues and continued to direct significant films, *L'Une chante, l'autre pas* (1977) and *La Vagabonde* (1987).

The *nouvelle vague* of the early 1960s encompassed a very disparate group of individuals who shared only a general, but new sensibility about film. While they were all highly conscious of the European and American film traditions, they expressed considerable ambiguity about them. On the one hand, they rejected the French *cinéma de qualité* and called for a new cinema. On the other hand, they praised prewar French cinema, especially the work of Renoir. Their adulation of Hollywood directors was boundless. Bazin and Truffaut transformed Alfred Hitchcock from a commercial master of suspense into a significant director of metaphysical depth. These Frenchmen taught Americans the artistry of Howard Hawks and John Ford. They propounded "*la politique des auteurs*": A film is a work of art, expressing the creativity of the director, its author; and the camera is the pen. Good directors express their personal stamp even in imperfect films, constrained by studio-imposed scripts.

This insistence on film as personal expression of the director's creativity encouraged a new style, expressionistic and spontaneous. Making a virtue of necessity, the early films of Truffaut and Godard were all shot on location with very few takes and very small budgets. Controls imposed by studio sets were abandoned for the moving or hand-held camera, and new, fast film stock allowing natural lighting. Godard in particular reveled in dislocating the narrative and the viewer with frequent jump cuts. Scripts were largely improvised. Even Resnais, who worked much more in the studio, rejected traditional narrative and through tracking shots and abrupt cuts recreated the process of memory.

Many of the films of the period were strongly autobiographical; Truffaut's best were all intensely personal. Movie making itself became a subject for the filmmaker, as in Truffaut's *La Nuit américaine* (1973). This self-consciousness about creativity and the medium introduced a modernist sensibility and presented perception itself as problematic. In the early 1960s the *nouvelle vague* was not particularly concerned with political issues. With the exception of Godard's *Le Petit Soldat* (1960, banned till 1963), there was little examination of the Algerian War. However, several of these new directors were treating relations between men and women as if they were political, and in many of their films there was a sometimes diffuse, sometimes sharp criticism of the comfortable bourgeois life. More important than content, the *nouvelle vague* communicated a new sense of the power of film, and this influenced all movie making. After Truffaut, Godard, and Resnais, the screen image had become infinitely more immediate, subjective, and kinetic.

By the late 1960s the *nouvelle vague* was increasingly less of a defined group. Many filmmakers were becoming less independent, less innovative, and were establishing their positions within commercial filmmaking. The events of 1968 had little effect on most of them, despite the fact that Truffaut led the successful disruption of the Cannes festival. Godard, the most productive and perhaps the most creative member of the *Cahiers* circle, was the one exception. His films of 1967, *La Chinoise* and *Weekend*, seemed to have predicted the student revolt of May and June. After 1968 Godard, with some desperation, sought to retreat entirely from commercial filmmaking, experimenting with new techniques, abandoning the artistic control of the director, and attempting to "*faire un film politiquement.*" In 1980 he began his return to more commercial films with *Sauve qui peut . . . (La vie),* in which the theme of prostitution, already treated in his films of the 1960s, stood as a metaphor for society and filmmaking.

Throughout the 1970s Truffaut continued to make fine films but without the breakthrough innovations of the previous decade. Among his most successful, studio and script reasserted their dominant place (*Adèle H*, 1975, and *Le Dernier Métro*, 1981). Resnais's work went into sharp decline. The new directors of the 1970s adopted the innovations of the early 1960s but now limited improvisation, relied more on scripts, sought more commercially viable themes, and required larger budgets. Among those who had begun during the period of the *nouvelle vague* was Louis Malle, whose stature grew during the 1970s, particularly with *Lacombe, Lucien* (1973). Constantin Costa-Gavras combined some elements of the *nouvelle vague* (especially its admiration for the *policier* genre) and the vaguely leftist sentiment of the post–1968 years creating commercially successful films. During the 1970s several new directors did appear, and the French government extended its policy of support. The most important has been Bernard Tavernier with his intimate portrait of family and social life in Lyon in *L'Horloger de Saint-Paul* (1974).

The 1970s could not match the previous decade in terms of energy, excitement, and innovation. As always the great mass of the cinema continued to be dominated by highly commercial ventures with conventional genre plots and star names. Although the number of films produced continued to increase in the 1970s, the size of the audience continued to shrink. Producers and theater owners found a facile solution to this problem in the mid–1970s: pornography. Censorship was relaxed in 1973, and by 1975 pornographic movies constituted 15 percent of all films shown. Under considerable pressure, the government created an X-rated category, banning entry to those under eighteen, relegating these films to certain theaters, and taxing receipts at 33 percent. By 1976 X-rated films represented only 5 percent of all films shown. Another effort to restore sagging movie attendance was Gaumont's aggressive management aimed at competing with Hollywood for an international market. In the early 1980s Gaumont produced a series of high-quality historical films with international casts and crew, such as *La Nuit de Varennes* and *Danton*. By 1985, however, Gaumont was in serious financial difficulty due to the enormous debt incurred by such expensive ventures.

Compared with many other European national cinemas, French Cinema was relatively well off in the mid 1980s. It had recovered slightly from the steepest loss of audience in the 1970s. The American share of the market held fairly steady at about 30 percent. Coproductions continued to flourish, *multi-salles* theaters maintained the more selective audience, the government continued to aid new directors and the industry as a whole, and there were commercial successes of serious movies, such as Louis Malle's *Au revoir les enfants* (1986). There were problems, however: The export of French movies continued its steady decline from its 1960s peak, relations with the government-controlled television stations of ORTF were never clearly elaborated, and the impact of the new commercial stations remained unknown. Truffaut's untimely death in 1984 seemed to mark the end of an era without any clear sense of what might follow. However, that same year Godard released his latest film, *Je vous salue Marie*, which demonstrated the continuing power of cinema and filmmakers.

R. Armes, *French Cinema since 1946* (London, 1970); *Les Cahiers du cinéma* (1951–), especially A. Bazin, "La Critique de la politique des auteurs" (1957), and the 1962 issue on *la nouvelle vague*; P. de Comes, M. Marmim, *Le Cinéma français, 1960–1985* (Paris, 1985); V. de Grazia, "Mass Culture and Sovereignty: The American Challenge to European Cinemas, 1920–1960," *Journal of Modern History* 61 (1989); J. Monaco, *The New Wave* (New York, 1976); J. Renoir, *My Life and My Films* (New York, 1974); F. Truffaut, *Le Cinéma selon Hitchcock* (Paris, 1966).

J. F. Stone

Related entries: CULTURAL POLICY; LEISURE; LITERATURE; SOCIAL TRENDS.

CLUB MOVEMENT, an effort to promote specific ideological points of view, especially under the Fifth Republic when the consolidation of the party system made it difficult to do so within individual parties. The tradition of political clubs began with the Revolution of 1789 and has revived time and again during France's recurrent periods of crisis. Relatively quiescent during the Fourth Republic, the clubs revived under the Fifth Republic.

Political clubs are organizations that individual French citizens, usually intellectuals, form in order to support particular political parties, or particular factions within the parties. Clubs meet, hear speakers, and hold debates on important topics of the day. Their significance and effectiveness usually rests in the personal prestige of their members, and not in the number of votes they can command. Some (e.g., the *Club Jean Moulin*), are very exclusive, whereas others (e.g., *Citoyens 60* or *Perspectives et réalités*) have welcomed large numbers into their fold.

Political clubs can be found on both the left and the right. Among the best known on the left were the *Club des Jacobins* and the *Club Jean Moulin*; the latter, founded in 1958 and now defunct, was roughly comparable to the British Fabian Society, leaning somewhat toward the center ideologically. Left-wing clubs have considered such questions as the problems associated with advancing technology, how to combat fascism (or Gaullism), and how to promote laicism. They have suggested a wide range of institutional and social reforms. In 1964 several socialist clubs banded together as the Convention of Republican Institutions (CIR), and it was as leader of this organization that François Mitterrand, the president of France, was able to form the Federation of the Democratic and Socialist Left (FGDS) and take its leadership. Although the FGDS did not succeed, it led eventually to the formation of the Socialist party (PS) and to Mitterrand's election to the French presidency in 1981. Throughout this period of socialist buildup, leading club intellectuals played key roles in Mitterrand's "shadow cabinet."

On the right the clubs have been preoccupied with such issues as the excesses of modern society, how to spread the Catholic doctrine, and how to combat socialism and communism. One of the strongest club movements in recent years has been that of "Perspectives and Realities." First founded in 1965, this movement grew to over fifty-five clubs with over five thousand members in the next five years. This rapid growth took place largely at the prompting of Valéry Giscard d'Estaing, to whose successful bid for the presidency this movement gave significant support in 1974. Gaullist clubs include the *Union des jeunes pour le progrès*, *Solidarité et liberté*, and *Club 89*.

Some clubs are strongly associated with particular parties, or even become components thereof. The Perspectives and Realities clubs and the *Mouvement démocrate socialiste de France* both belong to the Union for French Democracy (UDF), and the (CIR) eventually became a unit of the new Socialist party, as did CERES (Center of Socialist Study and Research).

Other clubs have been organized to support particular politicians, such as *Club 89* (Parisian Gaullists supporting Jacques Chirac), the *Comité d'études pour un nouveau contrat social*, established in 1969 by Edgar Faure (to support Edgar Faure), and *Socialisme et démocratie* (backing Alain Savary). In some cases, clubs have been taken over by individuals after their inception. Examples here include the takeover of the CIR by Mitterrand and Giscard's takeover of the Perspectives and Realities clubs in the late 1960s.

On the other hand, many clubs have been multipartisan or nonpartisan in their composition; examples include the *Club Jean Moulin*, which included Catholics and nonpolitical civil servants as well as socialists and radicals; the trade-unionist GROP (Worker and Peasant Research Group), the right-wing *Club d'horloge*, established in 1974 by businessmen and technocrats; and *Echange et projets*, a group intended to bring together like-minded socialists and businessmen.

Often referred to as the "*forces vives*" among French political associations, in recent years the clubs have played a key role in the transformation of outdated party structures. However, characteristically ideological, reformist, and often exclusive, it is doubtful they ever had the potential for developing into alternative mass movements that some would once have ascribed to them. Now, as French parties and politicians adopt more modern and more media-oriented styles of campaigning, the attention paid to the recommendations of the clubs has inevitably waned, and at present their influence is very much in decline. However, the clubs represent a venerable tradition in the French political system. Should their predilection for reform one day become focused on themselves, it seems reasonable to suggest that they may achieve yet another renaissance.

H. Ehrmann, *Politics in France*, 4th ed. (Boston, 1983); D. Hanley, *Keeping Left? CERES and the French Socialist Party* (Manchester, Eng., 1986); W. Safran, *The French Polity*, 2d ed. (New York, 1985); H. Waterman, *Political Change in Contemporary France* (Columbus, Ohio, 1969).

K. L. Lawson

Related entries: FEDERATION OF THE DEMOCRATIC AND SOCIALIST LEFT; INTELLECTUAL TRENDS; MITTERRAND, FRANCOIS; POLITICAL TRENDS; SOCIALIST PARTY (PS, SFIO).

COHABITATION, the period between 1986 and 1988 when socialist president François Mitterrand shared power with a conservative government headed by the Gaullist Jacques Chirac. It followed the narrow victory of the coalition of the Gaullist *Rassemblement pour la République* and of the center-right *Union pour la démocratie française* in the March 16 legislative elections. Despite Chirac's initial attempts to question the president's authority, compromises were quickly reached over the nominations of high-level civil servants and over the president's and prime minister's respective domains. Major institutional or policy clashes remained few. Following articles twenty and twenty-one of the constitution, Chirac ran domestic affairs and was free to implement a conservative program that emphasized the privatization of several state enterprises, the reform of labor laws, the elimination of proportional representation, the fight against crime and terrorism, and the control of illegal immigration. Mitterrand retained his preeminence over defense and key foreign policy areas such as East-West relations and European affairs.

Several reasons explain this relatively smooth process: (1) the relative popularity of the arrangement—by a large majority, the French wanted it to last until the 1988 presidential elections; (2) the growing political consensus expressed in the narrowing of the gap between left and right; (3) the proximity of the presidential elections, which, although it encouraged electoral positioning, also induced both leaders to adopt some restraint; (4) the divisions within the conservative coalition; and (5) as far as foreign affairs were concerned, systemic pressures toward continuity, the president's constitutional responsibilities, international legal stipulations, and a consensus on major foreign policy options (most evident in the adoption of the 1987 Military Planning Law and in the support for the Intermediate-Range Nuclear Treaty).

Politically, *cohabitation* rehabilitated the pre–1986 socialist government. The president cast himself as Father of the Nation and upholder of basic principles while distancing himself from the hard domestic decisions. His public declarations also helped weaken the government, for example during the winter 1987 strikes. Most important, along with the socialist victory of 1981, this period strengthened and finally legitimized the constitution. It demonstrated the public's opposition to a drastic weakening of the presidency and helped settle the separation of powers between the president in charge of defense and foreign affairs and the prime minister in charge of domestic ones. The impact of *cohabitation* on the national political culture therefore seemed profound. The French apparently like the balancing of power that it created and thus the obstacle to extremism. It showed that a wide gap no longer separated the left and the right since they could collaborate in the sharing of governmental powers. *Cohabitation* ended when Chirac failed to unseat Mitterrand and was replaced by the socialist Michel Rocard as head of a minority government in June 1988.

C. Debbasch, *La Guerre froide de la cohabitation* (Paris, 1988); M. Duverger, *La Cohabitation des français* (Paris, 1987); P. Le Prestre, ed., *French Security Policy in a Disarming World* (Boulder, Colo., 1989).

P. Le Prestre

Related entries: CHIRAC, JACQUES; CONSTITUTION OF THE FIFTH REPUBLIC; GAULLIST PARTY; MITTERRAND, FRANCOIS; POLITICAL TRENDS; ROCARD, MICHEL.

COHN-BENDIT, DANIEL (1945–), anarchist leader of the May 1968 Parisian student rebellion and a key figure in the March 22nd Movement at the University of Paris-Nanterre. Born in Montauban of German refugee parents, he opted for German citizenship at age eighteen. After completing his secondary education in Frankfurt, he entered Nanterre to study sociology. There he joined the anarchist *Noir et rouge* society and became a leader of student protests against the university system and the discipline of sociology, both of which he claimed supported and justified authoritarian capitalism. He became prominent nationally in January 1968, when he insulted the minister of youth and sports at the dedication of Nanterre's Olympic swimming pool. The government attempted, unsuccessfully, to expel him from France, only to see his popularity increase.

Using the ideas and tactics of the anarchist/surrealist Situationist International, Cohn-Bendit and his followers disrupted classes, attacked university administrators, and took over buildings in efforts to expose the repressive nature of the educational system and gain the support of the student body for revolutionary change. On March 22, 1968, during the takeover of a Nanterre administration building, he helped create the March 22nd Movement, a loose grouping of leftist activists engaged in confrontational tactics. During April, their calls for a student boycott of final exams polarized the university. On May 2 the Dean closed down Nanterre and had Cohn-Bendit and others summoned to appear before a disciplinary council at the University of Paris. The following day, at the courtyard of the Sorbonne, Cohn-Bendit and other student leaders held a protest meeting that led to police intervention, the arrest of hundreds of students, and the beginning of mass student agitation, which culminated in the ''Night of the Barricades'' on May 10 and the massive general strike of students and workers on May 13.

During the May events, Cohn-Bendit became a media figure, known to the French as Danny the Red. He exhorted the student revolutionaries to join forces with the working class to overthrow Gaullism, to establish local action committees as the base for democratic decision making, and to eschew compromise with political parties and trade unions. He refused to compromise his anarchist ideals for better bureaucratic organization, but he acted resolutely to avoid bloodshed on May 10 and he called for a general strike of all groups on the left for May 13. Eventually, however, his German citizenship, his Jewish background, and his strident anti-Gaullism and anticommunism made him into the *bête noire* of the forces of order on both the left and the right. On May 22, after a speaking engagement abroad, he was prohibited from returning to France. Although he reentered the country clandestinely in late May and was proclaimed ''existentialist man of the year'' by Jean-Paul Sartre, he never again resumed his prominence in the movement. As Cohn-Bendit recognized later, anarchist ideas encountered their limitations during the course of the May events. Today, he is an ecologist and a journalist in Germany.

D. Cohn-Bendit, *Le Grand Bazar* (Paris, 1975), *Obsolete Communism: The Left-Wing Alternative* (New York, 1968); H. Hamon, P. Rotman, *Génération*, vol. 1, *Les Années de rêve* (Paris, 1988); R. Johnson, *The French Communist Party versus the Students: Revolutionary Politics in May-June 1968* (New Haven, Conn., 1972).

T. R. Christofferson

Related entries: AUTOGESTION; DEMONSTRATIONS; ECOLOGY PARTY; EDUCATIONAL REFORM; JULY, SERGE; MARXISM; PEYREFITTE, ALAIN; POMPIDOU, GEORGES; STUDENT REVOLTS.

COMMON PROGRAM, an electoral campaign document elaborated in 1972 as the focus of a strategy to bring the socialist and communist parties to power in coalition. After the Algerian War, Charles de Gaulle's successes in various elections in 1962 persuaded socialist and communist leaders to overcome their traditional rivalry to prevent the Gaullists from ruling indefinitely. Joint campaigns in 1965–67 suggested a possible strategy. In 1971 François Mitterrand gained control of a profoundly renovated Socialist party (PS), intent on negotiating a Common Program with the Communist party (PCF).

Conceived in a period of sustained economic growth, assumed to be durable, the Union of the Left strategy drew on the progressive momentum generated by the upheavals of protest in May–June 1968. The relatively specific program reflected mutual mistrust, both partners viewing it as a means of both defeating the right and enhancing their own place on the left. Support from a breakaway group of Left Radicals (MRG), a counterweight to communist influence, reassured many centrist voters.

The difficult PS-PCF negotiations of 1972 produced many concessions, but ambiguity camouflaged major differences, especially in foreign policy. Building on an uneven distribution of wealth, the program promised an end to social injustice and the regime's "incoherence." Its most striking proposals were the elimination of France's *force de frappe* and the nationalization of the remaining private banks and insurance companies, as well as major chemical, electronics, aerospace, pharmaceutical, and petrochemical companies. Covering all areas of public policy in varying degrees of specificity, the program dealt with the economy (employment, purchasing power, workplace democracy, economic planning, industry, agriculture, foreign trade, small business, fiscal and monetary policies); societal issues (the family, women's rights, youth, Social Security, education and research, culture, sports, leisure); institutional reform (national and local government, public TV and radio, courts, the police); development issues (housing and urban renewal, transportation, the environment), and foreign/defense policies (East-West issues, disarmament, the Common Market, the Third World).

The Union of the Left narrowly lost the 1973 elections, but its 46 percent of the votes confirmed the strategy's viability. However, the onset of economic decline after the 1973 war in the Middle East undid its basic precondition, and after Mitterrand's defeat in the 1974 presidential elections, the alliance began falling apart. Several by-elections made clear to the communists that they were serving to legitimize and strengthen the socialists, thereby weakening their own chances of influencing an eventual government of the left. The socialists had also become suspicious of the PCF's motives.

Despite the left's remarkable success in the municipal elections of March 1977, negotiations that summer to update the program revealed deep divergence, and the alliance collapsed in September 1977, allowing the right to win the following spring's parliamentary elections. The program's spirit of unity remained useful to both the socialists and the communists, but no new preelectoral agreement was subsequently forthcoming. Despite short-term defeat, the failure of the Common Program enabled the socialists to demonstrate resistance to PCF pressures, facilitating Mitterrand's victory in the 1981 presidential elections

D. S. Bell, B. Criddle, *The French Socialist Party* (Oxford, 1988); O. Duhamel, *La Gauche et la V*[e] République (Paris, 1980); R. W. Johnson, *The Long March of the French Left* (London, 1981).

P. J. Godt

Related entries: ELECTIONS; FEDERATION OF THE DEMOCRATIC AND SOCIALIST LEFT; FRENCH COMMUNIST PARTY; LEFT RADICALS; MARCHAIS, GEORGES; MITTERRAND, FRANCOIS; SOCIALIST PARTY (PS); UNION OF THE LEFT.

COMPAGNIES REPUBLICAINES DE SECURITE (CRS), an elite corps of police who are at the disposal of the central government, to reestablish and maintain order in difficult situations, created either by demonstrations, strikes, or natural catastrophes. It numbers fourteen thousand, distributed in some sixty-three companies of 230 men stationed next to the major cities of France.

In 1947 they were used when the Communist party promoted insurrectional strikes. Several companies mutinied when ordered to charge demonstrators. As a result, Jules Moch, minister of the interior in the Robert Schuman government, dissolved the guilty companies with the agreement of parliament. Nothing as dramatic has happened since. The CRS intervened in many sit-down strikes during the Fourth Republic, in Algeria during the rebellion (1954–62), against the farmers' protests in the late 1950s and the early 1960s. They played an important role in the containment of the aborted revolution of May–June 1968, although they were a minority of the police that the students faced during these days. But for the students they were the archetypal police and they shouted "CRS equals SS" whenever they met any type of police. During all that time, even though they were attacked and sometimes seriously wounded by stones, paving blocks, and Molotov cocktails, they never used anything but night sticks and tear gas. No student died as a direct result of police (which includes CRS) intervention—a performance that speaks well for their professionalism.

Most of the time the CRS are engaged in public service activities: They police expressways, giving first aid when accidents occur; act as beach monitors and lifeguards; rescue mountain climbers; and their motorcycle sections accompany dignitaries, French and foreign, on their official trips. During the summer they organize day camps for idle youth, in the hope that the many activities will prevent them from drifting into vandalism and petty crime.

D. Monjardet, "Le Maintien de l'ordre: Technique et idéologie professionnelles des CRS," *Déviance et société* 12, no. 2 (1988); R. Pinaud, *Soldats sans victoires. Un Ancien Chef des CRS raconte* (Paris, 1986).

J. R. Pitts

Related entries: COHN-BENDIT, DANIEL; DEMONSTRATIONS; STUDENT REVOLTS.

CONFEDERATION FRANCAISE DEMOCRATIQUE DU TRAVAIL (CFDT), a noncommunist trade-union confederation usually associated with the Socialist party. The CFDT emerged from a split within the *Confédération française des travailleurs chrétiens* (CFTC) in 1964; about 80 percent of the CFTC joined the new, "deconfessionalized" organization. The CFDT filled a vital gap in the spectrum of trade unionism, between the orthodox communism of the *Confédération générale du travail* (CGT) and the rigid anticommunism of the *Force ouvrière* (FO). It rapidly became France's second-largest union confederation, a distant second behind the CGT. As an infant organization in the mid–1960s with a leftist and vaguely postcommunist ideology, the CFDT became a major New Left forum in the late 1960s and took a key leadership role in the revolt of May 1968.

The CFDT, like the two other small union confederations (FO and CFTC), survives largely due to France's trade-union pluralism—the fact that there is no law providing for exclusive representation by one union for a given category of worker. This situation has often given the CFDT a podium within a number of firms that would otherwise be dominated by the CGT. The CFDT negotiated for unity with the CGT both in the 1968 era and in the period of the common front (ca. 1977); yet unity was never achieved. However, the CFDT remains close to the independent teacher's union, the *Fédération de l'éducation nationale*.

During the Resistance era (1939–44), a secular humanist and progressive group, Reconstruction, began to develop the conceptions that would become the core of CFDT programs. Leaders of Reconstruction included Ferdnand Hennebicq (*Gaz-Electricité*), Charles Savouillan (*Métallurgie*), and Paul Vignaux (*Education*).

Generational tensions wracked the CFDT for some time, for it long maintained a large constituency of older, progressive-left Catholics and younger New Leftists. Nonetheless, internal unity rested on a consensus of *autogestion*, the belief that workers are competent to manage themselves, and that workers' self-management should be the starting point for a transition to democratic socialism. Many of the CFDT's beliefs in *autogestion* came from its members' interpretation of the Yugoslav council system in the late 1960s.

Like its occasional allies in the Socialist party, the CFDT had its major social support among white-collar salaried workers, particularly those in newer, technology-based activities and in the state sector. The CFDT's split from the CFTC represented in part a shift from a union of foremen and clerical workers to one of professional and technical employees.

Under the leadership of Edmond Maire for a number of years, the CFDT became the source of many new ideas for the rejuvenated Socialist party (PS). The CFDT's stresses on self-management, resistance to technocratic and capitalist rule, and on grass-roots democracy tended to mitigate the technocratic elitism and political opportunism of the PS. Unlike the FO, which is characterized by a strong pro-Americanism and an equally strong anticommunism, the CFDT tried to remain independent of Cold War rivalries, welcoming the emergence of Poland's Solidarity union in 1980 not as a harbinger of a capitalist, western Poland, but as the starting point for a socially democratic workers' state. Alone among major organizations in the Fifth Republic, the CFDT opposed both nuclear weapons and nuclear power. The CFDT did, however, strongly support the election victories of the socialists in 1981 and 1988.

The CFDT represented post–Cold War politics and unionism long before such an approach became fashionable. Rejecting the statism and authoritarianism of communism, the exploitation of workers under capitalism, and the statist traditions of French politics, the CFDT sought a third way between East and West, one characterized by democracy, social equality, and self-management.

R. Bonety, "La CFDT et la planification," *Revue d'économie politique* 81 (1971); P.

Vignaux, *De la CFTC à la CFDT* (Paris, 1980), *CFDT, les dégats du progrès* (Paris, 1977).

R. L. Frost

Related entries: AUTOGESTION; *CONFEDERATION FRANCAISE DES TRAVAILLEURS CHRETIENS*; *CONFEDERATION GENERALE DU TRAVAIL; FORCE OUVRIERE*; MAIRE, EDMOND; SOCIALIST PARTY (PS, SFIO); TRADE UNION MOVEMENT.

CONFEDERATION FRANCAISE DES TRAVAILLEURS CHRETIENS (CFTC), a Catholic union confederation that emerged out of the Catholic Workers' Circles founded by Albert de Mun in 1873. The Circles sought to minister the poor and working (particularly white-collar) classes in their own element, to offer an alternative to revolutionary Marxism and anarcho-syndicalism, and to develop an early version of liberation theology. These currents converged in the *Syndicat des employés du commerce et de l'industrie* (SECI) in 1887, and encouraged by the encyclical *Rerum Novarum* (1891) the roots of the CFTC were solidly set in the milieux of *employés* and shop-floor supervisors. By 1910 the SECI solidly affirmed the doctrines of Frédéric Le Play, and the long-term provincial concentrations of the later CFTC emerged—strong in the Nord, the Lyon region, the Stéphanoise, and in Laval, Le Mans, but weak in Bretagne and the center of France.

The modern CFTC emerged in 1919 guided by the three often contradictory attitudes: a wish to expand the CECI into the ranks of blue-collar workers, an attachment to the church and a militant faith, and a determination to develop a union movement free from all ideological attachments. Ultimately, the CFTC began to reflect the ''social Catholicism'' of the *Semaines sociales* and Marc Sangier. Nonetheless, many conservatives perceived the nascent CFTC as an alternative to the ''revolutionary'' *Confédération générale du travail* (CGT) of 1917 to 1920. The CFTC has indeed always been rent by cross-purposes, representing a leftist alternative among Catholics, but often perceived as a conservative alternative to Marxist unionism.

Vichy's insistence on a single nationwide ''union'' under the Labor Charter served to alienate many CFTC members from the right. In the tripartite era, the CFTC enjoyed an unhappy link with the Christian democrats (MRP). It participated in the MRP bloc, but retained its organizational autonomy from the MRP and some of its explicitly conservative members. Indeed, the CFTC strongly supported the nationalizations and planning, in contrast to many in the MRP.

With the onset of the Cold War in 1947–48, the CFTC attempted to remain aloof in the battles between the (CGT) and the *Force ouvrière* (FO). As a frequent mediator between the Cold War rival unions, the CFTC received no subsidies from the Soviet Union or the United States. In efforts to develop a stance above party politics, the CFTC might have developed a complementary relationship with the emerging technocracy in the Fourth Republic, but the CFTC's insistence on grass-roots democracy rejected the top-down managerial style. Nonetheless, some of the early nationalized firm managers had close links to the CFTC.

As France increasingly secularized after 1945, the confessional basis of the CFTC made little sense to leftist elements within the union. That element constituted the vast majority of the union, and they split off to form the *Confédération française démocratique du travail* (CFDT) in 1964. The CFTC today is essentially a moderate union of white-collar and supervisory personnel, and its overall influence on the labor movement remains minimal.

G. Adam, *La CFTC, 1940–1958* (Paris, 1964); M. Launay, *La CFTC* (Paris, 1986); J. Tessier, "Syndicalisme seulement," *Revue politique et parlementaire* 74 (1972).

R. L. Frost

Related entries: AUTOGESTION; CATHOLICISM; CHRISTIAN DEMOCRATS; *CONFEDERATION GENERALE DU TRAVAIL*; *CONFEDERATION FRANCAISE DEMOCRATIQUE DU TRAVAIL*; *FORCE OUVRIERE*; TRADE UNION MOVEMENT; TRIPARTITISM.

CONFEDERATION GENERALE DU TRAVAIL (CGT), France's largest and historically most important trade union. The CGT emerged after World War II with between five and six million members and as influential and powerful a position in French life as it has ever enjoyed. It collaborated with the French government in the politics of productivity, and France remained virtually strike-free until the Cold War began in 1947. The CGT had fallen heavily under communist influence during the Popular Front following its reunification with the communist CGTU (*Unitaire*). It was once again split following the Nazi-Soviet pact and reunified during the war; by 1945 the communists controlled the largest and most influential federations, and communist leader Benoît Frachon became joint general secretary with Léon Jouhaux, whose leadership went back to pre–World War I days. The noncommunists were restive under French Communist party (PCF) control, however, and led several successful strikes against the leadership during 1946, emerging as an independent tendency that took the name *Force ouvrière* (FO). Under the impact of the Cold War in 1947, with the PCF outside the government, the CGT returned to endorsing strikes, which it soon politicized, interpreting the massive wave of strikes of November–December 1947 as directed against the Marshall Plan, when the workers were clearly interested in higher wages. The strikes were defeated, the FO split over what it perceived to be quasi-insurrectionary communist tactics, and the CGT followed the (PCF) into isolation and relative decline.

During the PCF's sectarian years after 1947 the CGT was regarded in Leninist terms as a "transmission belt" from the party to the masses, and the PCF kept it in a subordinate role. The CGT followed political directives that placed Soviet foreign policy over the protection of working-class interests, and CGT militants could be seen collecting signatures to ban the atomic bomb rather than concentrating on trade-union work. In 1953, as a consequence, the CGT missed out on the largest number of strikes of the postwar period, which occurred in August of that year, and the government obligingly negotiated a settlement with the FO and the Christian unions, the *Confédération française des travailleurs chrétiens*

(CFTC). The CGT kept a plurality in elections to the French social security system and plant committees, but the pluralist mode of French unionism, and its ideological stance of challenge to the economic and political system, helped to reinforce the pattern of searching for state-imposed solutions to labor conflict. Frachon remained unhappy with the PCF's politicized and sectarian line, however, and in 1954 he succeeded in winning a relative degree of autonomy for the union, which enabled it to concentrate more on winning material improvement for workers and to seek entente with the CFTC, later the CFDT, and the FO, thus recouping its strength and support.

Yet, the CGT's ties to the PCF were always apparent, and its endorsement of the Soviet action in Hungary in 1956 and even Czechoslovakia in 1968 cost it adherents, even as it pursued solid and militant trade-union work. In 1963 the CGT led a successful coal strike against de Gaulle; but it was genuinely surprised by the 1968 student/worker upheaval, during which it negotiated a settlement with the government that the workers initially repudiated, and rejected entente with the students and the New Left. In the 1970s it put renewed emphasis on achieving material benefits for labor through political tactics rather than strikes, pursuing unity on the left, playing an active role in the negotiation of the Common Program in 1972, and campaigning for its support.

The CGT was forced to follow the PCF into breaking with the socialists after 1978, however, which hurt its efforts to foster growing cooperation with the more militantly leftist CFDT. The leadership, under Georges Séguy and then Henri Krasucki, remained suspicious of calls for *autogestion*, and rejected the "proposition force" strategy of reformers in its ranks, which would have allowed it to agitate in favor of constructive solutions to the epidemic of closings in traditional industries, which made up the union's base of support. In the meantime, heavy industry shrank as France assumed the characteristics of the modern postindustrial societies, with a larger tertiary sector. The use of immigrant labor in increasingly automated and robotized assembly-line industries in France further complicated the CGT's problems of adaptation. The CGT played virtually no role in the election of François Mitterrand in 1981. It backed the Auroux laws of 1982, which sought to modernize French labor relations by granting workers a greater say in plant conditions and guaranteeing them basic rights of expression on the job, but the reforms seemed to work to the benefit of management nevertheless. By 1980 the CGT was down to 1.63 million members, and further declines continued throughout the 1980s as French unionism languished generally with the active participation of fewer than 20 percent of the French labor force. Under Krasucki the CGT seemed relegated to defending outmoded industries, uncomfortably trying to integrate immigrant workers, and following the PCF into further decline.

M. Kesselman, ed., *The French Workers' Movement: Economic Crisis and Political Change* (London, 1984); Peter Lange, et al., *Unions, Change, and Crisis: French and Italian Union Strategy and the Political Economy, 1945–1980* (London, 1982); G. Ross, *Workers and Communists in France: From Popular Front to Eurocommunism* (Berkeley,

1982); W. Rand Smith, *Crisis in the French Labour Movement: A Grassroots' Perspective* (New York, 1968).

I. M. Wall

Related entries: FRACHON, BENOIT; FRENCH COMMUNIST PARTY; KRASUCKI, HENRI; SEGUY, GEORGES; TRADE UNION MOVEMENT.

CONSTITUTIONAL COUNCIL (1958–), the constitutional court of the Fifth Republic. Of all the political institutions established by the constitution of the Fifth Republic, none has evolved further from the founder's original intent than the *Conseil constitutionnel.* Originally conceived as a guarantor of executive mastery over the policy-making process, the Council has developed into a powerful policymaker in its own right, mostly at the expense of the executive. The Council certifies electoral results and ensures that law-making procedures conform to rules laid down by the constitution, but its constitutional review authority—the power to declare pending legislation unconstitutional, thereby blocking promulgation—is by far its most important role. Since 1981, its review activities have been the subject of periodic controversy, at times erupting into full-scale judicial-political confrontation.

The establishment of an official body charged with effective review powers constitutes an original institutional innovation. While the general prohibition against American-style judicial review in France remains in place, the founders of the Fifth Republic charged a special, nonjudicial organ to perform a similar function. The body is composed of nine members who serve nine-year terms; the president of the Republic, and the presidents of the Senate and the National Assembly each appoint one member every three years. Prior judicial training or expertise are not required for membership on the Council, and in fact judges and law professors are rarely appointed. Instead, former parliamentarians and/or ministers are most often recruited and have always made up a large majority of Council members. The Council is not attached to the greater judicial system and may not hear cases on appeal from other courts. Instead, legislation, after final adoption by parliament and before promulgation, is referred directly to the Council by politicians. Those empowered to make referrals are, exclusively, the president of the Republic, the presidents of the National Assembly and Senate, the prime minister, and, since 1974, any sixty deputies or sixty senators. Once petitioned, the judges have one month (one week if the government declares urgency) to rule on a bill's constitutionality. The Council's role in the policy-making process is supreme—a negative ruling prohibits the promulgation of offending provisions in any form, and decisions may not be appealed. Given these political attributes, it is worth emphasizing that the Council behaves like a judicial body in at least one crucial way: Its rulings are written and published in the form of judicial decisions and are based on judicial considerations.

The development of the Council can be divided into three periods. In the first period, 1959–71, the Council functioned as intended, as a means of protecting executive prerogatives in the "rationalized" policy-making process—ruling on the side of the executive against parliament on every instance of constitutional review. The second period, 1971–80, was dominated by two events, which in time served to transform the institution's role in the political system. In July 1971 the Council ruled against a government-sponsored bill for the first time, and in the same decision elevated to constitutional status two texts mentioned in the Preamble to the 1958 Constitution: the 1789 Declaration of the Rights of Man and the Preamble to the 1946 Constitution. These texts have come to constitute an extensive bill of rights to which legislation, in order to be valid, must conform. In October 1974 a constitutional amendment extended the power to refer bills to the Council to any sixty deputies or sixty senators. The impact on Council activity of expanded access and jurisdiction was extraordinary. In the first period, the Council was asked to make only seven rulings, after petitioners claimed violations of procedural rules; in the second period, petitioners asked the Council to make sixty-seven rulings, many on the grounds that legislation violated individual liberties enshrined in the preamble and the constitution. Whereas before 1971 the prime minister referred six of the seven bills to the Council for review, since 1974 the Council has been petitioned almost exclusively by opposition parliamentarians. In the third period, post–1981, the Council developed into a major policymaker and consequently into a significant obstacle to governments and their legislative program. From 1981 to 1987, the Council rendered 128 decisions. Even more striking, more than half of all bills referred to the Council were ruled to be in whole or in part unconstitutional as adopted. Moreover, virtually every major important piece of legislation passed during the 1981–87 period was referred, and many—including nationalizations and decentralization (1982), press and audiovisual reforms (1984, 1986), and legislation affecting the overseas departments and territories—were subject to important annulments, requiring extensive revisions on the part of the government to ensure eventual promulgation of a new bill.

The development of the Council's policy-making role has sparked a lively controversy among politicians and scholars. Since 1981 governments first on the left and then on the right have decried what they consider to be the Council's activism and have warned of an incipient or existing "government of judges." There is a certain cynicism to such protests, since once returned to opposition, former ministers may regularly refer legislation to the Council and cheer when the resulting decision goes against the new government. Scholars are generally divided into two camps: those (especially law professors) who see in the Council and its developing jurisprudence a positive foundation upon which to build regime stability and legitimacy, and those (more often political scientists) who focus less on the Council's unfolding jurisprudence than on its political behavior and impact on legislative processes.

L. Favoreu, *La Politique saisie par le droit* (Paris, 1988); L. Favoreu, L. Philip, *Les Grandes Décisions du Conseil constitutionnel* (Paris, 1990); J. T. S. Keeler, A. Stone, "Judicial-Political Confrontation in Mitterrand's France," in G. Ross, S. Hoffmann, S.

Malzacher, eds., *The Mitterrand Experiment* (New York, 1987); A. Stone, "In the Shadow of the Constitutional Council," *West European Politics* 12 (1989).

A. Stone

Related entries: BADINTER, ROBERT; DE GAULLE, CHARLES; GISCARD D'ESTAING, VALERY; MITTERRAND, FRANCOIS; POMPIDOU, GEORGES.

CONSTITUTION OF THE FOURTH REPUBLIC, approved by referendum on October 13, 1946, reaffirmed commitment to the primacy of parliament in French government. In its chief provisions (bicameral legislature, which selected the president), it was ironically much like that of the Third Republic, a conception of government overwhelmingly rejected by French voters only a year before.

In his Algiers decree of April 21, 1944, Charles de Gaulle, head of the government in exile, announced that after the Liberation he would call for a referendum to determine the future course of the nation. In the following year, on October 21, 1945, he honored his pledge by sponsoring elections for a constituent assembly and a referendum on the question of whether that assembly should have the power to construct a new regime. De Gaulle favored a regime based upon strong executive authority (with his own candidacy in mind). At the height of his popularity for his role in the Liberation, he was confident that his presidential model of government would be warmly received. Voters did give a strong endorsement (66.3%) to the proposal to create a new regime. But they returned an Assembly that had little enthusiasm for the model of government that de Gaulle advocated. Three parties of the left (Communist Party (PCF), 26.2% of vote, 161 delegates; *Mouvement républicain populaire* (MRP), 23.9%, 150; and Socialist party (SFIO), 23.4%, 143) dominated the Assembly, suggesting that popular support for de Gaulle was beginning to erode. The prospect of a powerful president conjured up too many memories of the authoritarian rule of Vichy.

While de Gaulle's historic role as military liberator had inspired universal confidence, his proposed role as political arbiter was not nearly as appealing. Sensing that his constitutional project had little chance of success in the constituent assembly, de Gaulle resigned as head of state on January 20, 1946 to take his case to the nation. The Assembly then followed the lead of the PCF in endorsing a Jacobin model of government that invested supreme power in a unicameral legislature. When presented to the electorate on May 5, 1946, however, this draft constitution was rejected by 10.6 to 9.5 million votes (52.7%).

On June 2, 1946 a second constituent assembly was elected. It again favored the left-wing parties, but in a configuration that gave the advantage to the MRP (28.2%, 169 delegates; PCF, 25.9%, 146; SFIO, 21.1%, 129), which was more sympathetic toward the principle of separation of powers. The document finally accepted was a compromise. This time the delegates opted for a bicameral legislature, while hoping that they might eliminate the worst features of the constitutional arrangements of the Third Republic. All parties heaped blame upon the Senate, bastion of the conservative interests of provincial France, for the ills that had beset that regime. The new constitutional document therefore lodged the power to initiate legislation exclusively in the lower house (formerly the Chamber of Deputies, renamed the National Assembly). The upper house (formerly the Senate, renamed the Council of the Republic), was given only a two-month suspensive veto over legislation passed by the lower house. Both houses elected the president of the Republic, who, while overseeing the proper functioning of governmental procedures, was expected to play a largely ceremonial role. To buttress further the sovereign authority of the National Assembly, the right of the premier to issue emergency decrees was rescinded. In a separate electoral law (October 5, 1946), a new procedure for legislative elections was inaugurated (*scrutin de liste*) to encourage the formation of larger parties, which the framers hoped would make the parliamentary system more efficient than it had been during the preceding regime.

If the political institutions proposed were reminiscent of the Third Republic, other provisions did signal new directions. The new constitution reaffirmed the liberties and rights guaranteed by the Declaration of the Rights of Man of 1789 but complemented these with a recognition of social and economic rights, thus establishing a moral imperative for implementing the welfare state. The preamble mentioned the right to work and to unionize, to free public education at all levels, to health care, to social security in old age, and to the basic amenities of life. Significantly, the right of women to vote and to hold public office was affirmed for the first time. The constitution also included elaborate provisions for the governance of France's overseas empire, renamed the French Union. A hierarchy of assemblies provided for self-government, and provisions were included to permit the eventual redefinition of overseas territories as departments. But while the ideal of self-government was proclaimed, that of independence was denied, and in retrospect it was this arrangement that brought the Fourth Republic to ruin.

On October 13, 1946 the draft constitution was approved by a popular vote of 9.1 to 8.0 million, but with 7.9 million abstentions (53% of ballots cast but only 36.4% of eligible voters). The constitution became the law of the land, but with such tenuous endorsement that Gaullist supporters at once launched a movement for its revision (*Rassemblement du peuple français*), a threat that shadowed the Fourth Republic throughout its twelve-year history.

The constitution was much maligned after the fall of the Fourth Republic in 1958. The parliamentary system never achieved the stability hoped for, and it foundered on its inability to deal with the crises in the overseas empire. Nonetheless, the constitution contributed to the ideal of social democracy enshrined in its preamble by establishing a framework for a government that provided more social services and greater prosperity than any of its predecessors.

R. Pierce, *French Politics and Political Institutions* (New York, 1968); D. Thomson,

Democracy in France since 1870 (Oxford, 1969); P. Williams, *Crisis and Compromise* (Hamden, Conn., 1964); G. Wright, *The Reshaping of French Democracy* (Boston, 1970).

P. H. Hutton

Related entries: CONSTITUTION OF THE FIFTH REPUBLIC; DE GAULLE, CHARLES; ELECTIONS; ELECTORAL SYSTEM; OVERSEAS DEPARTMENTS AND TERRITORIES; POLITICAL TRENDS.

CONSTITUTION OF THE FIFTH REPUBLIC, approved by referendum on September 28, 1958, owed much to the vision of Charles de Gaulle. Like the constitution of the Fourth Republic that it superseded, it carried forward the principle of separation of powers. The essential instruments of government (president, premier, council of ministers, bicameral legislature, and independent judiciary) were much the same as those in the preceding regime. But powers among them were reapportioned to favor president over parliament. The document also established and institutionalized relations with a French Community, an organization of the former colonies of the French Union, now granted political autonomy.

The constitution embodied a conception of government that de Gaulle had outlined more than a decade before in a speech at Bayeux (June 16, 1946) during deliberations over the constitution of the Fourth Republic. He had then for the first time called for the reconstruction of the executive branch of government around a presidency capable of providing leadership on national issues. His proposal was rejected by the constituent assembly, which remained loyal to the parliamentary model in the hope that it might be made more efficacious. De Gaulle's presidential model nonetheless became a cause for revisionists (*Rassemblement du peuple français*) through the troubled history of the Fourth Republic. Hobbled by ministerial instability and paralyzed by the prospect of civil war in Algeria, leaders of the Fourth Republic in the end turned to de Gaulle for assistance, knowing that his return to power meant the reconstruction of the Republic along the lines that he had earlier proposed. On June 1, 1958, he was elected premier of the Fourth Republic with a mandate to draft a new constitution.

The new constitution was de Gaulle's invention, but its text was not entirely of his making. He was aided in the task by his longtime friend and minister of justice, Michel Debré, who held strong views on the importance of separation of powers. The document drafted, therefore, was a hybrid, in which a greatly strengthened presidency worked with a ministerial council and a legislature that retained some measure of independence. Approved in a referendum by an overwhelming majority (79.2%), the constitution became law on October 4, 1958. The elections for the National Assembly in November returned a large Gaullist plurality (38% of seats), and in December de Gaulle was chosen president of the Republic by an electoral college of some 100,000 local officials.

The constitutional powers of the presidency that de Gaulle assumed were broadly defined and therefore capable of being expanded. Elected for a seven-year term, he was designated as the arbiter among public authorities and the guarantor of the national interest (Article 5). He appointed the premier and (on the latter's recommendation) the members of the ministerial council (Article 8), over whose meetings he presided (Article 9). He also possessed the right to dissolve parliament (after one year in session, Article 12) and to submit issues concerning the organization of the government or the Community to popular referenda (Article 11). He was chief of the armed forces (Article 15) and enjoyed wide powers of appointment to high civil and military posts (Article 13). Most far-reaching were the special powers he might assume in time of national emergency, with which he was authorized to suspend the ordinary conventions of government and to act alone, with the advice but not necessarily the approval of the premier and the parliament (Article 16).

The role of parliament, by contrast, was narrowly defined in comparison with that in the Fourth Republic. The legislature was bicameral: A National Assembly representing 487 single-member districts (four-year terms) was elected by popular vote; and a Senate of 279 members representing the departments (nine-year terms) was chosen by local electoral colleges. Parliament enacted the laws, but the rules it might legislate were specified in considerable detail, thus circumscribing its sphere of action (Article 34). Legislative sessions were shortened (Article 28) and staffs reduced. No longer might a member of parliament simultaneously serve on the council of ministers (Article 23). The National Assembly was primarily responsible for the budget, but was obliged to meet deadlines for its enactment (Article 47). A Constitutional Council was established to pass on the constitutionality of legislation enacted by parliament (Article 61).

Lodged ambiguously between president and parliament was the premier, with his council of ministers. Appointed by the president, this ministry was nonetheless responsible to parliament (Articles 20, 49, 50). The premier was designated as the chief policymaker. But the framers had created an office that worked best when the objectives of premier and president harmonized. Left undetermined were the rights of each in disputes over long-range directions in policy. This bifurcation of the executive sphere worried constitutional experts, but during de Gaulle's tenure the problem of ideological differences between president and premier (*cohabitation*) never presented itself. As president from 1959 to 1969, de Gaulle enjoyed a parliamentary majority and appointed premiers loyal to his viewpoint (Debré, Georges Pompidou, Maurice Couve de Murville).

In practice, de Gaulle gave an expansive definition to the powers of his office. Following his election, he spoke of his role as guide rather than arbiter, while his spokesman Jacques Chaban-Delmas advanced the proposition that the president was responsible for a *domaine réservé* of national defense, foreign affairs, and Community, where parliament ought not to intrude. Within the first four years of his tenure, de Gaulle had invoked all of the new presidential powers: He dissolved parliament (1962), invoked his special powers under Article 16 (Algerian crisis, 1961), and successfully sponsored three referenda (self-determination for Algeria, 1961; its independence, 1962; direct popular election of the president, 1962). Given de Gaulle's emormous popular support, his critics claimed that the line between his personal and institutional powers was beginning to blur. But de Gaulle won only a marginal victory in the presidential elections of 1965, and his popularity waned as his political pronouncements assumed a more arrogant cast over the following years. Riled by the student riots for educational reform in May 1968, he tested his authority in 1969 by sponsoring a referendum on the only element of his Bayeux proposal not yet incorporated into the constitution. His proposed constitutional amendment called for the transformation of the Senate from a parliamentary into a planning body, composed of representatives of the corporate interests of French society (business, family, education) and serving as a model for the creation of like regional planning bodies. But the Senate was the last refuge of the old parliamentary conception of the Republic, and voters were reluctant to see it disappear. The amendment was defeated (1969), and de Gaulle resigned.

Despite the fear that the constitution was too closely tailored to the personal aspirations of de Gaulle, it has since served as an effective governmental framework for presidents with differing ideological leanings and varying degrees of parliamentary support. The issue of *cohabitation* did not resurface until the presidency of Valéry Giscard d'Estaing in the mid–1970s, and it became a reality under that of François Mitterrand in the mid–1980s without provoking a constitutional crisis. The constitution epitomized the way in which a republican ideal first fashioned by the notables of the Third Republic was being reconceived by the managerial elite of the Fifth. Despite de Gaulle's old-fashioned authoritarianism, the regime that he and his supporters constructed was well suited to a nation that had accepted the need for more effective executive leadership to foster an unprecedented prosperity and political stability and to plan for a more complete integration into the European Economic Community and possibly a European political confederation beyond.

W. Andrews, S. Hoffmann, eds., *The Impact of the Fifth Republic on France* (Albany, N.Y., 1981); L. Derfler, *President and Parliament* (Boca Raton, Fla., 1983); R. Pierce, *French Politics and Political Institutions* (New York, 1968); D. Thomson, *Democracy in France since 1870*, 5th ed. (Oxford, 1969); J. Touchard, *Le Gaullisme, 1940–1969* (Paris, 1978); G. Wright, *France in Modern Times*, 4th ed. (New York, 1987).

P. H. Hutton

Related entries: ALGERIA, RELATIONS WITH; CHABAN-DELMAS, JACQUES; *COHABITATION*; CONSTITUTION OF THE FOURTH REPUBLIC; CONSTITUTIONAL COUNCIL; DEBRE, MICHEL; DE GAULLE, CHARLES; ELECTIONS; ELECTORAL SYSTEM; GISCARD D'ESTAING, VALERY; MITTERRAND, FRANCOIS; POLITICAL TRENDS; REFERENDA; STUDENT REVOLTS.

CORSICA, an island off the south coast of France, approximately 100 miles long and 50 miles wide. The island became part of the kingdom of France in 1769 and in 1789 was reorganized as a French department. In February 1983 the population was calculated to be 240,178, of which 40 percent live in the largest cities, Ajaccio and Bastia. It is estimated that presently only 140,000 of the inhabitants are native Corsicans.

Although becoming more and more French through cultural affinity after 1789, the people, because of their insularity and immutable social structure, remained distinctively Corsican. This tension between two identities, French and Corsican, remained in equipoise until well after World War II, probably the result of France's relatively slow development on the one hand as the so-called stalemate society, and on the other hand the static character of Corsica, this being the consequence of steady emigration to the mainland of France.

The result of emigration over a century and a half produced a situation that has been called the desertification of the interior of the island. Economic decline accompanied demographic decline, poverty and isolation intensified by the desire of the Corsicans to be left to themselves, and the unspoken policy of successive French governments to neglect the island. This compromise, rather like a paradox, started to break down with the advent of French decolonization in the 1950s and was hastened during the next decade once the Algerian question was resolved. Traditionally, the French colonies had furnished employment for Corsican youth, but, more than a career, such employment is a means to a comfortable retirement. While that opportunity was being lost, Corsica's economic decline continued.

During the Guy Mollet government in the 1950s Corsica's economic problems were addressed through the Regional Action Program, a plan devised to foster agricultural development and to create a tourist industry on the island consisting of SOMIVAC (*Société pour la mise en valeur agricole de la Corse*) and SETCO (*Société pour l'équipement touristique de la Corse*). The agricultural reforms did not succeed in the next few years, in part because they were instituted at a time when French Algerians (*pieds-noirs*), approximately 25 percent of them claiming Corsican origins, were settling on the island to become a new entrepreneurial class, taking a large profit from a plan that had been established to benefit the indigenous Corsicans. Nor did SETCO realize a great deal for the Corsican economy. Neither the infrastructure nor the superstructure of the island could furnish the materials and the personnel required. Underdeveloped Corsica only served to enrich the more prosperous France. While profits from tourism left the island, tourism produced changes in the island that the Corsicans deplored; for in their perception the natural beauty of the island was disappearing, and many feared that Corsica would become like the Balearic Islands, "balearicized" by all those developments that characterize tourism.

In 1956 a plan for regional cooperation was proposed in which France was to be divided into twenty-one regions. This gave a fillip to Corsican separateness at a time when agricultural and tourist experiments were not realizing their promises. In this milieu of disappointments, especially a growing awareness of Corsican poverty in contrast to the affluence of metropolitan France, a severe reaction occurred. Corsicans took a new interest in their heritage, and there was a revival of folk costumes, language, music, history, and so forth. These tendencies, in the aggregate cultural nationalism, were given a more exact expression with the formation of ARC (*Action régionaliste Corse*). On September 15, 1968 ARC issued a communiqué recommending that Corsica be "constituted as a separate regional area and be given its own statute." This call for Corsican autonomy was resisted by the national government; ARC then commenced "direct action." More extreme organizations appeared, the most violent among these being the Corsican National Liberation Front (FLNC). Many targets, from private residences to public buildings, were subjected to exploding bombs.

The 1970s were dominated by terrorism. Statistics gathered in 1983 revealed a greater number of violent incidents in Corsica than in Northern Ireland. In January of 1970 the French national government yielded, making Corsica a separate region. Then, in 1982 the socialist government in Paris granted Corsica a greater degree of autonomy than that allowed to other regions. Undoubtedly, Corsican nationalism had appeared and been partially gratified. Nevertheless, the 1980s witnessed continued terrorist activity by the outlawed FLNC, which was demanding independence. Yet, it is thought that the great majority of the Corsicans at present do not want to be cut off entirely from France.

R. Caratini, *Histoire de la Corse* (Paris, 1981); R. Ramsay, *The Corsican Time Bomb* (Manchester, Eng., 1983); P. Savigear, "Corsica: Regional Autonomy or Violence," in *Conflict Studies* (London, 1983).

I. C. Scott

Related entries: DECENTRALIZATION; DECOLONIZATION; REGIONS; TERRORISM.

COT, PIERRE (1895–1977), radical socialist and aviation minister in 1933 and under the Popular Front government of Léon Blum, who became increasingly leftist in his views after the war. Pierre Mendès-France regarded him as one of the bright young men who wished to avoid the errors of previous generations. He played a crucial role in the postwar debates over the constitution of the Fourth Republic, but his political views kept him from ministerial office.

In 1940 Cot left France for the United States, where he tried to alert Americans to the Nazi menace. In 1943 he joined the French provisional government in Algiers as a member of the consultative assembly. The following year he undertook a lengthy mission to the Soviet Union, where he was impressed by the suffering that the Nazi invasion had inflicted upon the country. His experience strengthened his advocacy of Franco-Soviet cooperation, and he developed a lifelong commitment to the peace movement.

In April 1946 Cot presented a constitutional proposal for a unicameral legislature with a weak executive, favored by the Socialist and Communist parties, to the Constituent Assembly. Although approved by a majority in the Assembly, voters rejected it, largely due to the opposition of the Christian democrats (MRP), the Gaullists, and the conservatives. The same year Cot broke with the Radical party to form the progressive Left Radicals (MRG). From this point Cot moved steadily to the left in his politics and often allied with the Communist party on a number of issues.

As the Cold War intensified, Cot opposed French participation in the Marshall Plan and NATO, which he considered to be instruments of American domination of France, and he also opposed German rearmament, whether under the European Defense Community (EDC) or NATO. He advocated a fully independent, neutralist France that would escape the pernicious influence of an American "way of life." In 1949 Cot collaborated with Frédéric Joliot-Curie to organize a World Peace Movement, and the same year he joined French intellectuals who insisted that accusations of Stalinist crimes and concentration camps were lies and fabrications. He warned against American use of atomic weapons in the Korean War.

An outspoken critic of imperialism, Cot criticized French wars in Indochina and Algeria, and he subsequently denounced American intervention in Vietnam. Following the events that brought down the Fourth Republic, Cot joined François Mitterrand, Pierre Mendès-France, François de Menthon, and Jacques Isorni in protesting the coup that brought general Charles de Gaulle to power. In the last years of his life he held an appointment as a sociologist in the international section of the *Ecole pratique des hautes études*, and he served as president of the International Association of Democratic Lawyers in 1960. Cot represented the progressive tendencies of those politicians and intellectuals who expected a neutralist and more socially democratic France to emerge from the experience of wartime resistance.

E. Fajon, et al., *Hommage à Pierre Cot* (Paris, 1979); J.-P. Rioux, *The Fourth Republic 1944–1958* (Cambridge, 1987).

J. K. Munholland

Related entries: DECOLONIZATION; EUROPEAN DEFENSE COMMUNITY; FRENCH COMMUNIST PARTY; LEFT RADICALS; MARSHALL PLAN; PEACE MOVEMENT; RADICAL PARTY.

COTY, RENE (1882–1962), second and last president of France's Fourth Republic, who had favored a stronger presidency and who intervened spectacularly in the political crisis of 1958 in order to bring General Charles de Gaulle back to power. Born in Le Havre into a republican family of schoolteachers, Coty took degrees in philosophy and law at the University of Caen, where he specialized in maritime law. He became active in local politics, was sent to the Chamber of Deputies in 1923, and was reelected in 1935 and 1941. He voted to give power to Marshal Pétain in 1940, but during World War II, at which time he lived in Normandy, he neither collaborated nor resisted. As a member of both constituent assemblies in 1945 and 1946, Coty opposed the return to parliamentary-dominated government and the ministerial instability it generated, and he voted against the new constitution establishing the Fourth Republic. He was elected senator in 1948, became one of its vice-presidents the following year, and remained faithful to moderate political stands.

After President Vincent Auriol finished his seven-year term of office in 1953, seven days of bitterly contested balloting were required to find his successor.

Only on the twelfth ballot was Coty, then a respected seventy-one-year-old conservative senator, put forward. A vice-president of the upper house and regarded as an expert on constitutional law, he was not, however, well known; it was said that he had spent three decades in parliament without making an enemy. Illness had kept him from taking sides in the debate over the European Defense Community, and with the support of Gaullists and Christian democrats he was narrowly selected on the next ballot as the chief of state. Though some observers credited his victory to voter fatigue, he was elected as the least conspicuous and most neutral of the candidates running, which offset the fears of those who found him too conservative. A return to a more limited electoral college, which ensured a more conservative Senate, also proved helpful. Nor had the publication of "Edwardian" photographs of Coty at the seashore in 1902 and cabaret songs about his wife's expansive dimensions hurt his candidacy.

His view of the office was traditionally Third Republic, believing as he did that the president had to submerge any personal views to those of the majority. Even his advocacy of a strengthened presidency had precedent: In his inaugural address he said that "a regime can defend itself only if it is able to reform itself." As a deputy he had favored constitutional revision and accordingly submitted a bill calling for proportional representation. He had come out for a strengthened presidency, supporting Poincaré's and Tardieu's efforts in this direction, and as a senator supported diverse proposals for reinforcing executive power, such as reestablishing the presidential right to dissolve the lower chamber. Unlike his predecessor, however, he was, with one exception (the return of Charles de Gaulle to power in 1958), to limit his presidential role to that specifically set forth in the constitution.

Much of his five-year tenure was taken up with colonial crises (the wars in Indochina and Algeria) and domestic political instability. Though a conservative, he tried to keep the Communist party within the republican framework, consulting with the leaders of its parliamentary delegation when searching for a premier; his rationale was that he was "president of all the French." If, during his presidency, he generally named the man who, in his view, was most likely to win a vote of confidence rather than fight for his personal choice, Coty did not indulge his preference for cautious senior statesmen, but brought to prominence a new generation of political leaders: Mendès-France, Faure, and Gaillard. On the other hand, fearing the reaction of settlers and the army in North Africa, Coty did not designate as prime minister the rising leader of the left opposition, François Mitterrand.

He showed less interest than had his predecessor Auriol in imperial matters: It was the government and not the president that now negotiated with Vietnam's Bao Dai. Nor did the Elysée respond to charges of French war abuses in Algeria. In foreign affairs, Coty showed sympathy for a Franco-German rapprochement, but initiated no action to further it. The lower chamber, the National Assembly, rejected the European Defense Community in 1954, but in 1957 ratified the Treaty of Rome creating the Common Market.

Greater initiative came in matters of constitutional reform. In his first Elysée address he asked for simplification of the procedures used in selecting a prime minister and for greater checks on the power of the lower house. He defended the presidential right of dissolution "in some cases," and the ouster of the prime minister only when a successor had been agreed on beforehand. Rising ministerial instability reinforced these concerns: There was to be a total of eight governments during Coty's five years of office. Several of these crises lasted for weeks, and during these five years France was without a government for no less than 127 days. Coty's technique was to consult first with the politicians who provoked the crisis, then with those responsible for prolonging it, but he was unable to promote greater stability.

Coty played a dramatic role in bringing to an end the final governmental crisis of his presidency—as well as an end to the Fourth Republic—in the aftermath of the army's mutiny in May 1958 and the threat of civil war. Coty, who had long favored a strengthened executive, had praised Charles de Gaulle in his inaugural address, and seven years earlier had supported the general's Bayeux constitutional program. Though denied by the president, there is evidence Coty was appealing for a Gaullist solution as early as May 5. After news of the Corsican insurrection, de Gaulle met with Prime Minister Pierre Pflimlin, and though the talks proved fruitless, the next day the general published his communiqué that he had undertaken the process of forming a new government. Pflimlin wanted to deny it publicly, but Coty, arguing that a war of denials would only aggravate the situation, implored him not to, and Pflimlin resigned the next day. Coty then asked the speakers of the two houses to meet with de Gaulle, and when that proved indecisive the president, on May 29, citing the threat of civil war, threatened to resign if the Assembly refused to invest de Gaulle as head of the government. He had put his authority and position in the balance, and de Gaulle, in return, agreed to seek parliamentary investiture. Seven months later, Coty's decision not to seek re-election meant that de Gaulle's victory as a constitutionally more powerful president was certain.

N. W. An, "A Study of the French Presidency under the Fourth Republic," (Ph.D. diss., University of Virginia, 1965); A. Dansette, *L'Histoire des présidents de la République. . . .* (Paris, 1960); L. Derfler, *President and Parliament* (Boca Raton, Fla., 1983); J. Massot, *La Présidence de la République en France* (Paris, 1977); M. Merle, "The Presidency of the Fourth Republic," *Parliamentary Affairs* 7 (1954).

L. Derfler

Related entries: DE GAULLE, CHARLES; PFLIMLIN, PIERRE.

COUVE DE MURVILLE, MAURICE (1907–   ), civil servant, diplomat, minister of foreign affairs, prime minister. He was born in Reims to a well-known Protestant family. He married Jacqueline Schweiguth, a painter known by the name of Vera Fabre, who was also a Protestant. (From the sixteenth century on, Protestants have played an impressive role in French life, a role out of proportion with their number.)

He studied in Paris where he was awarded a degree in literature and law, and a diploma from the *Ecole libre des sciences politiques* as well. In 1932 he passed the recruiting exam to the *Inspection des finances*, ranking first. From the early 1930s until 1943 he worked as a civil servant, but then political events collided with his career. In a dramatic breach of the French civil service tradition, the Pétain government, for political considerations, dismissed some employees of the government. Couve de Murville, who had stood aloof from the polemics, was compelled to take a stand. He became general secretary for the military authority in Algiers and a member of the *Comité national de la Résistance* (CNR). His career seemed to be moving toward diplomacy. In 1944 he served as a delegate to the Advisory Council for Italy, which included representatives from allied governments, including France. He was subsequently appointed ambassador to Rome.

During the early years of the Fourth Republic Couve de Murville worked at the Quai d'Orsay, becoming secretary general for political affairs. Among the numerous matters he had to deal with was the all-important German question. In 1949 he helped to define the official French attitude with regard to the creation of the Federal Republic of Germany. In the following year he left Paris for the post of ambassador to Egypt, where he remained for four years. In 1954 he was appointed a delegate to NATO and subsequently was appointed ambassador to Washington and Bonn.

The year 1958 marked a turning point in the career of Couve de Murville. Prior to this date he had been a distinguished civil servant without close ties to a political party. This changed with the return of general Charles de Gaulle to power and with the creation of the Fifth Republic. The general needed those he called "the faithful supporters," but he also wanted reliable specialists for his regime. In de Gaulle's vision, a future for France had to be based on three pillars: new institutions, a modernized army, and active diplomacy. Foreign affairs would be the means that de Gaulle would use to express French grandeur worldwide. The general chose Couve de Murville to serve as minister of foreign affairs. For ten years he remained in charge of foreign relations.

Like André Malraux, the minister of culture, Couve de Murville left his mark on French policy. Building on his prior experience, he guided his nation to conclude in 1963 a Franco-German treaty of cooperation. This special relationship with the Federal Republic of Germany was the first step toward consolidating a strong Paris-Bonn axis, one that characterizes the European Economic Community today. The successful decolonization of Africa south of the Sahara, and the conclusion of the Algerian War gave French diplomacy a greater freedom of action that it had lacked since 1945. Couve de Murville also facilitated de Gaulle's other bold moves, such as the withdrawal from NATO, the diplomatic recognition of China, and the adoption of a more pro-Arab policy in the aftermath of the 1967 six-day war in the Middle East.

May 1968 witnessed a shake-up of the Fifth Republic. Couve de Murville became economics and finance minister, keeping this portfolio only briefly. While he was defeated in a bid for a seat in the National Assembly in 1967, in

June of 1968 he was elected to the Assembly in de Gaulle's landslide victory that swept France as an aftershock that followed the student-worker revolt of the same year. In 1968 he was elected as a Gaullist deputy to the National Assembly, a position that he would also hold between 1973 and 1986. In July 1968 he was appointed prime minister and remained in this position until voters turned down de Gaulle's April 1969 referendum. In 1986 he was elected to the Senate. As a career civil servant he will be remembered for his competence and professionalism and for his long tenure as de Gaulle's skillful minister of foreign affairs.

M. Couve de Murville, *Une Politique étrangère, 1958–1969* (Paris, 1971); P. Viansson-Ponté, *Histoire de la République gaullienne* (Paris, 1970).

J.-R. Chotard

Related entries: ALGERIA, RELATIONS WITH; DECOLONIZATION; DE GAULLE, CHARLES; FEDERAL REPUBLIC OF GERMANY, RELATIONS WITH; FOREIGN POLICY; GAULLISM; THIRD WORLD, RELATIONS WITH.

CRESSON, EDITH (1934–), socialist politician, former head of several ministries—agriculture, foreign trade and tourism, industrial restructuring and foreign trade, and European affairs—and presently the first woman prime minister of France. She was born in the Paris suburb of Boulogne-Billancourt, the daughter of a civil servant. Raised partially by an English nurse, she speaks fluent English. Cresson has a degree in business from the Parisian business school *Hautes études commerciales* and also holds a doctorate in demography.

Her political career began in 1965 when she became a member of the *Convention des institutions républicaines* (CIR), assisting François Mitterrand in the election campaign that took him through to the second round against Charles de Gaulle. She remained in the leadership of CIR until 1971 when it was supplanted by the newly formed *Parti socialiste* (PS). Three years later, she was appointed national secretary of the new party. In 1975 she ran as a socialist candidate for a parliamentary seat in Châtellerault, a conservative bastion southwest of Paris. Although she lost this race, her vigorous campaign style earned her the title "the fighter" (*la battante*). The following year she published a book entitled *Avec le soleil* that focused on her commitment to the left. In 1977 she was elected mayor of Thuré; two years later, in 1979, she was elected to the European Parliament.

In June 1981, when the socialists formed the government for the first time in a generation, Cresson ran successfully for deputy from Vienne as the socialist candidate; in the event, however, she resigned her seat to become the first woman minister of agriculture (1981–83). While many farmers viewed her with contempt, and while she criticized the farm population as too conservative, her policies did help to increase the income of farmers by 10 percent in 1982. In the 1983 municipal elections she ran again for the mayor of Châtellerault and won, the only socialist to unseat a conservative mayor in a large town in these elections. Cresson's second ministerial office was as minister of foreign trade and tourism (1983–84, the first woman to hold this office), after which she served as minister of industrial restructuring and foreign trade (the first woman to hold this post as well), until the socialists were ousted from government in the legislative elections of March 1986. In the latter post she oversaw the restructuring of the ailing steel industry. As minister of foreign trade and tourism and as minister of industrial restructuring she was a pragmatist, supporting tax breaks for business in order to spur investment. Consequently, she had relatively good rapport with the business community. When the socialists were returned to power in the June 1988 legislative elections, in which Cresson was elected as a deputy from Vienne, she was appointed minister of European affairs in the cabinet of the right-wing socialist Michel Rocard. In this capacity, Cresson sought to further the interests of French business before the integration of the European Common Market at the beginning of 1993. She criticized Rocard, however, for what she thought was his failure to mobilize French industry in order to make the nation more competitive, especially vis-à-vis Germany and Japan, and resigned her position in October of 1990 and joined the electrical manufacturer *Groupe Schneider*.

President Mitterrand surprised many in France when he chose Cresson, one of his most loyal supporters within the PS, to replace Rocard as prime minister on May 15, 1991. Her main task includes: preparing France for the opening of European borders in 1993, reducing unemployment, rectifying social inequities, and strengthening the socialist position with the electorate as the 1993 legislative elections approach.

Known for her outspoken manner, she demonstrated it in her first appearance as prime minister when she said that she opposed the trade imbalance that existed between the European Community and Japan, charging that while the European Community was not protectionist, Japan was. Later she charged that Japan had taken over the world's photographic industry and had destroyed the American auto industry. To aid French competitiveness, she proposed merging the finance, trade, and industry ministries into one powerful ministry, similar to Japan's ministry of international trade and industry. Pierre Bérégovoy, the highly respected finance minister under Rocard, was appointed to this new super ministry.

Besides announcing that she intends to mobilize France industrially as European economic integration approaches, Cresson gave her government a more leftward tilt by including more socialists in her cabinet than Rocard had. Moreover, while Rocard pursued a policy of austerity and was criticized by some in the Socialist party as well as others for his lack of emphasis on social policy, Cresson will most likely pay more attention to social issues—especially unemployment, which was 9 percent when she assumed office. Her new government, too, includes a ministry for social affairs and integration; although the ministry of social affairs had existed before, integration became a new part of this ministry as her government tried to respond to the difficult problem of racism and the needs of the nation's immigrant population.

Regarding women's role in society, Cresson noted in a recent magazine interview that there are three places where women have been excluded: the military, religion, and politics. Today, according to France's first woman prime minister, females have the least access in politics. In the French National Assembly women hold 31 of 577 seats. With her new high-level appointment, Cresson is breaking important ground for women in France.

E. Cresson, *Avec le soleil* (Paris, 1976); D. Loschak, *La Convention des institutions républicaines* (Paris, 1971); *Le Monde*, May 17–20, 1991; *The New York Times*, May 16 and 20, 1991.

M. Maclean

Related entries: AGRICULTURE; CLUB MOVEMENT; ECONOMIC TRENDS; EUROPEAN ECONOMIC COMMUNITY (EEC), RELATIONS WITH; INDUSTRIAL POLICY; MITTERRAND, FRANCOIS; ROCARD, MICHEL; SOCIALIST PARTY (PS); WOMEN, CONDITION OF.

CULTURAL POLICY, state patronage of the arts and France's heritage. In the Fourth Republic as in the Third, this was conducted by the *Secrétariat d'état aux beaux-arts* within the Ministry of Education, whose traditional purpose was to preserve the national heritage (*patrimoine*), finance national institutions, and support artists. With a limited budget and powers, it was seen as a minor political appointment that largely favored conservation and academicism. The Liberation, however, saw a brief injection of new energy when the *Front populaire's* pledge to widen popular access to culture, delayed but refueled by the Occupation and the Resistance, resurfaced in 1946. Jeanne Laurent, in charge of theater at the *Secrétariat,* officialized an incipient regional-theater movement by creating five *Centres dramatiques nationaux*. In Paris she also revived the *Théâtre national populaire,* under Jean Vilar. After her dismissal in 1952, decentralization lay dormant until 1958.

Charles de Gaulle's presidency gave cultural policy its first broadly coherent doctrine, symbolized by the creation in 1959 of an autonomous Ministry of State for Cultural Affairs, under the visionary writer André Malraux, and the inclusion of a chapter on culture in the Fourth Plan. Recalling Laurent's voluntarism, the ministry's mission was to broaden access to the great works of humanity and the national heritage, and to encourage new work (*création*). With a budget averaging less than 0.45 percent of overall state spending during his ten-year term, Malraux restored many historic buildings and districts, contentiously modernized Les Halles and Montparnasse, strengthened the museum provision, and commissioned a ''general inventory'' of France's artistic riches. He also began reforms of specialized arts education and went some way toward promoting creativity through such schemes as the *avances sur recettes,* which gives aid to new film projects. But he is chiefly remembered for furthering democratization and decentralization. He sought to equip every *départment* with a *Maison de la culture* (MC), a huge multidisciplinary arts center jointly financed by central and local governments, intended to enhance France's international prestige, encourage creativeness and bring high art to the masses just as the Third Republic had done with education. The MCs were to be modern "cathedrals" substituting for a waning religious faith the unifying spiritual experience of art.

The MCs soon encountered problems. By 1969 only seven had opened, while by 1989, after various vicissitudes, only eleven remained. Their high running costs left little money for *création*; the oppositional stance of many of their directors antagonized municipal authorities; and their imposing size and overtones of elitism and national grandeur obstructed their mission to attract working-class audiences. In May 1968 many MCs were implicated in the uprising and a number of directors were sacked. But May also challenged Malraux's entire cultural ideology, which, claimed the insurgents, disseminated a single, repressive cultural model to passive and largely bourgeois "consumers," disdaining the daily experience of a vast "nonpublic."

Malraux's departure in 1969 brought a shift of emphasis. Although democratization remained central until 1974, the Sixth Plan, reflecting the demands of May, urged a move away from macroinstitutions toward work in local communities (*animation*), individual creativity, and the recognition of diverse cultural identities. Smaller, more adaptable regional units were set up, though the Pompidou era did see one particularly large-scale Parisian project, the contemporary arts center at Beaubourg. The year 1969 also heralded a period of instability as a succession of ministers took charge of culture (Michelet, Bettencourt, Duhamel, Druon, Peyrefitte). The Giscardian era (1974–81) saw the ministry reduced to a *Secrétariat d'état* under Michel Guy (1974–76) and Françoise Giroud (1976–77), twinned with environment under Michel d'Ornano (1977–78), and with communication under Jean-Philippe Lecat (1978–81).

The 1974 recession closed the first age of doctrinaire interventionism. No chapter specifically devoted to culture appeared in the Seventh or Eighth Plans, and emphasis shifted from state voluntarism to economic liberalism, exemplified in the freeing of book prices in 1979 and the promotion of cultural industries and private sponsorship (*mécénat*). Various other initiatives favored museums and monuments (1980 was declared *l'Année du patrimoine*), music and music education, new theater appointments (Jean-Pierre Vincent, Peter Brook, Antoine Vitez), and new creative work on television. Further decentralization came with Guy's "cultural charters" or contracts, which promoted cooperation between central and local governments on specific projects. However, with regional authorities assuming more responsibility for culture, Lecat subsequently declared state-initiated decentralization outdated.

Culture played an important part in the 1981 presidential campaign as previous policies were accused of incoherence, of sacrificing creativity to conservation, and above all of failing to allocate a workable budget. Central-government spending on culture had in fact reached 0.55 percent of the overall budget in the mid-1970s, but, despite an electoral undertaking in 1978 to work toward the 1 percent demanded by the left, had now dropped to 0.48 percent. The new socialist government promised to reverse these trends by giving culture priority. With the support of President Mitterrand, Culture Minister Jack Lang announced in November the doubling of his budget to 0.76 percent, a first step toward the promised 1 percent (almost attained before he left office in 1986). Although he commissioned a series of consultative reports on various sectors, Lang also had his own distinctive doctrine, presenting culture not as an ornamental accessory (Malraux's "*supplément d'âmé*") but an essential component of social welfare and even economic growth. Alongside the traditional arts and cinema, he supported previously excluded areas: rock music, cartoons, fashion, small amateur associations, even cooking. This was democratization of a kind but redefined according to May 1968's validation of cultural diversity. Other democratization measures included: extending decentralization via the innovative *Direction du développement culturel* (which reshaped Guy's contractual policy); creating festivals of music and cinema; and bringing culture to the workplace, prisons, and hospitals. Lang's apparent utopianism, however, was tempered by a growing acknowledgment of the importance of cultural industries, *mécénat*, and efficient financial management. He also demonstrated a shrewd sense of public relations, consciously provoking the attention of the media and the young. This was aided by Mitterrand's costly and much debated public building program for Paris, the *grands travaux* (Louvre Pyramid, Bastille Opera, etc).

Although successfully updating the ministry's activity and image, Lang was frequently and at times unjustly criticized: for *dirigisme*, for unselectively distributing resources and sacrificing the heritage, for failing to redress the budgetary imbalance between Paris and the provinces. A promised bill reforming arts education in schools did not materialize, while many saw the launch of two private television channels in 1986 as contradicting Lang's cultural ambitions for television.

A change of government in March 1986 restored a more pragmatic liberalism when the Republican leader, François Léotard, became minister of culture and communication. Determined to reduce Lang's interventionism, he also pursued or completed several of his predecessor's projects with a slightly reduced budget. He furthered commercial sponsorship, reduced taxes on cultural industries, and introduced a law on arts education in 1987. The heritage and the international role of French culture were his other priorities. After Mitterrand's re-election in May 1988, Léotard was in turn replaced by Lang, this time as minister for culture, communication, the bicentennial, and the *grands travaux*. Culture was again hailed as a priority but, in keeping with the new emphasis on *ouverture* and consensus, Lang moderated some of the more provocative aspects of his earlier actions. Still favoring mass culture (even appointing a junior minister for rock), he also consolidated Léotard's emphasis on *patrimoine*, education, and European cultural cooperation, while Mitterrand initiated plans for a new national library in Paris. The 1990 budget exceeded 10 billion francs for the first time, still some 0.15 percent short of the mythical 1 percent.

Despite changes of personality and ideology, there has been a degree of continuity in the main issues facing cultural policy since 1945: state intervention, decentralization, *création* versus conservation. In recent years, however, the considerable power still invested in the minister as ultimate decision maker has combined with growth in cultural consumption and a new concern with public image to bring about a greater politicization of such issues.

F. Bloch-Lainé, *La France en mai 1981*, vol. 3 (Paris, 1982); P. Cabanne, *Le Pouvoir culturel sous la V*[e] République (Paris, 1981); Council of Europe, *Programme expérimental d'évaluation des politiques culturelles: France* (Strasbourg, Fr. 1987); J. Forbes, "Cultural Policy: The Soul of Man under Socialism," in *Mitterrand's France*, ed. S. Mazey and M. Newman (London, 1987); D. Wachtel, *Cultural Policy and Socialist France* (New York, 1987).

D. L. Looseley

Related entries: ART AND ARCHITECTURE; DECENTRALIZATION; GIROUD, FRANCOISE; LANG, JACK; LEISURE; LEOTARD, FRANCOIS; MALRAUX, ANDRE; PEYREFITTE, ALAIN; POPULAR CULTURE; VILAR, JEAN.

D

DEBRAY, REGIS (1940–) a former revolutionary, a leading intellectual, and an adviser to President François Mitterrand. Debray was born in Paris on September 2, 1940, and lived a privileged youth with his affluent and conservative family. During high school he broke with his family's conservatism as a result of his opposition to French policy in Algeria. At the age of eighteen he attended the *Ecole normale supérieure*, where he came under the influence of Louis Althusser and Jean-Paul Sartre.

In 1961 he visited Cuba and volunteered to teach in a rural education program. Because of his connections with Sartre, he was given long interviews with Fidel Castro, after which he became a dedicated student and supporter of revolution in Latin America. In 1966 he was appointed professor of philosophy at the University of Havana and began writing extensively about the *foco* theory of revolutionary struggle, which rejected both Russian and Chinese models and called, instead, for the establishment of mobile, autonomous bands of guerillas.

In March 1967 he traveled to Bolivia to interview his revolutionary colleague and friend, Ernesto ''Che'' Guevara. Shortly thereafter, he was arrested and spent three years in a Bolivian prison. Guevara was captured and killed, and some critics claim that Debray was inadvertently responsible for allowing Bolivian troops to find his friend.

After his release in 1970, Debray went to Chile and interviewed the recently elected Marxist president of that country, Salvador Allende Gossens. As a result of that visit, Debray decided that it was possible to reform a society radically through the electoral and parliamentary systems, and in 1974 he joined the Socialist party (PS) headed by Mitterrand. In the same year he served as an adviser in Mitterrand's presidential election campaign.

For the remainder of the 1970s Debray dedicated himself to writing, publishing an average of more than a book a year. In those works Debray continued considering the prospects for revolution abroad, but also wrote novels about the lives of terrorists and critiques of what he thought was bourgeois domination of French cultural life.

On May 10, 1981 Mitterrand was elected president of the Republic, and three weeks later named Debray special assistant in the Office of the President, primarily responsible for policy in the Middle East and Latin America. The following year he also became Mitterrand's adviser on cultural affairs. Despite his newfound respectability, Debray remained a controversial figure and continued his critiques of conservative influence in French intellectual life. In 1985, Debray was appointed *Maître des requêtes* at the *Conseil d'Etat*.

R. Debray, *The Chilean Revolution* (New York, 1971), *Revolution in the Revolution* (New York, 1967), *Teachers, Writers, Celebrities* (London, 1981).

C. Hauss

Related entries: ALGERIA, RELATIONS WITH; ALTHUSSER, LOUIS; BROADCAST MEDIA; CULTURAL POLICY; DECOLONIZATION; ELECTIONS; LANG, JACK; MARXISM; MIDDLE EAST, RELATIONS WITH; MITTERRAND, FRANCOIS; PRESS; SARTRE, JEAN-PAUL; SOCIALIST PARTY (PS); STUDENT REVOLTS; THIRD WORLD, RELATIONS WITH.

DEBRE, MICHEL (1912–), a prominent Gaullist politician who was the primary architect of the constitution of the Fifth Republic and then served as its first prime minister from 1958 until 1962. Debré was born in Paris on January 15, 1912. His was a wealthy family of the intellectual *haute bourgeoisie*—both his parents were physicians. The young Debré had a typical Parisian bourgeois upbringing. Although the family had been Jewish, Debré was raised a Roman Catholic, a religion he continues to practice. He attended the prestigious *Lycée Louis-le-Grand* and the *Ecole libre des sciences politiques*. He received his doctorate in law from the law faculty of the University of Paris in 1934, when he joined the staff of the *Conseil d'Etat*.

In 1939 Debré was mobilized into the army, serving as a lieutenant until he was captured by the Germans. He escaped to Morocco in 1940 and immediately joined the Gaullist wing of the Resistance. Later, he returned to France to work in the underground, most importantly drawing up a list of prefects to serve in the provisional government after the liberation of France.

In 1945 Charles de Gaulle named him to a new commission to reform the civil service. Among other things, the commission established the *Ecole nationale d'administration* (ENA), which is credited for changing the training and outlook of French bureaucrats, many of whom have also gone on to political and business careers.

In 1946 Debré ran for the Chamber of Deputies but was defeated. However, in 1947 he was named to the Economic Mission in the Saar, and the following year he was named secretary-general for German and Austrian Affairs at the Ministry of Foreign Affairs. That year, he was also elected to the Senate from Indre-et-Loire, a position he held for the rest of the Fourth Republic.

During those years, Debré established his reputation as a constitutional lawyer and Gaullist loyalist. He was one of the Gaullists who was most critical of the Fourth Republic's concentration of power in the Chamber of Deputies, whose partisan divisions made effective government all but impossible.

When the Algerian War propelled de Gaulle back into the prime ministry in

May 1958, he named Debré minister of justice and head of the commission that drafted the constitution of the new Fifth Republic.

Debré had long been a supporter of British-style party government, in which a single party controls a firm parliamentary majority and can therefore implement its party program and use that legislation as the basis for coherent public policy making. De Gaulle, Debré, and their colleagues assumed that such a majority could not be forged in a society as divided as in France, and they therefore sought to write a constitution that would provide French executives with other means of achieving the degree of power exercised by British prime ministers.

The new constitution strengthened the presidency, attempting to make it the ''national arbiter'' able to stand above the squabbling parties and steer French policy as a whole, which de Gaulle had been insisting on since his famous speech at Bayeux in 1946. Under the new regime, the president of the Republic was given new powers, including the right to take certain issues directly to the people in a referendum (Article 11) and rule by decree in an emergency (Article 16). The president was also to be elected by an electoral college of over eighty thousand national and local officials, which would give him or her a broader mandate than Third and Fourth Republic presidents, who were chosen by the members of parliament, who invariably chose someone of limited talent and ambition.

The constitution also strengthened the prime minister's and cabinet's hands vis-à-vis parliament. Now, for example, the government can refuse to allow any amendments to a bill and force the parliament to vote directly on its draft. Similarly, severe limits are placed on the parliament's ability even to participate in the making of economic and foreign policy. Members of parliament who are named to the cabinet now have to give up their seats, thereby giving them more of a vested interest in sustaining the government.

After the constitution was ratified and de Gaulle was elected the Fifth Republic's first president, he named Debré its first prime minister, a position he held for over three years. Debré is best remembered for two things. First, along with de Gaulle, he was the primary architect of a new direction in French foreign policy that led to Algerian independence in 1962. Second, the two of them also eliminated much of the ambiguity in the constitution regarding the relationship between president and prime minister. From the beginning, it was clear to all that the Fifth Republic was to be a presidential regime, with the prime minister occupying a decidedly secondary position. That the president was dominant was made abundantly clear in April 1962, when in an unprecedented move, de Gaulle asked for and immediately received Debré's resignation.

In 1963 Debré was elected to the National Assembly from the first district of Réunion, an overseas department in the Indian Ocean. He has been reelected to the Assembly in each election since then. He was also elected mayor of Ambroise in 1966 and a member of the European Parliament in 1979. Since 1962 Debré has held a number of cabinet portfolios, including economic affairs and finance (1966–68), foreign affairs (1968–69), and defense (1969–73).

Debré is widely respected for his intellect and is the author of more than a dozen books on various political subjects. He has also received many of France's most prestigious honors, including the *Légion d'honneur*, the *Croix de guerre*, and the *Rosette de la Résistance*.

J. Charlot, *The Gaullist Phenomenon* (London, 1971); M. Debré, *Les Princes qui nous gouvernent* (Paris, 1957); S. Hoffmann, W. Andrews, *The Fifth Republic at Twenty* (Albany, N.Y., 1981); P. M. Williams, M. Harrison, *Politics and Society in de Gaulle's Republic* (New York, 1983).

C. Hauss

Related entries: BIDAULT, GEORGES; CHABAN-DELMAS, JACQUES; CHIRAC, JACQUES; CONSTITUTION OF THE FIFTH REPUBLIC; CONSTITUTION OF THE FOURTH REPUBLIC; CONSTITUTIONAL COUNCIL; DECOLONIZATION; DE GAULLE, CHARLES; ELECTIONS; ELECTORAL SYSTEM; GAULLISM; GAULLIST PARTY; GISCARD D'ESTAING, VALERY; POMPIDOU, GEORGES; REFERENDA; SOUSTELLE, JACQUES.

DECENTRALIZATION, administrative and political reforms proposed regularly by out-of-power politicians to transfer national government powers to elected local officials in order to reduce Paris's traditional domination of the provinces, considered excessive. Strong central authority developed in France as a consequence of overcoming locally entrenched feudalism during the process of state formation and national integration. Pursuing goals of democracy and equality, the Revolution of 1789 reinforced centralization by granting exclusive political power to nationally elected representatives and requiring that laws and institutions be uniform throughout the provinces. Later, Napoleon I made centralization more effective by appointing national officials, called prefects, to govern in local jurisdictions.

Following some democratization in the 1830s and 1840s, early Third Republic reforms granted more autonomy to the numerous towns, gradually and pragmatically extending their responsibility for local affairs under the central government's supervision (*tutelle*), exercised by the prefects. A delicate balance was achieved by incorporating local elites in policy making, and the basic pattern survived both the world wars and the depression. Economic modernization in the 1950s, however, created new administrative needs, and a regional framework was established to facilitate development planning. At the same time the national bureaucracies strengthened central influence by using regulatory powers or conditional subsidies to interfere with the managerial tasks of mayors.

De Gaulle's reforms of national political processes in the Fifth Republic met with opposition from local politicians, and his efforts to circumvent them by consulting economic interest groups (the "*forces vives*") in corporatist regional assemblies were unsuccessful. After the failed 1969 regional referendum, President Georges Pompidou suspended reform of center-periphery relations, a policy followed by his successor Valéry Giscard d'Estaing. Despite widespread recognition of the need for decentralization, the conservative governing coalition's dependence on local notables prevented change.

The socialist victory in 1981 cleared the way for some of the most significant reforms of the twentieth century. New legislation abolished the office of prefect, whose executive authority—and much of its administrative staff, now protected by territorial civil service status—was transferred to presidents chosen by popularly elected councils in the departments and regions. Most former prefects became *commissaires de la République*. In addition, all three local levels gained powers of economic integration to help promote employment. Local taxation was revised, simpifying state transfers and granting revenue-generating authority to local officials. Significant areas of jurisdiction, particularly in urban and territorial development, were also transferred. Finally, the traditional practice of multiple office holding at national and local levels was phased out, creating incentives to recruit new local elites.

On balance, decentralization in the 1980s represents a significant and pragmatic redistribution of national and local roles, although not a radical restructuring of center-periphery relations, and some problems still remain in local governance. The state's important regulatory and fiscal powers guarantee it opportunities to intervene in local affairs. The political class is undergoing renewal, and patterns of influence among national, regional, departmental, and municipal leaders are being reshaped

G. Bélorgey, *La France décentralisée* (Paris, 1984); P. J. Godt, "Decentralization in France," *The Tocqueville Review* 7 (1986); P. Grémion, *Le Pouvoir périphérique* (Paris, 1976); J. Rondin, *Le Sacre des notables* (Paris, 1985).

P. J. Godt

Related entries: DE GAULLE, CHARLES; PARIS REGION; PLAN; REGIONS; SOCIALIST PARTY (PS); URBANIZATION.

DECOLONIZATION, the process of relinquishing French colonies. In May 1931 the grandiose Colonial Exhibition at Vincennes featured a French Empire covering twelve million square kilometers and embracing some 100 million citizens. Thirty years—and several wars—later, the empire was no more.

Presided over by no fewer than three ministers (interior, foreign affairs, and colonies), these vast overseas territories were in effect run by a small number of senior (and permanent) civil servants, particularly in the Colonial Ministry. Before 1945 their fortunes were rarely discussed in parliament, nor were they of interest to the man in the street. Moreover, despite the periodic eruption of revolts in almost every part of the empire, the only organized domestic opposition to colonialism came from the French Communist party.

The disastrous impact of the economic recession in the 1930s gave rise to discussions over a new deal for the colonies and aroused hopes that the relatively liberal atmosphere of the Popular Front first stimulated and then dashed. Both processes helped foster a growing spirit of nationalism in the subject peoples. This spirit was intensified during World War II, both because the political position adopted in the colonial countries became crucial to the war effort (pro-Vichy in Indochina, eventually pro-Gaullist in Africa), but also because these positions, and the consequences stemming from them, were imposed on the colonial peoples with no consultation either from Paris or from local administrators.

The first sign that French officials recognized the need for change came at the Brazzaville conference in February 1944. Attended by the governors of France's African territories, the conference examined proposals for a new, postwar relationship between Paris and the colonies. While the wind of change was clearly discernible on the economic, social, and even administrative fronts, notably by talk of opening up positions to the local population and by conjuring up prospects of an economic and industrial plan, politically Brazzaville was little more than a reassertion of France's imperial pretensions, all notions of autonomy, self-government, or independence being explicitly ruled out in the final communiqué. Yet, by 1944 in all the colonies, independence and self-government had become the main objectives of the new nationalist movements emerging from the war. The Sétif riots in Algeria on VE-Day 1945, in which some 100 Europeans were massacred, was a timely warning of the changing mood.

Between 1944 and 1947 the future of France's colonies hung in the balance. A consensus existed within the political class in favor of retaining some form of international system based on the empire. Senior colonial administrators such as Laurentie conceived of a loose structure akin to the British Commonwealth. Gaullist constitution makers such as René Capitant spoke in terms of a federation. Most socialists and communists, still ideologically committed to *La République une et indivisible,* continued to think in terms of assimilation of colonial peoples into the republican polity. The political definition of French Union swung back and forth depending on the fortunes of the main political parties. As defined in the constitution of 1946, the French Union, although guaranteeing equality for individuals, ignored equality of collective entities. Articles 60 to 75 of that constitution made it clear that France would retain the dominant role and that integration, if not assimilation, would be the guiding spirit.

Yet, already major forces were opposed to any such development: the United States, the Soviet Union, the United Nations, and the Arab League to begin with, but also the leading political actors in the colonies, and a growing domestic lobby that questioned either the material value or the moral acceptability of colonialism (or both). But it was the institutional and political feebleness of the Fourth Republic that finally put an end to France's aspirations to renewed imperial status.

The first trial came from Indochina where, by September 1944, the essentially nationalist movement led by Ho Chi Minh had succeeded in liberating the northern part of the country. The proclamation in Hanoi of the Democratic Republic of Vietnam was not intended primarily as an act of rupture with France. Ho was not averse to some form of continued association with France. However, he had to contend with the determination of the colonial administrators in Saigon to return Indochina to French rule. A chapter of sabotage, including the interception in Saigon of telegrams from Ho to Prime Minister Léon Blum, ensured that the warmongers won out. The advent of the Cold War did the rest. France stumbled into a conflict it did not particularly want, could not afford, and certainly had no prospect of winning. The humiliating final defeat at Dien Bien Phu (May 1954) had several fundamental consequences. First, an example had been set to other colonial peoples. Second, the French army was thoroughly demoralized and aching for revenge against somebody. Third, the drain on resources, both human and financial, was yet another blow to the tottering Republic.

The politicians in Paris had nevertheless understood that, if something were to be salvaged from the ruins of empire, political change could not be avoided. Hence, the framework law (*loi-cadre*) of June 1956, which instituted universal suffrage in all the colonial territories and an elected assembly from which would derive an embryonic form of local government. With the exception of Algeria, where a new colonial war was already brewing, these concessions were sufficient to keep the different parties talking for a few more years. In Tunisia and Morocco, where French interests were less committed than in Algeria, the powerful movements in favor of autonomy achieved their objectives with minimum bloodshed. Both countries were granted independence in 1956.

In sub-Saharan Africa, matters were complicated by the strong personalities of Léopold Senghor (Senegal) and Félix Houphouët-Boigny (Ivory Coast), both of whom wished to retain close links with France. The advent of de Gaulle in 1958 and the abandonment of French Union in favor of a new concept of "community"—which was sufficiently vague to allow multiple interpretations—helped crystallize developments. No fewer than twelve states voted overwhelmingly in favor of participation in the Community (Madagascar, Central African Republic, Ivory Coast, Dahomey, Gabon, Upper Volta, Mauritania, Niger, Senegal, Sudan, Chad, Congo). And yet within a year the entire project was stillborn. When discussions over the new structure reached matters of detail, it transpired that "Community" smacked as clearly of colonialism as French Union. The wind of change was by now roaring through the continent, and the British colonies were all acceding to full independence. By 1962 the concept of community had given way to the more practical device of cooperation, which has prevailed ever since. All France's African colonies achieved full independence in the early 1960s.

This was also true of the most problematic territory of all, Algeria. The war that had raged since 1954 had, by 1958, reached an impasse. Neither side could either win or lose. De Gaulle had at first hoped that some kind of special political relationship could be arranged with Algeria that would satisfy the million-strong French community as well as the local population. The failure of all attempts to devise such a solution convinced him that independence was inevitable, the more so in that the war was destroying France's international credibility. His decision in favor of independence sparked off a civilian revolt (*barricades*) in January 1960, a military revolt (the generals' putsch) in April 1961, and a wave of terrorist attacks from the newly formed Secret Army Organization (OAS). The Evian agreements in March 1962 put an end to France's last colonial war and gave Algeria its independence. In April 90 percent of French voters approved the Evian agreements in a referendum, thus putting the final, unambiguous nail into the coffin of French imperialism. All that remained of the empire were the *Départements d'Outre-Mer* and the *Territoires d'Outre-Mer*, of which French Polynesia and New Caledonia in the South Pacific were to prove highly problematic in the 1980s and into the 1990s.

If France lost control of her overseas territories in the two decades after 1945, she did not relinquish her influence, particularly in Africa where commonality of language and a certain predilection for French culture on the part of the traditional elites helped to ensure a durable role. The concept of *francophonie* came to replace the former labels for empire, and French cultural *rayonnement*, fostered by educational and other exchange agreements, acquired growing recognition. Gradually, as the scars of battle healed, new trade agreements were signed and military treaties negotiated.

But the long-term sequel of empire had to await the passing of the generation of political leaders who had taken their countries to independence. By 1991 most were either dead or in their dotage. Their passing coincided with the emergence of new tensions throughout the Third World, which have opened a new chapter in the the story. The rise of Islamic fundamentalism, which had already rocked the former UN-mandate territories of Lebanon and Syria, began to rear its head in the Maghreb. Moreover, in sub-Saharan Africa, destabilization of the old regimes spread like wildfire in the wake of rising political forces whose roots predated the colonial presence. In Indochina the war that had begun in 1945 and had been taken over by the Americans between 1965 and 1972 continued unabated among rival factions of Vietnamese and Cambodians. The heady mixture of Europeanism, capitalism, and Christianity with which colonial peoples throughout the world were confronted in the nineteenth century has by no means ceased to influence the fates of the countries concerned.

J. Dalloz, *La Guerre d'Indochine* (Paris, 1987); R. Girardet, *L'Idée coloniale en France 1871–1962* (Paris, 1972); J.-P. Rioux, ed., *La Guerre d'Algérie et les Français* (Paris, 1990).

J. Howorth

Related entries: ALGERIA, RELATIONS WITH; DE GAULLE, CHARLES; DIEN BIEN PHU; FOREIGN POLICY; FRENCH UNION; INDOCHINA, RELATIONS WITH; NEW CALEDONIA; *ORGANISATION DE L'ARMEE SECRETE*; OVERSEAS DEPARTMENTS AND TERRITORIES; THIRD WORLD, RELATIONS WITH.

DEFENSE POLICY, supported by a national consensus on the Gaullist approach to external relations. At the end of World War II it was evident that France would be incapable, at least in the short run, of conducting an independent defense policy. France had been defeated militarily by Germany in 1940. The Free French armies of General Charles de Gaulle had depended on the financial and political support of Great Britain, and during the Liberation they operated largely as subordinate adjuncts of the Anglo-American military forces sweeping across the Western portion of the continent. After the liberation, the French economy was in shambles, scarcely capable of sustaining the formidable military establishment and ambitious defense policy for which France had been renowned for centuries.

Yet, within a few years of the capitulation of the German army on May 8, 1945, the emergence of the Cold War in Europe dictated that France maintain a large conscript army and develop a strategic doctrine suitable to a new international order that was characterized by two unprecedented features: the partition of Europe into a rigid bipolar system with each half dominated by one of the two non-European (or semi-European) superpowers, and the omnipresent threat of nuclear warfare that could obliterate the entire national territory of France in one apocalyptic moment. How France, weakened and dependent on external aid yet faced with a putative military threat from the East, would fit into this new international environment became the key question for French defense planners.

The first overt sign of France's loss of independence in defense matters after the war came on March 4, 1947 with the conclusion of the Dunkirk Treaty, a fifty-year security pact with Great Britain providing for consultation and joint action against a renewal of German aggression. But with Germany occupied and divided, it rapidly became evident that it was the Soviet Union that posed the only security threat to France on the continent. To meet that threat, the two signatories of the Dunkirk Treaty joined with the three members of the recently established Benelux customs union to establish on March 17, 1948 the Brussels Treaty Organization (BTO), a regional military alliance to repel an armed attack against any member.

The underlying objective of the BTO was to demonstrate to the United States that the nations of Western Europe were prepared to band together in the interests of collective defense, in the hope that American military assistance would be forthcoming. French foreign minister Georges Bidault and British foreign secretary Ernest Bevin took the lead in promoting the cause of a collective security system linking the United States and Canada with the five signatories of the Brussels Treaty and such other European states as might wish to join. The United States, Canada, and ten European states eventually signed the North Atlantic Treaty on April 4, 1949, pledging to come to the defense of any member subjected to armed attack and establishing the North Atlantic Treaty Organization (NATO) to coordinate the activities of the alliance. In the aftermath of the Korean War, American participation in, and dominance of, the Atlantic Alliance was formalized in a number of ways: the creation of an integrated military force under the unified command of an American general, the transfer of four divisions of American ground troops to the continent, and the explicit linkage of the American nuclear deterrent and NATO's defense through the deployment of American nuclear bombers and missiles on European territory.

France responded with ambivalence to the unprecedented American commitment to her defense. On the one hand, she benefited considerably from the flow of American military assistance, both in Europe and in Southeast Asia (where the United States was footing 80% of the bill for France's doomed military campaign against the Viet Minh). The presence of American military forces on French territory, together with the American pledge of extended nuclear deterrence, represented an entirely credible guarantee against any threat of aggression from the east at a time when American territory was exempt from the threat of Soviet nuclear retaliation. On the other hand, France's subordinate position in NATO caused resentment from the very beginning. During the negotiations for the North Atlantic Treaty, French foreign minister Bidault had vainly attempted to promote a tripartite military system within which France, Great Britain, and the United States would manage the alliance on the basis of total equality. Throughout the remainder of the 1950s, successive French governments would revive the idea of a tripartite "inner directorate" only to be rebuffed by Washington and London. The "special relationship" between the two English-speaking powers, particularly the sharing of nuclear intelligence and technology after Britain's entry into the nuclear club in 1952, engendered increasing bitterness in France, as did the unmistakable evidence of American and British domination of the alliance's military organs.

Another source of controversy for France in defense matters was the question of West Germany's role in the defense of Europe. After the outbreak of the Korean War, the Truman administration applied unrelenting pressure on the European members of NATO to agree to the rearmament of West Germany and its inclusion in the Atlantic Alliance. The French, still traumatized by their experience in the last war and unwilling to acquiesce in the revival of German military power, responded with a counterproposal of their own: the formation of an integrated European military force, throughout which national contingents—including West German ones—would be thinly dispersed, wearing "European" uniforms and taking orders from "European" commanders. But after the United States endorsed the project and all of the other European members of NATO ratified it, the French National Assembly rejected it as an unacceptable encroachment on national sovereignty. By May 1955, when West Germany was permitted to rearm and join NATO, the French plan for a supranational European Defense Community was dead. The Atlantic Alliance would remain a coalition of sovereign states under the undisputed domination of the United States, supported by the other English-speaking member of the nuclear fraternity. In the meantime, newly rearmed West Germany was assuming an increasingly important share of the conventional defense burden and developing its own special relationship with Washington. By the end of the Fourth Republic in 1958, discontent was already widespread in France concerning its political impotence and military dependence within the Western alliance.

After the advent of the Fifth Republic, General Charles de Gaulle gave expression to that frustration in ways that were to have lasting consequences for France's defense policy. After attempting one last time, again in vain, to obtain American acceptance of the three-power directorate concept, the new French chief executive proceeded to loosen the security ties that had bound France to the American-controlled Western alliance since the late 1940s. First, in order to break the "Anglo-Saxon" monopoly on nuclear weapons within the alliance, he authorized the testing of a nuclear device in 1960 and engineered a crash program that produced a rudimentary delivery system within a few years. Consisting of long-range bombers as well as land-based and submarine-based missiles, the new French *force de frappe* was entirely independent of NATO targeting schedules and under exclusive French national control. Second, in order to ensure total French independence in military decision making, de Gaulle withdrew French ground and air forces from NATO's integrated military command and expelled all non-French (i.e., American) military bases and personnel from French territory in 1966.

The basis for these controversial defense policies was not merely the provincial type of French nationalism of which de Gaulle has often been justly accused. They also reflected a realistic assessment of French security interests in light of what was widely viewed as the decline in credibility of the American pledge of extended nuclear deterrence. Once the Soviet Union had acquired the capability of delivering nuclear weapons to American territory by the late 1950s, many Europeans began to doubt that the American president would be willing to sacrifice tens of millions of his own countrymen to nuclear retaliation on behalf of Europeans three thousand miles across the Atlantic. Gaullist strategic doctrine emphasized the necessity of national control of nuclear weapons to enhance the credibility of the deterrent, since a state could be expected to risk nuclear devastation only if its own (rather than some distant ally's) vital interests were at stake. The relatively puny size of the fledging French *force de frappe* was discounted by the theory of "proportional deterrence," the theoretical underpinning of French nuclear strategy. According to this doctrine, a middle-sized state such as France requires only a modest retaliatory force because the damage it could inflict on a handful of Soviet population centers—probably as many casualties as were suffered in World War II—would be so far out of proportion to whatever gains Moscow might anticipate from the defeat of France as to represent a credible deterrent.

De Gaulle's successors, from the loyal heir-apparent Georges Pompidou to the socialist antagonist François Mitterrand, preserved and modernized the French *force de frappe*, reaffirmed the strategy of national nuclear deterrence, and retained France's independent position outside of NATO's integrated military command. A broad national consensus in France in support of Gaullist defense policy has contrasted sharply with the acrimonious debates over security issues in other NATO countries.

Nevertheless, some significant modifications of Gaullist defense policy have been apparent since the retirement of the general. Significant steps toward closer French cooperation with NATO began under the administration of Valéry Giscard d'Estaing in the 1970s and continued thereafter. Under Mitterrand in the 1980s, France took two steps away from the narrow Gaullist policies of the 1960s: The French president took the lead in promoting the cause of European defense cooperation under the auspices of the Western European Union, which had fallen into disuse since its creation in 1955. Second, Mitterrand intensified bilateral security links with the Federal Republic, including a joint defense council and a mixed Franco-German infantry brigade. The one issue that seemed likely to shatter the French security consensus in the future was the question of France's security relationship with West Germany: Should large French conventional forces be deployed in forward positions along the Central Front, treating the Elbe rather than the Rhine as France's eastern defense frontier? And should the French nuclear deterrent be extended to cover West German territory as well as the "national sanctuary"? An affirmative answer to those two questions would have constituted a decisive break with the Gaullist tradition of national independence in the security realm and would have heralded the advent of a genuinely supranational approach to European defense.

But in the early years of Mitterrand's second *septennat*, events in Eastern Europe and the Soviet Union appeared to render moot most of the old debates concerning French defense policy. The de facto disintegration of the Warsaw Pact, the end of Soviet hegemony in Eastern Europe, and the political, economic, and ethnic crises confronting the Soviet Union at the end of the 1980s removed the military threat that had determined French security policy since the beginning of the Cold War. With the reunification of Germany in 1990, fears of *economic* domination by France's premier EC partner replaced the old anxieties about Soviet *military* hegemony in Europe, thereby prompting a full-scale reassessment of France's defense needs.

P. Gallois, *The Balance of Terror* (Boston, 1961); J. Howorth, P. Chilton, eds., *Defence and Dissent in Contemporary France* (Beckenham, Kent, 1984); W. Kohl, *French Nuclear Diplomacy* (Princeton, 1971); P. Lellouche, *L'Avenir de la guerre* (Paris, 1985); W. Mendl, *Deterrence and Persuasion: French Nuclear Armament in the Context of National Policy, 1945–1969* (New York, 1970).

W. R. Keylor

Related entries: DE GAULLE, CHARLES; EUROPEAN DEFENSE COMMUNITY; FEDERAL REPUBLIC OF GERMANY, RELATIONS WITH; FOREIGN POLICY; GISCARD D'ESTAING, VALERY; GREAT BRITAIN, RELATIONS WITH; MITTERRAND, FRANCOIS; POMPIDOU, GEORGES; UNITED STATES, RELATIONS WITH; WESTERN EUROPEAN UNION.

DEFFERRE, GASTON (1910–1986), socialist politician. He was born on September 14, 1910 in Marsillargues (Hérault). After attending a *lycée* in Nîmes, he studied law in Aix-en-Provence, practicing in Marseille from 1931 to 1951.

During World War II Defferre was active in the French Resistance. In 1944–45 he was mayor of Marseille, and again from 1953 until his death. A deputy to the two constituent assemblies in 1945–46, he served as a socialist (SFIO) National Assembly deputy from the Bouches-du-Rhône department from 1946 to 1958, as senator from that department from 1959 to 1962, and was reelected by it to the National Assembly in 1962, 1967, 1973, 1978, 1981, and 1986. From 1951 until his death he was director of the Marseille daily *Le Provençal*, of which he was principal owner.

Defferre served in five governments of the Fourth Republic, his most notable post being as minister for overseas France in Guy Mollet's government in 1956–57, where he was responsible for the framework law that prefigured decolonization of French African territories.

In 1964 anti-Gaullist moderates backed him for the presidential campaign of 1965, but his candidacy was wrecked by the difficulty of uniting both moderates and leftists behind him and the lukewarm support he received from socialist leader Guy Mollet. Socialist candidate for the presidency in 1969, he received only 5 percent of the vote.

In 1971 Defferre aided François Mitterrand in becoming leader of the *Parti socialiste* (PS), remaining an important Mitterrand ally in subsequent years. After the socialist victory in 1981 he was named minister of state for the interior and decentralization. He devoted his major efforts to the latter task, which he saw as the crowning effort of his career. In 1984 he was shifted to become minister for planning and national development.

Socialist boss of Marseille for the last thirty-three years of his life, Defferre was challenged by party rivals late in life. He collapsed and died on May 7, 1986, shortly after making a speech defending his position. Although he supported the PS-communist alliance after 1972, Defferre was essentially a representative of the moderate social democratic tradition in French socialism. His most notable achievements were his work on decolonization and decentralization.

R. W. Johnson, *The Long March of the French Left* (New York, 1981); N. Nugent, D. Lowe, *The Left in France* (New York, 1982); G. Ross, S. Hoffmann, S. Malzacher, eds. *The Mitterrand Experiment* (New York, 1987).

J. W. Friend

Related entries: DECENTRALIZATION; DECOLONIZATION; MITTERRAND, FRANCOIS; MOLLET, GUY; SOCIALIST PARTY (PS, SFIO).

DE GAULLE, CHARLES (1890–1970), military and political leader who headed the Free French government-in-exile during World War II and who served as president of the Fifth Republic (1958–69). De Gaulle was born in Lille in 1890, the son of a literature and philosophy professor at a Jesuit *collège*. He received a traditionalist upbringing and education, with a strong emphasis on the classics and Catholic piety. As a young man he was attracted to the writings of Charles Maurras and the political doctrines of the neoroyalist *Action française* movement, which preached hatred of the parliamentary republic and called for the restoration of executive authority in the hands of the king or, failing that, a strong military leader. Following his graduation from the Saint-Cyr military academy in 1912, de Gaulle joined an infantry regiment under the command of Henri-Philippe Pétain and served with distinction in World War I. He was wounded at Verdun in March 1916 and spent time in a German prisoner-of-war camp. In the summer of 1920 he was attached to General Maxime Weygand's military mission in Warsaw during the Russo-Polish War. During the 1920s he taught military history at Saint-Cyr and served on Pétain's staff.

During the 1930s de Gaulle acquired a reputation as a trenchant critic of the reigning military orthodoxy championed by his superior Pétain, which emphasized the type of defensive strategy and tactics that inspired the construction of the infamous static fortifications along the Franco-German frontier known as the Maginot Line. In three books, *Le Fil de l'épée* (1931), *Vers l'armée de métier* (1934), and *La France et son armée* (1938), de Gaulle advocated the creation of mobile, mechanized divisions that could operate independently from the infantry in conjunction with air power to disrupt the enemy's lines of communication and sow confusion behind the front lines. Though the advocates of blitzkrieg-type warfare in Germany read these works and put them to good effect, de Gaulle was ignored by most military and political leaders in France.

The one exception was the conservative politician Paul Reynaud who, as prime minister during the German invasion of France in early June 1940, belatedly appointed de Gaulle undersecretary of state for war. When his old mentor Pétain replaced Reynaud and approached the Germans for an armistice, de Gaulle refused to concede defeat and fled to London. On June 18 he broadcast an appeal to his countrymen over the British Broadcasting Corporation, urging them to resume the struggle against the Germans. When no high-ranking French political or military official heeded his call, de Gaulle declared himself head of the ''Free French'' government in exile and obtained financial support and diplomatic recognition from the Churchill government in Great Britain. In the meantime Pétain's collaborationist government, established in the resort city of Vichy after capitulating to the Germans, sentenced de Gaulle to death in absentia.

During World War II de Gaulle consolidated his authority over the Resistance movement within France and the French colonial empire in West Africa. He skillfully elbowed aside his chief rival, General Henri Giraud, the hand-picked candidate of American president Franklin D. Roosevelt, who detested de Gaulle as an arrogant, would-be dictator. Although excluded from the planning and execution of the Allied amphibious landing in Normandy in June 1944, de Gaulle persuaded Supreme Allied Commander Dwight D. Eisenhower to grant Free French forces the honor of liberating Paris on August 25. Foiling a tentative American plan to occupy France militarily after the Liberation (thereby treating it as a defeated enemy rather than a fraternal ally), de Gaulle succeeded in transforming his Committee of National Liberation into a provisional government of the French Republic and got himself elected president.

Drawing on the revolutionary legacy of the Resistance, de Gaulle promptly inaugurated several radical economic innovations, such as the nationalization of basic industries, the promotion of social welfare schemes, and the development of elaborate plans for economic modernization. But once it became evident that the principal political parties of postwar France favored a return to the parliamentary political system that had collapsed in 1940, de Gaulle abruptly resigned in January 1946. In October, after French voters approved the constitution of the Fourth Republic, which reaffirmed the principle of parliamentary sovereignty and created a weak chief executive, de Gaulle retired to his country home to begin work on his memoirs.

But de Gaulle's taste for political power prompted him to assume control of a new political movement, the *Rassemblement du peuple français* (RPF), in the spring of 1947. Despite its strident criticism of the parliamentary regime of the Fourth Republic for its political impotence and subservience to the United States in foreign policy, the RPF failed to attract much public support, and de Gaulle abandoned it in 1953 to resume work on his memoirs. But his self-imposed internal exile was to be short-lived, owing to the disastrous colonial policies of the Fourth Republic. Following the humiliating military defeat in Indochina (1954), the French army faced a nationalist insurrection in Algeria that threatened the privileged position of the million French settlers there. In May 1958 military leaders joined with the European settlers to stage mass demonstrations against any concessions to the Algerian insurgents, and the nervous government in Paris summoned de Gaulle as the only national figure capable of preventing mutiny and civil war. On June 1 the National Assembly designated de Gaulle prime minister and accorded him emergency powers to cope with the crisis. Later in the year voters approved a new constitution that enshrined the principle of executive authority, and de Gaulle, whose new political party had won an absolute parliamentary majority in the legislative elections in November, was elected first president of the Fifth Republic.

Before addressing the multitude of internal and external challenges that France faced, the new chief executive was obliged to settle the Algerian problem that had brought the country to the brink of military insurrection and civil war. Between 1958 and 1962 de Gaulle shrewdly capitalized on his impeccable credentials as a soldier and patriot to facilitate the granting of independence not only to Algeria but also to the remnants of the French Empire in sub-Saharan Africa as well. Having divested France of the albatross of colonialism, he thereupon concentrated on completing the restructuring of the French political system. In the fall of 1962 he sponsored a referendum that approved an amendment to the constitution specifying the election of the president by direct popular vote. Three years later he was reelected to a seven-year term, while the Gaullist party controlled the National Assembly under the leadership of his prime minister and heir apparent, Georges Pompidou.

In the meantime, de Gaulle had inaugurated a foreign and defense policy that emphasized France's independence in international affairs. After exploding its first atomic bomb in 1960, France developed a rudimentary delivery system and embraced a doctrine of national nuclear deterrence that clashed with the reigning orthodoxy in the American-dominated North Atlantic Treaty Organization (NATO). When the United States refused to agree to de Gaulle's proposal for a tripartite governing structure for NATO (within which France, Great Britain, and the United States would have equal power), he took a number of steps that signaled France's dissatisfaction with the bipolar international system of the Cold War and America's leadership of the Western alliance: In 1963 de Gaulle concluded with West German chancellor Konrad Adenauer a bilateral treaty establishing a privileged relationship between Paris and Bonn that was designed to wean Bonn away from its dependence on Washington in defense matters and set the stage for an all-European defense system based on the French nuclear deterrent. In 1966 he withdrew all French land and air forces from NATO's integrated military command, expelled all American military personnel from French territory, and demanded the removal of NATO's headquarters from the Paris region. He also antagonized the "Anglo-Saxons" (as he derisively called them) by vetoing Great Britain's application for membership in the European Economic Community (EEC) on the grounds that it would serve as a Trojan horse for the United States in Europe, criticizing American military interventions in Vietnam and the Dominican Republic, and stirring up *québecois* nationalism in French-speaking Canada. De Gaulle also pursued détente with the communist bloc, visiting the Soviet Union and several Eastern European countries and calling for the creation of a "Europe from the Atlantic to the Urals" (whatever that meant).

In the spring of 1968 de Gaulle's domestic authority and international prestige were severely shaken by a worker-student insurrection in Paris that revealed widespread discontent within Gaullist France. Over a third of the French work force went on strike, while thousands of students occupied university buildings in the large cities. The workers protested the high cost of living and their exclusion from decision making in the workplace; the students agitated for reform of the antiquated academic facilities. Though de Gaulle skillfully exploited the fear of a communist revolution to win a resounding victory in the elections of June 1968, he never fully recovered from the May '68 events and the widespread dissatisfaction with his rule that they represented. In April 1969, when a referendum on constitutional reform that he had submitted to the voters was defeated, de Gaulle took the occasion to resign. He retired to his country home, where he worked on his memoirs until his death on November 9, 1970.

A. Crawley, *De Gaulle* (New York, 1969); E. Kolodziej, *French International Policy under de Gaulle and Pompidou* (Ithaca, N.Y., 1974); W. W. Kulski, *De Gaulle and the World* (Syracuse, N.Y., 1966); J. Lacouture, *De Gaulle* (Paris, 1969).

W. R. Keylor

Related entries: CONSTITUTION OF THE FIFTH REPUBLIC; DEFENSE POLICY; ELECTIONS; FOREIGN POLICY; GAULLISM; GAULLIST PARTY; POLITICAL TRENDS; REFERENDA; STUDENT REVOLTS.

DELORS, JACQUES (1925–), economic adviser to Jacques Chaban-Delmas (1969–72), minister of finance under the socialists (1981–84), and currently president of the Commission of the European Community. Born in Paris, the son of a Bank of France messenger, he passed the *baccalauréat* in math in 1943 and entered the Bank of France, where he rose rapidly to a managerial post. A devout Catholic advocate of reformist and personalist solutions to social, economic, and political problems, he adhered to Emmanuel Mounier's *personalisme communautaire*—the *via media* between communism and capitalism—joined the *Confédération française des travailleurs chrétiens* (CFTC) in the 1940s, and supported Pierre Mendès-France's reformist government. He remains a *mounieriste*, a trade-union militant (in the secularized *Confédération française démocratique du travail* [CFDT]), and a *mendésiste* reformer.

In 1962 Delors became *Chef des Affaires sociales* for the Plan. His emphasis on collective goods such as health, education, and culture was incorporated into the Fourth Plan. In 1969 Gaullist prime minister Chaban-Delmas chose him to be his adviser on social policy for the "New Society" program. Delors advocated more equitable distribution of goods and collective bargaining to achieve better salaries and working conditions. He was opposed, however, by the trade unions, which were suspicious of collective bargaining contracts.

Delors left government in 1972, but remained devoted to the ideals of the New Society. He joined the Socialist party (PS) in 1974, despite reservations about the Common Program. He was appointed socialist representative for international economic relations in 1976. In 1978 he sided with François Mitterrand against Michel Rocard, maintaining that Mitterrand alone could keep the socialists united. In 1979 he became a member of the *Comité directeur* of the party and was elected to the European Parliament. He served as Mitterrand's chief economic adviser in the 1981 election campaign and was appointed minister of finance in the new government.

As minister, Delors supported the *relance* of the economy, which included major increases in the minimum wage and social security benefits for the poorest, but he opposed massive nationalization and a *rupture* with capitalism. He emerged as a key advocate of rigor and modernization of French industry. In November 1981 his call for a "pause" in reforms sparked controversy in the party. In June 1982 he imposed wage and price controls as part of the second devaluation of the franc. In March 1983 he won a major victory when Mitterrand accepted his plan for increased rigor and austerity over the protectionist plans of the far left. In 1984 his ideas for restructuring industry were implemented. Delors believed that only a healthy private sector could provide the resources for reductions in the work week, higher social security benefits, and other redistributive programs.

In July 1984 Delors was not included in the Fabius government. He became president of the Commission of the European Community on January 1, 1985, where he is involved in preparing Europe for the 1992 dismantling of trade barriers.

P. Alexandre, J. Delors, *En sortir ou pas* (Paris, 1985); P. Bauchard, *La Guerre des deux roses: Du rêve à la réalité, 1981–1985* (Paris, 1986); J. Delors, *Changer* (Paris, 1975); G. Milési, *Jacques Delors* (Paris, 1985).

T. R. Christofferson

Related entries: CHABAN-DELMAS, JACQUES; CONFEDERATION FRANCAISE DEMOCRATIQUE DU TRAVAIL; CONFEDERATION FRANCAISE DES TRAVAILLEURS CHRETIENS; ECONOMIC POLICY; FABIUS, LAURENT; INDUSTRIAL POLICY; MAUROY, PIERRE; MITTERRAND, FRANCOIS; SOCIALIST PARTY (PS).

DEMOCRATIC AND SOCIALIST UNION OF THE RESISTANCE (UDSR), the most important of the minor parties under the Fourth Republic and the party of François Mitterrand during the early years of his political career. Created in 1945 from several Resistance groups, the UDSR officially became a party in 1946 and attracted support from various sources: non-Marxist socialists (Pierre Bourdan), Gaullists (René Capitant, André Malraux, Jacques Soustelle), and liberals (Jean Marin, Jean Legaret, Edouard Bonnefous). Functioning primarily as a group of leaders without mass support among the electorate, the UDSR served as a "hinge party" between the left and the right in postwar France. The party seldom had more than thirty deputies in the National Assembly. In its early existence the UDSR on several occasions stymied bids for power by the French Communist party (PCF) when the communists tried to capitalize politically on their role in the Resistance and when they attempted to form a Marxist coalition with the socialists. The UDSR also opposed tripartitism.

By the late 1940s the Gaullists in the party came under increasing attacks from within the UDSR, especially from Mitterrand, and left the party in 1949; this reduced the UDSR group in the National Assembly from twenty-seven members to fourteen. In the 1951 elections the UDSR won nine seats from metropolitan France and shortly thereafter added fourteen supporters from overseas. Also in 1951, at the UDSR congress in Marseille, Mitterrand became head of the party's parliamentary group in the National Assembly.

As one of the minor parties of the Fourth Republic, the UDSR was, as Philip Williams stated, "too well placed to be ignored, and too small to be feared." The party allowed Mitterrand to gain prominence as a young national leader under the Fourth Republic.

Les Cahiers de l'UDSR (Paris, archives of the FNSP); W. Northcutt, *Mitterrand: A Political Biography* (New York, 1992); P. Williams, *Politics in Post-War France*, 2d ed. (London, 1958).

W. Northcutt

Related entries: CAPITANT, RENE; ELECTIONS; FRENCH COMMUNIST PARTY; GAULLIST PARTY; MITTERRAND, FRANCOIS; POLITICAL TRENDS; SOCIALIST PARTY (SFIO); SOUSTELLE, JACQUES; TRIPARTITISM.

DEMONSTRATIONS, a form of grass-roots political expression in all societies, except totalitarian ones. In democratic societies they are a means whereby centers of power compete with one another for public favor and try to impress the legislative and executive (and occasionally the judicial) branches of government with the size of their groups, the urgency and the popularity of their demands, and the intensity of the feelings of their members. The demonstration also has a Durkheimian function: to reinforce the faith within the members of the group and its sympathizers and to serve a payoff function—that is, to bring a direct psychic income from participation, such as feelings of intensified solidarity, of excitement, and of moral righteousness. This payoff thus obviates to a certain extent the "free-rider" problem faced by all groups by rewarding activist participation immediately.

In France street demonstrations (*manifestations*, or *manifs* for short) have always played an important role in the equilibrium of political forces, partly because the centralization of political power in Paris makes the capital more vulnerable to street pressure and partly because the relative lack of confidence of the French citizen in the effectiveness and even legitimacy of the system of representation—until very recently the right having little or no respect for the Republican regime and the left believing that bourgeois democracy was a sham—makes obvious the advantages of bypassing parliament. Another factor is the sheer pleasure of the "unanimist jag" in an otherwise highly formalistic and segmented society.

In Paris alone, on the basis of requests for permits at the *Préfecture de Police* and police reports, there were 187 street demonstrations for the first six months of 1989. Demonstrations are commonplace in France.

Between 1789 and 1870 demonstrations, especially when militias and troops joined them, brought down four regimes. In the last sixty years demonstrations were responsible for the near-collapse of the Third Republic (on February 6, 1934) and for the fall of the Fourth Republic in May 1958. In May–June 1968 the combined student demonstrations and general strike nearly brought down the Fifth Republic and certainly hastened Charles de Gaulle's departure from power. In 1984 a massive demonstration called by Catholic action groups forced the majority socialist government to abandon attempts to legislate the integration of parochial schooling to the state system. Two years later, in November and December 1986, a series of massive student demonstrations, and especially the death of a North African demonstrator, forced the conservative Chirac government to rescind a project to reform the university.

Factors that have influenced demonstrations in the postwar era include:

1. The mass media has become more important in defining the demonstration. Radio and television coverage must be taken into account in planning its locale and timing.
2. While the means available to counter demonstrations have grown substantially during the twentieth century, the strength of public opinion has grown as well. This means that a demonstration that escalates to violence can become a trial of the government's legitimacy, and a battle won, especially against youth, can easily mean the loss of the war through the loss of the "moral edge" by the defenders of law and order (as in 1934, 1968, and 1986). In the Third and Fourth Republics this meant the resignation of the cabinet.
3. University students, those most active in demonstrations, have increased by a factor of seven since 1950, with a resultant "leftification" not seen in the first half of the century. In the Paris region alone there are more than 360,000 university students, to which must be added the last three grades of *lycée* students who consider participation in demonstrations a ritual of "adultification" in which they challenge the police and identify with university students. It is thus easy for the 0.5 to 1 percent of student activists to find their "critical mass."
4. The French Communist party, since 1920, has been a major source of demonstrations,

either directly or through its control of much of the trade-union movement. (Since 1975, however, it has lost half of its militants and half of its electorate.) In the past, the Communist party, except perhaps during the insurrectional strikes of 1947–48, exercised considerable control over its demonstrators. Today it cannot control or insulate the extreme left—Trotskyists, anarchists, anti-police militants—who sometimes engage in violence and looting when they join a mass demonstration that they are incapable of organizing by themselves.

5. While in the past the willingness of adults to demonstrate in the street was more typical of the working class, today white-collar, middle-class groups, and civil servants, are not loath to demonstrate for corporate or political goals and are often influenced by various political activists who hide their secret agenda while contributing their often considerable organizational and tactical know-how.

D. Assouline, S. Zappi, *Notre printemps en hiver, le mouvement étudiant de novembre-décembre 1986* (Paris, 1988); P. Favre, ed., *La Manifestation* (Paris, 1990); J. Pitts, ''Les Français et l'autorité,'' in *Français qui êtes-vous?* (Paris, 1982); C. Tilly, *The Contentious French* (Cambridge, Mass., 1986).

J. R. Pitts

Related entries: COMPAGNIES REPUBLICAINES DE SECURITE; FRENCH COMMUNIST PARTY; STRIKES; STUDENT REVOLTS.

DERRIDA, JACQUES (1930–), philosopher and critic. Born in Algeria, Derrida is a highly original thinker and dazzling experimental prose stylist with an international reputation. Closely associated with poststructuralism, his ideas are debated and discussed by a wide range of scholars in the humanities and other fields, as well as by persons in the arts and contemporary literature. To some extent Derrida, who currently divides his teaching duties between the *Ecole des hautes études en sciences sociales* in Paris and the University of California, Irvine, has a greater impact abroad than in France. However, with the removal of such major presences as Michel Foucault, Roland Barthes, Louis Althusser, and Jacques Lacan from the French intellectual scene, Derrida has enjoyed increasing prominence in recent years.

In 1967 Derrida was a relatively little-known teacher of philosophy at the *Ecole normale supérieure*. However, in that year he published three books: *De la grammatologie* (*Of Grammatology*, 1976), *L'Ecriture et la différence* (*Writing and Difference*, 1978), and *La Voix et le phénomène* (*Speech and Phenomena*, 1973). Together, these books constituted a formidable critique of structuralism and helped to define the post–1968 intellectual atmosphere in which the diverse theoretical and critical discourses known collectively as poststructuralism took shape. Significantly, Derrida was closely associated for a time with the journal *Tel quel*, whose editors embraced much of the immediate post–1968 mood in theory and criticism.

Derrida first attracted attention through his strong challenge to the structuralist insistence on the stability and systematic function of linguistic signs. He argued that, in keeping with what he designates as Western metaphysics, structuralists such as Claude Lévi-Strauss persist in a speech-centered (logocentric) notion of language. This logocentrism is marked by profound suspicion of writing, for writing, as Plato, Rousseau, and many other celebrated philosophers have realized, is no guarantor of meaning or authorial presence. Derrida has furthermore cited the patriarchal component in this preference, and this has influenced recent French feminist theorists considerably. In Derridean language, the opposition that favors speech over writing is, like patriarchal culture's preference for male over female, an unjustifiable one that will always be "deconstructed" through the workings of the text (which always implies other texts) itself. In the act of reading, unforeseen effects and linguistic operations manifest themselves so that authorial intention and univocality are compromised.

Derrida's often baffling terminology (e.g., *différence, trace, déconstruction*) stems from the effort to demonstrate the complex procedures attendant upon the act of reading. He takes reading very seriously, and the extraordinary nature of his very difficult texts derives from his habit of dramatizing, rather than simply explaining or theorizing, the ways in which textual meaning is produced and multiplied through reading. An important achievement of Derrida has been to temporalize the production of meaning in texts, employing and refining ideas previously suggested by such thinkers as Nietzsche, Heidegger, and Freud. Although the scholars and critics he has influenced have often failed to engage the temporal dimension implied by Derrida's approach to textual language, this aspect of his thought points to the would-be recovery by poststructuralism of what structuralism had most emphatically rejected: history.

J. Derrida, *De la grammatologie* (Paris, 1967); L. Finas et al., *Ecarts: Quatre essais à propos de Jacques Derrida* (Paris, 1973); P. Lacoue-Labarthe, J.-L. Nancy, eds., *Les Fins de l'homme: A partir du travail de Jacques Derrida* (Paris, 1981); C. Norris, *Derrida* (London, 1987).

J. A. Winders

Related entries: ALTHUSSER, LOUIS; BARTHES, ROLAND; FEMINISM; FOUCAULT, MICHEL; INTELLECTUAL TRENDS; LACAN, JACQUES; LEVI-STRAUSS, CLAUDE; LITERATURE; STRUCTURALISM; STUDENT REVOLTS.

DIEN BIEN PHU, a valley in North Vietnam close to the Laotian border that became the site of the final battle and defeat of French forces in the first Indochina War (1947–54). The battle occurred when commanders on both sides, General Navarre for the French and General Giap for the Vietminh, decided upon a test of strength in anticipation of an international conference scheduled for Geneva in the spring of 1954.

The French brushed aside Ho Chi Minh's last-minute offer to negotiate and sent parachute units into Dien Bien Phu, located three hundred miles northwest of Hanoi, in November 1953. Members of his staff warned Navarre that Dien Bien Phu would be difficult to supply by air, but the French commander predicted that Giap could not bring in heavy artillery to besiege the French garrison. On the other hand, Giap was determined to wipe out the French forces. He sent some of his best units into the hills around Dien Bien Phu and supplied them with siege artillery. The Vietminh attacked on March 13. Two key French defensive positions fell right away, and Vietminh bombardments put the airfield out of action. For the next six weeks Dien Bien Phu became, as one French historian described it, "hell in a very small place," an agony that ended with the surrender of the French garrison on May 7, 1954.

Both sides suffered heavy losses, but for the French Dien Bien Phu was a mortal blow to the Fourth Republic and a humiliation for the French Army. The defeat brought down the government of Joseph Laniel on June 12, 1954. Rather than carrying a victory to the bargaining table at Geneva, Laniel's successor, Pierre Mendès-France, accepted terms that gave Ho Chi Minh control over the northern half of Vietnam with a promise of elections for the whole country within two years. Officers who served in Indochina believed that they had been betrayed at home by politicians who denied them support for victory. A deep bitterness and alienation of many French officers from the civilian leadership of the Fourth Republic was a legacy of Dien Bien Phu that reappeared during the Algerian War (1954–62) and surfaced during the events that brought General Charles de Gaulle to power in 1958.

B. Fall, *Hell in a Very Small Place: The Siege of Dien Bien Phu* (Philadelphia, Pa., 1966); V. N. Giap, *Dien Bien Phu* (Hanoi, 1962); J. Roy, *The Battle of Dien Bien Phu* (New York, 1965).

J. K. Munholland

Related entries: FRENCH UNION; INDOCHINA, RELATIONS WITH; LANIEL, JOSEPH; MENDES-FRANCE, PIERRE.

DREYFUS, PIERRE (1907–), chairman of nationalized industries, political adviser on industrial affairs, minister of industry in the second Mauroy government (1981–82), Grand Officer of the *Légion d'honneur*. Born in Paris on September 18, 1907, the son of a banker, he studied at the *Lycée Janson-de-Sailly* before obtaining his doctorate in law at the Paris *Faculté de droit*. He joined the Ministry of Trade as technical adviser in 1935. Called up for military service in 1939, he fought in the Resistance movement after 1940.

Following the war Dreyfus headed the General Inspectorate of Trade and Industry and was chief adviser to the trade and industry minister, Robert Lacoste, from 1947 to 1949. He took over as president of *Houillères de Lorraine* in 1950 (until 1955) and joined the board of *Charbonnages de France* in 1954. Also in 1954 he presided over the Energy Commission of the Plan and became chief adviser to the trade and industry minister, Maurice Bourgès-Maunoury. Appointed vice-president of Renault in 1948, he took over as president of the company and kept this post until 1975. From 1976 until 1980 he was president of *Société financière et foncière* and *Société Renault-finance*.

In May 1981 the newly elected socialist president, François Mitterrand, appointed Dreyfus to his advisory staff. On June 23, 1981 Dreyfus was called into the second Mauroy government. As minister of industry he helped to define the government's nationalization program and introduced various aid measures to industry for modernization and the creation of new firms, but long-term policy had to give way to urgent problems such as those of the iron and steel industry. He was replaced by Jean-Pierre Chevènement in a cabinet reshuffle in June 1982 and rejoined Mitterrand's advisory team.

J.-F. Doumic, H. Lacharmoise, eds., *Le Guide du pouvoir* (Paris, 1989); P. Dreyfus, *La Liberté de réussir* (Paris, 1977).

S. Milner

Related entries: BOURGES-MAUNOURY, MAURICE; INDUSTRIAL POLICY; MAUROY, PIERRE; MITTERRAND, FRANCOIS; NATIONALIZATIONS.

DUCLOS, JACQUES (1896–1975), communist politician. He was born on October 2, 1896 in Louey-par-Juillan (Hautes Pyrénées) in a working-class family and was apprenticed to a pastry cook at the age of twelve. In World War I he was wounded at the battle of Verdun, and was taken prisoner in 1917.

Profoundly affected by his war experience, after its conclusion Duclos resumed work as a pastry cook but rapidly became active in the left-wing *Association républicaine des anciens combattants* (ARAC) and joined the new French Communist party (PCF), assuming increasingly important roles in the ARAC and in party work. In late 1924 Duclos was sent to the first PCF cadre school, marking his entry into full-time party work. In 1926 he became a deputy from Paris, entered the PCF Central Committee, and became deputy secretary of ARAC and director of several antimilitarist party newspapers. In 1927 he was sentenced repeatedly for inciting servicemen to disobedience. Freed to sit in parliament, he fled to escape sentences that by 1928 totaled forty-seven years in jail and included heavy fines. Reelected to the Chamber in 1928 (against Léon Blum), he worked in 1929 in the Comintern Western European bureau (WEB) in Berlin and its clandestine center in Brussels, and in 1930 was sent as a Comintern emissary to Spain. In 1931 Duclos was again in France, where he was elected to the PCF Politburo and Secretariat. Defeated in the elections of March 1932, he lost his parliamentary immunity and was also accused as an accessory in an espionage case. Sent back to Berlin in 1932, he worked in the WEB under Georgi Dimitrov, using the pseudonym Lauer. He was elected a member of the Comintern Executive Committee at the organization's seventh congress in 1935.

In November 1932 a noncommunist left government nullified Duclos's sentences, and he resumed his political activities in France. Continuously reelected to the Politburo for the rest of his life, member of the Secretariat until 1964, by 1935 Duclos had become the number-two man in the PCF after Secretary-General Maurice Thorez, while retaining his close ties with the Comintern apparatus. When the PCF was outlawed just before war broke out in 1939, Moscow ordered Thorez to desert and come to Russia. Duclos became the principal PCF leader in France, first in an antiwar phase until the Nazis invaded the Soviet Union, then in the Resistance phase.

After the war, Duclos was elected to the two Constituent Assemblies from the Seine department and again to all National Assemblies during the Fourth Republic. As number-two man in the PCF, he represented it at the founding of the Cominform in September 1947, where he made an autocriticism for PCF policy from 1944 to 1947.

During Thorez's illness and absence in the Soviet Union between October 1950 and April 1953, Duclos was acting secretary-general. He was arrested during the communist-inspired riots against new NATO commander General Matthew Ridgway in May 1952, but released. Duclos played a principal role in the PCF leadership purges of André Marty and Charles Tillon in this period. On Thorez's return, he and Duclos together opposed suggestions from Moscow that they begin de-Stalinization of the PCF, culminating in a refusal to recognize the existence of Nikita Khrushchev's secret speech of February 1956.

Thorez then began to move Waldeck Rochet into the number-two position, and he succeeded Thorez in 1964. After Thorez's death, Duclos, since 1959 a senator, led the old Stalinists in the party who wished to keep it ultrafaithful to Moscow. Despite his reputation as a confirmed Stalinist, the party chose Duclos as its candidate in the presidential election following Charles de Gaulle's resignation in 1969. In a campaign remarkable for oratorical brilliance, he came close to placing in the second round, obtaining 21.36 percent of the vote and far outdistancing socialist candidate Gaston Defferre.

Duclos's wit and the grandfatherly image he had acquired in the 1969 campaign improved his public image. However, his energies until his death in April 1975 remained devoted to promoting strict adherence to the Soviet doctrine of obedience, which marked his whole career in the communist movement.

B. Lazitch, M. Drachkovitch, eds., *Biographical Dictionary of the Comintern*, rev. ed. (Stanford, Calif., 1986); J. Maitron, *Dictionnaire biographique du mouvement ouvrier français* (Paris, 1971–85); P. Robrieux, *Histoire intérieure du parti communiste*, vols. 1, 2, 4 (Paris, 1980–84); I. Wall, *French Communism in the Era of Stalin* (Westport, Conn., 1983).

J. W. Friend

Related entries: DEFFERRE, GASTON; FRENCH COMMUNIST PARTY; ROCHET, WALDECK; THOREZ, MAURICE.

DUMAS, ROLAND (1922–), lawyer, journalist, deputy, and minister of foreign affairs under the Mitterrand presidency. Dumas was born in Limoges, where his father was a civil servant. After attending the *Lycée de Limoges*, he studied at the *Faculté de droit de Paris*, the *Ecole des langues orientales*, and the University of London. He holds degrees in law and political science as well as an advanced degree from the London School of Economics; he possesses excellent language skills. Beginning in 1950, he launched his law career, becoming known as a lawyer of artists and entertainment figures. As a journalist he has served as the political director of *Socialiste Limousin* and since 1967 in the same capacity for the weekly *La Corrèze républicaine et socialiste*.

His political career began, like that of his friend François Mitterrand, in the small hinge party in postwar France known as the Democratic and Socialist Union of the Resistance (UDSR), where he became a deputy to the National Assembly from Haute-Vienne (1956–58). He later served as deputy as a member of the Federation of the Democratic and Socialist Left (FGDS) from 1967 to 1968, serving as vice-president of the National Assembly from April to May 1968.

With the election of Mitterrand to the presidency in 1981, Dumas began to play a greater role in the political life of his nation as a member of the *Parti socialiste* (PS). In 1981 he was elected as a socialist deputy from the Dordogne. From 1983 to 1984 he was Mitterrand's minister of European affairs; in 1984 he was also spokesperson for the government. Dumas was appointed minister of external relations in 1984, where he remained until the election of a conservative government in 1986. Given Dumas's influence with Mitterrand as minister of external relations, one French newsweekly called him the "Vice-President." Although the 1986 elections returned a conservative majority, Dumas was elected to the National Assembly once again from the Dordogne. His election as president of the Foreign Affairs Commission of the National Assembly strengthened Mitterrand's position in foreign and defense matters as the nation experimented with power sharing (*cohabitation*) under Jacques Chirac's conservative government. Following Mitterrand's re-election in 1988, Dumas was sent to the National Assembly again by voters in the Dordogne, but gave up his seat when he was appointed minister of foreign affairs in the government of the right-wing socialist Michel Rocard (1988–91), a position that he retained in the cabinet of Edith Cresson (1991–).

He has authored a number of books, including *J'ai vu la Chine*, *Le Droit de l'information et de la presse*, *Plaidoyer pour Roger-Gilbert Lecomte*, *Le Droit de la propriété artistique et littéraire,* and *Le Peuple assemblé.* As a long-time confidant of Mitterrand, he has played key roles in sensitive positions under the Mitterrand presidency.

J.-F. Doumic, H. Lacharmoise (eds.), *Le Guide du pouvoir 89* (Paris, 1989).

W. Northcutt

Related entries: DEMOCRATIC AND SOCIALIST UNION OF THE RESISTANCE; FOREIGN POLICY; MITTERRAND, FRANCOIS; SOCIALIST PARTY (PS).

E

ECOLOGY PARTY, a political party, also known as *Les Verts,* formed in 1984 from the fusion of several Green movements in order to promote ecological issues and organize politically to this end. The wider movement grew out of the May 1968 events (*Amis de la terre,* 1970; *Verts-Confédération écologiste, 1981; Verts-Parti écologiste,* 1982, themselves often amalgamations of two or more groups). Present since 1973 at local, legislative, presidential, and European elections, the Green vote has been between 2 percent and 4.5 percent of the national vote (higher in some areas, such as Paris and Alsace, than in others), and rose to over 10 percent in the European elections of 1989.

The party has a membership of approximately five thousand. Membership is single party and individual. There is great stress upon decentralization within the party structure, and there is a collegiate leadership.

In the context of a growing national awareness of the importance and, in cases such as the ozone layer depletion and "greenhouse effect," the urgency of environmental issues, on the one hand and, on the other, the perceived failure of the post–1981 socialist government to implement Green policies, the "political" current within the movement vis-à-vis the "social" current was strengthened. Moreover, grass-roots pressure-group environmentalism was seen as necessary but politically inadequate. Concomitantly, the 1980s saw the increasing political autonomy of the party and, in particular, its resistance to Socialist party (PS) attempts to appropriate its policies, discourse, and electorate—a clear example being the appointment in 1988 of Brice Lalonde, the Greens' 1981 presidential candidate and an opponent of the subsequent party leadership, as environment minister. The most dramatic example of the rift between the governmental left and the ecologists was the sinking of the environmentalist pressure group's ship, Greenpeace's *Rainbow Warrior*, in which government complicity at some level was widely assumed.

The Greens' continuing success will depend largely upon whether they become accepted as a political party that voices social and political interests that are seen as enduringly relevant. *Les Verts* are vulnerable to the perception that they are an "issue" or "single-issue" party. Political victories, in the 1970s for example, concerning the military installation at Larzac and the nuclear power station of Plogoff, usually have a demobilizing effect once the single-issue victory has been won. And just as all political parties profess a concern for environmental issues, so too within the party and wider movement coexist a whole range of ideological tendencies. This finds reflection in a relatively diverse electorate, which to date has acted more as a protest vote than a true constituency.

The greatest political disadvantage the French Greens have when compared to their equivalent parties in West Germany, the United Kingdom, and elsewhere is the relatively wider acceptance among the electorate of the nuclear power industry and, for historical reasons, a strong commitment by the French and nearly all the French political parties of both right and left to France's military nuclear capability. Like all Green parties, *Les Verts* have affinities with the peace movement. In France, however, this latter has been traditionally dominated by organizations close to the French Communist party. This complicates further the Greens' relationship to both the issues and their own potential constituency.

S. Parkin, *Green Parties: An International Guide* (London, 1989); B. Prendiville, T. Chafer, "Activists and Ideas in the Green Movement in France," in *Green Politics I 1990,* ed., W. Rüdig (Edinburgh, 1990); W. Rüdig, P. Lowe, *The Green Wave* (London, 1990); A. Touraine, et al., *Anti-Nuclear Protest* (Cambridge, 1983).

J. Gaffney

Related entries: BOUCHARDEAU, HUGUETTE; ELECTIONS; GREENPEACE AFFAIR; HERNU, CHARLES; PEACE MOVEMENT; POLITICAL TRENDS; REGIONS.

ECONOMIC POLICY, a policy that has ranged from technocratic socialism to conservative neoliberalism under the Fourth and Fifth Republics. The Fourth Republic had constantly shifting policies and an ambivalent position for the state in the economy. Policies in the Fifth Republic have been largely consistent and favorable to a strong state role in the economy. The state has used fiscal, budgetary, and monetary policy, nationalized firms, planning, industrial subsidies, and price controls as its policy tools.

The Fourth Republic initially faced the problems of inflation, reconstruction, and modernization. After Antoine Pinay defeated Pierre Mendès-France's attempt at direct monetary reform, inflation control measures devolved to price controls, tariff measures, and efforts to reduce producers' costs and increase the supply of goods on the market. Inflationary pressures have been pervasive and almost intractable. Right-of-center anti-inflation policies relied primarily upon wage-restraint measures and private investment incentives. Left-of-center policies focused upon planning and nationalized firms to increase the supply of goods and services and also focused upon price controls. Rightists usually diagnosed labor costs and raw materials prices as the sources of inflation; leftists often focused upon profiteering and insufficient supplies of goods.

Most political leaders agreed that postwar reconstruction and modernization could proceed rapidly only if wages were restrained in order to augment the supply of capital available for productive investment. From 1944 to 1947, a combination of nationalizations and indicative economic planning were implemented so that investment capital would be efficiently allocated. Nationalizations focused upon primary and intermediary goods industries, those in which reductions in prices (due to modernization) would lower costs in downstream industries. Economic planning was to be voluntary for the private sector and mandatory for the public sector. The Monnet Plan (1946–51) targeted key sectors such as electricity, coal, steel, fertilizer, and farm machinery. Marshall Aid helped to fill financial gaps in pursuing the plan. Almost all of the plan's targets were met, but results remained largely invisible to the public—wages remained low and goods pricey or unavailable. Within the public sector and planning apparatus, France began to develop a corps of experts adept in economic management, technology analysis, economic modeling, and econometrics.

Elections in 1950 returned a conservative parliament determined to return France to a free-market economy. Nationalized firms could find little fresh capital, and planning activities fell largely into abeyance. At the same time, however, the modernization of key sectors was finally being translated into cheaper and more abundant goods. Trying to reduce the state's pervasive deficits, tax agents audited small businesses, fueling a tax revolt led by Pierre Poujade.

As cabinets shifted toward the center-left after 1954, the Socialist party (SFIO) sought a left Keynesian approach while the center remained resolutely neoliberal. Wage-driven inflation revived. Policymakers hoped that the European Economic Community (EEC), founded by the 1956 Treaty of Rome, would help them deal with inflation and high producer prices. More direct international competition would ostensibly force French producers to restrain their prices, seek productivity improvements, and keep wages down.

Early Fifth Republic economic policy was ambiguous. Charles de Gaulle solicited support from conservative business and erstwhile Poujadists, and his initial appointment of Pinay and Jacques Rueff reflected an apparent allegiance to economic liberalism. Meanwhile, the industrial and financial ministries adopted technocratic approaches, the plan was revived, and the appointment of Wilfred Baumgartner as finance minister signaled a modernist policy. Henceforth, the state encouraged *rentable* investments in both the public and private sectors, fostered oligopolies, and relied on international competition to tame inflation. Despite a temporary hiatus in the 1963 Stabilization Plan, the Gaullist regime allowed consumers a greater share of national income. France finally developed a concentrated and modern private sector; yet, the state maintained a strong role in economic management.

Presidents Georges Pompidou and Valéry Giscard d'Estaing extended the Gaullist approach, in part by phasing out price controls and adopting an aggressive nuclear power program for energy independence. After 1981 socialist governments initially attempted to extend the reforms of 1944–46. Yet, under the policies of Finance Minister Jacques Delors, the socialists reverted to Keynesianism by 1983. Emulating the economic liberalism of Ronald Reagan and Margaret Thatcher, the conservative Chirac government (1986–88) denationalized a number of firms and tried to return to early Gaullist policies. The socialist cabinets after 1988 largely continued Delors's policies.

France's postwar economic policy thus vacillated between statist socialist experiments and traditional liberalism. Nevertheless, two factors have remained constant, a decisive private sector and a state that takes essential responsibility for economic management and development.

J.-J. Carré, P. Dubois, E. Malinvaud, *La Croissance française, un essai d'analyse économique causale de l'après-guerre* (Paris, 1972); R. Kuisel, *Capitalism and the State in Modern France* (New York, 1983); J. Lecerf, *La Percée de l'économie française* (Paris, 1963); H. Rousso, ed., *De Monnet à Massé* (Paris, 1986).

R. L. Frost

Related entries: ATTALI, JACQUES; ECONOMIC TRENDS; EUROPEAN ECONOMIC COMMUNITY, RELATIONS WITH; GAULLISM; INDUSTRIAL POLICY; INFLATION; MARSHALL PLAN; MONNET, JEAN; NATIONALIZATIONS; PLAN; POLITICAL TRENDS; PRIVATIZATION; SCHUMAN PLAN; TAXATION.

ECONOMIC TRENDS reveal major change in the growth and structure of the economy over the postwar years. Following a period of rapid expansion, growth rates slowed substantially in the late 1970s and early 1980s, only to recover partially by the end of the decade; and, from a situation in the 1950s where agriculture and industry were the dominant sectors of the economy, tertiary activities have now become the principal employer and source of national wealth.

By the late 1980s the active population in France exceeded twenty-four million people, a total substantially above that observed in the early 1950s (19 million). Until the 1960s this working population had remained relatively stable, but from 1963 it began to increase rapidly, reflecting the influence of higher postwar birthrates. At this time unemployment was low: Throughout the 1950s and 1960s less than 300,000 people were out of work on average each year. By the early 1970s the jobless total was rising, although at the time of the first oil crisis (1974) there were still under 500,000 people out of work, representing less than 3 percent of the active population. From that date, however, unemployment rose sharply and continuously so that by 1987 more than 2.6 million people were without work, representing 10.7 percent of the labor force. Job losses were particularly heavy in industry, reaching a peak in the early 1980s when over 200,000 jobs were disappearing each year. After 1987, with an upturn in economic activity, the jobless total declined so that by 1989 2.5 million people (10.1% of the active population) were out of work.

The substantial rise in unemployment is partly explained by various structural influences, such as the large-scale entry of young people into the labor market each year, the result of past high birthrates, and technical progress in manufacturing processes, which have reduced or altered the demand for labor. At the same time changes in economic conditions have also played a role, notably the fall in demand during the years of recession (both within domestic and export markets), increased competition for foreign manufacturers, and a substantial rise in wage costs.

As the labor force has grown, so its composition has changed. For example, an increasing number of women are now in employment (over 9 million in 1988), with female activity rates increasing from 37 percent in 1962 to over 45 percent in 1988. Changes in occupational structure and attitudes to work explain this shift. More generally a basic sectoral shift of employment has occurred in favor of service activities. In 1946 agriculture employed nearly 37 percent of the work force, industry 29 percent, and the tertiary sector 34 percent. By 1968 a major restructuring was already evident: Only 16 percent of the labor force now worked in agriculture, employment in industry had peaked at just over 40 percent, and services, with 44 percent of the total, accounted for the largest proportion of the country's workers. By the end of the 1980s France's move toward a postindustrial society was confirmed: Only 7 percent of the work force had an agricultural occupation, 31 percent were industry, and 62 percent were employed in the service sector.

The rate of economic growth has varied considerably. For the greater part of the period from the late 1940s to the mid–1970s French gross domestic product rose to a high level, averaging 5.8 percent a year between 1960 and 1973, representing one of the highest growth rates among Western countries, ahead of Germany although still behind Japan. This period became aptly known as the *trente glorieuses*. Between 1974 and 1979, in the aftermath of the oil crisis, growth was cut substantially (to an average of 2.9% per annum), but remained higher than the average for all European Economic Community (EEC) countries. Subsequently, however, rates fell even further, averaging only 1.5 percent each year between 1980 and 1986, this time below the Community average. The French productive machine had failed to adapt sufficiently (in terms of modernization and the development of new markets) to the changed economic environment. It was only in the late 1980s that growth rates started to rise again, exceeding 3 percent per annum in both 1988 and 1989.

As these changes have occurred each sector of the economy has performed differently. In the agricultural field a significant decline in the size of the work force has occurred (with just over 1.4 million workers in 1988 compared with 5.1 million in 1954) and in the contribution to gross domestic product, which is now under 4 percent. However, widespread modernization and restructuring have occurred, resulting in fewer but larger holdings, a substantial increase in the use of intermediate products such as fertilizers, extensive mechanization, and an important rise in output and yields: Yields of cereals, for example, have more than tripled since the early 1950s.

In the case of industry, it was the remarkable expansion of this sector that for more than twenty years lay behind the postwar growth of the French economy. Between 1949 and 1963 industrial production rose by an average of 5.3 percent each year, rising to 5.8 percent between 1963 and 1973, rates unequaled by other West European countries. Productivity increased similarly. This period was also characterized by the growing technical and financial concentration of companies and the birth of a series of large, French-based multinationals. Such changes were actively encouraged by the French government, but were also stimulated by the opening up of the French economy to European and world markets. Since 1973 manufacturing output has slowed substantially, falling to a yearly average of 2.6 percent between 1973 and 1979 and only 0.4 percent between 1979 and 1984: Between 1981 and 1983 industrial production even declined, as French industry was particularly hard hit by the negative effects of recession. A corresponding decrease in industrial investment also occurred. However, since the mid–1980s investment and production have again increased, corresponding with the upturn in economic activity: Output rose by an average of 2.5 percent in 1987 and by 5.1 percent in 1988.

The tertiary sector now dominates the French economy, accounting for over 63 percent of gross domestic product. Growth was particularly vigorous in the 1960s and 1970s: For example, employment rose by 2.4 percent per annum between 1975 and 1979. In the 1980s, however, growth rates fell as a result of the recession; thus, between 1982 and 1988 jobs rose by a relatively modest 1.4 percent per annum. Over recent years, the growth of producer services has been particularly marked, encouraged by firms externalizing their demand for many services. In contrast, other branches have expanded less rapidly, partly as a result of technical change and computerization, leading to a reduced demand for labor (e.g., telecommunications and banking) and partly due to cuts in public expenditure (e.g., government administrative services).

Two further problems have recently characterized the French economy: high inflation and a balance of payments deficit. In the former instance inflation was already rising in the late 1960s and early 1970s (5.9% per annum between 1967 and 1972), but it was after the oil crisis that rates rose rapidly and substantially, reaching 14 percent by 1981. However, since then government austerity measures and a general world fall in price rises have produced a significant reduction in inflation—by the end of the decade the rate had been reduced to 3 percent per annum.

France's trade balance was also adversely affected by the oil crises of 1974 and 1979 and the much higher cost of imported energy products. The resulting balance of payments deficit persisted throughout the 1980s, exacerbated since 1987 by an important deficit in manufactured goods. This reflected reduced purchases by many of France's traditional trading partners (due to a drop, for example, in oil revenues as the price of crude oil fell), inadequate specialization in growth sectors such as capital goods, and a continuing lack of competitiveness in the face of the aggressive marketing tactics of newly industrializing countries. Foreign trade figures, therefore, illustrate the underlying weaknesses that still characterize the French economy.

J.-M. Albertini, *Bilan de l'économie française* (Paris, 1988); J. F. Eck, *Histoire de l'économie française depuis 1945* (Paris, 1988); *Le Monde*, *L'Economie française: Mu-*

tations 1975–90 (Paris, 1989); J. N. Tuppen, *France under Recession 1981–86* (New York, 1988).

J. N. Tuppen

Related entries: AGRICULTURE; ECONOMIC POLICY; INFLATION; LABOR FORCE; UNEMPLOYMENT.

EDUCATIONAL REFORM, dominated by two concerns: the age-old problem of the relationship between church and state, and the pressing new need to bring a greater proportion of each generation to higher levels of knowledge and technical competence. A related issue was the perpetuation of social differences through educational selection.

The Vichy regime passed several laws that compromised the secular identity of state schools. Members of religious orders were allowed back into the classroom and, for a few months, catechism became an elective in state schools. Students in private schools received the right to compete for state scholarships, municipalities were permitted to subsidize private schools, and in November 1941 the state allocated 400 million francs to the "*écoles libres.*"

These reforms were undone at the Liberation; the subsidies were halted in July 1945. When private schools languished, the Catholic parents' group APEL (*Associations de parents d'élèves de l'enseignement libre*) mobilized for the 1951 elections. At the price of the rupture of the "Third Force" alliance of Christian democrats (MRP) and socialists, the National Assembly passed two laws favorable to private schools in September 1951. The Marie law requalified private school students for state scholarships. The Baranger law provided for the quarterly allocation of 1,000 francs per child to schools—private or public—at the parents' discretion.

These measures permitted private schools to survive until more comprehensive reforms could be undertaken under the Fifth Republic. The Debré law (1959) offered subsidies to private schools willing to conclude contracts with the state. These contracts were made on the conditions of demonstrated public utility and acceptance of state supervision. Schools under contract were enjoined to respect liberty of conscience and to admit students irrespective of belief.

The role of the *écoles libres* in modern France goes well beyond religious instruction. By the same token their support extends beyond the Catholic community. *Ecoles libres* offer a second chance to students who perform poorly in public schools and are shunted off of tracks leading to the baccalaureate. They offer an alternative where lay schools are poor; as confidence in public schools declined after 1968, the *écoles libres* grew in popularity. Since low-income families cannot afford them, even though subsidized, they represent one of the ways that the educational system perpetuates social differences. And since 95 percent of immigrants' school-age children attend state schools, the *écoles libres* are also used to escape public schools where immigrant enrollments are high.

Perhaps an insufficient appreciation of these dimensions of the *écoles libres* led Alain Savary, the socialist minister of education from 1981 to 1984, to underestimate opposition to his reforms, which imposed stricter state control over private (mainly religious) schools. Supporters of the *écoles libres*, in a manner reminiscent of the banquet movement that presaged the overthrow of Louis-Philippe, staged demonstrations in provincial capitals starting in Bordeaux in January 1984 and building to a demonstration of 800,000 at Versailles in March. Savary's reforms—made law through the invocation of article 49–3 of the constitution—were in many ways advantageous to the Catholic schools: Henceforth, the state and the municipalities would assure their financial support. However, Catholics feared that shifting financial obligations to the municipalities would only "municipalize" the lay/Catholic debate. Moreover, municipal support would only be obligatory if at least half of private-school teachers were credentialed by the state, a clear and threatening extension of the supervisory powers of lay authorities. A monstrous demonstration of one million supporters of private schools in Paris on June 24—the largest demonstration in the history of France—forced the withdrawal of the Savary law and the resignation of Mauroy's socialist government.

University reforms centered around the issue of selection. The *baccalauréat*, or *bac*, serves as a sieve—it is both the "passing out" examination for *lycée* students and a prerequisite for university study. Attrition is fairly high. Typically 30 percent or more who take the *bac* fail to pass. Even so, the sheer number of students of the baby-boom generation qualified for university studies by the *bac* put an insupportable strain on the university system in 1968.

Edgar Faure's report on university reforms in the aftermath of the events of 1968 proposed limits on class size and a reorganization of the University of Paris into thirteen campuses. The old system of *facultés* was broken up and the *unité d'enseignement et de recherche* (UER) became the basic academic unit within the universities.

Prior to Faure's reforms, Minister of Education Christian Fouchet oversaw the creation of specialized versions, five in all, of the *baccalauréat*. These did not limit access to the university, but they did limit access to certain disciplines according to the version of *bac* one passed. They also imposed earlier and greater specialization on *lycée* students and greater coherence on the curriculum of secondary schools.

Higher education remained overburdened. In 1973 a new two-year degree, the DEUG or *Diplôme d'études universitaires générales*, was introduced. The DEUG was a response to a first-year dropout rate of 40 percent and continued ballooning of the university population. The DEUG would serve as a convenient terminal point for some students; for the rest it was a prequalification for the *licence*. Students viewed the DEUG with hostility, yet another selective barrier—a super-*bac*.

In 1986 Jacques Chirac's *ministre délégué* for research and higher education, Alain Devaquet, proposed reforms that would have enhanced the autonomy and selectivity of the universities, even allowing them to set their own admission standards, distribute their own degrees, and raise their fees. Protests followed and the legislation was fatally compromised when student-demonstrator Malek Oussekine died from blows delivered by police on December 5. Chirac withdrew the legislation, and Devaquet resigned.

C. Baudelot, R. Establet, *Le Niveau monte* (Paris, 1989); W.D. Halls, *Education, Culture, and Politics in Modern France* (Oxford, 1975); J. Moody, *French Education since Napoleon* (Syracuse, N.Y., 1978).

R. A. Jonas

Related entries: BIDAULT, GEORGES; CATHOLICISM; DEBRE, MICHEL; FAURE, EDGAR; MAUROY, PIERRE; SAVARY, ALAIN; STUDENT REVOLTS.

ELECTIONS (PRESIDENTIAL AND LEGISLATIVE), whose perceived systemic flaws in the Third Republic were never far from the minds of the politicians of the Fourth and Fifth Republics, although right and left differed on the nature of those defects and their remedies. The left had long been critical of the system of *scrutin d'arrondissement*, which created single-member constituencies from a system of two rounds of balloting, a system thought to give a distinct advantage to conservative local elites, the *notables*. The left preferred departmental electoral lists (*scrutin de liste*) accompanied by proportional representation, a system thought to favor issues and parties over personalities and patronage, and therefore favorable to disciplined parties rather than maverick deputies responsible only to narrow constituencies. For the right, the great institutional defect of the Third Republic was its weak chief executive. Under the Fourth and Fifth Republics both right and left sought to remedy the weaknesses of the preceding regime.

The left had its chance first in the 1945 and 1946 elections. Both the communists and the socialists manifested disciplined party behavior, as did the Christian democrats (MRP), and these parties dominated these early elections of the Fourth Republic. "Tripartite" cooperation ended in 1947, however, when both the communists and Gaullists went into opposition. Communist opposition began with their expulsion from the Ramadier government. The creation of the Gaullist *Rassemblement du peuple français* (RPF) in 1947 weakened the MRP, which had previously benefited from the anticommunist vote and the Gaullist vote—now the RPF was more likely to receive both. The result was a system much like that which had obtained under the Third Republic. Small parties and groups often became necessary to the formation of a majority government and therefore enjoyed an influence out of all proportion to their electoral strength.

The absence of a reliable, majority "Third Force" situated between the French Communist party (PCF) and the RPF inspired a revision of the electoral system for 1951. The new system allocated seats in a manner favorable to parties in electoral alliances. Since the intransigence of both the PCF and the RPF discouraged such alliances, the parties of the center were able to take 62 percent of the seats with only 51 percent of the vote. This center consisted of socialists, the MRP, radicals, and conservatives, who sought to constitute a so-called Third Force between the hostile Gaullists and communists.

The final legislative elections of the Fourth Republic were held in 1956, but the electoral system of 1951 produced much different results this time. A divided political center—socialists and the MRP had split over the issue of state aid to Catholic schools—made it much more difficult for Third Force parties to forge the electoral alliances that had rewarded so richly in 1951. The contestants had changed too. The Gaullist RPF no longer existed, though a Gaullist rump remained in the Social Republican party. Meanwhile, the Poujadist party successfully adopted the role, abandoned by the RPF, of radical opposition to the regime. Former Gaullist voters and former abstainers gave the Poujadist *Union et fraternité française* (UFF) nearly 12 percent of the vote.

The right had its opportunity to reshape French politics in 1958. De Gaulle insisted on constitutional revision when returned to power in the midst of the Algerian crisis. The constitution approved in the 1958 referendum brought back the *scrutin d'arrondissement* used for most of the Third Republic. The most significant innovation for legislative elections was the institution of the office of the presidency, because the race for the presidency, more than the electoral system itself, determined how successful parties and candidates behaved in legislative contests.

The president was not elected by popular vote in 1958. The constitution called for presidential election by an electoral college comprised of more than eighty thousand representatives, including both houses of the legislature, the *Conseillers généraux*, and representatives of the municipal councils and the *Territoires d'outre-mer*. In 1962 de Gaulle prepared to abandon this system. France was about to put behind itself the crises of the Algerian War and the army revolt, crises that had allowed de Gaulle to extract his presidency and constitution from the Third Force parties. Election by universal suffrage would give the presidency a kind of moral authority that, combined with the legal authority provided by the constitution, would allow de Gaulle to lead France in the period after Algeria. Moreover, the events in Algeria had persuaded many that in times of crisis it was necessary for someone to speak for all of France, and that someone should be more than simply the leader of the current parliamentary majority. Finally, Algerian *autodétermination* had removed the threat that a popularly elected presidency had heretofore held—namely that voters residing outside metropolitan France, more than 40 percent of the electorate in 1958, would someday impose their candidate on the ''Hexagon'' (i.e., France).

The legislative elections of 1958 had returned a majority favorable to de Gaulle and the new Republic. Gaullists of various stripes took close to one vote in five, beginning a period of Gaullist dominance that would last until 1981; the same elections registered a weakening of the left, which would prove equally durable. The legislative elections of 1962 were a kind of referendum in themselves in that they were necessitated by a dissolution of the Assembly following a confrontation over de Gaulle's use of the referendum to revise the constitution to allow popular election of the president. De Gaulle prevailed. The *Union pour la nouvelle république* (UNR) received over 5.8 million votes making the Gaullist party the most popular in France. A more numerous 8.6 million voters, perhaps moved by revulsion, confusion, or a sense of anticlimax, chose not to bother. This was to remain the high for abstentionism in postwar France until 1988.

Subsequent legislative elections showed the imprint of presidential ambitions. Presidential hopes could only be fulfilled by candidates who enjoyed the support of a broad alliance. Thus, in the presidential elections of 1965 François Mitterrand did well as the representative of the broad left including radicals, socialists, and communists, even though he was not himself a member of any of these parties. Conversely, de Gaulle failed to win a first-ballot victory because the voters on the right were split among the general, the MRP's Jean Lecanuet, and the anti-Gaullist Jean-Louis Tixier-Vignancourt.

In the legislative elections of 1967 Gaullists and Giscardiens presented joint candidates on the *Cinquième République* ticket. Mitterrand pursued a similar strategy when he worked to create his own vehicle on the center-left, the *Fédération de la gauche démocrate et socialiste* (FGDS), which eliminated first-round competition between socialists and radicals. Neither the communists nor the *Parti socialiste unifié* joined the FGDS; however, both announced their support of a single candidate of the left in the second round.

This spirit of cooperation on the left was unwittingly facilitated by de Gaulle's decisions to visit Moscow and to withdraw France from NATO—decisions that brought PCF positions on these issues much closer to the political mainstream. This boded well for the left, which had routinely garnered a majority of the vote in the elections of the Fourth Republic but whose indiscipline under the Fifth Republic had demoralized some of their supporters. A mobilized electorate brought the lowest rate of abstention under the Fifth Republic to date; the left, however, could not prevail at the polls. *Cinquième République* candidates garnered nearly 8.5 million votes, a record to date for political formations under the Fifth Republic.

While earlier elections had been dominated by issues of overwhelming importance—reconstruction, Indochina, Algeria—the legislative elections of 1967 were the first since the war to occur during a period of apparent calm. The calm broke in May–June 1968 as a university crisis quickly developed into a broad social and political crisis. Although discontent with Gaullism may have helped to spark the crisis, the general persuaded the voters, as he had in 1958, that he alone stood between France and chaos. De Gaulle dissolved the National Assembly and called new elections for June 23, 1968, thus getting politics out of the streets and factories and into the voting booth. The Union for the Defense of the Republic won a crushing victory with over ten million votes, more than 46 percent of those cast in the first round, eventually earning three of four seats in the Assembly. With only 41 percent of the vote, the left had reached its electoral nadir of the postwar period. As one observer put it, it was "Thermidor at the polls."

The elections of 1968 appeared to be an indisputable victory for de Gaulle. His defeat in the referendum of 1969 permitted a more nuanced conclusion—the 1968 elections had been a vote against the students' revolt, the strikes, the left, against the prospect of continued chaos. Moreover, Georges Pompidou's adroit handling of the events of May–June inspired many voters who had supported the general *faute de mieux* to see Pompidou as a potential successor. No longer fearful of the prospect of political life after de Gaulle, voters rejected de Gaulle's referendum and sent the general into retirement.

The Common Program of 1972 gave communists, socialists, and left radicals (MRG) a common basis for the legislative elections of 1973; they gained more than three points over their 1967 total, five points over that of 1968. These gains were illusory, in part, because the electorate itself had grown by 6 percent since 1968, thanks to the arrival of the leading edge of the postwar baby boom to voting age. Principal beneficiaries were the socialists, who received more votes (4.5 million) than at any time since 1945. However, the communists were still the dominant force on the left in 1973—for the last time in the history of France—with over five million votes. Although Trotskyist, PSU, and PCF voters backed socialists on the second round, they failed to outnumber voters who rallied behind UDR (Gaullist) candidates because they did not wish to see communists in a government of the left. The right retained its majority in the new Assembly.

Pompidou's death forced the scheduling of elections for May 1974. The third presidential election in the short history of the Fifth Republic brought several firsts. It was the first time that a woman, Arlette Laguiller of the Trotskyist *Lutte ouvrière*, stood as a candidate to the presidency. It was also the first time that a candidate of the left, François Mitterrand, led after the first round, a result as much attributable to the division of the right as the unity of the left. The quarrel between Jacques Chaban-Delmas and Valéry Giscard d'Estaing during the campaign left some doubt as to whether Giscard could prevail against Mitterrand; in fact, most Chaban-Delmas supporters backed Giscard. Giscard's narrow margin of victory over Mitterrand, barely 1 percent of the vote, may be attributable in the last analysis to the "gender gap" and to image. Women voters in the 1970s still favored conservative candidates by a margin greater than that by which men favored the left, though women's higher rate of abstention might have nullified much of the difference. As for image, presidential candidates in France had never appeared face-to-face on television before the Mitterrand-Giscard debate of May 10. Polls showed that Giscard had conveyed a more "presidential" image.

The legislative elections of 1978 were marked by the full arrival to political majority of the postwar baby boom. The electorate had grown by 15 percent since the election of Giscard, thanks to the combined effects of the demographic wave and the lowering of the voting age to eighteen in 1974. This boded well for the left because polls consistently showed a preference for the left among young men and women. In the first round of the 1978 elections the combined score of left candidates, from the radicals to the PCF, topped 50 percent (52%)

for the first time in the history of the Fifth Republic, a phenomenal political shift given that the left had languished since 1958 within a narrow range of 41 to 43 percent of the vote.

Why then did the left lose? The bitter collapse of the Common Program left many voters doubtful that the socialists and communists were prepared for power—only 21 percent of voters thought the left capable of forming a stable government. The margin of victory for the *Union pour la démocratie française* (UDF) and Gaullists was supplied by first-round abstainers and by new socialist voters who abandoned the PS on the second ballot.

The winners in 1978 were the ecologists, who received more than half a million votes, and the parties near the center. Both the new UDF and the PS captured more than their share of the new voters at the expense of the Gaullists and the PCF. For the PCF, the decline was relative—their vote had grown by only 12 percent when the electorate had grown by 15 percent—and concealed by an actual increase in deputies. For the Gaullists, the decline was absolute although the Gaullists remained the largest group in the Assembly.

Trends first identified in 1978 bore fruit in the presidential elections of 1981. Although Giscard led after the first round, left candidates collectively had attracted more than 51 percent of the vote. Giscard needed the support of all Gaullist voters and some renegade voters from the left to win—the formula for success in 1974. The formula was less likely to succeed in 1981 because of the bitter campaign between Chirac and Giscard. Chirac wounded Giscard and in the process supplied the left with battle-tested issues for the second round. Giscard, for his part, offended many Gaullists during the campaign; some of these voters turned to Mitterrand, while many more abstained. As for drawing left voters, here too conditions had changed. The communist share of the vote had declined steeply since 1978—Georges Marchais attracted a million fewer votes than PCF candidates in 1978, while the socialist vote had increased by a similar margin. This rendered remote the possibility of a socialist government beholden to the communists and thus reduced the fear factor among voters. Mitterrand prevailed.

The legislative elections of 1981 were justified on the grounds that Mitterrand's presidential mandate was more recent than that of the hostile legislature he faced. Five days after Mitterrand's election, the RPR and the UDF agreed to the formation of the *Union pour la nouvelle majorité* coalition and designated single candidacies in many constituencies. For all of that, the victory of the left was overwhelming with nearly 57 percent of the vote on the first round. After the second round, the PS had 285 of the 491 seats in the Assembly, enough to govern alone if it chose.

Confidence in socialist leadership had been badly shaken by 1986. In 1984 Mitterrand was the least popular president in the history of the Fifth Republic. The PS-dominated Assembly adopted a system of proportional representation so as to minimize their losses in the 1986 legislative elections. The worst fears of the socialists were not realized; the PS received more than 8.5 million votes, the second highest total in the history of the party. The left did lose its majority, thanks in part to the precipitous decline of the PCF. However, the major right-wing parties (UDF/RPR) failed to win a majority and were forced to govern with the support of smaller parties of the right, exclusive of the National Front (FN).

The public perception of Mitterrand improved considerably during the period of *cohabitation*. Mitterrand distanced himself from the details of government and presented an aloof, almost monarchical image of himself as ''above politics.'' Chirac, Mitterrand's Gaullist prime minister, failed to shake an image of partisanship and pettiness. Moreover, Chirac was challenged by the National Front on his right. Chirac's compensatory rightward drift made it easier for Mitterrand and the socialists to complete their bid to occupy the broad center-left of the French political spectrum. Mitterrand led second-place Chirac by 34 percent of the vote to 20 percent after the first round of the presidential elections in 1988. Chirac's apparent effort to stage dramatic political ''episodes'' involving hostages in Lebanon and New Caledonia succeeded only in making him look desperate, even reckless. On May 8, 1988 Mitterrand became the first president of the Fifth Republic to win re-election. De Gaulle's Republic suited Mitterrand so well that constitutional issues ceased to divide right and left.

Voter disenchantment was the outstanding theme of the 1988 legislative elections. The PS won a ''relative'' majority with 34 percent of the vote but, like the UDF/RPR in 1986, failed to secure an absolute majority. An abstention rate of over 34 percent on the first round was a new high for the Fifth Republic. Voters in 1988 were more likely than ever to abandon the mainstream ''gang of four'' parties: PCF, PS, UDF, RPR. The headline of the newsweekly *L'Express* declared, ''*Les Français et la politique: c'est le divorce*.''

F. Bon, J.-P. Cheylan, *La France qui vote* (Paris, 1988); A. Cole, P. Campbell, *French Electoral Systems and Elections since 1789* (Brookfield, Vt., 1989); P. Converse, R. Pierce, *Political Representation in France* (Cambridge, Mass., 1986); F. Goguel, *Chroniques électorales*, 3 vols. (Paris, 1983); A. Lancelot et al., *France de gauche, vote à droite* (Paris, 1981); H. R. Penniman, ed., *The French National Assembly Elections* (Washington, 1980).

R. A. Jonas

Related entries: CHRISTIAN DEMOCRATS; DE GAULLE, CHARLES; DEMOCRATIC AND SOCIALIST UNION OF THE RESISTANCE; ELECTORAL SYSTEM; FEDERATION OF THE DEMOCRATIC AND SOCIALIST LEFT; FRENCH COMMUNIST PARTY; GAULLIST PARTY; GISCARD D'ESTAING, VALERY; LEFT RADICALS; LE PEN, JEAN-MARIE; MITTERRAND, FRANCOIS; POLITICAL TRENDS; SOCIALIST PARTY (PS, SFIO); TRIPARTITISM; UNION FOR FRENCH DEMOCRACY.

ELECTORAL SYSTEM, the method by which French voters elect their national political representatives. Since 1945 French constitutions have tried to produce a legislature that accurately represents the electorate and to create a stable government. Unfortunately, governments have also frequently rewritten electoral law to maintain power in the short run. As a result France has had a half-dozen different legislative electoral laws and three presidential electoral systems since World War II.

In the Fourth Republic the president was elected by the legislature, as had been the case in the Third Republic. In the beginning of the Fifth Republic, the president was elected by an electoral college; in 1962 a national referendum established direct election by universal suffrage. This last reform has proved extremely popular with the French electorate, and it is unlikely to be changed.

No such consensus has emerged upon the best way to elect a legislature. Instead there have been two methods, that of runoff elections in single-member electoral districts and that of proportional representation of party slates elected in a single balloting. The Third Republic had operated according to the first system; the Fourth Republic instituted proportional representation; and the Fifth Republic has used both systems, single-member districts from 1958 to 1986 and again after 1987, and proportional representation from 1986 to 1987.

In the system of single-member districts, the country is divided into electoral districts of relatively similar population size, each district returning one deputy to the legislature. If, on the first ballot, no candidate wins a majority of the votes, a second balloting occurs in which the candidate with the highest vote wins the seat. In the Fifth Republic the first ballot has often served as a sort of primary; the less successful candidates usually withdraw, transferring their support to one of their opponents. In the Third Republic, this electoral system produced a multiplicity of small regional parties and many independent candidates. This has not been the case in the Fifth Republic, in which national party organizations have increasingly excluded fringe candidates from election.

A system of proportional representation was instituted after the Liberation in 1945. In proportional representation the electoral district is the department, with the number of seats proportional to the population. Within the district each competing party proposes a slate of candidates, and voters choose between slates rather than between single candidates. Seats are apportioned according to the percentage of the vote won by each slate. For example, if a district has five seats, a party winning 40 percent of the vote would win two seats, and the first two candidates on its five-candidate slate would be elected. Thus, in the system of proportional representation, election depends first upon the popularity of the party with the voters in the electoral district, and second upon the popularity of the candidate with the party organization that ranks the slate. Most parties have used the last positions on the slate to introduce new candidates to the voters.

The major changes in the electoral system in 1945 and in 1958 were intended to improve representation and political stability. However, less noble motives intervened in 1951, 1958, 1986, and 1987. In each of these cases, the government passed electoral legislation consciously intended to strengthen its own electoral position and weaken that of its opponents. In 1951 the Fourth Republic faced an election that would, in all probability, leave the centrist parties, the only parties committed to the constitution, in a minority. To avoid this, a center coalition government revised the system of proportional representation to award extra seats to small parties—like the many parties in the government's coalition. As a result the coalition managed to hold on to a bare majority in the 1951 elections.

In 1958, Charles de Gaulle restored single-member districts in order to make candidates less subservient to party organizations and more responsive to the voters. However, he also used the occasion to redistrict the country to reduce the voting strength of the left. As a result, the communist and socialist parties demanded a return to proportional representation. In 1981, François Mitterrand and his Socialist party (PS) proved that the left can win national elections with single-member districts. Nevertheless, in 1985 the socialist-controlled legislature voted to return to the system of proportional representation. At this point, however, it was less a matter of party principles than party advantage. The socialists hoped to increase the seats of the extreme-right at the expense of the center-right, their main opponents. In 1986, when a right coalition won a legislative majority, they voted to return to single-member districts.

Frequent changes in the electoral system—moreover, changes blatantly based upon political interest—have doubtlessly created cynicism about politics. Nonetheless, the French electorate has remained deeply committed to electoral politics. Since the consolidation of the Third Republic, voter turnout for legislative elections has rarely been lower than 70 percent; for presidential elections it has frequently been much higher. Whatever system has been adopted, the French electorate has been able to make its votes count.

P. Campbell, *French Electoral Systems and Elections since 1789* (Hampden, Conn., 1965); F. Goguel-Nyegaard, *Chroniques électorales: Les Scrutins politiques en France de 1954 à nos jours* (Paris, 1981–83); M. Larkin, *France since the Popular Front* (Oxford, 1988).

M. H. Darrow

Related entries: CONSTITUTION OF THE FIFTH REPUBLIC; CONSTITUTION OF THE FOURTH REPUBLIC; ELECTIONS; POLITICAL TRENDS; REFERENDA.

ELLEINSTEIN, JEAN (1927–), French publicist and historian. He was born August 6, 1927 in Paris. Joining the French Communist party (PCF) in 1944, Elleinstein became a functionary of the World Federation of Democratic Youth. In the late 1940s this and other party activities obliged him to lead a clandestine life, which led him to extensive reading. Receiving party permission to return to university studies, he became a *lycée* professor of history.

In 1970 Elleinstein was appointed deputy director of the PCF Center for Marxist Studies and Research (CERM). Striving to further gradual modernization of PCF views, in 1971–75 he published a four-volume history of the Soviet Union that attempted both to remain orthodox and to introduce a few changes of detail. During the brief PCF Eurocommunist phase in the 1970s, which Elleinstein strongly supported, he became the spokesperson for this policy in numerous articles and television interviews. He was criticized for showing too much personal initiative, and after the party line began to change in late 1977, found himself no longer a spokesperson for but a critic of his party. His articles and pronouncements continued in what the PCF regarded as "the bourgeois press." In early 1980 the PCF declared that he was not expelled but "had placed himself outside the party." Elleinstein's prominence as a spokesman for PCF Eurocommunism was as short-lived as that policy itself. He had invested too much hope for change in a party resistant to change.

P. Robrieux, *Histoire intérieure du parti communiste,* vol. 4 (Paris, 1984).

J. W. Friend

Related entry: FRENCH COMMUNIST PARTY.

EUREKA PROGRAM, a European research coordination agency that directs a program of industrial collaboration in high technology, first suggested by President François Mitterrand in April 1985. Originally intended as essentially Franco-German, it is currently one of the world's biggest research projects, grouping the European Commission, the twelve European Community nations, the European Free Trade Association, Finland, and Turkey. The sixteen hundred participating companies, universities, and research institutes are engaged in some three hundred research and development projects valued at 60 billion francs.

The genesis of the program lay in French reticence to contribute to the Strategic Defense Initiative (SDI) research and development organization as "subcontractors" for U.S. industry. EUREKA was intended to balance the stimulus to be given to U.S. science and technology by SDI with a civil cooperative industrial research program in the same crucial high-tech sectors. The program has gradually expanded into fields outside SDI such as biotechnology.

Institutionally, EUREKA should not be confused with European Community research programs; although the European Commission participates in the program, its activities are managed by national EUREKA coordinators, and the chairmanship of the program rotates annually between member nations. The deliberate absence of bureaucracy in EUREKA reflects both pressure from the United Kingdom and French abandonment of the massive state-led intervention in science and technology characteristic of the 1960s and 1970s.

EUREKA reflects traditional French concern about the existence of a "technology gap" between Europe and the United States, and the fear of political and economic dependence this might entail. Modeled on the *Ariane* and *Airbus* projects, EUREKA identifies current weaknesses in the application of research to industrial and commercial purposes.

"Les Ambitions d'Eureka," *Le Monde diplomatique* (August 1985); "Dossier spécial Eureka," *Sciences et techniques* 19 (October 1985).

H. D. Dauncey

Related entries: EUROPEAN ECONOMIC COMMUNITY, RELATIONS WITH; EUROPEAN SPACE PROGRAM; INDUSTRIAL POLICY; MITTERRAND, FRANCOIS; TECHNOLOGY.

EUROPEAN DEFENSE COMMUNITY, the abortive attempt to create an integrated European army that would include German divisions merged with French, Italian, and Benelux forces. Proposed in 1950 by Premier René Pleven as a way of controlling the reemergence of a strong German army within NATO, the "Plan Pleven" was adopted by the National Assembly on October 24, 1950, and the treaty was signed on May 27, 1952. But the French ratification debate lasted over two years, paralyzed governments, and divided parties except for the two most powerful opponents of the treaty: the Gaullists and the communists.

Some critics were opposed to the treaty's supranational character and charged that the European army would in effect be subordinated to the Pentagon. Others rejected any German rearmament. Supporters of the treaty not only saw in it a means of reconciling French fears of a resurgent Germany with American pressures for the rebuilding of the German army, but also approached it as a step toward European unification.

Premier Pierre Mendès-France having failed to obtain last-minute concessions from the allies, the treaty was defeated on a predebate procedural motion on August 30, 1954. Exactly four months later the National Assembly agreed to full German membership in NATO. Rather than striking a blow to European unity, the "quarrel" had made the French accept openly the unpalatable reality of an armed Germany pressed on them by the United States.

R. Aron, D. Lerner, eds., *La Querelle de la C.E.D.* (Paris, 1956); A. Grosser, *The Western Alliance* (New York, 1982).

P. Le Prestre

Related entries: AURIOL, VINCENT; CHRISTIAN DEMOCRATS; DEBRE, MICHEL; DEFENSE POLICY; FRENCH COMMUNIST PARTY; GAULLIST PARTY; MENDES-FRANCE, PIERRE; PLEVEN, RENE; SOCIALIST PARTY (SFIO).

EUROPEAN ECONOMIC COMMUNITY (EEC), RELATIONS WITH. French relations with the EEC have alternated between the supranationalist vision of a United States of Europe dear to Jean Monnet and Jacques Delors and the narrower, "soulless" (according to Raymond Aron) "*Europe des patries*" defined by Michel Debré, championed by Charles de Gaulle, and recently revived by Jean-Marie Le Pen.

Plans for a larger European Economic Community were made in the context of postwar European prosperity and out of a desire to promote Franco-German reconciliation after the war. In May 1950 French foreign minister Robert Schuman sponsored Jean Monnet's radical proposal for the creation of a European Coal and Steel Community (ECSC) founded upon the elimination of internal tariffs among member European states.

Because of British misgivings about European integration, the Community was limited to the "core" nations of continental western Europe—France, Italy, the Federal Republic of Germany, and the Low Countries. In April of 1951 they established the ECSC, the forebear of the EEC. The EEC was formalized in the Treaty of Rome in 1957.

Political integration began in 1949 when the statute of the Council of Europe was signed. The European Parliament was created two years later with representatives designated by the national parliaments. In 1979 the Community held its first direct elections to the European parliament; 110 million Europeans voted—61 percent of those eligible—demonstrating broad initial interest in the European Community, an interest that subsequent elections would show to be ephemeral.

Disagreements over agricultural policy, the budgetary independence of the EC Commission, and the impending turn to majority vote within the Council of Europe—slated for January 1, 1966—led de Gaulle to withdraw France's permanent representative to the EC in July 1965—the so-called empty-chair policy. De Gaulle's foreign minister, Maurice Couve de Murville, announced that "a community whose partners do not abide by their agreements has ceased to be a community," as much a commentary on French conduct as on the EC. In the compromise worked out in Luxembourg in early 1966, France made clear its intention to paralyze the EC once again if a majority decision taken by the Council violated its interests.

The oil crisis of the 1970s hampered the revival of momentum toward European integration. Instead, economic policy was often made according to strictly national criteria. The era's most significant innovation was the adoption of the European Monetary System (EMS) in 1978 at the urging of Valéry Giscard d'Estaing and Helmut Schmidt; member nations, with the exception of Britain, agreed to buy member currencies when they threatened established currency floors and ceilings.

With the economic recovery of the 1980s, the energetic leadership of Delors as president of the European Commission, and the new threat of Japanese economic strength, interest in common European solutions revived. In 1986 Delors, president of the European Council, promoted the adoption of the Single European Act, which amended the Treaty of Rome and provided for the free movement of persons, capital, goods, and services within the EC beginning January 1, 1993. In early 1989 a committee headed by Delors proposed full monetary union for Europe based on the European currency unit, ECU. The plan would rectify exchange problems within the EMS created by strong currencies, particularly the *deutschemark*.

For France the EC has always been primarily an economic vehicle for the achievement of political goals. In the 1970s and 1980s, politics remained paramount as the French hoped that the EC would prevent an uncoupling of German defense policy, in the name of *Ostpolitik*, from the Western alliance. Indeed, before the events of 1989 and the apparent collapse of communism, France was reassured when Chancellor Helmut Kohl explicitly linked *Ostpolitik* with European integration stating, in effect, that German reunification could take place only by transcending nationalism, through European integration.

Along with these important political considerations, the French increasingly see the EC as a vehicle for the realization of economic goals. As a businessman with North American interests, Jean Monnet was quite familiar with the United States and believed that competition within a European market of similar extent would have a bracing effect on France and the French. The GNP of the Twelve in 1984 was $2.5 trillion, second only to the United State. Since 1974 and the falloff of economic growth characteristic of the *trente glorieuses*, and especially since the failed economic policies of the socialist government in 1981–82, the French have looked to the EC for economic expansion through larger markets, new economies of scale, and reduced factor costs, including labor. In matters of culture and diplomacy, the EC holds the promise of renewed French influence through the general revival of European prestige and power (such as the Maastricht summit in December 1991).

S. Hoffmann, "The European Community and 1992," *Foreign Affairs* 6 (Fall 1989); H. Simonian, *The Privileged Partnership: Franco-German Relations in the European Community, 1969–1984* (Oxford, 1985); F. R. Willis, *France, Germany, and the New Europe, 1945–1967* (Stanford, Calif., 1968).

R. A. Jonas

Related entries: AGRICULTURE; DELORS, JACQUES; ECONOMIC POLICY; ECONOMIC TRENDS; IMMIGRANTS; LABOR FORCE; MONNET, JEAN; PEASANTRY; SCHUMAN, ROBERT; SCHUMAN PLAN.

EUROPEAN SPACE PROGRAM, managed by the European Space Agency (ESA), created in May 1975 under pressure from the French government by a merger of previous launcher and space science organizations. France has always played a leading role in ESA activities through the *Centre national d'études spatiales* (CNES), established in 1961, and the strong French space industry, which developed in parallel with the *force de frappe* in the 1950s and 1960s.

Grouping eleven countries, the program is exclusively civil, covering all aspects of space science and applications, including the independent European launcher *Ariane*, in which France plays the major part. Directed by CNES and launched from the French Guyana space center by CNES for the ESA, *Ariane* is the only ESA program not managed solely by ESA because of the preponderance of French investment and expertise in the project. The production and commercialization of the launchers is entrusted to the *Arianespace* company.

French industry also contributes substantially to the *Ariane V* heavy launcher, *Hermès* shuttle, and *Columbus* space laboratory as envisioned in the long-term ESA space plan of 1985. The French space industry employs some eleven thousand in CNES, *Aérospatiale*, *Matra*, *SEP*, and *Alcatel Espace* and the rest of the space sector. CNES also conducts national programs and bilateral cooperation with the United States and the Soviet Union and collaborates with the French Defense Ministry on the nascent military space program.

French participation in the European space program is seen as a means of safeguarding French and European independence in technology and defense.

CNES Annual Report 1988 (Toulouse, Fr., 1988); "*L'Espace: Un Défi pour la France, actes du colloque*" (Paris, November 1985).

H. D. Dauncey

Related entries: EUROPEAN ECONOMIC COMMUNITY, RELATIONS WITH; INDUSTRIAL POLICY; TECHNOLOGY.

EXISTENTIALISM, an important and influential philosophical orientation in postwar France that emphasized the concreteness of individual human existence rather than the general aspects of nature and the physical world. Though this revolt against traditional metaphysics is often traced back to Blaise Pascal and Søren Kierkegaard, and includes such important German thinkers as Friedrich Nietzsche and Martin Heidegger, existentialism gained its greatest prominence in France during the 1940s and 1950s with the thought of Jean-Paul Sartre, Simone de Beauvoir, Albert Camus, and Gabriel Marcel.

Sartre was the first to declare himself an existentialist in a lecture delivered in Paris in 1945; his novels and plays from the late 1930s already expressed the central existentialist theme of the anxiety and despair that follow the realization of absolute solitude and human contingency. For Sartre, there is no God and no fixed human nature; to put it in his most famous existentialist formula, "existence precedes essence." Rather than thinking of humans in terms of some fundamental concept that is derived from reason, Sartre considered it necessary to focus on living individuals in their actual preoccupations with themselves and the world. This attack on conceptual systems is characteristic of all existentialists. They argue that—however appealing such totalizing rational systems may be—reality always evades such conceptualization. The individual cannot be comprehended within an all-embracing set of necessary truths; existence, unfortunately, is more contingent, more absurd.

In Sartre's thought the concept of choice is central. An individual is not forced to act in a certain way; one is totally free and therefore entirely responsible for what one makes of oneself. It is exactly this confrontation with the reality of freedom, and with one's unmade future, that gives rise to experiences of dread, anxiety, and nausea. It is from within this experience of nausea that one must choose, must act. Choice is therefore a ubiquitous presence behind every action, and one's being is defined by the choices one makes.

Camus (who denied he was an existentialist) similarly focused on the isolation of humans as purely existing beings and on the centrality of choice. But his vision of human life, represented by the myth of Sisyphus, is both more tragic and more humanistic. Sisyphus was doomed eternally to roll a vast stone up a hill, but the stone would always roll back down the hill just as he was about to reach the top. The dignity of the life of Sisyphus derived from his refusal to give up, just as the dignity of humanity must come from its continual perseverance in projects for which the universe might offer no encouragement.

Gabriel Marcel, a leading Christian existentialist, stressed the centrality of key personal experiences and the inability of humans ever fully to understand or even conceptualize the general significance of these experiences. Unlike Sartre's and Camus's focus on dread, isolation, and nausea, however, Marcel emphasized the importance of human relationships and hope.

W. Barrett, *Irrational Man: A Study in Existential Philosophy* (New York, 1958); R. Grimsley, *Existentialist Thought* (Cardiff, Wales, 1960).

K. S. Vincent

Related entries: BEAUVOIR, SIMONE DE; CAMUS, ALBERT; INTELLECTUAL TRENDS; LITERATURE; SARTRE, JEAN-PAUL.

F

FABIUS, LAURENT (1946–), socialist politician and former prime minister. He was born in Paris on August 20, 1946. His father, André Fabius, was a prosperous art and antique dealer. Fabius attended the prestigious *Janson-de Sailly lycée*, the *Institut d'études politiques*, and both the *Ecole normale supérieure* and the *Ecole nationale d'administration*. In 1973, on graduation from the latter school, he was assigned to the *Conseil d'Etat*. In 1974 he joined François Mitterrand's *Parti socialiste* (PS), rapidly impressing the leader with his capacities. In 1977 he was "parachuted" into the safe socialist constituency of Le Grand-Quevilly, an industrial suburb of Rouen, to become deputy to its mayor, succeeding the mayor as a National Assembly deputy in 1978. He was reelected in 1981, 1986, and 1988 from the same constituency. In 1979, he became a PS national secretary. In the 1979 PS Nantes congress Fabius vigorously supported Mitterrand against the challenge mounted by Michel Rocard and Pierre Mauroy, lecturing Rocard on the meaning of socialism.

In 1981, after the socialist victory, Fabius was made a junior minister (*minister délégué*) for the budget. Though nominally under the supervision of Finance and Economics Minister Jacques Delors, Fabius used his credit with Mitterrand to report directly to the president. Since at that period his economic views were consistently to the left of Delors's own, there was friction between the two men. In 1983 Fabius initially sided with the Mitterrand advisers who urged France's departure from the European Monetary System, changing his mind once he learned the dangerously low level of French monetary reserves.

Appointed minister for industry and research in March 1983, Fabius began to demonstrate his new conviction that the PS must take a less ideological view of economics in order to combat the crisis and maintain its power. He succeeded in winning a measure of confidence from business leaders and advocated less government interference in the administration of nationalized industry.

In July 1984 Mitterrand chose Fabius to succeed Pierre Mauroy as prime minister. He thus became the youngest French prime minister since Elie Decazes in 1819. Fabius's appointment symbolized Mitterrand's commitment to a change in PS policy from its ideological phase in 1981–83 to one of restructuring run-down industry and industrial areas, including heavy cuts in employment. Great emphasis was placed on modernization, new investment, and continued fiscal austerity. Fabius's role in the 1985 Greenpeace affair remains unclear; he may not have been informed in advance of this French intelligence operation to sink the ecology group's ship.

In 1985 Fabius sought to use his position as prime minister to lead the party in the March 1986 elections. He was opposed by PS First Secretary Lionel Jospin, who was trying to bolster his own position and prevent Fabius from positioning himself as the obvious heir to Mitterrand. Although Fabius's position appeared strengthened at the PS congress in Toulouse in October 1985, he did badly in a much-discussed television debate with Rally for the Republic (RPR) leader Jacques Chirac shortly thereafter, and his standing in the polls went down sharply. In the event, Mitterrand himself was the most important single figure in the 1986 elections. Although the PS exceeded its expectations by winning 31 percent of the vote, the election resulted in a narrow conservative majority, and Fabius resigned immediately afterward.

During the period from March 1986 to Mitterrand's re-election in May 1988, Fabius attempted to strengthen his position as one of the major leaders of the PS, appealing to all those who believed that the party must stand for a modernized social democratic position. After the 1988 election Mitterrand favored Fabius to succeed Jospin as PS first secretary. However, he was defeated in a May 1988 vote in the PS directing committee, which elected his predecessor as prime minister, Pierre Mauroy. After the June 1988 parliamentary elections, Fabius became president of the National Assembly, the third-ranking post in French government.

Fabius remains an important figure in the PS, with strong ambitions to succeed Mitterrand when the older man retires. He is opposed in his own party, and to some extent in the country at large, by those who reproach him for an overly rapid conversion from ideological socialism to moderate social democracy.

J. W. Friend, *Seven Years in France* (Boulder, Colo., 1989); G. Ross, S. Hoffmann, S. Malzacher, eds., *The Mitterrand Experiment* (Oxford, 1987).

J. W. Friend

Related entries: DELORS, JACQUES; GREENPEACE AFFAIR; JOSPIN, LIONEL; MAUROY, PIERRE; MITTERRAND, FRANCOIS; ROCARD, MICHEL; SOCIALIST PARTY (PS).

FASHION, an industry whose growth and evolution was not greatly affected by World War I but was influenced enormously by World War II and its aftermath. The industry's financial foundations had deteriorated in the 1920s and 30s, but once the euphoria following the end of World War II had subsided new designers appeared in Paris (Fath, Dior, Castillo, Balmain, de Givenchy, Cardin), overshadowing older designers (Chanel in particular) whose association with the Germans had left them scarred. These years were marked by relatively fixed hemlines (between calf and ankle) and a search for pomp and splendor as an antidote to the lack of variety in styles worn during the Occupation. Even though young and older Parisian designers promoted luxury, the emerging ready-to-wear industry did not always follow their whims, and its productions exhibited a more sensible evolution. In 1958, Yves Saint-Laurent's designs, with their hemlines clearly above the knee, shook up the world of fashion and ushered in a new era focused on youth, paralleling to some degree the beginning of a rebellious age where the young would challenge the social and political mores of the time.

The 1960s did not constitute an era in French fashion where one style dominated, but the decade's importance for fashion cannot be overlooked, given the social and political changes of these years. Few fashion changes occurred between the years 1960 and 1963, but the emergence of the so-called tomboy style (Courrèges, Cardin, Saint-Laurent) in 1964 rocked the world of fashion because it was such a contrast to the more predictable and often more traditional styles of the postwar years. With the rise of consumerism during the early years of the 1960s, coupled with the deep social changes and political upheavals of the decade, a rift emerged between experimental fashion and everyday or popular clothing. Clothes became a part of the cultural, public, intellectual, and political persona of the wearer.

The divisions that emerged in the 1960s in the fashion industry continued during the 1970s. The social divisions within society were replicated to some extent in the world of fashion by the separation between high fashion and popular fashion. Moreover, the increasing involvement of designers in the ready-to-wear market and licensing (perfumes, make-up, accessories, etc.) could not hide major modifications in the buying patterns of their customers. There was a trend toward the acquisition of clothing whose practicality determined its success, as well as a tendency to focus on isolated accessories and items of clothing instead of buying total looks. Designers were progressively losing their positions as innovators and, instead of shaping popular taste, they were more and more influenced by it. The success of so-called second-line designers illustrated the competition that existed with the more-established and better-known designers.

These divisive trends led to a weakening of the influence of French fashion in the 1970s. Yet the early 1980s witnessed a rebirth of the cosmopolitan role of Paris in the world of fashion. The arrival of foreign designers (Kelly, Yamamoto, etc.) brought an international flair to Parisian styles, whose success is often influenced by the renown of the pop stars who buy them (Tina Turner or Grace Jones wearing Azzedine Alaïa designs, for example). The 1980s also witnessed a progressive emphasis on the "look"—the complete appearance of the individual, taking into consideration self-characterization as well as physical traits. Clothing became influenced by the appearance and lifestyle of the wearer. The increasing popularity of body-building, jogging, and health spas has led to a focus on physical appearance, a weakening of the role of established fashion, and more puzzling fashion statements.

At the beginning of the 1990s it is no longer possible to define the true social status of individuals by observing their clothes, because it is less and less easy to distinguish between *haute couture* productions and the ready-to-wear lines by second-line designers (Cros, Dedeyan). Also, given today's fashions, it is not possible to hide one's body beneath one's clothing due to the form fitting styles. These changes do not appear to signal the demise of the established fashion houses, nor their replacement by new designers, but they reflect the transformations that have marked the history of fashion as well as the social history of the French Fourth and Fifth Republics.

M. Delbourg-Delphis, *Le Chic et le look: Histoire de la mode féminine de 1850 à nos jours* (Paris, 1981); Y. Deslandes, F. Müller, *Histoire de la mode au XXe siècle* (Paris, 1986); M. Pagès-Delon, *Le Corps et ses apparences* (Paris, 1989).

A. J. M. Prévos

Related entry: SOCIAL TRENDS.

FAURE, EDGAR (1908–1988), twice prime minister and many times minister of finance during the Fourth Republic, and one of France's leading politicians in the post–World War II era. Born in Béziers, where his father was stationed as an army doctor, Faure came from a family of prosperous farmers, small-town lawyers, and government functionaries. After studying legal history at the Sorbonne and Russian at the *Ecole des langues orientales*, he was admitted to the Paris bar at age twenty in 1928. His legal practice focused on Russian émigrés, the food industry, and especially petroleum: He represented the oil importers and distributors of southwest France, wrote for the *Revue pétrolière*, and published a doctoral thesis on French oil policy in 1938. Rejected for military service because of a minor heart defect, Faure worked as a censor for *Agence Havas*, the French news service, in 1939–40, then returned to his legal practice in Paris. In the fall of 1942 he emigrated to Tunis and, following the Allied invasion of North Africa, joined the French provisional government in Algiers as chief of the legislative service and editor of the *Journal officiel*. Returning to Paris in October 1945, he served in the new Ministry of the National Economy under Pierre Mendès-France, a friend from his university days, then assisted François de Menthon, chief of the French delegation to the Nuremberg war crimes trials. Defeated for a seat in the second constituent assembly in June 1946, Faure was elected a radical deputy for the Jura in November. He sat in the National Assembly, either as deputy or senator, almost continuously from 1947 to 1980.

As budget director in the Bidault government of 1949–50, as finance minister under Laniel and Mendès-France in 1953–54, and as prime minister in 1955, Faure played a crucial role in formulating the economic and social policies of the Fourth Republic. In 1949, he led the government's effort to win funding of the Monnet Plan in the 1950 budget. To bring inflation under control, in 1953 he drastically cut expenditures in the public sector by eliminating jobs, even though this precipitated the worst strikes in France since 1936. With inflation contained, he then unveiled a wide range of government initiatives to stimulate economic growth in 1954. These included an ambitious program of housing construction and large wage increases for public employees, reduction of the discount rate from 4 percent to 3 percent and the creation of *Fonds pour développement économique et sociale* (FDES) to increase productive investment, and restructuring of the tax system to emphasize the value-added tax, which relieved industry of the taxation of both its raw materials and finished goods inventories. As a result, total invested capital in France rose 8.5 percent in 1954 over the previous year and 13 percent in 1955. In addition, Faure supported the preliminary steps taken in 1954–55 to organize the European Economic Community, which culminated in the signing of the Treaty of Rome in 1957.

Faure also played a crucial role in colonial affairs in 1955. Seeking accommodation with the Tunisian nationalists, he met with Habib Bourguiba in Paris in April and two months later signed accords granting Tunisia autonomy. Meanwhile, anti-French violence broke out in both Algeria and Morocco. Impressed by the growing popularity of the procolonial Poujadist movement on the right, Faure reluctantly adopted a hard-line policy in Algeria. But in Morocco he negotiated the return of the exiled sultan, leader of the nationalists, and in November signed an agreement granting Morocco "independence within interdependence." Seeking a stronger parliamentary majority to settle the Algerian imbroglio, Faure then tried to move legislative elections up from July to January. However, this maneuver met with opposition in Faure's own Radical party and precipitated a surprise defeat for the government on a vote of nonconfidence. Invoking a clause in the constitution allowing dissolution of the Chamber of Deputies when two governments were overturned by absolute majority votes within an eighteen-month period, Faure then dissolved the Chamber (for the first time since 1877) and scheduled elections for January 2, 1956. Expelled from the Radical party for this action, Faure led his followers into an electoral alliance with the conservatives. However, the Republican Front coalition of socialists and left radicals (led by Mendès-France) carried the day, and Guy Mollet, the socialist leader, formed the next government. Faure was out of power the remaining two years of the Fourth Republic except for a brief appearance in the Pflimlin cabinet that brought Charles de Gaulle back to power in May 1958.

In contrast to most of the leaders of the Fourth Republic, Faure did not suffer a political eclipse with the coming of the Fifth Republic. He was elected senator for the Jura in 1959 and deputy for the Doubs in 1967. Although Faure never joined the Gaullist party, he served de Gaulle as emissary to China in the early 1960s, as minister of agriculture in 1966–68, and, most important, as minister of education in the Couve de Murville cabinet formed in the aftermath of the events of May 1968. In 1968–69, Faure oversaw the drafting and passage of the Orientation Law on Higher Education, which provided the framework for a radical restructuring of the French universities in response to student discontent. Under the Faure law the existing twenty-three universities were broken up into some seven hundred UERs (*Unités d'enseignement et de recherche*) that were eventually regrouped into seventy-six new universities, while elected councils in both the UERs and universities assumed greater control over teaching, examinations, and faculty appointments.

When Georges Pompidou succeeded de Gaulle as president of the Republic in 1969, Faure returned to the National Assembly and served as its president from 1973 to 1978. He also took an active role in French and European regionalization, which he had first fostered in his 1955 government by creating *Circonscriptions d'action régionales*. After 1970 he headed the Eastern Renovation and Development Association, and in 1974 he became chairman of the council of the new Franche-Comté region. He worked for creation of a Council of Regions within the European Community and became its president in 1985.

Faure was a writer of repute and a cultural leader as well as a politician. Between 1930 and 1984 he published several novels, various philosophical tracts and commentaries on public affairs, two volumes of memoirs, and two notable historical studies: *La Disgrâce de Turgot* (1961) and *La Banqueroute de Law* (1977). In 1979 he was elected a member of the *Académie française*, and at the time of his death in March 1988 he was chairman of the French Revolution Bicentennial Commission. In sum, Faure contributed to the evolution of postwar France on a number of levels, most notably in economic and financial modernization, decolonization, regional development, and educational reform.

H. S. Cohen, *Elusive Reform: The French Universities, 1968–78* (Boulder, Colo., 1978); E. Faure, *Mémoires*, 2 vols. (Paris, 1982–84); J.-P. Rioux, *The Fourth Republic, 1944–1958* (Cambridge, 1987); P. M. Williams, *Crisis and Compromise: Politics in the Fourth Republic* (London, 1966).

M. S. Smith

Related entries: ALGERIA, RELATIONS WITH; ECONOMIC POLICY; EDUCATIONAL REFORM; MENDES-FRANCE, PIERRE; MOROCCO, RELATIONS WITH; RADICAL PARTY; REGIONS; TUNISIA, RELATIONS WITH.

FAUVET, JACQUES (1914–), journalist and political scientist, who served as director of *Le Monde*, France's most influential daily newspaper, from 1969 until his retirement in 1982. Fauvet was born in Paris on June 9, 1914, where he studied at the *Lycée Saint-Louis* and the Faculty of Law.

Fauvet's long, distinguished journalistic career began on the staff of *L'Est Républicain* of Nancy in 1937. At the end of World War II Fauvet joined the staff of the recently established daily, *Le Monde*. His forte was political journalism. In 1948 he was promoted to chief of the political department. Fauvet then rose quickly on the editorial ladder of *Le Monde*, becoming assistant editor in 1958, editor in 1963, and director in 1968, succeeding Hubert Beuve-Méry, the paper's founding director.

Under Fauvet's direction, *Le Monde* grew in editorial staff to two hundred and in circulation to 500,000 in 1980. Fauvet maintained the paper's independence from domination by any political party, but moved *Le Monde* perceptively to the left and supported the unsuccessful socialist candidate François Mitterrand against Valéry Giscard d'Estaing in the 1974 presidential elections. Increasing criticism from both readers and public officials, most notably Minister of Justice

Alain Peyrefitte, led to a return to a more centrist orientation in the last years of Fauvet's direction. Since his retirement from *Le Monde* in 1982, Fauvet has served on a number of distinguished national and international commissions.

Fauvet has also been a prolific, perceptive analyst of contemporary French politics. He has written critically acclaimed works on a wide range of topics, including the political parties of France, the Fourth Republic, and the French Communist Party.

J. Fauvet, *Les Partis politiques dans la France actuelle* (Paris, 1947), *La IVᵉ* République (Paris, 1959), *Histoire du Parti communiste français*, 2d ed. (Paris, 1977).

F. J. Murphy

Related entries: BOKASSA AFFAIR; PEYREFITTE, ALAIN; PRESS.

FEDERAL REPUBLIC OF GERMANY, RELATIONS WITH. Perhaps the most remarkable historical development of the post–World War II world has been the transformation in the relationship between France and Germany. After centuries of political hostility, economic rivalry, and military conflict, France and the western half of Germany that was established as an independent republic in 1949 became political and economic partners in the European Community and military allies in the North Atlantic Treaty Organization (NATO). Outside of these supranational organizations, these two erstwhile antagonists developed such mutually beneficial commercial ties and intimate bilateral security links that some observers began to speak of a Paris-Bonn axis as the dominant factor in the postwar European political scene.

The rapprochement between France and Germany did not begin immediately after World War II. On the contrary, bitter memories of the German occupation and the national obsession with preventing a repetition of the national disaster of 1940 prompted French leaders in the immediate aftermath of the Liberation to pursue a harsh, vindictive policy toward defeated Germany. During his brief tenure as head of the provisional government in 1944–46, Charles de Gaulle sought to achieve what extreme nationalists in France had failed to obtain after World War I: the political separation of the Ruhr and the Rhineland from Germany, a French protectorate over the Saar, and a reparations regime that would permanently cripple Germany economically to the profit of France.

France was in a good position to press its demands for a Carthaginian peace on its eastern antagonist, since it had joined the United States, the Soviet Union, and Great Britain as one of the four occupying powers in postwar Germany. From 1945 through 1947, France often clashed with the United States and Great Britain over reparations, joining with the Soviet Union in demanding a much harsher policy than the Anglo-Americans were prepared to tolerate. Paris also dragged its feet when it became evident that Washington and London were preparing to merge the three Western occupation zones into a single economic entity that would be an unmistakable prelude to a unified political unit. German political disunity seemed eminently desirable to French leaders who recalled the consequences of German unity for France since 1870.

But to the Americans, German disunity meant economic weakness, not just for Germany but for all of Europe, which needed German productivity to recover from the devastation of the war. The prospect of Europe permanently incapacitated prompted the Truman administration to regard the economic recovery and political fusion of the western zones of Germany as one of its highest priorities. By 1948 the United States, wielding the promise of economic assistance through the Marshall Plan and military aid through the Atlantic alliance then under discussion, persuaded France to abandon its reparation demands and its opposition to the economic (and by implication, the political) integration of western Germany. By acquiescing in the establishment of the Federal Republic of Germany in 1949, France had abandoned—once and for all as it turned out—the goal of partitioning Germany and dominating it economically and militarily.

The only suitable alternative to the policy of French domination of Germany, which American pressure precluded, was the policy of reconciliation. What once would have been deemed unthinkable was made palatable to the French people by two critical considerations: The first was the advent of the Cold War with the Soviet Union, which dictated that France and West Germany compose their differences in order to concentrate on defending Western Europe from the greater danger; the second was the prospect of economic opportunity: If the abundant natural resources and technological expertise of Germany could be tapped in the interests of the economic recovery of all of Western Europe, France could recover much more rapidly from the postwar economic malaise with which it was still afflicted.

The original basis for Franco-German reconciliation was to be achieved on the economic level, in a sector that had long been characterized by bitter rivalry between the two countries. On May 9, 1950 French foreign minister Robert Schuman proposed that the coal and steel production of France and West Germany be combined and supervised by a supranational authority. The ostensible objective of the Schuman Plan was deceptively modest: to achieve economies of scale in steel production through the combination of French iron ore with West German coking coal. However, it also intended to facilitate the political reconciliation of the two countries by increasing the points of contact between their respective businessmen, labor leaders, and public officials. After Italy and the Benelux countries joined France and West Germany to establish the European Coal and Steel Community in 1952, this modest step toward economic integration in the metallurgical sectors of these six states led to the formation in 1957 of the European Economic Community (EEC) and set in motion the movement toward full integration of all the sectors of the economies of the member states. France and West Germany became each other's most important trading partner and developed extensive financial links as well.

The military reconciliation of France and West Germany was more difficult to achieve. Once again, it was the United States that applied the pressure on France to accept the rearmament of West Germany and its inclusion in NATO, the military alliance system that had been established in April 1949 to counter what was perceived as a Soviet threat to the noncommunist nations of Western Europe. The outbreak of the Korean War in the summer of 1950 convinced American policymakers that German forces were needed to bolster the defenses of Western Europe during a period when a Soviet attack was deemed imminent. But the memories of the German occupation were still too fresh in the minds of the French for any government of the Fourth Republic to risk public displeasure by accepting the rearmament of the recent foe. In the fall of 1950 French prime minister René Pleven proposed an alternative: the establishment of a supranational military organization patterned on the Coal and Steel Community that would mobilize West German manpower but thinly disperse it among the youth of other European nations in a ''European'' army, so as to remove all vestiges of national loyalty. But after all the other European states endorsed the French proposal for a European Defense Community, the French National Assembly rejected it as an intolerable infringement on national sovereignty. By May 1955 France was finally prepared to accept the rearmament of West Germany and its inclusion in the Atlantic Alliance. As one of the occupying powers in Berlin, France consistently supported the West German position in the crises over that city's status from 1958 to 1961. In January 1963 de Gaulle and West German chancellor Konrad Adenauer signed a treaty of reconciliation formalizing the Franco-German rapprochement and providing for bilateral defense consultation and cooperation. When de Gaulle withdrew French military forces from NATO's integrated command in 1966, he was careful to prepare a special bilateral arrangement with the Federal Republic providing for the maintenance of French air and ground forces on German territory.

While West German chancellor Willy Brandt's pursuit of improved relations with the Eastern bloc during 1967 to 1974 engendered some fears in France that Bonn might loosen its increasingly intimate ties to Paris, Franco-German relations continued to improve throughout the 1970s. But the German *Ostpolitik* foundered by the end of the decade amid the controversy surrounding the Soviet deployment of a new generation of intermediate-range missiles and NATO's decision to counter them with Pershing II ballistic missiles on West German territory. In the meantime, Franco-German relations steadily improved, first under the joint stewardship of German chancellor Helmut Schmidt and French president Valéry Giscard d'Estaing, then under German chancellor Helmut Kohl and French president François Mitterrand. During the second half of the 1980s, the 1963 treaty of reconciliation was amended to establish a joint defense commission, plans were drawn up for a joint Franco-German infantry brigade, and cooperative projects of weapons production were launched. As the European Community advanced toward full economic integration, Paris and Bonn were poised to serve as the axis of the new supranational superpower that will emerge after 1992. But the rapid pace of events in the communist world toward the end of the 1980s radically transformed the balance of forces in Europe in general and between France and Germany in particular—the collapse of the Warsaw Pact and the internal disarray of the Soviet Union removed the rationale for closer Franco-

German military cooperation. The reunification of the two German states in 1990 raised the specter of a German economic superpower that would relegate France to a subservient position within the new Europe. As economic productivity seemed definitively to have supplanted military (and particularly nuclear) capability as the criterion of power in the post–Cold War era, the advantage that France had enjoyed over a militarily vulnerable, politically divided Germany since the end of World War II began to disappear.

K. Kaiser, P. Lellouche, eds., *Le Couple franco-allemand et la défense de l'Europe* (Paris, 1954); H. Simonian, *The Privileged Partnership: Franco-German Relations in the European Community, 1969–1984* (New York, 1985); F. R. Willis, *France, Germany, and the New Europe (1945–1967)* (Ann Arbor, 1968).

W. R. Keylor

Related entries: DEFENSE POLICY; DE GAULLE, CHARLES; EUROPEAN DEFENSE COMMUNITY; FOREIGN POLICY; GISCARD D'ESTAING, VALERY; MITTERRAND, FRANCOIS; POMPIDOU, GEORGES; WESTERN EUROPEAN UNION.

FEDERATION OF THE DEMOCRATIC AND SOCIALIST LEFT (FGDS), a limited electoral coalition that existed for only two years, 1967 and 1968. Nonetheless, it was a major way station in the unification of the left that culminated in the socialist victories in the 1981 presidential and legislative elections. By supporting single candidates in selected constituencies at the second ballot of the 1962 legislative elections and François Mitterrand as the sole left-wing candidate in the 1965 presidential elections, many left-wing politicians had come to see that only a strategy based on electoral cooperation could bring them to power.

Between 1965 and the 1967 legislative elections, Mitterrand and his Convention of Republican Institutions (CIR) convinced socialist (SFIO) and many radical politicians to form the FGDS. The Federation had two main purposes. First, it agreed on a single, noncommunist left-wing candidate in each constituency. Second, it negotiated an agreement with the communists (PCF) and the Unified Socialist party (PSU) that only a single left-wing candidate would stand at the second ballot.

In 1967 the FGDS did remarkably well, winning 19 percent of the vote. More important, as a result of the second ballot competition, the left as a whole won 192 seats and reduced the Gaullist majority to 6. However, in 1968 the FGDS, like the left as a whole, suffered in the backlash to the events of May 1968. Its vote was cut to 17 percent, and the left lost ninety-two seats.

The left failed to maintain its unity in 1969 when socialist, communist, PSU, and Trotskyist candidates all ran for the presidency. By 1971 the FGDS had become obsolete, its mission of unifying the left having been taken on by the new Socialist party (PS) headed by François Mitterrand.

R. Johnson, *The Long March of the French Left* (London, 1982); G. H. Simmons,

French Socialists in Search of a Role (Ithaca, N.Y., 1970); P. M. Williams, *French Politicians and Elections: 1851–1969* (Cambridge, 1970).

C. Hauss

Related entries: CLUB MOVEMENT; DEFFERRE, GASTON; DUCLOS, JACQUES; ELECTIONS; ELECTORAL SYSTEM; FRENCH COMMUNIST PARTY; JOXE, PIERRE; LEFT RADICALS; MENDES-FRANCE, PIERRE; MITTERRAND, FRANCOIS; MOCH, JULES; MOLLET, GUY; RADICAL PARTY; ROCARD, MICHEL; ROCHET, WALDECK; SOCIALIST PARTY (PS, SFIO); STUDENT REVOLTS; UNIFIED SOCIALIST PARTY; UNION OF THE LEFT.

FEMINISM, a term that, over the years, has been assigned various meanings in France. Even its historical usage is difficult to trace. For some contemporary French feminists the ideological thrust is paramount; others have a more personal view. There is a division between bourgeois intellectuals and the working class, between focus on theory or praxis in feminist activities. Simone de Beauvoir described feminism as a manner of living individually and a manner of fighting collectively. Women, she stated, were tired of always being right but never having their rights.

The recent (or neo-) feminist movement in France grew out of the events of 1968, which profoundly marked French society. In the course of meetings and demonstrations young women realized that they were assigned "traditional" roles, such as typing, and that their male colleagues were not willing to share equal responsibilities and equal rights. Women met among themselves for discussion and demonstrations. The term MLF (*Mouvement de libération des femmes*) was used by the press to describe a small group of women who demonstrated under the Arc de Triomphe in 1970, where they attempted to place a wreath on the tomb honoring "one more unknown than the soldier, his wife." This was the first of a number of demonstrations held to call attention to the concerns of women.

The newly emerging French feminist movement of the 1970s concentrated upon sexual issues, those concerning women's control of their bodies: sexuality, birth control, and abortion. Sexual politics brought women of diverse backgrounds together. In April 1971 a manifesto containing the names of 343 women who publicly admitted to having undergone illegal abortions was published. "*Choisir la cause des femmes*" was formed by Simone de Beauvoir, Gisèle Halimi, and biologist Jean Rostand to protect them and all other women accused of abortion. The highly publicized trial at Bobigny was used to try the law on abortion itself. Simone Veil, minister of health and family, was asked by President Valéry Giscard d'Estaing in 1974 to introduce a more liberal law on contraception; it passed successfully, and she quickly introduced a bill permitting abortion under certain conditions. In spite of stiff opposition from conservative quarters, French women representing the whole political spectrum rallied to ensure passage of the bill for a five-year trial period, and did so again to ensure its permanent adoption in 1979.

President Giscard set up the first Secretariat of the Feminine Condition (where was one for the masculine condition, French feminists asked) in 1974, calling attention to women's concerns. Because of political considerations, the importance assigned to the new post and the financing varied considerably in the following years. When the socialists came to power in 1981, Yvette Roudy was named minister of women's rights and given a large budget. Calling for ''positive discrimination'' for women, she made information one of the key areas of her ministry. During her five years in office she helped publicize the newly acquired rights of women.

As in the nineteenth and early twentieth centuries, journals and papers played an important role in disseminating the demands and aspirations of French women. Outside of the traditional mass-circulation French women's press, these feminist journals span the entire range of feminist positions: reformist and radical; Catholic and communist; heterosexual and lesbian; homemaker, intellectual, and worker. These reviews attest to the breadth and diversity of the contemporary French feminist movement, as well as to its divisions. In 1981 the small but well-financed group *Psychanalyse et politique* legally assumed the name *Mouvement de libération des femmes*. However, other French women's groups maintain that the name must continue to represent the ''thousand-and-one tendencies of the Movement for the Liberation of Women.''

C. Duchen, *Feminism in France: From May '68 to Mitterrand* (London, 1986); M. C. Weitz, *Femmes: Recent Writings on French Women* (Boston, 1985).

M. C. Weitz

Related entries: BEAUVOIR, SIMONE DE; HALIMI, GISELE; LABOR FORCE; POLITICAL TRENDS; ROUDY, YVETTE; SOCIAL TRENDS; WOMEN, CONDITION OF.

FOCCART, JACQUES (1913–), a Gaullist and an African specialist who served as an adviser for African Affairs under the presidencies of Charles de Gaulle and Georges Pompidou, and under Prime Minister Jacques Chirac (1986–88). Foccart was born into a family of the *grande bourgeoisie* in northwest France. From an early age he had contacts with French overseas territories, as his father had created a banana export business and married a Creole in Guadeloupe. During his youth he therefore traveled regularly between Mayenne and Guadeloupe. At the beginning of World War II he was a sergeant in the French army and, after France's defeat by Germany in 1940, he joined the Resistance under de Gaulle's banner. By the end of the war he had become a lieutenant colonel. He met de Gaulle in June 1944 after the liberation of Lavaland, marking the beginning of a long association between the two men that was to come to an end only with the death of de Gaulle in 1970.

After the war Foccart embarked on a business career. He was also closely associated with de Gaulle when he founded the *Rassemblement du peuple français* (RPF) in 1947, and he was an active member of the new party, both in France and abroad, and sat on its National Council from the outset. He became its deputy-general secretary, and subsequently general secretary in 1954. In 1953 he was responsible for organizing de Gaulle's visit to eighteen African countries, which enabled the latter to make contacts with leading political figures in French-speaking Africa that were to prove so important after 1958. During de Gaulle's period out of public office from 1946 to 1958, Foccart's exact purpose in his regular visits to France's colonies in Africa is unclear. What is certain is that, building on the contacts he had made during the Resistance, he cultivated good relationships with many of the future political leaders of francophone black Africa, the most influential of whom he knew personally. There are also unconfirmed reports that Foccart was a member of France's counterespionage services during this period.

On de Gaulle's return to power in 1958 Foccart was thus perfectly placed to become his special adviser on African affairs. In 1960 he became secretary-general of the French Community, and in 1961 secretary-general to the president with responsibility for African and Madagascan affairs. In this post he traveled regularly to the newly independent states of francophone black Africa and played a major role in maintaining France's good relations with this region of the world during and after the period of decolonization. He retained his post until the death of President Pompidou in April 1974. The incoming president, Valéry Giscard d'Estaing, no doubt feeling that Foccart was too closely associated with the Gaullist party, of which Foccart had remained an active member throughout this period, closed the offices of the Secretariat General for African and Madagascan Affairs. René Journiac, an associate of Giscard, was appointed to the office of Special Adviser to the President on African Affairs. However, unlike his predecessor who had run what was virtually a ministry for African affairs at the sumptuously appointed Hôtel de Noirmoutiers, Journiac was, until his accidental death in 1980, installed in modest offices at the presidential palace. The reconstituted Ministry of Cooperation took over many of the former responsibilities of Foccart's secretariat.

Throughout his life Africa has remained Foccart's primary interest and field of activity. By both political friends and foes, he has been associated with France's secret "networks," with its "alternative" police, with the secret agents, and with actual or attempted coups in Africa. He gained the confidence, however, of many of the leaders of newly independent francophone African states and was an intermediary between them and the French president. After 1974 his role in French political life was apparently at an end. He continued to retain an interest in francophone Africa, however, and traveled there frequently, either for his own business interests or as a representative for various French companies, such as Thomson CSF. After the victory of the right in the March 1986 parliamentary elections he made an unexpected return to French politics, when he was appointed by the new Gaullist prime minister, Chirac, as his personal adviser on African affairs. President Mitterrand had retained his son as his own adviser on African affairs, and Chirac clearly felt that Foccart's accumulated knowledge and experience of Africa would be invaluable to him in his dealings with francophone Africa during the period of *cohabitation* between a socialist president and a right-wing prime minister that was just beginning. With the defeat of Chirac in the presidential elections of 1988 and the return to a socialist-led majority in the National Assembly as a result of the subsequent parliamentary elections, Foccart's services were no longer required in Paris. However, he continues to visit the capitals of francophone Africa and reportedly continues to play the role of intermediary between the Gaullist party in France and those francophone African leaders with whom the party has traditionally maintained good relations, in particular President Félix Houphouët-Boigny of the Ivory Coast.

P. Péan, *Affaires africaines* (Paris, 1983), *Jacques Foccart* (forthcoming).

T. Chafer

Related entries: ARMS SALES; CHIRAC, JACQUES; DECOLONIZATION; DE GAULLE, CHARLES; FOREIGN POLICY; FRENCH UNION; *LA FRANCOPHONIE*; GAULLIST PARTY; OVERSEAS DEPARTMENTS AND TERRITORIES; POMPIDOU, GEORGES; THIRD WORLD, RELATIONS WITH.

FORCE OUVRIERE (FO), one of three major trade unions active on the French scene since World War II (with the *Confédération générale du travail* [CGT] and *Confédération française démocratique du travail* [CFDT]). The *Force ouvrière* can claim to be the most faithful to the founding traditions of the workers' movement in that it still scrupulously adheres to the political independence of trade unions as inscribed in the Charter of Amiens of 1905. The FO is also characterized by its commitment to political democracy and guaranteed representation for all the tendencies that adhere to it. The circumstances of its birth are set deep in controversy. When communist domination of the CGT seemed to be emerging prior to the war, a noncommunist tendency organized itself under the name *Syndicats*. Many of its leaders were compromised under Vichy, but the reunified CGT continued after the war to harbor several anticommunist tendencies that made their presence evident by successfully carrying on a number of strikes during the period of PCF (French Communist party) participation in government, when the CGT policy was to cooperate in encouraging labor productivity. Socialists, anarcho-syndicalists, Trotskyists, and independents eventually coalesced in 1946 to form the FO; the budding organization was immediately contacted and helped by the American Federation of Labor's representative in Europe, Irving Brown, who was to channel CIA funds to the union, an association it was not able to live down for a long time.

But the Americans never controlled the FO, and they played only a minor role in its split with the CGT that occurred in December 1947. FO militants were upset at unprecedented communist tactics in the November–December 1947 coal strikes, which invited nonunionized workers to vote on strike issues and confronted the government with unusual tenacity bordering on violence. They also rejected the CGT's interpretation of the strikes as directed against the Marshall Plan. The decision to split off from the CGT was taken in December 1947 and consecrated at the founding Congress of April 1948. Léon Jouhaux, the venerable prewar head of the CGT, led the new union at its birth, eventually giving way to Robert Bothereau, André Bergeron, and Marc Blondel. The FO immediately offered its cooperation in the implementation of the Marshall Plan, and it directed its attention to controlling prices rather than seeking higher wages, much to the annoyance of the Americans, who feared it was too timid to win the support of noncommunist workers. The FO's early support was among government workers, and it remains predominantly the union of *fonctionnaires* today. It came into its own by leading the August 1953 strikes, which began among government workers but quickly became general, and it was able to achieve a settlement with the Laniel government.

The FO has remained wedded to achieving economic gains for workers and is rigidly nonideological, advocating collective bargaining within a liberal democracy, although most of its militants and leaders have been close to the Socialist party. It has refused common tactics with the CGT in most instances and rejects union with the CFDT because it adheres religiously to an anticlerical posture. It was bypassed by the May 1968 events and ignored the Common Program of the left, spurning the new left rhetoric of *autogestion* (self-management). It maintained its distance from the Mitterrand government after 1981, in fact demonstrating greater militancy than either the CGT or CFDT, which sought early to cooperate with the socialists. For this reason it has improved its position in the 1980s, getting over the one million mark in membership, in contrast to the gradual decline of other unions.

A. Bergeron, *Ma Route et mes combats* (Paris, 1976); A. Bergounioux, *Force ouvrière* (Paris, 1975); J.-L. Validire, *André Bergeron, une force ouvrière* (Paris, 1984).

I. M. Wall

Related entries: BERGERON, ANDRE; *CONFEDERATION GENERALE DU TRAVAIL*; TRADE UNION MOVEMENT.

FOREIGN POLICY, arguably the most important feature differentiating the Fourth Republic from the Fifth. Between 1945 and 1958 diplomacy and foreign relations were marked by vacillation, drift, uncertainty, and, eventually, tragedy, leading directly to the collapse of the regime. From 1958 onward, they were characterized by strong, lucid, independent leadership that has served both to consolidate the domestic institutions of the regime and to restore France's standing in the world.

Two major problems faced foreign policy actors in the immediate postwar world. The first was the necessity to restore in some shape or form the shattered remnants of empire. The second was to contribute to the restructuring of the European order. These were tasks of the utmost complexity, requiring imagination, vision, sensitivity, and considerable diplomatic leverage. None of these was either available or even possible under the many-faceted prescriptions of the 1946 constitution. Nowhere does the constitution make clear who is in charge of foreign policy, the three articles on diplomatic treaties (Articles 26, 27, and

28) leaving this totally vague. By inference, the final decision rests with the one body least likely to be able to steer a clear course: parliament. As far as the president is concerned, he was merely to be "kept informed of international negotiations" (Article 31), and his every action was to be countersigned by the prime minister and by a minister (Article 38). The prime minister was to "supervise the armed forces and coordinate preparations for national defense," but all his foreign and defense policy decisions were also to be countersigned by a minister. In short, the constitution was the recipe for the very disaster that eventually took place.

Attempts to coordinate a clear sense of direction on the former empire fell foul of numerous conflicting vested interests, of which the most powerful and, ultimately, the most prejudicial to a successful outcome was the entrenched position of the local administrators, colonists, or armed forces. The war in Indochina (1946–54), far from reasserting France's role in the world, exacerbated the humiliation of 1940 at the same time as it thrust the country more and more into a dependency on the United States (by the end of the war, Washington was covering the vast majority of its cost). The war in Algeria (1954–62), while militarily less catastrophic, nevertheless highlighted the contradictions between ideological rhetoric and diplomatic/military practice, the left being, if anything, more determined than certain elements of the liberal right to maintain the North African enclave as an integral part of *La République une et indivisible*. That attempt led directly to the collapse of the Republic itself. On the first great issue facing postwar foreign policymakers, therefore, the picture is one of a glaring lack of any clear policy at all.

The same is not true for the European dimension. The outstanding problem facing the Quai d'Orsay in 1945 was the one that was to reemerge as its main concern forty years later: what to do about Germany. The immediate response was to forge new military and political alliances against any resurgent German threat. The first of these was signed, paradoxically but typically, by Charles de Gaulle in Moscow in 1944. More realistically, the general's successors, notably Léon Blum and Georges Bidault, placed their main hopes in a Franco-British treaty signed—symbolically—in Dunkirk in 1947. This was joined by the Benelux countries in the Treaty of Brussels (1948). However, already the goalposts were shifting position. Hardly was the ink dry on the Dunkirk parchment when Germany ceased to be the main threat. The Cold War offered up a new villain in the Soviet Union, a challenge that, sooner or later, was bound to involve a "reversal of alliances" whereby the wartime ally and the wartime adversary would be recast in opposite roles. That this happened sooner rather than later was largely due to the emerging superpower status of the United States. The signing of the North Atlantic Alliance in Washington in 1949 had two immediate consequences for France. The first was to underscore the client status of France in relation to the United States. The second was to render inevitable German rearmament and, as a consequence, to prompt a major struggle over the identity and structure of Europe's military defenses.

The latter problem was complicated even further by the nonmilitary dimension of European reconstruction. All French governments after the departure of de Gaulle in 1946 participated enthusiastically in the process of European economic cooperation, which was given a major boost by Marshall Aid and the establishment of the Organization of European Economic Cooperation (OEEC, later OECD). Visionaries like Jean Monnet and Robert Schuman were already committed to full European integration, to a United States of Europe. The Schuman plan for a European Coal and Steel Community was launched in 1950, just as the question of how to rearm Germany was becoming acute. The economic dimension of the Schuman plan was less important than the political significance of abandoning national sovereignty over such vital resources as coal and steel. Supported by the Socialist party (SFIO) and the Christian Democrats (MRP), the plan was opposed in principle by the communists and, on technical details (mainly concerning ultimate control), by the Gaullists. The debate already foreshadowed those of the next half-century over two conflicting visions of the structure of Europe: confederal or federal. But the large majority that ratified the plan in the National Assembly offered encouragement to those who sought to solve the security problem by a similar pooling of Europe's armed forces. The long drawn-out debates over the European Defense Community (EDC) brought home to the French just how narrow was their margin for maneuvering in foreign affairs. To accept the EDC was to end a thousand years of national control over defense. To reject it was to reinforce French dependence on NATO and to accept German rearmament. After four years of agonizing, it was the latter option that prevailed during a chaotic and inconclusive debate in the National Assembly, which did little more than rehearse the arguments to be heard a hundred times over the next few decades.

When de Gaulle returned to power in 1958, he therefore inherited a disintegrated empire, an integrated defense capacity (NATO), and an embryonic European Economic Community whose structures remained to be decided. On all this he was to impose a personal stamp that would mark French foreign policy for the rest of the century. His first task was to give constitutional backing to the presidential authority he sought to assert. The changes are not so much in the letter of the constitution (Articles 5, 15, 21, 35, 52, and 53 suggest a sharing of responsibility not that dissimilar from the terms of the Fourth Republic) as in the practice of presidential power underwritten by the constitution as a whole. Covered by that document and inspired by his own lucid vision of the postwar world, de Gaulle rapidly lanced the colonial abscess and shifted France's relations with the Third World to one of support for independence movements, for a multipolar (instead of a bipolar) international structure, and for a new economic deal offering serious development prospects for the "South."

Where European security and relations with the superpowers were concerned, the general rejected most aspects of the status quo—Soviet-American global condominium, American dominance of NATO, French security dependency on an increasingly questionable U.S. "deterrent," and American "open-door" economic and trade policy. The most significant features of his revolt involved his break with NATO (1966) and the development of an independent French nuclear strike force; his rejection of the blocs in the name of a confederal Europe "from the Atlantic to the Urals," a geographical area sufficiently vast and diverse to allow for the containment of German ambition and the balancing of Soviet might; an (unsuccessful) attempt to woo Bonn away from Washington's apron strings by a 1963 treaty of friendship whose military dimensions remained a dead letter until revitalized by François Mitterrand in 1983; and the extension of the hand of friendship to the Soviet Union's East European satellites. In practice the transcontinental vision (Atlantic to the Urals) proved premature, and de Gaulle is above all remembered for the independence of his foreign policy, backed by a growing nuclear arsenal.

In Western Europe, de Gaulle's firm stand against the architects of a federal structure and his insistence that no European Economic Community (EEC) decisions could be valid without unanimity, ensured that the fledgling Community's march toward integration would be long and tortuous. Above all, his repeated veto of British membership and his almost paranoid fear of American hegemony ensured that France was to dominate the politics of the EEC as long as he was in the Elysée. His departure in 1969 led to an acceleration of the integration process, President Georges Pompidou opening the door for British membership (1972), President Valéry Giscard d'Estaing promoting both direct elections to the European Parliament and a European monetary system (1979), and President Mitterrand fostering further extension of membership (Spain, Portugal, and Greece) as well as spearheading the move toward the Single European Act (1992) and exerting many pressures in favor of greater federalism.

On the security front, Giscard's hopes of edging France back into the NATO fold were scuttled by his parliamentary dependence on the Gaullists, while Mitterrand's attempts to appear more Gaullist than de Gaulle have been made against the backdrop of a rapidly shifting international security structure marked by the relative relaxation of superpower hegemony over both halves of Europe and the emerging need for the creation of an integrated European security system. Mitterrand's legacy will have been to keep all options open while historical forces continued to develop. But all presidents of the Fifth Republic have consolidated the general's heritage of restoring France's credibility and *rayonnement* throughout the world. In 1945 France's place as a permanent member of the United Nations security council was seen by many as a consolation prize for its loss of a world role. In 1990 its place on that council needs no further justification.

P. Cerny, *The Politics of Grandeur: Ideological Aspects of de Gaulle's Foreign Policy* (Cambridge, 1980); S. Cohen, M.-C. Smouts, *La Politique extérieure de Valéry Giscard d'Estaing* (Paris, 1985); A. Grosser, *La Quatrième République et sa politique extérieure* (Paris, 1961); F. Mitterrand, *Réflexions sur la politique extérieure de la France* (Paris, 1986)

J. Howorth

Related entries: ARMS SALES; DEFENSE POLICY; DE GAULLE, CHARLES; EUROPEAN DEFENSE COMMUNITY; EUROPEAN ECO-

NOMIC COMMUNITY, RELATIONS WITH; FEDERAL REPUBLIC OF GERMANY, RELATIONS WITH; GISCARD D'ESTAING, VALERY; GREAT BRITAIN, RELATIONS WITH; INDOCHINA, RELATIONS WITH; MIDDLE EAST, RELATIONS WITH; MITTERRAND, FRANCOIS; POMPIDOU, GEORGES; SOVIET UNION, RELATIONS WITH; THIRD WORLD, RELATIONS WITH; UNITED STATES, RELATIONS WITH.

FOUCAULT, MICHEL (1926–1984), social scientist, philosopher, archaeologist of thought, genealogist of power and knowledge, and self-styled historian of the present. One of the most influential thinkers of the twentieth century, Foucault is widely recognized as the most important figure in French philosophy since Jean-Paul Sartre. He is also regarded as one of the leading figures of structuralism, the intellectual movement that came to maturity in the mid–1960s and that was characterized by a preoccupation with the deep-seated structures that underlie and inform a variety of observed phenomena in the human sciences; however, *structuralist* was a label Foucault repeatedly refused. Such categorizations—later he was deemed to share with Jacques Derrida the leadership of poststructuralism—were shunned by a complex writer who proved forever ready to change focus and direction. Fundamentally pluridisciplinary in his outlook, Foucault married together history and philosophy, but annexed to these primary disciplines were others, including anthropology, linguistics, and psychology. His avowed aim was to question existing limits. Small wonder, then, that his work should elude classification.

Foucault was born into a well-to-do, middle-class family in Poitiers on October 15, 1926. His father was a surgeon by profession, but in addition to the house in Poitiers the Foucaults were owners of land, farms, and an imposing second home in nearby Vendeuvre. As a boy, Foucault attended the *Lycée Henri IV* in Poitiers; later he was sent to the prestigious *Lycée Henri IV* in Paris, where his teachers included the philosopher Jean Hyppolite. It was here that Foucault began, in 1943, the rigorous training required for admission to the *Ecole normale supérieure* (ENS). As a student he enjoyed a dazzling career. When he graduated from the *lycée* it was with the commendation "*élève d'élite*" in history and philosophy; then, aged only nineteen, he came in fourth in the entrance exam to ENS (albeit on his second attempt). There, and at the Sorbonne, Foucault studied under some of the leading intellectual stars of the day: Louis Althusser, Georges Canguilhem, Maurice Merleau-Ponty, and (again) Hyppolite. He was only twenty-three when he graduated as a *normalien*. He obtained a diploma in philosophy the same year, and in 1951 he tackled the *agrégation* and placed third. His education was not only in philosophy: He also studied psychology, then psychopathology, leading to the publication of his first book, *Maladie mentale et psychologie*, in 1954. Four years spent as a *lecteur* in French at the University of Uppsala were followed by shorter appointments at the French institutes of Warsaw and Hamburg. At the end of this period abroad, Foucault's study of the history of madness was complete, and in 1961 he was awarded the degree of *doctorat d'état*.

Foucault's academic career took off on his return to France in 1960, when he was appointed *maître de conférences*, and later professor in the department of philosophy at the University of Clermont-Ferrand. The following year saw the publication of his thesis under the title *L'Histoire de la folie à l'âge classique*. Here, Foucault examined the evolution of the concept of madness since medieval times, scrutinizing the historical need of a culture to define its limits in terms of what it admits, marginalizes, or excludes, and questioning the political ends such treatment may serve. Foucault's next book, *Naissance de la clinique, une archéologie du regard médicale* (1963), took a major step in the direction of structuralism, in that it sought to alter the standard way of thinking about intellectual history (essentially linear) through its insistence on "archeology" as method and the introduction of a spatial dimension. But it was *Les Mots et les choses* (1966) that brought him fame and a university appointment in Paris (first as head of the philosophy department at the University of Vincennes, then, from 1970, as professor of history and systems of thought at the illustrious Collège de France). This, probably Foucault's most important work, sets out to apprehend in terms of paradigms or "epistemes," the conceptual backcloth to the birth of the human sciences that took place during the nineteenth century. The key question it posed is this: How did man come to take himself as an object of possible knowledge? In *L'Archéologie du savoir* (1969), Foucault resumed this theme, conducting at the same time an intricate critique of his own writing and purpose.

In the last years of his life, Foucault embarked on a six-volume history of sexuality, only three volumes of which were completed. Some time after his death on June 25, 1984, it emerged that the philosopher had been a victim of AIDS. To have owned this publicly would have been to yield to the compulsion to speak the "truth" about himself, something Foucault had sought to resist all his life. He left behind a powerful and doubtless-enduring legacy: a discourse on power and the power of discourse that shatters accepted "truths" without offering itself in exchange; although this was a pitfall, it was difficult to avoid.

G. Deleuze, *Foucault* (Paris, 1986); D. Eribon, *Michel Foucault (1926–1984)* (Paris, 1989); J. G. Merquior, *Foucault* (London, 1985).

M. Maclean

Related entries: ALTHUSSER, LOUIS; BARTHES, ROLAND; DERRIDA, JACQUES; INTELLECTUAL TRENDS; LACAN, JACQUES; STRUCTURALISM.

FRACHON, BENOIT (1892–1975), Communist party and trade-union leader. Frachon was born near Saint-Etienne on May 13, 1893. His father was a miner, both literate and self-educated, and Frachon carried on in that tradition, rapidly becoming a stalwart of trade unionism in the Lyon area and participating in the founding Congress of the French Communist party (PCF) at Tours in 1920.

Frachon's rise in party and trade-union ranks was rapid, and by 1934 he was secretary of the *Confédération générale du travail unitaire* (CGTU) and a ranking member of the PCF's Central Committee, in which capacity he negotiated the unity of the CGTU and the *Confédération générale du travail* (CGT) in 1936. Frachon became a public figure for his prominent role in negotiating the Matignon agreements, which brought about a new charter of rights for French labor under the Popular Front, and he shared the leadership of the unified CGT with Léon Jouhaux until the communist faction was once again expelled following the Nazi-Soviet pact. When Maurice Thorez left France for the Soviet Union, Frachon became second-in-command in the Communist party to Jacques Duclos, playing a crucial role in the clandestine Resistance, and once again negotiating trade-union unity in 1943. At the war's end Frachon was once again general secretary of the CGT, in which communist influence was now paramount, alongside the aging Jouhaux, and he was one of the most popular figures in France. Although his union functions forbade his formal participation in the party's highest organs, virtually no PCF decision was made between 1944 and his retirement in 1975 in which he did not have an important role.

Frachon was a leading voice in the "battle for production" of the 1944–47 period and a vitriolic critic of the Americans during the height of the Cold War. He led the CGT through the bitter strikes of 1947, which led to the split with the *Force ouvrière*, and quickly denounced the rival union as a CIA-created tool of Washington. He politicized the CGT, making it a "transmission belt" of the PCF, and watched it decline as it subordinated working-class demands to the party-sponsored Peace Movement through the early 1950s. Frachon also appears to have been somewhat independent within the PCF: There is no record of his having a role in the purge of his fellow Resistance heroes André Marty and Charles Tillon, for example, and he confided that he found his party's antics "*pas toujours drôle*" on that occasion. Perhaps as a consequence he was required to criticize his own stewardship of the CGT at the PCF Congress in 1954, admitting that he had excessively politicized the union, something he certainly had not done without the agreement of the PCF leadership. Frachon emerged as a leading critic of Stalin's errors at the PCF Central Committee meeting of 1956, and he supported de-Stalinization of the party thereafter.

With the advent of the Fifth Republic, Frachon adamantly pursued a policy of trade-union unity, and he successfully negotiated a unity-of-action agreement with the *Confédération française démocratique du travail* (CFDT) in 1966. With this crowning achievement to his career he stepped up to the presidency of the CGT in 1967, leaving the everyday running of the organization to Georges Séguy. But the massive strike movement of May 1968 catapulted him once again to the center of events. He pushed hard for CGT participation in the twenty-four-hour strike of May 13 and then called for general walkouts when the spontaneous movement began days later. He was a critical figure in the negotiations of the Grenelle agreements on wages, as he had been in the Matignon accords thirty-two years before, but quickly backtracked when Renault workers rebelled against the agreements when they were presented by Séguy. Frachon may well have thus saved Séguy's career, and the CGT, on that occasion. He also showed that he could put autonomous trade-union concerns above the specific political considerations of the Communist party, a lesson that was not always followed by his successors after his retirement and subsequent death in 1975.

B. Frachon, *Au rythme des jours, retrospective sur 20 années de luttes de la CGT*, 2 vols. (Paris, 1967–73), *Pour la CGT: Mémoires de lutte, 1902–1939* (Paris, 1981); P. Robrieux, *Histoire intérieure du Parti communiste (IV), Biographies, Chronologie, Bibliographie* (Paris, 1984); G. Ross, *Workers and Communists in France: From Popular Front to Eurocommunism* (Berkeley, Calif., 1982); I. Wall, *French Communism in the Era of Stalin* (Westport, Conn., 1983).

I. M. Wall

Related entries: CONFEDERATION GENERALE DU TRAVAIL; DUCLOS, JACQUES; FRENCH COMMUNIST PARTY; SEGUY, GEORGES; THOREZ, MAURICE.

LA FRANCOPHONIE, an international francophone community comprising approximately three hundred million people that resembles the British Commonwealth. Under the leadership of the Mitterrand government, representatives from thirty-nine French-speaking nations met in Paris on February 17–19, 1986 for their first summit. At this first meeting the aim was to create a sense of identity among French-speaking nations and lay the groundwork for future joint action. Representatives in Paris made plans for the creation of an international television agency, the distribution worldwide of a twenty-minute French-language news program, the formation of an international network of French-language data banks to promote computer technology, the introduction of an international French-language book fair, and the publication of new paperback editions of French-language authors. Representatives also adopted a resolution condemning apartheid in South Africa.

The second meeting of the French-language community was held in Québec during the first week of September of 1987. At this summit a number of resolutions were passed on international issues, and representatives sanctioned 100 projects in the fields of communications, cultural exchange, education, scientific research, and agriculture. Plans were also made for the next summit in Dakar, Senegal, in March of 1989, and for sponsoring summer games—somewhat like the Commonwealth Games—in Morocco in 1989. What caught the attention of many observers of the meeting in Québec, however, was the problem of human rights abuses among a number of member states, such as Burundi (whose leader attended the summit but who was overthrown while attending the meeting), Somalia, Cambodia, and Vietnam. Although human rights abuses were not discussed in formal sessions at Québec, both President Mitterrand and Canadian prime minister Brian Mulroney assured the press that the issue was addressed in private sessions. Strains at the summit also arose because of French fears that Canada desired to challenge French commercial primacy in Africa and Asia in former French colonies. Strains, too, emerged between Canada and France because the conservative French prime minister, Jacques Chirac, said on the eve of the summit that Canada had General Charles de Gaulle to thank for overcoming the Québec problem (in 1967 while visiting Canada, de Gaulle had given impetus to an independent Québec by declaring, "*Vive le Québec libre*").

The third summit was held as scheduled in Dakar on May 23–25, 1989. Here, President Mitterrand announced that France would cancel the debt owed to it by the poorest African nations.

The hope of Mitterrand and others is that the French-speaking community can be developed into a powerful organization for promoting economic and technical aid among member states as well as promoting French language and culture in order to enhance France's position on the international scene.

French Embassy Press and Information Service, "News From France" (February 24, 1986, September 10, 1987, and May 16, June 14, 1989); *The New York Times* (September 3 and 6, 1987).

W. Northcutt

Related entries: ACADEMIE FRANCAISE; DECOLONIZATION; FOREIGN POLICY; MITTERRAND, FRANCOIS; THIRD WORLD, RELATIONS WITH.

FRANGLAIS, a blending of the words *français* and *anglais* to represent words borrowed from English into French, some undergoing slight morphological or orthographical alteration and others introduced wholesale into French. The word *franglais* was coined and popularized by a Sorbonne professor, René Etiemble, whose 1964 book *Parlez-vous franglais?* became a best-seller in France. Etiemble chided the French for abandoning their allegedly superior lexicon for the purportedly less aesthetic and insidiously corrupting vocabulary of American English.

It is estimated that there are some 2,260 English words in current use by speakers of French, equivalent to 2.5 percent of the words in the French vocabulary. In response to this growing trend, the *Académie française* has worked actively, yet relatively unsuccessfully, to halt the influx of Americanisms into French. The French government, too, has sought to discourage lexical borrowing from English, most notably by passing the Bas Law of 1977, designed to ban the use of foreign terms if suitable French terms exist, and the 1983 Law for the Enrichment of the French Language, which stipulated for those employed in government service when and where the use of French terms was absolutely mandatory. In 1970 President Georges Pompidou established a number of ministerial terminology committees whose task it was to identify lexical deficiencies in French in the areas of science and technology and to propose new French terms to replace the foreign borrowings. Thus, the French word *ordinateur* was proposed to replace the English word *computer*, and *stimulateur* was suggested to replace *pacemaker*. Nevertheless, violations of the language laws abound and go largely unpunished, and the infiltration of new foreign, mostly English, words continues.

J. Flaitz, *The Ideology of English: French Perceptions of English as an International Language* (Berlin, 1988); S. de Gramont, *The French: Portrait of a People* (New York, 1969).

J. J. Flaitz

Related entries: ACADEMIE FRANCAISE; CULTURAL POLICY; POPULAR CULTURE.

FRENCH COMMUNIST PARTY (PCF), a political party devoted to the principles of Leninist democratic centralism and solidarity with the Soviet Union as the fatherland of the world proletariat. The PCF emerged from World War II as the largest party in France, claiming 800,000 members (500,000 estimated real membership) and garnering over 28 percent of the popular vote in 1946. The important role the party played in the Resistance, and its strength in Departmental Committees of Liberation in August 1944, created the widespread fear that the PCF would seize power, but this was to reckon without the superior strength of General Charles de Gaulle, the presence of American troops in France, or the desire of Stalin not to antagonize the West. Party leader Maurice Thorez returned from the Soviet Union in November 1944, declared "one State, one Police, and one Army," and defined PCF policy as including full support for the provisional government and prosecution of the war, maximum productivity, and purging France of collaborators. The party entered the de Gaulle government, and following the October 1945 elections, five communist ministers held power, supervised by Thorez himself who became minister of state. This number grew to ten ministers under postwar tripartitism, during which the PCF collaborated in the construction of the modern French welfare state. De Gaulle would not, however, allow the party any of the "key" ministries of the interior, foreign affairs, or defense, and that prohibition stuck until the Cold War forced the ouster of the communists from the French government in May 1947. They were not to return until the victory of François Mitterrand in 1981, and then only for three years.

With the coming of the Cold War in 1947 the PCF became isolated and its fortunes declined, which, with very few exceptions, has continued since then. The isolation was in part self-imposed. With the creation of the Cominform in September 1947 the party adopted what was at the least a sectarian, and perceived to be revolutionary "class-against-class" line, characterized by attacks on the socialists as "principal supporters of the bourgeoisie," purge trials apparently aimed at cleansing itself of resisters, and quasi-hysterical indulgence in personality cults focused on Thorez and Stalin. PCF intellectuals were required to swallow the theories of the Soviet biologist Lysenko and to value the "socialist-realist" art of Fougeron over Picasso, notwithstanding the latter's communism. During the strikes of 1947 and 1948, interpreted by the PCF as directed against the Marshall Plan, insurrection was feared and the government, under a socialist minister of the interior, resorted to brutal repression. Internally in the PCF the strictest Stalinist discipline prevailed, which reflected the party's *ouvriérisme*, or workerism; by systematically promoting workers to positions of leadership the party retained its internal cohesion and maintained the belief that it alone was the party of the working class, capable of building a truly classless society.

Yet, the major activity of the PCF was to contest elections, and in terms of propaganda it focused on the question of peace; in 1950 and 1951 militants were mobilized in national efforts to get signatures on petitions to withdraw France from NATO and ban the atomic bomb (while the United States had a monopoly). And Thorez would seem always to have meant to return to a Popular Front policy and integration into the French body politic, although never at the price of sacrificing the party's revolutionary internationalism or internal workerist cohesion. Hence, the PCF's peculiar ambiguity: in international affairs, more sectarian than the Russians; in domestic affairs, internally Stalinist yet eager to pursue social-democratic politics.

From 1950 to 1953, while Thorez lay ill in the Soviet Union, rival factions contended within the Politburo for power, and purge trials rid the party of respected Resistance leaders and historic figures like Charles Tillon, André Marty, and Auguste Lecoeur. Thorez was able to return in March 1953 following Stalin's death, and he set the party on an internal integrationist path, seeking entente with the socialists, backing Pierre Mendès-France in 1954 when the latter settled the war in Indochina and Guy Mollet in 1956 because he promised to do the same in Algeria. Yet, in the international movement, Thorez intrigued with Vyacheslav Molotov and the Chinese against Nikita Khrushchev, and even tried to prevent knowledge of the latter's secret speech revealing Stalin's crimes from entering France. Still, the PCF was becoming a major factor in the Fourth Republic's politics, until brutally pushed back into isolation by the return of de Gaulle in 1958. Alone in campaigning against the constitution of the Fifth Republic, the party's vote total fell to near 18 percent, while the development of a New Left that solidarized with the Algerian nationalists and accepted their terrorism as the necessary complement to revolutionary struggle forced the party to miss completely the leftist generation of youth of the 1960s. In 1961 Thorez purged the pro-Khrushchev, New Left faction of Marcel Servin and Laurent Casanova. Internationally, however, Thorez had no choice but to rally to support Moscow against the Chinese.

With membership in decline and the Gaullist-enforced return to single-member electoral constituencies, Thorez's successor, the moderate Waldeck Rochet, led the party on a frankly reformist course after 1964. The PCF backed the candidacy of François Mitterrand against de Gaulle in 1965, declining to back its own candidate, and earnestly sought entente with the socialists. But the student demonstrations of 1968 were the occasion of another setback; the New Left ideology of the generation of the 1960s repelled the party, which denounced student leader Daniel Cohn-Bendit, anarchists, Trotskyists, and situationists. The massive strikes took the PCF by surprise; it was forced to rally to their support, negotiated a wage agreement with the government that the workers initially rejected, and prevented the establishment of an alternative government of the left when de

Gaulle briefly disappeared. This left the party no choice but to rally to de Gaulle's call for elections upon his return; de Gaulle repaid the party for its legalism by conducting a campaign against communist "totalitarianism," which reduced the PCF once again to its vote totals of 1962.

Waldeck Rochet fell ill in Moscow in 1969, and party leadership fell to the mysterious Georges Marchais, a figure very much in the Thorezian mold and a curious choice given his lack of a Resistance record, and a period of labor he undertook in Germany during the war that political opponents were able to show was voluntary rather than forced. Marchais negotiated a Common Program with Mitterrand's revived Socialist Party (PS) in 1972, and communist support for Mitterrand in the 1974 elections nearly resulted in the latter's victory. There followed the party's flirtation with "Eurocommunism," its apparent break with the Soviet Union, and doctrinal change at its twenty-second Congress of 1976, where the PCF abandoned the "dictatorship of the proletariat" and proclaimed its belief in a pluralist and democratic socialism characterized by liberties and a multiplicity of political parties. However, the PCF was increasingly uncomfortable with its new line; vote totals languished at the 21 to 22 percent level and membership rose only moderately, while the new dynamism of the socialists threatened to make them the hegemonic party of the French left. Marchais forced negotiations with the socialists to "update" the Common Program in 1977 and used the occasion to effect a break, in consequence of which the left lost the 1978 legislative elections. But the strategy failed. The PCF ran into an explosion of hostility; many intellectuals abandoned it, polemics against it increased, and when Marchais backed the Soviet invasion of Afghanistan in 1979 many simply wrote the party off. One quarter of the PCF electorate deserted in 1981, when the party received only 15 percent of the vote, and Mitterrand won despite the PCF and achieved a socialist majority in the National Assembly.

The 1980s seemed to threaten the party's disappearance as a major force in French political life. Three years of captivity in a socialist-led government did little to restore the party's image, although individual communist ministers, like Charles Fiterman in transport, distinguished themselves as capable administrators. Restive at the socialist return to austerity in 1983, the party quit the government in 1984 and accompanied its new line with an ideological turn that criticized its support for Mitterrand going back to 1965. Nor has the PCF been comfortable with Mikhail Gorbachev's reforms in the Soviet Union; the Soviets themselves criticized PCF secretarianism in 1988. The party claims a continued membership of 600,000; if the real figure is two-thirds of that it would still be the largest party in France in terms of numbers. But local elections have shown continued decline: The party received 9.8 percent of the vote in the legislative elections of 1986, while its presidential candidate, André Lajoinie, garnered under 7 percent against Mitterrand in 1988. The party rebounded to 11 percent in the legislative elections that followed, but lost many of its municipalities in March 1989 and fell back to 7.7 percent of the vote in the European elections of that year.

With the end of the Cold War in the 1980s it would appear difficult to conceive of an important future role for a party whose impact on France from its birth in 1920 to its decline in the 1980s has been enormous. The inability of the PCF's continued Stalinist internal practices to adapt to historically changed circumstances would seem to have prevented the integration it sought and forced its decline to a marginal role in French political life.

A. Kriegel, *The French Communists: Profile of a People* (Chicago, 1972); G. Lavau, *A quoi sert le Parti communiste français?* (Paris, 1981); P. Robrieux, *Histoire intérieure du Parti communiste*, 5 vols. (Paris, 1980–85); G. Ross, *The View from Inside: A French Communist Cell in Crisis* (Berkeley, Calif., 1984); R. Tiersky, *French Communism, 1920–1972* (New York, 1972); I. Wall, *French Communism in the Era of Stalin: The Quest for Unity and Integration* (Westport, Conn., 1983).

I. M. Wall

Related entries: COMMON PROGRAM; *CONFEDERATION GENERALE DU TRAVAIL*; ELECTIONS; FRACHON, BENOIT; MARCHAIS, GEORGES; MITTERRAND, FRANCOIS; POLITICAL TRENDS; ROCHET, WALDECK; SOCIALIST PARTY (PS); THOREZ, MAURICE; UNION OF THE LEFT.

FRENCH UNION, an association created under the constitution of the Fourth Republic (1946) to unite France and its former colonies. The association included the overseas departments and territories as well as the associated states and territories of Morocco, Tunisia, Indochina, Togo, and Cameroon. Black Africa representatives in the French Constitutional Assembly, including Lépold Senghor and Félix Houphouët-Boigny, accepted the creation of the French Union because they believed the narrow framework of this association would give them the opportunity to reach two goals: full legal equality and the recognition of a "Negro-African civilization," which would put an end to the pseudo-assimilation that had been the policy of the Third Republic.

The constitution brought about slow and rather insignificant modifications in the colonial situation. The attitude of the white settlers could not change quickly, and the laws that were to permit the application of the general principles written in the constitution were rather vague. It was only in 1956 that Gaston Defferre, minister of overseas France, helped by Houphouët-Boigny, then state minister in the French government and currently president of Ivory Coast, prepared the "*Loi-cadre*," which established the legal framework that could lead to administrative decentralization (universal suffrage, Africanization of the administration, and larger powers given to local assemblies). This was not yet independence, but for many in the French Union, such as the African member states, it was an irreversible step in that direction.

The collapse of the Fourth Republic in 1958 and its replacement by the Fifth brought General Charles de Gaulle back to power. The reemergence of de Gaulle and the end of the Fourth Republic were psychological shocks that prepared the way for the acceptance of new policies. Two years later twelve African states became independent and entered the United Nations. The French Union was a brief moment in the history of colonization, a transition of about twelve years between the colonial regime and the independence of black Africa. Its main function was to permit the granting of independence in a peaceful atmosphere and to avoid the type of bloody war fought in Indochina or Algeria.

P. Avril, G. Vincent, *La IVe République* (Paris, 1988); P. Williams, *Politics in Post-War France* (London, 1958).

J. Carduner

Related entries: CONSTITUTION OF THE FOURTH REPUBLIC; DE GAULLE, CHARLES; FOREIGN POLICY; INDOCHINA, RELATIONS WITH; MOROCCO, RELATIONS WITH; THIRD WORLD, RELATIONS WITH; TUNISIA, RELATIONS WITH.

FURET, FRANCOIS (1927–), French historian. He was born on March 27, 1927 in Paris. He studied at the *lycée Janson-de-Sailly* and the faculty of letters in Paris, taking the degree of *agrégé* in history. In his twenties Furet revolted against his middle-class background, becoming an active member of the French Communist party, but left the party after the suppression of the Hungarian uprising of 1956.

Furet's work has pulled the interpretation of the French Revolution away from the Marxist views that dominated academic historiography for sixty years. After 1917, French republican historians of the Revolution (the reigning academic school) began to see the French Revolution as prefiguring the Russian one. As Furet described this view in *Interpreting the French Revolution*, "the Bolsheviks had Jacobin ancestors, and the Jacobins anticipated the Communists." Furet maintains that the dominant extreme-left interpretation of the Revolution was not particularly that of Marx, who had not attempted a systematic analysis, but "the product of a confused meeting between Bolshevism and Jacobinism."

Part of Furet's work has been the rehabilitation in France of Alexis de Tocqueville, a figure revered in the United States but whose *The Old Regime and the Revolution* was little read and less understood in a France whose historians took sides either for or against the Revolution. His own history of the Revolution (with Denis Richet) appeared in 1965. In this, in his teaching at the *Ecole des hautes études en sciences sociales*, in much journalism, and in *Interpreting the French Revolution*, Furet—and with him the new school of nonleftist/nonrightist historians of this central event in modern French history—have in fact reinterpreted the Revolution and its tradition. French intellectuals have turned away from an uncritical and often adoring attitude toward revolutions of all descriptions, whatever their excesses. If in the bicentenary year 1989 it could be said that the Revolution was finally over, Furet and his school might claim some measure of credit for that.

F. Furet, *Interpreting the French Revolution*, trans. E. Forster (Cambridge and New York, 1981), *Marx and the French Revolution*, trans. D. K. Furet (Chicago, 1988); F. Furet; M. Ozouf, eds., *A Critical Dictionary of the French Revolution*, trans. A. Goldhammer (Cambridge, Mass., 1989); F. Furet, D. Richet, *The French Revolution*, trans. S. Hardman (New York, 1970).

J. W. Friend

Related entries: ANNALES SCHOOL; ARIES, PHILIPPE; LE ROY LADURIE, EMMANUEL; MARXISM.

G

GAILLARD, FELIX (1919–1970), radical-socialist deputy and penultimate prime minister of the Fourth Republic. Invested as premier on his thirty-eighth birthday in 1957, he was the youngest head of government since Napoleon. This was the crowning achievement of a meteoric political career that began eleven years earlier with Gaillard's election to parliament in 1946 and was cut short by the return to power of Charles de Gaulle in May of 1958.

Born in Paris on November 5, 1919 into a wealthy family with roots in the Charente cognac country, Gaillard had a brilliant academic career, earning a doctorate in law by the age of twenty. After the outbreak of World War II, he served briefly in the French army and then joined the Resistance, where he was a member of the underground finance committee. In examinations for appointment to the prestigious corps of *Inspecteurs des finances* in 1943, Gaillard took first place. The following year Jean Monnet named him his chief aide and took him to Washington for loan negotiations with American officials in December 1944. He later served Monnet as director of staff for the *Commissariat du plan*.

In 1946 Gaillard was elected to parliament as a radical-socialist deputy from the Charente, holding this seat until his death. For nearly a decade he served in junior ministerial posts, attaining ministerial rank for the first time in June 1957 when he entered the government of Maurice Bourgès-Maunoury as minister of financial and economic affairs. In this post he imposed orthodox financial measures that initiated a process of economic stabilization that would have its full flowering during the first years of the Fifth Republic. The Bourgès-Maunoury cabinet was overthrown after barely one hundred days in office on a proposal for limited home rule in Algeria. After a protracted parliamentary crisis that lasted thirty-seven days, Gaillard was able to form a government in November. Although he managed to secure passage of a watered-down version of his predecessor's home-rule bill, his ministry lasted less than six months. It was overthrown on April 15, 1958 in the wake of the international furor over the French aerial bombardment two months earlier of the Tunisian village Sakhiet that produced scores of fatalities.

The return of de Gaulle to power the following month effectively ended Gaillard's active political career, though in 1958 he assumed the presidency of the Radical-Socialist party, retaining that post until 1961. Thereafter he opposed the efforts of left-leaning radical-socialists to cooperate with the communists in forming an opposition united front. He was also a critic of the attempts by the controversial leader of the party in the mid–1960s, Jean-Jacques Servan-Schreiber, to give radical-socialists a revolutionary new image. By the time of his death in a yachting accident in July 1970, Gaillard had moved close to the Gaullist majority in parliament.

M. Candee, ed., *Current Biography Yearbook* (New York, 1958).

J. E. Reece

Related entries: BOURGES-MAUNOURY, MAURICE; RADICAL PARTY; SERVAN-SCHREIBER, JEAN-JACQUES.

GALLO, MAX (1932–), academician, writer, deputy in the European Parliament. Born on January 7, 1932 at Nice (Alpes-Maritimes) into a family of modest circumstances, he attended the local *lycée* and then studied at the *Faculté des lettres* and the *Institut d'études politiques* in Paris. The holder of doctorates in contemporary history and letters, he taught at the Nice *lycée* for five years and since 1965 has been an assistant lecturer at the *Faculté des lettres* at the University of Nice. A prolific writer, Gallo has published more than a score of historical studies and novels. He has also written extensively for the press and television and served as editor in chief of the daily newspaper *Matin de Paris* during 1985–86.

Gallo entered politics in June 1981 with his election to the National Assembly as a socialist deputy from Nice. He served in that body until 1983, resigning his seat in order to enter the government of Pierre Mauroy as secretary of state and official government spokesperson. His ministerial career was brief since President François Mitterrand replaced Mauroy with Laurent Fabius in July 1984. Gallo meanwhile had been elected the preceding month as deputy to the European Parliament, where he joined its socialist group and served as a member of the parliamentary committee on youth, culture, education, and sports. In 1988 he was named national secretary for cultural affairs of the French Socialist party.

M. Gallo, *La Troisième Alliance pour un nouvel individualisme* (Paris, 1984); *Who's Who in France, 1988–1989* (Paris, 1988).

J. E. Reece

Related entries: MAUROY, PIERRE; SOCIALIST PARTY (PS).

GARAUDY, ROGER (1913–), leading communist intellectual who broke with the party, eventually becoming France's most prestigious convert to Islam. Born in Marseille to a middle-class family whose income was lost when the father returned incapacitated from World War I, Garaudy owed his education to family sacrifices. *Agrégé* and *Docteur ès lettres* in philosophy, he taught in *lycées* and at the Universities of Clermont-Ferrand (1962–65) and Poitiers (1965–73).

Garaudy joined the French Communist party (PCF) in 1933 and, after war service that earned him the *Croix de guerre*, was arrested for clandestine activities in September 1940 and imprisoned in camps in North Africa until 1943. A leading (PCF) militant, he was deputy from the Tarn (1945–51) and from the Seine (1956–58), and senator from the same department (1959–62) as well as member of the PCF politburo (1956–70).

Garaudy blended Marxism with a Catholicism inspired by Maurice Blondel and created dialogues with left Catholics, encouraging the trends that became liberation theology. Garaudy distinguished between religion (which was alienating) and faith (which was not), and insisted that the kingdom of God, understood as both within this world and within history, was compatible with communism.

Garaudy broke with the PCF in 1970 over the events of 1968: the party's attitude to the student revolt and the Soviet invasion of Czechoslovakia. For the intellectual, the Soviet model was no longer adequate. The May revolt portended, in a confused way, the new revolution that would ally the middle classes and proletariat, and seek real workers' and technicians' control through decentralization supported by the computer revolution.

During the 1970s Garaudy extended his analysis to a crisis in Western civilization. Its unfettered productivism and will to power were leading to imminent destruction—nuclear or environmental. The causes were congenital defects in Western culture, notably the distinction between body and soul, spirit and matter of Plato, and the notion of mastery over nature expressed by Descartes. The solution lay in the reintroduction of truths cultivated by non-Western cultures, like the unity of being, consciousness, and the world expressed in Hinduism and Buddhism. Equally important was Zarathushtran and biblical "prophetism," both a moral exigency responding to social change and an affirmation of the ability to create the radically new, a freedom from the constraints of the "objectively" possible (the essence, for Garaudy, of the divine).

By 1981 Garaudy had turned to Islam. Not only did it combine faith with community, but its notion of divine unity (*tawhid*), according to Garaudy, prevented any sacralization of earthly power. The Islamic acceptance of earlier prophets (which Garaudy extended to non-Abrahamic religions) and Garaudy's conception of the Trinity as love (not paternity) permitted him to understand Islam as encompassing all his earlier positions.

R. Garaudy, *Appel aux vivants* (Paris, 1979), *Biographie du XXème siècle* (Paris, 1985), *Promesses de l'Islam* (Paris, 1981).

A. Douglas

Related entries: FRENCH COMMUNIST PARTY; MARCHAIS, GEORGES.

GAULLISM has been variously described as a set of beliefs, a state of mind, a program of action, and a way of thinking about France that differs from a systematic political doctrine or ideology. Born out of the experience of the Free French Resistance during World War II and often associated with the views and opinions of General Charles de Gaulle, Gaullism owes intellectual debts to currents of French nationalistic thought of the late nineteenth and early twentieth centuries and to elements of prewar, non-Marxist ideas of social reform. In his writings de Gaulle consistently referred to "a certain idea of France" as the foundation of his view of France and its place in the world. Certain key terms—*grandeur*, *authority*, *independence*, *resistance*, *unity*—provide guidance into Gaullism as a way of thinking about France. Gaullism also denotes a conception of relations between states in which national interests take precedence over ideological or other considerations.

In his memoirs and elsewhere de Gaulle insisted that France needed to stand in the front rank of the world's great nations and was not truly itself without a sense of greatness or *grandeur*, referring to a moral or cultural preeminence rather than to material strength. The notion of independence is closely tied to the Gaullist conception of grandeur, for only a fully independent state can offer its citizens true liberty. Associated with independence is Gaullist resistance to any external domination, whether the 1940 armistice that placed France under German control or a postwar imposition of an American hegemony in Western Europe. In Gaullist terms resistance means refusal to subordinate the interests of France. Finally, the state provides unity under a strong authority capable of defending national interests and providing stability and security to its people.

Gaullist nationalism seeks an escape from the divisions and debates over what is truly French by embracing the totality of French history, both the legacy of the Revolution and the traditions of the *ancien régime*. National interests precede personal or partisan ones. In this respect, Gaullism derives from Rousseau's conception of the general will. Political leadership comes from an individual or institution, such as a presidency, capable of rising above immediate, self-serving interest, and Gaullist political action emerges from a movement (*rassemblement* or rally) rather than the mediated interests of sectarian political parties. In style, the assertion of national interests involves deliberate confrontation with those whose interests differ from those of France, resulting in abrasiveness or intransigence as a characteristic of Gaullism, particularly in the realm of relations with other states. While often rigid and inflexible in defense of French interests, Gaullism also reflects a considerable degree of realism and pragmatism in the pursuit of those interests.

Gaullism contains elements of social responsibility that derive from aspects of Social Catholicism and nonconformist thought of the 1930s. The needs of society must be addressed no less than political interests. In this way Gaullism points toward social reconciliation rather than class conflict, and social unity becomes the touchstone of Gaullist views. This social dimension of Gaullism means that it cannot be readily placed on the right of a political spectrum.

In practice Gaullism has attracted diverse adherents and has found expression in the political institutions of the Fifth Republic. In its constitutional structure, the Gaullist state has established a balance of authority between parliament and the presidency. As to the Gaullists, three tendencies may be identified. There are the orthodox Gaullists, such as Michel Debré, Maurice Couve de Murville, or Pierre Messmer, who advocate a strong authority for the state, a firm commitment to an independent military and defense policy, and an opposition to compromise with centrists in domestic affairs. Liberal Gaullists, such as Jacques Chaban-Delmas or Olivier Guichard, tend to be less doctrinaire, are more progressive on social issues, and support French cooperation in the construction of a new Europe. Left Gaullists favor worker participation, and during the rigorous era of the Cold War they preferred a more neutral role for France. These differences within Gaullism became apparent following de Gaulle's resignation as president in 1969 and contributed to subsequent divisions and quarrels within the Gaullist ranks. Many Gaullists have deplored the tendency away from what might be termed a Gaullist mystique toward an attempt to create a Gaullist orthodoxy since 1970.

J. Charlot, *Histoire politique du gaullisme* (Paris, 1983); F.-G. Dreyfus, *De Gaulle et le gaullisme* (Paris, 1982); S. Hoffmann, section 3, ''De Gaulle,'' in *Decline or Renewal? France since the 1930s* (New York, 1974); J.-C. Petitfils, *Le Gaullisme*. 3d ed. (Paris, 1988); J. Touchard, *Le Gaullisme 1940–1969* (Paris, 1978).

J. K. Munholland

Related entries: CATHOLICISM; CHRISTIAN DEMOCRATS; CONSTITUTION OF THE FIFTH REPUBLIC; DEFENSE POLICY; DE GAULLE, CHARLES; FOREIGN POLICY; GAULLIST PARTY; INTELLECTUAL TRENDS; POLITICAL TRENDS.

GAULLIST PARTY, currently called the Rally for the Republic (RPR), created in 1976, but the movement has in fact a much longer history. The original Gaullist movement was the Gaullist Union, founded in July 1946 by René Capitant. This party, formed by a small band of persons eager to see General Charles de Gaulle carry on the leadership he had offered in forming and leading the Free French during World War II, won ten seats in the legislative elections of November 1946. It was, however, almost immediately superceded by a more ambitious organization, the Rally of the French People (*Rassemblement du peuple français*, RPF) formed by the general himself. The purpose of the RPF, according to de Gaulle, was to create a movement capable of rising above all the petty differences of opinion contained in individual parties and to make ''a great effort for the common good and a profound reform of the state.''

Although not intended to be a party, the RPF in fact soon became exactly that. Its principal themes were reform of the state, cooperation between employers and workers, hostility to German rearmament, maintaining the French Empire, and fighting communism. It was characterized by a highly disciplined and quasi-military form of organization. In the municipal elections of 1947 the party won 40 percent of the vote in towns of over nine thousand inhabitants and gained control of the thirteen largest cities in France. In the legislative elections of June 1951 it won 16.5 percent of the vote, taking 117 seats. This success, while impressive, was inadequate to force the dissolution of parliament and create the hoped-for constitutional reform. Furthermore, the RPF deputies soon showed themselves ready to play more traditional parliamentary party politics, and many voted for the investiture of prime ministers drawn from other parties. The party lost ground in the municipal elections of April 1953 and lost its chief in July 1955 when de Gaulle, disillusioned by its failure to resist the temptations of ordinary politics, announced his retirement from public life. In the legislative elections of January 1956 the party won only twenty-two seats.

The RPF was dying, but the Gaullist movement soon rose again in another form. In 1958, when dissenting military leaders refused to obey civilian rule and instead formed committees of public safety in Algiers, Oran, and Corsica, the still-loyal followers of the general were convinced that only he could save France from civil war. Others soon agreed and the Union for the New Republic (UNR) was formed from the remnants of the RPF and various other minor groups that had rallied to the leadership of General de Gaulle during the period of crisis. The UNR presented itself as the one movement selflessly dedicated to serving the general. It campaigned for the constitution establishing the Fifth Republic, for the election of de Gaulle as president, and for its own candidates in the first legislative election of the new regime (electing 198 of them). The comeback of the Gaullist movement was thus remarkable. However, de Gaulle, still stung by the failure of the RPF and not wishing to be beholden to any single party, formed a coalition government composed of representatives of several parties, including but not limited to the UNR. The general maintained his distance from the party throughout his presidency, and was emulated in this regard by his immediate successor, Georges Pompidou, to whom the party also gave its unqualified support. Nevertheless, throughout the terms of office of both men, members of the party held most of the key ministries in the French government.

In 1968, in response to the crisis provoked by student riots and a near general strike, the party changed its name to Union for the Defense of the Republic (UDR) and backed President de Gaulle and then Prime Minister Pompidou in their efforts, eventually successful, to negotiate a conclusion to *les événements*. In the legislative elections held that year, the party did better than ever before and won an absolute majority of seats in the National Assembly. In 1974, however, the UDR suffered its first serious defeat, as Valéry Giscard d'Estaing won the presidency; however, Giscard's victory had been partly engineered by UDR leader Jacques Chirac, who was then rewarded with the position of prime minister. Unhappy with the direction the Giscard presidency was taking, and with this role of prime minister, which proved to be extremely limited as the president relied more on close friends than on him, Chirac resigned in 1976, took the leadership of the UDR, and called for an elaborate reform of the party. It was in this 1976 reorganization of the party that it took its present name, Rally for the Republic.

The current Gaullist movement is one of the best-organized political parties in Europe, with an elaborate structure of local branches, departmental offices, and national headquarters. At every level there are numerous functional offices as well as the usual party secretary and staff. Youth, women, seniors, veterans, workers, businessmen, and teachers all have their special organizations within the party. The party claims to be democratically organized, because local party secretaries and executive committees are all elected. However, departmental secretaries are appointed from above, and they in turn appoint their own committees. Local leadership is normally co-opted, even though the party goes through the pro forma steps of an internal election. Furthermore, national headquarters maintains absolute power to decide candidacies for elective office, although it is true that such choices are almost always made in full consultation with the local constituencies.

At the national level, a large central committee meets rarely and normally endorses the decisions of a much smaller executive committee, which meets once a week and is completely dominated by the president of the party. The secretary-general of the party is always a trusted supporter of the president and operates under his or her guidance.

A key characteristic of party ideology is commitment to leadership. This means not simply allowing a leader to do what he or she wishes, but also engaging actively in carrying out the purposes of the leader. The RPR is a pragmatic party, interested above all in achieving power and keeping it. It is committed to certain principles as well: free enterprise, modernization, an important role for France in the world of nations, the maintenance of French independence, and respect for the institutions of the Fifth Republic. Its commitment to free enterprise was at first tempered by a strong tradition of *dirigisme*, but since the midseventies the RPR has become increasingly liberal in its stance on economic affairs, a tendency accelerated by the socialist victory in 1981 and by the near-mutinous insistence of younger leaders within the party that it move in that direction in the mid 1980's. The RPR has become increasingly pro-Europe in the past decade and is in this and other respects more and more difficult to distinguish ideologically from its rival and sometime coalition partner, the Union for French Democracy (UDF). Like the UDF, the RPR is plagued by internal dissent on the questions of how to handle the problem posed by a large immigrant population and the electoral competition of the far-right National Front, itself unashamedly anti-immigrant and racist.

The party is the second most important party (after the Socialist party) in France in terms of electoral support. It took only eighty-eight seats in the legislative elections of 1981, but gained sixty more in 1986, giving it, with its coalition partner the UDF, a very slim majority in the Assembly, returning Chirac to the prime ministership, and forcing France into two years of government divided between a leftist president (François Mitterrand) and a parliament located distinctly to the right. However, in the presidential elections of 1988, Chirac took only 46 percent of the vote (having made it into the runoff with only 20%), and in the subsequent legislative elections the party's candidates gained only a little more than 19 percent of the votes. The RPR was once again in opposition, although still second in rank among the parties of France. In 1990 the RPR and the UDF announced the formation of a confederation known as the *Union pour la France*. For the first time in French politics, the two parties will use primaries to select a single candidate to represent them in the presidential election in 1995.

J. Charlot, *Etude du pouvoir au sein d'un parti politique* (Paris, 1967); P. Crisol, J.-Y. Lhomeau, *La Machine RPR* (Paris, 1977); P. Habert, C. Ysmal, *Le Figaro/Etudes politiques, Elections législatives 1988* (Paris, 1988); K. Lawson, "The Impact of Party Reform on Party Systems: The Case of the RPR in France," *Comparative Politics* (July 1981); C. Ysmal, *Les Partis politiques sous la Vᵉ République* (Paris, 1989).

K. L. Lawson

Related entries: CAPITANT, RENE; CHABAN-DELMAS, JACQUES; *CO-HABITATION*; DE GAULLE, CHARLES; FOCCART, JACQUES; GAULLISM; MALRAUX, ANDRE; MESSMER, PIERRE; PALEWSKI, GASTON; PASQUA, CHARLES; POLITICAL TRENDS; POMPIDOU, GEORGES; PONIATOWSKI, MICHEL; SEGUIN, PHILIPPE; SOUSTELLE, JACQUES.

GENET, JEAN (1910–1986), moralist, poet, and avant-garde novelist and playwright. Much of Genet's early life is shrouded in mystery due to his early immersion in the criminal lower depths of society, prison life, and the secret world of pederasty and retributive myths. A ward of the National Foundling Society in Paris where he was born, Genet, illegitimate and abandoned by his mother, was raised by a simple peasant family at Le Morvan in the Massif Central. Here he lived an early, alienated double life: Beneath the mask of a docile, church-going model student he matured into an angry, deceptive outsider who transformed himself by dreams into a member of the royal family.

This inner rebellion led, by the age of ten, to a pattern of thefts, punishments, and pardons by his peasant family and friends. But in 1926 he was sent to the Mettray Reformatory in the Loire where he was exposed for the first time to gangs of hoodlums with whom he soon found adequate chances to prove his own powers of deception and sadism. Here it was, for three years, that he found consolation and revenge in the excitements of betrayal and homosexual intimacies. Finally, in 1929, like many of his fellow prisoners, he was allowed to join the French Foreign Legion. He deserted after a few days, choosing instead to wander over Europe as a beggar, smuggler, thief, and male prostitute until 1942, when he was arrested in France by the Vichy police for desertion and forging passports.

In Fresnes prison that year he wrote his first poems and *Our Lady of the Flowers*, which led Jean Cocteau to attempt to have him pardoned in 1943. Remarkable works followed in which he revealed his "tons of hatred" and deep involvement with myth and the condemnation of middle-class values. Led by Sartre, whom he met in 1944, literary and stage successes such as *Funeral Rites*, *Quarrel of Brest*, *Death Watch*, *The Maids*, and *The Thief's Journal* finally brought him a presidential pardon in 1948.

During the next two decades successful productions of plays such as *The Balcony* (1957), *The Blacks* (1959), and *The Screens* (1961) gave a greater degree of credibility to Sartre's sanctification of him in the two-volume *Saint Genet*, published in 1952 as the beginning of the publication of an edition of

Genet's complete works. But wealth from royalties only made the vagabond life easier for Genet's next two decades. In 1970 he toured the United States where he spoke in support of the imprisoned Black Panther leaders. He lent his name to the Palestinians and to the German anarchists in 1976, befriending their imprisoned leader Ulrike Meinhof.

Perhaps Genet summarized his life best in his posthumous work, *A Captive of Love*: "My life was thus composed of inconsequential gestures, inflated ever so subtly with audacious acts." Found dead of throat cancer in a hotel room in Morocco, he is buried in an abandoned Spanish Catholic cemetery next to many French colonists, whom he so detested.

P. Brooks, J.Halpern, eds., *Genet: A Collection of Critical Essays* (New York, 1979); B. L. Knapp, *Jean Genet* (Boston, 1989); J.-P. Sartre, *Saint Genet,* trans. B. Frechtman (New York, 1963).

M. Siegel

Related entries: LITERATURE; SARTRE, JEAN-PAUL.

GIROUD, FRANCOISE (1916–), journalist, film critic, and politician. Giroud (Gourdji) was born in Geneva on September 21, 1916. Her father was director of the Ottoman Telegraph Agency. She studied at the *Lycée Molière* and the *Collège de Groslay* in Paris before beginning her career as script girl for Marc Allégret and Jean Renoir, then working as an assistant director. In 1945 she became editorial director of *Elle* magazine, serving in that capacity until 1953 when she cofounded the weekly *L'Express* with Jean-Jacques Servan-Schreiber. She occupied various administrative positions with that magazine and the Express Group until 1974 when President Valéry Giscard d'Estaing appointed her secretary of state for the newly formed Secretariat for Women's Status. She held that position until 1976 when she was appointed secretary of state for culture under Raymond Barre's cabinet, a position she held until 1977. Since 1983 she has been on the editorial staff of the *Nouvel observateur*. With several friends she founded and presided over AICF (*Action internationale contre la faim*), a humanitarian organization for which she now serves as honorary president. She has received honorary degrees and distinctions, including one from the International Medicis Academy of Florence. Her works include: *Le Tout-Paris* (Paris, 1952); *La Nouvelle Vague, portrait de la jeunesse* (Paris, 1958); *Si je mens* (Paris, 1972); *La Comédie du pouvoir* (Paris, 1977); *Ce que je crois* (Paris, 1978); *Une Femme honorable* (Paris, 1981); *Marie Curie* (Paris, 1981); *Le Bon Plaisir* (Paris, 1982); *Alma Mahler* (Paris, 1988); and adaptations for the cinema.

F. Giroud, *Le Bon Plaisir* (Paris, 1982), *Ce que je crois* (Paris, 1978), *Si je mens* (Paris, 1972).

M. C. Weitz

Related entries: CINEMA; CULTURAL POLICY; GISCARD D'ESTAING, VALERY; WOMEN, CONDITION OF.

GISCARD D'ESTAING, VALERY (1926–), a civil servant who pursued a distinguished career as a politician, governmental official, minister of finance (1962–65; 1969–74), and president of the Fifth Republic (1974–81). A deputy at age twenty-eight, minister at thirty-five, and president at forty-eight, he compiled a record of accomplishment in public affairs conspicuous for its early success and long-range promise. In the eyes of many of his contemporaries, however, his tenure as president failed to meet expectations.

Born in Koblenz, Germany (where his father was an administrator with French forces of occupation in the Rhineland), he was descended from a family of cultivated provincial notables. His mother had distant ties with French royalty, while his father was a high official in the civil service. Hailing from a background of wealth, culture, and privilege, the young Giscard earned an exceptional record of academic achievement. From his entry into the *Lycée Janson-le-Sailly* to his graduation from the *Ecole polytechnique* and the newly created *Ecole nationale d'administration*, he ranked near the top of his class. Like his father, he entered the highly prestigious corps of the inspectorate of finance.

Giscard's first posting was to the *Banque de France*. But he soon made a hitherto rare transition from the administrative to the political side of government. Winning the notice of future prime minister Edgar Faure, he was invited to join the Ministry of Finance in 1950. During the 1950s he ascended through a succession of important posts in that ministry, culminating in his selection as minister of finance in the Faure government in 1962. His colleagues admired his competence and his masterful presentations of budgetary issues to the National Assembly.

Success confirmed Giscard's intuition that he was destined for high office. While climbing the echelons of the governmental ladder, he simultaneously embarked on a quest for elective office. In 1956 he won a seat in the National Assembly from the Puy-de-Dôme long held by his maternal grandfather. Over the following decade, he consolidated his political position by winning local elections in that department (departmental council, mayoralty of Chalmières). Like his grandfather, Giscard called himself an ''independent republican'' and affiliated with the tiny Independent and Peasant party (CNIP). But he voted with the larger Gaullist coalition, backing President Charles de Gaulle on the critical issues of independence for Algeria and the popular election of the presidency. Elegant in manner and eloquent in speech, he began to acquire a national following.

Giscard fell from Gaullist favor in 1965. As minister of finance, he had devised a program of fiscal austerity that contributed to de Gaulle's declining popularity, and so he was dismissed. He nonetheless used his retreat from government to lay the groundwork for his own bid for the presidency. He concentrated his political efforts in the National Assembly, where he worked to transform the Independent Republicans from a parliamentary caucus into a more effective political party. A practitioner of the new politics of image making, he used television to woo the electorate. Wonderfully articulate, he was able to project an image of leadership that blended informality, self-confidence, and intelligence. Although regarded by his colleagues as a moderate, he presented himself as a progressive who might transform France into what he characterized as an ''advanced liberal society.'' In his message as in his style, he provided a contrast to de Gaulle, by then viewed by the public as a cranky authoritarian. Tactfully, Giscard began to distance himself from de Gaulle's positions. Thus he weathered the years of loyal opposition of the late 1960s, his reputation intact and his popularity rising. He ingratiated himself with Georges Pompidou, the new president, who invited him to resume his former position as minister of finance (1969–74).

When Pompidou died in 1974, opinion polls revealed that Giscard was the most likely candidate among the moderates to fend off the bid of François Mitterrand, the socialist candidate of an emerging left-wing coalition, for the presidency. In the highly competitive election that followed, Giscard bested his opponents of right and center (Faure, Jacques Chaban-Delmas, and Pierre Messmer) on the first ballot (32.9%), and Mitterrand by a narrow margin on the second (50.7% to 49.3%).

In his early years as president, Giscard outlined his high-minded ambitions for France in the late twentieth century. Although elected by a constituency of the right and center, he formulated a left-leaning agenda. In his widely read book, *Démocratie française* (1976), he called for an alternative to the classical liberalism of the United States and the authoritarian Marxism of the Soviet Union. Giscard never spelled out what he had in mind with much precision. In general terms, he advocated the making of an open, pluralistic society with wider opportunities for all citizens. In specific terms, this translated into a number of enlightened political and social reforms. Among the most important were the extension of the franchise to eighteen-year-olds, liberalization of the divorce law, and legislation permitting abortion and the distribution of information about birth control. Through his education minister, René Haby, he sought to modernize the educational system. He also loosened restrictions on programming for state-sponsored radio and television, which had been tightly controlled during the Gaullist years. Giscard, however, had the misfortune to embark upon his presidency in an era of economic recession. The oil crises of 1973 and 1978 fueled inflation, obliging him to turn to a policy of economic austerity that dashed much of his reformist agenda and whittled away his popularity over the years.

In foreign affairs Giscard departed from Gaullist policy by promoting greater cultural and economic cooperation among the West European nations. He was instrumental in the formation of the European Economic Council, the annual meeting of the leaders of the nations participating in the Common Market. He also worked to implement the European monetary system. His cordial relations with West German chancellor Helmut Schmidt enabled him to deepen cultural ties between their countries. But in the face of the rivalry of the superpowers, Giscard followed the course set by his Gaullist predecessors by clinging to the notion of France as an independent force in world politics—a near-great if no longer a great power. He did little to ameliorate Franco-American relations, lukewarm since de Gaulle's days. He ignored the plight of President Jimmy Carter during the Iran hostage crisis (1979) and shunned Carter's request for a boycott of the Moscow Olympic Games (1980) as a protest against the Soviet invasion of Afghanistan. At the same time, he made overtures to Soviet leaders to improve diplomatic and economic relations. In Africa he held fast to de Gaulle's vision of a community of francophone people and pursued a policy of intervention in the affairs of nations that had once been French colonies.

As president, Giscard affected an easygoing, populist style. Fighting the criticism that he was personally aloof, he sought out informal contacts with the public, the most celebrated being his dinners with ordinary families. He continued to use the television effectively to share his ideas with the nation. His relaxed manner notwithstanding, Giscard had no compunctions about using his presidential powers forcefully. Like de Gaulle, he acted as his own policymaker. But unlike him, Giscard lacked the backing of a strong political party. As president, he hoped to build a broad-based centrist coalition of his own. His overtures to the left were rebuffed, however, while the Gaullist constituency that had elected him was alarmed by his social policies. His vigorous leadership riled Gaullist party leaders, particularly his own premier Jacques Chirac. Relations between the two worsened until Chirac resigned in 1976 and ran successfully for the newly created office of mayor of Paris. Resuscitating the Gaullist party (*Rassemblement pour la République*), Chirac used his office as a forum from which to criticize Giscard's policies, burdened by the deepening economic recession.

In the last years of his presidency, Giscard grew more discouraged and remote. He was disappointed in his inability to sustain interest in his progressive agenda or to win tolerance for the measures of economic austerity that he and his premier, Raymond Barre, deemed necessary. Scandals within his entourage also tarnished his regime. The rivalry of Gaullists and socialists in the legislative elections of 1978 managed to forestall a defeat for his government. Even so, Giscard was reconciled to sharing power with a premier of an opposition party (*cohabitation*), a situation that would have raised the ambiguous constitutional issue of the respective powers of president and premier.

Running a half-hearted race for re-election in 1981, Giscard was defeated by Mitterrand. Still young for a politician (fifty-five), he ignored the precedent of his predecessors, who typically had chosen genteel retirement. He returned to the National Assembly in 1984 and subsequently became involved in the regional council of his home province of the Auvergne. While no longer principal spokesperson for the opposition, he continued to play an important role in public life.

In his distinguished career Giscard reveals the ambiguity of liberalism redesigned in the late twentieth century. In his values he blended the old style of the Orleanist with the new style of the technocrat. Able and eloquent in the tradition of nineteenth-century liberals, he was a master of the complexities of economic management in the manner of their twentieth-century counterparts. Yet he failed in his ambition to mold public policy to his conception of what an advanced liberal society might be. Circumstances worked against him as president, but so too did the vagueness of his own political rhetoric. As a vision of the good society for the late twentieth century, Giscard's doctrine was never quite focused.

J. Ardagh, *France in the 1980s* (New York, 1982); L. Derfler, *President and Parliament* (Boca Raton, Fla., 1983); J. Frears, *France in the Giscard Presidency* (London, 1981), "Giscard d'Estaing," in *Biographical Dictionary of French Political Leaders since 1870*, ed. D. Bell et al. (New York, 1990); V. Giscard d'Estaing, *Démocratie française* (Paris, 1976).

P. H. Hutton

Related entries: BARRE, RAYMOND; BOKASSA AFFAIR; CHABAN-DELMAS, JACQUES; CHIRAC, JACQUES; *COHABITATION*; CONSTITUTION OF THE FIFTH REPUBLIC; DE GAULLE, CHARLES; FAURE, EDGAR; GAULLIST PARTY; MESSMER, PIERRE; MITTERRAND, FRANCOIS; NATIONAL CENTER OF INDEPENDENTS AND PEASANTS; PINAY, ANTOINE; POMPIDOU, GEORGES; PONIATOWSKI, MICHEL.

GOUIN, FELIX (1884–1977), socialist politician who served briefly as president of the provisional government of the French Republic after Charles de Gaulle's resignation from that post in January 1946. The son of middle-class schoolteachers from Provence, Gouin was born at Peypin (Bouches-du-Rhône). A scholarship student at the *lycée* of Marseille, he later studied law in nearby Aix-en-Provence and was admitted to its bar in 1907. He joined the Socialist party in 1904 and spent the next decade establishing himself as a successful, politically ambitious lawyer. Gouin volunteered for military service in 1914 and served throughout the war as a private, resuming his law practice in 1919. Five years later the voters of Aix sent him to the Chamber of Deputies where he aligned himself with the right-wing socialists. He was easily reelected to parliament in 1928, 1932, and 1936. Gouin's considerable parliamentary skills brought him to the leadership of the socialist group in the Chamber during Léon Blum's Popular Front government. Upon the outbreak of war in 1939, he was appointed chairman of a parliamentary oversight subcommittee on armaments and war production.

After the fall of France in June 1940, Gouin courageously refused to vote full powers to Marshal Pétain. He then joined the Resistance at Marseille. In the spring of 1942 he helped defend Léon Blum at the Vichy-instigated Riom trial. Gouin was subsequently designated socialist representative to the Gaullist Free French movement in London. Escaping to London via Spain in mid–1942, he joined de Gaulle's committee of national liberation. In September 1943 he accompanied the French Resistance leader to Algiers where in November he was elected president of the recently convened consultative assembly. Gouin remained in that post after de Gaulle transferred his provisional government to Paris following the liberation of the French capital in August 1944.

In October 1945 Gouin was sent by Marseille to the Constituent Assembly, where in November he was overwhelmingly elected its president. The high regard in which he was held by his colleagues was soon after confirmed when he was selected to succeed de Gaulle as head of France's provisional government. But

Gouin's cabinet was intended only as a transitional device to get France through the upcoming June 1946 parliamentary elections. His cabinet accordingly resigned immediately afterward, with Gouin entering the new ministry headed by Georges Bidault. He was also part of subsequent Blum and Ramadier cabinets. Meanwhile, his political career had been gravely damaged when in July 1946 he was accused of complicity in a wine procurement scandal. Although eventually exonerated of any wrongdoing, he never regained his political standing.

Gouin's Marseille constituents nevertheless continued to send him to the National Assembly throughout the life of the Fourth Republic. He formally retired from politics in 1958 and died in Nice two decades later at the age of ninety-two.

Current Biography Yearbook 1946 (New York, 1947); *Dictionnaire de biographie française*, vol. 16 (Paris, 1982).

J. E. Reece

Related entries: BLUM, LEON; SOCIALIST PARTY (SFIO).

GRANDES ECOLES, the elite branch of French higher education that prepares students for careers in applied science, business management, and public administration. Some three hundred schools lay claim to this status, although only a few dozen have a national and international reputation and bestow the prestige generally associated with the name. The most famous are the *Ecole polytechnique*, the *Ecole nationale d'administration* (ENA), the *Ecole normale supérieure*, and the *Ecole des hautes études commericales*. Although most of the *grandes écoles* are run by the state, they are not part of the university system. The *Polytechnique*, for example, is under the supervision of the Ministry of Defense rather than the Ministry of Education. All of the *grandes écoles* have considerably more autonomy than the universities, including setting the curriculum and selecting students.

The first of the *grandes écoles* were founded by the Old Régime monarchy to provide specialized military and technical training for government service. The prestigious *Ecole des mines*, founded in 1778, is one example. The Revolution and Napoleon favored the *grandes écoles* over the universities and founded new ones such as the *Ecole polytechnique* to train military engineers and the *Ecole normale supérieure* to train secondary-school teachers. In the nineteenth century the state established special schools to promote technical advances in agriculture and industry, such as schools of agronomy, chemistry, and mechanics. By the end of the nineteenth century, with the growth of big business, commercial education came to the fore. In 1881 the Paris Chamber of Commerce founded the *Ecole des hautes études commericales*. The *grandes écoles* have continued to multiply in the twentieth century, especially since World War II. Currently the most prestigious and sought-after school is the ENA, which was founded in 1945. More recent arrivals include the *Ecole nationale supérieure de l'électronique et de ses applications* founded in 1975, which specializes in electronics and telecommunications, and the *Centre météorologique Toulouse-Mirail* founded in 1982, which trains meteorologists.

The *grandes écoles* are small, averaging only four hundred students. Entry is by competitive examinations, which are extremely rigorous. Students who hope to attend one of these schools must first pass the *baccalauréat*, usually the mathematics and physics option. They must then be accepted into one of the special two- or three-year preparatory courses offered by only a few of the most elite *lycées*, such as the *Collège Louis Le Grand* in Paris. These courses are universally acknowledged to be far more demanding than students would face in university or even in the *grandes écoles* themselves. After completion of the course, applicants take the examination for the school of their choice; only about one in ten succeed.

The courses of study within the *grandes écoles* are generally two to three years long and oriented toward specific careers. Often the school is connected with a specific industry such as the *Ecole nationale supérieure de l'aéronautique et de l'espace* in Toulouse, which supplies scientists and engineers to the French aerospace industry. Students often spend part of their training in internships in industry or the civil service. Graduates are much in demand and have little difficulty finding prestigious and high-paying jobs. The *Polytechnique*, founded to train military engineers, now sends its graduates mainly to top-level management positions in industry and government. Graduates of the ENA move directly into the upper ranks of the civil service. The *grandes écoles* have also been a favorite route to a career in politics. In the Third and Fourth Republics, the *Ecole normale supérieure* was the most prestigious political credential; Jean Jaurès, Léon Blum, and Georges Pompidou were all *normaliens*. In recent years, the *Polytechnique* and ENA have gained in political clout; Valéry Giscard d'Estaing was a graduate of both. Jacques Chirac and Michel Rocard are both *énarques*, that is, graduates of ENA. Graduates of the *grandes écoles* maintain close ties all their lives and depend upon one another for advice and assistance.

The *grandes écoles* educate a small elite, graduating less than 100,000 students a year. The vast majority are from the upper-middle class, and their parents are often also *grandes écoles* graduates. The left has frequently criticized the *grandes écoles* and demanded their democratization, but the socialist ascendancy to power in 1981 has triggered no major reforms. There is general agreement that unlike the university system, which is constantly in crisis, the *grandes écoles* have performed well. They have provided and continue to provide the specialists and technocrats who are increasingly important in the postmodern age.

J.-L. Bodiguel, *Les Anciens Elèves de l'ENA* (Paris, 1978); H. D. Lewis, *The French Education System* (New York, 1985); B. Magliulo, *Les Grandes Ecoles* (Paris, 1982); J. Shinn, *L'Ecole polytechnique* (Paris, 1980).

M. H. Darrow

Related entry: EDUCATIONAL REFORM.

GREAT BRITAIN, RELATIONS WITH. Britain and France have found it possible to cooperate effectively on issues in which they share a sense of common external danger, but their fundamentally different understanding of their real positions during much of the postwar period has hindered other forms of co-operation. With their country weak and divided, the French sought strength and unity. Since 1945 French foreign policy has chiefly aimed to consolidate domestic political consensus, whether through the pursuit of material resources and security under the Fourth Republic, the pursuit of a policy of grandeur by Charles de Gaulle, or a combination of the two approaches by de Gaulle's successors. Britain emerged from the war numbering itself among the victors. In seeking to preserve this special status through the magnification of its relations with the Commonwealth and the United States, Britain long kept continental nations at a distance. When French and British paths occasionally crossed they were as often as not at odds.

A military alliance might have seemed a natural link between the two chief European democracies. The presence of communists in the Tripartite government delayed the forging of this link. The Dunkirk Treaty (March 1947) limited their joint commitments to repressing German aggression and organizing some sort of Europe between the superpowers. The intensification of the Cold War compelled greater cooperation. British foreign minister Ernest Bevin worked steadily during 1948 to encourage a Western union, based on Franco-British agreement, which would draw in American support against the Soviets. This mounting fear of the Soviet Union led to the Brussels Treaty (March 1948) and to the North Atlantic Treaty Organization (NATO, April 1949). Britain remained reluctant to commit much of its military manpower to a permanent garrison on the continent because this would limit its ability to project power outside of Europe in an emergency touching some part of its global interests. This hesitation bred French distrust of British intentions. France sought to guarantee its future security by a two-track policy of reconciliation with Germany on the basis of equality and international control of the immense productive power of the Ruhr.

Britain also refused to support actively closer integration after centrist and conservative parties returned to power on the continent. The predominance of advanced social policy, a concern for its status as a global power if it submerged itself in European union, and strong links to the non-European Commonwealth all worked to hold Britain back from the policy pursued across the Channel. With most British trade oriented outside of Europe, and feeling little enthusiasm for the supranational schemes proposed by continental governments, Britain met French suggestions of a European Coal and Steel Community with reserve, just as it had suggestions of a customs union and policy coordination. British belief that the talks would come to nothing proved mistaken; the same error occurred over the proposed European Economic Community (EEC). Soon afterward, French efforts to reconcile German rearmament with French security through a European army under strong supranational controls were torpedoed when Britain refused to participate and the proposed controls were largely removed in negotiation. Eventual grudging British agreement to maintain forces on the continent within the context of an expanded Western European Union provided an escape from this impasse but did not signal a fundamental improvement of relations between the two countries.

Egypt's nationalization of the Suez canal and Gamal Abdel Nasser's support for the Algerian rebels aligned British and French interests during 1956. Since public support for a strike against Nasser appeared much stronger in France than in Britain, the British insisted upon disguising their subornation of an Israeli attack upon Egypt as Western intervention in a local quarrel that threatened freedom of navigation. The initial military successes failed to compensate for the brutal pressure applied by the two superpowers. The most notable example of Anglo-French cooperation in the postwar period soon collapsed in failure.

De Gaulle's return to power in 1958 continued traditional lines of French policy within the changing international environment at the end of the immediate postwar era. The new president conceived of an active policy of enhancing France's international position as the means by which to unite the French in a common cause. This policy proved far more effective in its domestic purposes of reconciliation than it did in the external purpose. By the end of the 1950s Britons were becoming alarmed at their relative decline since World War II, especially in terms of a comparatively stagnant economy that robbed Britain of the resources needed to maintain its great-power status. Recognizing Britain's decline, Harold Macmillan tried to reorient its relations with other states by drawing closer to Europe without, however, abandoning the special tie to the United States.

De Gaulle regarded too close a reliance upon the Americans as debilitating and desired to lead the European states toward a greater independence. Since Britain desired a close association with the United States as a means of buttressing its position in world affairs, de Gaulle distrusted Macmillan's belated conversion to a "European" position in 1961. He saw in Britain a Trojan horse for the perpetuation of American ascendancy. France and Britain also differed on how to divide up European agricultural markets and over cooperation on nuclear weapons. The French feared that cheap Commonwealth food imports and subsidized British food would hold down British labor costs to such an extent that French manufacturers could not compete, even as French farmers were also undercut. Macmillan's decision at the Nassau Conference with President John F. Kennedy (December 1962) to depend on the Americans to preserve Britain as a nuclear power finally decided de Gaulle. He twice rejected British application for membership in the EEC on the grounds that Britain showed an insufficiently European orientation (January 1963, November 1967).

In the later 1960s foreign policy reverses—China's rejection of a special connection with France, a financial crisis in the aftermath of May 1968, the humbling visit of Richard Nixon to Paris, and French acceptance of American nuclear doctrines—all seemed to indicate that de Gaulle's independent course had failed. Suffering from a stagnant economy, Britain also cut many of its international pretensions in 1967. By the early 1970s it began to seem that closer cooperation on defense issues would be possible between Britain and France.

As British interest in the Common Market revived, de Gaulle gave way to Georges Pompidou, who then found it expedient to accept British membership as a counterweight to the growth of German economic power. Britain finally joined the EEC in January 1973. After Pompidou's death, Valéry Giscard d'Estaing concentrated upon drawing the maximum profit from the EEC through benefits for French farmers and obstructing budget reform at the expense of Britain.

The socialist government that took power in 1981 expressed a deeper commitment to fostering European cooperation than had its predecessor, but had to deal with Prime Minister Margaret Thatcher's dislike of European solutions. Resolution of her demands for reform of EEC financing practices in 1984 failed to improve markedly what remains a troubled relationship. The survival of differing national perspectives in two of the chief Western European states indicates the difficult obstacles that will remain to be overcome in the European union after 1992.

C. J. Bartlett, *A History of Postwar Britain, 1945–1974* (London, 1977); P. Cerny, *The Politics of Grandeur: Ideological Aspects of de Gaulle's Foreign Policy* (Cambridge, 1980); M. Larkin, *France since the Popular Front* (Oxford, 1986); N. Waites, ed., *Troubled Neighbors* (London, 1970).

J. S. Hill

Related entries: DEFENSE POLICY; DE GAULLE, CHARLES; EUROPEAN DEFENSE COMMUNITY; EUROPEAN ECONOMIC COMMUNITY, RELATIONS WITH; FOREIGN POLICY; SCHUMAN PLAN; SUEZ CRISIS; UNITED STATES, RELATIONS WITH; WESTERN EUROPEAN UNION.

GREENPEACE AFFAIR, a political and military scandal involving the French government and the environmental organization Greenpeace. Late in the evening on July 10, 1985, two bombs that had been placed by frogmen on the hull of the Greenpeace flagship *Rainbow Warrior* tore huge holes in the vessel's side and sent it to the bottom of Auckland harbor. A Portuguese photographer, Fernando Pereira, died in the attack. The *Rainbow Warrior* had been preparing to leave New Zealand for a protest campaign around the French nuclear testing ground at Mururoa Atoll in Polynesia.

Within a week, New Zealand police had arrested two French secret service agents, Major Alain Mafart and Captain Dominique Prieur, who were masquerading as Swiss tourists under the false name of Turenge. For several weeks the "Turenges" protested their innocence and succeeded in concealing their true identities. The French government strenuously denied all knowledge of or involvement in the affair. On August 7, 1985, however, two French weekly magazines, *VSD* and *L'Evénement*, reported that the couple were in fact agents of the *Direction générale de la sécurité extérieure* (DGSE). A beleaguered President François Mitterrand instructed Prime Minister Laurent Fabius to instigate an official inquiry, and a venerable Gaullist counselor of state, Bernard Tricot, was wheeled in to oblige.

The Tricot report, published on August 26, while admitting that two teams of French agents had been in New Zealand to keep tabs on Greenpeace, effectively exculpated the DGSE and the government from direct involvement in the bombing. The report was met with universal skepticism. Its findings were directly challenged by the investigative journalism of *Le Monde*, and in particular by its special reporter Edwy Plenel who, on September 17, revealed the existence of a third team of DGSE agents, this time involving explosives experts and frogmen trained at a special base in Corsica.

The only question that remained was to establish how far up the chain of command the finger of responsibility would point. The president and the prime minister, whom over 50 percent of French people believed to have been involved, were spared by the sacking of the defense minister, Charles Hernu, and the head of the DGSE, Admiral Pierre Lacoste. In November 1985 the two arrested agents were each sentenced to ten years imprisonment, a fate that was subsequently commuted, after intense diplomatic and commercial bargaining between Paris and Wellington, to three years' ''exile'' on a French South Pacific atoll. Prime Minister Jacques Chirac subsequently reneged even on this deal by repatriating both agents in an attempt to reap electoral mileage. The final act of the Greenpeace affair was played out in May 1990 when France, which had already paid compensation to Greenpeace, was formally condemned by an international tribunal to contribute $2 million to a fund to improve relations with New Zealand.

J. Derogy, J. M. Pontaut, *Enquête sur trois secrets d'état*, (Paris, 1986); J. Dyson, *Sink the Rainbow* (London, 1986); R. Shears, I. Gidley, *The Rainbow Warrior Affair* (London, 1986).

J. Howorth

Related entries: FABIUS, LAURENT; HERNU, CHARLES; MITTERRAND, FRANCOIS.

H

HALIMI, GISELE (1927–   ), lawyer and feminist. Born in Tunisia where she was a brilliant high school student, she went to Paris to study philosophy, political science, and law. Halimi became a lawyer in 1948 and passed the Paris Bar exam in 1956. She became identified with the war of decolonization and more generally with the politics of the left. She was the principal lawyer for the National Liberation Front of Algeria and caught the attention of the public by her passionate defense of the Algerian cause. She published her first book, *Djamila Boupacha* (1962), about a young Algerian woman she had defended during a well-publicized trial. Her book was a strong attack on the use of torture by the French army in Algeria.

Halimi is also a noted leader of the women's liberation movement in France. After the end of the war in Algeria, she directed her energy toward the promotion of birth control and the legalization of abortion. In 1973 she published *The Cause of Women* and in 1978 *The Common Program of Women*, a work whose title echoed the Common Program of the left signed earlier by the communist Georges Marchais and the socialist François Mitterrand and that represented a giant step toward the political triumph of Mitterrand in the 1981 presidential election.

She ran for election to the National Assembly in 1981 in the department of Isère and became a member of the huge socialist majority that governed France from 1981 to 1986. Halimi resigned in 1984 in order to become ambassador and permanent delegate of France at UNESCO. In this capacity she became a controversial figure during a difficult period in the life of the UNESCO (the United States had just withdrawn from the organization and a year later Britain followed). Halimi was seen by the Western allies of France as a vocal if somewhat clumsy supporter of the Third World, and for a while their relations with France were rather cool. Eventually the controversial director general of UNESCO, Amadou Mahtar M'Bow, was replaced and the situation improved. In 1986 Halimi returned to private practice. She remains an ardent advocate of feminism and a vigorous enemy of racism.

G. Halimi et Choisir, *Quel président pour les femmes?* (Paris, 1981).

J. Carduner

Related entries: ALGERIA, RELATIONS WITH; FEMINISM; IMMIGRANTS; WOMEN, CONDITION OF.

HERNU, CHARLES (1923–1990), journalist, socialist politician, minister of defense. Hernu was born in Quimper, the son of a former army volunteer who subsequently became a gendarme. In 1943, ignoring a Vichy summons to report for compulsory labor, Hernu joined the Resistance and finished the war with the First Army in its drive to Cologne. His early life thus predestined him to achieve what was to become the crowning fulfillment of his career: the reconciliation of the French army with the Socialist party.

In postwar Lyon, Hernu embarked on a journalistic career while throwing himself into radical politics by way of the *Club des Jacobins* of which he rapidly became a leading light. An ardent supporter of Pierre Mendès-France, he was elected in the Seine department for the *Front républicain* as the youngest deputy in the 1956 parliament. Convinced that the pursuit of a military solution in Algeria was doomed, Hernu's first contact with François Mitterrand came, ironically, in an article in *Le Monde* calling on Guy Mollet's minister of justice to resign.

The two men subsequently made their peace in opposition to de Gaulle. Hernu, after a brief sojourn in the Unified Socialist party (PSU), became one of Mitterrand's closest and most loyal supporters. Having lost his parliamentary seat in 1958, it was not until 1978 that he was reelected, this time for Villeurbanne, the city of his early youth, of which he had become mayor in 1977.

Throughout his political career, Hernu specialized in defense and security issues. He deplored the divorce between the army and the nation that had begun with the colonial wars and had been exacerbated by de Gaulle's nuclear elitism. He deplored in equal measure what he called the "strange intellectual paralysis" afflicting the Socialist party's (SFIO) attempts, in its dying years, to come to grips with the problem of national defense. Hernu, more than any other socialist, waged a relentless campaign within the Mitterrand entourage and subsequently within the Socialist party to elaborate a left-wing nuclear defense policy. Confident, from as early as 1969, that Mitterrand himself had "converted" to the politics of deterrence, Hernu finally succeeded, at a special party conference in 1978, in aligning socialist (PS) defense policy with "Gaullism."

In parallel with his propaganda within the Socialist party, Hernu also sought to foster links with left-leaning military officers. After the events in Chile in 1974, he founded the *Conventions pour l'armée nouvelle*, whose objective was to revitalize the spirit of Jean Jaurès in late twentieth-century mode and to ensure that, whenever the left did come to power, significant sections of the officer class would support the new government.

This long-term strategy paid off handsomely when Hernu was appointed minister of defense on May 22, 1981. In that office he ensured perfect continuity with existing defense policy, presiding over a massive program of nuclear weapons' modernization, reasserting on every occasion the independence of French military options and waging a relentless campaign to maintain the level of the military budget. At the same time he fostered Franco-German defense cooperation and made major strides toward the development of a European security system.

His style was flamboyant and pugilistic, his forte the impromptu visit, in full battle dress, to French forces throughout the world. For *Le Monde's* cartoonist, Plantu, Hernu was the archetypal paratrooper, ever ready to take on anybody who dared utter a word against any aspect of a defense policy now enjoying the support of a broad national consensus. His confidence that, at the end of the day, the requirements of national defense were answerable to nobody became his undoing. Whether or not Hernu himself gave the order for the sinking of the Greenpeace vessel *Rainbow Warrior* in Auckland harbor in July 1985, the archives may one day tell. It was this incident that finally led to Hernu's resignation on September 20, 1985. For some he became a national hero and, in semiretirement, was even touted as a potential presidential candidate. He continued as an active mayor of Villeurbanne until his death of a heart attack on January 17, 1990.

C. Hernu, *Défendre la paix* (Paris, 1985), *Soldat-Citoyen* (Paris, 1975); J. Howorth, P. Chilton, eds., *Defence and Dissent in Contemporary France* (London, 1984); P. Krop, *Les Socialistes et l'armée* (Paris, 1983).

J. Howorth

Related entries: DEFENSE POLICY; GREENPEACE AFFAIR.

HERRIOT, EDOUARD (1872–1957), a leading radical-socialist politician during the Third Republic. He had a significant, if negative, impact on the formation and first decade of the Fourth Republic. Herriot began his political career in 1905 as mayor of Lyon, a position he retained until his death except for a brief interruption during the Vichy regime. In the interwar years he served twice as premier, heading fragile electoral and parliamentary coalitions of radical-socialists and socialists. From 1919 to 1935 he was annually elected as president of the Radical-Socialist party. In 1936 the beleaguered Chamber of Deputies elected him president, a post from which he officiated over the demise of the Third Republic in July 1940. By then Herriot was regarded as the personification of the dominant Radical Party: committed to the parliamentary system, defender of provincial small property owners, wary of social and economic change, and unable to resolve the economic and diplomatic crises of the 1930s.

In the first months following the 1944 liberation from German occupation, Herriot seemed a relic of a thoroughly repudiated regime. Not only was he intimately associated with the defeated Third Republic, but also his stance from 1940 to 1944 was sharply criticized by many Resistance veterans. Herriot had abstained on the decision to dissolve the National Assembly in July 1940. While he protested Vichy policies, he refused to join the Resistance whose resort to "illegality" he rejected. From 1942 to 1944 he was placed under house arrest. At the end of the war he participated in discussions organized by a desperate Pierre Laval about the revival of the Third Republic under U.S. patronage. The Germans cut these short and deported Herriot to a sanatorium outside Berlin.

In the spring of 1945 the seventy-three-year-old politically isolated Herriot embarked on a series of apparently futile efforts: to preserve the Third Republic, to revive an almost defunct Radical party, and to curb General Charles de Gaulle's power. He consciously set out to act as a brake against precipitous change in postwar France. From his perspective, the new political forces threatened individual liberties and republican traditions. By 1950 Herriot's aims had at least been partially realized. This success was less the result of his personal intervention than the conjuncture of postwar developments and his powerful presence as a symbol of the past.

The marginal Radical party had called for the repudiation of both drafts of the new constitution in 1946, joining more powerful opponents, first the Christian democrats (MRP) and then the Gaullists. While not replicating the Third Republic as Herriot wished, the institutions of the Fourth Republic resembled their predecessor more than anything else. Herriot himself was elected to both constituent assemblies and then to the National Assembly. By the end of 1946 Herriot was a key parliamentary leader of a group of seventy deputies, forty-five of whom were radicals and the rest allied liberals to their right. This unanticipated revival of Herriot and radicalism was recognized in Herriot's election to his old position as president of the National Assembly in January 1947, marking a return to prewar party politics. Further amplifying his image as the symbol of traditional republicanism, Herriot was elected to the *Académie française* for his work on literary criticism in June 1947. His prestige within the Radical party became increasingly impregnable; elected as president in 1945, he held the post until his death. In the 1950s the elderly and ailing Herriot combined the prestige and importance of his positions as mayor of Lyon, parliamentary leader, president of the Assembly, and head of the Radical party to serve as mentor of the new regime, tying the Fourth Republic to the past.

However, Herriot's efforts to maintain the ideology and the political structure of prewar France were fraught with contradictions. The electoral viability of the radicals depended on alliances with politicians to their right and increasingly with the Gaullists. Personally and politically opposed to de Gaulle's ambitions, Herriot urged the Radical party to disassociate from Gaullism in 1951, thus weakening the party's electoral position and provoking a split among radicals. Four years later in one of his last speeches to the Radical party, Herriot endorsed Pierre Mendès-France, leader of the party's left wing, preparing the way for yet another damaging split of the Radical party in 1957. As with the Third Republic, the parliamentary system of the Fourth, with its fragile coalition governments, was unable to respond to complex economic and international crises. Herriot's bitter opposition to the rearmament of West Germany contributed to the failure of a supra-European defense organization, but West German rearmament occurred nonetheless under the auspices of NATO. His persistent support of French colonialism and particularly the interests of French colonists in North Africa foreshadowed the radicals' inability to deal with the Algerian crisis. At the time of his death, March 1957, both the Radical party and the Fourth Republic were on the brink of dissolution.

S. Berstein, *Edouard Herriot ou la République en personne* (Paris, 1985); E. Herriot,

Jadis, 2 vols. (Paris, 1948); S. Jessner, *Edouard Herriot, Patriarch of the Republic* (New York, 1974); M. Soulié, *La Vie politique d'Edouard Herriot* (Paris, 1962).

J. F. Stone

Related entries: CONSTITUTION OF THE FOURTH REPUBLIC; ELECTORAL SYSTEM; EUROPEAN DEFENSE COMMUNITY; RADICAL PARTY.

HERSANT, ROBERT (1920–), a controversial right-wing politician and newspaperman whose press group owns, among many others, the influential right-wing daily *Le Figaro*. A leading political figure now largely associated with Jacques Chirac and the conservative Rally for the Republic (RPR), Hersant owes his fame (some would call it infamy) to his press empire. By 1986, after fifteen years of aggressive buyouts and legally questionable takeovers, the Hersant group controlled nineteen news dailies, five news weeklies, more than a dozen leisure magazines, eleven radio stations, a press service, an advertising agency, and the largest share of the newly privatized television station *La Cinq* (TV5). The percentage of the total French newspaper market that Hersant controls today is greater than that controlled by any press group in any Western democracy, leading some to nominate Hersant as "the most powerful man in France."

Hersant has been at the center of controversy since the late 1930s, when he joined a number of groups sympathetic to fascist causes. During the war, he led a German-sponsored, collaborationist, and anti-Semitic youth corps, and was accused of extorting the property of Parisian Jews and of managing an extensive black-market ring. When the war ended, Hersant was convicted of collaboration and sent to prison, but was released in the general amnesty of 1952. In 1956 he was elected deputy from Oise. That election was invalidated by his colleagues in the Assembly on the basis of his wartime activities, but his constituency refused to turn him out, and he retook the seat in the subsequent election. He has served as a deputy, except for brief periods, ever since.

By the late 1950s Hersant had amassed a fortune publishing automobile magazines and managing his own advertising agencies. Beginning in the early 1970s he turned his sights on general-interest news weeklies and dailies. From 1971 to 1978, aided by Chirac and former banking associates of Georges Pompidou in charge of state-controlled banks, his holding company was able to acquire a number of important regional papers, including *Paris-Normandie*, and the national dailies *Le Figaro*, *l'Aurore*, and the paper with the largest circulation in France, *France-soir*. Once under his control, these papers' staffs were purged and then replaced by editors and writers who shared Hersant's political beliefs: support of a law-and-order agenda, the free market, and virulent animosity toward the Giscardien center as well as the left. The pattern established during these years—of takeover, purge, and ideological reorientation—was replicated after other newspaper acquisitions.

Hersant and his press empire were at the center of a nearly continuous legal battle from 1975 to 1986. The group's acquisitions had certainly violated French antitrust laws governing the press sector, but the fluidity and the complexity of the ownership and management structure, which Hersant had purposely erected to disguise his ownership and control, succeeded in forcing lengthy delays. Indeed, because Hersant rotated ownership among friends, employees, and family members in dummy corporations, and because Hersant refused to cooperate with the authorities, it took one court nearly three years of investigation simply to prove that he was the legal owner of three papers in Lyon and Grenoble.

In 1983, after two years of what *Le Monde* called the Hersant group's "systematic political obstruction," the socialist government of Pierre Mauroy introduced legislation that would have in effect dismantled the Hersant group. In October 1984 the Constitutional Council struck from the bill those provisions that would have applied to Hersant, ruling that the bill's antitrust provisions could only apply to future acquisitions. In January 1986 Hersant acquired *Le Progrès* of Lyon, France's fifth largest newspaper, violating a number of provisions in the 1984 legislation. "Sometimes," he wrote in *Le Figaro* the next day, "in order not to be late for the war [a reference to the 1986 elections], it is better to be in advance of a law." The Chirac government abrogated the 1984 press law a few months later in a bill that many characterized, not unfairly, as a "Hersant amnesty bill." For the foreseeable future, at least, there is virtually no likelihood that Hersant's dominance of the print medium will be challenged, and his influence in the newly decentralized audiovisual communications industry will almost certainly be extended.

N. Brimo, *Le Dossier Hersant* (Paris, 1977); *L'Evénement du jeudi* (special issue on Hersant, February 13–19, 1986); D. Pons, *Dossier H . . . comme Hersant* (Paris, 1977).

A. Stone

Related entry: PRESS.

I

IMMIGRANTS, called to join the work force of industrialized France for over a century, have played a significant role in this nation traditionally plagued by a chronic low birthrate and wartime attrition. In the early 1950s France experienced rapid economic growth, which required an influx of foreign manpower similar to that of the 1920s, when workers from Belgium, Italy, and Poland comprised up to 7 percent of the French population. In the following forty years the fate of the immigrants on French soil was closely allied to the ups and downs of French industry and to the attention they received from the French government.

In 1945 the French government broke the monopoly exercised by the heads of industry in recruiting foreign workers by creating the National Immigration Office (ONI). Foreseeing the coming economic prosperity, it wanted to bring some control over hiring practices, and used immigration as a powerful tool in foreign policy.

From 1945 to 1960 the first wave of foreign workers came mostly from other European countries where the economic recovery was slow to arrive. The national census reported 1.8 million aliens in 1954. Italy, Spain, and Poland contributed the biggest share (61.5%), followed by Belgium, Germany, Portugal, and Yugoslavia. Only 13 percent came from Africa (including 12% from Algeria), and some 5 percent from Asia and the Americas. The immigrants, who came with their families, blended rapidly with the French population, but the great majority went back home after two or three years in the French work force.

After 1962 the number of European immigrants decreased as the economic recovery in their countries demanded more hands. Only the Portuguese continued moving to France in great numbers. By 1975 this group had become the largest, with 758,900 persons. The year 1982 found nearly 92 percent of them still residing in France and holding jobs as skilled or specialized workers. Encouraged by their government to emigrate but keep close financial ties with their homeland, many plan to retire there. Their children, born and/or raised in France, have integrated easily into French society, often marrying French nationals. Other nationalities have not fared so well.

Moreover, after 1962 the French government, wishing to strengthen its ties with the former colonies, signed agreements (especially with Algeria) that facilitated the immigration process. Allowed to bypass the ONI, the *Office algérien de la main-d'oeuvre* (ONAMO) sent close to thirty-five thousand workers to France annually until 1973. This practice fostered a large number of illegal entries, which in the short term benefited French industries, which enjoyed the hiring and firing flexibility. The Algerian immigrants would work for two to three years in France, then be replaced by others, equally reluctant or ill-prepared to integrate into French society, which treated them like outcasts. Fearing that this source of unhappy working hands would soon dry up, the French government began inviting their families to settle in France, thus offering more incentives to prospective foreign workers. These policies led to a drastic change in the profile of the alien population. Of the 3.7 million foreigners reported in 1973, more than one million had come from North Africa alone, eighty-two thousand from black Africa, and fifty-one thousand from Turkey. Seventy percent of them were male, 90 percent were in the work force, 70 percent were under thirty-five years old, and close to 90 percent were blue-collar workers. They were also locked into jobs requiring little or no qualifications. All were particularly vulnerable to economic fluctuations.

The economic recession due to the oil crisis of 1973 curtailed the need for imported labor, and in July 1974 President Valéry Giscard d'Estaing officially closed the French borders to new immigrants (with some provisions for political asylum and the regrouping of families). Illegal entries were curbed by stiffer laws, and serious efforts, including financial incentives, were made to encourage foreign workers to return to their home countries. But the attempt was not successful, as few North and West Africans took the opportunity to leave, not only because they were hoping for better times, but also because their families were, by now, very much settled in France. Moreover, their return to their former countries, which were faced with failing economies and fast-growing populations, offered less hope than staying in France, even if unemployed. Thus the number of immigrants has remained at close to four million. The alarming rate of unemployment and the concentration of immigrants in the depressed areas has led to strong and sometimes violent hostility on the part of the French working class, who resent the growing number of Muslims born on French soil.

By 1982 it became clear that the recession affected foreign workers most: 14 percent (22% for the Algerians) were unemployed compared to 8.4 percent for the French. They held jobs in the most severely affected industries (steel, automotive, construction) and had no flexibility due to their lack of skills. Unnoticed, but foreseeable, xenophobia had crept from the workplace into the political arena: Faced by a worsening employment picture and mounting pressure from its electors, who saw the immigrants as responsible for the economic and social crisis and the increasing crime rate, the French government, under Prime Minister Jacques Chirac, in 1984 implemented measures designed to facilitate the deportation of illegal aliens. Furthermore, in 1986 Justice Minister Albin Chalandon proposed (but failed) to modify the naturalization laws (*code de la nationalité*) to make naturalization more difficult. A decade of dramatic unemployment figures finally forced the French government and its citizenry to face up to the impact of the non-European immigrants in the workplace and on French society as a whole.

A current of strong xenophobia (often mixed with overt racism aimed especially at the North Africans) found its speaker in Jean-Marie Le Pen, head of a rightist party, the *Front national*. The meteoric success of his political career took him to the presidential primaries in 1988 and his racist rhetoric shocked many French on the eve of the Bicentennial and the celebration of the *Droits de l'homme et du citoyen*. It was no surprise to the immigrants, who cannot yet fit into the mainstream due to difficulties that are grounded in their cultural differences—a difference the French are not ready to accept, and that the immigrants are not always willing or able to forget.

The immigrants came to France to work, to join a family member, or to find political asylum. Their profile is very different from that of the French. They have a very high working rate (56% compared to 44% for the French), with 1.5 to 1.7 million people employed or seeking employment (in 1987), and women, except for North Africans, are enrolled in the work force in higher numbers. The male to female ratio is reversed: 61.5 percent are male compared to 48 percent among the French. The immigrants are younger: They have a much higher birthrate (3.1 compared to 1.8 for the French), and few individuals have yet reached the retirement age (when they do, they often choose to return home with their pensions).

Immigrants make up the lower working class: 77 percent are blue-collar workers (40% unskilled), compared with 37 percent for the French. The majority of them work in building and road construction; a somewhat smaller group holds jobs in automotive, rubber, plastic, and textile industries. The women hold low-paying jobs in nursing, housekeeping, the garment industry, commercial and custodial services. They are mostly hired in small- or medium-size companies, which offer lower salaries and fewer social benefits, and where unionization is very low. More docile in the workplace, immigrants are also the first to lose their jobs in an economic crunch. Particularly vulnerable are the young (sixteen to twenty-five years old) non-European workers; in the late 1980s 35 percent of them were jobless and their rate of unemployment was 10 percent higher than for their French counterparts.

The immigrants are concentrated in large urban, industrial settings: Until the last few years, more than half of them lived in Paris and its immediate suburbs, making up almost 14 percent of the city's population. Many favor Marseille and the Mediterranean coast, the Rhône valley, the Jura, Alsace and Lorraine. Others reside in the North-Pas de Calais, in Haute-Normandie, and Champagne, where large industrial parks are located. Recently, a growing number of immigrants have accepted work in the west and in rural areas, where smaller companies offer a variety of jobs, but still few secure positions. Nonetheless, a deconcentration of the foreign population may alleviate the feeling shared by many French of being overrun in their own country by immigrants whose parents fought France in their war for independence.

Improvements in the socioeconomic status of immigrants may not lead to better integration, as cultural habits, customs, and religious beliefs (Islam is today the second religion in France, with 4 million followers) create a gulf and presage social unrest. But two factors may calm the xenophobic feelings of the French population and lead to a more harmonious society: A slow but definite economic recovery in France, with the creation of more jobs in the western regions, is under way; and the coming-of-age of a new group of vocal electors, the children of the immigrants or the *Beurs* (a friendly slang word for French-born Arabs). They are French, they have rallied around *SOS Racisme*, they publish novels and essays on their life experience, and many are successful. They want to be recognized for their achievements as well as their specific needs. They want to be part of France's future, fully integrated but not assimilated; they see value in their differences; they long for a pluralistic society that will give to each a chance to bloom. The immigrants have worked at making France a rich, industrial country; they now want it to become a more diverse, more generous society.

A. Begag, *Le Gone du Chaaba* (Paris, 1986); H. Désir, *Touche pas à mon pote* (Paris, 1985); F. Gaspard, C. Servan-Schreiber, *La Fin des immigrés* (Paris, 1984); P. George, *L'Immigration en France, faits et problèmes* (Paris, 1986); *INSEE, Données sociales* (Paris, 1978, 1981, 1987); M. Verdie, ed., *L'Etat de la France et de ses habitants* (Paris, 1989).

L. J. Haenlin

Related entries: ALGERIA, RELATIONS WITH; DEMONSTRATIONS; LABOR FORCE; LE PEN, JEAN-MARIE; MINORITIES, PROBLEMS OF; NATIONALITY CODE; PARIS REGION; POPULATION TRENDS; *SOS RACISME*; UNEMPLOYMENT.

INCOME DISTRIBUTION, traditionally one of the most inegalitarian in all major industrialized countries. The tribulations of war and reconstruction tended to mitigate income inequality, yet income differentials widened steadily until socialist policies, beginning in 1981, began to reverse the trend. State policies often exacerbated income disparities, as fiscal and budgetary mechanisms largely benefited the wealthy—until 1981, the prefisc (before the state's influence) income distribution was more egalitarian than postfisc income distribution. The state's reliance on consumption taxes (which take a larger bite out of lower- than higher-income earners) is a major cause of income maldistribution. Yet tactical decisions on labor's part, weak unions, and sharp demarcations among social strata also play a part in the problem.

State economic policy from 1945 to 1962 actively encouraged a policy of deferring consumption (and hence, keeping incomes low for many) and allocating marginal increases in national income to public and private investors. This strategy was intended to augment France's productive apparatus so that in time, the economy could afford more consumption among the lower-income deciles. Consumption taxes, investment incentives, and wage restraints were all pursued as part of this approach. When wage restraints were loosened in the mid–1960s and popular consumption was encouraged, the tax structure remained regressive and the wealthy retained the political power needed to maintain a maldistribution of income. Tax reform, governmental largesse, and better access to education and training after 1981 began to reduce inequality.

Inflationary pressures also oddly mitigated against reductions in income inequality. Price inflation followed wage increases in 1936, 1944–46, 1956–57, and 1968–69, largely annihilating them. As a consequence, labor opted for institutional gains that were impervious to price changes, in particular, paid vacations. Thus, while money income inequality remains strong, nonmoney income in the form of vacations tends to reduce differences in compensation.

A low rate of unionization in the French labor force—rarely greater than 20 percent—meant few institutional pressures for higher wages. In addition, the absence of exclusive representation legislation has meant that several unions can exist within the same work force and that employers can capitalize upon political rivalries among unions to divide labor and maintain low wages.

While the distinctions in social strata have remained less sharp in France than in Britain, access to avenues of social mobility have remained limited. Though education has, since Napoleon I, offered the promise of social ascent based on personal merit, rates of matriculation are generally proportional to income levels. When universities opened admission more broadly in the 1960s, the elite developed new signs of educational superiority to maintain the old stratification. Language usage also represents a mark of social difference, and those who speak working-class French are rarely hired in anything but working-class jobs. Patterns of residential class segregation have also reinforced social differences and allowed little interaction across the social chasms. Immigrant workers have always remained a racially distinct subproletariat with little hope of upward social mobility.

Income inequality has thus remained pervasive in postwar France, and appeals to social solidarity have rarely found a sizable audience. Reforms by the state since 1981 have, nonetheless, begun to close some of the gaps.

P. Bourdieu, *La Distinction: Critique sociale du jugement* (Paris, 1979); J.-J. Carré, P. Dubois, E. Malinvaud, *La Croissance française, un essai d'analyse économique causale de l'après-guerre* (Paris, 1972); J. Lecerf, *La Percée de l'économie française* (Paris, 1963); A. Przeworski, B. Rubin, E. Underhill, "The Evolution of the Class Structure in France, 1901–1968," *Economic Development and Cultural Change* 28 (1980).

R. L. Frost

Related entries: COMMON PROGRAM; CONSTITUTION OF THE FOURTH REPUBLIC; ECONOMIC POLICY; ECONOMIC TRENDS; INFLATION; LABOR FORCE; MINIMUM WAGE; MINORITIES, PROBLEMS OF; TAXATION.

INDOCHINA, RELATIONS WITH. After World War II the French Empire was redefined as a "French Union," which was meant in principle to resemble the British Commonwealth of Nations. Indochina provided a test case of the sincerity of French intentions in guiding the peoples under its tutelage to independence. A nationalist movement existed there in the 1930s, and communist leader Ho Chi Minh was already then prominent within it. The abject surrender of Indochina by Vichy to the Japanese discredited the French administration; a guerilla movement arose against Japanese occupation, and the Japanese, before they evacuated Indochina in 1945, installed a puppet emperor, Bao Dai. The area was liberated under allied agreement by the Chinese in the north and the British in the south, but it was already under de facto control of the Vietminh when these forces arrived. The French returned on the heels of the British, but were forced to recognize the new authority, and the Vietminh, for its part, showed great moderation, declaring its readiness to accept independence within the context of the French Union. In March 1946 Jean Sainteny, on behalf of the French, signed a protocol with Ho Chi Minh recognizing the independence of Vietnam within the French Union, and when Ho arrived in France in the summer to negotiate the final details, he was greeted as a head of state.

By the summer, however, the French were no longer prepared to live up to the protocol; they separated Laos and Cambodia from Vietnam and within the latter sponsored a separate Cochin Chinese regime independent of the north. The negotiations at Fontainebleau failed to reach an accord, and Ho Chi Minh returned to Vietnam in September with only a modus vivendi, continuing the status quo pending further talks. These were not to occur. French high commissioner Thierry d'Argenlieu decided to seize control of customs, and when clashes occurred with Vietnamese irregulars, he ordered fleet bombardment of the harbor at Haiphong, causing thousands of civilian deaths. Ho still hoped for compromise, sending a telegram to the new French interim premier, Léon Blum. It was held up in transmission, however, and failing a response General Giap was given approval to attack the French in Hanoi. The Blum government regarded this attack as the causus belli opening the way to a full French effort at reconquest.

Despairing of any agreement with a communist-led opposition, the French tried to created a nationalist alternative under Bao Dai, whom they thought to be more compliant. In December 1947 a protocol was signed provisionally recognizing his rule, and in June 1948, at the Bay of Along, France agreed to reunify Vietnam and recognize its independence within the French Union. Ratification of the agreements took many more months, however, and the French retained control of Vietnamese military, foreign, and economic affairs, as they did in the other two "associated states" of Indochina. Meanwhile the war escalated. The French were unable to penetrate the countryside although they controlled the cities, and the October 1949 seizure of power by the Chinese communists in Beijing altered the political landscape. The Soviet Union recognized the government of Ho Chi Minh; fearing Chinese involvement in the struggle, the French turned to Washington for help.

The Americans had resisted becoming involved in what they regarded as a French war of colonial reconquest, but they were convinced by the Bao Dai "solution" that a noncommunist alternative to the Vietminh could be created, and when the Russians recognized Ho they did likewise with Bao Dai, following up with some military aid. With the coming of the Korean War in June 1950 this rapidly escalated, and the French were quickly able to convince Washington that the Korean and Indochinese struggles were two linked "hot" fronts in the otherwise Cold War pitting the "free world" against communism. The French suffered further reverses in battle late in 1950; with Washington now looking over their shoulder, they appointed the famous de Gaulle associate, General Jean de Lattre de Tassigny, as commander and high commissioner, and his forceful personality brought new confidence to their effort, holding out the hope that the war could be turned around. The French commitment extended to about 200,000 troops of whom 90,000 were actually French. These were volunteers and legionnaires, however, for the French were never willing to commit regular draftees to the conflict for fear of the political consequences at home.

De Lattre convinced the Americans to step up their aid and started to build an indigenous Vietnamese army, negotiating with the Americans for their financial support. But he fell ill with cancer and died in January 1952, and the war degenerated into a stalemate for the remainder of the year. The Republican administration in Washington, in January 1953 resolved to force the hand of the French toward victory. President Eisenhower demanded a victory plan from Premier René Mayer during the latter's visit to Washington in March 1953, and the latter responded with the Navarre plan for an offensive in the north following "pacification" of the south by the new Vietnamese army. The Americans committed $385 million to the plan, in addition to a subsidy of another $400 million to the French military budget and various categories of miscellaneous assistance, bringing the total American involvement to over one billion dollars per year and 80 percent of the war's cost. It was the French, however, who watched their casualties mount and their military preparedness in Europe suffer due to the loss of a third of each year's graduating officer class from Saint-Cyr.

Pressure for a negotiated solution to the war meanwhile grew in Paris, and in June 1953 Pierre Mendès-France narrowly failed to win investiture as premier. Washington pressured the Laniel government to push on to victory, and Navarre launched a parachute drop on the isolated outpost of Dien Bien Phu. The Americans were initially pleased, but the fortress was quickly surrounded, and when the Vietminh succeeded in bringing up heavy artillery, defeat loomed. The Indochina conflict was also on the agenda of the forthcoming international conference at Geneva in April, where Korea was to be discussed; a French defeat at Dien Bien Phu would make pressures for negotiations irresistible. In desperation Laniel and Bidault pressed Washington for B-29 air strikes to save the fortress, but the Americans were not prepared to use their own forces to fight in Indochina. On May 7 the outpost fell. Washington insisted loss of a battle was not loss of the entire war and tried to negotiate terms for a joint Franco-American prosecution of the struggle, but the French could not get satisfaction that the Americans intended to put in ground troops. With negotiations at a standstill, the Laniel government fell, and Mendès-France took power with a promise at Geneva to end the war within a month, or resign with a recommendation that draftees be sent in.

Despite Washington's opposition, a favorable international environment enabled France to get an honorable settlement. Laos and Cambodia were left independent under noncommunist regimes, the Vietminh took power in the north, and the French regrouped in the south, provisionally under the rule of Ngo Dinh Diem, pending elections in 1956. Mendès-France hoped to retain a foothold in the south and nurture it along under French influence with American support in the hope of winning the elections in 1956, while hedging his bets and negotiating a modus vivendi with the north that would permit the maintenance of French interests there. But Washington quickly pushed the French aside in the hope of consolidating the south for an evenual reconquest of the north, clashing with Paris on the suitability of Diem as leader, and the respective roles that France and the United States would play in Vietnam. With the European Defense Community going down to defeat in August 1954, the Americans lost all interest in cooperating with Mendès-France and cut off aid. Following an internal crisis in the south that pitted the two against each other in 1955, the French were forced to evacuate altogether, as Paris turned its attention to another colonial conflict in Algeria, where seven more years of war ended in similar defeat and negotiated withdrawal in 1962.

The French attempt to keep a foothold in Indochina resulted in the squandering of enormous economic resources (the whole of Marshall Plan aid and more by some counts), the poisoning of the army against the regime, humiliating dependence on Washington—to which the war was ''sold'' as a means of balancing the French trade deficit with the dollar zone—and the continued strength of communism and ''neutralism'' at home. De Gaulle wrongly thought that Dien Bien Phu might bring him to power in 1954; in the event, it required the additional push of Algeria. But the contradiction of a democracy seeking to fight a colonial war against national self-determination resulted only in useless bloodshed, defeat, the eventual decline of the Fourth Republic, and the near-collapse of democracy itself.

D. Artaud, L. Kaplan, *Dien Bien Phu: L'Alliance atlantique et la défense du Sud-Est Asiatique* (Lyon, 1989); P. Devilliers, J. Lacouture, *End of a War: Indochina, 1954* (New York, 1969); R. E. M. Irving, *The First Indochina War* (London, 1975); D. Lancaster, *The Emancipation of French Indochina* (New York, 1975); E. Rice-Maximin, *Accommodation and Resistance: The French Left, Indochina and the Cold War, 1944–54* (New York, 1986).

I. M. Wall

Related entries: DIEN BIEN PHU; FOREIGN POLICY; FRENCH UNION; MENDES-FRANCE, PIERRE; UNITED STATES, RELATIONS WITH.

INDUSTRIAL POLICY, a field in which there is a strong tradition of government intervention, related to modernizing industry, reinforcing specific branches of manufacturing, and modifying location patterns. The modernization of French industry was a central feature of the country's early five-year plans, notably the

First Plan (1947–52) in which priority was given to investment in key industries such as coal, electricity, cement, and agricultural machinery. In the early years of the Fifth Republic priority was again accorded to industry, especially during the period of the Fifth Plan (1966–70). Emphasis was placed on creating a series of large French multinationals and on directing investment toward specific growth sectors, particularly aerospace, nuclear energy, professional electronics, and computing.

Under President Valéry Giscard d'Estaing (1974–81) such policies continued. However, the government reduced its interventionist role and promoted increased competition, notably by adopting a more liberal attitude to foreign investment. But with the recession, an urgent need arose to provide financial assistance for a growing number of ailing industries, notably steel. The new socialist government (1981–86) introduced further changes. A comprehensive series of restructuring and modernization plans was formulated to cover a wide range of industries, such as *plan textile, plan informatique, plan machine outil.* In addition, a major program of nationalization was carried through (1982) that included five large industrial groups (CGE, Thomson-Brandt, St. Gobain, Rhône-Poulenc, and Péchiney-Ugine-Kuhlmann).

The succeeding Chirac administration favored reducing state intervention and initiated a program of privatization, which included the two industrial groups St. Gobain and CGE. With the further change of government in 1988, policy changed little. The idea of specific plans for individual industrial branches had already been abandoned, but financial aid for selected industries remained important. With respect to the role of the state sector, President Mitterrand declared in 1988 that he favored neither more nationalizations nor more privatizations.

Government policy designed to modify the spatial distribution of industry dates from the mid–1950s and was directed originally at reducing the overwhelming concentration of French manufacturing in the Paris region. From 1955 it became necessary to obtain government approval (through a development permit known as an *agrément*) for any new factory exceeding five hundred square meters of floor space. This measure has remained in place ever since (although in 1972 the threshold was raised to fifteen hundred square meters) and was partly responsible for an important movement of decentralization in the 1960s and early 1970s.

From the mid–1950s measures were also introduced to encourage industrial investment in certain industrial "problem regions" (e.g., Nord-Pas-de-Calais, Lorraine, Le Creusot-Montceau, and St. Etienne). Then in 1964 a more extensive range of areas qualifying for financial assistance was defined, covering much of western and southwestern France, the Massif Central, and industrial areas of northern and northeastern France. This demonstrated the government's desire to promote new development not only in traditional manufacturing centers but also in many of the country's predominantly agricultural regions. The majority of these areas still qualify for government assistance, now paid in the form of a regional development grant (*prime à l'aménagement du territoire*, PAT) which can cover up to 25 percent of industrial costs.

During the 1960s other spatial policies were pursued. In 1964 eight counterweights (*métropoles d'équilibres*) to Paris were defined to favor investment in major provincial cities such as Lyon, Lille, and Strasbourg. Then in 1968 five major port-industrial zones were designated, including Le Havre, Marseille-Fos, and Dunkerque, aimed at attracting heavy industry to these areas. To coordinate these different policies a special government agency known as the Datar (*Délégation à l'aménagement du territoire et à l'action régionale*) was created in 1963.

After the mid–1970s government policy was increasingly oriented to assisting industrial areas badly hit by the recession. In 1984 fifteen industrial conversion zones were established in which additional aid was provided, such as retraining programs. The towns concerned included Lille, Dunkerque, St. Etienne, Le Creusot, Montluçon, and Valenciennes. Then in 1986 three enterprise zones were set up at Dunkerque, La Ciotat, and La Seyne (in which companies are exempted from tax on their profits) to offset the closure of shipyards. At the same time grants were increased for the rehabilitation of derelict land.

Apart from these measures, there has been a general decline in the importance attached to regional industrial policy in the 1980s. For example, in 1985 the *agrément* procedure was greatly relaxed, and subsequently expenditure on regional grants was substantially reduced by the Chirac government. In part this reflects the difficulty of maintaining a regional policy in periods of low growth, but it also results from revised government thinking, favoring less direct intervention in the economy.

P. De Roo, *Atlas de l'aménagement du territoire* (Paris, 1988); J.-P. Laborie, et al., *La Politique française d'aménagement du territoire de 1950 à 1985* (Paris, 1985), "La Politique industrielle," *Les Cahiers français* 212 (1983); J. Monod, Ph. de Castelbajac, *L'Aménagement du territoire* (Paris, 1987).

J. N. Tuppen

Related entries: ECONOMIC POLICY; ECONOMIC TRENDS; NATIONALIZATIONS; PLAN; PRIVATIZATION.

INFLATION has reflected since 1945 the larger movements of the French economy. Between 1950 and 1970 annual growth averaged 5.05 percent, inflation 4.7 percent. Between 1970 and 1979, average growth fell to 3.9 percent while inflation soared to 8.8 percent. Similarly, real wages grew at an average of 5.45 percent between 1953 and 1973, then slowed to an average of 3.8 percent between 1973 and 1982. France tolerated inflation during the first three decades after World War II because it was bound up with rising prosperity. All sorts of long-term investments—whether by industry or the individual consumer—were encouraged by the impact of continuing moderate inflation on debt. During the *trente glorieuses* inflation thus stimulated investment and consumption, and therefore employment, without becoming intolerable. Furthermore, increases in real incomes served as a powerful cement in a badly divided society. Finally, "bracket creep" and growth also generated substantial state revenues without resort to a painful public vote on additional taxation. Tolerance has diminished since the mid–1970s because inflation has been linked to relative economic stagnation.

In the immediate aftermath of the war the imbalance of supply and demand produced a wage-price spiral that engendered political instability. Revived production and American aid broke the back of the worst stage during 1949. Postwar industrial modernization carried with it the double need for heavy investment followed by heavy consumption, both of which could be facilitated by a moderate inflation. Close cooperation between the Finance Ministry and the *Commissariat au Plan* gave modernizing industries easy access to investment capital. Wages were formally linked to the price index from 1951. When combined with heavy military spending and weak authority over taxes and wage-price controls, this heavy investment resulted in continuing inflation. Inflation deteriorated the balance of payments by raising the price of exports on foreign markets and reducing the price of imports. The Fourth Republic met this problem with repeated devaluations. The inability to control inflation contributed to the impression of weakness that eventually undercut support for the Fourth Republic.

General Charles de Gaulle returned to power determined to avoid the policies that had sapped the prestige of the Fourth Republic. The substantial devaluation of 1958 established a solid base for continued expansion: Thereafter de Gaulle preferred to rein in the economy whenever inflation threatened to get out of control, as in 1963 and 1967. Two of the chief achievements of postwar society were already storing up trouble for this strategy. First, the growth of the welfare state dragged on economic performance, because it is labor intensive and the taxes needed to finance it reduced savings and forced up interest rates. Second, full employment had become so integrated into expectational structures that it formed a commanding political goal. These factors hindered adaptation of the French economy when international economic conditions interrupted the great postwar boom.

Since the mid–1970s France has been harmed by the shift in terms of trade with primary-product countries because of its dependence on imported energy and raw materials, by the rise of new industrial nations employing the most modern techniques within the context of low labor costs and aggressive national economic strategies, by stagnant investment, and by the difficulty of mobilizing political consensus supporting painful adaptation in a still deeply divided society. France has not been able to master inflation under governments of either the right or the left. Valéry Giscard d'Estaing and Raymond Barre showed the same preference for stability as had de Gaulle, but could not get inflation down to a tolerable level or restore French competitiveness. After 1980 the socialists seriously misunderstood economic realities. The policies that they introduced exacerbated many problems and compelled a sharp change in course within a year after taking power.

It now seems likely that the achievements of France's postwar modernization disguised a continuing failure to adapt fully to an increasingly competitive world economy. The 1970s demanded more intense competitiveness and flexibility just when the French economy had begun to lose its vigor. Moderate inflation between 1945 and 1973 facilitated economic growth and rising incomes; more severe inflation since 1973 has reflected the economic and political conflicts arising from stagnation.

J. and G. Brémond, *L'Economie française face aux défis mondiale* (Paris, 1985); J.-J. Carré, P. Dubois, E. Malinvaud, *French Economic Growth* (Stanford, Calif., 1975); H. van der Wee, *Prosperity and Upheaval* (Berkeley and Los Angeles, 1987).

J. S. Hill

Related entries: ECONOMIC POLICY; ECONOMIC TRENDS; INCOME DISTRIBUTION; INDUSTRIAL POLICY; MARSHALL PLAN; MENDES-FRANCE, PIERRE; MIMIMUM WAGE; PINAY, ANTOINE; PLAN; UNEMPLOYMENT.

INTELLECTUAL TRENDS can be usefully seen in three periods, each indicated by a dominant mode of thought and central thinkers: from the end of the war through the 1950s, (Marxist) existentialism, Jean-Paul Sartre and Maurice Merleau-Ponty; in the 1960s, structuralism and Claude Lévi-Strauss; through the 1970s to the present, poststructuralism, Michel Foucault, and Jacques Derrida. The concerns of intellectuals in the first period were shaped by the experiences of the Resistance during the Occupation and Liberation. During the Occupation, intellectuals, like others, experienced life in situations of extreme stress, when every act and word could seem to carry the burden of a decision between trust and deceit, honor and betrayal, life and death. Reduced to the essentials, people found meaning in the defiance of the tragic circumstances surrounding them. Creating dignity by the decision not to allow the meaningfulness, or meaninglessness, of life to be determined by the actions of others, but only by, and in, one's own actions, even if that action was limited to deciding one's attitude toward one's own death, became a generative figure during and after the war.

The experience of the Resistance and the early months of Liberation created hopes for a radical social and political renewal founded on equality and embodying a distinct ethical vision. However, the lack of a concrete program or experience of political maneuvering, infighting among would-be leaders, the general conservatism of the population as it turned its efforts to the rebuilding and maintaining of life in familiar local contexts, doomed these hopes, and the preexisting framework of party politics and factional interests was soon back in place. The restrictive weight of historical patterns and institutionalized divisions and conflicts, the character of historical change, and the character—past, present, and possible—of grounds for radical historical and political change became central issues for postwar intellectuals.

These issues were depicted in literature and drama by a variety of intellectuals, some of whom invented new artistic forms to match the ambiguity, incoherence, and meaninglessness that threatened and provoked decisive action. Jean-Paul Sartre's prescient novel, *Nausea* (1938), Albert Camus's novels *The Stranger* (1942) and *The Plague* (1947), Sartre's plays *No Exit* (1944) and *Flies* (1943), and Jean Anouilh's *Antigone* (1944) all dramatized the situations of individuals shaped by their choices in uncertain and tragic circumstances. Later in this period novels and plays, which embodied in the very structure and language of the artistic works themselves the lack of a stable point of view, the lack of internal connections and wholistic point, and the lack of meaningful conclusions, were produced by the creators of the "*nouveau roman*," Michel Butor, Nathalie Sarraute, Alain Robbe-Grillet, and Claude Simon, and by the creators of the Theater of the Absurd, Samuel Beckett and Eugène Ionesco. Beckett's *Waiting for Godot* (1952) has become the emblem of this work.

But the dominant intellectual current of the period, becoming the reference point for contemporaries and for succeeding generations, was Sartre's existentialism, or more precisely, the project of an existential Marxism into which his initial philosophical orientation was soon transformed. Sartre's early literary and philosophical works, *Nausea* and *Being and Nothingness* (1943), had been expressions of his distinctive appropriation of Edmund Husserl's phenomenology. Husserl's philosophical project had been to describe, bracketing all metaphysical presuppositions about the ultimate nature or cause of things, the appearing of meaningful entities (numbers, material objects, concepts, persons) strictly in terms of the evidence given in their appearing to consciousness. Husserl's disciplined return to the "phenomena themselves" then correlated modes of the appearing of entities of all kinds with the modes of mental apprehension of these entities, and thus sought to disclose the basic types of subject-object knowledge structures that constituted the objects, fields, horizons, and validities of meanings of all actual and possible kinds.

Sartre had encountered Husserl's work, and that of his younger associate Martin Heidegger, in Germany in 1933–34. In *Being and Time* (1927) Heidegger had sought to go beyond Husserl's analysis of specifically knowledge-constituting structures and to describe the fundamental and general structures of understanding and engagement that constituted the very sense of existence for humans. In a similar vein, Sartre sought, with philosophical acuteness in literary forms and with dramatic vividness in philosophical works, to describe the full structure and texture of consciousness in the experiences of decision, from the mindless fleeing from decision in everyday habits to the life-and-death decisions in extreme situations, in which the meaningfulness of individuals' existences were forged. His rich and striking descriptions of value creating, or failing to create, individuals, gave paradigmatic figure to the "existentialist" actor and situation, proposing the possibility, even the necessity, of individuals creating and embodying values in a world otherwise without them.

In 1945, with Simone de Beauvoir, Merleau-Ponty, and some others, Sartre launched a journal, *Les Temps modernes*, as a vehicle for the integration of the meaning-creating existential protagonist with a critically reconstructed Marxism, the only existing social-political orientation that they took as having appropriable and revisable theories of history, conflict, and revolutionary struggle. For the following decade the project of exploring the range and types of meaning-creating human action, examining the enabling and the restrictive features of actual and theoretical social and political situations, and attempting to articulate a defensible path of political conduct, centered the intellectual discourse of France. Sartre's *Qu'est-ce que la littérature*? (1947), *Baudelaire* (1947), *Saint Genet* (1952), *Les Communistes et la paix* (1952–54), de Beauvoir's *The Ethics of Ambiguity* (1947) and *The Second Sex* (1949), and Merleau-Ponty's *Phenomenology of Perception* (1945) and *Humanism and Terror* (1947) generated continuous controversy.

By the late 1950s and early 1960s, however, the situation engaging intellectuals had changed. The project of existential Marxism had produced a number of striking works, but neither by personal example nor theoretical synthesis had provided a base for effective political organization and action. The Russian invasion of Hungary and the authoritarian, and sometimes brutal activities of various communist regimes dimmed many intellectuals' hopes that Marxism could inspire progressive change. Merleau-Ponty left the journal and the project in 1953 to take a new look at the experiential resources for the creation, and for the creative transmission, of meaning. The actions of France in Vietnam and through the course of the Algerian War seemed to many to be just continuations of colonial stances forced into new guises. The task for many intellectuals now came to be to understand the transindividual and transgenerational structural forces and patterns whose persistence seemed to nullify, or at least to restrict severely, the effect of particular, self-conscious, radical actions.

In the 1960s, then, rather unhelpfully lumped together under the rubric of "structuralism" by the increasingly pervasive and reputation-creating popular media, there were a wide variety of intellectual projects arguing for the importance, positively or negatively, of systems of meaning that were not centered in or by consciousness or individual action. The chief example of the new structuralist orientation was the work of the anthropologist Claude Lévi-Strauss. Basing his approach on the earlier work of the Swiss linguist Ferdinand de Saussure, Lévi-Strauss developed a structuralist theory of South American tribal myths, suggestive of all similar systems of signs. Lévi-Strauss treated myths as expressions of a single closed system of signs structured around pairs of opposed elements. These opposed elements represented choices of basic dramatic figures and relations. The choices within a given system were hierarchically organized into sets. An analytically derivable set of operational rules plotting the possible variations and resulting configurations of the elements and relations of the system then revealed to the myth theorist the intelligibility and the range of meanings governed by that sign system.

Insofar as there were similarities among the approaches generally called structuralist, it was the focus on closed systems of meaning within which changes followed analytically specifiable transformation rules and thereby assured a unity of meaning to the phenomena examined and a "scientific" character to the analyses revealing the laws governing the changes in the phenomena. Work roughly sharing these characteristics was carried out in the 1960s by A. J. Greimas and Gérard Genette in the theory of narrative; by the early Roland

Barthes in the theoretical manifesto *Elements of Semiology* (1964); by the *Annales* school of historians, most notably in Fernand Braudel's analyses of transformations of material culture over the "long duration"; by Louis Althusser in Marxist theory, a reconstruction that promised to free the "scientific" Marx from romantic subjectivism; by the work of psychoanalyst Jacques Lacan, whose treatment of Freud's unconscious as a language operating according to internal rules was taken as analogous to Lévi-Strauss's work on myth; and by the early works of Michel Foucault, particularly *The Order of Things* and *The Archaeology of Knowledge*, which focused on the configurations of elements, relations, and rules constituting the discursive practices of distinctly modern fields of knowledge.

Parallel with intellectuals' focus on nonconscious systems, French society experienced the steady expansion and systematization of Gaullist bureaucratic practices, and the university system began to face a postwar student population whose numbers and expectations it could not satisfy. The events of May 1968 brought to visibility and gave impetus to intellectual currents loosely called poststructuralism or deconstructionism, radically questioning the validity of the very notion of "scientific" understandings of intellectual and political systems of meaning. This questioning has ranged from Jean Baudrillard's examinations of the degradation of meanings and of meaning itself in consumerist and self-referring sign systems, to Gilles Deleuze and Félix Guattari's provocative explorations of the limitations of traditional logical categories relative to the specific political horrors, and psychological pleasures, of twentieth-century experience.

The poststructuralist work that has generated the most promise of a new constructive as well as critical orientation are the later studies of Foucault and the project of Jacques Derrida. In *Discipline and Punish* (1975) Foucault investigated how in penology, education, and medical and juridical procedures, normative disciplines of knowledge and behavior-directing institutional practices reciprocally constituted the practical forms of the modern self, and of the "truths" of that self. In his three-volume work entitled *The History of Sexuality* (vol. 1, 1976; vols. 2 and 3, 1984) he began to trace through successive Western cultural forms the "political technologies of the body" exercised by social systems' practices enveloping sexuality.

Derrida, in a series of works exhibiting a rarely matched blend of technical complexity and novel form, has undertaken the project of interrogating from within and from without the claims and practices of philosophy itself. In exactingly close readings of texts of Plato, Hegel, Husserl, and Heidegger, Derrida has in each case shown features of the experience of the world presupposed and necessary for the meanings articulated in the texts, but necessarily displaced, repressed, or denied in the textual presentation in order to claim a completed unity of meaning. In inventive readings and writings across texts and genres he has sought to resituate seemingly incommensurable textual meanings in new, more complex, unfinished, and uncentered, inter- and extratextual fields, which the activity of thinking always appropriates and yet is outstripped by. Derrida's work reminds philosophy and its truths of the multiform "Others" to which they are inextricably tied.

The thought of French intellectuals since the war has made the issues of structural presuppositions, rhetorical form, institutional contexts, and power inescapable aspects of the perennial issue of the character and status of critical thinking.

E. Bannet, *Structuralism and the Logic of Dissent* (Chicago, 1989); A. Boschetti, *Sartre et "les Temps Modernes"* (Paris, 1985); P. Bourdieu, *Homo academicus* (Paris, 1984); R. Debray, *Le Pouvoir intellectuel en France* (Paris, 1979); M. Frank, *What Is Neostructuralism?* (Minneapolis, Minn., 1989).

J. Kirkland

Related entries: ALTHUSSER, LOUIS; BARTHES, ROLAND; BEAUVOIR, SIMONE DE; BECKETT, SAMUEL; BRAUDEL, FERNAND; CAMUS, ALBERT; DERRIDA, JACQUES; FOUCAULT, MICHEL; LACAN, JACQUES; LEVI-STRAUSS, CLAUDE; LITERATURE; NEW PHILOSOPHERS; SARTRE, JEAN-PAUL; STRUCTURALISM.

IONESCO, EUGENE (1912–), Romanian-born playwright and man of letters. Ionesco spent most of his early years in France, returning to Romania at the age of thirteen. With his wife, he fled Romania in 1938, escaping the fascist epidemic he was to satirize in his famous play *Rhinocéros* (1959). He has remained in France since the late 1930s.

His first play, *La Cantatrice chauve* (1953, *The Bald Soprano*), premiered in 1950 and shocked and scandalized the audience, beginning one of the most celebrated careers of any twentieth-century French dramatist. Ionesco's themes of the impossibility of communication and the banality of conventional opinions and attitudes, as developed in such later plays as *La leçon* (1953, *The Lesson*), *Rhinocéros* (1959), and *L'Homme aux valises* (1975, *Man with Bags*), have earned him the reputation of a playwright of the "absurd." However, as one realizes from the allegorical *Rhinocéros* and from his journals, short stories, plays, interviews, and essays, Ionesco is a profoundly political, even moral, writer. He despises the orthodoxies of left and right alike, insisting always on the absolute creative freedom of the artist. Ionesco lends a metaphysical cast to much of his writing; yet there remains a spirit of outrageous fun, reminiscent of Alfred Jarry and the *Collège de pataphysique* that honors his memory. Indeed, Ionesco is a member of this group. He has also, with his elevation to the *Académie française* in 1971, taken his place among the ranks of France's leading living writers. Ionesco is known for his accessibility, generously granting interviews and participating in conferences devoted to his work.

E. Ionesco, *Notes et contre-notes* (Paris, 1962), *Journal en miettes* (Paris, 1967); *Ionesco: Situation et perspectives/Colloque de Cerisy* (Paris: 1980); M. Lazar, ed., *The Dream and the Play: Ionesco's Theatrical Quest,* (Malibu, Calif., 1982).

J. A. Winders

Related entries: BECKETT, SAMUEL; INTELLECTUAL TRENDS; LITERATURE; NEW PHILOSOPHERS.

J

JOBERT, MICHEL (1921–), minister of foreign affairs under Georges Pompidou and minister of foreign trade under François Mitterrand. Born in Meknès, Morocco, he entered the *Ecole libre des sciences politiques* in Paris in 1939, fought in the Italian campaign, completed his studies after the war at the *Ecole nationale d'administration* (ENA), and in 1949 took a position at the *Cours des comptes*. He held administrative staff positions in several ministries, including that of Pierre Mendès-France in 1954–56, and was chief of staff for the high commissioner of the Republic in French West Africa from 1956 to 1958. He became the *directeur de cabinet* of Georges Pompidou in 1963, who was at that time prime minister; in 1969, when Pompidou was elected president of France, Jobert became *secrétaire général* of the Elysée Palace.

Named minister of foreign affairs by Pompidou in April 1973, he became highly visible due to his much-publicized confrontations with Henry Kissinger, most notably at the conference on energy in Washington in February 1974. Jobert acquired the reputation of being anti-American; he claimed that he wished to deny the hegemony of the superpowers and had to defend the national independence of France. Kissinger, in *Years of Upheaval*, praised Jobert for his intelligence but surmised that Jobert's efforts to thwart U.S. policy were designed to enhance his image with voters in France. Jobert, however, denied that he ever intended to run for the presidency following Pompidou's death.

After Valéry Giscard d'Estaing's election to the presidency in 1974, Jobert lost his ministerial post; he had publicly supported Jacques Chaban-Delmas in the first round of the presidential elections, preferring him to Giscard. Soon afterward, he founded a new political party, the *Mouvement des démocrates*, based on the principles of national independence and refusal of the dichotomy between left and right.

Following a long absence from the political scene, Jobert was named *ministre d'état chargé du commerce extérieur* in Pierre Mauroy's socialist government in 1981. He was most noted for his effort to reduce the importation of Japanese videocassette recorders by forcing all imported VCRs to be routed through Poitiers for customs inspection beginning in October 1982, where the bureaucratic delay proved to be very lengthy and consumers waited for months for VCRs.

He resigned from the Mauroy government in March 1983, and in April the measure regarding VCRs was rescinded.

Jobert remains an enigmatic figure, and it is difficult to categorize his political ideology. He found absurd the division of France into two ideological blocs, and his participation in the governments of both the right and the left witnesses his effort to transcend ideological boundaries. He constantly defended France's independence, even at times when international events, in particular the energy crisis provoked by the oil embargo, seemed to require increased cooperation among Western nations. He has never avoided controversy.

M. Jobert, *L'Autre Regard* (Paris, 1976), *Mémories d'avenir* (Paris, 1974), *Par trente-six chemins* (Paris, 1984); H. Kissinger, *Years of Upheaval* (Boston, 1982).

H. B. Sutton

Related entries: POMPIDOU, GEORGES; UNITED STATES, RELATIONS WITH.

JOSPIN, LIONEL (1937–), politician, head of the Socialist party (PS) between 1981 and 1988, vice-president of the Socialist International (1981–88), minister of education (1988–), and now a presidential contender. Jospin was educated at the *Fondation nationale des sciences politiques* (1956–59) and the *Ecole nationale d'administration* (ENA, 1963–65). He did his military service in Germany between 1961 and 1962, attaining the rank of second lieutenant. As a student and a left-winger, Jospin supported Algerian independence. However, he would not join the French Communist party (PCF) because of the events in Hungary, nor the Socialist party (SFIO) because of the government's involvement in the Suez (both 1956). In 1960 he joined the new *Parti socialiste unifié*.

After leaving ENA, he worked for the Foreign Ministry until 1970 when, unhappy with the life-style of the upper civil service, he left to teach economics (University of Paris XI), where he remained until 1981.

Jospin joined the PS in 1971 after the Epinay Congress and was elected to the party's Executive Bureau in 1973, joining the Secretariat in 1975. He was encouraged to join the party by Pierre Joxe and was singled out early on by François Mitterrand, in particular for his report on PS-PC relations in 1975.

He was elected as a Paris councillor in 1977, as a Paris deputy in the 1981 socialist landslide, as a member of the European Parliament in 1984 (he led the Socialist party's campaign), and as a Toulouse deputy in 1986 (whereupon he resigned both as deputy and councillor in Paris).

Jospin was prepared for the leadership of the PS before 1981, chairing the National Secretariat and Executive Bureau from 1979, when Mitterrand was absent. In January 1981, when Mitterrand became a presidential candidate, Jospin was elected as first secretary. As first secretary from 1981 until the socialists regained power in 1988, Jospin's position was uncontested for several reasons: He managed to seek compromises between the various factions, often taking on the role of conciliator rather than leader; he did not rival any of the *présidentiables* within the party; he was unequivocally Mitterrand's representative; and—in spite of the last point—he believed in keeping the party from becoming an American-style presidentialist party (this causing tension between himself and Mitterrand by 1988), thus generating sympathy and respect, if not great allegiance, among party activists.

Jospin resigned from the leadership of the party to take the education portfolio (widened to include research and sport, and thus reflect Mitterrand's concern for these issues during his 1988 election campaign) in Michel Rocard's 1988 government. He was also appointed minister of education in Edith Cresson's cabinet (1991–).

In spite of his marked ability in containing the leadership rivalries in the PS during the 1980s and his central role between 1981 and 1986 (even though not a minister, as leader of the PS his role was crucial to the smooth running of government), he was generally regarded as a political lightweight when compared with figures such as Laurent Fabius and Rocard. After 1988, however, as both a minister and a *courant* leader with a great deal of sympathy inside the party, he became independent from Mitterrand and a prime ministerial hopeful and/or presidential contender on a par with others. By the late 1980s, the former Mitterrandist *courant* (which now also included Pierre Mauroy's *courant*) sported several potential *courants* and *courant* leaders, the most significant being Jospin and Fabius. Jospin, the former conciliator, was forced henceforward into the kind of maneuvering and self-positioning vis-à-vis Rocard, Fabius (there had been some tension with Fabius during the 1986 legislative election campaign), and others that for seven-and-a-half years he had presided over and, generally speaking, attenuated.

His self-depiction after becoming such a contender was that of a figure capable of keeping the party united and identifiably socialist while being able, nevertheless, to come to terms with the realities of the political arithmetic (the PS's apparent inability to achieve a parliamentary majority on its own). His relationship to the party was therefore his advantage over Rocard and, to a lesser extent, Fabius. His new national prominence as education minister, however, involved attempting to complement this advantage with popularity on a wider, national scale.

Ironically, as a young activist, as a party leader after 1981, and as a government minister after 1988, Jospin has shared with his potential rival, Rocard, the same troubled preoccupation with the relationship between politics and ethics, political idealism and power. Politically, Jospin's strengths have been his weaknesses, that is, his authority was rarely contested in the party between 1981 and 1988 because he was acceptable to all (he was Mitterrand's representative, not his *dauphin*) and therefore threatening to none; by the same token, as a *courant* leader and, after 1988, potential presidential contender, just as he had aroused little opposition before, he was not the kind of figure to arouse passion or allegiance, after having served so long as Mitterrand's loyal and self-effacing servant.

D. Bell, B. Criddle, *The French Socialist Party* (Oxford, 1988); L. Jospin, "Les Relations PS-PC," *Le Poing et la rose* 70 (April-May 1978).

J. Gaffney

Related entries: COMMON PROGRAM; EDUCATIONAL REFORM; FABIUS, LAURENT; JOXE, PIERRE; MITTERRAND, FRANCOIS; ROCARD, MICHEL; SOCIALIST PARTY (PS); UNIFIED SOCIALIST PARTY; UNION OF THE LEFT.

JOXE, PIERRE (1934–), one of the chief members of the Socialist party (PS), the former minister of the interior and then of defense in the cabinet headed by Michel Rocard (1988–91), and minister of defense in the government of Edith Cresson (1991–). Joxe was born in Paris on November 28, 1934, into one of France's leading intellectual families. His father, Louis, was one of General Charles de Gaulle's first and most loyal supporters, is a former ambassador, and served as a cabinet minister during the first years of the Fifth Republic. Despite their political differences, the family remains close, sharing the same house on the banks of the Seine where the younger Joxe grew up.

Joxe has had a typical career for a Fifth Republic politician, whether from the left or the right. He attended the *Lycée Henri IV*, received a law degree, and then graduated from the prestigious *Ecole nationale d'administration* (ENA) in 1962. At that point he joined the *Cour des comptes* and held a series of important bureaucratic positions during the 1960s and early 1970s.

He also joined François Mitterrand's *Convention des institutions républicaines* (CIR) and was its deputy secretary-general in the years before it became a part of the new Socialist party in 1971. He was first elected to the National Assembly in 1973 from the the Saône-et-Loire, a department he has represented ever since.

From 1981 until 1984 and then again from 1986 until 1988, he was head of the Socialist party group in the National Assembly. In 1984 Laurent Fabius named him minister of the interior, a position he held until the socialists lost the 1986 legislative elections. Rocard named him to that same position when he formed two cabinets after the presidential and then legislative elections in 1988. In January 1991 he was appointed minister of defense replacing Jean-Pierre Chevènement who resigned because of his opposition to allied objectives in the Persian Gulf War (1991). Joxe retained the important defense portfolio in the Cresson government, which was formed in mid-May, 1991.

B. Brown, *Socialism of a Different Kind* (Westport, Conn., 1982); G. Ross, S. Hoffmann, S. Malzacher, eds., *The Mitterrand Experiment* (New York, 1987); D. Singer, *Is Socialism Doomed*? (New York, 1988).

C. Hauss

Related entries: DEMOCRATIC AND SOCIALIST UNION OF THE RESISTANCE; ELECTIONS; FABIUS, LAURENT; FEDERATION OF THE DEMOCRATIC AND SOCIALIST LEFT; LEFT RADICALS; MAUROY, PIERRE; MIDDLE EAST, RELATIONS WITH; MITTERRAND, FRANCOIS; ROCARD, MICHEL; SOCIALIST PARTY (PS, SFIO); UNION OF THE LEFT.

JULY, SERGE (1942–), journalist and television executive. He was born in Paris on December 27, 1942 into a typical lower-middle-class family of liberal persuasion. He studied art history and was for a time a French teacher at the *Collège Sainte-Barbe*. In his youth he was vice-president of the National Union of Students of France (UNEF). From 1961 to 1962 he was a journalist for *Clarté*, the monthly of the *Union des étudiants communistes* (UEC). Prior to 1968, he launched a short-lived theater review called *Calliop*. From 1969 to 1972 he was a deputy leader of *Gauche prolétarienne* (GP), a Maoist spin-off from the French Communist party, in the wake of the May 1968 student revolt. The spring of 1970 saw July in charge of the relations of the GP with the press. On April 11, 1970 he signed an article in *Le Monde* in defense of the GP and its periodical, *La Cause du peuple*, which the government harassed. This extended his connections within the leftist intelligentsia, including such personalities as Jean-Paul Sartre, who became the nominal publisher of *La Cause du peuple*, Maurice Clavel, and Michel Foucault.

Since 1973 July has played a key role in running the new-left daily, *Libération*, a newspaper he founded with Philippe Gavi, Jean-René Huleu, Jean-Claude Vernier, and Sartre. From its founding, he has been the central figure in the evolution of this newspaper, one that is somewhat similar to the U.S. underground press with its use of humor, expressionistic style, and personal classified ads. *Libération's* goal was to be a nonpolitical and nonideological paper giving a stronger voice to the problems and the demands of alienated people. The collective management of the paper, however, did not stand the test of time. As editor in chief since 1973, publisher from 1974 to 1975, and director since 1981, July has guided *Libération* through a series of reorganizations that jettisoned most of the original principles of the paper. He introduced paid advertisements, the hierarchical principle of management, unequal compensation, and technological modernization, making *Libération* one of the most commercially sound and politically influential French papers. In the meantime, July became a well-known media personality, becoming executive director of *Télélibération '84* and appearing frequently on the most popular French television talk shows, which often solicit his opinion on the state of the world.

July has also written a number of books on French political life. He coauthored a book with A. Geismar and E. Morane entitled *Vers la guerre civile* (1969), published a collection of the pieces he wrote for *Libération*, including *Dis, maman, c'est quoi l'avant-guerre?* (1980), *Les Années Mitterrand* (1986), and *La Drôle d'année* (1987). He has also published a portrait of French political leaders entitled *Le Salon des artistes* (1989).

F. M. Samuelson, *Il était une fois Libération* (Paris, 1979).

P. Aubery

Related entries: COHN-BENDIT, DANIEL; DEMONSTRATIONS; FOUCAULT, MICHEL; FRENCH COMMUNIST PARTY; PRESS; SARTRE, JEAN-PAUL; STUDENT REVOLTS; UNIFIED SOCIALIST PARTY; UNION OF THE LEFT.

JUQUIN, PIERRE (1930–), communist dissident and presidential candidate. The son of a railway worker, he made his way up the educational ladder to obtain the prestigious *agrégation* in German. He joined the French Communist party (PCF) in 1953. Although he was very orthodox at first, he became identified with liberal strands in the party and became a leading dissident who ran as a presidential candidate in the 1988 elections.

In the PCF his ascension was steady: nominated to the Central Committee in 1967, a Political Bureau member in 1979 and in charge of the Press and Information Office. In 1967 he was elected deputy for Essonne (third district), a seat he lost in 1968 but regained in 1973 and held until 1981. Always media conscious, he became a minor celebrity in 1976 when he shook hands with Leonid Plyushch, the Russian human rights campaigner.

Despite these signs of official favor, ''comrade taboo'' (as PCF chief Georges Marchais called him) increasingly differed from the party's leadership. In 1982 at the twenty-fourth party congress he was stripped of most responsibilities but emerged as the leading publicist for communist dissidents (''renovators'') and criticized the leadership at the twenty-fifth congress in 1985. When André Lajoinie was nominated to run as a presidential candidate under the communist banner, Juquin started his own campaign and was excluded from the PCF on October 14, 1987.

Juquin's presidential campaign was supported by a heterogeneous group of renovators, PSU (Unified Socialist party) supporters, Trotskyists, and ecologists on a feminist, antiracist, antinuclear platform. The outcome, 606,017 votes (1.99%), was well below expectations, and the coalition disintegrated. Juquin still campaigns with other renovators but is now a relatively marginal figure. He has returned to teaching.

P. Juquin, *Autocritiques* (Paris, 1987).

D. S. Bell

Related entries: COMMON PROGRAM; ECOLOGY PARTY; FRENCH COMMUNIST PARTY; LAJOINIE, ANDRE; MARCHAIS, GEORGES; SOCIALIST PARTY (PS).

K

KRASUCKI, HENRI (1924–), labor leader and communist party official who has served as secretary-general of the *Confédération générale du travail* (CGT) since 1982. Born in Poland in 1924, he fled with his family from prewar pogroms to France. During World War II young Krasucki, already a member of the *Jeunesse communiste*, joined the Resistance. Following his arrest in 1943, he was deported to labor camps in Germany.

Upon his return to France in 1945, he became a metal worker and a militant in the CGT. In 1950 he became secretary of the CGT for the Department of the Seine. Krasucki rose rapidly in the hierarchy of both the CGT and the French Communist party (PCF). In 1960 he was elected to the secretariat of the CGT and became director of its weekly newspaper, *Vie ouvrière*. In 1956 he was elected to the Central Committee of the PCF and since 1961 has been a member of its *Bureau politique*. Succeeding Georges Séguy, in 1982 Krasucki became secretary-general of CGT.

Krasucki embraces a left-wing view of industrial relations as a conflict of irreconcilable class differences. This view has proved increasingly less effective among France's growing cadres of white-collar workers. Although the CGT is still the largest French labor union, with approximately 1.5 million members in 1989, it has suffered substantial setbacks during the recession of the 1980s. As a result, membership has continued to decline, further weakening the CGT's bargaining power. Despite differences of doctrine, the communist-dominated CGT often works with other unions and is not always the most militant. Serious change in either the direction or the prospects of the CGT is unlikely under Krasucki's leadership.

H. Krasucki, *Syndicats et socialisme* (Paris, 1972), *Syndicats et unité* (Paris, 1980), *Un Syndicat moderne? Oui!* (Paris, 1987); N. Tandler, *Un Inconnu nommé Krasucki* (Paris, 1985).

F. J. Murphy

Related entries: CONFEDERATION GENERALE DU TRAVAIL; STRIKES; TRADE UNION MOVEMENT.

L

LABOR FORCE from 1954 to 1961 had been stable at about 19 million, and from 1962 to the end of 1987 grew to 24.4 million (including 2.5 million unemployed), an increase of 28.4 percent, the largest growth in the European Economic Community (EEC). Otherwise, France has in common with the EEC an increased percentage of the labor force that is salaried (65% in the mid-1950s, 85% in 1987); an increase in the percentage of the employed labor force devoted to tertiary activities (54% in 1977, 62% in December 1986); a decline in the percentage occupied in agriculture (from 25% to 6.5%) and manufacturing; a decrease in the effective work week (from a peak of 47 hours in 1964 to 39 hours in 1986; a fifth week of paid vacation mandated by law in 1981); later entrance into the work force, due mainly to increased education; earlier retirement; an increased feminization of the work force; an increase in the use of foreign workers, especially of Third World origin, until the oil shocks of 1973 created unemployment; the tendency of the labor force to divide into those who have continuing contracts with benefits and those who have limited-duration contracts or no contracts (*interim*) with few if any benefits and protections, with a dichotomization of the labor force into stable occupations requiring continued education, high capacity to communicate, and high responsibility, and occupations of low education, low responsibility, and unstable employment.

Demography

The major source of the increase in the labor force was the baby boom, which in France began during the Occupation, reached a peak of births in 1965 (net reproduction rate [NRR] 134.5), and ended in the early 1970s. In 1975 the NRR fell to 91.8, where it has more or less remained until now. As a result, until the year 2000, past demographic trends will contribute to an increase in the labor force.

In the period 1984–87 the labor force has increased by an average of 152,000 per year. But if the effects of earlier retirement and later entry into the labor force are deducted, the average increase in the effective labor force is 117,000, mainly contributed by an increase in female employment.

Women

The participation of women in the labor force has always been high in France due to the many farms, retail and artisanal establishments where the wife operated the cash register while the husband worked in the cellar or the back office, and due to the importance of the textile industry and domestic service. In 1906 women made up 36 percent of the labor force. Until 1968 a female contribution to the labor force was a status disability, and with the increasing standard of living in the 1950s and 1960s, the decline of farms, of the textile industry, and of the retail and artisanal establishments, the percentage of women in the labor force fell to 34.9 percent in 1968 before climbing back to 36 percent in 1975.

During the 1980s the status disability vanished. Middle-class women sought employment, and this, combined with the growing availability of jobs in education, health, social services, business offices, and electronics, and with the decline of male participation, made women 44 percent of the labor force in 1989. Two-thirds of women with two children worked in 1988 as against 46 percent in 1975. Women make up 76 percent of the employés, 51 percent of the civil service, 62 percent of the teachers, but only 7 percent of the engineers. Women comprise 28.8 percent of the "*cadres* and superior intellectual professions." In "intermediary professions" they are already at 42.6 percent. They also contribute to "off-the-books" work, since their husbands' Social Security gives them the health benefits they need. They are thus cheaper to employ by some one-third than "declared" workers. Meanwhile, within the working class (21% women) they tend to occupy the least skilled occupations (37% women).

Immigration

France has always been a society of immigration, especially after World War I when immigrants from Italy, Poland, Belgium, and Spain came to replace the war dead. They represented 6.5 percent of the population in 1931, and 6.78 percent in 1982, with a range of 43,000 to 55,000 being naturalized every year to compose 2.6 percent of the population. Until 1962 European immigrants dominated the flow. In the census of 1982 the European immigrants, mainly Portuguese, Italians, and Spanish made up 47.6 percent of foreigners, while Africans (especially North Africans) made up 42.8 percent.

Actually, the most significant immigration was the repatriation of the French families of Algeria (*pieds-noirs*) in 1962 to 1965, a total of some 860,000 people—modern farmers, white-collar workers, *cadres*, and professionals—who contributed substantially to the economic expansion of the 1960s.

Foreign immigrant labor is concentrated in the lower-paid categories of the working class, especially in construction and public works, where it makes up 17 percent of the work force. There are many factories and building sites where a foreign labor force operates the machines under the supervision of native French engineers and foremen.

The French government, after the first shocks of the oil crisis, like after the onset of the depression in 1931, tried to send back many foreign workers. In

1975 to 1985 the methods were somewhat softer than in 1931. The results have been that in the period 1975–82 net immigration slowed to ten thousand a year—and has had a zero balance in the period 1982–87. Illegal immigration (estimated at one million) is significant and is supported by employment off the books in construction, in the garment trades, and in the unskilled services.

A specific aspect of the French labor force is its dispersion among many small establishments, often located in villages or small towns of less than twenty thousand. Approximately 27 percent of industrial workers live in villages, where small family firms have a monopoly over the local labor pool.

Finally, the French labor force, in its proletarian sector, suffers from a lack of educational qualification—one-third of French students leave school to enter the labor force without adequate training. Efforts are being made to remedy this deficiency.

Annuaire statistique 1987; *Comptes de la nation 1988*; *Données sociales 1974, 1990, INSEE*; D. Gambier, M. Verniäres, *L'Emploi en France* (Paris, 1988); R. Klatzman, *Le Travail noir* (Paris, 1982); *Recensement 1982: Les étrangers, INSEE.*

J. R. Pitts

Related entries: IMMIGRANTS; POPULATION TRENDS; TRADE UNION MOVEMENT; UNEMPLOYMENT; WOMEN, CONDITION OF.

LACAN, JACQUES (1901–1981), psychiatrist and psychoanalyst, disciple and interpreter of Sigmund Freud, and one of four leading structuralists in France in the 1960s. Lacan saw the purpose of his work as that of a "return to Freud"—to pursue and defend his teachings, and elucidate his concepts—and made relatively few claims regarding its originality. The most important of his essays are published in the collection *Ecrits* (1966), where he explored the themes of language, desire, alterity, the unconscious, and the ideal. For almost three decades, Lacan gave regular seminars in Paris (first in his apartment in the rue de Lille, then at the *Hôpital Sainte-Anne*, next at the rue d'Ulm, and finally in the law faculty at Paris I) on every aspect of psychoanalysis. By the 1960s, these seminars had become a Parisian institution, referred to elliptically as *le séminaire*. Lacan's greatest discovery is perhaps that of the "mirror phase," a stage that occurs when, faced with his or her reflection in the mirror between the ages of six and eighteen months, the infant first conceives of himself or herself as an autonomous and coherent entity. For Lacan, the significance of this primal moment of self-identification lies in the fact that it exemplifies a permanent tendency on the part of the individual, who needs the illusion of wholeness readily accessible to him or her in the mirror image in order to mask those elements of *manque* endemic in life itself. Lacan was the founder both of the *Ecole freudienne de Paris* (1964) and of the *Ecole de la cause freudienne*, which replaced the *Ecole freudienne* in 1980.

Lacan was born in Paris on April 13, 1901. As a pupil at the *Collège Stanislas*, his ambition from the age of fifteen was to be a doctor. In 1920 he went to medical school and six years later chose to specialize in psychiatry under the neurologist Henri Claude at the *Hôpital Sainte-Anne* and began to publish his first articles. In 1928 Lacan studied at the *Infirmerie spéciale des aliénés de la préfecture de police* under Clérambault, who, together with Kraepelin and Freud, can be seen as one of three major pillars in the subsequent development of his ideas. Four years later he was awarded a *doctorat d'état* for a thesis entitled "La Psychose paranoïaque dans ses rapports à la personnalité." Here, the more traditional world of psychiatry, as represented by Kraepelin, merges with the new world of psychoanalysis to which Lacan had been initiated by the writings of Freud.

By 1936 Lacan was a fully fledged doctor working both in the psychiatric hospitals of Paris and in his own private practice. In July of that year he attended the fourteenth meeting of the International Psychoanalytical Association (IPA) in Marienbad, where he presented a paper on the concept of the mirror phase. The ideas it contained were elaborated and presented afresh at the IPA's sixteenth international congress in Zurich thirteen years later, under the title: "*Le Stade de miroir comme formateur de la fonction du Je.*" Here, taking as his starting point this primal vision of the self as a comprehensive whole, Lacan distinguished between the ego (*moi*), the ideal self created by the individual and imagined to be essential and unchanging, and the subject (*sujet*), which can only be apprehended in its relation to external stimuli, and which cannot therefore be reduced to an essence since it is constantly refashioned anew. Lacan's seminar on "*La Lettre volée*," the opening article in the collection *Ecrits* and one of his most fundamental texts, pursued this point, revealing the subject to be decentered and itinerant, and irrevocably determined in its actions and destiny by the signifier, in this case the stolen letter. Language, of course, is the medium of psychoanalysis, and Lacan's most important essay is perhaps his manifesto, "*Fonction et champ de la parole et du langage en psychanalyse*," presented to the Institute of Psychology at the University of Rome in September 1953. His belief was that the unconscious bears the structure of a language and consequently, borrowing from the discoveries of modern linguistics and Ferdinand de Saussure in particular, that the subject is constituted by the symbol. The fundamental symbols for Lacan (as clarified in "*La Signification du phallus*," presented in May 1958) are the phallus and the primordial Other, the father within the Oedipal triangle. Lacan expresses the father's symbolic function as primal legislator by the term *le nom du père*, simultaneously implying both authority and prohibition (*nom* = *non*). The father guarantees the indestructibility of desire by ensuring that its goals (in this case comforting sexual relations with the mother) are never satisfied. This too, for Lacan, is a primal instance of a mechanism repeatedly triggered throughout life: It is "the Other" that incapacitates the subject for plenitude through his initiation of *manque* within the self.

Lacan died on September 9, 1981. It is perhaps too soon to pronounce judgment on his work, which during his lifetime stimulated both controversy and adulation, and much of which—including the majority of the texts presented during his seminars—remains to be published.

M. Bowie, "Jacques Lacan," in *Structuralism and Since*, ed. J. Sturrock (London, 1982); G. Miller, ed., *Lacan* (Paris, 1987); B. Ogilvie, *Lacan: La Formation du concept de sujet (1932–1949)* (Paris, 1987); J.-M. Palmier, *Lacan* (Paris, 1972); E. Roudinesco, *Jacques Lacan & Co.: A History of Psychoanalysis in France, 1925–1985*, trans. J. Mehlman (Chicago, 1990).

M. Maclean

Related entries: FOUCAULT, MICHEL; INTELLECTUAL TRENDS; STRUCTURALISM.

LAJOINIE, ANDRE (1929–), son of a peasant farmer from the Corrèze, who joined the French Communist party (PCF) at the age of nineteen, a man of impeccable orthodoxy and the lackluster communist candidate in the 1988 presidential elections. Lajoinie's steady climbing in the party hierarchy was a function of his closeness to Georges Marchais and his ability in handling agricultural questions. In 1956 he became federal secretary of the Communist Farmers' Union of the Corrèze and a party employee shortly afterward. In May 1958 he was injured in a clash with police and went to Czechoslovakia for treatment of head injuries. He was made editor of the party weekly *Le Travailleur de la Corrèze* and then in 1963 went to Paris to work on the PCF's farmers' weekly *La Terre*.

It is possible that Lajoinie was at some time in the 1960s a student at the Lenin International College in Moscow; what is certain, however, is that in 1972 he became a substitute member of the Central Committee of the PCF and secretary of the peasant farmers' division, in 1976 a substitute member of the Political Bureau, and in 1977 editor of *La Terre*. He was elected deputy for the third district of l'Allier in 1978 (and has been returned since then) and became leader of the communist group in the National Assembly in 1981. Lajoinie became a full member of the party's Political Bureau in 1979 and a member of the Secretariat in 1982.

Lajoinie's promotions in the 1970s coincide closely with Marchais's increasing grip on the party machine. However, he was neither an organizational genius nor a politician of outstanding talent—he was, in fact, a rather obscure *apparatchik*. The choice of Lajoinie by Marchais to run as the party's candidate for the 1988 presidential election was an unhappy one, but understandable. Unlike the former PCF ministers, Lajoinie posed no challenge to Marchais even if he did do well in the polls. But Lajoinie was ill at ease with the hustings, and he was a lamentable figure. The PCF's issues in the campaign itself were singularly ill-judged, but he was not responsible for that. The outcome was a humiliation for the party. Lajoinie polled only 2,055,995 votes (6.76% of the vote), the lowest communist vote since the war and another milestone in the party's plunge into marginality.

The presidential campaign had revealed an introverted character who, in the national political competition, was a bit like a checkers player who had wandered inadvertently into a chess tournament. He was really at ease only among the communist farming community, discussing livestock prices; it was to his credit as a local personality that he increased his vote (relative to the presidentials) in the Assembly elections that followed by 15 percent.

Lajoinie is the author of an unrevealing book, *A coeur ouverte*, written in the form of an interview with a communist journalist.

A. Lajoinie, *A coeur ouverte* (Paris, 1987).

D. S. Bell

Related entries: AGRICULTURE; FRENCH COMMUNIST PARTY; JUQUIN, PIERRE; MARCHAIS, GEORGES; PEASANTRY; ROCHET, WALDECK.

LANG, JACK (1939–), university professor, media producer, and minister of culture in Mitterrand's socialist governments. Born September 2, 1939 in Mirecourt (Vosges), Lang is the son of Roger Lang, the industrialist, and Marie-Luce Boucher. He studied at the *Lycée Poincaré* in Nancy, where he graduated in 1957. He then enrolled in the Nancy Law School and studied acting at the Nancy Conservatory for Dramatic Arts (in 1958 he was awarded a second prize for elocution and a second prize for comic acting). Lang graduated in 1961 from the Paris Law School and from the Political Science Institute. He received his doctorate in law from the Nancy Law School, completing a dissertation on "The Theater and the State." *Agrégé* in public law in 1970, he was appointed professor of international law and elected dean of the Nancy Law School in 1977.

In 1963 he founded the International Festival of Student Theater that he directed until 1972, when he was appointed to head the National Theater of Chaillot. His innovative style at Chaillot generated heated controversies that caused him to be fired in 1974 by Maurice Druon, a Goncourt Prize–winning novelist and minister of cultural affairs at the time.

In 1958 Lang joined the Radical party, left it to follow Pierre Mendès-France in the *Parti socialiste autonome* (PSA), later becoming the *Parti socialiste unifié* (PSU), and eventually joined the Socialist party (PS) renovated by François Mitterrand. Lang officially began his political career with his election to the Paris City Council in 1977; one year later he became a special adviser to Mitterrand, the first secretary of the Socialist party. He served as a campaign manager for the socialists in the 1979 European elections. Following the election victory of Mitterrand in 1981 as president, Lang was appointed minister of culture (1981–86), and he was reappointed to the same post in the governments of Michel Rocard (1988–91) and Edith Cresson (1991–).

In July of 1982 Lang delivered a speech in Mexico City at a meeting of UNESCO that brought him to the attention of the American public. He blasted the alleged "cultural imperialism" of the United States, exemplified by such television programs as "Dallas." As minister of culture, he considered putting quotas on the number of American films, television programs, and tapes admitted into France. This unfortunate manifestation of cultural protectionism backfired, but it did not slow down the progress of Lang's career. He was reappointed minister of culture and communication in 1988 following the brief interlude of Jacques Chirac's conservative government (1986–88). In March 1989 he was elected mayor of the city of Blois, defeating the right-wing incumbent, Pierre Sudreau, a former chief of French counterintelligence. Lang has also supervised the official celebrations under the socialist governments, such as Mitterrand's 1981 installation-day ceremony at the Pantheon and the 1989 bicentennial festivities.

P. De Plunkett, *La Culture en veston rose* (Paris, 1982); J. Lang, J. D. Bredin, A. Vitez, *Eclats* (Paris, 1978); Interview in *Playboy*, July 1981.

P. Aubery

Related entries: ARAGON, LOUIS; ART AND ARCHITECTURE; ATTALI, JACQUES; MALRAUX, ANDRE; MITTERRAND, FRANCOIS; POPULAR CULTURE; SOCIALIST PARTY (PS); UNIFIED SOCIALIST PARTY; VILAR, JEAN.

LANIEL, JOSEPH (1889–1975), industrialist, conservative deputy, and nineteenth prime minister of the Fourth Republic. Born in Vimoutiers, Normandy on October 12, 1889 into a wealthy and powerful family of textile manufacturers, Laniel followed the family tradition of combining careers in industry and politics.

After distinguished service in World War I as an artillery officer, for which he won the Legion of Honor and the *Croix de guerre*, Laniel began his political career as mayor of Notre-Dame-de-Courson and general councillor of Calvados. In 1932 he assumed the seat in the Chamber of Deputies representing Lisieux (Calvados) that had been held by his father, Henri Laniel, since 1896. Reelected in 1936, he served as under-secretary of state for finance under Paul Reynaud's 1940 government and was one of eighty deputies who voted against granting full powers to Marshal Pétain.

Laniel became a leader in the Resistance, helping to found the Council of National Resistance and serving as its vice-president. Refusing to run his textile factory for the Germans, Laniel withdrew to his farm in Bellerive-sur-Allier, which became an important Resistance headquarters. At Liberation, he entered Paris beside General Charles de Gaulle and was later awarded the Resistance medal.

After serving as vice-president for both constituent assemblies, Laniel was elected in 1946 to the National Assembly representing Calvados, a post that he held continuously until 1958. In 1947 Laniel was chosen vice-president of the National Assembly, but resigned to become the president of the parliamentary group for the *Parti républicain de la liberté* (PRL), a conservative party that he helped found. He later joined the Independent Republican party.

Known as an expert in economic and financial affairs, Laniel was named secretary of state for finance in the government of André Marie (July-August 1948), and after briefly serving as minister of posts, telegraphs, and telephone in 1951 under René Pleven, held the position of minister of state from September 1951 to February 1952 under both Pleven and his successor, Edgar Faure.

Laniel became prime minister in June 1953, ending a month-long crisis during which seven other candidates failed to win parliamentary approval. With his exemplary war record and his reputation as a dynamic, but socially responsible businessman, Laniel was able to win support from the left and right. Thanks to that broad support his government lasted a full year (June 1953–June 1954), surviving economic recession, a bitter, week-long general strike that paralyzed France in August 1953, the rise of the Poujadist movement, and a deteriorating situation in Indochina.

Against the backdrop of the debacle at Dien Bien Phu, Laniel began negotiations in Geneva to end the war in Indochina, but by then his government was discredited and internally divided. It finally fell in June 1954, leaving his successor, Pierre Mendès-France, to conclude the talks. Laniel retired from politics in 1958. He died on April 9, 1975.

C. Bourdache, *Les Années cinquante* (Paris, 1980); J. Laniel, *Jours de gloire et jours cruels, 1908–1958* (Paris, 1971).

R. D. Moore

Related entries: BIDAULT, GEORGES; DECOLONIZATION; DIEN BIEN PHU; EUROPEAN DEFENSE COMMUNITY; FAURE, EDGAR; FRENCH UNION; MENDES-FRANCE, PIERRE; PLEVEN, RENE; POUJADISTS; STRIKES.

LECANUET, JEAN (1920–), politician who has served in a variety of positions in several administrations during the Fourth and Fifth Republics, most noted for his unsuccessful bid for the presidency in 1965. Lecanuet was born in Rouen on March 4, 1920. Upon completion of his studies at the Faculty of Letters in Paris, he taught briefly before entering the Resistance in 1943. After World War II, he entered government service and was elected to the National Assembly (1951–55) and the Senate (1959–73, and since 1977) from the department of Seine-Maritime. He has also served as mayor of Rouen since 1968, as an elected member of the European Parliament since 1979, and in several ministerial positions since 1946. He was one of the founders of the *Mouvement républicain populaire* (MRP).

After breaking with President Charles de Gaulle in 1963, Lecanuet devoted his efforts to building a democratic alternative to both Gaullism and any kind of alliance with communism. Although unsuccessful, his presidential candidacy in 1965 forced President de Gaulle into a second round. Because of his relative youth and media appeal, Lecanuet was often compared during that campaign to U.S. President John F. Kennedy. From 1965 to 1974 Lecanuet was frustrated in his efforts to construct a center party, but faithfully pursued that goal successively through the MRP, the Democratic Center, and the Reformers' Movement.

Lecanuet rallied to the successful presidential campaign of Valéry Giscard d'Estaing in 1974 and held several important ministries during the Giscard presidency. Since 1976 Lecanuet has been president of the centrist party, Union for French Democracy. He has been a consistent advocate of the European Community and a very effective mayor of Rouen.

J. Lecanuet, J.-J. Servan-Schreiber, *Le Projet réformateur* (Paris, 1973); W. Safran, "Centrism in the Fifth Republic," in *The Fifth Republic at Twenty,* ed. W. Andrews and S. Hoffmann (Albany, N.Y., 1981).

F. J. Murphy

Related entries: CHRISTIAN DEMOCRATS; GISCARD D'ESTAING, VALERY; SERVAN-SCHREIBER, JEAN-JACQUES; UNION FOR FRENCH DEMOCRACY.

LEFT RADICALS (*Mouvement des radicaux de gauche*, MRG), first emerged as a dissident group within the Radical party in 1971, becoming an independent party in December 1973. Following the leadership of René Fabre and René Billères, who had been active in internal party discussion groups during the 1960s, strong opposition was voiced to the political strategy of the Radical party's new president, Jean-Jacques Servan-Schreiber. Servan-Schreiber sought to end the radicals' electoral alliance with the socialists and shift the party to the center of the political spectrum. He was convinced that declining radical strength would be revived by the creation of a centrist "third force" coalition clearly distinct from both socialists on the left and Gaullists on the right. The majority of radical deputies and members strongly disagreed. They boycotted the June 1971 party congress and demanded the continuation of electoral and parliamentary alliances with the socialists, despite losses in the 1969 legislative elections.

This group of dissidents, now identifying itself as the MRG, negotiated with the newly formed Socialist party (PS) and established an alliance for the 1973 legislative elections, the *Union des gauches socialistes et démocratiques*. These same left radicals then accepted and added their signature to the historic Common Program, which had been worked out the previous year between socialists and the Communist party. The elections, a vital turning point for the socialists, brought modest gains for the newly formed MRG; their twelve deputies joined the strengthened socialist group in the National Assembly. In December of that year the MRG became a formal political party, adopting almost the identical statutes that had governed the Radical party since 1901 and were still being used by their centrist rivals who had retained the label *radicals*.

The MRG drew on the traditional strength of the Radical party in the rural, less economically advanced southwest. In the early 1970s radical deputies from departments such as the Dordogne, Lot, and Charente-Maritime, feared twin electoral perils—opposing a reinvigorated alliance of socialists and communists or the equally dangerous situation of facing center-right opponents without the support of socialist or communist allies. Such concerns led some key radical deputies, such as Maurice Faure and Georges Bonnet, to support and join the MRG. In addition, younger radicals, like Michel Crépeau, the mayor of La Rochelle, viewed the MRG as a means to reaffirm the traditional commitment of radicalism to the left and to adapt that tradition to post–1968 France.

Since 1973 the political fortunes of the MRG have been largely tied to the successes and failures of the Socialist party. For many outside the MRG, the left radicals are indistinguishable from the socialists. They appear as a tiny group of individual politicians who, for various idiosyncratic reasons, choose not to adopt the label socialist while adhering to the Socialist party's principles and actions, including support of the Common Program launched by the socialists and communists in 1972. However, within the MRG, despite its limited political clout, members view themselves as distinct from both the other minuscule Radical party on their right and their giant partner to the left. Left radicals stress their dedication to parliamentary democracy, civil liberties, and social reform. As representatives of the "little people," they criticize big capital and large bureaucracies. Speaking for the radical, humanist left they intend to serve as a "third force" countering the influence of the communists.

There was certainly enough political life within the MRG to support a series of internal controversies and rifts. In 1978, following electoral defeats, the party president René Fabre disavowed the left alliance and called for a shift to the center. He, in turn, was repudiated and forced to resign. Michel Crépeau, deputy from the Charente-Maritime, was elected party president and reaffirmed the alliance with the socialists, but internal tensions between a right and left wing remain.

Through the 1970s and early 1980s the MRG maintained a small but noticeable presence in the National Assembly. However, since 1986 their already reduced numbers have further declined. In 1973 the MRG had twelve deputies, in 1978 ten, in 1981 fourteen, in 1986 two, and in 1988 nine, always sitting with the socialists. In 1981 the left radicals mounted an independent presidential campaign for Michel Crépeau, gaining 2.2 percent of the vote on the first round. The socialists have recognized the left radical's electoral and parliamentary support and awarded them positions in the socialist governments of 1981 and 1988. Between 1981 and 1986 Crépeau served as minister of environment (perhaps an acknowledgment of the left radicals' sensitivity to the nuclear issue); as minister of commerce, small business, and tourism; and briefly as minister of justice.

The increasing polarization of French politics under the structural pressure of a presidential system with national election campaigns would seem to doom the ever-more-marginal MRG to oblivion. However, the continuation of an important parliamentary arena and a group of voters who identify themselves with a non-socialist left may continue to sustain this small political formation. The left radicals have embodied the characteristic central to French radicalism since at least 1901: its commitment to social reform, but its deep uncertainty about the consequences of change.

M. Crépeau, *L'Avenir en face* (Paris, 1981).

J. F. Stone

Related entries: CENTRIST PARTIES; COMMON PROGRAM; ELECTIONS; FEDERATION OF THE DEMOCRATIC AND SOCIALIST LEFT; RADICAL PARTY; SERVAN-SCHREIBER, JEAN-JACQUES; SOCIALIST PARTY (PS).

LEISURE, an important social, economic, and political issue in France today. Defined as the portion of time that is not devoted to work and commuting, or to home chores and physiological needs (eating, sleeping, ailing, etc.), leisure time is directly affected by legislation governing workload. In 1936 a standard work week of forty hours and two weeks of paid vacation was established. From 1946 to 1970 the industrial work force had to average eight hours a week overtime per person to meet the high demand for goods in postwar France. A third week of paid vacation was granted in 1956, and a fourth one in 1969. There were, however, large differences between the various economic sectors in the 1970s. Construction workers averaged fifty hours, while workers in energy industries rarely worked more than forty-three hours. These differences tapered off with the 1973 economic crisis and mounting social pressure for reforms. In January 1982 the legislature set the work week at 39 hours, limited overtime to 130 hours per year, and increased paid vacation to five weeks. This was an attempt to equalize workloads between the various industries, small and large companies, and male and female workers. For the same reason, retirement age was set at age sixty for all.

Today, the amount of an individual's free time is still linked to age, sex, and type of employment. The married working woman has an average low of 2.5 hours of daily leisure (given her heavier load of household chores), the self-employed man 3.3 hours, the male employee 4.1 hours, the nonworking or retired woman 4 hours, and the nonworking or retired male 5.5 hours.

With a little over seven hours a day on the job and less than half of their life span spent at work, the French have entered the leisure era. What they do with their added free time depends again on their sex and age, but also on their social status, locale, and level of education rather than their income.

By 1988 watching television had become the preferred leisure activity in France, where 94 percent of the families owned a set. The amount of time devoted to television has increased at the expense of other leisure activities. In 1986 the French spent 3.3 hours watching television each day and more than 8 hours on the weekend. It is the rural, less educated, and older person who watches television most, and the young, intellectual city person who watches the least. Still avid film viewers, the French now prefer to watch movies on television or on videotape, rather than at theaters, which sold only 133 million tickets in 1987, compared with 400 million in 1953. Well equipped with cassette players and hi-fi equipment, the French have declared that listening to music remains their favorite pastime. They rely much less on the radio to be informed or entertained. Similarly, time spent reading daily newspapers has decreased sharply since 1945. However, weeklies and the specialized press have grown tenfold, the most successful being television magazines. Books are published in increasing numbers, but with fewer copies per title. Novels have the highest readership, made up mostly of nonworking women under sixty, pink-collar workers (low-paid office personnel, mainly women), and Parisians.

Three leisure activities evidence a profound change in life-style in France today: sports, gardening, and *bricolage* (tinkering, pottering). The French are increasingly involved in sports: 53.7 percent of adults between age twenty and fifty-nine and 86 percent of the fifteen to nineteen age group participate in at least one sport regularly. Educated middle-class men and women under fifty living in the Paris region are the most sports-oriented. They favor individual sports: walking, swimming, and aerobics first, followed by biking and tennis. In rural areas people prefer team sports, but few are actively engaged in them. Soccer, the national sport, is practiced by only 14 percent of the twelve- to thirty-five-year-old age group, but it remains the sport most watched on television.

The combination of more leisure, higher income, and the use of individual cars led, starting in the late 1950s, to a new trend: the acquisition of a vacation home by urban dwellers. With 2.5 million *résidences secondaires* (12% of all households), France has the highest such ratio in the world. Of late, the rapid increase of suburban individual housing has curtailed this trend, but has increased the amount of free time the French spend gardening and fixing their homes and cars. In 1988, thirteen million households were in this category.

Since 1945 the number of people spending vacation away from home has steadily increased, to reach 57.5 percent of the population in 1985. The most notable change occurred in 1975 when people started to go on vacation outside of the traditional July–August period. In 1984 only 51.5 percent of the vacationers chose to leave home in the summer. The fifth vacation week is most often used after Christmas, or during the February school holiday, somewhat offsetting the traditional French leisure calendar. Yet, despite the legislation, serious inequities remain between urban and rural dwellers, rich and poor, young and old, Paris and the rest of France, in terms of the number of days spent away and the ability to leave for winter vacation.

Where the French go for their vacations is less clearly linked to their social status than to their income. Close to half spend their vacation at parents' or friends' houses, the rest choosing almost equally between hotels, apartments, camps, or their vacation home. They prefer the Atlantic seashore in the summer, and the Alps in the winter. Still, few go to a foreign country, and most are in the sixteen to thirty age group. Wherever they are, French vacationers are increasingly participating in sports and cultural activities rather than sunbathing, another new departure.

Leisure greatly affects everyone's budget in France. The portion of income each household spends on leisure activities and equipment varies according to age, family size, profession, and locale. It averaged 10 percent in 1986; non-married people under thirty-five spent twice as much as single people over sixty-five, and Parisians 4 percent more than the national average.

Leisure activities have far-reaching implications for all sectors of the economy. For instance, tourism, with a yearly raw income of 155 billion French francs, is a flourishing industry that dictates the construction of theme parks, seashore developments, highways, public transportation, and so forth. Together with sports and cultural activities, it affects the domestic industrial production of consumer goods as well as the country's trade balance. The importance of leisure on the political arena is clear with three ministers (of culture, youth and sports, and social affairs) and one state secretary (for tourism) in charge of legislating, organizing, funding, or developing every known aspect of leisure. Possibly more than in any other country, leisure has changed the French way of life.

Haut-Comité de la jeunesse, des sports, et des loisirs, *Compte-rendu d'assemblées plénières* (Paris, 1981); INSEE, *Données sociales* (Paris, 1988); G. Mermet, *Francoscopie* (Paris, 1989); Secrétariat d'état à l'environnement, *Rapport sur l'aménagement du temps libre* (Paris, 1976); M. Verdie, ed., *L'Etat de la France et de ses habitants* (Paris, 1989).

L. J. Haenlin

Related entries: BROADCAST MEDIA; CINEMA; CULTURAL POLICY; POPULAR CULTURE; PRESS; SOCIAL TRENDS; SPORTS.

LEOTARD, FRANCOIS (1942–), politician, leader of the *Parti républicain* (PR), and would-be contender for the presidency of the Republic in 1995. Educated at the *Fondation nationale des sciences politiques* (degree in law) and prestigious *Ecole nationale d'administration*, Léotard became a subprefect (Dordogne) in 1975, having worked in the Foreign Office (1968–71) and Ministry of the Environment (1973–75).

His entry into politics took two forms. After Valéry Giscard d'Estaing's election to the presidency in 1974, his administrative ability was noticed by Michel Poniatowski, then minister of the interior, who asked him to lead *Agir pour l'avenir*, a coordinating organization for future Giscardian candidates in local and national elections. In response to a more personal commitment, in 1977 he campaigned and won the local elections of March, becoming mayor of Fréjus. He regarded this as a kind of symbolic vindication of the memory of his father, who had also been mayor of Fréjus but had been the victim of a whispering campaign, and who had died in 1975. Léotard was a founding member of the Giscardian PR in May 1977. He was elected as deputy (*Union pour la démocratie française, UDF/Parti républicain*) in the legislative elections of 1978 (from the Var region), and *conseiller régional* of Provence-Côte d'Azur. The following year he was also elected *conseiller général* of the canton of Fréjus.

In the legislative elections of June 1981, Léotard was reelected on the first round, and this, as in 1977, against the national trend toward the left. In November 1981 he became deputy general secretary of the PR, and in September 1982, general secretary. By the time he became leader of the PR, his many successes between 1977 and 1981, his media popularity, youth, and dynamism meant that he, in part, symbolized the renewal of the right after its 1981 defeat. He therefore incurred the suspicion of the two main representatives of the non-Gaullist right, Raymond Barre and Giscard, and through the 1980s maintained a respectful but unenthusiastic relationship with them (he became vice-president of the UDF in 1983). His objective ally became Jacques Chirac. When the right won the 1986 legislative elections, Léotard, whose PR was the largest constituent element of the UDF, gave Chirac his support (thus precluding the possibility of appointing an alternative prime minister such as Simone Veil or Jacques Chaban-Delmas), and became minister of culture and communication (1986–88), a high-profile ministry (thanks, in part, to his immediate predecessor, Jack Lang), but one that perhaps failed to endow Léotard with the prestige he would have derived from, say, the Defense Ministry, which he had wanted. The most significant initiative of his ministry was the privatization of the television channel TF 1.

After the return of the socialists to power in June 1988, Léotard's action was twofold: to impede any drift of the new opposition to the center (and, therefore, into possible alliances with the minority socialist government), and to embark, with his supporters, on a period of ideological self-evaluation and strategic reappraisal.

Léotard and the PR represent a modernist, economically liberal, and moderate right (he is often considered as more left-leaning than his entourage and supporters), which would have itself an activist party, that is, more like the *Rassemblement pour la République* and less like the traditional cadre parties of the center-right.

Personally, Léotard has used the media to great advantage. His own interests are philosophy and literature, and he occasionally gives the impression of being too reflective and pensive for political life. Before his military service, which he spent as a teacher in Lebanon, he spent a year in a monastery (1963–64). Léotard both represents a French political tradition, the non-Gaullist, moderate right, and illustrates the Fifth Republic's personalization, presidentialism, and media utilization of French political parties and their leaders.

F. Léotard, *A mots découverts* (Paris, 1987), *Culture: Les Chemins de printemps* (Paris, 1988), *La Ville aimée* (Paris, 1989), *Pendant la crise le spectacle continue* (Paris, 1989).

J. Gaffney

Related entries: BARRE, RAYMOND; BROADCAST MEDIA; CHABAN-DELMAS, JACQUES; CHIRAC, JACQUES; *COHABITATION*; CULTURAL POLICY; GISCARD D'ESTAING, VALERY; LANG, JACK; PONIATOWSKI, MICHEL; PRIVATIZATION; UNION FOR FRENCH DEMOCRACY; VEIL, SIMONE.

LE PEN, JEAN-MARIE (1928–), a political activist who in recent years has given the radical right its most important electoral penetration since the Liberation. Born in the Breton fishing port of La Trinité-sur-Mer, Le Pen became a "national orphan" when his fisherman father was lost at sea in 1942. After a Jesuit education, he studied law in Paris, where he became president of the law students' "corporation" and began his career of radical rightist, anticommunist activity. Le Pen left his studies to enroll in the elite First Foreign Paratroop Battalion and serve in the final months of the Indochina campaign. Back in Paris, he came to the notice of the shopkeeper-turned-radical-right-politician Pierre Poujade, on whose list he was elected deputy for the Seine (1956, reelected

1958–62). As a deputy, Le Pen returned to his unit in 1957, serving in the Battle of Algiers (which led to specific accusations against him of torture) and the Suez expedition.

Le Pen worked for "French Algeria" as orator on the summer 1957 caravan that visited the vacation beaches. In 1965 he served as secretary-general of the ill-fated presidential election campaign of Jean-Louis Tixier-Vignancour.

To support himself during the dry years in the 1960s when he was out of Parliament, Le Pen founded a company to sell historical recordings. An historical appreciation (stressing the popular and legal character of the Nazi rise to power) that he wrote for a set of documentary recordings led to his conviction for "apology for war crimes" in 1968. (Le Pen's financial woes eased when he married the former wife of a theatrical impresario and when Le Pen and his wife received a substantial inheritance, in 1976, from an industrial heir with radical right sympathies.)

In 1972 Le Pen became president of the National Front (FN), an organization designed to reunite the French radical right and which included many former members of the violent neofascist organizations *Occident* and *Ordre nouveau*. In maneuvers with more "revolutionary" components of his party, Le Pen gained increasing control and steered the FN to electoralism and legalism while drawing on the clientele of more intransigent groups. Unlike its rival, the *Parti des forces nouvelles*, however, the National Front eschewed alliances with parties of the respectable right. Despite this, neither the FN nor Le Pen achieved more than derisory electoral results. In 1981, he could not even get on the presidential ballot.

The advent in 1981 of a socialist president and a government with communist participation, along with the continuing recession, gave the National Front its chance. Le Pen responded by concentrating on, and linking, the issues of immigrant workers (really the North African minority) and "insecurity" (law and order). In first-round municipal elections in 1983 Le Pen received 11 percent of the vote in Paris (eleventh *arrondissement*), and the National Front won 17 percent in the left municipality of Dreux, forcing its way onto the united right list for the second round (more recently over a third of the local electorate voted for the FN). The 1984 European Parliament elections, using proportional representation, gave the Front 11 percent, ten deputies (including Le Pen), and major media coverage. Further elections confirmed the Front's penetration, with results depending on the use of proportional representation (e.g., the 1986 legislative elections gave the FN thirty-five deputies) or majoritarian two-round consultations (e.g., in the 1988 legislative elections the FN won only one seat). Le Pen himself captured slightly more than 14 percent of the vote in the first round of the 1988 presidential elections. The FN's greatest strengths have been in the Midi, with its strong *pied-noir* vote, the Paris area, and districts with a high immigrant population. Its voters come from across the spectrum, from the right (RPR and UDF) through the socialists, but more rarely the communists, despite that party's concomitant decline. While the left vigorously opposes Le

Penism (though its policy of proportional representation favors it), the RPR and UDF have been divided between principled condemnation and the need for local electoral alliances.

Le Pen denies being fascist or racist and sues, usually successfully, anyone who publicly calls him such. His ideology draws most from the reactionary tradition of the French right, from Maurras through Pétain, updated to be Republican and legalist, and with neoliberalism replacing corporatism. Though his lieutenants include many with neofascist or anti-Semitic backgrounds, his periodic lapses into language that approaches anti-Semitism, or a less-than-systematic hostility to Nazism, can be understood as the real man showing through or as calculated scraps thrown to the more extremist among his followers.

J. Algazy, *L'Extrême-Droite en France de 1965 à 1984* (Paris, 1988); J.-M. Le Pen, *Les Français d'abord* (Paris, 1984); E. Plenel; A. Rollat, *L'Effet Le Pen* (Paris, 1984).

A. Douglas

Related entries: ANTI-SEMITISM; ELECTIONS; IMMIGRANTS; MINORITIES, PROBLEMS OF; POLITICAL TRENDS; POUJADISTS.

LE ROY LADURIE, EMMANUEL (1929–), leading figure in the *Annales* school of historiography, specialist in the agrarian and rural history of southern France during the medieval and early modern periods. Born in a village in Normandy (Calvados), Le Roy Ladurie was nurtured in the rural traditions and Catholic piety of the French countryside until his departure for a *lycée* in Paris following World War II. In the cosmopolitan world of the capital he became active in politics, joining the Communist party (PCF) in 1949, the same year he gained admittance to the elite *Ecole normale supérieure*. There he focused on historical studies, earning his degree in 1953. From 1955 to 1963 he lived and taught in Montpellier, first at a *lycée*, then at the university. His residence in the south of France inspired research for what would become his *thèse d'état* and influential first book, *Les Paysans du Languedoc* (1966, abr. Eng. trans. 1974).

Committed intellectually to Marxism, he initially sought, by studying the *compoix* (land registers) of the Languedoc, to trace the emergence of agrarian capitalism. But his extensive investigation of these documents failed to turn up support for the Marxist model of economic development. Instead he gradually discerned a great agrarian cycle, marked by successive phases of demographic growth and decline, that lasted from the fifteenth to the eighteenth century. Not Marx but Malthus best explained the fundamental dilemma of inelastic agricultural productivity that resulted in recurrent subsistence crises. This shift in historical explanation paralleled Le Roy Ladurie's own increasing disenchantment with communism, and he resigned from the PCF in 1956.

Increasingly, too, Le Roy Ladurie's historical thought came under the influence of *Annales* ideas, particularly those of Ernest Labrousse and Fernand Braudel, and in some respects *Les Paysans* is the most successful attempt to compose the *histoire totale* of a society to which the *Annales* aspired. Like Braudel, Le Roy

Ladurie was convinced that material and biological conditions exercised fundamental influences on premodern history, but he also stressed the importance of culture—language, religion, and especially psychological factors. The technological immobility of rural southern France stemmed as much from cultural stumbling blocks as from the forces of nature.

In 1963 Braudel offered Le Roy Ladurie a position in the *VIème section* of the *Ecole pratique des hautes études*, and from this point on he assumed increasing prominence in the *Annales* school. Appointed professor at the University of Paris VII in 1970, he has also held since 1973 the chair of the history of modern civilization at the Collège de France. In 1987 he was appointed director of the *Bibliothèque nationale*. While Paris was now his home and place of work, southern France remained the focus of his historical study, with *Les Paysans* providing the seedbed for much of his subsequent research. Considerations of the influence of climate on agriculture led to his *Histoire du climat depuis l'an mil* (1967; Eng. trans. 1971), with its extensive treatment of the dates of wine harvests and the advance and retreat of Alpine glaciers as evidence of past climatic fluctuations. A brief treatment of a Mardi Gras riot in *Les Paysans* in turn became the subject of a whole book, *Le Carnaval de Romans* (1979; Eng. trans. 1979).

During the 1960s and early 1970s, Le Roy Ladurie was a leading advocate for the empirical and quantitative investigation of the past, arguing that only this form of history was scientific. But in 1975 he published *Montaillou: Village occitan de 1294 à 1324* (abr. Eng. trans. 1978), which drew from anthropology and semiotics notions for recreating the mental and emotional universe of peasants and shepherds living in a remote medieval village in the Pyrenees. Ecological circumstances continued as the basic economic and social framework of rural life, but Le Roy Ladurie used the testimony of the villagers as preserved in inquisitorial registers to reconstruct their attitudes toward such matters as sex, death, and the condition of women, and to reconstitute their religious belief system. Anthropological and semiological approaches similarly mark *Le Carnaval de Romans* as well as two subsequent books, *L'Argent, l'amour et la mort en pays d'Oc* (1980; Eng. trans. 1982) and *La Sorcière de Jasmin* (1983; Eng. trans. 1987). Each of the latter takes as its starting point a fictional work, written in Occitan, the native language of the French south, and uses this as a springboard to reveal the traditional folk culture of the rural Midi. The topics covered include the language of money in peasant mentality, the symbolic codes of love and marriage, the subconscious obsessions with death, and the unconscious fears of witchcraft.

In his inaugural lecture at the Collège de France (1973), Le Roy Ladurie spoke of an "immobile history" of medieval and early modern times, in which fundamental ecological and demographic forces established a nearly stable society, without significant change. Recently he has begun to reassess this conclusion. In essays devoted to the "baroque state" and the monarchical regime of Louis XIV he has denoted important changes in political and religious institutions that demarcate the seventeenth century.

By the late 1980s Le Roy Ladurie was established as one of France's most influential and prolific historians. Throughout his career he has stood at the forefront of the *Annales* effort to apply the methods and insights of social sciences to understanding the past, particularly of people and places neglected in earlier historiographical traditions.

G. Iggers, *New Directions in European Historiography*, 2d ed. (Middletown, Conn., 1984); E. Le Roy Ladurie, *Paris-Montpellier, P.C.-P.S.U., 1945–1963* (Paris, 1982), *Le Territoire de l'historien*, vol. 1 (Paris, 1973; Eng. trans. Chicago, 1979), vol. 2 (Paris, 1978; Eng. trans., *The Mind and Method of the Historian*, Chicago, 1981).

C. L. Stinger

Related entries: ANNALES SCHOOL; BRAUDEL, FERNAND.

LEVI-STRAUSS, CLAUDE (1908–), ethnologist and social thinker, famous as an exponent of structuralism and for arguing the importance and sophistication of primitive thought. Born in Brussels, where his painter-father was temporarily employed, Lévi-Strauss grew up in Paris in a middle-class family of Alsatian-Jewish origin. As a student he was active in the Socialist party (SFIO), especially its Constructive Revolution wing, which preached greater attention to trade-union and cooperative organization.

After studying both law (*licence*) and philosophy (*licence* and *agrégation*), Lévi-Strauss chose ethnology as his area of specialization. Attracted by the possibility of doing fieldwork, he accepted a position at the University of Sao Paulo in Brazil from 1935 to 1937. During school vacations and again in 1938–39, Lévi-Strauss organized expeditions into the Brazilian interior to study the Bororo, Nambikwara, and other Indian groups.

Mobilized during 1939–40, Lévi-Strauss was spirited out of France following the defeat by a Rockefeller Program to save prominent Jewish intellectuals. In New York from 1941 to 1945, he taught in the New School for Social Research, and on a second stay in 1946–47 served as French cultural officer. During the war Lévi-Strauss joined a community in exile in the United States dominated by leading surrealists and became close friends with André Breton and Max Ernst.

After holding positions at the National Center for Scientific Research, the *Musée de l'homme*, and the *Ecole pratique des hautes études*, Lévi-Strauss was elected to the Collège de France in 1959 where he directed a laboratory of social anthropology until his retirement in 1982. The *Académie française* elected him to membership in 1973.

Lévi-Strauss's first major theoretical work, *The Elementary Structures of Kinship*, appeared in 1949, followed by *Tristes tropiques* (combining autobiography, travel narrative, and ethnographic analysis) in 1955. *The Savage Mind* (1962) extended Lévi-Strauss's ethnographic explanations into a general theory of culture, while the two volumes of *Structural Anthropology* (1958, 1973) and the four of *Mythologiques* (1964–71) deal respectively with theoretical issues and myth analysis.

Lévi-Strauss's thought assumes that the apparent variety of cultural phenomena can be understood as a set of permutations of a smaller number of universal patterns. Working from a structural linguistic model derived from Ferdinand de Saussure (through Roman Jakobsen and the Prague School), Lévi-Strauss organizes data into binary oppositions. Treating ethnographic data as "speech," he seeks to generate the system of which this speech is an expression. Hence, his models function like grammars; and the fundamental, and hence universal, level of cultural reality is not the ritual, name, or other datum but the empty system of potential combinations and categories.

Applied to kinship and marriage systems, Lévi-Strauss's analysis defines society as a system of the circulation of women. In *Savage Thought*, the French anthropologist emptied totemism of biological or economic specificity and reduced it to a system of classifications that become applicable to cultural phenomena in advanced societies as well, from names to culinary rules and dress codes. Similarly, *Mythologiques*, while interpreting myths from South America to North America, aims at a universal logic of myth, applicable to all world myths and accessible only when the individual stories are combined into cycles.

Lévi-Strauss's connection to the main trunk of linguistic structuralist thought is far more direct than that of Michel Foucault, Jacques Lacan, and Roland Barthes, who, along with him, helped to make structuralism fashionable in the 1960s and 1970s.

Lévi-Strauss's insistence on the sophistication of the thought processes of primitive peoples, combined with his respect for their technological contributions, is associated with a hostility to any sense of Western cultural superiority and a Rousseauian preference for neolithic social organization. Such "cold" human societies are as important as the "hot" technologically dynamic ones of the West.

While preaching tolerance of diversity on a global scale, Lévi-Strauss has also defended the rights of French society to its own particularisms. A certain resistance to the changes in life-styles wrought by immigrants is therefore natural and defensible. Finally, relying on the "scientific" nature of his enterprise, Lévi-Strauss denies that the practice of social anthropology assumes or necessarily generates power or superiority over the primitive societies he describes.

C. Lévi-Strauss, *La Pensée sauvage* (Paris, 1962), *Tristes tropiques* (Paris, 1955); C. Lévi-Strauss, D. Eribon, *De près et de loin* (Paris, 1988).

A. Douglas

Related entries: ACADEMIE FRANCAISE; BARTHES, ROLAND; FOUCAULT, MICHEL; INTELLECTUAL TRENDS; LACAN, JACQUES; STRUCTURALISM.

LITERATURE assumed many forms in postwar France. In 1946 literature was slowly recovering from the war. Some renowned authors had died, while others were, voluntarily or not, exiled. The remaining writers were divided between the collaborators and those engaged in the Resistance. While punishment met the former, the latter were adulated. The most immediate effect of peace on literature was paradoxically the publication of many eye-witness accounts inspired by the war, especially the horror of the great battles and the concentration camps. Yet these writings were not the most lasting literature.

The literature that was to prevail for the next decade emerged from two thinkers, Jean-Paul Sartre (1905–1980) and Albert Camus (1913–1960). Both were labeled existentialists, a title they never claimed but resigned themselves to accepting. According to existentialism, humans are aliens in the world and are confronted with the void of nothingness and the absurdity of life. Thus, for the existentialists conscious action gave meaning to life. Sartre, for instance, stressed political engagement. Both Sartre and Camus wrote in various genres and subgenres: fiction, drama, essays, literary criticism. Sartre also published his autobiography, *Les Mots* (1964, *The Words*). What differentiated the two writers was their vision of the world. Friends after the Liberation and admirers of one another's work, Camus and Sartre split in 1952 because of their divergences concerning political commitment in general and Russian communism in particular. Camus received the Nobel Prize for Literature in 1957, but Sartre refused his in 1964 because he, as a writer, did not want to become an institution.

Another important existentialist was Simone de Beauvoir (1908–1986), who was always associated with Sartre, her lifelong companion. In 1954 Beauvoir received the prestigious Goncourt Prize for *Les Mandarins* (*The Mandarins*), a term she used to designate the leftist intellectuals questioning their political commitment. Parallel to her career as an existentialist writer, Beauvoir became a cult figure of feminism with her study *Le Deuxième Sexe* (1949, *The Second Sex*). Her famous statement that "one is not born a woman, one becomes a woman" implies that the education and formation women receive put them in a position of inferiority compared to men.

A contemporary of the existentialists, Boris Vian (1920–1959), novelist, poet, playwright, and jazz musician, stands out as the incarnation of postwar youth. Vian chose the realm of the fantastic to denounce war and its absurdity, as well as issues of intolerance and injustice.

New ideas and techniques invaded French literature in the 1950s with a cluster of writers grouped under the label *nouveau roman* (new novel), although these authors always denied that they were part of a literary school. What did they share? First, they felt that the existentialist novel or more generally speaking the *roman engagé* (committed novel) was no longer suited to contemporary society. They also all wrote essays on the novel as they envisioned it: a narrative deprived of traditional characters and lacking a plot. Unable to identify with nontraditional protagonists or to rely on a (chrono)logical plot, the reader would not be distracted or entertained and could thus actively participate in the making of the novel. The leading proponents of the new novel are Nathalie Sarraute, Claude Simon, Alain Robbe-Grillet, and Michel Butor. They all continue to write to this day. In 1983 Sarraute published her autobiography, *En-*

fance (*Childhood*). In 1985 Simon received the Nobel Prize for Literature for *L'Invitation*. (*The Invitation*). In 1988 Robbe-Grillet published *Angélique ou l'enchantement*, the second volume of *Romanesques*, and his autobiographical trilogy started in 1985. Also in 1988, Butor published two works, *Avant-goût II* and *Le Retour du boomerang*, in which he explains himself to his public. Marguerite Duras is sometimes associated with the new novel. In 1984 she won the Goncourt Prize for *L'Amant* (*The Lover*). In addition to novels, she also writes plays and movie scripts.

Many writers who do not belong to a specific literary current must be cited. Georges Bataille (1897–1962) and Michel Leiris (b. 1901) were both early supporters of surrealism. Author of often erotic and violent fiction and of poetry, Bataille remained obscure until the late sixties when the structuralists, deconstructionists, psychoanalysts, and others became interested in his work. It has been only recently that Leiris has won a large audience. Marguerite Yourcenar (1903–1987), often remembered as the first woman to join the *Académie française* (1981), is an unusual historical writer whose work constitutes a meditation on the destiny of mankind. Her death prevented her from finishing her trilogy, *Labyrinthe du monde*.

The 1970s were marked by an explosion of women's movements that influenced certain currents of contemporary literature. Whereas Simone de Beauvoir had earlier refused the notion that women were inherently different at birth, contemporary feminists insisted on their differences and singularities. Their specificity, they claimed, lied in their bodies, desires, pleasure, and suffering, especially that of giving birth. Consequently, women writers addressed their discourse to other women and not to men, always suspected of sexism. Thus, they created their very own language, *l'écriture féminine* (feminine writing), the aim of which was to deconstruct everything masculine in the commonly used language made by and for men. What writers such as Beauvoir, Christiane Rochefort, the sisters Benoîte and Flora Groult, Françoise Mallet-Joris, and Françoise Sagan had touched upon was developed by Marie Cardinal, Hélène Cixous, Chantal Chawaf, Annie Ernaux, Luce Irigaray, Annie Leclerc, and Monique Wittig.

As far as the current state of the novel is concerned, the difficulty lies in determining what styles and genres will endure. The following, nevertheless, merit our attention. Michel Tournier's work appears poised between the security of the traditional and the risks of the postmodern. His latest work, *Le Médianoche amoureux* (1989), a best-seller in France, is a collection of tales and short stories. Georges Perec (1936–1982) was an innovative writer who experimented with language; *La Vie mode d'emploi* (1978) is regarded as his masterpiece. Akin to writers of the new novel, Jean-Marie Gustave Le Clézio has been writing for the last twenty years. Widely read, Patrick Modiano has received three major literary awards (including the Goncourt Prize) between 1968 and 1978. His latest novel, *Vestiaire de l'enfance*, came out in 1989. Modiano is haunted by the war, as is the Jewish writer Elie Wiesel, who received the Nobel Peace Prize in 1987 for his work. Philippe Sollers, cofounder of the literary review *Tel quel*, also deserves to be cited.

The dramatic genre has also evolved, especially since the 1950s. Classic authors such as Henry de Montherlant (1896–1972) and Jean Anouilh (1910–1987), who gave priority to psychological analysis, were soon replaced by Samuel Beckett (1906–1989), Arthur Adamov (1908–1970), Jean Genet (1910–1986), and Eugène Ionesco (b. 1912). These proponents of a new theater, often referred to as the theater of the absurd, opposed the traditional plays where plot, psychology, and language were predominant. They preferred minimal action and limited scenery. They also depersonalized their characters, who were given no social identity and often no name. Instead, human beings became anonymous abstractions, unable to communicate with one another, illustrated in the lack of true and meaningful dialogues that are often replaced by monologues. The most famous absurdist play is Beckett's metaphysical *En attendant Godot* (1953, *Waiting for Godot*). Fernando Arrabal, Spanish by birth, continues to write in the same vein.

Poetry is not as homogeneous in its evolution as the other genres, where definite trends can be identified. However, World War II and the Resistance produced a politically committed poetry. The poets Paul Eluard (1895–1952) and Louis Aragon (1897–1982) were surrealists at the beginning of their careers and joined the Communist party and expressed their political engagement in their poetry. Several older poets were especially productive after the war: Pierre-Jean Jouve (1887–1976) and Saint-John Perse (1887–1975) are two examples. Other poets concentrated on less traditional lyricism. Unconventional is probably the best way to describe the work of Jacques Prévert (1900–1977) and Raymond Queneau (1903–1976), both influenced by the surrealist school. Prévert is probably the best-known French poet, not only because of his innovative and accessible poems, many of which were made into songs, but also for his work in cinema. Queneau, for his part, should be remembered for his use of language, especially with regard to vocabulary, spelling, and syntax, which make his work (which includes novels) inventive and humorous.

Among the other contemporary poets who have strived for a new poetry (also labeled antipoetry), are Francis Ponge (1899–1988), the Belgian-born Henri Michaux (1899–1984), and René Char (1907–1988). Ponge's hermetic poetry describes objects in an objective manner. Michaux, also a painter, was an existentialist whose work reflects upon the anguish of being. Char, also a surrealist, concerned himself with the mysterious relationship between human order and cosmic sensations. The poets of the last two decades are mainly interested in the permutations of language. The meaning of their poems often lies in their textuality. The foremost poets of the postwar period, in addition to those mentioned, are Yves Bonnefoy, André du Bouchet, and Denis Roche. Poetry, like the other literary genres, reveals that what one writer once referred to as the unity of the *Eglise littéraire* of France has been broken in the postwar era.

J. Bersani, et al., *La Littérature en France depuis 1945* (Paris, 1970); B. Vercier, J. Lecarme, *La Littérature en France depuis 1968* (Paris, 1982).

D. S. Thévenin

Related entries: ACADEMIE FRANCAISE; ARAGON, LOUIS; BARTHES, ROLAND; BEAUVOIR, SIMONE DE; BECKETT, SAMUEL; CAMUS, ALBERT; DERRIDA, JACQUES; EXISTENTIALISM; FEMINISM; FOUCAULT, MICHEL; INTELLECTUAL TRENDS; IONESCO, EUGENE; LACAN, JACQUES; LEVI-STRAUSS, CLAUDE; MALRAUX, ANDRE; SARTRE, JEAN-PAUL; STRUCTURALISM; WOMEN, CONDITION OF; YOURCENAR, MARGUERITE.

LUCHAIRE AFFAIR, an affair originating in the illegal sale of 450,000 artillery shells to Iran by the French armaments firm Luchaire, apparently with the tacit approval of highly placed officials in the Defense Ministry close to the then socialist minister, Charles Hernu. The arms exports occurred over the period 1982–86 and were first revealed by the press in February 1986, the Defense Ministry itself referring the matter to the courts before the March legislative elections. After the return of a conservative government, the Defense Ministry commissioned the Barba Report (completed in June 1986 and immediately classified as confidential), which suggested that Hernu and even President François Mitterrand had tolerated the breaking of the embargo in return for Luchaire contributions to Socialist party (PS) funds.

In June 1989 the case against Luchaire was rejected for lack of evidence, there being no proof of payments to the PS and the accused having believed with reason that their activities were approved by the Defense Ministry. This decision, taken under the socialist government of Michel Rocard, was seen by the right as a political whitewashing of the affair, especially since the Ministry of Justice accused the Ministry of Defense of withholding evidence.

The exports to Iran occurred at a time of declining sales for the French arms industry, and the affair itself was revealed during the uncertain period of *cohabitation*. Known as "the French Irangate," the Luchaire affair combined the machinations of the military-industrial complex and of party politics, renewing fears of the former and culminating in doubt over the independence of the judiciary from political pressure.

E. A. Kolodziej, *Making and Marketing Arms* (Princeton, 1986); P. Marion "Le Danger du complexe militaro-industriel," *Le Monde*, November 28, 1987.

H. D. Dauncey

Related entries: ARMS SALES; *COHABITATION*; GREENPEACE AFFAIR; HERNU, CHARLES.

LYON, the second largest city in France, with a population of over 1.2 million inhabitants and offering more than 500,000 jobs. It has a long history as a major center of industry, business, and commerce, dominating economic activity throughout the wider region of Rhône-Alpes (5 million inhabitants).

For most of the period between 1950 and 1970 the major problem facing Lyon was how to cope with strong demographic growth and the related expansion of economic activity. By the early 1960s the city's population was increasing by over 2 percent per annum, largely due to a heavy inflow of residents from surrounding rural districts and other regions of France. At the same time, as industry expanded rapidly an increasing number of foreign migrants (mainly from North Africa) settled in Lyon, accompanied in the early 1960s by a large number of repatriates from Algeria. Currently, over 12 percent of the city's population is of foreign nationality.

This influx of population, accompanied by an acute shortage of housing, led to a major building program, predominantly in the form of large peripheral apartment complexes, mostly built on the eastern fringes of the city. The rapid urbanization of these communes and the associated industrial development helped accentuate the spatial contrast that has long characterized the city's socioeconomic structure. The western sector of Lyon, benefiting from a hilly and attractive environment, has developed as a predominantly middle-class residential area with few industrial activities. In contrast, to the east in the floodplain of the Rhône, the extensive outward expansion of the city has been dominated by widespread industrial development and the growth of a working-class population. By the 1960s decentralization had become an important force explaining the rapid growth of many peripheral communes.

Over the last two decades growth has slowed and Lyon's population is no longer increasing. However, a contrast exists between the central and inner areas where there is a marked decline, and the outer suburbs where growth is still strong. As the demand for new housing has eased, growing emphasis has been placed on improving areas of older property (like the inner city) or, increasingly, on rehabilitating the *grands ensembles* (vast housing developments), too hurriedly built in the 1960s and increasingly rejected as a form of urban living. Les Minguettes (26,000 inhabitants), on the southeastern perimeter of the city, is typical of such estates.

Lyon has long been known as a manufacturing city, but since the early 1970s industrial employment has fallen sharply, affecting all major branches of activity, notably mechanical and electrical engineering, vehicles, textiles, and chemicals. Many job losses resulted from the rationalization programs of major groups such as Rhône-Poulenc and Renault Véhicules Industriels, forced to adapt to a highly depressed market in the recession years of the late 1970s and early 1980s and to increased competition. Not all activities have been characterized by a reduction of employment and production: The parachemical industry, notably pharmaceuticals, and its related research laboratories (e.g., Pasteur, Mérieux) remain a particularly dynamic sector of activity. Other high-tech fields such as biotechnologies demonstrate similar features, and their development has been encouraged by the designation of three science parks within the city.

While industrial jobs have declined and factories closed, the tertiary sector has expanded rapidly, even if the rate of growth eased during the years of recession; in the late 1980s employment in services was increasing by around 1.6 percent each year, only half the rate recorded in the early 1970s. Part of the strength of this sector derives from Lyon's administrative functions as a major city responsible for the provision of a wide range of public services and as head of the department of Rhône and the region of Rhône-Alpes. In addition, Lyon's long tradition as a business and commercial center has led to the development of a significant banking sector, employing over thirteen thousand people and involving more than sixty companies. However, over the last decade the most dynamic branch of the tertiary sector has been the diverse group of business or producer services, covering fields such as publicity, accountancy, financial and legal services, consultants in computing and engineering services—over forty thousand people now work in such occupations.

Unlike the industrial sector, the majority of service employment remains concentrated in the city center, although there is evidence of growing decentralization, notably to the western, more attractive suburbs. The main weakness of this sector is the absence of headquarter offices of major national or international companies, depriving Lyon of important decision-making centers and their valuable multiplier effects. Despite the decentralization over recent years of a number of important organizations (e.g., Interpol, *Ecole normale supérieure*), head offices have continued to leave the city in favor of Paris.

The substantial transformation of Lyon's economy has been accompanied by a series of major infrastructural works and development schemes, relating particularly to the improvement of accessibility and to the provision of new business and commercial facilities. The first trend may be illustrated by the city's metro transit system (first opened in 1978 and subsequently extended) and by the building of the new railway line (for the *train à grande vitesse*, TGV) linking Paris and Lyon: Since 1984 the journey time between the two cities has been reduced to two hours, compared with four previously. The second trend is reflected in the creation of the major central retailing and office complex at Le Part-Dieu (covering over 30 hectares) and opened progressively from the mid–1970s. Over fifteen thousand people now work in the center, which offers nearly 400,000 square meters of office floorspace and over 250 shops. Further development has occurred with the creation of additional office floorspace (70,000 square meters) adjacent to the new Part-Dieu main-line station opened in 1983, primarily for the city's TGV traffic.

In a political context the mayor of Lyon has played an influential role in the city's development (the commune of Lyon is by far the largest in the agglomeration with over 400,000 inhabitants). Since 1957 three people have held this office: Louis Pradel (1957–76), Francisque Collomb (1976–89), and Michel Noir (1989–). While Lyon is traditionally known for its moderate conservatism, in the two former instances both mayors preferred to remain outside the major political parties. In Michel Noir's case, although a member of the Gaullist *Rassemblement pour la République* (RPR) and former minister of Jacques Chirac, he has again sought to develop the consensus politics advocated by his predecessors.

Within the city there has long been a political divide between the center and western communes (center/right wing) and the eastern suburbs (socialist and communist). However in 1969, to facilitate management of the urban area, the majority of the city's communes agreed to form a joint body, the Courly (*la communauté urbaine de Lyon*), to enable the more rational administration of a wide range of services (e.g., transport, water supply, police) and, above all, to ensure the effective overall planning of the city. The president of the Courly has traditionally been the mayor of Lyon.

Over the last three decades changing patterns of development have also been linked to modified policies. Until the mid–1970s priority was accorded to coping with rapid expansion, notably in terms of new housing and infrastructure. Since the 1980s, in the context of more modest expansion, greater priority has been placed on resolving problems resulting from past growth and, in an effort to attract new investment, on enhancing the city's European, rather than purely French image.

J. Bonnet, "Lyon et son agglomération," *Notes et etudes documentaires* 4836 (1987); A. Latreille, ed., *Histoire de Lyon et du lyonnais* (Toulouse, Fr., 1988); R. Lebeau, *Atlas et géographie de la région lyonnaise* (Paris, 1976); J. N. Tuppen, "Core-periphery in Metropolitan Development and Planning: Socio-economic Change in Lyon since 1960," *Geoforum* 17 (1986).

J.N. Tuppen

Related entries: HERRIOT, EDOUARD; IMMIGRANTS; NOIR, MICHEL.

M

MAIRE, EDMOND (1931–), one of France's most powerful and respected trade-union leaders who served as secretary-general of the *Confédération française démocratique du travail* (CFDT), the second largest and most innovative trade-union federation. Maire was born on January 24, 1931 in Epinay-sur-Seine, a suburb of Paris. His father was a railroad engineer. Maire's full-time education ended with *Lycée Jacques-Decour* in Paris, and he continued taking evening courses in chemistry at the *Conservatoire national des arts et métiers*. He began his professional career with a paint company in 1949 and became a chemist at one of the Péchiney corporation's research centers in 1954.

In 1958 he became a full-time union official with the CFDT's federation of chemical workers in the Paris region. Six years later he became secretary-general for the CFDT's national federation of chemical workers. He became a member in 1970 of the CFDT Executive Committee, responsible for its professional and social activities. Then, in 1971 he assumed the position of secretary-general of the entire CFDT, a post he held until 1988.

In his nearly forty-year union career, Maire was one of the people most responsible for the transformation of the CFDT. Until 1964, it was a Catholic federation of unions, *Confédération française des travailleurs chrétiens* (CFTC), known for its moderate and apolitical stands. That year, it dropped its confessional ties, although a small group broke with the new CFDT and still calls itself the CFTC.

The union gradually began to move to the left. Its members were at the heart of many of the factory occupations during the events of May 1968 and more often than not proved more militant than their colleagues from the *Confédération générale du travail* (CGT), the communist-dominated federation that at the time was France's largest and most militant union.

In the next decade the CFDT grew in membership and influence as it became more militant and took on many of the causes and ideas first given widespread discussion during 1968. For example, it was the trade-union federation that most supported specific proposals to give workers more control over their jobs and the more general idea of *autogestion* or a decentralized self-managed form of socialism. The CFDT also became more militant, leading, for instance, the famous Lip "strike" of 1973 in which workers took over a factory the owners had closed and continued to manufacture and sell watches for more than a year. The union also made significant inroads among technicians and white-collar workers who had not previously been organized in any substantial number by the union movement.

Although the CFDT maintained its independence from all political parties, by the late 1970s the union found itself in agreement with the Socialist party (PS) on many important issues, and CFDT members played an active role in the revival of the party and its twin victories in the presidential and legislative elections in 1981. For the first two years of François Mitterrand's presidency, the union supported the social and economic reforms implemented by the socialist government. Since then, the union and Maire himself have been far more critical of the more moderate economic strategy the PS has been following.

Maire was a central participant in everything the CFDT did. Although he never craved personal power, his writing, frequent appearances on television, and strong leadership of the union made him both widely known and widely respected.

In 1988 he retired from the leadership of the CFDT and is now deputy director of *Villages-Vacances-Familles*.

C. Hauss, *The New Left in France* (Westport, Conn., 1978); G. Ross, S. Hoffmann, S. Malzacher, eds., *The Mitterrand Experiment* (New York, 1987); D. Singer, *Is Socialism Doomed*? (New York, 1988); W.R. Smith, *Crisis in the French Labor Movement* (London, 1987).

C. Hauss

Related entries: AUROUX LAWS; CATHOLICISM; COMMON PROGRAM; DEMONSTRATIONS; *CONFEDERATION FRANCAISE DES TRAVAILLEURS CHRETIENS*; *CONFEDERATION GENERALE DU TRAVAIL*; ECONOMIC POLICY; ECONOMIC TRENDS; *FORCE OUVRIERE*; FRACHON, BENOIT; FRENCH COMMUNIST PARTY; INCOME DISTRIBUTION; INDUSTRIAL POLICY; KRASUCKI, HENRI; LABOR FORCE; MARXISM; MINIMUM WAGE; MITTERRAND, FRANCOIS; NATIONAL COUNCIL OF FRENCH EMPLOYERS; ROCARD, MICHEL; SOCIALIST PARTY (PS); SOCIAL SECURITY; STRIKES; STUDENT REVOLTS; TRADE UNION MOVEMENT; UNEMPLOYMENT; UNIFIED SOCIALIST PARTY.

MALRAUX, ANDRE (1901–1976), writer, art critic, politician, minister of culture under Charles de Gaulle. He was born in Paris into a bourgeois family. When his parents separated in 1906, he remained with his mother but lived under his father's influence. After successful studies in the *lycée*, he attended courses at the Institute of Oriental Languages. In the early 1920s he began writing and publishing in literary reviews. He also began to travel during this period. In October 1921 he married Clara Goldschmidt and together they wandered through southern Europe, paying special attention to Italian museums. It was in East Asia, however, that he had a rendezvous with destiny. Arrested for discovering, and stealing, Khmer sculptures from the Bantai-Srey temple in Cambodia, he was sentenced to three years in jail, but thanks to a group of friends that included François Mauriac and Gaston Gallimard, he was released. Asia did not reward him with fortune but with fame and knowledge about cultures. His work, *La Tentation de l'Occident* (1926), analyzed how civilizations meet and, occasionally, clash. Further stays in Indochina and China exposed him to the revolutionary activities of communists and provided material for his novels. *La Condition humaine* (1933) earned him the Goncourt Prize and official recognition. In the 1930s Malraux's literature was associated with the leftist politics of the era. He denounced colonialism and insisted on the danger of fascism. Each year he took part in writer's congresses to protest the extreme right-wing trends in Europe. An observer and participant in the Orient, he become an actor with the Spanish Civil War: To buttress the military resistance of the Republic, he organized an airplane squadron. Malraux returned from Spain with a novel completed—*L'Espoir*—and a few months later a film with the same title was released.

The wartime period, especially from 1941 through 1943, is not a well-known period in Malraux's life. Drafted in 1939, he was eventually taken as a prisoner of war. Liberated, he settled on the Côte d'Azur where, separated from his wife, Malraux cohabited with Josette Clotis. Somewhat aloof from the events of the day, he spent two years in seclusion near Nice. Toward the end of the war he emerged on the military front. After the liberation of Paris, he formed a brigade that fought along with the Allies.

A new Malraux appeared by 1944–45. Prior to the war he was relatively close to the communists. Never a Marxist himself, he had admired their sense of purpose in China and was a "fellow traveler" in Spain, but only for a few months. Like George Orwell, he witnessed the slaughter of the anarchists by Soviet agents. In January 1945 he returned to Paris and began to speak out passionately against the current trend in favor of a unity with the communists in peacetime. He argued that renewal or revolution are not restricted to the proletariat but to the national community as a whole. Before the war he had been a speaker in conference halls and for the intellectual elite. He now became on orator for large audiences. Meanwhile, the decisive *rencontre* that left its mark on Malraux for the rest of his life was his encounter with General Charles de Gaulle, who may have appeared to him like someone out of his own novels. Both men impressed and needed one another. In de Gaulle's provisional government he was appointed minister of information, but resigned when the general stepped down.

In the late 1940s politics and art dominated his attention. As a Gaullist, he supported the general's endeavors for a comeback and was active in the creation of the *Rassemblement du peuple français* (RPF). He also pursued his long interest in art and civilization. From 1947 to 1949, Skira Publishers released his three-volume *Psychologie de l'art*. By 1951 they were released under a new title, *Les Voix du silence*.

As a writer, Malraux now began to address important themes in the history of humankind. However, he did not cut himself off from events, and the Algerian drama brought out his anticolonialist leanings. The collapse of the Fourth Republic in 1958 saw Malraux returning to the world of politics. Minister of culture under de Gaulle, he was part of every cabinet from 1958 until the general's resignation in 1969. As minister of culture, he believed that politics and art could coexist. In spite of tight budgets, he revived a tradition that the Republic had abandoned, the glorification of art and culture. For instance, besides creating the *maisons de la culture* for various regions, state honors were given to artists who died, such as Georges Braque and Le Corbusier, and a number of artists received state commissions, like André Masson for the ceiling of the Odéon theater or Marc Chagall for the Opera. A few important works were also undertaken at the Louvre, the Notre Dame cathedral, and the Grand Trianon, while a thorough cleansing of Paris facades helped to brighten the French capital. Additional funding, too, was given to the theater. As with de Gaulle, May 1968 and the student-worker revolt surprised him. When de Gaulle used his unsuccessful April 1969 referendum as an excuse to resign, Malraux, too, ended his political career. Art prevailed as his long-lasting interest.

Malraux's complex personality remains difficult to comprehend. His *Antimémoires*, published in the early 1970s, provide little help. As a man he was attracted to both art and politics; yet, his early years were characterized by leftist leanings, while his later life was characterized by Gaullist nationalistic proclivities.

J. Lacouture, *André Malraux* (Paris, 1973); A. Malraux. *Antimémoires* (Paris, 1967).

J.-R. Chotard

Related entries: ALGERIA, RELATIONS WITH; CULTURAL POLICY; DE GAULLE, CHARLES; GAULLISM; GAULLIST PARTY; INDOCHINA, RELATIONS WITH; SPAIN, RELATIONS WITH.

MARCHAIS, GEORGES (1920–), communist militant. Since 1972, he has served as secretary-general of the French Communist party (PCF). As representative for the Val-de-Marne (first district: Arcueil, Villejuif) in the red belt south of Paris, he has been continuously elected to the National Assembly since 1973. He has also been a member of the regional council of the Ile-de-France (1976–81) and the European Parliament (1979–89). In 1981 he ran unsuccessfully for the presidency of the Republic.

Marchais was born in La Hoguette (Calvados), the son of a miner. A metalworker by trade, he took a job as a plate fitter in the aeronautical industry in France in 1940, and in 1942 was sent to Germany to work in the Messerschmitt factory. After the war he became active in the trade-union movement in the industrial suburbs of Paris, and in 1946 he joined the PCF. Between 1946 and 1956 he advanced from local (Issy-les-Moulineaux) to regional (greater Paris) positions of leadership within the metalworkers' union.

Thenceforth he turned his attention to politics. He joined the PCF's Federation of the South Seine, home section of party boss Maurice Thorez, whose favor he earned. Named secretary of the Federation in 1956, he advanced quickly into the higher echelons of the party: He was appointed to the Central Committee in 1956 and to the Politburo in 1959. During the 1960s he served as secretary of the organization of the PCF. In 1970 he became adjunct secretary-general, effectively the party's leader because of the deteriorating health of the aging Waldeck Rochet. He was promoted to the post of secretary-general two years later.

In his patient rise to party leadership, Marchais was but one among a number of aspiring party bureaucrats, and his success might not have been foreseen. He was neither an intellectual nor a war hero in a party that had an abundant supply of both. Some observers thought he was an unfortunate choice. Opponents within the party even accused him of having volunteered for his wartime tour of labor in Germany. But Marchais enjoyed the patronage of the party's hierarchy, the approval of Soviet leaders, and the affection of the party faithful.

As secretary-general, Marchais was conspicuous for the verve with which he used television to advance his party's cause. Energetic, forthright, sometimes entertaining, he appeared frequently on the screen in debates or on talk shows, and thus became the icon of his party in households throughout France during the 1970s. But if Marchais cut an image that pleased the public, that appeal was not reflected in the elections. The PCF made no headway at the polls in the 1970s, and in the 1980s its electoral support steadily declined. Favor shifted to the Socialist party (PS) led by François Mitterrand, who, while willing to work with the PCF, treated it as a junior partner.

The keynote of Marchais's early tenure as party leader was the accord he struck in 1972 with Mitterrand of the PS and Robert Fabre of the Left Radicals (MRG) for a Common Program that would serve as the basis for an electoral union. But it was one thing to announce an agenda and another to negotiate its details. Amid endless skirmishing, the accord unraveled by 1977, leaving all parties embittered. In 1981 Marchais ran against Mitterrand for the presidency, but with a poor showing on the first ballot (only 15.3% of the votes), backed the PS leader on the second.

For some observers, Marchais had been outwitted by Mitterrand, who could not have won the presidency without communist support. But Marchais may have outwitted himself in believing that he could find a common ground with the PS. As party leader, his political instinct had been to rejuvenate the PCF with overtures to other parties on the left. He professed to be a proponent of a revisionist communism, more democratic and less beholden to the Soviet Union. In Italy this stance was being called Eurocommunism; Marchais dubbed it "socialism in the colors of France." Commentators made much of his proposal at the twenty-second congress of the party (1976) to drop the phrase "dictatorship of the proletariat" from the lexicon of party objectives. But Marchais's pronouncements about the democratization of the PCF contained more rhetorical flourish than substance. Trained as a party bureaucrat, he clung to the pieties and traditional loyalties of the PCF. The causes of the new left passed him by.

Though an ardent spokesman for the working class, he had less to say about the plight of immigrants from former French colonies, the importance of women's issues, or the concern of the young about environmental problems. He was openly contemptuous of the students' protest for educational reform in May 1968, and he despised the humanist Marxist intellectuals within the party (notably Roger Garaudy, whose expulsion he supervised). Like his predecessors, Marchais rallied to the defense of some of the worst projects of the Soviet Union, for example its occupation of Czechoslovakia in 1968 and Afghanistan in 1978. If he was not an *apparatchik* as opponents charged, he was nonetheless the product of the sectarian environment in which he had made his way to prominence.

Highly touted as a modern image maker, Marchais offered images of the PCF that were timeworn. As party leader he is likely to be remembered as a typical careerist, distinguished mainly for having presided over his party's slide toward obscurity.

M. Adereth, *The French Communist Party* (Manchester, Eng., 1984); F. Fejto, *The French Communist Party and the Crisis of International Communism* (Cambridge, Mass., 1967); P. Holmes, "Marchais," in *Biographical Dictionary of French Political Leaders since 1870*, ed. D. Bell et al. (New York, 1990); R. Johnson, *The Long March of the French Left* (New York, 1981); F. Wilson, *French Political Parties under the Fifth Republic* (New York, 1982).

P. H. Hutton

Related entries: COMMON PROGRAM; FAUVET, JACQUES; FRENCH COMMUNIST PARTY; GARAUDY, ROGER; MARXISM; MITTERRAND, FRANCOIS; POLITICAL TRENDS; ROCHET, WALDECK; THOREZ, MAURICE; UNION OF THE LEFT.

MARIE, ANDRE (1897–1974), lawyer and radical-socialist politician who was prime minister for a month in 1948. Born into a family of schoolteachers at Honfleur in Normandy, he attended the *lycée* at Rouen where he was called up for military service immediately upon graduation in 1915. An artillery lieutenant, he was awarded the *Croix de guerre* for distinguished service in action. After the war he studied law and was admitted to the bar of Rouen. Active in local politics since 1919, Marie was elected to the Chamber of Deputies in 1928 as a radical-socialist, representing the same Seine-Inférieure constituency throughout the remaining interwar period. He was a junior minister in two short-lived governments during the early 1930s. When war erupted again in September 1939 he volunteered for military service and received the rank of artillery captain. Taken prisoner by the Germans in June 1940, Marie was released the following year after promising to refrain from politics. He nonetheless joined and took an active role in the Resistance until arrested by the Gestapo in September 1943. Deported to Germany for imprisonment at Buchenwald, the gravely ill Marie was liberated by the American Third Army in April 1945.

Quickly recovering his health, he resumed his former political career, though the prospects of the Radical-Socialist party were not bright. Elected to both postwar constituent assemblies and thereafter to the National Assembly of the

Fourth Republic, Marie was elected president of his party's parliamentary group. He held the Ministry of Justice in the first two governments of the new Republic, headed by Paul Ramadier and Robert Schuman respectively. Few thought that a radical-socialist would anytime soon lead a French cabinet, but party maneuvering in the summer of 1948 gave Marie his chance, and in July President Vincent Auriol called upon him to form a government. His was the first frankly conservative cabinet since the war, signaling that the heroic period of Resistance-inspired state interventionism was at an end. Irreconcilable internal divisions, however, soon doomed Marie's government and forced its resignation at the end of August.

Marie joined the succeeding cabinet as minister of justice and then was minister of education in five different governments during the early 1950s. In the latter capacity he sponsored a bill in September 1951 that granted state subsidies to clerical schools. This made Marie unacceptable to mainstream radicals, now under the leadership of Pierre Mendès-France, and contributed to his failure to form a second government in June 1953. In October 1956 he resigned from his longtime party and helped constitute, with former premier Henri Queuille and other dissident radicals, the right-wing *Centre républicain*, which supported the *colons* in the Algerian war.

André Marie survived the collapse of the Fourth Republic, holding his seat from Seine-Inférieure through the first parliament of the new Gaullist Republic. After failing to retain it in the 1962 parliamentary elections, however, he retired from active politics and died twelve years later at Barentin, where he had been mayor since 1945.

Current Biography Yearbook 1948 (New York, 1949); *Obituaries from the Times 1971–75* (Reading, Eng., 1978).

J. E. Reece

Related entries: MENDES-FRANCE, PIERRE; QUEUILLE, HENRI; RADICAL PARTY.

MARSEILLE, the third largest city in France and the leading port. The city's economy emerged devastated from World War II, the result of allied bombing raids and German destruction of the port. Yet by 1949 the port surpassed all previous records for tonnage and passengers. Oil was the main factor in this revival, comprising 73 percent of all imports in 1950, a percentage that has remained virtually constant since then. As a result, Marseille developed industries in the petrochemical sector; by 1980 oil products and chemicals comprised over half of the port's exports.

The traditional industrial sector, which included food processing, building materials, and soap, did not fare well after 1945. The decline of the French Empire, which was the main export market for these industries, was one factor in their demise, but not the most important one. With the exception of the sugar industry, they failed to concentrate and consolidate production to meet growing competition from European and American conglomerates. By the early 1960s few traditional industries remained in the city.

Such outside forces as the Algerian War (1954–62) and the Treaty of Rome (1957) played major roles in Marseille's economic and social evolution after 1945. Approximately 130,000 *pieds-noirs* (repatriates from Algeria) settled in the city in the 1960's, causing the fastest population boom in its history, and the state intervened directly in the local economy in order to protect and readjust it in light of the collapse of colonial markets and competition from the Common Market. The Gaullist state funded massive public works and housing projects in the 1960s. It also encouraged the development of the city's high-tech sector by creating two new campuses for the *Faculté des sciences*, establishing a new tropical medicine center, and creating numerous research institutes, including a *Centre national de la recherche scientifique* (CNRS) branch and an economic research unit. Heavy industry, in contrast, was developed to the west of Marseille, at Fos, the center of the petroleum and chemical industry. In 1969 the state decided to build one of the nation's largest steel manufacturing complexes at Fos and to encourage the relocation of other heavy industries to the area.

State intervention, combined with pressures to modernize the local economy, changed Marseille profoundly. The building boom of the sixties led to a massive influx of North African construction workers, increasing the Algerian population alone from five thousand in 1955 to thirty-four thousand in 1975. The local Chamber of Commerce lost control over the port in 1966, when the *Port Autonome de Marseille* was created, directly under Parisian jurisdiction. The center of port activity moved outside of the city, to the west. Changes in shipping technology, such as containerization, led to a drop in the number of dock workers. Between 1954 and 1975 industrial jobs declined from 70,641 to 61,795, despite an almost 50 percent increase in the city's population. By 1982, five of the seven largest industrial firms in the department were located in the Fos area; only two were in Marseille. All of them were either nationalized industries or multinational firms. By 1982 over two-thirds of exports went to Europe or the United States, a total reversal from the pre–Common Market, colonial era.

The city prospered during the 1960s and 1970s, but the 1980s brought major problems. Unemployment increased rapidly, reaching 14 percent by 1986. Industry and commerce both stagnated, in part because the Fos project created only ten thousand new industrial jobs by 1985, compared with expectations for almost thirty-seven thousand, but also because the national economy stagnated, reducing the demand for oil and chemicals. Port activity rose from 75 million tons in 1971 to 109 million in 1979, but declined to 100 million in 1982. The city's population, which had grown from 636,000 in 1946 to 662,000 in 1954, before exploding to 889,000 in 1968 and reaching a peak of 914,000 in 1975, dropped to 879,000 in 1982. By 1989 many prophets of doom saw Marseille as a city in irreversible decline, beseiged by crime, drugs, racism, economic stagnation, and political instability. The same had been said on numerous occasions in the past.

Politics in Marseille has tended to reflect economic factors. In the immediate postwar period, the socialists and the communists emerged as the dominant forces, mainly because of their role in the Resistance against the Germans and the collaborationist city government of Simon Sabiani. They won control of the municipal council in 1945, but failed to reconcile their differences. In 1947, with the left alliance in shambles, the Gaullists gained control over the government for the first and last time. In 1953 Gaston Defferre, who had been a leading figure in the socialist resistance movement and mayor of Marseille in the immediate postwar period, formed a coalition of socialists and centrists that took over city government and maintained control over city politics until 1977, when the Common Program between socialists and communists brought an end to such alliances. Defferre would continue as mayor of Marseille until his death in 1986.

Defferrism excluded both communists and Gaullists from power, dividing up municipal government between the liberal *hommes d'affaires*—the *négociants* of the Chamber of Commerce, real estate developers, construction contractors—and the Marseille socialist machine, which was comprised of *Force ouvrière* union members and middle-class bureaucrats. Defferre's machine controlled about fifty thousand jobs by 1964, while the liberals controlled the city's urban renewal projects. Social programs were relatively neglected by Defferre, who was more interested in *grands travaux* and competent management. The communists accused him of neglecting industry, the port, and the working-class quarters of the city in favor of a quasi-Gaullist program that favored the middle class.

In elections to national office, however, the communists were the dominant force. Under the Fourth Republic, they won four out of nine Marseille seats in every legislative election, gaining 70 percent or more of the working-class vote. Under the Fifth Republic this pattern continued until 1981, with the exception of the 1958 and 1968 elections. The socialists, in contrast, won only two or three seats in most elections. Because of de Gaulle's Algerian policy, Gaullist candidates won few seats in Marseille. In 1962 Marseille was one of two cities of more than 100,000 population to vote No on the Algerian independence referendum.

In the 1980s Marseille politics underwent major changes. In the 1981 legislative elections, the socialists won five seats to only one for the communists, precisely reversing the 1978 results. The Communist party has not yet recovered from this catastrophe: In the 1988 elections they won only one seat, compared to four for the socialists. As the communists declined, a new party, the xenophobic, racist National Front (FN), gained strength, obtaining 21.42 percent of the vote in the 1984 European elections, more than either the socialists (18.42%) or the communists (16.96%) received. In the 1986 legislative elections, the FN came in second with 24.37 percent of the vote, and in the first round of the 1988 presidential elections its candidate, Jean-Marie Le Pen, finished first in Marseille with 28.34 percent of the vote. Since then, however, the FN has lost ground, winning no seats in the 1988 legislative elections and receiving only 14.14 percent of the vote in the 1989 municipal elections. In those elections, the Defferrist coalition of socialists and centrists was successfully revived by Robert Vigouroux, whose dissident socialist group swept all eight local council elections, while Michel Pezet's regular Socialist party, allied with the communists, received only 12.2 percent of the vote.

E. Baratier, et al., *Histoire de Marseille* (Toulouse, Fr., 1973); D. Bleitrach, et al., *Classe ouvrière et social-démocratie: Lille et Marseille* (Paris, 1981); Y. Lacoste, ed., *Géopolitiques des régions françaises*, vol. 3: *La France du Sud-Est* (Paris, 1986); M. Wolkowitsch, *Provence-Alpes-Côte d'Azur* (Paris, 1984).

T. R. Christofferson

Related entries: DEFFERRE, GASTON: IMMIGRANTS; LE PEN, JEAN-MARIE; REGIONS; URBANIZATION.

MARSHALL PLAN, U.S. Secretary of State George Marshall's proposal for massive economic aid to Europe made on June 5, 1947. Behind it lay the need to restore the European economy on a self-sustaining basis, the desire to anchor Germany into the Western camp, and the perception that sustained instability could render governments vulnerable to Soviet influence or even communist takeovers in France and Italy.

Emergency interim aid was given to those countries most in need (France among them) prior to Congress passing the European Recovery Act on April 3, 1948. The aid, which eventually totaled $13 billion, was to be allocated among sixteen European countries by the Organization for European Economic Cooperation created for that purpose on April 16. The privileges granted the United States and the economic conditions included in the Franco-American agreement signed on June 28 implied some U.S. intervention in French internal affairs and were violently denounced by the *Parti communiste français*.

Between 1948 and 1952 France received $2.6 billion, mostly in the form of grants. Although half of the investments in transportation, electricity, cement, coal, or steel that were made between 1947 and 1951 came from U.S. aid, various domestic political reasons later contributed to French reluctance to acknowledge its contribution to their economic and political stability. Military aid took over when the Marshall Plan ended in 1952.

A. Grosser, *The Western Alliance* (New York, 1982); S. Hoffmann, C. Maier, eds., *The Marshall Plan* (Boulder, Colo., 1984); M. Hogan, *The Marshall Plan* (New York, 1987); C. Mee, *The Marshall Plan* (New York, 1984).

P. Le Prestre

Related entries: BIDAULT, GEORGES; ECONOMIC POLICY; FRENCH COMMUNIST PARTY; UNITED STATES, RELATIONS WITH.

MARXISM, once the ideology of the labor movement, became in the contemporary age a philosophical discourse among left-wing intellectuals. Formulating a theory of class struggle within an emerging capitalist society, Karl Marx in the mid-nineteenth century forecast the coming of a collectivist society, to be ushered in by an uprising of the industrial working class. During the Third Republic, Marxism became the official doctrine of the Socialist (SFIO) and subsequently the Communist parties (PCF). During the Fourth and Fifth Republics, however, the contexts for appreciating Marxism diversified, as new realities superseded those that Marx had analyzed and as philosophers tried to accommodate Marx's teachings to new trends in social thought. Out of the earlier political tradition of Marxist ideology, a variety of Marxist theories emerged, from the dogmatic Stalinist doctrine of Communist party leaders to the speculative interpretations of literary critics and historians. As a general trend, Marxism was of waning importance for the labor movement, whose objectives no longer turned on overthrowing bourgeois governments but rather on molding the emerging welfare state. Without critical importance for policy making by statesmen (even the socialists among them), Marxism became a self-reflective endeavor of intellectuals. As such, it retained a surprising vitality from the end of World War II until the 1970s.

Despite the anti-intellectualism and subservience of its leaders to Soviet directives during the 1950s and 1960s, the PCF remained the primary forum for the discourse of Marxist intellectuals. After World War II students and young idealists flocked to the party, lured by its record of heroism during the Resistance and the image of the egalitarian society it promised to seek. But many found the party's leaders dogmatic and its routines stultifying. It was difficult to apologize for the brutality of Soviet politics during the Stalinist era, reaffirmed in the repression of the revolutions in Hungary in 1956 and Czechoslovakia in 1968. By the late 1960s, no one in the PCF any longer believed that the Soviet Union was the classless society that Marx had prophesied, and even party leaders turned to the rhetoric of Eurocommunism to distance themselves from Soviet politics. Over the years, therefore, defections among the intellectuals were ongoing. For some, however, Marxist philosophy was intertwined with causes of the Communist party they were reluctant to disown. Through the 1960s, therefore, the leading discussions of Marxist theory were conducted by intellectuals identified with the party, or by those sympathetic to it. In the end, most of them resigned or were expelled, thereby widening the divide between the practice of communist politicians and the theorizing of Marxist intellectuals.

In contemporary France, no single theorist emerged to provide a unifying interpretation of Marxism, as had Gyorgy Lukács in eastern Europe before the war. Instead, a succession of theories was put forth to explain the enduring relevance of Marx's thought in light of trends in contemporary philosophy. The first such interpretation to emerge was a humanist Marxism. Based upon a reconsideration of Marx's debt to Georg Hegel, it signified a break with the pseudoscientific Marxist-Leninism of PCF leaders. The interest in this approach was inspired by the discovery and publication (1931) of economic and philosophical manuscripts (1844) of the young Marx. These writings revealed how Marx had turned to Hegel for the philosophical method that enabled him to explain how human alienation could be transcended and human potential fulfilled through revolutionary struggle against bourgeois capitalism. This approach was reinforced by the acquaintance of French intellectuals with Lukács's brilliant analysis of these Hegelian foundations of Marx's thought. For Marx, Lukács explained, philosophy permitted not only critical insight into the contradictions of economic processes, but also an imaginative grasp of how they might be overcome. Far from being a mere epiphenomenon, philosophical inquiry was an active, imaginative expression of human freedom and as such an integral part of revolutionary praxis. Through the lectures and writings of Auguste Cornu, Alexandre Kojève, and Jean Hyppolite this Hegelian reading of the work of the young Marx made some headway in academic circles before the war.

After the war interest quickened, in part because of the immediacy of the parallel between Marx's struggle against the tyranny of bourgeois capitalism and the PCF's own against the Nazi Occupation. The problem of alienation displaced that of economic production as the central theme of Marxist discourse, while leading exponents of this new turn in Marxist philosophy initiated a more open, even speculative inquiry into cultural issues hitherto judged irrelevant. Henri Lefebvre was acclaimed for his studies of the culture of everyday life, Lucien Goldmann for his critique of themes in the history of philosophy, Roger Garaudy for the dialogue he launched with Christian leaders, Albert Soboul for his historical studies of the democratic vision of the *sans culottes* during the French Revolution.

Aligned with this inquiry but somewhat apart was Jean-Paul Sartre. Sartre was already a celebrity for his existential writings of the prewar era, and his efforts to arrive at a blend of the two philosophies aroused interest far beyond the intellectual confines of the PCF. Sartre's Marxism, however, was an idiosyncratic formulation. He shared with the humanists a belief that Marxism was a critical philosophy in the struggle for human liberation. The problem of alienation had served as his own point of departure in his earlier, existential phase. Sartre's interest in the subjectivity of the human predicament stemmed from his reading of René Descartes rather than Hegel, and he had little interest in its relationship to the objective conditions of historical development that had always been integral to Marxist thought. For Sartre, Marxism was important for the ideological role it played in the present as the shibboleth of the struggle against oppression.

Sartre's efforts to synthesize Marxism and existentialism inspired a much-publicized debate about the extent to which he may have succeeded. But pro or con, it was a debate among academicians, signifying the degree to which Marxist theory had, by the late 1950s, become a self-absorbed endeavor. Historically, Marxism had been an ideology to raise the consciousness of workers so that they might rally to the class struggle. With Sartre it became part of the recondite discourse of those who wrote for the little magazines of the Parisian literary scene.

In the mid–1960s, Louis Althusser interjected a countervailing interpretation into this rarefied milieu of Marxist theorizing. A professor at the *Ecole normale supérieure* and a member of the PCF, he repudiated the humanist reading of Marx's authorship, together with the significance of his early writings. Althusser's interest was in Marx the scientist, not the activist, and accordingly he refocused attention on Marx's mature writings, particularly *Capital* (1867). He sought to show how Marx had moved beyond his youthful musings to arrive at a systematic science of political economy deeper than all of the ideological uses to which his doctrine has since been put. Bracketing Marx's intentions, he engaged in a close analysis of his texts, seeking to sift through levels of symbolic reading (economic, political, ideological) to uncover the deep structure of capitalist processes that Marx had purportedly discovered. Althusser's interpretation of Marx was widely discussed both inside and outside Marxist circles, in part because it drew upon the structuralist conceptions then of topical interest in Parisian intellectual life. But the appeal of Marxism had always been grounded in its prophetic message, and there were limits to the interest that such an abstruse analysis of economic structures could sustain. Althusser's work was a kind of scholasticism, in which he tried to do for Marxism what Thomas Aquinas had done for Christian theology. Althusser's accomplishment, therefore, was not in convincing his colleagues that Marxism was a science, but rather in systematizing the reflective posture into which Marxism had by then retreated. As a theory, Marxism had become a philosophy by and for intellectuals. For all the attention that such theorizing received, it had little impact beyond the cognoscenti.

This lively endeavor in Marxist theorizing notwithstanding, the essential tenets of Marx's teachings had long since been absorbed into the mainstream of social thought. As an enduring legacy for politics, sociology, and history, Marxism provided insight into the underlying power of economic processes, respect for the rational analysis of social complexities, a method for unmasking ideological pretensions, and a moral exhortation to create a more egalitarian society. But by the 1980s so thoroughly had such propositions become part of a consensus about progressive social thought that labeling them Marxist added little to their meaning. The ties with nineteenth-century Marxism had become tenuous, and contemporary Marxist exegesis arcane. Such was the verdict of Michel Foucault, a philosopher with left-wing sympathies that Marxists wanted to claim for their own. In fending off efforts to reduce his philosophy to Marxist dimensions, Foucault paid homage to Marx's originality as a thinker. But he also suggested that the task was to emulate his creativity, not to enshrine his philosophy.

T. Judt, *Marxism and the French Left* (Oxford, 1986); M. Kelly, *Modern French Marxism* (Baltimore, Md., 1982); G. Lichtheim, *Marxism in Modern France* (New York, 1966); M. Poster, *Existential Marxism in Postwar France* (Princeton, 1975).

P. H. Hutton

Related entries: ALTHUSSER, LOUIS; FOUCAULT, MICHEL; FRENCH COMMUNIST PARTY; GARAUDY, ROGER; SARTRE, JEAN-PAUL.

MAUROY, PIERRE (1928–), socialist politician and former prime minister. Born July 5, 1928 in Cartignies (Nord), son of a primary schoolteacher whose ancestors had all been woodcutters, Mauroy plunged early into socialist politics. He studied at the *Ecole normale nationale d'apprentissage* and briefly became a professor of technical education. National secretary of the socialist youth movement from 1950 to 1958, he was also secretary-general of the technical education teachers union within the *Fédération d'éducation nationale* from 1952 to 1959.

Elected federal secretary of the socialist (SFIO) federation for the department of the Nord in 1961, Mauroy became a member of the national bureau in 1963, and in 1966, deputy secretary-general. Disappointed in his hopes to succeed Guy Mollet as secretary-general when the latter stepped down from this post in 1969, Mauroy associated himself with François Mitterrand at the 1971 Epinay-sur-Seine congress of the Socialist party—since 1969 renamed the *Parti socialiste* (PS). Mitterrand, leading his own small group from the *Convention des institutions républicaines* (CIR) into the PS, became the new first secretary; Mauroy was his deputy. In 1971 he also became first deputy to his patron Augustin Laurent, mayor of Lille, succeeding him in 1973 in a post he has held ever since. In that year he was also elected a deputy to the National Assembly from the Nord, and reelected in 1978, 1981, 1986, and 1988.

Tensions inside the PS after the 1977 split in the Union of the Left and the loss of the 1978 parliamentary elections allowed Michel Rocard to challenge Mitterrand's authority at the 1979 PS congress in Metz. When Mauroy and his friends backed Rocard they were defeated, as Mitterrand shifted internal party alliances and moved left. Nevertheless, when Mitterrand was elected president in 1981 he made Mauroy—a senior figure of the old SFIO faction—his prime minister.

Mauroy's three years in this office divide into two phases. In the first, his government rapidly attempted to implement a leftist program of extensive nationalizations, increased social legislation, and decentralization. Economic difficulties consequent on France's attempt at reflating its economy in the midst of a general world recession brought reconsideration, three devaluations of the franc, and a crisis in March 1983 during which Mitterrand considered withdrawing from the European Monetary System and possible resumption of French tariff barriers. Opposing this program, Mauroy submitted his resignation, but once the President concluded that the idea was economically infeasible he asked Mauroy to remain in office, forming what was technically his third government.

In the second phase of his prime ministership Mauroy was not comfortable with the pace of an economic restructuring that demanded extensive cuts in aging industry, and he sought to emphasize socialist ideas in other ways, pushing a bill to curb the power of press lord Robert Hersant and a reform of government subsidization of private (largely parochial) education. Protests against socialist amendments that upset the balance of a delicate compromise on the school question ultimately led Mitterrand to withdraw the bill. Education Minister Alain Savary resigned, and Mauroy, whose popularity ratings had fallen sharply, chose also to submit his resignation on this issue in July 1984.

During his prime ministership Mauroy's often overly optimistic speeches and his flowery rhetorical style led to much criticism and some ridicule. However, he retained the respect of most elements in the PS. In June 1988, after Mitterrand's re-election, he was chosen first secretary of the PS, beating out Mitterrand's apparent candidate, former prime minister Laurent Fabius.

Mauroy had remained the chief of a faction within the PS whose members saw themselves as steadily upholding the best of an old, basically social democratic tradition against other party factions that until 1983 they had seen as opportunistically too far left and then considered opportunistic in their newfound moderation. Despite Mauroy's intermittent disagreements with Mitterrand, their relations remained good, and in 1987 his faction in the PS merged with the core of Mitterrand's followers.

P. Mauroy, *C'est ici le chemin* (Paris, 1982), *A gauche* (Paris, 1985); T. Pfister, *La Vie quotidienne au Matignon au temps de l'Union de la gauche* (Paris, 1985).

J. W. Friend

Related entries: EDUCATIONAL REFORM; HERSANT, ROBERT; MITTERRAND, FRANCOIS; SAVARY, ALAIN; SOCIALIST PARTY (PS, SFIO).

MAYER, DANIEL (1909–), journalist and socialist statesman. Born in Paris on April 29, 1909, Mayer is the son of Emile Mayer, jewelry salesman, and Lucie Weil, schoolteacher. A genuine self-educated intellectual, Mayer left school at age fourteen. In the wake of the uproar that followed the execution of Sacco and Vanzetti (August 1927), he joined the League of the Rights of Man (September 1927) and the Socialist party (SFIO). A very articulate SFIO speaker, he was put in charge of socialist youth membership development for the Paris area. In 1933 he was recruited by Léon Blum to join the staff of the socialist paper *Le Populaire*. He covered the labor movement and became acquainted with the economic issues of the depression years. An enthusiastic supporter of Blum, he noted later that the Popular Front government did more in a very short time to transform the living conditions and the status of the workers in France than the Russian Revolution of 1917 did in Russia.

He shared the anxieties of most liberals during the Spanish civil war and felt acutely the shame of the Munich accords that led to World War II. After his discharge from the army in 1940, he worked underground to rebuild the badly divided Socialist party and to bring out a clandestine edition of *Le Populaire*.

He served as general secretary of the SFIO from 1943 to 1946 and as a member of the National Council of the Resistance. In this last capacity he met with General Charles de Gaulle in London in 1943. Mayer appreciated de Gaulle as a symbol of the unity of the French Resistance but had serious misgivings as to his understanding of democratic procedures and his obvious lust for power.

After the end of the German Occupation Mayer was successively a delegate to the provisional consultative assembly (1945), a member of both constituent assemblies (1945–46), and was elected to the National Assembly as a representative of the Seine department, then reelected in 1951 and 1956. He was minister of labor and social security in 1946, minister of social affairs in 1947, minister of labor in 1948–49, and he was president of the foreign affairs committee of the National Assembly (1953–57). He resigned his mandate on April

29, 1958 and left the SFIO in September 1958 when he, as a staunch democrat and anticolonialist, felt he could no longer hope to influence French colonial policies and the de Gaulle monocracy from the inside. In 1958 he became president and later president emeritus of the League of the Rights of Man. He presided also over the executive committee of the Organization of Rehabilitation Training (ORT, 1958–78), was a member of the national committee of the Unified Socialist party (PSU), was president of the International Federation of the Rights of Man (1977–83), was president of the committee for the history of the Resistance, was a member of the supervisory council of the judiciary (1982–83), and was president of the Constitutional Council (1983–87).

Mayer acknowledges that his Jewish roots might have something to do with his dedication to freedom and justice. As a fifth generation Parisian, however, he thinks that there is no such thing as a Jewish vote in France, since what differentiates people is not their ethnic origin but their position in the class struggle.

Mayer wrote *Etapes yougoslaves* (1962), *Les Socialistes dans la Résistance* (1968), *Pour une histoire de la gauche* (1969), *Socialisme: Le Droit de l'homme au bonheur* (1976).

C. Juin, *Liberté . . . justice . . . Le combat de Daniel Mayer* (Paris, 1982).

P. Aubery

Related entries: ALGERIA, RELATIONS WITH; AURIOL, VINCENT; *CONFEDERATION GENERALE DU TRAVAIL*; CONSTITUTION OF THE FIFTH REPUBLIC; CONSTITUTION OF THE FOURTH REPUBLIC; DEFFERRE, GASTON; GOUIN, FELIX; INDOCHINA, RELATIONS WITH; MAYER, RENE; MOCH, JULES; MOLLET, GUY; RAMADIER, PAUL; SOCIAL SECURITY; SOCIALIST PARTY (SFIO); STRIKES; TRADE UNION MOVEMENT; TUNISIA, RELATIONS WITH; UNIFIED SOCIALIST PARTY.

MAYER, RENE (1895–1972), a leading proponent of economic modernization. Born into a wealthy, prominent family, educated in law at the University of Paris, Mayer seemed destined for positions of power. After serving in World War I, Mayer rose rapidly on the *Conseil d'Etat*. Immediately noted for his abilities and powerful intellect, he served in several ministerial cabinets and gained expert knowledge of complex large-scale transportation systems from his work for the port of Strasbourg and as secretary-general of the *Conseil supérieur des transports*. Mayer became a director of private railroads in 1928. His support for the modernization and coordination of French railways in a single network gave him a leading role in the creation of the *Société nationale des chemins de fer français* (SNCF). Mayer also helped develop the French electrical and air transportation industries. His intimate knowledge of some of interwar France's most forward-looking, internationally oriented enterprises shaped Mayer's ideas.

So too did the German problem. Mayer recognized German industrial power from negotiations with the Rhenish coal barons in 1930, and he headed the Armaments Ministry mission to Britain until July 1940, which demonstrated the degree to which that power had been converted into military might. After fleeing the German Occupation of the southern zone, Mayer initially aligned himself with Henri-Honoré Giraud and took charge of transportation and communications. He soon made his peace with General Charles de Gaulle, who continued Mayer in his post in the first provisional government.

Whereas Mayer had avoided all political involvement before World War II, he established himself as a leading radical after the war. In politics Mayer sought to maximize French strength and prosperity through modernizing the economy and mastering the German problem. In foreign policy this meant increasing French strength relative to that of Germany. Within France he sought to dismantle the barriers that he believed were raised by state intervention in the economy.

Defeated in an initial bid for office (October 1945), Mayer oversaw German and Austrian affairs for seven months before becoming the deputy for Constantine (November 1946). A year later Robert Schuman named him finance minister. Mayer implemented a plan for financial stabilization that balanced the budget, dismantled economic controls, and devalued the franc. Both as justice minister (October 1949–July 1951) and as finance minister (1951–52), Mayer continued to exert great influence over economic policy. Despite reservations about some aspects of their policy, Mayer strongly supported Jean Monnet and Schuman in the creation of the European Coal and Steel Community (ECSC). Mayer recognized that Germany must inevitably recover its power and believed that measures like the ECSC were the sole means of preventing it from becoming the arbiter of Western European affairs.

Mayer finally got his chance to lead as prime minister (January–May 1953). Before his government fell over his request for decree powers to use against inflation, Mayer introduced the draft law on the European Defense Community (EDC). Mayer saw in the Atlantic Alliance a means of countering the potential danger from Germany as well as the current danger from the Soviet Union. Persuaded that Germany would be rearmed, he supported the EDC to prevent the reconstitution of a German national army. Mayer sought substantial American aid as a means of keeping France fully active in Indochina while still maintaining an army superior to that of a rearmed Germany in Europe.

After Mayer succeeded Monnet as president of the ECSC's High Commission in 1955, he muted supranationalism in favor of fostering cooperation among states. Resolutely liberal in his vision, Mayer avoided any more intervention in the effects of free competition than political and social stability required, and then chiefly through consultation. Mayer sought agreement by all interested parties to a policy before he began to implement it. This required continuous negotiation with unions, businesses, and governments. Mayer wanted the High Authority to mediate between the various communities, enhancing its authority by its usefulness. He retired in 1957 to devote himself to his private business interests. Mayer possessed little flair for electoral politics or parliamentary maneuvering, but his administrative ability and vision of a modernized France number him among the elite group that brought about so much change after 1945.

V. Auriol, *Mon septennat* (Paris, 1970); F. Caron, "Le Plan Mayer," *Histoire, économie, et société* 3 (1982); G. Elgey, *La République des contradictions* (Paris, 1968); D. Mayer, *René Mayer* (Paris, 1983).

J. S. Hill

Related entries: ECONOMIC POLICY; RADICAL PARTY; SCHUMAN, ROBERT; SCHUMAN PLAN; TRIPARTITISM.

MEHAIGNERIE, PIERRE (1939–), agronomist, centrist deputy, and president of the *Centre des démocrates sociaux* (CDS), one of France's centrist parties grouped in the *Union pour la démocratie française* (UDF). Born in Balaze (Ille-et-Vilaine) on May 4, 1939 into a bourgeois Catholic family, he studied in Brittany and then in Paris, where he graduated from the *Ecole nationale supérieure des sciences appliquées* and became an agricultural engineer. Interested in politics from his youth, he adopted the ideas of the *Mouvement républicain populaire* (MRP), the dominant party in Brittany in the 1950s.

After serving as a technical counselor in Tunisia from 1965 to 1967, he worked as an engineer in Bordeaux from 1967 to 1969, and then was appointed *chargé de mission* in the Ministry of Agriculture under Jacques Duhamel (1969–71). His next appointment was as a technical adviser in the Ministry of Cultural Affairs (January 1971–July 1972). In March 1973 he was elected deputy for Ille-et-Vilaine. In 1976 Prime Minister Jacques Chirac chose him as secretary of state for agriculture and a year later appointed him minister of agriculture. Then, in 1977 he was elected mayor of Vitré (Ille-et-Vilaine).

Following the 1981 election victory of François Mitterrand, Méhaignerie played a role in the opposition. From 1981 until 1986 he was regularly reelected to his posts as deputy, mayor, president of the General Council of Ille-et-Vilaine, and, of course, president of the CDS (a post he had held since 1982). In 1986 when the defeat of the Socialist party forced Mitterrand into *cohabitation* with a conservative government headed by Chirac, Méhaignerie was appointed minister of *Equipement, du logement, de l'aménagement du territoire et des transports.* After the re-election of Mitterrand in May 1988 to a second term in office and the return of a socialist government under Michel Rocard, Méhaignerie found himself once again in the opposition. Disillusioned by the defeat of the candidate that he had supported in the 1988 presidential campaign, Raymond Barre, Méhaignerie claimed the right to independence for his party within the opposition and advocated a policy of openness to the Rocard government; some members of his party even agreed to serve in the new socialist government when Mitterrand launched an "opening to the center" at the beginning of his second mandate. In the 1989 European Parliament elections he supported the centrist Simone Weil and not Valéry Giscard d'Estaing, the candidate of the rightist parties. Again his candidate was defeated. In the post–1988 election period, Méhaignerie ostensibly sympathized with the ideas of a number of young "renovators," a group of talented and ambitious junior deputies from the *Rassemblement pour la République* (RPR) and

UDF demanding changes of methods and possibly leaders within their respective parties. Since 1988 he has served as president of the *Union du Centre* in the National Assembly. Méhaignerie's strategy is to work for the emergence of a large centrist party capable of governing the nation.

J.-F. Doumic, H. Lacharmoise, eds. *Le Guide du pouvoir* (Paris, 1989).

R. Viton

Related entries: CENTRIST PARTIES; CHRISTIAN DEMOCRATS; *CO-HABITATION*; TRIPARTITISM; UNION FOR FRENCH DEMOCRACY.

MENDES-FRANCE, PIERRE, (1907–1982), left-leaning radical politician who led the government for 245 days in 1954–55 and who acted as the conscience of the democratic left during the Fourth and early Fifth Republics. Born into an assimilated Jewish family in Paris in January 1907, Pierre Mendès-France received a secular republican education at the *Lycée Turgot* and the *Lycée Louis-le-Grand*, followed by studies at the Faculty of Law and the *Ecole libre des sciences politiques*. In 1924 he helped found the *Ligue d'action universitaire républicaine et socialiste* (LAURS), an antifascist student organization.

The early fame of Mendès-France was a result of his work in economics and finance, including a 1928 thesis, a 1929 article, and a 1930 book entitled *La Banque internationale*. These publications criticized individualist law and argued that modern economic difficulties required international solutions and, therefore, international organizations.

In 1932 Mendès-France was elected deputy for the city of Louviers (Eure). Though a member of the Radical party, he was considered a "young Turk," along with Jacques Kayser, Pierre Cot, Gaston Bergery, Jean Zay, and Gaston Mannerville. In May 1935 he was elected mayor of Louviers, a position he held, except for the interruption of the war, until 1958. He devoted himself to financial and economic matters: In the National Assembly, he spoke in favor of government loans to farmers and was a member, then chair, of the Customs Committee; as a lawyer, he defended peasants; as mayor in Louviers he oversaw the installation of public utilities and the provision of social welfare.

A strong proponent of the Popular Front strategy, Mendès-France was reelected to the National Assembly in 1936. He was critical of the government's reluctant devaluation of the franc, favoring instead immediate devaluation, and he opposed the policy of nonintervention in the Spanish civil war. He nonetheless remained a vocal supporter of the government's record of reform and in 1938 entered Léon Blum's second government as undersecretary of the Treasury. With Georges Boris he authored the first French planning program, but before implementation could proceed, the government fell.

Mendès-France joined the air force when war broke out in 1939. Assigned briefly to the Levant, he was back in France when the German invasion began. After receiving a shrapnel wound, he traveled south and gained passage to Casablanca on the ship *Massilia*. This "flight" became one target for the charge of desertion trumped up by the Vichy government. Arrested on August 31, 1940,

Mendès-France was transferred to Clermont-Ferrand where he was tried, convicted, and sentenced to six years in prison. After a failed appeal, Mendès-France escaped from prison (June 1941). He lived underground for several months, mostly in Grenoble, and then escaped to London on March 1, 1942 to join de Gaulle and the Free French. He rejoined his squadron in England and flew about a dozen bombing operations.

In November 1943 Mendès-France moved to Algiers and became the commissioner of finance in the French National Liberation Committee (CFLN). In this capacity he prepared for reconstruction and represented Free France at the international meeting at Bretton Woods that established the World Bank and the International Monetary Fund (IMF). Following the Liberation, he was appointed minister of national economy in de Gaulle's first government. He urged a policy of austerity, including the reduction of the volume of inflated currency in circulation, restriction of consumption, wage and price controls, the freezing of bank accounts, tax on capital gains, and state-imposed discipline on some production and exchange. De Gaulle rejected his advice in favor of the more laissez-faire policy advocated by Minister of Finance René Pleven, and as a result Mendès-France resigned in April 1945.

Mendès-France returned to his duties as mayor of Louviers and was elected deputy, first to the constituent assembly in 1946 and then to the National Assembly in 1951. He also taught courses at the *Ecole nationale d'administration* on the fiscal and budgetary problems posed by planning and reconstruction, was a member of the Executive Committee of the IMF and World Bank, and became France's representative, from 1947 to 1951, on the Economic and Social Council of the United Nations.

The issue that catapulted Mendès-France to the center of French politics was not economic policy, however, but colonial policy. After 1950 he became a vocal public advocate of a negotiated settlement in Indochina that would entail the gradual evacuation of French troops, free elections, and national independence for Vietnam. This campaign, coupled with his calls for dialogue with North Africa and his program for fiscal and economic reform, made Mendès-France the statesman of choice for many young technocrats and intellectuals.

His brief tenure as premier began on June 18, 1954, in the midst of the debacle of Dien Bien Phu. Mendès-France moved quickly to open direct negotiations with the Vietminh in Geneva and succeeded in arranging the armistice that halted the fighting. Simultaneously, he traveled to Carthage to begin the negotiations that led to the internal autonomy of Tunisia. Finally, Mendès-France oversaw, after the French rejection of the European Defense Community, the London Agreements that led to German rearmament and English attachment to continental security. While Mendès-France was occupied with foreign policy issues, economic policy was left in the hands of the more moderate Edgar Faure, and by the time Mendès-France himself took over control of the Finance Ministry on January 20, 1955, opponents were preparing to bring down the government; it fell on February 2, 1955.

Mendès-France next turned his attention to consolidation of power for his progressive faction within the Radical party. He was instrumental in forming the Republican Front, which brought together the parties of the noncommunist left: progressive radicals, SFIO socialists (Guy Mollet), the *Union démocratique et socialiste de la résistance* (UDSR) (François Mitterrand), and social republicans (Jacques Chaban-Delmas). The coalition won the elections of December 1956, and Mendès-France served briefly as minister without portfolio in the government of Guy Mollet. He resigned in May 1957 because of his opposition to the hard-line Algerian policy of the SFIO leader. Mendès-France became spokesperson for the democratic opposition on the left: He was critical of government policy in North Africa; he warned against the consequences of the Suez adventure; he voted against the Treaty of Rome establishing the Common Market; he opposed de Gaulle's return to power in 1958. He was so out of step with national opinion that he lost the support of his constituency in Louviers in the elections of November 1958. The following year Mendès-France broke with the Radical party, declared himself a socialist, and aligned himself with the *Parti socialiste autonome* (PSA), a splinter group from the SFIO that was attempting to distance itself from the policies of Mollet.

In 1967 he was elected deputy for Grenoble (Isère), and his brief return to the center of national politics occurred during the crisis of 1968 when he sympathized with the striking workers and students, attended the demonstration in Charléty, and suggested—during de Gaulle's dramatic disappearance—that he might lead a provisional government. In the Gaullist landslide that followed, Mendès-France lost his Assembly seat. In 1969 he and Gaston Defferre ran a campaign against Georges Pompidou and the Gaullist system. They were badly defeated, and for all practical purposes Mendès-France passed from active political life. He died on October 18, 1982.

J. Lacouture, *Pierre Mendès-France* (Paris, 1981; Eng. trans. 1984); J. Nantet, *Pierre Mendès-France* (Paris, 1967); A. Werth, *The Strange History of Mendès-France* (New York, 1957).

K. S. Vincent

Related entries: ELECTIONS; EUROPEAN DEFENSE COMMUNITY; FOREIGN POLICY; INDOCHINA, RELATIONS WITH; MITTERRAND, FRANCOIS; POLITICAL TRENDS; RADICAL PARTY; TUNISIA, RELATIONS WITH.

MESSMER, PIERRE (1916–), minister of defense under Charles de Gaulle and prime minister under Georges Pompidou. Messmer rallied to the forces of Free France in 1940. He saw considerable action in various African campaigns and in the Liberation of Europe. In 1945 an ill-fated mission to Tonkin led to his imprisonment by the Vietminh. A colonial civil servant by training, Messmer notably served as *Directeur de cabinet* for the French high commissioner in Indochina (1947–48). Later shifting to Africa, he was successively appointed governor of Mauritania in 1952 and of the Ivory Coast in 1954. As Gaston Defferre's *Directeur de cabinet* in 1956, he assisted the minister of overseas France in the preparation of his crucial framework law for African autonomy.

Back in the field, Messmer held the post of high commissioner in Cameroon (1956–58), French Equatorial Africa (1953), and French West Africa (1958–59). During the *Treize mai* crisis of 1958, he publicly supported a return to power by General de Gaulle.

Messmer was appointed minister of the armies in succession to Pierre Guillaumat on February 5, 1960, immediately after the week of the barricades in Algeria. During his tenure as minister, the nuclear *force de frappe* became the cornerstone of French defense. Relatedly, the French military came increasingly to rely on a highly trained, technically proficient core of professional soldiers (*l'armée de métier*). The initiative in each case clearly flowed from de Gaulle; Messmer's role was essentially one of implementation and explanation. His departure from office followed shortly after that of the general in 1969.

Reelected to the National Assembly seat he had first won in 1968, Messmer was a founder of the militantly orthodox *Présence et action du gaullisme*. In 1971 he was named minister of state for the overseas departments and territories. On July 5, 1972 he rather unexpectedly succeeded Jacques Chaban-Delmas as prime minister. Besides dissipating a whiff of scandal, Messmer's appointment also marked a decisive break with Chaban's "new society." President Pompidou clearly wished both to reassert his own authority and to reassure Gaullist militants.

The first Messmer government was largely preoccupied with the March 1973 legislative election. The prime minister set out the response of the presidential majority to the left's *Programme commun* in a lengthy speech at Provins on January 7, 1973. In the event, his leadership proved successful; the government parties retained a solid, if reduced majority.

The second Messmer government was formed at the beginning of April 1973. It long found itself haunted by the "Lip Affair," which involved the illegal takeover of a watch factory by its employees. Nevertheless, the political agenda was dominated by Pompidou's visibly failing health and the power vacuum that this appeared to create. Most particularly, Messmer himself faced a barrage of criticism for a seeming failure to give firm direction to the government. *Le Point* called for his departure in a December 19, 1973 cover story, while in January and February of 1974 *L'Express* repeatedly raised "the question of confidence."

The deteriorating state of affairs finally prompted Messmer's resignation on February 27, 1974. He was, however, immediately reappointed by Pompidou in an orchestrated demonstration of renewed presidential support. Shortly after its investiture the third Messmer government announced a major new energy policy predicated on the rapid acceleration of nuclear power plant construction (sometimes referred to as the Messmer Plan). After Pompidou's death on April 2, 1974 Messmer succumbed to considerable pressure and announced on April 9 that he would stand in the ensuing presidential election. However, when the other declared candidates of the right refused to step down unanimously for the prime minister, he definitively withdrew from the contest. His candidacy had only lasted some eight hours.

A deputy from 1974 until his surprising defeat in 1988, Messmer most importantly served as parliamentary leader of the *Rassemblement pour la République* during the legislature of *cohabitation* (1986–88). He was also mayor of Sarrebourg from 1971 until 1989. A faithful servant of the French state who rose to the highest levels of government under the Fifth Republic, Messmer nevertheless proved either unwilling or unable to leave a distinctive personal imprint on the course of events.

A. Conte, *Les Premiers Ministres de la Ve République* (Paris, 1986); P. Messmer, "L'Atome, cause et moyen d'une politique militaire autonome," *Revue de défense nationale* 24 (1968), "The French Military Establishment of Tomorrow," *Orbis* 6 (1962).

R. A. Harmsen

Related entries: CHABAN-DELMAS, JACQUES; DECOLONIZATION; DEFENSE POLICY; DE GAULLE, CHARLES; GAULLISM; GAULLIST PARTY; POMPIDOU, GEORGES.

MIDDLE EAST, RELATIONS WITH. Two phases characterize this relationship, the first dominated by decolonization and the second by commercial and, to a lesser degree, strategic concerns. Independence for the Syrian and Lebanese mandates, first proposed by the Léon Blum government in 1936 but not ratified by parliament, and promised by General Charles de Gaulle in 1941, was only granted in 1945, and after a combination of nationalist agitation and British pressure. The borders of the new state of Lebanon had been created to assure a Maronite majority.

More important for relations with the Arab world were the close ties created with Israel even before statehood. Inspired by tremendous post-holocaust sympathy for the plight of the Jewish people and hostility to British policy, Frenchmen in and out of government cooperated in the clandestine emigration effort organized by Zionist groups like the Haganah. Though France voted partition, it was not among the very first to recognize the new state. Nevertheless, France quickly developed a relationship of close cooperation with Israel as well as becoming its chief arms supplier. Under the heavily socialist governments of the Fourth Republic, close working relationships with the labor-dominated Jewish state were formed on so many bureaucratic levels that they effectively escaped open foreign policy debate.

The beginning of the Algerian revolt in 1954 added a strategic dimension to these ties. Impressed by the considerable verbal and slight military support for the rebellion by Nasser's Egypt, French government circles blamed the revolt on pan-Arab nationalism directed from Cairo and concluded that toppling Nasser was essential to security in Algeria. The ultimate expression of this strategy was the Anglo-Franco-Israeli military attack on Egypt during the Suez crisis of 1956. In response to Nasser's nationalization of the canal (which appeared to threaten British and French financial, and Israeli strategic, interests), in a secret meeting in Sèvres the three governments agreed to the following charade: Israeli troops invaded the Sinai, followed by British and French forces, which arrived as ostensible peacemakers. Despite military victory, the three powers gained little politically. In a solution imposed by the United Nations (with the United States and the Soviet Union in uncommon agreement), the canal remained in Egyptian hands, all foreign forces had to withdraw, and, most important, Nasser emerged strengthened.

Algerian independence and the coming of the Fifth Republic paved the way for a reversal of French policy in the region. De Gaulle saw a closer relationship with the Arab states both as essential for French commercial interests and as a necessary part of his global strategy to weaken the domination of the two superpowers and escape the constraints of a bipolar system. The 1967 war allowed for the first manifestation of the new policy. France condemned Israel as the aggressor and insisted that no claim could result to any of the territories occupied in that conflict. An arms embargo (started just before the conflict) blocked Israeli purchases, including those already paid for, while declining to release the funds laid out by the Jewish state. Israeli agents, with the cooperation of some in the French military, seized some of ''their'' embargoed ships in Cherbourg in 1969, and agreement was not reached over repayment until 1972. Massive arms sales were permitted, however, to non–front line Arab states like Libya, Iraq, and Saudi Arabia.

France led the European Economic Community in its gradual rapprochement with the Palestine Liberation Organization (PLO) and the Palestinian movement (the PLO office in Paris in 1975 was the first in Western Europe). Similarly, France rejected the agreements that followed the 1973 war, culminating in the Camp David accords (1978–79), and has consistently called for an international conference to restore peace and the rights of the Palestinians, in contrast with American and Israeli preference for separate negotiations between the parties. Nor does France accept the American and Israeli interpretation of UN Resolution 222 as permitting the retention of some lands occupied in 1967. Many thought that the election of François Mitterrand and the Socialist party in 1981 would lead to a less anti-Israeli policy, but French policy choices remained essentially the same despite cosmetic changes. One reason was the consistency of French commercial interests, the other the growing sympathy with the Palestinians on the French left. French governments, both Gaullist and socialist, have also promoted the idea of a North-South dialogue and a more just international order, as well as trying to block the formation of a united front of oil importing nations, with the United States, and against the Organization of Petroleum Exporting Countries (OPEC).

These positions have had material rewards. France received the most favored treatment of any Western state during the 1973 oil boycott, and commercial relations have boomed with Arab states, which have effectively replaced Israel as the biggest market for French arms exports. Under President Valéry Giscard d'Estaing (and especially his prime minister, Jacques Chirac) an especially close relationship was created with Iraq, which in return for guaranteed oil supplies purchased a nuclear reactor (1976, destroyed by Israel in 1981) and many modern arms. Despite French claims of neutrality, it continued to supply Iraq during the war with Iran (1980–88), and French pilots appear to have flown combat missions. One result was a terror bombing campaign in Paris organized by pro-Iranian groups. In the fall of 1990, however, President Mitterrand sent troops to the Middle East to join a U.S.-led multinational force to oppose Iraq's invasion and annexation of Kuwait. When war broke out with Iraq early in 1991, French forces were put under U.S. military command. Following Iraq's defeat in the Gulf War, Mitterrand continued to cooperate closely with President Bush in opposing Saddam Hussein, especially on the issue of the development of nuclear facilities in Iraq.

The civil war that began in Lebanon in 1975 witnessed the destruction of the Maronite-dominated, pro-Western state France had done so much to create. A French offer of military intervention to restore peace was rejected in 1976, and French participation in international peacekeeping forces only increased the targeting of French interests and personnel by radical Islamic groups. Attempts to influence successive rounds of fighting have had little result, though many believe that the French government was among the backers of the Christian general Michel Aoun. The French government is now seeking to normalize its relations with Iran.

A. Grosser, *Affaires extérieures, la politique de la France 1944–1989* (Paris, 1989); G. Lenczowski, *The Middle East in World Affairs* (Ithaca, N.Y., and London, 1980); C. Saint-Prot, *La France et le renouveau arabe* (Paris, 1980).

A. Douglas

Related entries: ARMS SALES; DECOLONIZATION; DEFENSE POLICY; FOREIGN POLICY; TERRORISM; THIRD WORLD, RELATIONS WITH.

MINIMUM WAGE (SMIC, *Salaire minimum interprofessionnel de croissance*), which was first established under the 1950 law on collective bargaining as the SMIG (*salaire minimum interprofessionnel garanti*). The legislation aimed to provide low-paid workers with a physical minimum as wage control gave way to free collective bargaining. Because of the failure of collective bargaining to set actual wage levels, the minimum wage became a major element of wage determination, an instrument of economic and social policy, and bone of contention in political debate and the class struggle.

Under the 1950 law the government fixed the wage after considering the economic situation and a basic working-class budget decided by representatives of unions, employers, and consumers on the Higher Commission on Collective Agreements. This family budget, drafted after a walkout by employers, allowed for merely a kilogram of meat per family each month. Governments circumvented a 1952 provision indexing the wage to the cost of living by allocating bonuses and manipulating the index. With the possible exception of Pierre Mendès-France, who conducted periodic consultations, governments ignored union complaints and allowed the SMIG to lag seriously behind average wage levels, contributing to the gross inequalities and accumulating tensions in French society.

The gap was filled by the general strike of May-June 1968, which imposed a raise of 35 percent in the minimum wage, an end to abatements for low-wage regions, and led to the adoption of a new formula, the SMIC, which took into account national growth and the average level of wages. Reformist governments of the right, wishing to assist the low-paid, regularly augmented the SMIC in the 1970s as did the socialist-communist government of Pierre Mauroy. Because of the atrophy of collective bargaining since the economic crisis, a growing proportion of employees has become dependent on the SMIC—perhaps 10 percent who receive the bare minimum and another 10 percent whose wages are affected by it—which now exceeds contractual minimums for almost all workers in industry.

J.-P. Courthéoux, *Le Salaire minimum* (Paris, 1978); G. Lyon-Caen, *Le Salaire* (Paris, 1981); F. Sellier, A. Tiano, *Economie du travail* (Paris, 1970); J.-J. Wagner, ''Les Salaries au SMIC en juillet 1984,'' *Dossiers statistiques du travail et de l'emploi* 17 (1985).

B. H. Moss

Related entries: ECONOMIC POLICY; INCOME DISTRIBUTION; LABOR FORCE; TRADE UNION MOVEMENT.

MINORITIES, PROBLEMS OF, the difficulties facing religious, regional, and ethnic subcultures in France, which are related to their status as minorities in the national population. The preamble to the constitution of the Fourth Republic, adopted in October 1946 and perpetuated in constitutional law by the constitution of the Fifth Republic, guarantees ''the sacred and inalienable rights'' of all citizens, ''without distinction by race, religion, or belief.'' These rights include the liberties guaranteed by the Declaration of the Rights of Man of 1789 (e.g., freedom of speech), as ''completed'' by the preamble of 1946, which added ''political, economic, and social principles necessary in this era'' (e.g., the equality of women and the rights of trade unions).

These constitutional guarantees notwithstanding, minorities have faced persistent problems during the Fourth and Fifth Republics. The definition of French minorities varies, but it includes at least three broad categories: (1) religious minorities, chiefly Moslems, Protestants, and Jews; (2) regional ethnic groups, which may constitute a local majority yet form a small minority of the national population, such as Bretons or Corsicans; and (3) minority nationalities, chiefly immigrants or resident aliens from former French colonies.

Approximately 8 percent of the population of France belongs to religious minorities. From the Calvinist reformation of the sixteenth century until the Fifth Republic, the largest minority was Protestant, chiefly Calvinists in the Reformed church plus a smaller population of Lutherans concentrated in Alsace and the Pays de Montbéliard. The French census does not identify religious beliefs, but Protestants today number well over one million, approximately the same 2 percent of the population that they have constituted for two centuries. The Jewish population of France includes both Sephardic Jews of Mediterranean ancestry and Ashkenazim of East European ancestry. They total between 600,000 and 700,000 people, slightly more than 1 percent of the population; this is the largest Jewish community in Europe outside of the Soviet Union. Since the 1960s, Protestants and Jews have been overshadowed by the arrival of a large Moslem minority from North Africa. The Moslem population in 1988 was estimated at approximately three million, roughly 5 percent of the population.

The problems of religious subcultures are related to France's history of intolerance toward religious minorities: French Protestants and Jews experienced centuries of persecution. Article Ten of the Declaration of the Rights of Man guaranteed religious freedom, but anti-Protestantism and anti-Semitism have persisted in modern French opinion; both were underscored by the behavior of the Vichy government of 1940–44. Religious minorities have received greater acceptance during the Fourth and Fifth Republics. Protestants face only subtle anti-Protestant attitudes, most recently seen during the celebration of the tricentennary of the revocation of Edict in Nantes in 1985. Michel Rocard's Protestantism presented no obstacle to his appointment as premier (1988–91) or the inclusion of five other Protestants in the cabinet, but this striking prominence of Protestants caused widespread discussion.

France has also had Jewish premiers since 1945, notably Léon Blum and Pierre Mendès-France during the Fourth Republic. Anti-Semitism, however, has remained a virulent force in France, frequently revealed by international questions involving Israel or by issues awakening discussion of the Vichy government, such as the trial of Klaus Barbie. A wave of anti-Semitic violence began in 1978, with bombings aimed at Jews in Avignon, Marseille, and Paris. Attacks became frequent in the late 1970s and early 1980s, including the bombing of a student restaurant, the vandalism of Jewish cemeteries, and the murder of a Jewish writer. The largest incidents were the bombing of a synagogue in Paris in October 1980 and a massacre at a Parisian delicatessen in August 1982. Moreover, in the spring of 1990 a Jewish cemetery was desecrated at Carpentras in southern France. The anti-Semitism of the 1980s and early 1990, however, has won little acceptance in the French press or in politics, in contrast to the widespread anti-Semitism expressed there in the 1930s.

The Moslem population of France similarly confronts great hostility. The problems of this religious subculture, however, are a smaller feature of the racism directed against the North African population, discussed below.

The Fifth Republic has also witnessed serious problems for regional ethnic minorities. Both the monarchical tradition of the old regime and the republican tradition of the French Revolution gave France an exceptionally centralized system of government that directed local affairs from Paris. Distinct regional populations, often with their own languages or dialects and differing cultures, steadily lost their distinct identity during the nineteenth and twentieth centuries. This produced a variety of campaigns for local rights and decentralization, and sometimes movements for autonomy or independence. Especially strong sentiments have existed among the Bretons of northwestern France, the Alsatians in the east, the Basques in the southwest, and on the island of Corsica.

The problems of these regional minorities have chiefly been cultural (the threat to their distinct identity) and economic (the underdevelopment of their region). The Deixonne Law of January 1951 addressed the cultural issue by permitting the study of a local language (but not other instruction in it). Such reforms did not defuse the regional issue, however, and autonomist movements appeared by the late 1960s. This launched a debate that resulted in a law of July 1972 dividing metropolitan France into twenty-two regions. Alsace, Brittany, and Corsica all became separate regions by this legislation, but autonomist agitation did not cease.

The Corsican minority (a population of less than 250,000) has been the most vehement. Breton nationalists attempted a few, isolated terrorist attacks in the early 1970s, but the Corsicans launched a larger movement. Starting with a series of bombings in January 1974, Corsican nationalists began a decade-long campaign of violence. In 1975–76 Corsican ''liberation fronts'' made more than five hundred bomb attacks. Their program for dealing with Corsican problems ranged from the obligatory teaching of the Corsican language and the replacement of French civil servants with Corsicans to the removal of ''all instruments of colonialism'' such as the French army and bureaucracy, plus the right of self-determination. The response of the government, however, was the outlawing of autonomist movements in January 1974 and virtual military operations against Corsican nationalists, such as *Opération Ile Morte* of September 1975.

The greatest minority problems in France, however, have been those of minority nationalities. In the early twentieth century, foreign laborers (especially Belgians and Italians) and ethnic minorities (such as gypsies) faced severe discrimination. The economic reconstruction of France after 1945 and the breakup of the French colonial empire, particularly after the Algerian War, however, drew an immigrant and migrant population including large numbers of North African Arabs and West African blacks who have experienced racism.

During the 1950s over 100,000 immigrants a year entered France. In 1954, this population totaled 1.7 million; by 1974, when the government suspended immigration rights on the grounds of high unemployment, the total had passed 4 million, nearly 8 percent of the population. In 1973 alone, 846,000 Algerians entered France. The majority of this population is concentrated in the Paris, Marseille, and Lyon regions. Marseille has nearly a 15 percent immigrant population, and some working-class suburbs of Paris (such as Gennevilliers) reach 30 percent. Over 80 percent of the immigrant population is concentrated in unskilled and semiskilled labor.

The problems of the Arab and black African minority cover a wide range: Government studies have found that 60 percent have difficulty with the French language, 24 percent live in substandard housing (plus another 45% in hotels), and morbidity and infant mortality are far above the national average. Academic studies have identified a wide range of racism, manifested in paternalism, prejudicial treatment, derision, and hostility. An explicit Law Against Racism, adopted in July 1972, has neither eliminated these problems nor prevented violent attacks on Arabs and blacks, such as took place in the race riot at Marseille in August 1973.

The foremost problem confronting the immigrant minority is that the lack of citizenship deprives them of many constitutional rights and guarantees. Trade-union rights, judicial rights, and social rights (such as welfare) are limited for noncitizens. They have no political rights and must explicitly adopt ''political neutrality'' or face expulsion from France.

F. Malino, B. Wasserstein, *The Jews in Modern France* (Hanover, Ger., 1985); P. Maurcours, *Les Français et le racisme* (Paris, 1965); G. Noiriel, *Le Creuset français: Histoire de l'immigration, XIXe-XXe siècles* (Paris, 1988); R. Ramsay, *The Corsican Time Bomb* (Manchester, Eng., 1983).

S. C. Hause

Related entries: ALGERIA, RELATIONS WITH; ANTI-SEMITISM; BARBIE, KLAUS; CORSICA; DECENTRALIZATION; IMMIGRANTS; LE PEN, JEAN-MARIE; NATIONALITY CODE; *SOS RACISME*; TERRORISM.

MITTERRAND, FRANCOIS (1916–), Resistance figure, minister in numerous governments under the Fourth Republic, resolute opponent of Charles de Gaulle, and president of France. Mitterrand was born into a devout middle-class Catholic family in Jarnac in southwestern France. After attending secondary school in Angoulême, he enrolled at the Sorbonne and at the *Ecole des sciences politiques* in Paris where he pursued and obtained degrees in law and political science. As a young university student in the 1930s, he seemed more destined for a career as a lawyer or a journalist than a politician.

The outbreak of World War II and his experiences in it transformed this shy, bookish, provincial Catholic student into an organizer and strategist who would play a major role on the French political stage after 1945. He began his military service in 1938 and was a sergeant when the war began. In May 1940 he was wounded by mortar fire near Verdun and taken prisoner. Escaping his Nazi captors after three tries, he made his way to Vichy and found a job in the Commission for War Prisoners, and shortly thereafter he joined the Resistance. He met General Charles de Gaulle, head of the Free French forces, for the first time in Algiers in 1943. The general sought ways to coordinate the Resistance effort from abroad. Mitterrand balked at the suggestion that he merge his group with one led by the general's nephew. Mitterrand later pointed out that he was suspicious of a man trying to lead a Resistance effort from abroad while others were on French soil actively opposing the Nazis. Eventually, Mitterrand did merge his group with the one of the general as well as with another led by the communists, eventually emerging as head of this new organization. During the war years he also met his wife, Danielle Gouze, who came from a family of socialist schoolteachers from Burgundy. After the Liberation of Paris, Mitterrand remained head of the war prisoners' movement, an organization that he had founded earlier.

After dabbling in journalism following the war, he launched his political career by joining a small "hinge party" known as the Democratic and Socialist Union of the Resistance (UDSR) and quickly became a young political star of the Fourth Republic (1946–58). This party originally included Gaullists, socialists, and moderates like himself. He lost his first election in 1946 but shortly thereafter was elected a deputy to the National Assembly from the rural department of the Nièvre in Burgundy. In 1947 at the age of thirty he became minister of veterans' affairs in the government of Paul Ramadier. Under the Fourth Republic he gained valuable political experience by serving in eleven different governments, as minister of overseas territories (1950–51), minister of the interior (1954–55), and minister of justice (1956–57). The career of this emerging young politician was interrupted by the return of de Gaulle to power in 1958 as France found itself in crisis as a result of the Algerian independence movement.

Mitterrand opposed de Gaulle's return to power as well as the constitution of the new Fifth Republic with its strong executive. He later charged that the general's return was simply a *coup d'état*. Losing his seat in the National Assembly in the 1958 legislative elections for the new Gaullist Republic, Mitterrand ran for the senate in 1959 and won; in 1959 he was also elected mayor of Château-Chinon in Burgundy. In 1962 he made a successful bid for the National Assembly, where he remained until elected president in 1981.

His animosity toward the right was strengthened by two scandals in which he was embroiled, the *affaire des fuites* of 1954 and the *affaire de l'Observatoire* in 1959. These scandals, inspired by his enemies on the right, only encouraged him to oppose de Gaulle and his supporters. Mitterrand realized that to defeat de Gaulle and the right he would need the support of the *Parti communiste français* (PCF), which normally claimed approximately 25 percent of the vote. In the 1965 presidential election he ran as the common candidate of the Federation of the Democratic and Socialist Left (FGDS), an alliance of noncommunist leftist parties. The PCF, pursuing a popular front strategy at the time, also backed the common candidate of the FGDS. Mitterrand gave de Gaulle a scare in the election by winning almost 45 percent of the vote in the second round. It was clear that a united left could challenge the domination of the right.

Mitterrand also realized that he could keep his name before the French public and underscore his opposition with the power of his pen. He has authored more than ten books, mainly political reflections and critiques, that have often appeared on the eve of major elections. For example, he published an indictment of the Gaullist regime entitled *Le Coup d'état permanent* (1964) and a critique of the Giscard years under the title *Ici et maintenant* (1980).

The electoral fortunes of the left, however, suffered a setback as a result of the student-worker revolt of May–June 1968. Mitterrand himself appeared as an opportunist when he tried to take advantage of the crisis by calling for a new government headed by Pierre Mendès-France, without first consulting him, and by announcing that he himself would run for president. When the left suffered a large setback in the June 1968 legislative elections that served as a referendum on de Gaulle's policies, Mitterrand resigned as chairman of the FGDS and decided not to run in the 1969 presidential elections.

The 1970s saw the rise of a new organization in France under Mitterrand's leadership. After heading a group known as the Convention of Republican Institutions (CIR), Mitterrand was chosen in 1971 to become the first secretary of the *Parti socialiste* (PS), which had emerged two years earlier to replace the old bankrupt Socialist party (SFIO). Ironically, he had joined the PS only a few days before taking over the leadership of the party. Because the new PS was a catchall party that cut across class lines and comprised three major tendencies, Mitterrand had to play three factions against one another to maintain his leadership. These three groups were represented by Mitterrand's radical tradition, Jean-Pierre Chevènement's revolutionary socialism, and Michel Rocard's social democracy. Mitterrand and the PS agreed to a Common Program in 1972, an electoral alliance and program of government between the socialists, communists, and left radicals (MRG). Mitterrand declared several days after signing the agreement that he wanted to use the Common Program to reconquer an important part of the communist electorate. In the presidential elections of 1974 Mitterrand launched his second try for the Elysée Palace as the common candidate of the left and almost defeated Valéry Giscard d'Estaing by capturing more than 49 percent of the votes cast.

In 1981 Mitterrand ran once again for the presidency and was victorious. His win over incumbent Giscard was aided by a number of factors: Giscard's imperial image, the need for economic and social reform, and the twin problems of growing inflation and unemployment. Mitterrand's election triumph was important because it ended twenty-three years of right-wing domination; it showed that *alternance* (alternating governments) was possible under the Fifth Republic, and it helped the socialists win an absolute majority of seats in the legislative elections that followed the presidential contest. To reward the PCF for its support and to help carry out the Common Program, four communist ministers were appointed to the new government.

Under socialist prime minister Pierre Mauroy, the Mitterrand government introduced a long series of reforms and a reflationary economic policy. The government carried out a nationalization program aimed at the takeover of nine industrial groups, launched social reforms (reduced the work week to thirty-nine hours; gave workers additional rights in the workplace; lowered the retirement age to sixty; extended vacations to five weeks; increased allocations for the elderly, women living alone, and the handicapped; raised the minimum wage; provided reimbursements for abortions), and introduced a wealth tax. The government also created approximately 100,000 jobs in the public sector. In addition to these measures, it attempted to strengthen social justice when it created a Ministry of Women's Rights, abolished the death penalty, eliminated the ad hoc security court, amended laws against homosexuals, tried to regularize the status of France's nearly four million immigrants, and instituted decentralization to restore regional power. The socialist government also launched significant reforms in broadcasting policy.

During the first year of his presidency Mitterrand believed that pump priming, heavy state spending, would help pull France out of the recession so troubling to the Western world at the time. He also mistakenly believed, as did others at the time, that the United States would soon reflate its economy and the recession in the West would soon end. His reflationary policy, coupled with a refusal to devalue the franc immediately after assuming office, heightened inflation and the balance of payments deficit, and created serious problems for the new socialist government. The economic situation forced him to launch an austerity program in 1982 and 1983. The turn to austerity and the subsequent rise in unemployment, aided by industrial restructuring to make France more competitive, quickly sapped the popularity of the government. The largest demonstration against the government, however, grew out of education and not economic policy. When the government tried to increase control over the ten thousand private and mainly Catholic schools, protest erupted, with more than one million demonstrating at the Bastille in Paris on June 24, 1984.

Confronting rising discontent and protests—not to mention socialist setbacks in the 1983 municipal elections and the June 1984 European Parliament elections—Mitterrand decided to move his government to the center. On July 12 he addressed the nation and said he would withdraw the Savary law for private schools (named after Education Minister Alain Savary) and desired to consult the public in the future with a series of public referenda. He then picked a new prime minister, Laurent Fabius, a young and loyal *Mitterrandiste* technocrat. When Fabius announced that he would continue austerity, the communists withdrew from the government. The move toward the center allowed Mitterrand to prepare for the 1986 legislative elections and beyond. The Socialist party would later mirror that turn to the center at their 1985 congress of Toulouse, the Bad Godesberg of the PS where the socialists revealed their new social democratic colors.

While the economy began slowly to show improvement under the new prime minister, Mitterrand confronted two major problems prior to the 1986 legislative elections. One problem was the *Rainbow Warrior* affair involving the sabotaging by French secret agents of a Greenpeace vessel in the South Pacific that was protesting nuclear testing. Mitterrand insisted that he was not fully informed about the details of the operation. Nevertheless, Minister of Defense Charles Hernu had to resign, and the head of the French external security agency (DGSE) was dismissed in order to "terminate" the affair. The other major problem was the independence movement in far-away New Caledonia that threatened to explode and that the right could easily exploit. It was finally decided that the island community would be given more autonomy and that a referendum would be held in the future on the status of New Caledonia.

Despite the socialist president's relatively active role in the 1986 legislative campaign and the adoption of a proportional-representation voting system to save PS seats and to divide to right, voters returned a new conservative majority. Mitterrand appointed his old Gaullist nemesis, Paris mayor Jacques Chirac, as the new prime minister, as France experienced *alternance* once again and its first experiment under the Fifth Republic with *cohabitation*, power sharing between a socialist president and a conservative government.

Politically, *cohabitation* allowed Mitterrand to restructure and diversify his image, appearing as a president of all the French rather than simply one of leftist voters. He did this by staying above the day-to-day political fray and intervening to defend what he considered the national interests. Power sharing allowed him to project the image of an arbiter and unifier. One factor that gave additional life to *cohabitation* was a wave of terrorist attacks in Paris in September of 1986 that forced unity of action on the part of the president and his prime minister. *Cohabitation* remained popular with the electorate until the massive student revolt of late 1986 and the rising threat of a serious public-sector strike revealed some of the difficulties of power sharing. The nationwide student revolt, a response to Chirac's attempt to reform universities, forced the conservative government to announce a "pause" in its legislative agenda. While *cohabitation* advanced political democracy in France by showing that the left and the right could share power, and while the nation lost its exceptionalism vis-à-vis other Western countries, power sharing was driven by the presidential politics of both Mitterrand and Chirac.

In the 1988 presidential elections, Mitterrand won a landslide victory over Chirac, 54 percent to 46 percent. "Mitterrand II," as he was called in France, began his second term by calling for an "opening to the center." When the 1988 legislative elections failed to produce a majority for either the left or the right, he appointed the right-wing socialist Michel Rocard to lead a minority cabinet that included socialists and centrists. The new centrist orientation of France was clearly reflected in the bicentennial celebrations in 1989, in which Mitterrand and his advisers emphasized the unity of the nation.

At the beginning of Mitterrand's second term he had to confront a rising wave of racism and anti-Semitism, the growing popularity of his new prime minister while the PS itself experienced disunity, and a new European challenge. The emergence of a durable extreme right in France led by Jean-Marie Le Pen and his National Front (FN) helped to encourage racism and anti-Semitism, the most alarming example being the desecration of a Jewish cemetery in Carpentras in the spring of 1990.

Somewhat unexpectedly, Rocard's popularity remained very high after his appointment as prime minister. This concerned Mitterrand, because Rocard has been his nemesis within the Socialist party. Moreover, at its March 1990 congress at Rennes the PS experienced a fratricidal duel among two contending heirs to the president's throne (Fabius and Lionel Jospin) that strengthened the possibility that Rocard would emerge as the best placed socialist candidate in the next presidential elections. Yet, after three years of Rocard at the helm, the prime minister's anti-inflationary and deficit-reducing policies had led to increased unemployment, criticism among some socialists and others that Rocard was too conservative and that social policy was being ignored, and difficulty in piecing together majorities in the National Assembly. Consequently, Mitterrand decided once again to change the image of the government, and on May 15, 1991 he appointed one of his loyal followers, the socialist Edith Cresson, to replace Rocard. This appointment made Cresson the first woman in French history to hold the post of prime minister. Mitterrand announced this change shortly after celebrating his tenth year in power. While it was thought that Mitterrand had requested Rocard's resignation, both suggested publicly that it was a mutually desired divorce. Nevertheless, Cresson's appointment gave the government an image that was quite different from Rocard's prime ministership. Politically, Cresson is to the left of Rocard, and she formed a government with a more leftward tilt; moreover, she announced shortly after taking office that she wanted to strengthen France industrially as the Common Market prepared for its rendezvous with economic integration in 1993, and she lashed out at Japan for its protectionist trade policies. As Mitterrand had said in a public address after her appointment, the objective for France was now meeting the challenge of 1993, when Europe dismantled its economic borders. But another objective for Mitterrand, unannounced but obvious to many, was the approaching 1993 legislative elections.

Dealing with the European challenge, the reform movement in Eastern Europe, the collapse of the Berlin Wall, and the decline of Soviet power and influence posed new problems for the president: how to keep European integration on track and how to ensure French and European security. Given the new situation in Europe, Mitterrand called for a European confederation from the Atlantic to the Urals that was reminiscent of de Gaulle's earlier vision, a speed-up of EEC integration, the formation of a reconstruction and development bank to aid Eastern Europe, German guarantees for the existing German–Polish border, and a stronger role for the Conference on Security and Cooperation in Europe in security matters.

The foreign and defense policy of Mitterrand's presidency has been pragmatic and Gaullist in approach, allowing him to maintain a consensus in these domains while attempting reform at home. Like de Gaulle, he has supported the development of the French nuclear arsenal. With the Soviet Union he has pursued a policy of containment and cooperation. Prior to 1984 when the PCF was part of his government, the emphasis was on containment; he even launched a crusade in Europe for the need to deploy new NATO missiles on the continent late in 1983. After the PCF left the socialist government in 1984, Mitterrand began to emphasize cooperation, especially following the climax of the reform movement in Eastern Europe and new Soviet reforms under Mikhail Gorbachev. While Mitterrand has promoted solidarity with NATO members, namely the United States and Germany, he has, like de Gaulle, carefully guarded French autonomy in foreign and defense matters. For instance, he refused to give the United States permission to fly over French territory during the former's raid on Libya. The French president has supported the revival of the Western European Union, an organization created in the 1950s to promote the coordination of defense and foreign policy issues of member states, in order to enhance European autonomy in security matters. He has also tried to maintain French influence in the Third World, even sending troops and material to Chad to protect that nation from Libyan aggression and arming Iraq during its long war (1980–88) with Iran. He has tried to promote a North–South dialogue and has criticized U.S. policy in the southern hemisphere, notably in Latin America.

In the Middle East, Mitterrand has tried to play a more even-handed role in the region compared to de Gaulle. Shortly after taking office in 1981, he visited Israel and became the first French president to do so since the creation of the Israeli state in 1948. Prior to the outbreak of the recent war with Iraq, Mitterrand advocated a non-military solution to the crisis in the Persian Gulf following Iraq's takeover of Kuwait, including an international conference on the Middle East. Once the war commenced in mid-January of 1991, Mitterrand placed 10,000 troops and almost one hundred French aircraft in Saudi Arabia under U.S. command, which played a significant role in evicting Iraqi troops from Kuwait. He supported President George Bush in opposing Saddam Hussein in the aftermath of the war, especially on the issue of the development of nuclear facilities in Iraq. He is now attempting to normalize France's relations with Iran.

During his long political career Mitterrand has become the leading figure on the left in late-twentieth-century France. He has reconstructed the Socialist party, rebalanced the forces of the left and the right, and marginalized the PCF. Mitterrand has played a key role in transforming the political landscape of his nation and creating a centrist Republic. He has transformed the face of Paris with his *grands projets*, large new monuments for the capital that include the pyramid at the Louvre, the Opera at the Bastille, the arch at La Défense, the Musée d'Orsay, the center for science and industry as well as a music center at La Villette, the *Institut du monde arabe*, and the Ministry of Finance at the Quai de Bercy. In the history of postwar France, Mitterrand may be remembered as a centrist revolutionary.

F-O. Giesbert, *Le Président* (Paris, 1990); F. Mitterrand, *Ma part de vérité* (Paris, 1969), *Politique*, 2 vols. (Paris, 1977, 1981); C. Nay, *Le noir et le rouge* (Paris, 1984); W. Northcutt, *Mitterrand: A Political Biography* (New York, 1992); G. Ross, S. Hoffmann, S. Malzacher, eds., *The Mitterrand Experiment* (New York, 1987).

W. Northcutt

Related entries: ART AND ARCHITECTURE; BROADCAST MEDIA; *CARREFOUR DU DEVELOPPEMENT* AFFAIR; CHIRAC, JACQUES; CLUB MOVEMENT; *COHABITATION*; COMMON PROGRAM; CULTURAL POLICY; DEFENSE POLICY; DE GAULLE, CHARLES; DEMOCRATIC AND SOCIALIST UNION OF THE RESISTANCE; ECONOMIC POLICY; ELECTIONS; EUROPEAN ECONOMIC COMMUNITY, RELATIONS WITH; FABIUS, LAURENT; FEDERATION OF THE DEMOCRATIC AND SOCIALIST LEFT; FOREIGN POLICY; FRENCH COMMUNIST PARTY; GISCARD D'ESTAING, VALERY; GREENPEACE AFFAIR; IMMIGRANTS; LUCHAIRE AFFAIR; MARCHAIS, GEORGES; MAUROY, PIERRE;

MENDES-FRANCE, PIERRE; POLITICAL TRENDS; ROCARD, MICHEL; SOCIAL TRENDS; SOCIALIST PARTY (PS, SFIO); STUDENT REVOLTS; TERRORISM; UNION OF THE LEFT.

MOCH, JULES (1893–1985), prominent socialist deputy and minister during the Third and Fourth Republics. Moch was born in Paris into an assimilated Jewish family. His father had been a *polytechnicien*, army officer, and *dreyfusard*. Jules also attended the *Ecole polytechnique*, but saw his education interrupted by the outbreak of World War I. During the conflict he was cited for bravery in battle. After the armistice he employed his engineering skills to rebuild northern France. Elected to the Chamber for the first time in 1928, Moch became a close collaborator of the socialist leader Léon Blum. He served in the first Blum government, 1936–37, and then became minister of public works and transports in 1938.

In 1940 Moch was one of the eighty deputies to vote against Marshal Pétain and was imprisoned at the end of the year. Liberated in 1941, he participated in the Resistance in France and joined Charles de Gaulle in London in 1943. After the Liberation, he served as minister of public works and transportation from 1945 to 1947, when he again devoted himself to rebuilding France's shattered infrastructure. However, Moch's most important ministry was that of interior, which he filled during 1947–48, and he had a large role in suppressing the strike waves of those years. During this period of social unrest fueled by economic difficulties, Moch acted eagerly to protect the "right to work." The socialist minister was not reluctant to throw the full weight of the state's repressive forces against striking workers. He reorganized the *Compagnies républicaines de sécurité* (CRS) and instituted a nationwide system of "*ignames*" (*inspecteurs généraux de l'administration en mission extraordinaire*) who were charged with coordinating the police and the military to restore order. Confronting another strike wave in 1948, Moch acted equally firmly to impose state authority. He charged that the 1948 wave was communist inspired and had the aim of executing a "coup de Prague" that would transform France into another Czechoslovakia.

Moch then became the minister of defense in the Pleven government (1950–51). Firmly Atlanticist and anticommunist, he nevertheless opposed American plans to rearm Germany. In 1952 he became the French representative for disarmament, a goal that he pursued within the framework of the Western alliance. In 1958 he was again appointed minister of the interior. Even though he eventually rallied unenthusiastically to de Gaulle's May 1958 candidacy as the lesser of various evils, he was forced to uphold the laws of the Fourth Republic at a time when, as he recognized, it had lost legitimacy among wide sectors of the administration and population.

A socialist parliamentarian, his authority and influence inevitably declined during the Gaullist and presidential Fifth Republic. He lost his seat in the Assembly in 1958 by refusing an agreement with the communist candidate. He was elected again as deputy in 1962 but resigned in 1967 because he considered the Assembly to be devoid of real power. He campaigned against the *force de frappe* and, as a member of the Second International, generally opposed the Gaullist nationalism of the late 1960s. In the early 1970s he became increasingly alienated from his own Socialist party (PS). He attacked the "revolutionary verbalism" of the young radicals who had joined the party and regarded certain Parisian universities as "a nest of savages." He opposed the socialist leadership's alliance with the French Communist party (PCF). He resigned from his party in 1974 and returned to his engineering studies, specifically to a project for a tunnel under the English Channel. Moch was a prolific author and wrote dozens of books, pamphlets, and newspaper articles.

J. Moch, *Une si longue vie* (Paris, 1976).

M. Seidman

Related entries: BLUM, LEON; *COMPAGNIES REPUBLICAINES DE SECURITE*; DEFENSE POLICY; PLEVEN, RENE; SOCIALIST PARTY (PS, SFIO).

MOLLET, GUY (1905–1975), socialist militant and governmental leader of the Fourth Republic. He served as secretary-general of the Socialist party (SFIO) from 1946 to 1969. He was premier of the Republic from 1956 to 1957 and participated in several ministries, including that of Charles de Gaulle at the inauguration of the Fifth Republic.

He was born in Flers (Orne) to parents of modest means. A scholarship student, he earned a bachelor's degree in English at the University of Lille. He tutored in that subject in Le Havre and Lisieux before obtaining a teaching position first at the college and subsequently at the *lycée* in Arras. But politics was his vocation, and he was active in youth groups and local sections of the SFIO from an early age. He regarded Alexandre Desrousseaux (Bracke), a founder of the party, as his intellectual mentor, which helps to explain his doctrinaire Marxism and his conception of the party as an agency of class struggle. Mollet served in the French army from the beginning of World War II, was wounded, captured, and interned. Released in 1941, he returned to Arras, where he participated in the Resistance. Immediately following the war, he was elected mayor of that city, a position he held until his death.

At the outset of the Fourth Republic, Mollet made a meteoric rise to national prominence, both within the party and the government. He was a member of a faction of younger SFIO militants that repudiated the accommodating socialism of the party's venerable leader, Léon Blum. Mollet and his colleagues preferred a more exclusive role for the Socialist party, a stance reminiscent of the party's Guesdist beginnings. At the party's thirty-seventh congress (March 1946), this faction led a successful campaign to oust its secretary-general, Daniel Mayer, Blum's confidante and protégé. Mollet was elected to replace him and held the post for twenty-three years. Mollet had little use for theoretical discussions of Marxist ideology, and he was intransigently opposed to working accords with the Communist party. Under his leadership, the SFIO stressed organizational discipline and solidarity. Some contemporaries saw him as humorless and inflexible, but all admitted he was an effective organizer.

Mollet's rise to prominence in parliamentary politics was equally spectacular. He was elected to both the first (1945) and second (1946) constituent assemblies, where he served on the drafting committees. In 1950–51 he was named minister of state in a tandem of left-wing coalition governments (René Pleven, Henri Queuille), before forming his own in 1956. Inflexible as a party leader, he proved more adaptable in his ministerial role, where he was obliged to work within parliamentary coalitions. As premier, Mollet had an agenda of labor (annual paid vacations) and social reform (improved old-age pensions) that he was able to advance. Equally successful were foreign policy initiatives that furthered Franco-German understanding (the return of the Saar to West Germany) and European economic cooperation (the inauguration of the Common Market). But civil strife in Algeria intensified during his tenure, despite his efforts to effect compromise, and his commitment of French troops to the occupation of the Suez canal aroused widespread disapproval within his own party. Unable to persuade parliament to raise taxes to fund military operations in Algeria, he resigned from office in May 1957.

Mollet was among that entourage of left-wing politicians that turned to de Gaulle to save the Republic during the Algerian crisis of 1958. Backing de Gaulle's plan for constitutional revision, he served in his cabinet during the transition between regimes. By 1962, however, he had severed his association with the Gaullist coalition in order to back the efforts of his socialist colleagues to build a viable left-wing opposition movement. Acceding to this change of direction within his party, he was never enthusiastic about the overtures to the Communist party that it entailed. He retired from politics in 1969 when the SFIO was absorbed into the Federation of the Democratic and Socialist Left.

As a leader of the SFIO, Mollet invites comparison with Jules Guesde, the party's founder in the early Third Republic. For both, Marxism was a creed to be accepted, not a philosophy in need of ongoing interpretation. Their emphasis was always on the organization of the party, to which they were totally devoted. Both were patriots, and when faced with a choice between their socialist and nationalist ideals, they tended to put the latter first: Guesde in World War I, Mollet during the Cold War.

The career of Mollet provides insight into the implications of the retreat of the SFIO during the Fourth Republic from Blum's vision of a popular front to further the goals of social democracy. Mollet preferred a return to the older notion of the SFIO as a party dedicated to social action on behalf of the working class. Admittedly, Mollet's forte was political action, not theory. But his unreflective allegiance to the socialist ideal of an earlier age limited his vision of what the party might do at a time when socialist theorists were turning their attention from the problem of class struggle to that of the welfare state. Tied to the conventions of the past, Mollet was eventually displaced by a younger generation of socialists with more generous attitudes toward other politicians of the left and wider ambitions for building a broad-based party that might direct the future course of French social democracy.

G. Codding et al., *Ideology and Politics: The Socialist Party of France* (Boulder, Colo., 1979); D. Graham, "Guy Mollet," in *Biographical Dictionary of French Political Leaders since 1870*, ed. D. Bell et al. (New York, 1990); H. Simmons, *French Socialists in Search of a Role, 1956–67* (Ithaca, N.Y., 1970); J. Touchard, *La Gauche en France depuis 1900* (Paris, 1977).

P. H. Hutton

Related entries: BLUM, LEON; DEFFERRE, GASTON; DE GAULLE, CHARLES; MARXISM; MAYER, DANIEL; MITTERRAND, FRANCOIS; SOCIALIST PARTY (SFIO); SUEZ CRISIS.

MONNET, JEAN (1888–1979), architect of the Monnet Plan (1946–51), and, more significantly, the recognized father of the coal-steel pool and the Common Market (EEC). The French of the Fifth Republic might live under Charles de Gaulle's political system but they also live under Monnet's economic system. That system is characterized by an essentially depoliticized technocratic and ostensibly open-ended management of the economy with the goals of economic prosperity and technological development. Monnet's genius lay in his ability to appeal to his compatriots "above" petty politics, allowing and encouraging each participant, whether a union, an industrial trade association, or a foreign ministry of finance, to seek his or her own corporate self-interest within the context of concerted action.

Son of a cognac salesman, Monnet first came to prominence as an expert within the League of Nations. In the Liberation era his apolitical approach (which, by default, gave autonomous state organs considerable power) dovetailed well with the agenda of de Gaulle, who appointed him to head up the national planning apparatus in 1945. To allay suspicions of a strong state, Monnet made the planning process participatory and indicative: Representatives from each group within an industry would meet in a commission (as the Steel Commission, etc.) and simply draw up production targets. The private sector was encouraged to conform to the plan, but the nationalized sector (consumer of well over one-half of the investment capital between 1946 and 1951) had to comply.

The Monnet Plan miraculously met almost all of its targets, but with considerable (if not decisive) financial help from the Marshall Plan. Most significant, the Monnet Plan and its methods of execution gave the French private sector the confidence to break from its traditionalism and invest in growth-oriented and sometimes risky ventures. Monnet taught them that the state was not an enemy, that indeed, each franc taxed and spent by the state ultimately found its way to the private sector, and that the state provided essential infrastructure at a very reasonable price.

The lessons of the Monnet Plan, particularly those concerning apoliticism and enlightened self-interest, were soon applied to the development of the coal-steel pool. Recognizing that the French, Luxembourgeois, Belgian, and German border region potentially comprised a single ferrous metals zone, Monnet appealed to all parties to rise above old nationalist rivalries and develop solidarity by a collective pursuit and management of wealth—rather than squabbling over the shares of the zone's wealth, he had the partners cooperate to increase its output.

Having encouraged cooperation first among classes and sectors, then among a limited group of nations, Monnet then turned to fostering cooperation among western Europeans as a whole, acting to draw up the Treaty of Rome in 1956, the foundation of the EEC. Again, his approach shone forth, to table political issues as long as possible so that confidence could be developed through dealing successfully with practical material questions. Monnet's legacy does remain the object of criticism among both economic liberals and those opposed to the increasingly technocratic and "Eurocratic" character of Monnetist organisms.

J. Bouvier, "Le Plan Monnet et l'économie française, 1946–1952," *Cahiers Internationaux d'Histoire, Economique et Sociale* 15 (1983); R. Kuisel, *Capitalism and the State in Modern France* (New York, 1981); J. Monnet, *Mémoires* (New York, 1978).

R. L. Frost

Related entries: ATTALI, JACQUES; AURIOL, VINCENT; DE GAULLE, CHARLES; ECONOMIC POLICY; EUROPEAN ECONOMIC COMMUNITY, RELATIONS WITH; FEDERAL REPUBLIC OF GERMANY, RELATIONS WITH; INDUSTRIAL POLICY; MARSHALL PLAN; MENDES-FRANCE, PIERRE; NATIONALIZATIONS; PLAN; TECHNOLOGY; TRANSPORTATION; WESTERN EUROPEAN UNION.

MOROCCO, RELATIONS WITH. After a protracted struggle for independence, Morocco became an effective French ally in Africa. American sympathy expressed at the allied meeting in Casablanca in 1942 raised Moroccan hopes for an end to the protectorate created by the 1912 Treaty of Fes, whose unequal application had effectively relegated the country to colonial status. A quiet alliance gradually developed between the Sultan (later King Muhammad V) and the nationalist Istiqlal party with the common goal of independence. The Quai d'Orsay was only able to maintain a relatively weak control over the Resident, the French-appointed official in Morocco, who dictated policy and handled relations with the Sultan. Most of the Residents worked closely with the considerable French colony and the important French economic interests in the country. When they did not, members of the local French administration, closely linked with colonial groups, effectively tied their hands.

A rapprochement begun between General Charles de Gaulle, who suggested a more flexible policy in North Africa, and the Sultan ended with the former's resignation in 1946. The reformist policies and political overtures to the Istiqlal by Eirik Labonne (Resident from 1946 to 1947), were brought to nought by opposition of colonist groups including the Civil controller Philippe Boniface, who apparently was not above creating bloody incidents (like those of 1944 and 1947) when conciliatory policies threatened to bear fruit.

Under the generals Alphonse Juin and Albert Guillaume (Residents from May 1947 to August 1951 and August 1951 to August 1953), the considerable French colony in Morocco sought a "democratization" of the regime, which they saw as a means of weakening the Sultan's theocratically based power in favor of a form of cosovereignty that would give them (and clearly not the natives) civic rights in a country in which they were legally foreigners. The Paris government effectively refused the Sultan's requests for a renegotiation of the Treaty of Fes. The conflict was insoluble; and the hesitations of the government in Paris forced Muhammad V and the nationalists into a tighter alliance. In this struggle the Sultan's chief weapon was his refusal to countersign "reforms."

Muhammad met the Resident's claims of reform by endorsing the Istiqlal's calls for a true democracy, representing the Moroccan people. For allies, this left the French with only the most reactionary and corrupt elements. The government responded to the Sultan's growing intransigence with a first version of a tactic renewed later. The Glaoui, feudal potentate of Marrakech, spokesman of the pro-French notables and no friend of the Sultan, was persuaded in early 1951 by Juin and Boniface to lead a revolt of local notables and Berber horsemen (recruited with the assistance of the French administration) against Muhammad V, accused of working with the "communist" Istiqlal. Though Paris, under American pressure, declined to back a deposition, the Sultan was forced to accept a number of alleged reforms.

Strikes and demonstrations in December 1952, which were met with brutal repression and massive arrests, began to create sympathy for the Moroccan cause in France and internationally. Further resistance from the palace and increased restiveness led to a replay, in 1953, of the 1951 revolt of the Glaoui. Muhammad was deposed in the name of Islam and replaced by a French puppet who went forward with Guillaume's plans for Franco-Moroccan cosovereignty. The Moroccans resisted with terrorism and guerilla warfare, bringing the usual cortege of repression, torture, and colonial counterterrorism. After mounting domestic and international opposition, the Sultan was returned from exile in November 1955, and the independence of the country was recognized in March 1956.

Despite two brief squalls, the first caused by the skyjacking of a Moroccan plane by French services in 1956, the second by possible Moroccan involvement in a political assassination in Paris in 1965, relations between the two countries have been good; and France, despite technical neutrality, has been sympathetic to Morocco in its battle over the Sahara, even aiding Mauritania militarily against the Polisario in 1977. France imports Moroccan phosphates and workers, and the two countries cooperate in international ventures like the intervention in Zaire in 1977.

S. Bernard, *Le Conflit franco-marocain, 1943–1956* (Brussels, 1963); A. Grosser, *Affaires extérieures, la politique de la France 1944–1989* (Paris, 1989).

A. Douglas

Related entries: DECOLONIZATION; FOREIGN POLICY; THIRD WORLD, RELATIONS WITH.

MUSEUMS, repositories for French history and culture, have become increasingly central to French perceptions of national identity. France supports over thirteen hundred museums, including the art and natural history museums so dear to those of the nineteenth century, as well as museums of science, technology and industry, folklore, and popular culture that have become increasingly popular since World War II. Virtually every sizable town has a municipal museum, usually combining an art collection with local history exhibits. Many towns also support natural history museums and ethnographic collections, the latter often installed in old buildings, thus displaying the artifacts of daily life in a contemporary setting. Towns famed for particular industries or products have established museums dedicated to them, while others have museums to commemorate local events that have had national or worldwide significance. One such is Caen's new Peace Museum located not far from the D-day landing beaches. Many national monuments, such as *châteaux* and abbeys, are also museums, housing collections of art or furnishings.

Although France is well stocked with museums, Paris is without doubt the museum capital, with over eighty public collections; Lyon, the nearest rival, has only fourteen. And, although many Parisian museums are small and narrowly focused, Paris is best known for its large national art museums—the Louvre, the Pompidou Center, and the new Orsay Museum.

Most museums in Paris and throughout the country are under the direction of the Ministry of Culture, which allows them to draw upon the stocks of the great national collections. Nonetheless, centralized decision making and administration has tended to concentrate the national museums in Paris and to direct the majority of funding to them. André Malraux, Charles de Gaulle's minister of cultural affairs, declared his mission was to make French culture available to all citizens, but with regard to museums his tenure is best remembered for a few spectacular exhibits and international exchanges, such as the Mona Lisa's American tour in 1963. The domination of Parisian institutions continued under his successors. Although the recession of the 1970s cut the cultural budget, President Valéry Giscard d'Estaing completed the Pompidou Center and pushed ahead with the project for the Orsay Museum. President François Mitterrand and his popular minister of culture, Jack Lang, have substantially increased funding for culture in general, up from less than half of one percent of the national budget to more than 1 percent. In the early 1980s Lang favored new provincial projects, such as the comic-strip museum in Angoulême. By the middle of Mitterrand's term, Paris returned to the forefront with the completion and opening of the Orsay Museum in 1986 and the renovation of the Louvre, completed in 1989.

Since de Gaulle, each French president has left a distinctive mark upon the national heritage with a major museum project in Paris. In 1969, President Georges Pompidou decided to include a grandiose multipurpose cultural center in the redevelopment of the Halles district. The new facility, eventually named the Georges Pompidou National Center of Art and Culture, houses libraries, research institutes, and a children's workshop, as well as a modern art museum. Its architecture, dominated by huge multicolored utility ducts and snakelike escalators, evokes industrial society. Inside, the focus is on *animation*, programs and activities in which visitors participate. Controversial when it first opened, the Pompidou Center quickly won popular approval; thousands visit it every day.

Less than six months after the Pompidou Center opened in May 1977, President Giscard embarked on his own project, a new Parisian museum of nineteenth-century art to be housed within the disused Orsay train station and hotel across the Seine from the Louvre. The enormous turn-of-the-century white elephant had been slated for demolition in the 1960s but was rescued and designated an historic building. Discussion of its ultimate fate proceeded until Giscard officially approved the museum proposal in October 1977. Opened in 1986, the museum displays paintings from the romantic period to the Post-impressionists, as well as sculpture, decorative arts and architecture, photography, and films. Like the Pompidou Center, it includes facilities for film showings, concerts, and children's programming. Like the Pompidou Center, the museum building is itself on display; the renovation incorporates the huge iron and glass vault of the former train hall and the rococo decor of hotel reception rooms as part of the exhibit. The Orsay Museum has been a popular and critical success from its opening.

In 1983 President Mitterrand initiated his own museum project, a major renovation of the Louvre. Completed in 1989, the renovation includes a new entry lobby in the main courtyard under a seventy-foot-high glass pyramid. The need to improve the traffic flow and provide services and storage space within the Louvre is generally acknowledged, but nonetheless the project has been much criticized. First, Mitterrand has been attacked for choosing Chinese-American architect I. M. Pei, rather than a French architect. Second, many argue that the pyramid clashes with, rather than complements, the seventeenth-century facades that embrace it. It is too early to judge if this contribution to French culture will ultimately be as well received as those of Mitterrand's predecessors.

Recent years have seen more modest but nonetheless significant new museums. In 1985 a new Picasso museum opened in Paris, based on a collection of works donated by the artist's heirs in lieu of paying estate taxes. Another new museum devoted to a single artist is Claude Monet's home in Giverny. Not only has his house been restored, but also the beautiful gardens and water-lily pond that inspired so much of Monet's later work. Interest in restoring or preserving the environment as well as the objects of culture informs another new departure for French museums, the *écomusée* or museum park. The first opened in 1971 at the Creusot ironworks to preserve and demonstrate the technology and history of the foundry and its workers. Recently, other *ecomusées* have been established in Finistère and the Vendée, dedicated to local agriculture, industry, and popular culture.

G. Barnaud, *Répertoire des musées et collections publiques de France* (Paris, 1982); J. Jenger, *Orsay, The Metamorphosis of a Monument* (Paris, 1987); D. Wachtel, *Cultural Policy and Socialist France* (New York, 1987).

M. H. Darrow

Related entries: ART AND ARCHITECTURE; CULTURAL POLICY; LANG, JACK; MALRAUX, ANDRE; PICASSO, PABLO.

N

NATIONAL CENTER OF INDEPENDENTS AND PEASANTS (CNIP), a loose right-wing political formation that emerged in 1951 when the Independent parliamentary group joined Roger Duchet's *Centre national des Indépendants* (created in 1949). It became a major political force in the Fourth Republic (with Antoine Pinay, prime minister, 1952; René Coty, president, 1953–58), with more than a hundred parliamentarians. Keen on keeping Algeria French, the group supported General Charles de Gaulle's return to power in 1958, but the majority were disappointed by his Algerian policy and opposed his constitutional change of 1962 making the presidency of the Republic a directly elected office. A minority left the movement with Valéry Giscard d'Estaing to form the *Républicains indépendants*.

The movement lost much of its influence in the 1960s, achieving a slight revival in the 1970s (modernizing its image, rule-book changes in 1973, reversed in 1980) and the 1980s, giving support to right-wing coalitions. The election of the socialists in 1981 further weakened the movement, which became increasingly (and willingly) the object of a takeover by extreme right-wing activists (Alain Robert, Bernard Anthony, Pierre Sergent, Yvon Briant). The CNIP has managed to attract a former armed-forces chief of staff, Jeannou Lacaze, and has attracted disaffected Le Pen supporters and elected representatives, changing the political composition of several regional councils. It rejects Nazi and fascist labels and claims to be a more respectable alternative ''third force'' on the right (backing Jacques Chirac's 1988 presidential bid), akin to British Conservatives or American Republicans. It also claims Pinay as its spiritual father and wants to be known as *Conservateurs nouveaux et Indépendants*, keeping the CNI acronym.

Under Philippe Malaud (1980) it had forty parliamentarians and five thousand local councillors, but was characterized by leadership conflicts between Raymond Bourgine and Maurice Ligot (1980), Malaud and Michel Junot (1986), and between Jacques Féron and Briant (1989). Its program included withdrawal from the European Monetary System, strong support for restoring the death penalty, promotion of free enterprise, encouragement of higher birthrates, and opposition to strikes and immigration.

In 1990, under former National Front parliamentarian Briant (president) and J. A. Giansily (general secretary), it had six parliamentarians and was situated to the right of the two major right-wing groups (but allied to them). It also edited a monthly journal, *France indépendante*.

F. Borella, *Les Partis politiques en Europe* (Paris, 1984); *Le Monde, dossiers et documents: L'Extrême Droite en France* (Paris, 1984); A. Rollat, *Les Hommes de l'extrême droit* (Paris, 1985); P. M. Williams, *Crisis and Compromise* (London, 1964).

M. Khane

Related entries: ALGERIA, RELATIONS WITH; CHIRAC, JACQUES; COTY, RENE; DE GAULLE, CHARLES; GISCARD D'ESTAING, VALERY; LE PEN, JEAN-MARIE; PEASANTRY; PINAY, ANTOINE.

NATIONAL COUNCIL OF FRENCH EMPLOYERS (CNPF), the principal professional organization of French businessmen, founded in 1946 on the model of the *Confédération générale de la production française* (CGPF), which represented French industry and commerce in the interwar years. As in the case of its predecessor, the CNPF (*Conseil national du patronat français*) was the capstone of a complex pyramid of patronal organizations. Its membership consisted not of individual firms but of hundreds of trade associations. Its purpose was to encourage solidarity among employers, large and small, to promote "the efficacy of the patronal function," and, above all, to represent the interests of business vis-à-vis the government, especially on matters of economic and social policy. In theory, the CNPF was governed by a general assembly made up of delegates from the member associations, but because the general assembly met only every other year, real power rested with the president, executive committee, and the study committees on economic and social policy.

Under its first president, Georges Villiers, a small-scale metal fabricator and mayor of Lyon, the CNPF proved to be much more flexible and progressive than its predecessor. After a 1950 law strengthened the position of labor unions, the CNPF relaxed its long-standing opposition to collective bargaining and started seeking a modus vivendi with noncommunist unions. In the realm of economic policy, it abandoned its traditional ultraprotectionism and supported more forward-looking, growth-oriented policies, including the Monnet Plan, the Marshall Plan, and a European Common Market. It opposed the Schuman Plan in 1950 only because the plan centralized power in a high authority and banned *ententes* and cartels. However, once the French Assembly had approved the Schuman Plan, the CNPF cooperated in the launching of the European Coal and Steel Community. Its support for modernization of French industry, expansion of French exports, and integration of France in a larger European community remained consistent throughout the Fourth and Fifth Republics.

The CNPF was ambivalent about Charles de Gaulle's return to power in 1958 because of the general's stand on Algerian independence and his apparent willingness to countenance close supervision of the economy by government "technocrats.'' Accordingly, the CNPF's 1965 charter was defensive, denouncing government interference and demanding greater freedom for private enterprise. In the realm of labor relations, the CNPF initially resisted concessions to striking workers during the crisis of May-June 1968, but eventually it accepted the Grenelle accords, which gave workers a fourth week of paid vacation, substantial pay increases, and other benefits. From 1968 onward, the CNPF was increasingly dominated by the social progressives of the *Entreprise et progrès* group, such as Antoine Riboud, who wanted to heal the long-standing breach between management and labor. Under the leadership of François Ceyrac, who succeeded Paul Huvelin as president in 1973, the CNPF negotiated an unprecedented series of ''grand accords'' with the unions on various aspects of wages and benefits policy, all without the usual prompting from government. However, when the oil price hikes of 1973–74 pushed the French economy into recession, the CNPF tempered this policy of ''social innovation'' with a ''give-and-take'' approach whereby new concessions by business had to be balanced by concessions by workers to maintain productivity gains.

Its accommodation of labor notwithstanding, the CNPF remained committed to classically liberal, laissez-faire economics in the late 1970s. It disliked the *dirigiste* tendencies of Valéry Giscard d'Estaing, but supported Giscard against the left in the elections of 1978 and 1981 as much the lesser evil. The CNPF expected the worst in 1981 when François Mitterrand was elected president and a socialist majority took over the National Assembly. Yet, under its new president, Yvon Gattaz, founder of a small, dynamic electronics firm (Radiall), the CNPF kept lines of communication to Mitterrand open in the hopes of wearing down the socialist reform program. Indeed, it succeeded in softening the terms of the new nationalizations and in defeating Mitterrand's efforts to shorten the work week significantly. It also managed to turn the *groupes d'expression*, mandated in all large plants by the Auroux laws of 1982–83, into Japanese-style quality circles under management rather than union control (the number of quality circles in France rose from 3,000 to 10,000 in 1983–84).

Despite its considerable success in working with the socialists, the CNPF welcomed the victory of the right in the 1986 parliamentary elections and the subsequent advent of Jacques Chirac as prime minister. Chirac shared the CNPF's neoliberal philosophy, and his government quickly enacted several planks in the CNPF platform, including reduction of business taxes and loosening of established government controls on layoffs. Meanwhile, long-standing personal rivalries within the CNPF leadership came to the fore in 1986 with a bitter feud between Gattaz and Yvon Chotard, head of the social policy committee and heir presumptive to the presidency, a feud that reflected an equally long-standing rivalry between big business and small business for control of the organization. Ultimately, big business prevailed as François Perigot of Unilever France was elected president in December 1986. However, this seems to have reinforced the CNPF's commitment to the modernization and expansion of French business as the European Community has prepared for full economic integration in 1992.

H. Ehrmann, *Organized Business in France* (Princeton, 1957); I. Kolboom, *La Revanche des patrons* (Paris, 1986); G. Lefranc, *Les Organisations patronales en France* (Paris, 1976); H. Weber, *Le Parti des patrons* (Paris, 1986).

M. S. Smith

Related entries: AUROUX LAWS; ECONOMIC POLICY; INDUSTRIAL POLICY; SCHUMAN PLAN.

NATIONALITY CODE, a document defining circumstances and conditions of French nationality. The existing *Code de la nationalité française* (CNF), systematized for the first time in 1945, became controversial in 1986 and 1987. Debate on immigration/race encouraged the conservative government of Jacques Chirac (threatened electorally to some extent by the anti-immigrant views of Jean-Marie Le Pen's National Front, FN) to propose recasting the code. The result was wider-ranging inquiries into the nature of French identity/nationality.

Traditionally, the majority of the 100,000 people acquiring French citizenship annually have to do so in two major ways: either through *jus sanguinis* or through variations of *jus soli*, where children in France born of foreign parents, having lived there for at least five years, automatically acquire French nationality on reaching adulthood provided that they do not have serious criminal records.

The October 1986 proposals of the Chirac government sought to abolish automatic conferral by making the process a formal request—*une acte volontaire*—and to extend the notion of criminality. Although the bill's more reactionary elements were dropped, controversy abounded because it was perceived that the measures were radically weighted against the Magrebian population. However, nationwide student demonstrations in late 1986 forced the right to call for a "pause" in its overall legislative program. Eventually, Justice Minister Albin Chalandon convened a nonpolitical *Commission des sages* to hold televised hearings to report on the question of nationality. Hearings continued throughout the autumn of 1987. Chirac finally decided that there would be no new legislation before the 1988 presidential elections (which he lost to François Mitterrand). The Commission's recommendations, less rigorous than governmental proposals, welcomed "opting for" citizenship but severely criticized the criminality clauses. Other proposals were rejected. The code was an important element in the political debate during *cohabitation*; however, while immigration is still a major issue in France, efforts to revise the nationality code faded with the outcome of the 1988 elections.

A. Hargreaves, "The French Nationality Code Hearings," *Journal of Modern and Contemporary France* 38 (1988).

J. Bryant

Related entries: CHALANDON, ALBIN; CHIRAC, JACQUES; *COHABITATION*; LE PEN, JEAN-MARIE; STUDENT REVOLTS.

NATIONALIZATIONS, played a role in the postwar politics of both the Fourth and Fifth Republics. There were two periods of intense nationalization in the post–1940 period: immediately after the Liberation in 1945–48 and during the first year of the Mauroy government, 1981–82. The post-Liberation nationalizations differed from one another and from those of the 1980s in their aims and extent.

Nationalizations were among the demands announced by the National Council of Resistance in its "Charter of Resistance" of March 1944. The partisans of nationalization offered numerous justifications, not all of them political. First of all, there were historical precedents for state investment and management on behalf of efforts beyond the means or will of the private sector. Much postwar economic reconstruction, including the repair or replacement of obsolete or war-damaged material, fit this category. Next, private ownership of important basic industries had, in the past, placed national sovereignty at the mercy of narrow private interests; nationalization would help to limit these inroads on the exercise of sovereignty. Finally, there were punitive goals. Some business leaders had collaborated with the enemy; workers were reluctant to produce for individuals who had compromised themselves. Such problems hampered postwar economic recovery. Moreover, a significant portion of public opinion favored punishment through expropriation for those who had willingly sacrificed the national interest for private profit.

General Charles de Gaulle restrained post-Liberation plans for immediate and ambitious nationalizations with the argument that such actions could only be undertaken by a duly elected government. Only compelling economic and political demands justified the creation of *Houillères nationales du Nord et du Pas-de-Calais* as a public corporation in December 1944, the nationalization of Renault in the *Régie nationale des usines Renault* in January 1945, and the nationalization of the *Société anonyme des moteurs Gnome-Rhône* in the *Société nationale d'études et de construction de moteurs d'aviation* (SNECMA) in May 1945. The first of these actions helped get postwar coal production under way while the latter satisfied demand for punitive nationalizations against prominent collaborators. Other actions would have to follow the elections of October 1945.

The Bank of France and the four largest deposit banks were nationalized in December 1945. *Electricité de France* and *Gaz de France* were created with the nationalization of the gas and electricity utilities in early April 1946. In March and April the Assembly also debated and voted to nationalize the largest insurance companies and the Bank of Algiers. None of the nationalizations was confiscatory in that former owners were compensated, typically with long-term corporate bonds paying 3 percent annually, after determination of market value. Plans to nationalize air carriers in order to create Air France were scrapped in 1948 in favor of a public/private partnership in which the state possessed a majority of voting shares. Similar arrangements were employed in maritime transport and shipping.

The nationalizations of 1982 were conducted in vastly different circumstances. The victory of François Mitterrand in the second round of presidential elections of May 10, 1981 and the subsequent victory of Socialist party candidates in the June legislative elections put the socialists and their communist allies in a position to act on their ambitious proposals to reshape French society. While their opponents threatened that nationalizations would give France ''Europe's only Latin American economy,'' under the nationalization law of February 13, 1982 the left carried out the nationalization of major sectors of the economy including virtually the entire banking sector and the largest industrial groups including chemicals, steel, electronics, aviation, and telecommunications. The larger firms undergoing nationalization included *Paris-Bas*, *Compagnie financière de Suez*, *Usinor-Sacilor*, *CGE*, *Thomson-Brandt*, *Rhône-Poulenc*, *Saint-Gobain*, and *Péchiney*.

Just as in 1945–46, there were several justifications for nationalization. Various points had been made during the electoral campaign, each revealing the Marxist, Jacobin nationalist, Saint-Simonian technocratic, and Proudhonian *autogestionnaire* influences circulating within the modern French left. Socialists had spoken of using nationalizations to ''re-equilibriate social forces'' in France—a euphemism for dispossessing the wealthy. They also faulted the inadequacies of laissez-faire, citing the timid investment tastes and habits of French investors, and spoke of using an enlarged public sector to set an example of aggressive business investment. Public sector firms would also demonstrate effective models of labor/management relations to be imitated by a private sector heretofore dominated by patriarchal forms. Mitterrand himself played on fears of foreigners and foreign takeovers with the remark that ''If we don't nationalize, they [foreign corporations] will internationalize.'' The nationalizations were to be part of a new state-led industrial policy that would galvanize the French economy, thus creating jobs, reducing unemployment, winning back the domestic market, and generally enhancing the quality of life in France.

With few exceptions (Dassault, Matra), the nationalizations were total. Partial nationalization, leading to mere controlling interest on the Air France model, was ruled out because the shares remaining in private hands would continue to trade, thus maintaining a tradable price, which would in turn make any subsequent attempt at denationalization easier. It also raised the vexed question of which shareholders to expropriate, one certain to raise objections of discrimination within the *Conseil constitutionnel*. However, such measures did not prevent privatizations after the left lost power in 1986, while the inability of publicly owned corporations to sell shares hampered their ability to raise the funds necessary to prepare for the intense competitive battles of post-1992 Europe.

Before 1981 nationalized industries produced 16.8 percent of France's industrial GNP. After the 1982 nationalizations, nationalized industries produced 30 percent of industrial GNP. In some areas public ownership was nearly total: Deposits in government-controlled banks constituted some 91.5 percent of total funds on deposit.

C. Andrieu, L. Le Van, A. Prost, *Les Nationalisations de la Libération* (Paris, 1987); P. Bauchard, *La Guerre des deux roses* (Paris, 1986); R. Kuisel, *Capitalism and the State in Modern France* (Cambridge, 1981); M. Massenet et al., *La France socialiste*

(Paris, 1983); D. Pinkney, "Nationalization of Key Industries and Credit in France after the Liberation," *Political Science Quarterly* 62 (1947).

R. A. Jonas

Related entries: AUTOGESTION; COMMON PROGRAM; CONSTITUTIONAL COUNCIL; INDUSTRIAL POLICY; MAUROY, PIERRE; MITTERRAND, FRANCOIS; SOCIALIST PARTY (PS); UNION OF THE LEFT.

NEW CALEDONIA, a mineral-rich island in the South Pacific that French explorers first colonized in 1853. Since 1946 New Caledonia has been an Overseas Territory (TOM) with political representation in the National Assembly. Since 1968 New Caledonia has become the scene of violent confrontations between native Melanesians, or Kanaks, seeking independence, and the French settler population, determined to preserve their economic and political domination.

World War II had a profound impact upon New Caledonia and shook it out of its colonialist slumber. The island rallied to General Charles de Gaulle's Free French movement in 1940 after the fall of France. When war erupted in the Pacific, the island became a major staging point for Allied operations in the Solomons, and a massive American presence during these years brought an influx of wealth and habits that prepared the way for a liberalization of French control in the postwar era.

At the end of the war the French government ended a system of indentured labor on the island, broadened the franchise to include women, gave considerable local power to the Territorial Assembly, and ended the *indigénat*, or system of restrictions that had confined the Melanesians to reservations. Postwar reforms included the extension of voting rights to male Melanesians who had served in the armed forces, and in 1951 nearly all adult Melanesians received the vote. These reforms opened a new era in Caledonian politics and enabled the Caledonian Union (UC), a progressive, reformist multiethnic party, to represent both the Kanaks, who made up nearly one-half of the island's population, and the small farmers and shopkeepers, who opposed the large landowners and the wealthy commercial and nickel interests. The Caledonian Union's slogan, "Two colors, one people," expressed the party's ethnic ideal. Under the leadership of Maurice Lenormand, the UC gained control of the Territorial Assembly in 1953 and remained in control until 1968.

The politics of ethnic cooperation began to unravel as a result of both a conservative attack, supported by the Gaullists, upon the UC and the militancy of younger Melanesians, who demanded an independent Kanaky after 1968. Passage of the *loi-cadre* or basic law of 1956 alarmed French nationalists, who feared a Kanak-dominated New Caledonia under the UC. On the other hand, the events of 1968 brought a desire for Kanak identity to Melanesians who had been educated in France and had participated in the student uprising. Elections during the 1970s saw a proliferation of political parties in New Caledonia as various Kanak groups split away from the UC, which was considered too moderate on the issue of independence. On the other hand, liberal white supporters of the UC moved toward the pro-French Gaullist party led by Jacques Lafleur. As Caledonian politics became increasingly polarized, the ethnic origins of the island's population assumed political significance.

By the early 1960s no single ethnic group constituted a majority in New Caledonia, as the percentage of Kanaks fell below 50 percent. By 1974, following an influx of immigrants from France and other parts of the French Empire, notably the Pacific territories, the European population was slightly less and the Melanesians slightly more than 40 percent of the population. The 20 percent balance reflected Asian or Polynesian peoples who had come to New Caledonia to work in the mining industry. This population began to side with the pro-French settlers. The ethnic division was also geographic, with Kanaks dominating the sparsely populated interior regions and the offshore Loyalty Islands, and the settlers and their Asian or Pacific supporters in control of the populous southern district.

These divisions reached a crisis with the election of a socialist government in France in 1981. The Kanaks pressed for independence and formed an Independence Front, and they joined the UC, which belatedly came out for independence, to gain control of the Territorial Assembly. Opponents rallied behind Lafleur's Rally for Caledonia within the Republic (RPCR). In 1983 the government tried to appease both sides with a proposal that offered Kanaks the right of self-determination but created a territorialwide electoral system that favored the anti-independence majority that was centered in the heavily populated region around Noumea. Violence erupted late in 1984 on the eve of new elections when militant advocates of independence engaged in an ''active'' boycott of the elections, including smashing ballot boxes and creating roadblocks in the countryside. An attack upon European settlers brought retaliation when ten Kanaks were ambushed near the town of Hiénghène, and at the beginning of 1985 a police officer shot Eloi Machero, a leader of the boycott movement.

The crisis brought the minister for overseas France, Edgard Pisani, to New Caledonia, and a compromise agreement provided for an electoral system that would assure the Kanaks control of three of four electoral districts, but the concentration of anti-independence voters in the heavily populated southern district assured them control of the Territorial Assembly. Unable to win an overall majority in territorial elections, independence advocates resumed boycotts during the 1986 legislative elections and the September 1987 referendum on independence. Abstentions ran just over 40 percent, but they assured the RPCR New Caledonia's seats in the National Assembly and opened the way to a 58 percent vote against independence in 1987.

This impasse brought violence on the eve of the 1988 presidential election when Prime Minister Jacques Chirac ordered security forces to free hostages that independence elements had seized on Lifou Island, leading to the deaths of several Kanaks. Shortly afterward, a respected leader of the independence movement, Jean-Marie Tjibaou, was assassinated. New Caledonia seemed headed for a new round of bloodshed when the new prime minister, Michel Rocard, proposed a ten-year cooling-off period that held the possibility of eventual independence. Both sides accepted this proposal and in recent years New Caledonia seems to have returned to relative calm. New Caledonia's history under the Fourth and Fifth Republics illustrates the often tragic side of ethnic politics in an era of decolonization.

J.-M. Colombani, *L'Utopie calédonienne* (Paris, 1985); M. Dornoy, *Politics in New Caledonia* (Sydney, 1984); M. Spencer, A. Ward, J. Connell, eds., *New Caledonia: Essays in Nationalism and Dependency* (St. Lucia, Queensland, 1988).

J. K. Munholland

Related entries: DECOLONIZATION; GAULLIST PARTY; PISANI, EDGARD; REFERENDA.

NEW PHILOSOPHERS, a mid-1970s movement composed primarily of disillusioned Marxists who had studied with such professors as Louis Althusser, Jacques Lacan, and Michel Foucault during the 1960s, had participated in the May 1968 student rebellion, and had been greatly influenced by the writings of Alexander Solzhenitsyn on the Gulag Archipelago. The publication of Bernard-Henri Lévy's *La Barbarie à visage humain* and André Glucksmann's *Les Maîtres penseurs* in 1977, along with the authors' appearance on Bernard Pivot's television program "Apostrophes" in May 1977 to debate the question of whether or not the New Philosophers were on the left, made the movement widely known and talked about in France, although the term *New Philosophers* had been coined and talked about in 1976 by Lévy in an article in the June edition of *Nouvelles littéraires*.

For the most part, the New Philosophers were unoriginal popularizers of philosophical ideas. They condemned power in all of its forms, whether it be the Gulag or Western capitalism. They were skeptical of all political systems. They rejected all masters, Big Brothers, and manipulators who tried to control the individual. They viewed revolution with skepticism, as part of the process of power. But their responses to the crisis of the twentieth century were not uniform. In some cases, notably in Jean-Paul Dollé's *L'Odeur de la France* (1977), they expressed profound pessimism about the present and nostalgia for a lost utopia. In other cases, such as Michel Le Bris's *L'Homme aux semelles de vent* (1977), they argued for a regionalist, decentralized, carnivalesque solution to the problems of power and statism. At times, as in Bernard-Henri Lévy's *Le Testament de Dieu* (1979), they advocated Maurice Clavel's belief that man can find meaning in the world only through faith in God and used this belief in novel ways to justify individual resistance to totalitarianism. At other times, as in Jean-Marie Benoist's *Un Singulier Programme, le carnaval du Programme commun* (1978), they adopted blatantly political positions, in this case on the right against French leftist "totalitarianism."

By 1981 the New Philosophers had disappeared from public consciousness as a group of thinkers. In the 1980s, leading New Philosophers such as Lévy, Glucksmann, and Benoist moved increasingly to the right, condemning the socialist government for introducing the Gulag to France. The final verdict on the movement might well be that it was primarily an intellectual rightist reaction to the Union of the Left and denigrated politics while upholding the values of laissez-faire libertarianism in both the public and private spheres. As intellectuals the New Philosophers were primarily derivative thinkers.

S. Bouscasse, D. Bourgeois, *Faut-il brûler les nouveaux philosophes?* (Paris, 1978); J.-M. Domenach, *Enquête sur les idées contemporaines* (Paris, 1981); K. Reader, *Intellectuals and the Left in France since 1968* (New York, 1987).

T. R. Christofferson

Related entries: ALTHUSSER, LOUIS; FOUCAULT, MICHEL; INTELLECTUAL TRENDS; LACAN, JACQUES; STRUCTURALISM.

NOIR, MICHEL (1944–), neo-Gaullist politician and since 1989 mayor of Lyon. He was born into a working-class family in Lyon. His father, active in a Gaullist Resistance network, was arrested and deported to Mauthausen but survived the war. Noir received scholarships to attend a *lycée* and the *Institute d'études politiques*, first in Lyon, then in Paris. After working for the Gaullist party in 1966–68, he spent six years in private industry. Returning to full-time political work in 1974, he backed the presidential campaign of Jacques Chaban-Delmas, but later rallied to support Jacques Chirac in the renamed *Rassemblement pour la République* (RPR). Noir was elected a municipal councillor in Lyon in 1977 and a National Assembly deputy from the Rhône in 1978, and was reelected in 1981, 1986, and 1988. He strongly backed Chirac's candidacy for the presidency in 1981.

After the conservatives returned to power in 1986 Noir became minister for foreign trade under Chirac. After Chirac's defeat, Noir and other young RPR leaders pressed for changes in party structure and appeal. These "*rénovateurs*" did not assume that Chirac was still the RPR's best presidential candidate. Noir also declared that the RPR would do better to lose elections than to "lose its soul" by making electoral alliances with Jean-Marie Le Pen's racist National Front. In 1989, Noir won an upset victory to become mayor of Lyon, and as its deputy-and-mayor became an important figure on the French political scene. Criticizing the structure and the evolution of the RPR, in December of 1990, Noir announced his resignation from the Gaullist party and from his position as a deputy in the National Assembly.

T. Desjardins, *Les Chiraquiens* (Paris, 1986).

J. W. Friend

Related entries: CHIRAC, JACQUES; GAULLIST PARTY; LYON.

NOUVELLE CUISINE, a culinary movement whose aesthetic was said to be defined by the chef's commitment to the use of the freshest products, lightness and exactitude of preparation, pleasing visual presentations on the plate, and digestibility. The term *la nouvelle cuisine* was coined in 1972 by the team of restaurant critics Henri Gault and Christian Millau, who sought to identify and then to champion a group of younger French chefs under that banner. The movement took hold, swept France and the world, and eventually succeeded in transforming *haute cuisine*. Virtually every well-known cook working today has been associated with the movement, including Paul Bocuse (who later noisily defected from the movement), Michel Guérard, the Troisgros brothers, Alain Senderens, Jacques Maximin, Joel Robuchon, and Guy Savoy, among many others. Beginning in the early 1980s, *la nouvelle cuisine* fell out of favor, and the term has lost its commercial value.

The movement can be evaluated from a number of viewpoints. First, its success led to a chef-dominated restaurant world. In 1960 chefs were little known, and few major restaurants in France were chef-owned; today chefs are superstars, and more than 80 percent of France's three-star restaurants are chef-owned. Second, the movement can be understood as *haute cuisine*'s reaction to and process of adaptation to modernity: Improvements in food distribution, storage, and the greater availability of a wider and more exotic range of ingredients encouraged experimentation, as did developments in kitchen technology; further, a dramatic change in public awareness of health issues and the importance of diet threatened *haute cuisine*—which based its reputation on a certain richness—with extinction failing significant change. In the end, a general weariness with the constant pressure to innovate and public dissatisfaction with small portions and high prices led to a counterrevolution. By the mid–1980s no major chefs called their cooking *nouvelle*; most instead were scrambling to fill up plates and to offer (albeit updated) versions of old favorites.

R. Courtine, "Nouvelle Cuisine," *Larousse gastronomique* (Paris, 1984); H. Gault, C. Millau, *Gault et Millau se mettent à table* (Paris, 1977).

A. Stone

Related entry: SOCIAL TRENDS.

O

***OCCITAN* MOVEMENT,** a separatist initiative undertaken by those wishing to preserve the culture and language of Occitanie or what is now called Languedoc, part of southwestern France occupying an area roughly from Limoges in the north to the Mediterranean and from Nice to the Atlantic coast. The name Languedoc initially referred to the language of the inhabitants of Occitanie whose word for *yes* was *oc*.

Until the sixteenth century Occitan language and culture had flourished independent of French assistance or influence for nearly ten centuries. Its economy was based on a traditional agrarian life-style and the contributions of various craftsmen. One of the most impressive remnants of its bygone greatness may be seen in the rich literary tradition that was begun during the emergence of the troubadors and which has in recent years experienced a renaissance of sorts, largely attributable to the efforts of Occitan scholars in such centers of Occitan literature as Toulouse, Nîmes, and Montpellier.

The movement by these intellectuals to revive the Occitan language soon attracted the attention of the public. This in turn served to broaden the movement by including in it the defense not only of the Occitan language but also of the Occitan way of life. In addition, as the advocates of an "*Occitanie libre*" began to look back nostalgically to a more dignified and prosperous past, their resistance to efforts by Paris to modernize the region began to increase proportionately. Today scores of organizations exist whose aims vary in the degree to which they advocate a revival of Occitan ways, independence for the region, and violence as a means to achieve their goals.

Y. Barelli, J.-F. Boudy, and J.-F. Carenco, *L'Espérance occitane* (Paris, 1980).

J. J. Flaitz

Related entries: BASQUE QUESTION; CULTURAL POLICY; LITERATURE; REGIONS.

ORGANISATION DE L'ARMEE SECRETE (OAS), secret French army organization that resisted Algerian independence. The Algerian Revolution began in November 1954. By early 1958 France had made little headway in suppressing the revolt. After internal disturbances in Algeria in May 1958, the government of the Fourth Republic brought General Charles de Gaulle to power as its last premier. De Gaulle began, as head of the new Fifth Republic, to end what he termed the "sterilizing obsession": the war for French Algeria. The European settlers and the military leadership had misjudged de Gaulle's intentions. As it became clear that de Gaulle was moving toward negotiations with the National Liberation Front (FLN), resistance grew. In April 1961 four generals, the most famous of whom was General Raoul Salan, led a revolt against de Gaulle in Algeria; the revolt failed. As conspirators were arrested or fled, resistance to de Gaulle's policies took form. The OAS was born in Madrid in February of 1961. Acts of violence, bombings, and assassinations were directed against Algerians and those French who supported de Gaulle's policies in Algeria and in France, and by December 1961 the OAS had reached the peak of its power. As Algeria moved toward independence, the OAS carried out a scorched-earth policy in Algeria. In July 1962 the nation formally became an independent state, and, with many OAS leaders killed or imprisoned, the movement slowly died out. Many of the leaders of the OAS who were imprisoned were granted an amnesty by de Gaulle in 1968, and today many have returned to France.

A. Harrison, *Challenging de Gaulle* (New York, 1989); P. Henessart, *Wolves in the City* (New York, 1970); A. Horne, *A Savage War of Peace* (New York, 1977).

J. J. Cooke

Related entries: ALGERIA, RELATIONS WITH; BEN BELLA, AHMED; CONSTITUTION OF THE FIFTH REPUBLIC; DE GAULLE, CHARLES; FOREIGN POLICY.

OVERSEAS DEPARTMENTS AND TERRITORIES (DOM-TOM), refers to categories of the French Empire created after World War II as part of the Fourth Republic's reforms that established a French Colonial Union. Hopes for a colonial reform that would give greater voice to the peoples of the French Empire were first raised at the Brazzaville Conference in January 1944 when General Charles de Gaulle proposed a new French Federation. The postwar provisional government, responding to these expectations, created a new and presumably more liberal structure, the Colonial Union, in 1946. However, the debates leading up to the formation of the French Colonial Union revealed difficulties in finding a formula for governance of the empire that would concede something to indigenous desires for self-government (independence was ruled out) yet retain French control of overseas territories. The Union was to be less centralized than the old empire and more "federal" in its structure, but in reality, despite provisions for regional governments and limited representation in the National Assembly, the Colonial Union was a complex organization that left the realities of political power in the hands of French politicians and administrators.

Under the Colonial Union French overseas possessions fell into three main categories: Overseas Departments (DOM), Overseas Territories (TOM), and Associated States and Territories. The Overseas Departments consisted of the older colonies of Guiana, Guadeloupe, Martinique, and Réunion, which received departmental status in March 1946. Algeria, which had traditionally been considered part of France politically insofar as the European population elected delegates to parliament, was again divided into three departments—Oran, Algiers, and Constantine—by a special law passed on September 20, 1947. These departments elected representatives on the basis of limited franchise (70,000 assimilated Moslems out of a total electorate of over 500,000 for all of Algeria had the right to vote in the national elections) to the National Assembly. The administration of DOM came under the jurisdiction of the Interior Ministry.

The former colonies that had been administered directly by the Colonial Ministry became Overseas Territories (TOM) under a newly created Ministry for Overseas France. They included the older colonies, such as Saint-Pierre and Miguelon, the Comoro Islands, the Pacific possessions (Oceania, New Caledonia, New Hebrides, Wallis, and Futuna), Cochin China, the Indian settlements, Madagascar, French Somalia, and the states of the West and Central African Federations (Senegal, Mauritania, Guinea, Sudan, Niger, Upper Volta, Ivory Coast, Dahomey, Congo, Gabon, Chad, and Ubangi-Shari). Although technically called Associated Territories, the former League of Nations Mandates, Togo and Cameroon, were treated as if they were Overseas Territories. The Overseas Territories sent representatives to the National Assembly. Of the 619 delegates elected to the National Assembly in November 1946, 75 came from DOM-TOM.

Morocco, Tunisia, the states of Vietnam (Tonkin and Annam), Laos, and Cambodia had been established as French protectorates during the era of imperial expansion. They came under the administration of the Foreign Ministry, and the constitutional reforms of 1946 designated them Associated States. They did not send delegates to the National Assembly, but were represented in other institutions of the Colonial Union.

The governance of the Colonial Union was no less cumbersome than its structure. Some Overseas Territories were allowed territorial assemblies, such as New Caledonia, which were elected on the basis of a relatively broad franchise. The major political institutions of the Colonial Union consisted of a president, who was the president of the Republic, a High Council, which was formed by delegates appointed from metropolitan France and from the Associated States, and an Assembly with half of its membership elected from DOM-TOM and half appointed from France. The powers of the council and assembly were limited to advice to the French government, thus disappointing indigenous leaders who quickly realized that the Colonial Union offered only the appearance of local political power and opportunity for a measure of self-rule. Even provisions for local assemblies, which were part of the first Colonial Union constitution, were further limited in the second version that came into effect with the second referendum creating the Fourth Republic. Disappointment over the final form of the Colonial Union contributed to the outbreak of war in Vietnam late in 1946. The institutions of the Colonial Union ultimately proved insufficient either to satisfy or to contain pressures for national independence.

Along with political reforms the Fourth Republic offered prospects for economic development for overseas France with the creation of a Fund for Economic and Social Development (FIDES). This fund seemed to fulfill earlier proposals for an economic new deal for the French Empire, but the results proved disappointing. Much of the construction and transportation development benefited French colonial enterprises, and the monies for public housing tended to be spent for urban development in Dakar or Saigon.

The postwar Colonial Union began to unravel almost immediately with the outbreak of war in Indochina. By the early 1950s the French position in Indochina seemed increasingly threatened by Vietminh forces, now supported from China, and nationalists demanded independence in Morocco and Tunisia. The political leadership in France hesitated to accept the risks of decolonization, but increasingly public opinion favored some settlement of the colonial dilemma. With the French defeat at Dien Bien Phu in 1954, the era of decolonization for France in Asia could no longer be avoided. That same year Pierre Mendès-France undertook initiatives that would culminate in independence for Morocco and Tunisia two years later, but by this time the French army was locked in a struggle over Algeria that would prove fatal to the Fourth Republic.

In 1956 Gaston Defferre, then minister for overseas France, proposed a basic law (*loi-cadre*) to liberalize and decentralize the Colonial Union by granting territories locally elected assemblies and governing councils. The Defferre law took a significant step toward autonomy and eventual independence for many territories in Africa with the singular exception of Algeria, where conditions of war prevented holding elections for the National Assembly in 1956.

The impasse over Algeria came to a climax in May 1958 with an uprising of European settlers, backed by units of the army, in Algiers and the eventual call to General de Gaulle to form a government. Although long believed to be an advocate of France's colonial mission, by the time he became president of the Fifth Republic de Gaulle was convinced that decolonization was inevitable and attempts to hold the empire, even in Algeria, weakened France. While pursuing a carefully calculated policy that led to a negotiated end to the war and independence for Algeria in 1962, de Gaulle moved quickly toward fulfillment of the promise of the *loi-cadre* in sub-Saharan Africa. In August and September of 1958 he toured French possessions in Africa and offered a referendum in which the inhabitants of French Overseas Territories could choose between an autonomous status within a French Community and outright independence. Only Guinea chose the latter, and de Gaulle promptly severed all political and economic ties with the former colony. Under the Community France maintained control over key areas such as foreign policy, defense, financial policies, education, and justice.

In the elections for the 1958 National Assembly of the Fifth Republic, DOM-TOM sent sixteen delegates to Paris; alongside the sixty-seven representatives from Algeria and the Sahara, they constituted 15 percent of the delegates in the National Assembly. Despite the limitations in those areas that France still controlled, the choice for membership in the French Community became a preparation for full independence in black Africa. The reality of full independence came when Article 86 of the Fifth Republic's constitution was changed to allow members of the French Community to become fully independent without a complete break with France. Between June and November, twelve former member states of the Community (Madagascar, Mauritania, Senegal, Mali, Ivory Coast, Dahomey, Upper Volta, Niger, Central Africa, Congo-Brazzaville, Gabon, and Chad) joined the former Associated Territories of Cameroon and Togo in gaining admission to the United Nations. They all retained strong economic and cultural ties with France so that by 1985 there were more French in these new nations, serving as teachers, government advisers, or business representatives, than during the days of the Community.

These rapid changes led de Gaulle to announce in 1961 that the Community no longer existed. With the agreement on Algerian independence in 1962 the days of the French Empire seemed over. What remained were the so-called confetti of that empire, notably DOM (Martinique, Guadeloupe, Réunion, and Guiana) and the seven TOM (French Polynesia, New Caledonia, French Somaliland, the Comoro Islands, Saint-Pierre and Miguelon, the Southern Antarctic Territories, and Wallis and Futuna). In 1980 the curious Anglo-French condominium in the New Hebrides ended when these islands became the new state of Vanuatu.

About 1.5 million overseas inhabitants of DOM-TOM constitute the remainder of a French Empire that apologists once boasted was not just 40 but 100 million strong. From the grand but unrealistic vision of the Colonial Union to the modest DOM-TOM of today, the Fourth and Fifth Republics grappled more or less successfully with the problems of decolonization, yielding either with some grace in black Africa or to the force of opposition, as in Algeria and Vietnam. The issue of decolonization still remains for some overseas territories, notably New Caledonia and other islands where autonomist or nationalist movements continue. Whether further steps toward decolonization will occur for DOM-TOM remains uncertain. The Greenpeace affair revealed a determination to hold onto colonial rights in the Pacific in the name of national interest. However reduced in size, DOM-TOM enables the last of the French colonial nostalgics to claim that the sun still has not fully set upon France overseas.

J.-J. Becker, *Histoire politique de la France depuis 1945*, 2d ed. (Paris, 1988); R. Betts, *Tricouleur: The French Overseas Empire* (London, 1978); F. Borella, *Evolution juridique et politique de l'Union français depuis 1946* (Paris, 1958); H. Grimal, *La Décolonisation* (Paris, 1965); B. D. Marshall, *The French Colonial Myth and Constitution Making in the Fourth Republic* (New Haven, Conn., 1973); J.-P. Rioux, *The Fourth Republic 1944–1958* (Cambridge, 1987); M. Rosenblum, *Mission to Civilize: The French Way* (New York, 1986).

J. K. Munholland

Related entries: ALGERIA, RELATIONS WITH; DECOLONIZATION; DEFFERRE, GASTON; DE GAULLE, CHARLES; FRENCH UNION; GREENPEACE AFFAIR; INDOCHINA, RELATIONS WITH; NEW CALEDONIA; THIRD WORLD, RELATIONS WITH; TUNISIA, RELATIONS WITH.

P

PALEWSKI, GASTON (1901–1984), Gaullist politician. After his studies at Paris and Oxford, Palewski joined the staff of Marshal Lyautey in Morocco (1924–25). Subsequently, he became one of Paul Reynaud's closest collaborators from 1928 until 1940. It was during this period that he also first met Charles de Gaulle. In December 1940 Palewski was appointed as director of political affairs for Free France. Following a stint as commander of the Free French Forces in East Africa (1941–42), he served as de Gaulle's *Directeur de cabinet* from 1942 to 1946. Palewski was a founding member of the *Rassemblement du peuple français* (RPF). He was elected as an RPF deputy in 1951. In 1955 he joined the Faure Government as minister delegate for atomic affairs, the Sahara, and defense coordination. His brief ministerial tenure saw a major expansion of both civil and military nuclear development. Defeated in the 1956 election, Palewski was appointed as ambassador to Italy the following year. Returning from Rome only in 1962, he served as minister of state for scientific research and atomic and spatial questions in the first two Pompidou governments. Palewski was then president of the Constitutional Council from 1965 to 1974; a new institutional assertiveness marked the latter part of his mandate. A *mondain* as well as a statesman, Palewski's social ease was the ideal complement to the studied aloofness of General de Gaulle.

Espoir 50 (1985); G. Palewski, *Hier et aujourd'hui* (Paris, 1974), *Mémoires d'action, 1924–1974* (Paris, 1988).

R. A. Harmsen

Related entries: CONSTITUTIONAL COUNCIL; DE GAULLE, CHARLES; GAULLISM; GAULLIST PARTY; REYNAUD, PAUL.

PARIS REGION, an area that has undergone vast changes over the last forty-five years in administration, population, economy, and urban development. The three administrative changes that led to a better governmental and territorial organization of the metropolitan area were accomplished in three steps. First, in 1964 the two existing *départements* of Seine and Seine-et-Oise were divided into seven smaller *départements* (Paris, Hauts-de-Seine, Seine-Saint-Denis, Val-de-Marne, Val-d'Oise, Essonne, and Yvelines), functioning like the other ninety *départements* of continental France. Then, in July 1976 they were grouped with Seine-et-Marne to form the *Région d'Ile de France*. Finally, in 1977 Paris became an autonomous municipality for the first time since 1871.

These administrative changes gave the local government agencies more independence vis-à-vis the central administration. The region, placed under the authority of a *préfet de région*, is run by a regional council that works on four major areas: transportation, health care, sanitation, and environmental protection. Paris, with its dual function of city and *département*, is run by a mayor as are other French cities, but has kept its *préfet de police*. The mayor, elected for six years by the City Council, insures the application of the laws and supervises the bureau of vital statistics and the board of election. The mayor's main responsibilities are to prepare the budget and oversee urban development. He or she is helped by eighteen deputy mayors, chosen from among the members of the council, and numerous appointed city clerks. Given the size of the city and its population, the mayor delegates many responsibilities to the council members of the twenty *arrondissements* and works closely with the *commissions d'arrondissements*, which are composed of elected representatives, municipal officers, and members of the City Council. Jacques Chirac, elected first mayor of Paris in March 1977, was reelected in 1983 and 1989.

These administrative changes were designed to answer the needs of a region whose population was growing at an unprecedented rate. Today, its 1,278 cities and villages harbor more than 10 million people, an absolute increase of 7.7 million since 1945. During the same period the Parisian population decreased steadily from 3 million in 1939 to 2.2 million in 1985, where it has stabilized. As a result, the immediate suburbs, with some 4 million inhabitants, are as densely populated as Paris. Further out of the city, 3.8 million people are gathered in urban centers interspersed with large expanses of farm and forest land.

Two aspects of this population are equally shared by Paris and its region: the high percentage of people in the work force (over 4.1 million), and the concentration of foreigners (twice the national average of 6.8%). However, the Parisian population sets itself apart in three ways. First, the Parisians are older; 18.5 percent are sixty-five and over. Second, women outnumber men by 17 percent. Third, 58.4 percent of all Parisian women under sixty-five are employed. In the suburbs, the population is notably younger than in Paris (the birthrate is higher), only 44 percent of the women are employed, and the ratio of men to women is reversed because of the large number of single male factory workers and foreigners.

The changes in the population mirror those of the Parisian economy. Paris has lost most of its factories to its suburbs. The percentage of its blue-collar jobs declined from 34 percent in 1950 to only 17.6 percent in 1985. However, finance companies, state and local administration, commerce, and transportation employ an increasing number of white- and pink-collar workers (low-paid office personnel, mainly women), who made up 34.5 percent of the work force in 1985, compared with 24.2 percent in 1975. Today, with its heavy concentration in the chemical, aviation, automotive, pharmaceutical, optics, and construction industries, the region offers one-fourth of the nation's industrial jobs and nearly 30 percent of its office employment.

The leading role of the capital in the intellectual and cultural life of the country has remained, while spilling over to its suburbs. The most notable changes since 1945 are the creation or relocation of some of the *grandes écoles* and the opening of new university centers in Paris and in Ile de France.

The new industrial and residential role of the suburbs has brought about pressing housing needs and increasing congestion on the roads and in public transportation. To address these issues the *Ministère de la construction* developed, in 1960, the *Plan d'aménagement et d'organisation générale de la région parisienne*. Once its proposals for zoning, area rehabilitation, modernization, and expansion of highways and public transportation were approved, thirty years of urban development followed, changing dramatically the face of the city and its region.

This development saw two phases: From 1950 to 1970 high-rise housing units were built in an attempt to meet the urgent needs of a fast-growing population; after 1970 urban planners paid more attention to the integrity of the construction, the integration of the new within the traditional, and the quality of life offered to the residents.

In Paris, during the first phase, an abundance of buildings sprang up celebrating modern technology and offering more spacious apartments, more office space to accommodate a growing tertiary economy, more hospitals, schools, and universities. This effervescent urban renewal happened mostly in the thirteenth, fifteenth, nineteenth, and twentieth *arrondissements*.

In 1970, after the erection of the controversial *Tour Montparnasse*, the need for concerted and coherent planning was apparent. The *Atelier parisien d'urbanisme* (the city planning office) was created to study the *plan d'occupation des sols* (a very detailed land-use map) and make recommendations for the rehabilitation and transformation of areas needing improvement. The hotly debated Pompidou Center and the Quartier des Halles bear the marks of the previous tendencies, but the renovation of the area along the Canal Saint-Martin, for instance, testifies to the new focus on harmonization of styles and the effort to improve the quality of life in the city. The transformation of the Gare d'Orsay into a museum, the renovation of the Louvre, the opening of the Bastille Opera and a science center in La Villette Park, to name only the most spectacular, show the attention paid to the cultural life of the Parisians and the gentrification of the city. The opening of new sports facilities at Bercy and new parks in Vaugirard and Javel make the city even more enjoyable for the visitors who flock to Paris every year, making the tourist industry one of the most profitable in the country.

In the suburbs urban development took three forms during the first phase: individual homes on small lots, medium-size housing projects (most often run by the city as rent-controlled units), and vast housing developments called *grands ensembles* as in Sarcelles. In spite of industrial nuisances, many housing projects were built near factories and workshops. Little thought was given to the environment and the need for communal life.

The second phase after 1970 saw a new vision of urbanization lead to the construction of five new cities: Evry, Cergy-Pontoise, Saint-Quentin-en-Yvelines, Marne-la-Vallée, and Melun-Senart. These *villes nouvelles* were to solve the problems inherent in the "bedroom communities" built earlier: The environment was carefully conceived to bring to the new city dweller a true sense of community. It is also the time when a very ambitious project was undertaken at the *Rond Point de la Défense* (on the city limits of Nanterre, Puteaux, and Courbevoie) to provide many square miles of needed office space in dozens of skyscrapers. The decisions of the urban planners rarely met with the approval of the population, which generally preferred living in suburban subdivisions. At present, a strongly regulated zoning imposed on the entire region allows for a more traditional urban landscape with limited industrial parks, greater room for individual homes, and better-located administrative and commercial centers.

Suburban development also prompted the construction of major expressways and divided highways to and from Paris, to shorten commuting time in the region. Nonetheless, a beltway at the city limits and a divided highway along the Seine are not sufficient to curb the congestion at rush hours in Paris. The traffic between suburbs is just as bad since there are more people commuting from one suburb to another than to and from Paris; nevertheless, few superhighways link the towns surrounding the capital.

Improvements in public transportation, however, are many: In the subway, comfortable trains reach deeper into the suburbs, and a new fleet of buses runs a notably expanded route. But what has greatly improved the transit system in the last fifteen years has been the construction of a rapid subway system, the *Réseau express régional* (RER). The RER offers direct connections to the subway lines, the railroads, and the bus lines in and out of the city. It has placed the center of Paris less than thirty minutes away from its farthest suburb, but again favors the Paris-suburb direction rather than the lateral movement that is numerically more important. The use of a monthly pass (*carte orange*) allowing for unlimited travel on the whole network has simplified the ticketing process and fosters greater use of trains and buses.

The region is well equipped for air travel with an expanded Orly airport and a new airport, Charles de Gaulle. The latter, located in Roissy-en-France where construction began in 1972, now has two of its three passenger terminals completed.

In recent decades supplying the region with food, water, and energy became a major and difficult task given the sudden population growth and the limited access roads in Paris and the surrounding towns. Important steps have been taken to solve the problems of distribution of goods, the most notable one being the transfer of the Central Market to Rungis near Orly airport.

Furthermore, the urbanization of the region has triggered a need for recreational facilities and green space. Since the population has stabilized and concern for the environment has increased, the regional offices are working closely with the *Agence des espaces verts de la Région d'Ile de France* to improve living conditions, notably by expanding and protecting the remaining green areas (forests, parks, riverbanks, and lakes) so necessary to the quality of life in the large metropolis.

Finally, in recognition of the need to solve commuting problems and to redress the widening inequities between the region's east and west sides in terms of municipal income, concentration of population, and general land use, Prime Minister Michel Rocard reopened the debate on regional development in July 1989. In keeping with the spirit of decentralization, the municipalities will have a much greater input in the drawing of the next urban development plan (*schéma directeur d'aménagement urbain*, SDAU). The regional planners seem ready to meet these new challenges to surpass thirty years of population growth and economic changes that have reaffirmed the leading role of Paris and its region in France today and increased the city's attractiveness and stature among world capitals.

Atelier parisien d'urbanisme, *Paris projet* (Paris, 1969–88); J. Bastie, *La Croissance de la banlieue parisienne* (Paris, 1964); M. Carmona, *Le Grand Paris, l'évolution de l'idée d'aménagement de la région parisienne* (Paris, 1980); Documentation française, *Paris* (Paris, 1985); P. Lavedan, *Nouvelle histoire de Paris* (Paris, 1975); J. Steinberg, *Les Villes nouvelles d'Ile de France* (Paris, 1981).

L. J. Haenlin

Related entries: CHIRAC, JACQUES; DECENTRALIZATION; ECONOMIC TRENDS; FASHION; IMMIGRANTS; LABOR FORCE; MUSEUMS; PLAN; POPULATION TRENDS; REGIONS; TRANSPORTATION; URBANIZATION.

PASQUA, CHARLES (1927–), Gaullist politician and minister of the interior in the government of *cohabitation*. Born in Grasse (Alpes-Maritimes) to Corsican parents, Charles Pasqua joined the "Tartane" Resistance network while still only fifteen. After the war, the young veteran drifted for several years until he entered and climbed through the ranks of the Ricard pastis firm. A Gaullist of unshakable faith, Pasqua was an ardent member of both the *Union gaulliste* and the *Rassemblement du peuple français*. Later, from 1962 until 1969, he emerged as a central figure in the *Service d'action civique*, the shadowy security corps (*service d'ordre*) of the reborn Gaullist movement. During the *événements* of 1968, he was instrumental in organizing the *Comités de défense de la République* and the massive progovernment counterdemonstration of May 30.

Pasqua was elected to the National Assembly in June 1968, ousting an incumbent communist deputy in the "red suburbs" of Paris. Defeated in the 1973 legislative election, he served as the president of the *Conseil général* of the Hauts-de-Seine from 1973 to 1976 (regaining the post in 1988). In 1974, Pasqua played a key role in imposing Jacques Chirac at the head of the *Union des démocrates pour la République* (UDR). A trusted lieutenant of the new Gaullist leader, from 1974 to 1979 he held senior positions in both the UDR and its successor, the *Rassemblement pour la République* (RPR). In 1981 (as in 1988), he was one of the principal organizers of Chirac's presidential campaign.

First elected to the Senate from the Hauts-de-Seine in 1977, Pasqua became the leader of the Gaullist group in the Palais Luxembourg four years later. It was from this position that he first rose to national prominence, spearheading the opposition in 1984 to the socialist government's education and press legislation. He also violently attacked the government's handling of events in New Caledonia.

As minister of the interior from 1986 to 1988, Pasqua was responsible for the reintroduction of two-ballot majority voting for elections to the National Assembly. His ministerial tenure was also marked by tragic incidents of police brutality, an overzealous political exploitation of the *Carrefour du développement* scandal, and an involvement in negotiations leading to the release of French hostages held in Lebanon. More generally, by staking out a strong law-and-order position and suggesting the existence of common values, Pasqua sought to woo voters away from the National Front.

After the right's defeat in 1988 Pasqua returned to the Senate and reassumed the leadership of the Gaullist group. Primarily preoccupied by matters of internal party reform, he formed an alliance with Philippe Séguin prior to the February 1990 national convention of the RPR. A rare combination of inspired populist orator and astute backroom operator, Pasqua remains a highly controversial figure who has not yet emerged completely from the shadows.

P. Boggio, A. Rollat, *Ce terrible Monsieur Pasqua* (Paris, 1988); C. Pasqua, *L'Ardeur nouvelle* (Paris, 1985).

R. A. Harmsen

Related entries: BARZACH, MICHELE; *CARREFOUR DU DEVELOPPEMENT* AFFAIR; *COHABITATION*; CHIRAC, JACQUES; *COMPAGNIES REPUBLICAINES DE SECURITE*; ELECTORAL SYSTEM; FOCCART, JACQUES; GAULLISM; GAULLIST PARTY; LE PEN, JEAN-MARIE; NOIR, MICHEL; SEGUIN, PHILIPPE; STUDENT REVOLTS; TERRORISM.

PEACE MOVEMENT, organized group(s) campaigning for the reduction and/or elimination of nuclear weapons. The French peace movement has always been weak, even before 1977 when the left still resisted the Gaullist nuclear program. The *Mouvement de la paix* (MDP), appearing after 1945, is the oldest peace group. Organized initially around Charles Tillon, his plan was to foster an independent movement but this proved unacceptable to the *Parti communiste français* (PCF), which expelled Tillon and assumed direction over it. Subsequently, sections within the MDP (some journalists, professors, and Catholic priests) have sought to redefine the movement outside any political line, but the PCF has, by and large, made the MDP its own.

Since 1958 additional groups have appeared. In 1962 the *Mouvement contre l'armement atomique* (MCAA) was born—partly out of the belief that France needed further stimulus and partly as a response to the British Campaign for Nuclear Disarmament (CND) and the International Confederation for Disarmament and Peace's demand for a group espousing nonalignment. In 1968 the MCAA transformed into the *Mouvement pour le désarmement, la paix, et la liberté* (MDPL), recruiting heavily from the *Parti socialiste unifié* (PSU). Membership in the MDPL rose to ten thousand.

The year 1962 saw the birth of a second new movement, the *Ligue contre la force de frappe* (LCFF), jointly headed by former minister Jules Moch (Socialist party, PS) and former communist deputy Maurice Kriegel-Valrimont. The LCFF and the MDPL coordinated their efforts until organizational problems resulted in the LCFF's eclipse a few years later. The short life span of the LCFF was not unproductive since an umbrella organization, the *Comité contre la force de frappe* (CCFF), was another 1962 development, coordinating with the MDP, the PCF, the MDPL, the *Confédération générale du travail* (CGT), some PS federations, and the *Confédération française democratique du travail* (CFDT) to organize demonstrations against French and Soviet weapons.

May 1968 and the decade of the seventies represented a period of crisis and demobilization for French peace politics. With the prospect of initiating widespread domestic changes, many peace campaigners momentarily abandoned international problems, and in the aftermath of the revolt of 1968 many *soixante-huitards* never resumed activity. Those who did concentrated on U.S. involvement in Vietnam. Most significant perhaps, political developments on the left encouraged the peace movement to relax. The Mitterrand courtship of the PCF culminated in the nuptial pact of 1972—the common program of government—which, among other things, called for the abolition of French nuclear weapons. The peace movement congratulated itself and waited for the left's victory.

In the late 1970s the peace movement was seriously weakened when the left changed its stance and accepted the *force de frappe*. The MDP nearly disappeared; many left, utterly disillusioned. For the next few years the independent groups simply tried to remain active. The major event in the 1980s has been the creation in late 1981 of an umbrella organization, *Comité pour le désarmement nucléaire en Europe* (CODENE), which has brought together over twenty groupings—the MDPL, ecologists, feminists, the PSU—into something resembling Britain's Environment Near Death (END). In May 1982 the "*Appel des cents*" was launched with an appeal signed by representatives of France's professional and cultural elites, although its demands—summed up by its slogan "*J'aime la paix*"—were rather weak.

The reasons for the weaknesses of the French peace movement are manifold. France has a long military tradition, which is still much revered domestically. Notions of pacifism have assumed derogatory overtones that, since the fall of France in World War II, have lingered in the popular memory. Moreover, when the peace movement is condemned for being pro-Soviet and pacifist, the second challenge is as debilitating as the first. The close MDP-PCF link and the ''illogical'' position of criticizing French weaponry but (usually) remaining silent about Soviet hardware has further damaged credibility. There is no major non-nuclear political party that the movement can adopt as a useful vehicle for its ideas. The left and the church have not played a central role in French peace politics as in Britain and West Germany. In France both the left and the church at times express themselves in nationalistic, even militaristic terms, which is in keeping with their historical roots and traditions. Ultimately, the *force de frappe* has, since its inception, been equated with French grandeur, rank, and independence and continues to be the source of considerable national pride. Its war-preventing facets are repeatedly underlined, and dissent from this consensus has been successfully marginalized by the state. Finally, the 1960s withdrawal of American missiles from France removed a target that has been extremely mobilizing in other states where strong peace movements exist.

P. Cerny, *The Politics of Grandeur* (New York, 1980); J. Howorth, P. Chilton (eds.), *Defence and Dissent in Contemporary France* (New York, 1984); P. Le Prestre, *French Security Policy in a Disarming World*, (London, 1989).

J. Bryant

Related entries: COMMON PROGRAM; DEFENSE POLICY; ECOLOGY PARTY; UNIFIED SOCIALIST PARTY.

PEASANTRY, France's farm population, which has declined rapidly since World War II. The peasantry includes two overlapping groups, one including all farm families, the other referring only to small farmers living a traditional, insular life close to the subsistence level: In 1939, 35 percent of the population was peasants, and most fell into the latter category. A revolution within the peasantry during the 1950s and 1960s has greatly raised the living standards of farm families, so that only a few traditional peasants remain, mostly old people in isolated hill regions. At the same time, the farming population has decreased in size to less than 8 percent of the population.

Many people in France perceive the peasantry as essential to French civilization and culture. Most political parties have been committed to preserve small- and medium-sized farmers and independent family farms, even at the cost of higher food prices. During the Third Republic, the Méline tariffs of 1892 protected the French peasantry from international competition. Marshal Pétain's Vichy regime claimed to return France to its peasant roots and to defend the rural way of life. Since Liberation, fringe movements like the Poujadist movement continued this ''peasantist'' tradition, but most politicians have argued that the best way to protect the peasantry is through judicious modernization. The Pisani Law of 1962 is a good example; it created pension funds to induce old peasants to retire, encouraged cooperative production and marketing, and set up agencies to improve and regroup land into more efficient farms.

Since World War II what some historians have termed a ''rural revolution'' has radically altered the peasantry's political, economic, and social position within France. But, while there is general agreement that in politics and the economy these changes have been all to the good, many peasants are concerned by the decline of peasant society.

In prewar France, the peasantry had little direct impact upon the government. As a group, peasants were poorly educated with little experience outside their own villages. They depended upon a rural elite of large landowners, priests, notaries, and schoolteachers to represent them in the legislature and to organize programs for them, such as mutual aid societies or purchasing syndicates. After the war this deference faded as leaders began to emerge from the peasantry itself. Some, like Pierre Tanguy-Prigent, the Fourth Republic's first minister of agriculture, came from the Resistance; some, like René Blondelle, powerful leader of the *Fédération nationale des syndicats des exploitants agricoles* (FNSEA), had experience in Vichy's corporative organizations; and many, like Blondelle's rival and successor, Michel Debatisse, came from the Catholic youth organization, the *Jeunesse agricole chrétienne*. Tanguy created the FNSEA as a peasants' union whose members were required to be active farmers. Through it, the peasantry became a powerful lobby in the National Assembly and also, perhaps more important, active participants in the government's economic Plan and in negotiations within the European Economic Community (EEC). Because of the importance of the European market for French agricultural products and also because of the EEC price support system, in recent years peasant politics and activism have been directed more at Brussels than Paris.

Before World War II, French agriculture stagnated. Many peasants worked tiny plots of land, often by hand. Their living standard was sharply lower than that of city dwellers. Peasants lived as much as possible upon their own products, using small cash crops to pay their taxes and to buy the few essentials, such as tobacco or coffee, that they could not grow or make. After the war, the Fourth Republic and the FNSEA embarked upon a major modernization program to make tractors, fertilizer, and other modern technology available at low cost. The Fifth Republic continued these efforts, and has also supported cooperative production and marketing and improved technical education. Farms today are larger—the average size has increased from thirty-five acres to eighty acres—and considerably more productive; so productive, in fact, that France is becoming swamped with surplus butter, wine, and other products. Peasants are often members of a co-op, to share equipment or to process and market their crops. Peasant living standards are now close to those of urbanites, and they have cars, televisions, freezers, and home computers. However, increased acreage and technology have come at the price of much-increased operating expenses and heavy debt.

Until the 1940s, peasant villages were largely self-sufficient, with their own artisans and retailers, their own active social life, and even their own languages. Most villages organized festivals, dances, and concerts while groups of neighbors met in the traditional *veillées*, evening gatherings to work, tell stories, and play games. Since the 1950s and the advent of the automobile and the television, village-based social life has drastically declined. Where it still exists or has been revived, it is often as folklore, sometimes aimed mainly at tourists. Peasant dialects have died out with increased education and the influence of the standard French broadcast by radio and television. Traditional regional languages such as Breton and Occitan are now taught as second languages in school rather than learned at home.

The peasantry is no longer the class apart that it once was. Much smaller, but much better off, the peasantry has entered the mainstream of French politics and society. But this transformation has had its costs, particularly in community life. Although few peasants would want to return to the harsh conditions of prewar life, many regret the increasing suburbanization of the countryside and the loss of a distinct peasant culture.

J. Ardagh, *France Today* (London, 1987); H. Mendras, *The Vanishing Peasant* (Cambridge, Mass., 1970); G. Wright, *Rural Revolution in France* (Stanford, Calif., 1964); F. Zonabend, *The Enduring Memory* (Manchester, Eng., 1984).

M. H. Darrow

Related entries: AGRICULTURE; EUROPEAN ECONOMIC COMMUNITY, RELATIONS WITH; NATIONAL CENTER OF INDEPENDENTS AND PEASANTS; PISANI, EDGARD; PLAN; POUJADISTS; REGIONS; URBANIZATION.

PEYREFITTE, ALAIN (1925–), diplomat, writer, and politician. Peyrefitte is a good example of the way in which France recruits and trains its elite. His parents were both teachers. He was a brilliant *lycée* student who prepared for the competitive exam for the prestigious *Ecole normale supérieure*, succeeded, and became a "*normalien*." Now, he was well on his way to the upper ranks of society. Like many ambitious young men in 1945, he was among the first group of students to enter the National School of Administration (ENA), which Charles de Gaulle had just established in order to develop top civil servants for the new Republic. Upon graduation in 1947, he chose a career in the Foreign Service, which led him to be first a junior diplomat in the French Embassy in Bonn (1949–52), later a consul general in Krakow (1954–56), and then after various assignments (e.g., member of the French delegation to the Brussels Conference on the Common Market), a delegate to the General Assembly of the United Nations (1959–61 and 1969–71). By then his political career was well under way. He had become a Gaullist representative in the National Assembly from the Seine and Marne district. Since 1965 he has been the mayor of the city of Provins. He entered the Georges Pompidou government as minister of information from 1962 to 1966, of scientific research from 1966 to 1967, and had the misfortune of being minister of education from 1967 to May 1968 during the period of widespread student protest. From 1972 to 1973 he was general secretary of the Union of Democrats for the Republic (the name of the Gaullist party at the time). His government career resumed under the presidency of Valéry Giscard d'Estaing where he served as minister of justice from 1977 to 1981.

In 1977 he was elected to the French Academy, having already published seven books, including two important best-sellers: *Quand la Chine s'éveillera* (1973), which sold 670,000 copies, and *Le Mal français* (1977), which sold 400,000 copies. *Le Mal français* was a very liberal analysis of the difficulties of an over-centralized country. But when Peyrefitte was minister of justice, his actions were anything but liberal and he fell victim to the syndrome he had analyzed so well. When the law called "Security and Freedom," better known then as the Peyrefitte law, was approved in December 1980, it had become the symbol of the opposition between the left and the right. It was the type of "law and order" legislation that seemed to signal a basic shift in the penal policy followed since 1945. Since François Mitterrand was elected in May 1981 and since his new justice minister, Robert Badinter, proposed the abolition of the law and of the death penalty, the Peyrefitte law never had a chance to be applied. Nevertheless, it had been perceived as one of the most visible signs of the conservative shift of the Giscard presidency, and as such played its part in the socialist victory.

Peyrefitte is now known as the very conservative editorial director of *Le Figaro* and as an expert in Chinese history; his latest book on China (1989) was a phenomenal success.

J.-F. Doumic, H. Lacharmoise, eds., *Le Guide du pouvoir* (Paris, 1989).

J. Carduner

Related entries: DE GAULLE, CHARLES; EDUCATIONAL REFORM; GAULLISM; GAULLIST PARTY; GISCARD D'ESTAING, VALERY; POMPIDOU, GEORGES; STUDENT REVOLTS.

PFLIMLIN, PIERRE (1907–), Christian democratic (MRP) politician and former premier at the time of the Army's mutiny in Algeria in May 1958, which led to Charles de Gaulle's return to office. Born February 5, 1907 in Roubaix, Pflimlin studied at Strasbourg University and the Catholic Institute in Paris and prepared to practice law. He was elected to the Strasbourg Municipal Council in 1945 (and would serve as mayor of the city beginning in 1959). As a Christian democrat he sat in the two constituent assemblies (1945–46), was elected a deputy from the Bas-Rhin department in 1946, and reelected in 1951 and 1956. He held junior and then senior cabinet posts in several Fourth Republic governments, including those of Georges Bidault, Robert Schuman, André Marie, Henri Queuille, René Pleven, Edgar Faure, and Félix Gaillard.

Asked by President Coty to form a new government, Pflimlin planned to present his cabinet to the National Assembly May 13, 1958. French settlers in Algiers feared that he would negotiate with the rebels seeking independence. The settlers' demonstration turned into a riot, and government buildings in Algiers were sacked. Gaullist Generals Jacques Massu and Raoul Salan stated their support for the uprising, ignored Coty's appeals to have the soldiers return to duty, and called for a committee of public safety headed by de Gaulle. The seizure of Corsica on May 24 by Gaullist supporters intensified pressure on the government. Rumors of an Algiers-led paratroop attack on Paris spread, and the "Gaullist solution" gained more ground. On May 26 de Gaulle met with Pflimlin to discuss the latter's resignation, but the talks proved fruitless. De Gaulle, in a communiqué, nevertheless created the impression that negotiations were under way for a change in government. A furious Pflimlin wanted to deny it publicly, but was persuaded not to by President Coty, who feared the outbreak of civil war. Pflimlin, despite having won a vote of confidence in his government, submitted his resignation on the night of May 27.

Pflimlin served as a minister of state in the de Gaulle government of 1958–59 and in the Pompidou government of 1962. He was reelected as a deputy by the Bas-Rhin voters in 1958 and 1962. He continued to play an active role, particularly in European affairs, representing France at the Council of Europe and then on the European Parliament between 1959 and 1967. Between 1956 and 1959, he served as MRP president. He has published books on the industry of Mulhouse and on the economic structure of the Third Reich.

J. Chapsal, A. Lancelot, *La Vie politique en France depuis 1940* (Paris, 1975); L. Derfler, *President and Parliament* (Boca Raton, Fla., 1983).

L. Derfler

Related entries: COTY, RENE; DE GAULLE, CHARLES.

PIAF, EDITH (1915–1963), stage name of Edith Gassion, France's most popular singer from the late 1930s to the 1950s. Beginning her career as a street singer, Piaf captured in her ballads the experiences and emotions of the poor, the marginal, and the insecure. With her voice, staging, and lyrics, and in her own life, she embodied the determination of "little people" to find love and to endure pain. Among her most famous ballads are: "*L'Accordéoniste*," the story of a streetwalker whose lover, the accordionist at the local dance hall, is killed in the war; "*Bravo pour le clown,*" the portrait of a circus clown, entertaining the crowd even though his own life is in shambles; and "*Milord*," which recounts the efforts of a taxi dancer to cheer up her gentleman patron. Piaf's two most famous love songs, "*La Vie en rose*," which she wrote herself, and "*Non, je ne regrette rien*," her 1960 comeback hit, express her optimism and her reckless defiance of the lessons of bitter experience.

Born in 1915 in Paris, Edith traveled with her father, an itinerant acrobat, soon learning to sing for her supper. In 1935 cabaret owner Louis Leplée heard her singing on a Paris street corner. He employed her, trained her, and gave her her stage name, Piaf, the Parisian slang for sparrow. In the 1930s Piaf passed from nightclub singing to headlining in shows, cutting records, and singing in films. She was well received by audiences and by the press from the start. By the 1940s she was able to choose her own material and projects. Songwriters such as Raymond Asso, Marguerite Monnot, Henri Contet, Michel Emer, and later Georges Moustaki and Charles Dumont wrote material for her. In 1940 she starred in a one-act play, *Le Bel indifférent,* written especially for her by Jean Cocteau. She made her New York debut in 1947 and earned an enthusiastic reception, particularly after she began to perform some songs in English, such as "Autumn Leaves." Her success continued to grow in the 1950s; Piaf made her last recording, "*L'Homme de Berlin,*" in April 1963, only six months before she died.

Piaf's creative, productive, and immensely successful career contrasted with her hectic and self-destructive personal life. Her professional self-confidence was bought, from the first, at the price of dependence upon alcohol, a string of lovers, a coterie of hangers-on, and finally, drugs. Piaf married twice, first to singer Jacques Pils in 1952 (divorced 1957) and, in 1962 when she was already dying, to Theophanis Lamboukas, a young hairdresser. In Piaf's mind and in the mind of her public, however, the love of her life was Marcel Cerdan, the middleweight boxing champion. His death in a plane crash in 1949—he was flying to New York to see her—plunged her into the first of increasingly debilitating "black periods." An auto accident in 1951 left her addicted to painkillers. After several years spent in and out of hospitals, always on the verge of collapse, Edith Piaf died of a massive internal hemorrhage on October 10, 1963. She was buried in Père Lachaise cemetery in Paris where her tomb has become a pilgrimage site for her thousands of still-adoring fans. In 1981 Paris commemorated her life by dedicating the place Edith Piaf in the twentieth *arrondissement*.

Edith Piaf was part of a long tradition of French popular singers who rose from street entertainers to cabarets and music halls, capturing the audience with raw emotion as much as with musicality. Like Yvette Guilbert before her, Piaf's songs and her life together tell a story of struggle and express an indomitable will to survive that, in the post war years not less than during the Occupation, the French took to their hearts.

M. Crosland, *Piaf* (New York, 1985); E. Piaf, *The Wheel of Fortune* (Philadelphia, Pa., 1965).

M. H. Darrow

Related entry: POPULAR CULTURE.

PICASSO, PABLO (1881–1973), Spanish painter, sculptor, ceramist, graphic artist, dramatist, and poet, who spent most of his creative years in France. His phenomenal productivity spans seven decades. Known for his technical skills, his versatility, and his powerful originality, his most significant influence in the development of modern art was the stylistic breakthrough of his painting *Les Demoiselles d'Avignon* (1907), which abandoned traditional use of perspective and space and deliberately rejected classical beauty for simplified masklike planes. During the subsequent decade, Picasso worked closely with Georges Braque to explore the conceptual and artistic implications of this new Cubist "war against positivism."

Acutely sensitive to the violence and beastliness of war, Picasso painted his first openly political canvases during the civil war in his native Spain. The most famous was *Guernica* (1937), which expressed his rage and shock over the premeditated cruelty of the bombing of this small unprotected Spanish town by

German planes in the service of General Francisco Franco. Imagery of cruelty and anger was common in Picasso's paintings during the next few years, as the defeat of Republican Spain was followed by the outbreak of World War II and the defeat of Republican France.

During the war Picasso remained in occupied Paris, and at the time of Liberation in August 1944 he came to symbolize the artist in defiance of Nazi barbarism. In October 1944 he joined the French Communist party. At the opening of the *Salon d'Automne* the same month, an entire hall was devoted to Picasso's wartime works. This was the first time that this honor was bestowed upon a foreign artist; however, organized groups of reactionaries disrupted the show and attempted to destroy some of his paintings.

Though already in his sixties when World War II ended, Picasso continued to produce a phenomenal number of works for another three decades. In addition to numerous new canvases and sculptures, he painted "translations" or reinterpretations of works of Poussin, Courbet, Velázquez, and Manet, and he painted a huge mural for the UNESCO building in Paris (1958). He also did innovative work in lithography and ceramics, and in 1947 alone produced some two thousand ceramic pieces.

Picasso attended the 1948 Congress of Intellectuals for Peace held in Poland and the subsequent Peace Congresses in Paris (1949), Sheffield (1950), and Rome (1951). His continuing political concerns were evident in some of his postwar paintings, such as *Le Charnier* (1945), *Massacre en Corée* (1951), and the two large compositions entitled *Guerre* and *Paix* (1952).

Most of his final years were spent on the southern coast of France—in Antibes, in Vallauris (where he did much of his work in ceramics), in Cannes at his villa *La Californie*, and further inland at the Château de Vauvenargues near Aix-en-Provence, which he purchased in 1958. In 1961 Picasso moved to a villa near Mougins; here he continued to work vigorously until his death on April 8, 1973 at the age of ninety-one.

P. Daix, *Picasso* (New York, 1965); F. Gilot, C. Lake, *Life with Picasso* (New York, 1964); R. Penrose, *Picasso: His Life and Work*, 3d. ed. (Berkeley, Calif., 1981).

K. S. Vincent

Related entry: ART AND ARCHITECTURE.

PINAY, ANTOINE (1891–), a pillar of postwar French conservatism. Pinay built a modest political career in the Third Republic as a mayor, deputy, and senator on a reputation for astute business management, professions of faith in sound public finances, and warnings of the danger posed by the socialist-communist left. He recaptured his place in politics, unscathed by any substantial penalties at the Liberation for having voted full powers to Marshal Pétain in 1940, by winning election in 1946 to the second constituent assembly and to the National Assembly. As the governments of the Fourth Republic evolved to the right after 1947, Pinay became secretary of state for economic affairs and minister of public works and transportation.

In the early 1950s the inability of the Third Force to sustain coherent governmental majorities and the erosion of the intransigent Gaullist refusal to participate in government produced a reconfiguration of French politics by enhancing the strength of the right. This period witnessed a general preoccupation with enjoyment of rising living standards, which did not entirely mask a discontent with the ineffective political regime. When the Korean War stockpiling boom renewed the harrowing inflation that had troubled France from the Liberation until 1949, it proved difficult to form a government capable of dealing with the problem. Pinay surprised many people by succeeding in forming a cabinet in March of 1952 that was acceptable to parliament.

Pinay attacked the psychological roots of inflation by halting government borrowing from the Bank of France, freezing utility prices, and driving down some food prices. He chose to pare nondefense spending rather than raise taxes. Given the preponderance of indirect taxes in state revenue and the natural tendency to shift these to consumers by higher prices, Pinay judged that higher taxes would stimulate inflation rather than reduce it. Pinay also wagered on public confidence in a government pursuing sound management by issuing a loan—indexed to the price of gold to prevent depreciation—to raise badly needed funds. Potential malcontents on either flank were conciliated by indexation of wages to prices and an amnesty for tax evaders. These measures helped break the inflationary psychology, while the fall in world raw material prices reduced the upward pressure on costs. Rising living standards so dominated the concerns of ordinary Frenchmen in the 1950s that Pinay's success won him lasting credit with voters, a reflection of the low esteem in which most politicians were held. His cabinet came under fire from the Christian democrats (MRP), however, for its lack of progress on the intractable problems of the empire and fell just before Christmas 1952. Pinay did not return to office until he became foreign minister in the government of Edgar Faure (February 1955–January 1956), where he struggled to solve the thorny issue of the Saar.

Pinay entered a cabinet for the final time as Charles de Gaulle's finance minister (June 1958–January 1960). Pinay's policy resembled his earlier program: another loan, import controls, working down consumer prices through cajoling and coercion, and imposing temporary taxes to raise additional revenue. The Rueff-Pinay report on the structure of the French economy (December 1958) led to a blizzard of decrees devaluing the franc, removing most restrictions on trade, raising taxes on personal incomes, corporate profits, and mass consumption items such as alcohol, tobacco, and energy. State spending was redirected from subsidizing consumer prices toward investment. The reductions in consumer incomes implied by all these measures aroused much criticism from the left.

Chosen principally to encourage confidence in the new regime, Pinay adapted with difficulty to the more authoritarian political style of the Fifth Republic's government. De Gaulle's distancing of France from the Atlantic Alliance and the multiplying interventions of the state in economic affairs increasingly disturbed him. Pinay refused any further participation in national politics after leaving the government, despite talk of his candidacy for president in 1965. His service as France's first official mediator (January 1973–May 1974) constituted an acknowledgment of the deep faith in his integrity held by a whole generation of the French. It speaks volumes to the problems of the Fourth and Fifth Republics that a man of modest abilities could build so successful a career solely on the public belief that he did not lie.

S. Guillaume, *Antoine Pinay* (Paris, 1984); J.-P. Rioux, *La France de la Quatrième République*, 2 vols. (Paris, 1980–83).

J. S. Hill

Related entries: DE GAULLE, CHARLES; ECONOMIC POLICY; FAURE, EDGAR; INFLATION; NATIONAL CENTER OF INDEPENDENTS AND PEASANTS; POLITICAL TRENDS; QUEUILLE, HENRI.

PINEAU, CHRISTIAN (1904–), socialist deputy and minister. Born in Chaumont (Haute-Marne), he attended the *Ecole alsacienne* in Paris. He received degrees in law (*licence*) and in political science (*diplôme*). In the 1930s, while working for the Bank of France and the *Banque de Paris et des Pays-Bas*, he became involved in the trade-union movement, and between 1934 and 1936 he was secretary of the Economic Council of the *Confédération générale du travail*. In this period he also founded and directed the review *Banque et bourse*. When France fell in 1940 he was among the first French leaders to join the Resistance movement. In November 1940 he started publishing *Libération*, and together with other trade-union leaders he issued a Resistance manifesto. When he organized his own Resistance *réseaux*, called *Phalanx*, he was arrested and deported to Buchenwald. He was released in 1945. For his role in the Resistance he received numerous decorations such as the *Légion d'honneur*, the *Croix de guerre 1939–45*, and the *Rosette de la Résistance*.

In 1945–46 he was a member of the Fourth Republic's constituent assemblies and was then elected as a socialist deputy to the National Assembly from 1946 to 1958. In the immediate postwar period he participated actively in the nationalization and reorganization of credit and banking. He occupied the following posts: member of the *comité directeur* of the Socialist party (SFIO); minister of *ravitaillement* (1945); president of the *Commission des finances* at the National Assembly (1945–47); minister of public works (1948 and 1949); and minister of foreign affairs (1957 and 1958). In February of 1955 he was asked to form a cabinet but was not confirmed by the National Assembly as premier.

Throughout his career as a socialist deputy he grew increasingly interested in foreign affairs and in France's role in Europe and the world. He was a staunch supporter of the European Defense Community—especially as a guarantee of German rearmament within a European-wide context—and he supported many initiatives to further European economic integration. As minister of foreign affairs he promoted closer ties between Western and Eastern Europe, aided in granting independence to Morocco and Tunisia, and approved sending French troops to the Suez canal area in 1956. In 1958 he opposed Charles de Gaulle's plans to create the new Fifth Republic. He remained a prominent socialist leader until the early 1970s.

Besides publishing several storybooks for children, he is also the author of several essays, such as *La Simple Vérité* (a history of the Resistance), *Khrushchev*, and *1956: Suez*.

A. Gazier, *Les Socialistes et l'Europe* (Paris, 1962); *The New York Times*, March 3, 1956; *Qui est qui en France, 1979–80* (Paris, 1979); R. Quilliot, *La SFIO et l'exercice du pouvoir, 1944–1958* (Paris, 1972).

C. Esposito

Related entries: CONSTITUTION OF THE FOURTH REPUBLIC; DECOLONIZATION; EUROPEAN DEFENSE COMMUNITY; FOREIGN POLICY; SOCIALIST PARTY (SFIO); SUEZ CRISIS.

PISANI, EDGARD (1918–), civil servant and cabinet minister, architect of agricultural reform in the 1960s, and a key figure in the crisis over New Caledonia in 1984–85. Born and raised in Tunis, Pisani was educated at the *Lycée Louis-le-Grand* and the *Faculté de droit* in Paris. He served the Liberation government as subprefect of police in 1944 and the Fourth Republic as prefect of the Haute-Loire and the Haute-Marne. In 1954 he was elected to the Senate for the Haute-Marne and took a seat with the democratic left (*gauche démocratique*). In 1961, amid massive demonstrations by farm syndicalists frustrated with the slow pace of agrarian change, Pisani joined the cabinet of Michel Debré and prepared new legislation to give force to the farm reform law of 1960. The resulting Pisani Charter, which became law in August 1962, increased the capacity of the state-run Land Management Society (SAFER) to purchase land and to make it available to modernizing farmers. It also created Social Action Funds to provide retiring farmers with supplementary pensions, thereby freeing yet more land for young farmers, and it authorized the formation of producer cooperatives to market crops. The Pisani Charter is widely credited for much of the improvement in French agriculture in the 1960s and 1970s.

Pisani stayed on as minister of agriculture in the Pompidou government in 1962–66, working to implement agrarian reform and defending the interests of French agriculture in the negotiation of the Common Agricultural Policy of the European Economic Community. In the cabinet shuffle following Charles de Gaulle's close call in the presidential election of 1965, Pisani moved to the Ministry of Transportation but resigned in 1967 in protest over Pompidou's use of emergency decree powers to enact economic and social reforms. His estrangement from the Gaullists continued the following year when, as deputy for the Maine-et-Loire, he voted to censure the government for its handling of the "events of May." He completed his political migration in the 1970's when he joined François Mitterrand's new Socialist party (PS). As a socialist he was again elected senator for the Haute-Marne in 1974.

After 1981 Pisani served the Mitterrand government in a number of capacities, first as French representative to the Commission of European Communities, and later as high commissioner and minister for New Caledonia. New Caledonia, France's nickel-rich island colony in the South Pacific, erupted in ethnic violence in the fall of 1984 as the native Kanaks sought independence. In December, Pisani was appointed high commissioner and charged with drafting a plan to give New Caledonia "self-determination." That plan, unveiled in January 1985, called for a referendum on independence by July. But in the face of further violence and the dispatching of one thousand French troops to the islands to maintain order, Pisani repeatedly modified his recommendations, ultimately settling on a bill calling for a four-part administrative division of the colony and creation of a new Territorial Assembly. As minister for New Caledonia, Pisani successfully shepherded this bill into law in August 1985 (it would be set aside by the Chirac government a year later). In November 1985 he resigned his cabinet post to become president of the *Société internationale du développement* while remaining *chargé de mission* for President Mitterrand. Never a major political figure in the traditional sense, Pisani was among the most prominent of the new breed of "technocrats"—nonideological technical experts and pragmatic problem solvers—who have had so much influence on policy making during the Fourth and Fifth Republics.

Pisani's published works include *La Région: Pour quoi faire* (1969), *L'Utopie foncière* (1977), *Socialiste en raison* (1978), and *La Main et l'outil* (1984).

J.-F. Doumic, H. Lacharmoise, eds., *Le Guide du pouvoir* (Paris, 1989).

M. S. Smith

Related entries: AGRICULTURE; MITTERRAND, FRANCOIS; NEW CALEDONIA; SOCIALIST PARTY (PS).

PLAN, or rather a series of plans, each covering a span of approximately four to five years, that have guided French economic development ever since 1947. In 1989 the Tenth Plan was published to cover the period until 1992. The dates of the earlier Plans are as follows: First Plan, 1947–53; Second Plan, 1954–57; Third Plan, 1958–61; Fourth Plan, 1962–65; Fifth Plan, 1966–70; Sixth Plan, 1971–75; Seventh Plan, 1976–80; Eighth Plan (prepared for the period 1981–85 but never submitted to parliament); Interim Plan (replacing Eighth Plan), 1982–83; Ninth Plan, 1984–88.

French planning has been characterized by its indicative rather than compulsory nature, aiming to complement rather than replace market forces. However, since its inception the nature of the Plan and its broad orientation have changed considerably. Thus, initially the prime goal was to ensure the modernization and reconstruction of the French economy in the immediate postwar period. Then, from the Third to Sixth Plans the main objective was to promote the strong growth of the economy. For the next three Plans, the principal concern was how to manage the economy during a period of recession, while the underlying theme for the Tenth Plan has been France's integration into Europe. Moreover, since the Seventh Plan there has been a move away from fixing rigid growth targets in favor of outlining broad growth strategies. Similarly the importance attached to the Plan has greatly diminished. In part this reflects an ideological shift favoring less state direction in the economy, but it also results from the increased difficulties of accurately forecasting growth as the French economy has become far more dependent on external forces.

P. Bauchet, *Le Plan dans l'économie française* (Paris, 1986), "Planifier aujourd'hui: Le X Plan 1989–1992," *Les Cahiers français* 242 (1989).

J. N. Tuppen

Related entry: INDUSTRIAL POLICY.

PLEVEN, RENE (1901–), businessman and politician who served with Jean Monnet on a purchasing mission to the United States in 1939–40. After the fall of France in 1940, Pleven responded to General Charles de Gaulle's appeal and held important positions in the Free French movement, including colonies, finance, and foreign affairs. After presiding over the Brazzaville Conference in January 1944, Pleven became minister for overseas France in the French provisional government of 1944 (subsequently Colonial Ministry) and then finance minister in 1945. In this latter post, differences with André Philip, his colleague from the Resistance and war years, and with Pierre Mendès-France, then minister of the national economy (MEN), led to the latter's resignation in April 1945 and a rejection of Mendès-France's austerity proposals for a strict control of currency to curb postwar inflationary pressures. After Mendès-France's resignation de Gaulle incorporated MEN into the Finance Ministry, and under Pleven's guidance the Fourth Republic's economic policies became less *dirigiste* and more liberal. Pleven argued for policies that would encourage investment, industrial modernization, and increased productivity, and at one time he claimed that for France it was either modernization or death. He was supported in his economic policies by other liberals, such as René Meyer and Emmanuel Monick, governor of the Bank of France.

After a period of ministerial instability that followed the formation of de Gaulle's Rally of the French People (RPF) in April 1947 and the dismissal of the communist ministers from the government in May of that year, Pleven urged a rapprochement between the Third Force parties of the center and center-left and the Gaullist RPF, a suggestion that evoked considerable skepticism among leaders of the Third Force parties, who feared de Gaulle's ambitions.

Pleven is perhaps best known for his proposed European Defense Community (EDC). When Pleven became prime minister on July 11, 1950, the Korean War had just erupted, intensifying the Cold War in Europe. With military forces committed to land operations in Asia, the U.S. government insisted upon strengthening Europe's defense by allowing the newly formed Federal Republic of Germany to rearm. The prospect of Germany again under arms frightened the French public, and Pleven sought a way to reassure his compatriots. On October 24, 1950 he proposed the formation of a European army under a European defense minister who would be under the control and supervision of a European assembly. German armed forces would exist only within an integrated

European military structure. Proponents considered the EDC to be a companion to the Schuman Plan in making possible West Germany's further integration into a Western European Community. After overcoming initial doubts in Washington, in London, and within the NATO command, the Western allies initialed the treaty in 1952. Although the Schuman Plan was ratified during Pleven's second ministry in 1951, by the time the EDC treaty reached the French Chamber of Deputies for final ratification in 1954, political circumstances had changed. East–West tensions had eased following Stalin's death, and the proposal itself had become greatly watered down during the negotiations from 1950 to 1952. The government of Mendès-France, preoccupied with liquidating the war in Indochina, refused to support ratification of EDC, and a combination of communist, Gaullist, and nationalist votes defeated the proposal.

Pleven held ministerial posts in several governments during the final years of the Fourth Republic, including foreign affairs in the very last government of May 1958. Pleven's rivalry with François Mitterrand for leadership of their left-of-center political party, the Democratic and Socialist Union of the Resistance (UDSR), was symptomatic of the confusion, political fragmentation, and paralysis that marked the last days of the Fourth Republic. Pleven continued to sit in the Chamber of Deputies under the Fifth Republic, although he never attained ministerial rank during de Gaulle's presidency. From 1958 to 1969 he served as a parliamentary representative to the Council of Europe in Strasbourg. After de Gaulle's retirement in 1969, Pleven became justice minister and keeper of the seals during the ministries of Jacques Chaban-Delmas and Pierre Messmer. In the parliamentary elections of March 1973, Pleven suffered a narrow defeat (51 votes) at the hands of the socialist candidate. Although Pleven continued to be active in local politics in Brittany until 1976, his national career ended with the 1973 defeat, after many years of honest, honorable, and solid service to his country.

J. Julliard, *La Quatrième République* (Paris, 1968); J. Pascal, *Les Deputés bretons* (Paris, 1983); J.-P. Rioux, *The Fourth Republic 1944–1958* (Cambridge, 1987).

J. K. Munholland

Related entries: DEMOCRATIC AND SOCIALIST UNION OF THE RESISTANCE; EUROPEAN DEFENSE COMMUNITY; FEDERAL REPUBLIC OF GERMANY, RELATIONS WITH; MITTERRAND, FRANCOIS; SCHUMAN PLAN.

POHER, ALAIN (1909–), longtime Christian democratic senator who, as the Senate's presiding officer, acted as president of the Republic after Charles de Gaulle's sudden resignation in 1969 and again after Georges Pompidou's death in 1974, and who was an unsuccessful candidate for the presidency in 1969. Born in Ablon-sur-Seine in the Seine-et-Oise department, Poher gathered both a law degree from the Paris Faculty of Law and an engineering diploma. He became *chef-de-cabinet* in the 1946 Schuman government, and beginning in 1946 was repeatedly elected to the Senate from the Seine-et-Oise. He served as secretary of state for finance in both the Schuman and Queuille governments in 1948–49, and presided over the Christian democratic group in the Senate (1954–57, 1959–60, 1966–69). Poher developed an interest in European integration and served on the European Committee for Iron and Coal (1954–55), presided over the Committee of the Common Market (1955–57), and after 1958 was a delegate to the European Parliament, which he presided over between 1966 and 1969. As president of the Senate (1968), he successfully led the opposition to de Gaulle's referendum proposing a lessened role for the Senate and the strengthening of regional administrative structures. He exercised the duties of the president of the Republic after de Gaulle's departure (April 28–June 19, 1969). As candidate for the presidency, he was defeated by Pompidou, who said that a Poher victory would return the country to the impotence experienced under the Fourth Republic. After Pompidou's death, Poher again acted as temporary president of the Republic (April 2–May 27, 1974). He was re-elected to the Senate by voters in the Val-de-Marne department in 1977.

J. Chapsal, A. Lancelot, *La Vie politique en France depuis 1940* (Paris, 1975).

L. Derfler

Related entries: ELECTIONS; POMPIDOU, GEORGES.

POLITICAL TRENDS, shaped in large part by Resistance leaders who also remembered the debilitating economic crises of the 1930s. From across the political spectrum as a generation, these political leaders agreed that national security and economic prosperity (as the foundation for military security) were the highest priorities of government. France struggled with a wide variety of constitutional institutions and many political parties after World War II compared to other European powers. Yet, the primary political goals of security and prosperity have largely been achieved for the generation from Charles de Gaulle to François Mitterrand. The viability of that political generation was not written so much in their constitutions as in the deep and broad domestic prosperity where for the first time in nearly a century the French population grew by almost a third, while life expectancy and income per capita rose at unprecedented rates. Moreover, despite real differences the established political parties from the Gaullists in government to the socialists and communists in opposition threw their lots together in defense of the Fifth Republic in its hour of greatest challenge in May of 1968.

After the Liberation in 1944 de Gaulle formed a provisional government from the leadership of the three major Resistance movements. Ranging from Christian democrats (MRP) and other Catholic resisters loyal to himself to communist militants who had carried a major share of the guerilla war against the Vichy regime and who only reluctantly gave up their guns and their own revolutionary aims late in 1944, to socialists, radicals, moderates, and conservatives who were steeped in the old politics of the late Third Republic, they all held in common the desire to provide for the military security of a France that had been invaded twice in living memory, and to avoid returning to the bleak impoverishment of the depression years. Even while these factions quarreled over the constitution of the Fourth Republic, they agreed to create the *Commissariat général au plan* (CGP) in 1946 under Jean Monnet, which would in the long run shift deeply divisive issues of economic policy from the realm of ideological political debate in the National Assembly to a more bureaucratic framework. These fundamental decisions to restore a republican style of government and to create a form of controlled, even governed capitalism, in effect settled the postwar political fate of the French Communist party (PCF), which was the largest and best-organized movement to emerge from the Resistance period. In agreeing to abandon the old communist goal of overthrowing the French republican and capitalist state in favor of a Soviet-style regime, the PCF cast itself as the major player in the loyal opposition during much of the Fourth and Fifth Republics. After these two fundamental compromises, the PCF faced a difficult struggle to distinguish its appeal from the openly reformist socialists. As a republican party the PCF had as much to gain or to lose as any of the other mainstream movements from the viability and stability of constitutional institutions.

The MRP introduced a second draft of the constitution and succeeded in gaining a popular majority in the referendum of October 1946, despite the opposition of de Gaulle in his famous Bayeux speech. Shortly afterward, tripartitism collapsed when inflation and massive labor strikes shook France. In May 1947 the communist ministers left the government, and the party went into the opposition in the National Assembly.

In 1946 France had as many peasants as industrial workers, but by the end of the Fourth Republic (1958) the number of farmers had fallen by over half, and in the next decade farmers declined to around 10 percent of the active labor force. Since conservative peasants in the Catholic west and other rural regions made up the greatest electoral block for the conservative parties, their political fortunes waned along with small-scale farming. Shops and similar small businesses also declined as waves of prosperity and commercial consolidation at the hands of the CGP swept over France. Briefly, the displaced shopkeepers found a champion in Pierre Poujade, the former Doriot-style fascist who appealed to France's ''little'' people. While the Poujade movement in itself was not a serious threat to the Fourth Republic, it did underscore the futility of traditional conservative political movements in the 1950s.

Radicals under Premiers Edgar Faure and Pierre Mendès-France rode the rightward drift to power during the later Fourth Republic, but like the conservatives their movement was rapidly losing constituencies and potential new leaders to Gaullists who took away the radical base in municipal government during the 1940s and early 1950s. The relentless movement of the population from tiny rural villages to large towns and cities across the postwar period meant that the historic dominance of the old conservativelike radical and traditional elites of the Third Republic and before was coming to an end.

France during the Fourth Republic had six major political groups: the conservatives and radicals, who faded with the fundamental demographic and economic changes in the country and the electorate; the socialists and the communists, already urban parties with the ability to adapt to the new political climate; and two new parties, the Christian democrats and de Gaulle's own loyal following, which eventually absorbed much of the momentum of the MRP as the Fourth Republic gave way to the Fifth. The new Gaullist Republic of the late 1950s simplified the political landscape with two primary political coalitions: on the right, the Gaullist party for the government with their constellation of minor conservative factions; and on the left, the Socialist and Communist parties. What all these new political movements of the Fifth Republic held in common was their growing prosperous urban electoral bases and the shared struggle of the Resistance.

Algeria tested the strength of the old political parties and the institutions of the Fourth Republic until they broke. In the face of a potential military coup, French president René Coty made General de Gaulle the last premier of the Fourth Republic in May 1958. De Gaulle acted quickly to put down any threat of rebellion by the disgruntled generals of the Algerian campaign and proposed a new constitution along the lines of his Bayeux speech of 1946. Voters approved the measure by a wide margin in September 1958, and de Gaulle became the founding president of the Fifth Republic.

De Gaulle built a mandate for his regime by placing the difficult issue of ending the colonial presence in Algeria before French voters in the referenda of January 1961 and April 1962 and by proposing in another referendum of October 1962 the direct election of the French president. In the 1965 presidential elections de Gaulle defeated the common candidate of the left, François Mitterrand, and seemingly placed the Fifth Republic on a stable course highlighted by calm detachment from colonial entanglements, independence in foreign policy and in economic policy, which produced a substantial improvement in the French standard of living. The goals of de Gaulle's generation were largely met in this period from 1962 to 1968.

The crisis of May 1968 proved to be the turning point for the Gaullist movement during the Fifth Republic. It played a critical role in reviving the stagnant Socialist party, which was far quicker in responding to the new political currents of the late 1960s than the PCF, which still was hamstrung by its orthodox and Stalinist leadership. Massive student demonstrations and wildcat strikes in Paris and throughout the country shocked de Gaulle's government and much of French society of the general's generation, which saw itself as at peace and relatively prosperous. After weeks of disorder, de Gaulle brought the episode to a close by calling for new elections in June 1968, which transformed the political discourse of the streets into a fairly traditional electoral contest between the two major political coalitions. Fearing a loss of deputies from a splintering of the electorate in many fringe left parties, the Communist party rallied its voters in defense of the Republic and its institutions. The results of the June elections largely favored the Gaullist coalition. Emboldened by this apparent show of support, de Gaulle proposed two constitutional amendments in the spring of 1969 in hopes of rebuilding his government's mandate just as he had done in the early 1960s. But French voters, and some members of his own coalition, such as future president Valéry Giscard d'Estaing, rejected the measures. Upon hearing the results, de Gaulle offered his resignation on June 20, 1969. He died in the following year.

The presidencies of the Gaullist Georges Pompidou and the conservative Giscard regime were marked by the rise of a new Socialist party (PS) and by growing economic difficulties. In May 1974 at the height of the oil crisis, the longtime finance minister Giscard narrowly defeated Mitterrand, once again the common candidate of the left, for the presidency. Despite a 1972 electoral alliance between the socialists and the communists, considerable rivalry between the PS and the PCF hampered their ability to campaign together in the late 1970s. While the leadership of both leftist parties remained firmly in the hands of leaders who derived their political standing in large part from their wartime records, the socialists managed to attract younger political leaders like Michel Rocard who attempted to weave linkages between the basic political objectives of the generation that fought the war and formed the Republics, and the young critics of the 1960s who were intensely concerned about the environment and bureaucratic excess.

In 1981 Mitterrand finally defeated the incumbent, Giscard, and became president of France, ending twenty-three years of right-wing control of government. In the subsequent legislative elections, Mitterrand's Socialist party won an absolute majority of seats. The new president appointed a socialist-dominated cabinet that also included four communist ministers. As the right splintered several smaller factions rose briefly in the 1980s to claim the attention of conservative and moderate voters. Giscard attempted to rally his Independent Republicans in the National Assembly as the Gaullist factions scrambled to lead the opposition to Mitterrand. Jacques Chirac, mayor of Paris, tried with limited success to build a new movement of conservative *notables* in big and small cities. His efforts reached their high point during the period of "shared governance" (*cohabitation*), when a conservative opposition won control of the National Assembly after the 1986 elections and forced the socialist Mitterrand to accept the conservative Chirac as premier. This power-sharing experiment ended in 1988 when the legislative elections of that year failed to give either the right or the left an absolute majority of seats, motivating Mitterrand (reelected in 1988) to appoint a minority cabinet headed by the socialist Rocard. As the socialist-dominated left revived its mandate in the late 1980s, the Gaullist and conservative coalition began to weaken further. On the far right was the challenge of the former *Poujadiste* Jean-Marie Le Pen, who launched his National Front (FN) on an appeal to exclude foreign and former colonial French workers from France in a campaign that was reminiscent of Vichy propaganda. While the FN appealed to some Gaullist supporters and some former communists, young reformers emerged in both Chirac's and Giscard's political formations that challenged the leadership of the old guard in the Gaullist and conservative camps in post–1988 France. Attempting to respond to these challenges, Chirac's *Rassem-*

blement pour la République (RPR) and Giscard's *Union pour la démocratie française* (UDF) announced in 1990 the foundation of a confederation called the *Union pour la France*. For the first time in history, the two parties will use a system of primaries to select a single candidate to represent them in the 1995 presidential elections. Thus, the Fifth Republic, unlike the Fourth, has witnessed the development of a presidential regime, the rise of a strong Socialist party under Mitterrand, the marginalization of the PCF, and the emergence of a centrist Republic.

For the generation of World War II, the Fourth Republic, and to a far greater extent the Fifth, provided for the national security and general prosperity that had eluded their parents' generation. What will emerge in France during the last decade of the twentieth century is a taking-up of political power by younger leaders and voters whose own historical experiences are radically different from those who laid out the foundations of the current political system.

J. Chapsal, *La Vie politique sous la Ve République* (Paris, 1981); P. Converse, R. Pierce, *Political Representation in France* (Cambridge, Mass., 1986); P. Williams, *Crisis and Compromise* (London, 1964).

P. A. Phillips

Related entries: CENTRIST PARTIES; CHRISTIAN DEMOCRATS; CLUB MOVEMENT; *COHABITATION*; COMMON PROGRAM; CONSTITUTION OF THE FIFTH REPUBLIC; CONSTITUTION OF THE FOURTH REPUBLIC; DE GAULLE, CHARLES; ECONOMIC TRENDS; ELECTIONS; ELECTORAL SYSTEM; FEDERATION OF THE DEMOCRATIC AND SOCIALIST LEFT; FRENCH COMMUNIST PARTY; GAULLISM; GAULLIST PARTY; GISCARD D'ESTAING, VALERY; LEFT RADICALS; LE PEN, JEAN-MARIE; MITTERRAND, FRANCOIS; POMPIDOU, GEORGES; POPULATION TRENDS; POUJADISTS; SOCIALIST PARTY (PS, SFIO); STUDENT REVOLTS; TRIPARTITISM; UNION FOR FRENCH DEMOCRACY; UNION OF THE LEFT.

POMPIDOU, GEORGES (1911–1974), premier and second president of France's Fifth Republic. Pompidou was born July 5, 1911 at Montboudif, in the Auvergne region of central France. He chose an academic career and excelled in classical languages and in philosophy at the prestigious *Ecole normale supérieure* and political science at the *Ecole libre des sciences politiques*. While a *lycée* professor, he entered military service in 1939. In 1944 he joined Charles de Gaulle's staff and the personal cabinet of the general's provisional government. Pompidou became a member of the Gaullist *Rassemblement du peuple français* (Rally of the French People, RPF) and was active in its executive, but in 1953 advised de Gaulle to disown the movement and remain aloof from Fourth Republic politics. He refused government positions himself. In 1955 he took a post with the Rothschild bank and within a year became its chief director.

The uprising of 1958 returned Pompidou to political life, first on de Gaulle's staff (where in 1961 at de Gaulle's request he opened contacts with the Algerian rebels in Switzerland), then on the Constitutional Council, until he was asked in April 1962 to form a government. Though his lack of political experience initially aroused hostility among Gaullists, who recollected that he had not been among the general's original supporters in London or active in plots aimed at overthrowing the Fourth Republic, he was successful. As prime minister, he readily acknowledged the supremacy of the president and worked to assure himself a leadership position within the Gaullist party.

De Gaulle appeared baffled in handling the May 1968 rising of students and workers, and it was Pompidou who opened negotiations with the trade unions, persuaded the president to abandon (temporarily) his proposed referendum on labor's ''participation in management'' and dissolve the National Assembly instead, and to campaign hard in the subsequent election. Accordingly, Pompidou was perceived as the architect of the subsequent electoral victory. In July, de Gaulle nevertheless replaced him as head of the government and Pompidou withdrew from active politics until April 1969, when de Gaulle resigned his presidency after his proposals to restructure the Senate and provide greater regional autonomy were defeated in a national referendum.

Pompidou emerged as the Gaullist candidate in the presidential election of 1969. In a well-organized and intense campaign, he placed stress on ''continuity in change'' and on the presence of the Gaullist majority already seated in the National Assembly. On the second ballot he defeated his chief competitor, the centrist candidate Alain Poher, and, by amassing more votes than had de Gaulle in the previous presidential election, demonstrated that the Fifth Republic could survive without the general.

During his five years in office and in part because of his need to develop his own base of authority by reaching out to centrists, Pompidou furthered presidential domination over the government. He could not claim, as had de Gaulle, to stand above the fray. He appeared more friendly and more available than his ''remote and regal'' predecessor. The Elysée became more accessible, the work load of its staff was reduced, more vacations were taken by the president, his press conferences were less formal, and, though he traveled extensively, he preferred small and well-planned appearances to de Gaulle's huge crowds. His choice of prime minister, Jacques Chaban-Delmas, had fought as a ''companion'' to de Gaulle, but had also been a member of the Radical party and Fourth Republic minister. Veteran non-Gaullists sat in the government, and this movement toward the political center meant less need for reliance on the Gaullists. Within two years, Pompidou asserted his right to exercise full presidential power, insisted that his jurisdiction extended to all state interests, and that as head of the legislative majority he was the effective head of the government, not the arbiter called for by the constitution. Like de Gaulle, Pompidou did not hesitate to dismiss his prime minister abruptly in January 1972, even though Chaban-Delmas had won a large vote of confidence from the Assembly the previous June, replacing him with the more subservient Pierre Messmer. The belief that the prime minister derived his power from the president and not from the constitution or the Assembly was now firmly rooted in the Fifth Republic because Pompidou as well as de Gaulle had put it into practice.

Pompidou saw as his chief goal the full modernization and industrialization of France. Most outstanding, if not most appreciated, were the commercial complex at *La Défense* outside Paris and the Center for Contemporary Art, a museum and library complex open to the public at place Beaubourg in central Paris. In the realm of foreign affairs, Pompidou appears to have differed most from his predecessor. Unhappy when de Gaulle had vetoed the British application for entry into the Common Market, Pompidou as president approved the admission of Britain, Denmark, and Ireland. Yet, like de Gaulle, the president opposed broadening the powers of the Community's executive council and rejected any movement toward political integration. Also like his predecessor, Pompidou showed no interest in returning France to NATO's military arm. Nor did any change take place in either the *force de frappe* (France's nuclear deterrent system) or the country's pro-Arab policy, as shown in the 1970 sale of Mirage fighter planes to Libya. One conspicuous defeat was the president's inability to marshal adequate support for a proposed constitutional reform reducing the presidential tenure from seven to five years, the same term of office as for deputies. Other losses included government bills on administrative reform and veterans' pensions, which were severely amended or withdrawn.

Like de Gaulle, Pompidou saw the president as solely responsible for the nation's foreign policy. He announced his own decisions here (e.g., France's support for the British entry into the Common Market) without going through his ministers, though not as spectacularly as de Gaulle. Pompidou called for seven European summit meetings; he hosted the Soviet chiefs twice and twice visited the Soviet Union and he traveled to French Africa and China. But aside from his devaluation of the franc and approval of Britain's entry into the European Economic Community, he reversed none of de Gaulle's policies or practices.

Pompidou intervened actively in the legislative election of 1973, in which a left-wing victory had appeared quite possible thanks to an agreement reached by socialists and communists on a "common program." In formally opening the campaign on February 8, the president predicted that a leftist victory would "completely upset the institutions of the Fifth Republic." He participated more actively after the first round of votes, describing the contest as one between "Marxists" and "all the others" and (on television) as threatening a loss of freedom if the left won, and was able to take some credit for the majority's sixty-seat plurality. Aware of his debt to his centrist allies, Pompidou moderated his policies and took fewer initiatives in what proved to be his final year of office. For example, the government took no official stand during Israel's Yom Kippur war. Pompidou remained personally popular, with over 50 percent of those questioned expressing satisfaction with him. He continued to give television interviews, offering opinions on art and architecture as well as politics.

The government kept Pompidou's failing health a secret for at least a year, but toward the end of March 1974 the president told his closest advisers that he suffered from a rare and fatal cancer. He died on April 2.

G. Aubray, *Georges Pompidou, un portrait* (Paris, 1969); J. Chapsal, A. Lancelot, *La Vie politique en France depuis 1940* (Paris, 1975); L. Derfler, *President and Parliament: A Short History of the French Presidency* (Boca Raton, Fla., 1983); S. Rials, *Les Idées politiques du président Georges Pompidou* (Paris, 1977); P. Rouanet, *Pompidou* (Paris, 1969).

L. Derfler

Related entries: CHABAN-DELMAS, JACQUES; CHIRAC, JACQUES, GAULLIST PARTY; GREAT BRITAIN, RELATIONS WITH; MESSMER, PIERRE; PARIS REGION; POHER, ALAIN; URBANIZATION; WESTERN EUROPEAN UNION.

PONIATOWSKI, MICHEL (PRINCE) (1922–), minister of the interior under Valéry Giscard d'Estaing and Giscard's closest political adviser in the 1970s. Born into a noble family of Italian and Polish extraction, Poniatowski went to Algiers during World War II, joined a Free French battalion of paratroopers, and was parachuted into France during the invasion of Provence. He studied law following the war and entered the *Ecole nationale d'administration* (ENA) in 1946.

From 1949 to 1952 he was the *chef du cabinet* of the director of finances in Morocco, was financial attaché in Washington, D.C. in 1956, and took the post of *directeur de cabinet* of Giscard from 1959 to 1962. First general secretary, then president of the *Républicains indépendants* (RI) from 1967 on, Poniatowski was deputy from the Val d'Oise and was mayor of the Isle-Adam in the 1970s. He was elected to the European Parliament in 1979.

Under Prime Minister Pierre Messmer, Poniatowski became minister of public health and social security in 1973, when Georges Pompidou was president. Upon Giscard's election in 1974, he was named minister of the interior under Prime Minister Jacques Chirac, and he continued in his post until March 1977, when he was replaced by Christian Bonnet. In 1977, Giscard appointed him as his personal "roving ambassador." He has returned to his writing career since leaving politics and has written several works on Charles Maurice de Talleyrand, a distant relative.

Poniatowski was vilified by the left as a repressive minister; he had publicly complained that judges were too lenient in France and that the police should have the right to enter any building, including churches and universities, if necessary. He ordered the police to evacuate several churches that had been occupied by prostitutes, notably in Lyon.

He angered some magistrates by publicly declaring his support for the death penalty for the murderer Patrick Henry, thereby breaking the tradition of "separation of powers" by appearing to influence the judicial branch. He organized police patrols in the *métro* that included identity checks of foreigners, prompting accusations by the left that such measures were racist. At the same time, he reduced the number of authorized telephone wiretaps and ended the practice of requiring clients to fill out police registration forms when checking into hotels.

He also had his disagreements with the Gaullists. In 1971 at a congress of the RI, he had called for the creation of a great "federation of the center," of right and left. When Chirac was prime minister, Poniatowski was known as the *premier des ministres*, and disagreements between the two were common. He had previously denounced the Gaullist monopoly on state posts, deriding *les copains et les coquins*. He remained a fervent supporter of Giscard, and the two maintained a close relationship.

X. de la Fournière, *Michel Poniatowski à la recherche de l'avenir* (Paris, 1979).

H. B. Sutton

Related entry: GISCARD D'ESTAING, VALERY.

POPULAR CULTURE, a complex of widespread forms of living and thinking (references and values), much of which is regularly represented in the mass media, is urban in origin and inspiration, and—especially since the 1950s—is oriented to youth. The more traditional popular cultures of local work group, family, and community life have continued their long decline or have disappeared along with the peasants and artisans who sustained them for centuries. In its contemporary forms particularly, popular culture is not cleanly divorced from culture associated with an elite; borrowings and cross-influences are common. It is generally an unstable mix of various social groups' cultures, often in tension if not conflict. A large part of contemporary popular culture is shaped and mirrored by cinema, radio, and television and centers on the consumption of industrial products and commercial leisure activities. This part is often called *mass culture,* a term now frequently used without its original connotations of uniformity and unmitigated dominance by the powerful. Radio and television, for example, remain the two most important mass media, but have clearly become more diversified and less tightly controlled by the state in the 1980s.

The postwar era opened to the sounds of jazz. In late 1945 Paris youth flocked to *caves* and cafés of Saint-Germain-des-Prés to dance *le be-bop* and *le jitterbug* and to listen to new songs. There the careers of Juliette Greco, Francis Claude, Léo Ferré, and the Frères Jacques took off. Radio and records—especially the new long-playing record from 1949 on—spread their songs throughout France. Outside the Latin Quarter such new stars as Yves Montand, Charles Aznavour, and Gilbert Bécaud ("Monsieur 100,000 volts") also helped revitalize French song, in part through fresh jazz effects.

Such singers became idols for their crowds of fans, and concerts in the late 1950s and 1960s became rites of collective delirium for youth, especially with the introduction of American rock and roll in the late fifties. In 1960 teenager Johnny Hallyday made his Paris music-hall debut and quickly became the first French rock or *yé-yé* idol.

Of the media, radio was the one most thoroughly woven into the fabric of everyday life. Since the last years of the Third Republic it was a commonplace consumer item and source of news and entertainment and has remained so. At the end of 1945 over 5,345 million radios were in use in France. In 1958 there were twice that number. Programming that was most popular consisted of pop music, game shows, and serials. Around 1960 an airwaves club called ''*Salut les copains*'' strengthened the group consciousness of youth and brought them quantities of the latest rock music, their generational touchstone.

For cinema, too, a new era was opening. In 1956 Roger Vadim's *Et Dieu créa la femme* (And God Created Woman) became a commercial success that made Brigitte Bardot the leading model of erotic beauty and heralded an emergent youth subculture. In the late 1950s Alain Resnais, Jean-Luc Godard, Claude Chabrol, and François Truffaut initiated their celebrated new wave of innovative films, many of which became popular with the public at large. At the same time older-style comedies and *policiers* continued to draw large audiences. Then in the 1960s movie attendance declined sharply as television spread: Between 1957 and 1966 annual cinema attendance fell from 411 to 232 million. Yet, cinema has remained the most frequented paid-admission entertainment.

Television was slower to spread in France than in West Germany and Britain. In 1955 only 260,508 sets existed. In 1957 only a third of the territory—and 50 percent of the population—was able to receive television. Televisions in cafés, however, multiplied the number of spectators. During the Fifth Republic the number of sets soared to eleven million in 1973 and almost sixteen million in 1980. In the 1980s the French spent more time viewing television than in any other free-time activity. Films have generally drawn the largest audiences. The American serial ''Dallas'' became a mass favorite during much of the 1980s. The popularity of ''*Apostrophes*'' (1975–90), a weekly discussion of books, not only showed the continuing prestige of print culture, but also helped to strengthen the otherwise competing leisure activities of book buying and reading.

Until the 1960s these cultural changes did not stem from growing amounts of leisure time. In the era of postwar reconstruction the work week increased for most people. Although in the 1950s the full weekend of free time became widespread for workers (but not for schoolchildren), the working hours per week remained high. The biggest advance was the granting of a third week of annual paid vacation to workers in 1956.

The late 1960s and 1970s brought most working people significant gains in free time along with dramatic increases in consumption. From 1960 to 1979, as household consumption doubled in value, the part of household expenses devoted to culture and leisure rose from 5.5 percent to 7.6 percent. The average workweek shortened from 45.2 hours in 1960 to 40.8 in 1980. Workers gained a fourth week of annual paid vacation in 1965. One flourishing expression of the vacation ideal was the rapidly expanding *Club Méditerranée*, which Gérard Blitz founded in 1950.

A Ministry of Culture was created for the first time in 1959 by the new Fifth Republic. The first minister, André Malraux, worked to give more people access to the arts, long associated with cultural and social elites. Rarely did the cultural elite recognize achievement in popular culture, as it did in 1967 when the *Académie française* gave Georges Brassens its *Prix de poésie*.

In the 1960s modern-style folk songs and protest songs became popular.

Brassens, Jacques Brel, and Ferré, notably, gave voice to the spirit of *contestation*. Stars rooted in an earlier era were passing on (Edith Piaf died in 1963; Maurice Chevalier retired in 1968). A remarkable exception was Charles Trenet, a star of the 1930s who continued his career into the 1980s without being hopelessly *démodé*.

The student rebellion of the spring of 1968 challenged not only wielders of power in universities, business, and government but also the dominant culture sustained by them and in particular the state-controlled media. Rallying around the themes of imagination and individual liberation, the 1968 movement grew out of and furthered a counterculture that heightened awareness of the environment and quality of life as opposed to technocratic and productionist values and a modernist urbanism. In the aftermath some urban youth moved to the country and attempted to live their values there. In the early 1970s the Breton Alain Stivell and other regionalist folksingers gained a large following.

The election of socialist François Mitterrand as president in 1981 brought conspicuous changes in cultural policy. His first minister of culture, Jack Lang, favored more cultural diversity and was more accepting of contemporary popular culture than his predecessors, although he kept control of monies allocated for regional productions. Under his leadership the state created a *musée de la bande dessinée* (comic strip museum) at Angoulême, founded a circus school at Chalons, and constructed a two-thousand-seat concert hall in Paris, the *Zénith*, designed primarily for rock concerts. The new socialist government also reduced the legal work week to thirty-nine hours and introduced a fifth week's paid vacation for workers in 1982.

In the same year new legislation governing the audiovisual system opened the way to the creation of dozens of *radios libres*, many of which almost continuously played American and English rock music. Within a few years there were some nine hundred "free" radio stations, catering to specialized, local audiences drawn together by specific political, ethnic, religious, or cultural interests. Radio in recent years has thus gone strikingly counter to the theoretical model of mass culture as a world of more or less uniform and passive audiences consistently taking in standardized messages.

The expansion of the audiovisual has not been consistently at the expense of reading as a leisure activity. The number of newspapers and their circulation have declined sharply since 1945, but the buying and reading of books have not. Tops in reading choices are contemporary novels. In 1978 Harlequin romance novels were launched in France and quickly became the best-selling collection. Magazines for various cultural niches and cartoon albums (*bandes dessinées* or BDs)—not just for youthful readers—have also thrived in recent decades. *Télé 7 Jours*, launched in 1960, quickly became the best-selling periodical. Popularized history magazines and books have also enjoyed a large readership unmatched in the United States and Great Britain.

Spectator sports have been important through the entire period as a business and a leisure activity for millions. The annual *Tour de France* has long drawn the biggest following—in person along the roads and via the media. World Cup soccer matches have occasioned record-setting large television audiences. In the 1980s the number of participants in sports increased dramatically, particularly individual sports such as *le jogging*, tennis, skiing, and squash.

Since the late 1950s, American rock and then American television have had a large impact in France. And American films continued to enjoy box-office success in France as they had for most of the time since World War I. In the 1980s Minister Lang repeatedly attacked such importations as "cultural imperialism." His critiques to date, however, have not had a notable effect. At the end of 1992 the new Europe will become the arena for grappling with this problem of preserving national identity while remaining open to other cultures.

J. Ardagh, *France Today* (London, 1988); R. Barthes, *Mythologies* (Paris, 1957); M. Crubellier, *Histoire culturelle de la France, XIXe-XXe siècle* (Paris, 1974); J. Dumazedier, A. Ripert, *Loisir et culture* (Paris, 1966); P. Ory, *L'Entre deux-mai, histoire culturelle de la France* (Paris, 1983).

C. Rearick

Related entries: BROADCAST MEDIA; CINEMA; CULTURAL POLICY; LANG, JACK; LEISURE; PRESS; SOCIAL TRENDS; SPORTS.

POPULATION TRENDS, a great concern of various governments in postwar France. During the thirty "glorious years" between 1945 and 1975, the French population grew at historically unprecedented rates, jumping from 39.7 million to 52.7 million, an increase of almost one-third. Growth came from a wide variety of forces, which are often attributed to rapid modernization. Birthrates increased while death rates declined. French prosperity attracted many immigrants from former colonies and from other parts of Europe. Yet, after the change in life-styles that accompanied the May movement in the late 1960s and early 1970s and with the return of economic distress in the mid-1970s, French birthrates began to decline dramatically. Despite continued declines in mortality and persistent immigration, total population growth slowed considerably. By 1988 the French population had risen only to fifty-six million. Yet, at that rate of growth, 0.4 percent in 1987, France might be expected to represent a larger portion of the total European population by the end of the century than its even slower-growing European neighbors, such as the United Kingdom.

The baby boom in France actually began during World War II when under the Occupation French families remained intact while the war divided families in most of the rest of Europe. From the war period to 1964 the number of children born to French mothers (the measure of fecundity) jumped from 1.82 to 2.9, and across those years the additional births in effect replaced the losses attributed to the deaths in the Great War and to the low birthrates of the entire period since the Franco-Prussian War (1870). After 1976, however, the rate of fecundity fell back to 1.83, initiating the period dubbed the "baby crash." Explanations for the drop in births include economic hard times after the oil crisis in 1973, longer years of schooling for women, a dramatic increase in divorce rates (under 6%

in 1913, and nearly 40% in 1985) and life-style choices in which young couples live together for a period before marriage, but without children. In addition, today the majority of families have one or two children, sharply contrasting with the 45 percent of families that had four or more children in 1911.

Death rates declined across the twentieth century, with a sharp drop during the post–World War II period. Over the near half-century between 1936 and 1982, death rates fell by over 50 percent. On the eve of the Great War, male life expectancy was 48.5 years, and female expectancy was 52.4. In 1988 men lived on average to 74 and women to 80, with the most common age of death being considerably higher (80 for men and 84 for women). These changes reflected the sharp decline in infant mortality, general prosperity, and advances in medical technology. In 1911 over a third of the population was under twenty, despite the very high infant mortality rates of that period, but only 12 percent were over sixty. In 1988 the segment of the population under twenty had fallen by 5 percent and the segment over sixty had increased by virtually the same amount. The middle segment from twenty-one to sixty remained unchanged. Because of the greater numbers of male wartime deaths and general survival rates, far more French women than French men are among the elderly population. Declining death rates and great survival rates contributed to the general increase in the population in the second half of the twentieth century.

Immigration from the former French colonies in Asia, North Africa, and sub-Saharan Africa contributed also to the growth in the French population and has posed a variety of problems for French society. According to the 1982 census, at least 6.6 percent (1,556,000) of the active work force came from abroad. Legal immigration accounts for about a third of the foreign population residing in France, another one-third are the children of foreign workers who claim both proper French citizenship and sometimes standing in the country of their parents' origin, and there are many illegal immigrants, possibly equaling the number of legal, invited foreigners. Differences in language, religion, family, and cultural mores have produced a sharp segregation of immigrants in French society. The perception that the foreign population in France is growing at a rapid rate and in ways different from the patterns of France as a whole has produced considerable social and political tension, especially in the 1980s and early 1990s.

Since the end of World War II, population trends have become national, with a handful of exceptions, such as Corsica and Brittany. Urbanization has contributed to muting of differences as France approached the mark of a 75 percent urban population in the 1980s. Urban growth has been especially strong in the Paris basin, along the northern and southern coasts, and at cities designated as "poles of attraction" (Bordeaux, Nantes, Lyon). Much of the movement to urban areas has taken place in systematically planned suburban ZPIUs (*zones de peuplement industriel et urbain*).

France has been very much like its Western European neighbors in most of these trends in population growth, changing family life, age structures, and immigration patterns during the postwar period. The overarching change in those years, however, has been the far more rapid growth of the rest of the world's population, especially in poorer and more distant countries. Before the Great War, Europe of the Twelve represented around 11 percent of the world's population, but today it constitutes less than 7 percent. As a mere 11 percent of the total European population, France like Britain may face challenges over its position on the Security Council of the United Nations and in other international matters, if worldwide population growth produces comparable shifts in economic and political power.

J. Dupaquier, ed., *Histoire de la population française*, vol. 4 (Paris, 1988).

P. A. Phillips

Related entries: ECONOMIC TRENDS; IMMIGRANTS; LABOR FORCE; MINORITIES, PROBLEMS OF; POLITICAL TRENDS; SOCIAL TRENDS; URBANIZATION.

POUJADISTS, supporters of Pierre Poujade, who led a revolt of small shopkeepers and artisans in the 1950s that symbolized resistance to economic modernization and France's diminished role on the global scene. Poujade, a shopkeeper, was born in Saint-Céré (Lot) in 1920. In 1953 he founded the *Union de défense des commerçants et artisans* (UDCA), which protested *les contrôles fiscaux* and taxes by launching a tax revolt. His right-wing and antiparliamentary movement played to the "*petits*" against the rich and the bureaucrats, as well as the provinces and victims of economic change against the authority of the state. In many ways the Poujadist movement was a reaction to new and significant changes in the postwar world: industrial modernization and the rise of the large firms, decolonization (e.g., Indochina and Algeria), and the decline of French power and prestige. A chauvinistic and imperialistic nationalism characterized the Poujadists.

In the January 1956 parliamentary elections the Poujadists campaigned under the banner "*Sortez les sortants*" and captured more than 11 percent of the vote, giving them fifty-two deputies in the National Assembly who formed a group known as *Union et fraternité françaises*. Yet, beginning in 1957 Poujadist strength declined as a result of the rise of Gaullism in France. Both Poujadist deputies and electors voted for the return of General Charles de Gaulle to power in 1958. The president of the UDCA, however, was strictly opposed to the Algerian policy of the general and did not rally behind de Gaulle's new Fifth Republic until 1966.

A number of *Organisation de l'armée secrète* (OAS) members and supporters were former Poujadists. Jean-Marie Le Pen, head of the racist and chauvinistic National Front in France today, was also once among the ranks of the Poujadists, elected as a Poujadist deputy in 1956.

Grand dictionnaire encyclopédique Larousse (Paris, 1984); S. Hoffmann, *In Search of France* (Cambridge, Mass., 1963); *Le Mouvement Poujade* (Paris, 1956).

W. Northcutt

Related entries: ECONOMIC TRENDS; ELECTIONS; LE PEN, JEAN-MARIE; POLITICAL TRENDS.

PRESS, general-interest newspapers and magazines. The French are avid consumers of general-interest newspapers and magazines, which in turn reflect the broad range of ideological orientations found in the body politic. In few other Western democracies are politicians, political parties, and the advocacy or opposition to party programs as intimately associated with the press as they are in France. Individual newspapers are often vital elements of national political identity, but also of the machinery by which regional *notables* have ruled their fiefdoms. Obvious examples include or have included the national daily *L'Humanité,* the official organ of the Communist party (PCF); the *Provençale* empire radiating out of Marseille, controlled for decades by the long-time mayor of that city, the socialist Gaston Defferre; and the press group of the right-wing politician Robert Hersant, whose flagship paper, *Le Figaro,* led that group's virulent opposition to socialist rule in the 1980s.

In general terms, the ideology of journalistic objectivity has never found firm roots in France. The ideology is even actively resisted, and this resistance constitutes an accepted "rule of the game" governing the interplay of French journalism and politics. Unlike the Anglo-American press, newspapers in France do not have an editorial page; facts and commentary are instead freely mixed. Since the 1970s, the press industry has undergone rapid and dramatic transformation, as bankruptcies, mergers, and takeovers have concentrated ownership in the hands of large press groups, most notably that of Hersant. Not surprising, given the political stakes involved, government attempts to regulate this and other aspects of the industry have been deeply divisive; in the 1980s, for example, only the politics of nationalizations and privatizations were more salient or controversial.

Approximately five hundred newspapers, of which about ninety are general interest dailies, and nearly twenty-five hundred periodicals are published in France today. Parisian dailies, which collectively constitute the "national press," include the following (with recent but only approximate circulation figures):

- *Le Figaro* (433,000), *France-soir* (410,000), *L'Aurore* (variable), all of which were acquired by the Hersant press group between 1976 and 1978. *Le Figaro,* one of France's oldest newspapers (founded in 1828), remains the most influential conservative daily in France. Once well known as the forum for such intellectuals as Raymond Aron, both the paper's quality and respect for it in elite circles seriously declined after the Hersant takeover. Due to the fact that it is distributed free of charge by the tens of thousands, its circulation figures are inflated. *France-soir* focuses more on human interest stories and entertainment than it does on current affairs. *L'Aurore* lost its autonomy in 1978 after having been acquired by Hersant, and it is today published by the staff of *Le Figaro* as a twin of that paper.
- *Le Monde* (362,000), journal of record, the most prestigious French daily, and the paper most widely read by politicians, intellectuals, and other elites. *Le Monde* has a tendency to lean leftward, but diversity of opinion is tolerated within the organization and actively solicited in the form of regular guest commentaries.
- *Le Parisien,* formerly *Le Parisien libéré* (339,000), a paper appealing to a broad audience.

- *Libération* (165,000), an unabashedly left-wing daily aimed at a younger audience. Its circulation has climbed steadily since its founding in 1973.
- *L'Humanité* (117,000), the official paper of the Communist party. Founded in 1904 by Jean Jaurès, *L'Humanité* was published as the organ of the Socialist party (SFIO) until 1920, when the PCF was formed. Its circulation has declined with Communist party membership.
- *La Croix* (113,000), France's Catholic daily, and *Le Quotidien* (75,000), which leans to the right, are the remaining general-interest national dailies (the left-leaning *Le Matin* declared bankruptcy in 1988). The leading national financial daily is *Les Echos* (73,000).

The provincial press is today dominated by large press groups, the most important of which are the Hersant group, which owns papers in the north of France and, more important, enjoys an absolute monopoly in the nation's largest multipaper regional market, the Rhône valley (since Hersant's achievement of this monopoly position in 1986, *Le Monde* and *Libération* have published Lyon editions); and the Hachette group, which now dominates the market in the Provence-Marseille region.

Among all nations, France is second only to the United States in total number of periodicals published. The increasingly conservative *L'Express*, with a circulation of about 600,000, is the biggest-selling prestige weekly, followed by the socialist-leaning *Le Nouvel Observateur* (420,000) and *Le Point* (335,000).

State regulation of the industry has structured the development of the French press. In the twentieth century, governments have sought not to censure written expression, but to regulate issues concerning ownership and control. The press law of July 29, 1881, which remains on the books, established what was probably the most liberal license to print anywhere in the world, by virtually interdicting state regulation of the industry. Thus encouraged, newspapers proliferated. But between the wars, a dramatic consolidation of the industry by large financial and business concerns took place. Newspapers, reflecting the politics of the day, polarized between left and right, and fierce polemical battles were waged in the press over social politics. By the 1930s, vicious defamation campaigns against rival politicians became the rule; libel actions, however, were seriously hampered by the fact that the identities and financial profiles of newspaper owners and publishers were carefully held secrets. The short-lived Léon Blum government proposed legislation to force papers to divulge their financial and management structures, but the government fell before the bill was passed.

Under the Occupation major newspapers continued to be published as organs of Nazi propaganda. With the Liberation, many of the established press groups of the Third Republic were dismantled, their property confiscated along with their rights to publish. These were then distributed among Resistance groups and to publishers who had chosen to close down their newspapers rather than print under Nazi tutelage and censorship. Of the thirty-one dailies published in Paris in 1939, only ten were allowed to begin publishing in 1944, also the date when several important new papers, including *France-soir*, *Le Monde*, *Le Parisien libéré*, as well as a majority of present-day provincial papers were founded.

In 1944 as well, the National Council of the Resistance adopted an *ordonnance* designed to insure the long-term success of this restructuring. The *ordonnance* sought to regulate the industry in two ways. First, it established the right of readers to know who owns and manages the newspapers and magazines they read, and from where their financial resources come; in the process the text forbade the use, extensive before the war, of fronts—bogus names and organizations—to disguise true ownership. Second, the *ordonnance* forbade any one person from owning more than one publication, the so-called one-man/one-newspaper rule.

Until 1984, the 1944 text constituted the main antitrust provision governing the industry. But the rules it contained were never applied. Politicians and publishers were more comfortable not applying the provisions than either enforcing them or seeking to create a new regime. For most of the 1945–70 period the French press was nevertheless among Europe's most vital and diverse.

During the 1970–86 period, the newspaper industry was transformed by business failures and the formation of large press groups. The figures are striking: In 1946, there were 28 Parisian and 175 regional dailies; today, there are 9 Parisian dailies and fewer than 80 regional papers. This dramatic development is due to a number of factors, including ever-rising printing costs and increased competition from information sources such as radio and television. In political terms, however, even more important have been the activities of one man, Robert Hersant, whose group aggressively entered the newspaper market in the early 1970s, and by 1986 controlled 38 percent of the national (i.e., Parisian) and 26 percent of the regional markets for dailies.

By 1979 intense political pressure led then prime minister Raymond Barre to promise new legislation to update or replace the 1944 text as a means, not least, of halting the Hersant group's relentless expansion. No bill was produced by the Barre government, however, and after the *alternance* of 1981 the issue was left to the socialists to resolve. Proposition 95 of the socialists' 1981 electoral manifesto declared that the 1944 *ordonnance* would be applied, but in 1983 the government of Pierre Mauroy sponsored legislation to replace it. The ensuing legislative debate was the most rancorous in the history of the Fifth Republic, breaking records for length of debate and for the use of obstruction tactics by the opposition. In essence, the bill as finally adopted required papers to divulge details of their ownership and management structure and forbade any one person or group from owning multiple papers if their combined share of the market (national or regional) surpassed 15 percent; its most spectacular effect would have been to dismantle the Hersant group. Upon adoption, the opposition referred the bill to the Constitutional Council, which in October 1984 ruled that the legislature could use such fixed market ceilings to protect what it called "press pluralism," but that it could not apply these ceilings to "preexisting situations," that is, to Hersant. Hersant's dominance was thus frozen, since no other group could surpass the 15 percent ceilings (which were below the share controlled by the Hersant group).

Even before the 1986 elections the right-wing majority in the Senate wrote and passed a bill to abrogate the 1984 press law. Upon taking office in 1986 the conservative Chirac government threw its support behind the bill, which was adopted in July 1986. During these debates the new government and its majority argued that concentration had actually strengthened diversity in the industry (since otherwise weak dailies would have failed had they not been absorbed by stronger groups); it therefore opposed the fixed ceilings as counterproductive. Fear that the Constitutional Council would require some form of antitrust provision to protect press pluralism, however, led the majority to replace the ceilings, albeit raised to 30 percent of the total market, thus accommodating, but just barely, the Hersant group. The Constitutional Council accepted the ceilings but not the abrogation of the 1984 provisions that sought to prevent the use of fronts to disguise ownership; the government was thus forced to rewrite these provisions in accordance with the Council's ruling.

Despite legal reforms, the economic situation that publishers will confront in the 1990s will be even less favorable than it has been in the past two decades. Most important, private radio and television stations have proliferated in recent years, increasing competition for public attention and advertising revenue. Further concentration in the industry is therefore probably inevitable.

P. Albert, *La Presse* (Paris, 1988); Documentation française, *Notes et études: La Presse française* (Paris, 1985); J. W. Freiberg, *The French Press* (New York, 1981); M. Jamet, *La Presse périodique en France* (Paris, 1983); M. Mathieu, *La Presse quotidienne régionale* (Paris, 1985).

A. Stone

Related entries: HERSANT, ROBERT; POLITICAL TRENDS.

PRIVATIZATION, the effort of the Chirac government (1986–88) to privatize a large segment of state-owned industry. In the 1980s, governments of different political persuasions in countries at different stages of development, and for a whole host of different reasons, questioned the role of the state in the economy. With widespread and increasing indebtedness, many turned to the public sector as a major source of savings. During the period of *cohabitation* (1986–88), France embarked on the most ambitious privatization program to be drawn up by any West European country. Finance Minister Edouard Balladur made even the nationalizations of 1982—themselves unprecedented in any developed country—look small-scale by proposing to privatize, in the short space of five years, sixty-five major companies with an overall value of 275 billion francs. That the program was prematurely cut short first by the stock market crash of October 1987, then by the electoral defeat of the French right-wing majority in the legislative elections of June 1988, left Britain as the undisputed front-runner in this worldwide dash to privatization.

If the sheer scope of the French project was bewildering, privatization itself came as no surprise to anyone. It had featured as a *loi-cadre* in the 1986 election manifesto produced jointly by the two principal right-wing parties, the *Rassem-*

blement pour la République and the *Union pour la démocratie française*. Moreover, the general disenchantment with state ownership, the replacement under a socialist regime of traditional left-wing values by a new focus on the firm, together with a growing recognition that the government's room to maneuver was ultimately constrained by market forces, suggested that even the socialists, had they been reelected in March 1986, would have been prepared to countenance some measure of denationalization. The socialists had, after all, been accused of privatization by the back door: In the course of the socialist quinquennium (1981–86), the capitalization of the Paris *Bourse* had increased as much as in the previous twenty years, largely due to the "participatory shares" and "investment certificates" introduced in 1983 by Industry Minister Laurent Fabius as part of an investment development drive. Thus, individuals and private-sector companies were able to buy nonvoting shares in nationalized industries, a useful means of increasing available state funds without any loss of state control.

The sixty-five firms selected in September 1986 for privatization by March 1, 1991 comprised thirty-eight banks, thirteen insurance companies, four finance companies, one communications agency, and nine industrial giants. By October 1986 the short list of candidates for the opening sale had been narrowed to just three: the elitist commercial bank *Paribas*, the glass manufacturer *Saint-Gobain*, and the insurance company *Assurances générales de France*. In the event, *Saint-Gobain* was chosen, perhaps because, of the three, she was clearly the most deeply rooted in the French *patrimoine*, having been in operation since the days of Colbert and numbering among her creations the *galerie des glaces* at Versailles and the light-reflecting windows of *La Défense*. And the Chirac government wanted privatization to be perceived first and foremost as a giving-back of France to the French. Other equally ambitious claims were made for privatization, namely that it would effect a fundamental change in attitudes toward all aspects of business and the market, thus paving the way for the single European market in 1992; and that it would break down the age-old oppositions of capital and labor.

The success of the French privatization program was mixed. On the one hand, a staggering seventeen million applications for shares helped to swell the ranks of the so-called popular shareholding body from less than two million to almost seven million small investors. Employee share ownership widened considerably: Between 50 percent and 80 percent of the employees of newly privatized companies (500,000 in all) rose to the bait. Moreover, the proceeds from privatization amounted to some 71 billion francs, even though less than a quarter of the program had been effected.

But this success was mitigated by the political damage done to the Chirac government by the controversy surrounding the composition of the notorious "hard cores" (*noyaux durs*) of investors. These were formed by Balladur to give a measure of stability to newly privatized firms following their change of status, and generally between 18 percent and 25 percent of the equity released in each flotation was reserved for them, in return for a small premium over and above the issue price. But the French institutional investors and industrial companies selected to form the *noyaux durs* were said to be dominated by personal acquaintances of Chirac and Balladur. Thus, Balladur became accused of selling off state assets cheaply to his friends. ''Black Monday'' marked the first nail in the coffin of the French privatization program. Another setback was the electoral defeat suffered by Chirac and French right-wing parties in 1988. Whether or not the privatization program will be revitalized at a later date remains to be seen.

E. Balladur, *Je crois en l'homme plus qu'en l'Etat* (Paris, 1987); A. Bizaguet, *Le Secteur public et les privatisations* (Paris, 1988); R. Fraser, *Privatisation* (Paris, 1988); A. Hamdouch, *L'Etat d'influence* (Paris, 1989).

M. Maclean

Related entries: BALLADUR, EDOUARD; CHIRAC, JACQUES; *COHABITATION*; ECONOMIC TRENDS; NATIONALIZATIONS.

Q

QUEUILLE, HENRI (1884–1970), a distinguished yet ineffective Third and Fourth Republic politician who was almost always a cabinet member and served as prime minister in 1948 and 1949 and again for five months in 1951. Queuille was born on March 31, 1884 in Neuvie d'Ussel in the department of Corrèze in central France. He was a physician and served in the medical corps during World War I.

He was first elected to Parliament from the Corrèze in 1914. Like most politicians of his day, Queuille maintained close ties to his constituency, concerning himself primarily with rural questions and serving as mayor of his hometown and as a member of the departmental General Council. He was first named to the cabinet in 1920 when he became under-secretary of state for agriculture. Between then and 1953 Queuille served in more than thirty different governments. More often than not, he was minister of agriculture, although he also served as minister of health, telecommunications, and food supply during the interwar years.

Queuille was part of the majority of French politicians who underestimated the power Hitler would have and the threat Nazi Germany would pose to Third Republic France. There is still disagreement about Queuille's role in the debates leading up to the Armistice and France's capitulation.

There is no debate about his role in the Resistance. He returned to Neuvie where he supported himself as a timber merchant and worked actively for the Resistance. He resumed his governmental career in 1943 when General Charles de Gaulle named him *Commissaire d'état*, and in the general's absence he ran the *Comité français de la Libération nationale* from Algiers for the next two years.

In 1946 Queuille was again elected to the Chamber of Deputies from the Corrèze and was also elected leader of the Radical-Socialist party group in Parliament. In 1948 he was named minister of state in the short-lived government of André Marie.

Nineteen forty-eight was an especially difficult year for France. A wave of strikes crippled French industry. There were shortages of food and housing in the cities. There was a severe budgetary deficit. Meanwhile, the government was trying to find a new equilibrium following the collapse of tripartitism and the onset of the Cold War. Marie's government fell quickly, having proved unable to end a wave of strikes, provide food for the cities, or deflect opposition from both the Gaullists and communists. Following Marie's resignation, the former premier, Robert Schuman, could not secure a parliamentary majority for his proposed government. President Vincent Auriol then turned to Queuille to form a government that reflected the viewpoints of the various center-left and center parties. That government turned out to be the second most durable government in the entire history of the Fourth Republic.

Queuille was not known as a decisive man. Nonetheless, he was able to bring the strikes to an end gradually, increase the revenue and buying power of urban workers, and use Marshall Fund money for industrial investment. Most important of all, his ability to remain in power kept General de Gaulle from making a stronger and possibly successful attack on the new Republic. His government was finally defeated thirteen months later when it split over wage policy.

He was also premier of the shortest-lived government. On March 3, 1951, the Chamber of Deputies elected him premier, largely as a result of support from the socialists (SFIO). Five days later, the SFIO withdrew its support when it saw that Queuille had chosen a cabinet dominated by conservatives.

Despite the success of his first government, Queuille is known as the father of *immobilisme*, the term used to describe the constantly shifting coalitions and ineffectual governments of Third and Fourth Republic France. He was known as a cautious and moderate politician who did not take risks, even though bold initiatives may well have been needed to solve France's many social and economic problems. As the eminent political scientist Philip Williams put it, "Queuille believed, like Stanley Baldwin, that 'the art of statesmanship is to postpone issues until they are no longer relevant.' "

Queuille died on June 16, 1970.

N. Leites, *On the Game of Politics in France* (Stanford, Calif., 1959); D. MacRae, *Parliament, Politics, and Society in France* (New York, 1967); P. M. Williams, *Crisis and Compromise* (London, 1964).

C. Hauss

Related entries: AGRICULTURE; AURIOL, VINCENT; CENTRIST PARTIES; CHRISTIAN DEMOCRATS; DE GAULLE, CHARLES; ECONOMIC POLICY; ELECTIONS; PEASANTRY; PINAY, ANTOINE; STRIKES; TRIPARTITISM.

R

RADICAL PARTY, the oldest party in France (1901) and once a mainstay of the politics of the Third Republic, it played a diminished role in the Fourth and a marginal one in the Fifth. The values of the party were derived from the early nineteenth-century revolutionary tradition. Radicals were champions of republicanism, patriotism, lay education, parliamentary democracy, and the civil rights of ordinary citizens. The party never abandoned this orientation. But in a stable republic that had institutionalized these goals by the early twentieth century, the orientation itself acquired a more conservative cast. By then the party had shifted the base of its political operations from Paris, the place of its revolutionary tradition, to small towns and villages, places of its newfound electoral support. There the party defended the interests of the provincial petty bourgeoisie—farmers, shopkeepers, artisans, country lawyers, and doctors. In the mid-nineteenth century, radicals had epitomized the political avant-garde; by the mid-twentieth century, they were regarded as a bulwark against social change. Through it all radicals retained their suspicion of big government. Loyal to their local constituencies and fiercely independent-minded, their leaders exercised enormous influence in the parliaments of the Third Republic, where they were renowned for their skill at negotiation.

Well adapted to the political needs of the Third Republic, the radicals of the Fourth Republic were less well positioned to lead a society committed to a greater measure of governmental planning, a larger role in European economic cooperation, and a wider distribution of the entitlements of the welfare state. The reputation of the party, moreover, had been tarnished by its role in the fall of France in 1940 and by the compliance of many of its leaders with the policies of the Vichy regime during the war. The party was only marginally represented in the constituent assemblies convened in 1945 (28 of 586 delegates) and 1946 (32 of 586).

Between 1946 and 1956 the party nonetheless made a surprising comeback. It retained considerable power in local politics in some regions, and its parliamentary leaders, though few, found a prominent place in the ministries of the Fourth Republic. As members of a minority party of the political center, radicals often held the keys to viable ministerial coalitions, whose configurations changed as rapidly as the issues and events Parliament was required to consider. Radicals participated in all twenty-seven of the ministries of the Fourth Republic and headed fourteen of them. Indeed, if all the ministerial positions held during this regime are tallied, the Radical party was better represented than any other. Yet the governmental role of the party's leaders is deceptive as a measure of its strength. During the Fourth Republic, it never commanded more than 15 percent of the electorate, nor more than 12 percent of the seats in the National Assembly. The party was as much a route to power for ambitious politicians as it was an agency for advancing policies based on its principles. Its official programs possessed little substance; its membership in the National Assembly was modest (75 of 596 seats at its apogee in 1956); its electoral support was unreliable (fluctuating between a high of 3.2 million [1956] and a low of 1.7 million [1958] in the general elections).

Party leaders, moreover, were deeply divided among themselves. A contingent of survivors from the Third Republic rallied around Edouard Herriot, who continued to enjoy much personal prestige at the outset of the Fourth Republic. But this group was no longer the backbone of a party reaffirming its values and traditions. Several factions coexisted in uneasy alliance, and they gravitated toward opposing ends of the political spectrum. The loyalty of the left-wing faction was tenuous, and most of its members defected within a few years. A faction of "neoradicals" advocated ties with business and banking interests in a manner reminiscent of the Progressists of the turn of the century. Another faction flirted with the Gaullists, while a contingent of "managerial" radicals (*radicaux de gestion*) were openly opportunistic. Representing too broad a range of opinion to act consistently on principle, the party was distinguished by its pliable response to particular issues.

To this congeries of interests, Pierre Mendès-France sought to provide unity in the mid–1950s, and for a moment offered the prospect of party renewal. He served as premier in 1954–55, and as general secretary of the party from 1955 to 1957. He was distinguished by his style, and notably by his commitment to his principles. The prodigy of radical politics in the 1930s, a participant in Léon Blum's Popular Front, a hero of the Resistance and a pilot with Charles de Gaulle's Free French forces in England during the war, Mendès-France brought to his party his talent as a financier, his verve, and his idealism. As premier, he had some support for the program of economic austerity that he proposed. But he was also burdened with the responsibility of disengaging French forces from a humiliating defeat in Indochina and the ongoing strife in Algeria, and his government fell amidst the complex problems of disestablishing a far-flung colonial empire. Within his party Mendès-France continued to inspire intellectuals and youthful reformers. But his style annoyed the party veterans, who engineered his downfall there as well.

Radicals had turned the political institutions of the Fourth Republic to their advantage, but the institutions themselves were inadequate for carrying out the tasks facing French government. Once powerful as kingmakers in Parliament and secure as defenders of the prerogatives of local electoral committees, the radicals of the Fifth Republic found the base of their power deinstitutionalized by the provisions of the new constitution, which favored president over parliament and fostered the creation of larger, more centralized parties. Sandwiched between the triumphant Gaullist party and the emerging left-wing coalition of François Mitterrand, the radicals were crowded out of contention. Some party leaders (Edgar Faure) joined the Gaullists, while a left-wing faction defected to form a separate party (Movement of Left Radicals) in concert with Mitterrand's Federation of the Democratic and Socialist Left. By the late 1960s the party was bankrupt and threatened with eviction from its offices in Paris.

The demise of the party was forestalled by the election of Jean-Jacques Servan-Schreiber as secretary-general in 1969. He was the editor of a popular news magazine and a practitioner of the new techniques of publicity. An admirer of Mendès-France, he hoped to provide the party with new energy and a new image, one borrowed from American entrepreneurial practice. But his party continued to be torn by its conflicting allegiances to the left and the center, and his efforts to make the party the nucleus of a larger movement of opposition to the Gaullists failed. By 1973 the party was in disarray. Here and there a radical politician survived, proclaiming the independence of mind for which radicals had always been famous. But the days when radicals were an effective force in French politics were gone.

The decline of the Radical party since World War II mirrors long-range changes in the dynamics of French politics. The extension of the powers of the presidency in the Fifth Republic worked to the disadvantage of a party committed to the primacy of Parliament. Equally significant was a growing popular commitment to the moral imperatives of the welfare state, with which radicals, spokespersons for a bygone ideal of individual autonomy, were never comfortable. The values of the radicals were humane, but their political concerns were outmoded. With their radical flair, Mendès-France and subsequently Servan-Schreiber seemed to their respective contemporaries to augur the party's renewal. In retrospect, they appear only to have orchestrated its recession.

H. Coston, ed., *Dictionnaire de la politique française*, 4 vols. (Paris, 1967–82); F. de Tarr, *The French Radical Party from Herriot to Mendès-France* (London, 1961); J. T. Nordmann, *La France radicale* (Paris, 1977); J. Touchard, *La Gauche en France depuis 1900* (Paris, 1977); P. Williams, *Crisis and Compromise* (London, 1964); F. Wilson, *French Political Parties under the Fifth Republic* (New York, 1982).

P. H. Hutton

Related entries: BOURGES-MAUNOURY, MAURICE; CENTRIST PARTIES; FAURE, EDGAR; GAILLARD, FELIX; HERRIOT, EDOUARD; LEFT RADICALS; MARIE, ANDRE; MAYER, RENE; MENDES-FRANCE, PIERRE; POLITICAL TRENDS; QUEUILLE, HENRI; SERVAN-SCHREIBER, JEAN-JACQUES.

RAMADIER, PAUL (1888–1961), a leading socialist of the Fourth Republic. Born at La Rochelle, educated at Toulouse and in law at Paris, the young attorney made his mark representing cooperative societies. Ramadier worked for Minister of Armaments Albert Thomas after being badly wounded in the first months of World War I. Already a socialist, Ramadier won election as mayor of Decazeville in 1919 and later to Parliament (1928–40). Ramadier stood on the right of the badly factionalized interwar Socialist party (SFIO). He supported participation in coalition governments, voted for the defense budget when the threat from Germany mounted, and wished to adapt socialist ideology to changing conditions. Holding firmly to his principles, Ramadier split from the mainstream to join the neosocialists around Pierre Renaudel and Adrien Marquet (November 1933), became an under-secretary of state for public works (1936), sought to preserve the forty-hour week as minister of labor (January–August 1938), and opposed the grant of full powers to Marshal Pétain (1940).

Ramadier returned to the Socialist party after the war without jettisoning his basic ideas. Deeply committed to social justice and increasing prosperity, he pursued these goals pragmatically but often had to preside over periods of injustice and hardship. As minister of food supply in November 1944 he soon earned the sobriquet "Ramadan."

When he was appointed the first prime minister of the Fourth Republic (January 1947), Ramadier took office at a moment of crisis for France's laborious recovery. His cabinet grouped an unstable coalition of communists, socialists, and Christian democrats (MRP). Bloody fighting had erupted in Indochina in December 1946, and the fitful aid provided by the United States after the war had fallen into remission. The government soon broke with both Gaullism and communism while trying to master a desperate economic situation. Excessive public spending, uncontrolled wage increases, a cancerous payments deficit, industrial bottlenecks, and the failure of the 1947 wheat crop militated against the growth in production necessary to stabilize the political situation. The bread ration plummeted as farmers held back much of their limited crop. The erosion of their purchasing power provoked the workers into repeated strikes, which Ramadier saw as communist-orchestrated. Ramadier's state of mind, like that of many other Frenchmen in the spring of 1947, responded to the atmosphere fostered by the onset of the international Cold War and by fears of some sort of domestic coup from the right or left.

Ramadier expelled the communist ministers from his cabinet after they refused to endorse his economic policies (May 1947). This act marked a decisive rupture in the postwar political coalition governing France. Thereafter, the inability to choose between the *dirigiste* and liberal policy alternatives advocated by the opposing extremes still contained within the coalition set policy drifting from one expedient to the next. Inflation accelerated as workers extracted the additional wages necessary to compete for the limited food stocks coming in from the countryside. In June the announcement of the Marshall Plan offered hope of sustained and adequate American assistance. The October 1947 municipal elections revealed that French voters now divided evenly between communists, Gaullists, and a potential Third Force in which the moderate right would predominate over the moderate left. Ramadier quickly bought the support of the moderate right by purging his cabinet of some of the more doctrinaire socialists. Within a month, however, he had to yield power to Robert Schuman.

Ramadier returned to office as Henri Queuille's minister of defense (September 1948–October 1949). The Revers-Mast affair, involving an allegation that two French generals had given a confidential report on the situation in Indochina to the Vietminh, broke just after he had left office; the subsequent inquiry, however, found he had acted in the national interest by dropping the investigation. Defeated in the general election of 1951, Ramadier regained his seat in 1956 and occupied the Ministry of Finance and Economic Affairs in Guy Mollet's cabinet (February 1956–May 1957). As had been his misfortune in earlier positions, Ramadier had to preside over a period of difficulties. The economic burden of the Algerian War destabilized the French economy so badly that the unpopular taxes he sponsored could not restore the situation. Opposed to calling General Charles de Gaulle back into power, Ramadier permanently retired from national politics upon his defeat in the 1958 general election. Ramadier possessed tenacious integrity and drive but often found himself saddled with responsibilities that would have tested a man of even greater abilities.

V. Auriol, *Mon septennat, 1947–54* (Paris, 1970); R. Quilliot, *La SFIO et l'exercice du pouvoir, 1944–1958* (Paris, 1972); J.-P. Rioux, *La France de la Quatrième République*, 2 vols. (Paris, 1980–83).

J. S. Hill

Related entries: DEFENSE POLICY; ECONOMIC POLICY; INDOCHINA, RELATIONS WITH; MARSHALL PLAN; POLITICAL TRENDS; QUEUILLE, HENRI; SCHUMAN, ROBERT; SOCIALIST PARTY (SFIO); STRIKES; TRIPARTITISM; UNITED STATES, RELATIONS WITH.

REFERENDA, used to ratify the constitution of the Fourth Republic, by President Charles de Gaulle to demonstrate popular approval for his policies (including the founding of the Fifth Republic and independence for Algeria), and by both Presidents Georges Pompidou and François Mitterrand. Opposition leaders charged that the Gaullist referenda were intended largely to circumvent the regular legislative processes of the National Assembly. These critics pointed to use of referenda by nineteenth-century Bonapartist and Orleanist regimes to undermine the legislatures of their own day. The political traditions of the referendum underwent a profound change in the late 1960s when the rebels of May 1968 called for more salient methods of popular participation in governance at a time when the increase in the number of televisions made it possible for opposition groups to mount effective campaigns against the government's position on a particular referendum. As the risks of a popular vote of nonconfidence in the government's policies grew, Gaullist enthusiasm for referenda waned and the procedure was largely abandoned in the 1970s.

The Fourth Republic's constitution was presented to French voters in two referenda of May and October 1946. The May referendum failed to win the approval from a majority of French voters, some of whom were probably frightened by the extremely vigorous communist campaign in favor of the constitution. Despite the open opposition of de Gaulle in his historic Bayeux speech, the October version carried with a small margin. In the referendum of September 28, 1958 voters approved the constitution of the Fifth Republic with its stronger executive powers as proposed by de Gaulle by a wide margin.

Historically in France the head of state has possessed enormous advantages in defining referendum questions, in controlling information (and thereby limiting debate), and in collecting the votes. De Gaulle made full use of those advantages in the referenda of January 8, 1961 on self-rule in Algeria, of April 8, 1962 on the Evian Accords, and on October 28, 1962 with the creation of a direct presidential election, a generalized form of referendum. Opposition leaders were never able to overcome the government's position in the early 1960s, even though up to a quarter of the electorate abstained, which the opposition claimed to show a lack of confidence in the government's policies on the part of many French voters.

May 1968 proved to be the breaking point in the Gaullist strategy of seeking popular approval within a carefully structured referendum process. A fraction of the abstentions were mobilized by the opposition and brought to polls to cast votes against the government's position in the referendum of April 27, 1969 to restructure the Senate on a more corporatist basis and to create regional governments. De Gaulle chose to make these questions an implicit vote of confidence in his own mandate to govern. When voters rejected the measures by a margin of 53 to 47 percent, de Gaulle resigned. He died in the following year.

On April 23, 1972 French voters overwhelmingly approved the entry of Great Britain, Denmark, the Irish Republic, and Norway into the Common Market in a referendum posed by Pompidou's government. Yet the striking result of the poll was the nearly 40 percent of the electorate that heeded the socialist, and belatedly the communist, call to abstain in a show of nonconfidence in the government. Pompidou did not define the referendum as a personal vote of confidence and did not follow de Gaulle's example. Having recognized at the outset the implicit risks of defining referenda as votes of confidence in an age when nine out of ten households had televisions (compared to less than one in ten in 1958), the Gaullist Pompidou and his successor, Valéry Giscard d'Estaing, never enjoyed enough personal electoral success in presidential elections to gamble their own political futures on the referendum process.

Under the Mitterrand presidency a referendum was held on November 6, 1988 on the status of New Caledonia. Despite an abnormally high abstention rate in this referendum, voters supported the government's plan to divide the Pacific territory into three provinces, each with an assembly elected for a six-year term, to use the assemblies to constitute a legislative body, and to continue to entrust executive power in a high commissioner appointed by the state. This law will remain in effect until 1999 when a referendum on self-determination is scheduled. Mitterrand suggested on various occasions during his presidency that he desired more referenda in order to enhance public liberties; yet, with the exception of the vote on New Caledonia, this has not occurred. Under the constitution of the Fifth Republic the initiative for a referendum is supposed to originate with either the government or Parliament, but for the most part direct democracy in the form of referenda has come from the Elysée, in part to recharge presidential authority.

J. Chapsal, *La Vie politique sous la Vᵉ République* (Paris, 1981); P. E. Converse, R. Pierce, *Political Representation in France* (Cambridge, Mass., 1986).

P. A. Phillips

Related entries: ALGERIA, RELATIONS WITH; CONSTITUTION OF THE FIFTH REPUBLIC; CONSTITUTION OF THE FOURTH REPUBLIC; DE GAULLE, CHARLES; EUROPEAN ECONOMIC COMMUNITY, RELATIONS WITH; MITTERRAND, FRANCOIS; NEW CALEDONIA; POLITICAL TRENDS; POMPIDOU, GEORGES.

REGIONS, from modest origins in the 1950s, have grown to become a third tier in French local government. There has long been a strong regional component to the organization of French life (embodied in the country's former provinces), but it was only in 1955 that a formal set of regions was first created. In that year twenty-one "programming regions" (*régions-programmes*) were recognized, formed from groups of existing departments. Initially their role was extremely limited, confined to producing a regional development plan. At a national level these different plans were intended to help reduce problems of regional imbalance, thus complementing and adding a limited spatial dimension to the National Plan.

In 1964 the region took on greater significance, becoming an integral part of the French administrative structure rather than remaining simply a forum for the discussion of issues related to regional development. A prefect was nominated at the head of each region, supported by an advisory commission for Regional Economic Development (CODER, *Commission de développement économique régional*). This body brought together representatives from the regions' different business and administrative communities and advised on matters such as social and economic development and spatial planning. In 1970 the number of regions increased to twenty-two: Corsica was detached from Provence-Alpes-Côte d'Azur and became a separate region.

More important changes occurred in the early 1970s as a partial response to the growing demand for devolution. Instead of remaining a purely administrative framework, the region became a political reality with the law of July 5, 1972. It was given the status of a public authority (*Etablissement public*), controlled by the prefect and a newly formed regional council, nominated by the different councillors of the region's communes and departments. This executive was assisted by a consultative council, the *Comité économique et social*, which replaced the former CODER. The region also now had a small budget, derived from various local taxes. Such resources were used to provide limited financial help to communes or departments with their programs to build new infrastructure or facilities such as swimming pools. However, the region's principal functions still remained the formulation of regional development plans and advising central government on such matters. Despite this reform the region's effective powers and independence from central government remained limited, due largely to the weakness of financial resources and the control exercised by the prefect.

A new identity and more influential role was given to the region in 1982 within the context of the then socialist government's legislation on decentralization. Change occurred in various ways. First, the region's legal status was modified, so that it became an institution equivalent to the commune or department, freed from the direct control of Paris. As a result the regional council was to be directly elected by a system of proportional representation, with councillors serving for a period of six years (the first elections took place in 1986). More significant, control of the council and of its decisions was transferred to the president of the council (elected by the council members). Previously the prefect had assumed this role. The preexisting consultative body, the Economic and Social Committee, remained in place. (In the case of Corsica, and in view of the island's special economic and political problems, further changes were also made.) A second area of change was represented by the increase in the region's budget. To the traditional sources of funding were added a special grant made by the government to cover additional expenditure resulting from the transfer of responsibilities, and the income derived from the provision of vehicle registration documents. Unlike the commune and the department, the larger part of the region's budget is spent on investment rather than on current expenditure, emphasizing one of the specific roles of the region, namely to assist in the funding of new infrastructure and amenities. However, overall regional budgets remain far less significant than those of the country's communes or departments.

A third major change occurred with new responsibilities being transferred to the region; in most cases this took place progressively between 1982 and 1986. Thus, the region is now responsible for a range of activities in the fields of education and vocational training. In the former instance, for example, the building, equipment, and maintenance of *lycées* (for the school population of 14 to 17 years of age) is now administered by the regional council, which also has similar responsibilities concerning special education. In the case of vocational training, the administration of different training programs and apprentice schemes is also now a regional matter.

In the fields of strategic planning and social and economic development the functions of the region were redefined and strengthened under the 1982 legislation. The regions, therefore, continue to play a consultative role in the formulation of the country's national plan. They are also now required to prepare a regional plan, which is negotiated with the government. Other new areas of responsibility include transport policy, housing strategy, regional parks, and tourism.

Since 1982 the regions have also been given the opportunity to intervene far more directly in the economic development of their respective areas. The regional council is able to offer various forms of grants to firms prepared to invest within the region. Two main forms of subsidy exist, the *Prime régionale à la création d'entreprises* (the regional grant for company creation) and the *Prime régionale à l'emploi* (the regional employment grant). The value of these grants is limited and depends in general on the number of jobs that are created. Various forms of indirect aid also exist, notably in the form of guarantees for loans taken out by a firm. Similarly the region is empowered to help companies in difficulty. It is able to offer such firms direct assistance in the form of grants or loans, or indirect help such as the purchase of its land or buildings, advice on management, or guidance in the training or retraining of personnel. Despite the wide range of these measures, all are not available in every region; moreover, in general they are designed to assist firms that are too small to qualify for assistance under the government's national program of regional aid.

Although the activities and responsibilities of the region have become more diversified over time, one of its key functions remains the design and implementation of strategic planning and development policy. Since 1984 this role has been reinforced by the system of contractual planning launched by the socialists. The aim was to produce a combined investment program between the government and the region lasting over a period of five years. This innovative approach was designed as a two-way process: The regions, in the formulation of their plans, were expected to take account of the government's investment priorities set out in the national plan, while the government was under a similar obligation to incorporate into this plan proposals emanating from the regions.

The first round of these contract plans (*contrat de plan Etat-région*) ran from 1984 to 1988. Over this period the main fields of investment were communications and transport, agriculture and related industries, the rehabilitation of rundown urban areas, and the development of research and education. Quite obviously, however, not all regions had the same priorities. Thus, certain areas of western France such as Aquitaine, Midi-Pyrénées, and Bretagne gave preference to the improvement of agriculture or to the diversification of their rural economies; in other cases, notably Rhône-Alpes, Alsace, and Provence-Alpes-Côte d'Azur, greater emphasis was given to promoting high-tech industry. In Ile-de-France two-thirds of expenditure was allocated to improving transport infrastructure, particularly the road network, with the aim of diverting traffic away from the congested inner areas of the city. Certain problems arose with this first series of contracts (notably concerning their vagueness and the lack of rigor in their costing), but overall the experience was adjudged positive.

As a result it was decided in 1987 to launch a new generation of regional contracts for the period 1989–93. Following two years of negotiation directed by the various regional prefects, the different plans were all finally signed by May 1989, committing investment of 52 billion francs from the state and 43 billion francs from the regions. Following the earlier experience, an effort was made to ensure that these second-generation plans were not only more selective, focusing on a narrower and more precise range of objectives, but also easier to implement with fewer administrative procedures.

From the many different proposals adopted, a limited number of major priorities for investment may be distinguished. Most expenditure is to go to infrastructure improvements, particularly roads, reflecting previous inadequate investment in this field as well as the need to improve access to those areas still poorly served by motorways, such as the southern Massif Central. Research and vocational training represent a second priority, with in the former case the specific aim of diverting such activity away from the Paris region. Emphasis is also placed on promoting economic development and technology transfers, especially in favor of small and medium-sized businesses. In order to provide additional assistance to a limited number of small areas experiencing particular problems (e.g., severe industrial decline, rural depopulation, or urban decay), a number of special investment programs are envisaged known as *Programmes d'aménagement concerté du territoire* (PACT). Thus, in Lorraine four such programs have been designated corresponding with the main areas in which industrial jobs have been lost, such as Longwy and the Vosges textile towns. As with the first-generation plans, priorities also vary with different regions; for example, a special effort to promote training or retraining programs is apparent in many regions of northern France and the Paris Basin, generally corresponding with areas of industrial decline. Similarly in Nord-Pas-de-Calais, the anticipated impact of the Channel Tunnel has led to major expenditure on transport infrastructure.

After more than thirty years of existence the region has become an established feature of the French institutional and administrative framework. A progressive increase in responsibilities has occurred since the decentralization legislation of 1982. However, throughout the life of the region, its special role has been to advise on strategic planning and social and economic development, areas in which the regional council is now able to intervene directly due to its increased resources and powers and to the innovative system of contract-plans.

"Les Collectivités territoriales," *Les Cahiers français* 239 (1989); "La Décentralisation en marche," *Les Cahiers français* 220 (1985); M. Keating, P. Hainsworth, *Decentralisation and Change in Contemporary France* (Aldershot, Eng., 1985); J. Monod, P. de Castelbajac, *L'Aménagement du territoire* (Paris, 1987), "Contrats de plan Etat-Régions, deuxième génération," *La Lettre de la Datar* 124 (1989).

J. N. Tuppen

Related entries: DECENTRALIZATION; PLAN; TRANSPORTATION.

REYNAUD, PAUL (1878–1966), unconventional conservative who was both deputy and minister during the Third and Fourth Republics. In the 1930s, Reynaud was known for his anti-Nazism and his desire for an alliance with the Soviet Union. Throughout his political career he was also a defender of economic liberalism. Named minister of finances by Edouard Daladier in November 1938, Reynaud issued a series of decrees that terminated the Popular Front coalition of radicals, socialists, and communists by effectively ending the forty-hour work week and restoring the confidence of investors. His team at the Finance Ministry included Alfred Sauvy and Michel Debré.

In March 1940 he replaced Daladier as prime minister but resigned in June, leaving the way open for Marshal Pétain. During the war he was imprisoned, first in France and later in Germany. Reynaud opposed the constitution of the Fourth Republic because of what he considered its "ultraparliamentarism" and encouragement of governmental instability. Nevertheless, as deputy and sometime minister, he participated in it actively. He again fought for policies that reflected his economic liberalism and thus earned the enmity of the left. In 1948 Reynaud argued for a longer workweek and wage stability to promote French production and competitiveness. A firm Atlanticist, he struggled in 1953 for parliamentary approval of a common European defense against the opposition of communists and Gaullists. As an early postwar advocate of European unity, he favored reconciliation with Germany and proposed, in 1948, a European parliament elected by universal suffrage. He supported General Charles de Gaulle's return to power in 1958, but in the early 1960s criticized the regime for what he perceived to be its anti-Europeanism, anti-Atlanticism, and antirepublicanism.

E. Demy, *Paul Reynaud: Mon père* (Paris, 1980); P. Reynaud, *In the Thick of the Fight* (New York, 1955), *The Foreign Policy of Charles de Gaulle* (New York, 1964).

M. Seidman

Related entries: DE GAULLE, CHARLES; ECONOMIC POLICY; EUROPEAN DEFENSE COMMUNITY.

ROCARD, MICHEL (1930–), Socialist politician, former leader of the *Parti socialiste unifié*, prime minister of France from 1988 to 1991. Michel Rocard was born into a professional middle-class Parisian family. His mother—a convert to Protestantism—was a teacher, his father a professor of physics at the *Ecole normale supérieure* and, later, joint creator of the French atomic bomb. As a young adolescent during the Occupation, Rocard joined the Protestant scout movement and imbibed from this experience the ideals of the Resistance, which his father—a conservative, lapsed Catholic—had joined in 1941. Rocard himself claims that his later political tolerance stemmed from his recognition that the spirit of the Resistance was as strong in men like his father as it was in communists or socialists.

After an unremarkable schooling at *Louis-le-Grand*, during which he showed as much interest in the scout movement as he did in his studies, he abandoned plans, fostered by his father, to enter the *Ecole polytechnique* and opted instead for the *Sciences-Po* (*Institut d'études politiques*). It was, in part, his interest in European integration, but also his acquaintance with the anti-totalitarian writings of Kravchenko, Koestler, and Merleau-Ponty, that steered him unequivocally away from the Communist party and into the arms of the socialist student movement, of which he became the Paris secretary in 1950 and the national secretary in 1954. But his student activism (which was already geared to the task of creating a united student left dominated by socialists rather than by communists, and to combating the strong-arm tactics of the right-wing student leader Jean-Marie Le Pen) resulted in his failing—twice—the entrance exams for the *Ecole nationale d'administration* (ENA).

He was finally admitted to ENA in 1955, while completing his military service in the air force. The Algerian War was the political issue on which he rapidly began to distance himself from the Socialist party (SFIO) of Guy Mollet and to identify with the opposition led by Alain Savary, whose new party, *Parti socialiste autonome* (PSA, later PSU), he was to join in 1959. For Rocard, the PSU offered the prospect of a new, modern party, capable both of galvanizing the progressive forces on the left around an end to the Algerian War and of developing an alternative economic policy that would allow the left to manage the consequences of France's unparalleled economic growth and combine liberal economics with a clear social program.

At the same time, he embarked on a career as *Inspecteur des finances*, rising, by 1965, to a position of real political influence within the Finance Ministry. It was in this double capacity, as party activist and professional economist, that Rocard gradually began to promote the new ideas of libertarian socialism (*autogestion*, decentralization, and the promotion of social movements) that was already the hallmark of the former Catholic trade-union, the *Confédération française démocratique du travail* (CFDT), and with which the PSU, under his leadership after 1967, would be identified. Above all, he wished to break with the ideological straitjacket in which much of the French left continued to find itself, bogged down in "quantitative" issues of statism and nationalization. It was precisely his defense of an alternative "qualitative" vision of socialism that led him to the leadership of the PSU in 1967 against Gilles Martinet, who had proposed that the party absorb itself into François Mitterrand's *Fédération de la gauche démocratique et socialiste*. In the same year, Rocard fought his first parliamentary election campaign, being narrowly outdistanced, in the Yvelines, by the Communist party candidate.

It was the PSU's role at the heart of the issues generated by May 1968 (particularly its analysis of the new types of strike activity and of the situation in the universities) that brought Michel Rocard's name to national prominence, the more so in that the "historic" leader of the PSU, Pierre Mendès-France, repeatedly (1965, 1967, and 1968) refused to rise to the opportunities presented by the political developments. In the wake of the events of May 1968, Rocard saw two major political tasks: The first was to translate the energies and enthusiasm revealed that May into a coherent and responsible political movement, and the second was to eliminate the influence, within the PSU, of the wilder *gauchiste* elements still dreaming of something they called revolution. In pursuit of the former task, Rocard stood as presidential candidate in 1969 after de Gaulle's surprise resignation. His 3.7 percent of the vote said more about national voting habits than about the actual popularity of this rising young politician. Rocard's real impact could be judged by his parliamentary election immediately afterwards, to a seat in the Yvelines, where he defeated de Gaulle's former prime minister, Maurice Couve de Murville.

Rocard's struggle against the *gauchistes* occupied the greater part of the period 1969–73, during which his continuing vision of the PSU as the spearhead of a new, modern, united left blurred his analysis of what was happening to the old Socialist party, rapidly transmogrifying itself, under François Mitterrand, into a credible political force. Too late did he recognize that the fiercely squabbling sects within the PSU were, all too often, happier with ideological debate than with political action. By 1973 he felt that the future of the socialist left as a whole—not to mention his own future—demanded the fusion of the PSU with the new PS. After defeat in the 1973 parliamentary elections, he resigned the leadership of the PSU and, in 1974, threw himself into support for Mitterrand's presidential bid. But only a minority (40%) of the PSU followed him, at the important *assises du socialisme* in November 1974, into the Socialist party.

The advent of the Rocard troops allowed Mitterrand to wrest himself free of the Jacobin-based majority with which he had run the party since 1971. At the Socialist party congress at Pau in 1975, he formed a tactical alliance with Rocard to eliminate Jean-Pierre Chevènement's CERES (Center of Socialist Study and Research) from the leadership. Rocard entered the PS national secretariat at the same time and fought a running battle from within the party to shift its dominant culture toward his vision of liberal democratic socialism. In 1977 he provided himself with a political base, becoming mayor of Conflans-Sainte-Honorine (Yvelines), and in 1978 he was returned to Parliament for the same constituency. But his personal victory was coupled with a televised outburst of fury against the Communist party, which he held responsible for the defeat—and the continuing archaism—of the entire left.

Rocard now emerged as the popular champion of the "modern" left, the scourge of the Communist party and the apostle of openness (*ouverture*) toward the more socially conscious elements of the liberal center. He was preferred to Mitterrand as a potential president, in a succession of opinion polls, by margins as high as two to one. Simultaneously, however, his popularity within the party slumped. Mitterrand chose to drop him from the leadership in 1979, conferring on Rocard's archrival, Jean-Pierre Chevènement, the task of giving the party a program for the 1980s. Rocard's ill-conceived presidential bid in October 1980 inflamed relations with Mitterrand who, on being elected to the Elysée in 1981, offered him the poisoned chalice of planning, a ministry where clearly the apostle of a more market approach to the economy was bound to be relatively powerless in a government whose key economic posts were all held by dedicated statists. In a cabinet reshuffle in 1983, Rocard was offered the hugely problematic portfolio of agriculture, which he nevertheless turned into a personal success. However, when Mitterrand was forced to abandon state socialism and embrace the market in 1984, Michel Rocard received no credit for having been "right" a decade before everyone else. Increasingly disillusioned with what he regarded as governmental opportunism, he sought to give himself a free hand by resigning on the issue of proportional representation (April 1985).

Rocard continued for the next few years to preach his version of liberal democratic socialism and of *ouverture*. His opinion poll ratings continued to soar. By 1987, Mitterrand knew that he had little alternative in the event of a second term but to appoint Rocard prime minister. He consequently chose him as special adviser during his successful presidential campaign in 1988. Nobody in France was surprised when, on May 9, 1988, the champion of *ouverture* finally became prime minister. Rocard's performance in that post confirmed his reputation as by far the most credible left-wing presidential candidate in France.

On May 15, 1991, after three years in office, Rocard resigned his post as prime minister, and the president quickly appointed the socialist Edith Cresson to the post, making her the first female prime minister in French history. The resignation was portrayed as a mutual decision by Rocard and Mitterrand. While some speculated that Mitterrand had requested Rocard's resignation following a campaign-financing scandal involving the government and following problems piecing together majorities—not to mention rising unemployment, a sluggish economy, and social inequities—Rocard's newfound ''freedom'' permits him to devote his energies to the 1995 presidential campaign. Rocard will also have the ''luxury'' of not leading France as the 1993 legislative elections approach, elections in which the socialists may not fare too well according to recent polls.

K. Evin, *Michel Rocard ou l'art du possible* (Paris 1979); H. Hamon, P. Rotman, *L'Effet Rocard* (Paris, 1980); M. Rocard, *Parler vrai* (Paris, 1979), *Le Coeur à l'ouvrage* (Paris, 1988); *Un Pays comme le nôtre* (Paris, 1989).

J. Howorth

Related entries: AUTOGESTION; CRESSON, EDITH; MITTERRAND, FRANCOIS; POLITICAL TRENDS; SOCIALIST PARTY (PS); UNIFIED SOCIALIST PARTY.

ROCHET, WALDECK (1905–1983), communist politician and secretary-general of the French Communist party, 1964–72. He was born April 5, 1905, in Sainte-Croix (Saône-et-Loire). His unusual given name derived from his shoemaker father's admiration for republican leader Pierre Waldeck-Rousseau. Rochet joined the French Communist party (PCF) at nineteen. Catching the attention of higher-ups, he was sent in 1930 to the Comintern school in the Soviet Union. After graduation he became regional secretary for the Lyon region, in 1932. Two years later he was appointed head of the Central Committee farmers' section, moving to Paris. In 1936 he became a nonvoting member of the Central Committee, was elected deputy from Colombes-Nanterre in May 1936, and in 1937 became a full Central Committee member and director of the PCF farmers' newspaper *La Terre*.

Arrested when the PCF was outlawed in 1939, he was imprisoned first in France, then in Algiers. After the Allied landings, he represented the PCF at General Charles de Gaulle's London headquarters. In 1944 he resumed his duties at *La Terre* and the farmers' section, becoming a nonvoting member of the Politburo in 1945 and a full member in 1950. Deputy for the Saône-et-Loire department in the two constituent assemblies and in the National Assembly from 1946 to 1956, he then represented the Seine department for the rest of his active life.

More impressed by Nikita Khrushchev than was Maurice Thorez, Rochet nevertheless remained on good terms with the latter, who promoted him in the party. He entered the Secretariat in 1959, became deputy secretary-general in 1961, and secretary-general in May 1964. Thorez became party president, dying three months later.

Attempting to introduce new policies, Rochet encountered opposition both from PCF Stalinists and the Soviets. PCF support for François Mitterrand's 1965 presidential campaign drew an implicit rebuke in a *TASS* article supporting President de Gaulle. In 1968 Rochet apparently attempted to mediate between the Czech communists and an increasingly hostile Soviet leadership. When the Soviets invaded Czechoslovakia, the PCF first reproved, the next day merely disapproved, their action. Rochet was now under heavy pressure from his more rigid comrades and the Soviets. His health deteriorated and he was diagnosed as having Parkinson's disease. Although by late 1969 he could no longer function as secretary-general, the party maintained an air of mystery on his health, and he was reelected in 1970, with Georges Marchais as his deputy and de facto party chief. His condition degenerated into total loss of cognition. In 1972, after Marchais became secretary-general of the PCF, Rochet was made honorary party president. He died in February 1983. Rochet's hopes of gradually moving the PCF from its rigid and pro-Soviet line failed because of strong opposition and his own physical collapse, but also because of his own caution and fear of splitting the party.

B. Lazitch, M. Drachkovitch, eds., *Biographical Dictionary of the Comintern*, rev. ed. (Stanford, Calif., 1986); P. Robrieux, *Histoire intérieure du parti communiste*, vols. 1, 2, 4 (Paris, 1980–84).

J. W. Friend

Related entries: FRENCH COMMUNIST PARTY; MARCHAIS, GEORGES; MITTERRAND, FRANCOIS; THOREZ, MAURICE; SOVIET UNION, RELATIONS WITH.

ROMILLY, JACQUELINE (DAVID) DE (1913–), academician. Born in Chartres, she studied in Paris as a pupil of the Nation (her father, a professor of philosophy, was killed in combat at the beginning of World War I), first at the *Lycée Molière* and then at the *Ecole normale supérieure*, receiving the *agrégation* in geography and the doctorate in letters. Romilly has devoted her entire professional life to teaching except for the period from 1940 to 1945 when she was prohibited by the Vichy statute on Jews. Beginning in 1939 she taught the preparatory classes for the *grandes écoles* at several *lycées*. After a year at both the University of Bordeaux and the Sorbonne, she became professor at the University of Lille in 1949 and remained there until 1957 when she was appointed professor at the Sorbonne. In 1976 she was the first woman named to the Collège de France, where she held the chair in "Greece and the Formation of Moral and Political Thought" until her retirement in 1984. Romilly was the also the first woman chosen to belong to the *Académie d'inscriptions et belles lettres*, thus becoming the first woman elected to the *Institut de France* (1975). She was elected to the French Academy, another of the five academies that constitute the Institute, in 1989. Her distinguished academic career has brought many other awards and honorary degrees, both French and foreign, including the Grand Prize of the French Academy for the ensemble of her work (1984). The majority of her writings focus on Greek civilization, history, and literature: *Thucydide et l'impérialisme athénien: La Pensée de l'historien et la genèse de l'oeuvre* (Paris, 1947); *Thucydides* (Paris: vol. 1, 1953; vol. 2, 1962; vols. 4–5, 1968; vols. 6–7 [with L. Bodin], 1955); *Histoire et raison chez Thucydide* (Paris, 1956); *La Crainte et l'angoisse dans le théâtre d'Eschyle* (Paris, 1958); *L'Evolution du pathétique, d'Eschyle à Euripide* (Paris, 1961); *Time in Greek Tragedy* (Ithaca, N.Y., 1968); *La Tragédie grecque* (Paris, 1970); *La Loi dans la pensée grecque, des origines à Aristote* (Paris, 1971); *Magic and Rhetoric in Ancient Greece* (Cambridge, Mass., 1975); *Problèmes de la démocratie grecque* (Paris, 1975); and *La Modernité d'Euripide* (Paris, 1986). Her lifelong concern with education is expressed in *Nous autres professeurs* (Paris, 1969) and *L'Enseignement en détresse* (Paris, 1984).

J. Romilly, *Nous autres professeurs* (Paris, 1969), *L'Enseignement en détresse* (Paris, 1984); *Who's Who in France, 1990–1991* (Paris, 1990).

M. C. Weitz

Related entries: ACADEMIE FRANCAISE; ANNALES SCHOOL.

ROUDY, YVETTE (1929–), deputy minister charged with the Rights of Women from 1981 to 1985 and minister of women's rights from 1985 to 1986 under French president François Mitterrand. An activist born of working-class parents in Bordeaux, Roudy has been a longtime champion of women's rights and socialism. After completing the requirements for a high school diploma through a correspondence course, she moved to England with her husband and learned to speak, read, and write English so well that she embarked on a career as a translator. Her first major work of translation was Betty Friedan's *The Feminine Mystique* (1965), followed by translations of *My Life* by Eleanor Roosevelt (1967) and *Women's Place in a Man's World* by Elizabeth Jeannewan (1969). She was later to author four books on the status of women, namely *La Réussite de la femme* (1969), *La Femme en marge* (1975), *Les Métiers et les conjoints* (2d ed., 1981), and *A cause d'elles* (1985). Her work on behalf of feminism also included a term as secretary-general of the *Mouvement démocratique féminin* (1964) and as the founder and editor in chief of the popular magazine *La Femme du XXe siècle*.

Roudy's political career as an advocate of socialism formally began in 1965 when she became a member of Mitterrand's Convention of Republican Institutions. In 1978 she stood as a Socialist party candidate for election to the National Assembly, and in 1979 was elected as a deputy to the European Parliament. During her tenure as deputy she headed the European Parliament's Commission on the Rights of Women.

After President Mitterrand appointed her to the post of deputy minister and then minister of women's rights, Roudy concentrated her efforts on strengthening the rights of women in the workplace through the design and enforcement of "catch-up" measures and through the establishment of the Supervisory Council for Professional Equality, a watchdog organization charged with the task of ensuring women equal access to professional training. Roudy also launched a series of national media campaigns to increase public knowledge about birth control. In addition, some 140 National Centers for Information on the Rights of Women were established under her leadership. These centers offered advice and counseling on such matters as professional training, wife abuse, rape, and prostitution. One of Roudy's most notable battles was fought over what was commonly called the *loi Roudy*, proposed legislation that would ban sexism in advertising. The *loi Roudy* was modeled after the Law of 1972, which banned racism in advertising. While the bill was approved by the Council of Ministers in March 1983, it lost in the National Assembly after a prolonged and bitter conflict over possible violations to freedom of expression and after almost daily public ridicule of the minister of women's rights.

Roudy left office after the socialists lost their majority in the National Assembly in 1986 and the new conservative prime minister, Jacques Chirac, reconstituted the cabinet. She was subsequently elected to the National Assembly as a Socialist party delegate from Calvados in 1986, and was reelected for a second term in 1988, serving as vice-president of the Commission for Social Affairs of the National Assembly. She was also appointed the Socialist party's National Secretary for Women's Rights in 1988.

W. Northcutt, J. Flaitz, "Women, Politics, and the French Socialist Government," *West European Politics*, 8 (October 1985); Y. Roudy, *A cause d'elles* (Paris, 1985).

J. J. Flaitz

Related entries: FEMINISM; LABOR FORCE; SOCIALIST PARTY (PS); WOMEN, CONDITION OF.

S

SARTRE, JEAN-PAUL (1905–1980), philosopher, dramatist, novelist, critic, and political activist, who became the most famous exponent of postwar French existentialism. Though consistently hostile to bourgeois culture, he had been born into a bourgeois family and received an elite education at *Lycée Henri IV* and *Lycée Louis-le-Grand* and at the *Ecole normale supérieure* (1924–28). After passing his *agrégation* in 1929, he taught philosophy in *lycées* in Le Havre and Neuilly, studied the works of Edmund Husserl and Martin Heidegger, and spent a year (1933–34) at the French Institute in Berlin.

Sartre always stood apart, however, and he was brutally critical of the bourgeois world in which he was economically and professionally integrated. As a youth he befriended Paul Nizan, and while at the *Ecole normale supérieure* they formed a *bande à part* (which later included Simone de Beauvoir) that ridiculed teachers and conventions. In his teaching posts Sartre adopted an open and relaxed style—in sharp contrast to tradition—that endeared him to many of his students. His first published writings focused on notions that seemed to meet the mood of the times—radical pessimism, revolt, insubordination, absolute solitude. He explored the frustrated rationalist aspirations of man as purely existing being, and the hollowness and meaninglessness of modern life. In *Nausée* (1938), for example, the protagonist Roquentin finds existence in a universe that is not rigid and predictably terrifying. Contingency plunges him into "a horrible ecstasy," and he recognizes that he must find his own reason for living. This focus on individual choice was a central theme in Sartre's writings: Choice was inherent in every action; by choice an individual defined his/her being; and only by careful choice could one avoid being adrift in a life devoid of commitment.

In his early writings Sartre's attack on the uncommitted life lacked specific political content. He reasoned that salvation could be attained through art, and that his own existence was justified by creating beautiful books. This changed with the outbreak of the war in 1939, which forced Sartre to confront politics and historicity. As Simone de Beauvoir recalled, "His new moral attitude, based on the notion of authenticity . . . demanded that man 'assume' his situation . . . by engaging in action." This new engagement in politics was reinforced by the experiences of war: He was mobilized into the French Army as a private and sent to Lorraine where, on June 21, 1940, he was captured by the Germans. After eight months as a prisoner, he was released and he returned to Paris to teach philosophy and to write plays and books, as well as articles for the underground paper *Les Lettres françaises*. He was briefly active in the Resistance, creating a circle called *Socialisme et liberté* with Beauvoir and Maurice Merleau-Ponty.

Sartre's preoccupation with choice was evident in his wartime publications such as *Les Mouches* (1943) and *Huis clos* (1944). In *L'Etre et le néant* (1943), the most famous of his philosophical works, he denounced bad faith, appealed to authenticity and responsibility, and made the now-famous distinction between being *en-soi*—that is, being deprived of consciousness and therefore representing all that is not freedom—and being *pour-soi*, voluntaristic being that strives to assert its liberty through intentional acts that confer life with meaning.

It was after the war that Sartre became the personification of existentialism. He was successful enough by 1944 to give up teaching. But the pivotal year was 1945, during which Sartre published the first two volumes of *Les Chemins de la liberté*, delivered and published a lecture entitled "*L'Existentialisme est un humanisme*" that many in Paris regarded as the cultural event of the year, and created the immensely influential review *Les Temps modernes*, with a stellar editorial staff that included Beauvoir, Merleau-Ponty, and friends like Michel Leiris, Albert Ollivier, Jean Paulhan, and Raymond Aron. The review was devoted to the discussion of political and literary questions from a generally existentialist point of view, and it came quickly to be dominated by Sartre, especially as relations among the editors deteriorated during the late 1940s and early 1950s.

This corresponded with the increasing hostilities of the Cold War. Sartre initially was critical of both the East and the West, and he tried, unsuccessfully, to help found a new political movement—the *Rassemblement démocratique et révolutionnaire* (RDR)—on the noncommunist left. But by 1950 he was blaming the United States for the Korean War, and by 1952 he had become a visible and vocal defender of the French Communist party (PCF). In 1954, following a trip to the Soviet Union, he expressed a naive enthusiasm for the beauties of the Soviet regime. This political itinerary led to acrimonious public breaks with many of his former friends and colleagues—first Aron, and then Albert Camus, Merleau-Ponty, Claude Lefort, and others. The alliance between Sartre and the PCF remained an uneasy one, however, and with the repression of the Hungarian Revolution of 1956 it came to an end.

That Sartre continued to view himself as a Marxist is clear from his book *Critique de la raison dialectique* (1960), which attempted to reconcile a Marxian theory of history with existentialism. Moreover, Sartre's various public interventions—such as the campaign for Algerian independence and his support of the students in 1968—continued to situate him on the left. Often referred to as "synthetic anthropology," Sartre's mature politics combined an aggressive anticolonialism with his philosophy of existential ethics.

His principal publications after 1960 were devoted to reflection and literary analysis. In 1963 he published his autobiography, *Les Mots*, to almost universal acclaim. He was awarded the Nobel Prize in the same year, but refused it because as a writer he did not wish to become an institution. His last major publication was an extensive investigation of Flaubert's childhood, entitled *L'Idiot de la famille* (vols. 1–2, 1971; vol. 3, 1972). The final two volumes on Flaubert's mature years were never completed, because Sartre became blind in 1973. He died in Paris on April 15, 1980.

A. Cohen-Solal, *Sartre 1905–1980* (Paris, 1985; Eng. trans., 1987); J.-P. Sartre, *Les Mots* (Paris, 1963; Eng. trans., 1964).

K. S. Vincent

Related entries: BEAUVOIR, SIMONE DE; CAMUS, ALBERT; EXISTENTIALISM; INTELLECTUAL TRENDS; LITERATURE.

SAVARY, ALAIN (1918–1988), socialist politician. He was born on April 25, 1918 in Algiers. In June 1940 the young naval officer was one of the first to join Charles de Gaulle's Free French, and he became governor of Saint-Pierre-et-Miquelon when they took control of the islands from Vichy in 1941.

A member of de Gaulle's *Compagnons de la libération*, Savary was elected a socialist (SFIO) deputy to the National Assembly from Saint-Pierre-et-Miquelon in 1956. State secretary for Moroccan and Tunisian affairs in Guy Mollet's government, he played a leading role in the 1956 negotiations reestablishing Morocco as a sovereign state and according independence to Tunisia. He resigned in October 1956 to protest Mollet's acquiescence to French capture of a Moroccan airplane carrying Algerian rebel leaders.

Leaving the SFIO in 1958 when Mollet supported de Gaulle, Savary helped to form the *Parti socialiste autonome*, merging in 1960 with other small left groups to form the *Parti socialiste unifié* (PSU). He later headed a group called *L'Union des clubs pour le renouveau de la gauche* (UCRG). In 1969 Savary's and other left groups (but not François Mitterrand's *Convention des institutions républicaines*, CIR) united with the SFIO to form a renewed *Parti socialiste* (PS), and Savary became first secretary but was not master of the new party. A new unification congress in 1971 at Epinay-sur-Seine ended with an alliance among the CIR, parts of the old SFIO, and young left-wingers, which elected Mitterrand the new first secretary.

Savary was elected to the National Assembly by the Haute-Garonne department in 1973, retaining this seat in the 1978 and 1981 elections. After Mitterrand won the presidency in 1981, Savary became minister of national education in Pierre Mauroy's government. His principal challenge was legislation fulfilling Mitterrand's electoral promise to establish "a unified and secular public education system" while conciliating adherents of the private schools (largely parochial), where teachers were paid by state funds. In patient negotiations lasting over two years, Savary and his team achieved a delicately balanced compromise satisfying most elements in the episcopate, anxious to end the church-state quarrel once and for all. However, this compromise did not satisfy PS secularists, nor many in the Catholic camp, and socialist amendments to Savary's education bill upset the balance. Resulting demonstrations against the bill drew more than a million people in a Paris protest march in June 1984. After some hesitation, Mitterrand withdrew the bill without previously informing Savary, who felt he had been disavowed and resigned, precipitating Mauroy's resignation as well.

More a diplomat than a strong political leader, Savary was widely admired as a man who had always followed his conscience. He died on February 17, 1988.

R. W. Johnson, *The Long March of the French Left* (New York, 1981); J. Poperen, *L'Unité de la gauche 1965–1973* (Paris, 1975); *Who's Who in France* (Paris, 1981).

J. W. Friend

Related entries: EDUCATIONAL REFORM; MAUROY, PIERRE; MITTERRAND, FRANCOIS; MOLLET, GUY; MOROCCO, RELATIONS WITH; SOCIALIST PARTY (PS, SFIO); TUNISIA, RELATIONS WITH.

SCHUMAN, ROBERT (1886–1963), lawyer, politician, minister, author of the Schuman Plan, and early supporter of European integration. Schuman was a man from two cultures: French and German. Born in Luxembourg, he grew up in Metz when it was under German control and attended the universities of Bonn, Munich, and Berlin, completing his legal studies in 1912. Shortly after 1918 when Lorraine and Alsace were returned to France, Schuman was elected deputy from Metz. For twenty years he paid special attention to a bilingual constituency that readapted itself to the French rule. In 1940 he was minister for the refugees and displaced persons. While his conservative leanings made him sympathetic to Pétain, during the Occupation he managed not to be involved in the Vichy regime.

As member of the new Christian democratic party, the *Mouvement républicain populaire*, he was appointed minister of finance in June of 1946. He insisted upon the need for economic liberalism. When the Cold War intensified he stood resolutely for a close association with the United States. In November of 1947, when many feared civil turmoil because of deep divisions in postwar France, he became prime minister and remained in this position until July of 1948. During his term "stopgap aid" was voted by the U.S. Congress, legislation that helped the French government to stay afloat until the Marshall Plan was adopted to aid Western Europe. Then, Schuman went to the Ministry of Foreign Affairs where he remained until January of 1953.

As minister of foreign affairs, one of his key priorities was the strengthening of the alliance with the United States. In regular contacts with the American ambassador Jefferson Caffery, he supported significant American initiatives: the European Recovery Program and formation of the Atlantic Alliance. In July of 1949 he went before the French Parliament to present a strong case in favor of NATO and easily won ratification for the treaty.

Europe was another concern for Schuman. Given his familiarity with both French and German culture, he understood the necessity of building European unity. In the aftermath of World War II, the German question was controversial in France. Schuman relied on economic necessity to draw the two nations together to prevent war. He prepared a bold scheme to pool basic commodities, German coal and French steel. The technical plan for this effort was prepared by Jean Monnet, who consulted with American experts on a regular basis. In order to avoid the polemics, Schuman informed Parliament about the plan only briefly on May 9, 1950. The plan was formally approved by the French Assembly on December 13, 1951 (later expanded into the European Coal and Steel Community that included Italy, Belgium, the Netherlands, and Luxembourg, the basis of the European Economic Community). The integration of two economic sectors had a political dimension as well. Over time it shifted the emphasis of French foreign policies away from a close association with the British toward an understanding with Germany. The European Coal and Steel Community (ECSC) was much more than an economic scheme. It encouraged French diplomacy to develop a strong relationship with Germany, while Great Britain tried to preserve a special partnership with the United States. Yet, Schuman wanted France to be a reliable partner of the United States and a supporter of Atlantic policy. However, at times he might have had some doubts about U.S. policy; for instance, he was lukewarm about any extension of the Korean War. Even in Europe he saw some limits to military developments under NATO. He did support the contested Pleven Plan for a European Defense Community that would include German regiments. The bitter debate over and defeat of the Pleven Plan led to his resignation as minister of foreign affairs. On the question of colonial issues, he supported flexible arrangements that would one day end the semicolonial status of Morocco and Tunisia.

In 1955 he became minister of justice, but then faded from the political scene with the return of Charles de Gaulle in 1958. His last important position was as chairman of the European Parliament in Strasbourg, an appropriate symbol for a man who worked for European economic cooperation and integration.

A. Grosser, *La IVème République et sa politique extérieure* (Paris, 1961); R. Schuman, *Pour l'Europe* (Paris, 1951).

J.-R. Chotard

Related entries: ECONOMIC POLICY; EUROPEAN DEFENSE COMMUNITY; EUROPEAN ECONOMIC COMMUNITY, RELATIONS WITH; INDUSTRIAL POLICY; MARSHALL PLAN; SCHUMAN PLAN.

SCHUMANN, MAURICE (1911–), writer, chief spokesperson for the Free French in London during World War II, founding chairman of the Christian democratic *Mouvement républicain populaire* (MRP) from 1945 to 1949, and member of government during both Republics. From D day until the liberation of Paris, Schumann assisted the Allied Expeditionary Forces, and he was decorated with the *Compagnon de la Libération*, *Légion d'honneur*, Order of Leopold, and the *Croix de guerre*. Schumann's enormous prestige and popular recognition resulted in his selection as a member of the provisional consultative assembly under Charles de Gaulle in 1944 and 1945, and in his membership in the constituent assembly in 1945 and 1946, which drafted the constitution of the Fourth Republic.

In the National Assembly Schumann represented the politically volatile department of the Nord during the critical years of 1945, 1958, 1967, and 1968. He served as minister of foreign affairs from 1951 to 1954 when France negotiated the Schuman Plan (after Robert Schuman) for the Franco-German coal and steel industry. After the early 1950s the electoral strength of the MRP waned, though Schumann's own support remained strong among Catholics and conservative Resistance movement voters. He was loyal to de Gaulle and to the Gaullist agenda in foreign policy, which argued for negotiating from positions of French strength and striving for independence from American domination. In 1967 and early 1968 Schumann was the minister of state for scientific research. After the May 1968 crisis he became minister of social affairs, where he helped formulate the traditional, conservative, and Catholic social agenda (some have called it the Gaullist corporatist agenda), which was the core of the 1969 referenda whose defeat in turn brought about de Gaulle's resignation. Under the Gaullist president Georges Pompidou, Schumann served as minister of foreign affairs from 1969 to 1973. In 1974 he was elected to the *Académie française*. He retired to the Senate where he has voted with the conservative and Catholic bloc. He has written four novels and ten works of nonfiction, including *Angoisse et certitude*, which won the *grand prix catholique de littérature* in 1978.

J.-F. Doumic, H. Lacharmoise, eds., *Le Guide du pouvoir* (Paris, 1989); P. Williams, *Politics in Post-War France* (London, 1958).

P. A. Phillips

Related entries: ACADEMIE FRANCAISE; CATHOLICISM; CHRISTIAN DEMOCRATS; DE GAULLE, CHARLES; POMPIDOU, GEORGES.

SCHUMAN PLAN, announced by the French foreign minister, Robert Schuman, in 1950 to integrate the coal and steel resources of France and Germany, subsequently expanded to include Italy, and Belgium, the Netherlands, and Luxembourg (Benelux). In a now-famous speech of May 9, 1950, Schuman proposed that French and German coal and steel resources be integrated into a single, common market by eliminating tariff and transportation barriers in the coal and steel region astride the French-German frontier. In making this proposal Schuman broke a deadlock in the debate over West Germany's reintegration into a Western European community. There were economic and political considerations behind the plan. Schuman argued that a pooling of these vital industries would benefit both German and French steel industries, sustain the momentum of European recovery, foster European cooperation, and resolve the age-old opposition between France and Germany by making war between the two countries both unthinkable and practically impossible.

The plan called for creation of a European Coal and Steel Community (ECSC) that would be governed by a high authority representing the participating states. This high authority had extensive powers of regulation and control. Jean Monnet, also an advocate of integration, became the first president of the High Commission. The success of the ECSC led the Inner Six to move quickly toward formation of a common market in other areas, culminating in the agreements that produced the European Economic Community (EEC) or Common Market by 1958.

W. Diebold, *The Schuman Plan, A Study in Economic Cooperation* (New York, 1959); A. S. Milward, *The Reconstruction of Western Europe* (Berkeley, Calif., 1984); R. Poidevin, *Robert Schuman: Homme d'état 1886–1963* (Paris, 1986).

J. K. Munholland

Related entries: EUROPEAN ECONOMIC COMMUNITY, RELATIONS WITH; FEDERAL REPUBLIC OF GERMANY, RELATIONS WITH; MONNET, JEAN; SCHUMAN, ROBERT.

SEGUIN, PHILIPPE (1943–), a rising Gaullist politician. Séguin was born in Tunis; after studies at Aix-Marseille and the *Ecole nationale d'administration*, he joined the *Cour des comptes* in 1970. From 1973 to 1974 he served as a *chargé de mission* to the secretary-general of the presidency. He was later the *Directeur de cabinet* of the secretary of state for relations with Parliament (1977) and a *chargé de mission* in the office of Prime Minister Raymond Barre (1977–78). First elected as the deputy for Epinal in 1978, Séguin has won re-election in every subsequent contest. He has also been the mayor of the city since 1983.

From 1981 to 1986 Séguin served as a vice-president of the National Assembly and proved to be one of the opposition's most effective orators. Yet, an avowed nonconformist, he strongly criticized the right's "*libéralomanie*." As minister of social affairs and employment in the government of *cohabitation* (1986–88), Séguin followed a basically moderate course. Nevertheless, he was responsible for two markedly controversial measures: the abolition of prior administrative authorization for worker redundancies and the partial deregulation of working hours. Since the 1988 elections Séguin has been an active, if conspicuously cautious proponent of "renovation" within the right. Clearly one of France's ascendant political stars, Séguin appears to have plotted his future trajectory essentially within the context of a reformed *Rassemblement pour la République*.

T. Desjardins, *Les Chiraquiens* (Paris, 1986); P. Séguin, *Réussir l'alternance* (Paris, 1985); P. Séguin, P. Servent, *La Force de convaincre* (Paris, 1990).

R. A. Harmsen

Related entries: BARZACH, MICHELE; CHIRAC, JACQUES; *COHABITATION*; GAULLISM; GAULLIST PARTY; NOIR, MICHEL; PASQUA, CHARLES.

SEGUY, GEORGES (1927–), communist trade unionist who led the *Confédération générale du travail* (CGT) from 1967 to 1982, when he retired to make way for Henri Krasucki. Jovial and genuinely popular, Séguy devoted his life to the French Communist party (PCF). A print worker born in Toulouse, Séguy was involved in the Resistance after the German invasion of Russia in 1942. He was arrested and sent to a concentration camp, from which he was later released. Séguy then became an electrician for the French railroad (SNCF) and was quickly promoted in the hierarchy of the union. In 1954 he was nominated a substitute member of the PCF's Central Committee and in 1956 a substitute member of the Political Bureau. Séguy was made secretary-general of the communist rail workers' union in 1961, and in 1964 made a member of the CGT's confederal bureau. At the thirty-sixth CGT congress, he was made secretary-general of the communist unions in succession to Benoît Frachon, who became president.

Séguy's career was highly orthodox. His first challenge as leader of the CGT was to end the strike movement of May 1968. In conformity with the prevailing party line, he negotiated across-the-board wage increases. Séguy, like others, had been taken aback by the strike movement but suffered the further humiliation of seeing the terms rejected by strikers in Billaincourt. Nevertheless, the terms became the basis for the eventual settlement of the strike. He became an enthusiastic supporter of the socialist/communist alliance and used his union organization to promote the cause. During the mid–1970s, he grew in stature and was associated with reformist currents in the PCF. However, the PCF's change of line, its closing up, and its rejection of the socialists, which began in 1977, was much less to his taste. Nonetheless, with exemplary discipline, he fully accepted the new strategy.

The fortieth congress of the CGT in 1978, which could have seen a loosening of the CGT's internal structure, was abruptly curtailed and Séguy fell out of favor with party leadership. He was probably worried that the emphasis on union (particularly local strike) action and the transfer of cadres from the CGT to the party would damage the union. The PCF's action to defend its position in the 1978 legislative elections had already led Séguy to call on workers to vote communist. This ended the fiction that the party and the union were quite independent and was damaging, according to some, to the CGT. However, Séguy dutifully stepped up attacks on the rival union, the *Confédération française démocratique du travail* (CFDT), for its rightward drift (a carbon copy of the PCF's attacks on the socialists), and flung the CGT into the front line of the social battle.

Séguy was still regarded as insufficiently enthusiastic about new CGT militancy vis-à-vis the socialist government, and he was retired in 1982 to make way for the more reliable Henri Krasucki. However, Séguy retained a capital of popularity (ironically deriving from association with the high noon of the union of the left and liberalizing communism), which the party continued to exploit. For example, he headed the party's disarmament campaign in the mid-

1980s and was mentioned as a possible leader of the 1984 communist list for the European Parliament elections. He was also frequently mentioned as a potential supporter of communist dissidents—first the ''renovators'' and then the ''reconstructors''—but he preferred to keep his own counsel.

G. Séguy, *Le Mai de la CGT* (Paris, 1972), *Lutter* (Paris, 1978).

D. S. Bell

Related entries: BERGERON, ANDRE; COMMON PROGRAM; *CONFEDERATION FRANCAISE DEMOCRATIQUE DU TRAVAIL*; *CONFEDERATION GENERALE DU TRAVAIL*; *FORCE OUVRIERE*; FRACHON, BENOIT; FRENCH COMMUNIST PARTY; KRASUCKI, HENRI; MAIRE, EDMOND; MARCHAIS, GEORGES; STRIKES; TRADE UNION MOVEMENT.

SERVAN-SCHREIBER, JEAN-JACQUES (1924–), journalist, intellectual, social critic, and political maverick with a capacity for dramatizing, often in flamboyant style, important political issues of the Fourth and Fifth Republics. A graduate of the prestigious *Ecole polytechnique*, Servan-Schreiber first gained prominence in the early 1950s as cofounder (with Françoise Giroud) and editor of the then left-of-center political weekly, *L'Express*. He represented a strain of reform-minded opinion within the postwar left that gained the admiration of progressives. In 1954 he served on the staff of Pierre Mendès-France, providing liaison with the press and intellectuals.

A decorated fighter pilot for the Free French during World War II, Servan-Schreiber gained fame and notoriety as an outspoken opponent and critic of the war in Algeria. Recalled to service as a reserve lieutenant, Servan-Schreiber denounced the army's widespread use of torture during the battle for Algiers in 1957 in both *L'Express* and his best-selling *Lieutenant en Algérie*, causing the Ministry of Defense to charge Servan-Schreiber with undermining the army's morale. The antiwar movement in France gained momentum with publication of a ''Manifesto of 121'' intellectuals in 1960, which called for a refusal of military service and led to arrests of some who had signed this antiwar protest.

Servan-Schreiber won further fame with publication of another sensational book, *Le Défi américain*, that predicted an American economic domination of the European Common Market. Although intended as a call for European unity in the face of an American threat, the book's alarm proved premature, but it strengthened French opinion against American investments.

A longtime critic of Charles de Gaulle and Gaullism (he is reported to have said that the day of de Gaulle's resignation in 1969 was one of the happiest of his life), Servan-Schreiber developed political ambitions. He saw himself as a candidate who could unite the noncommunist left and centrist elements against the conservative Gaullists with a program of reforms, including decentralization, worker participation, the ''democratizing of opportunity,'' and a European policy that would be less nationalistic. He became secretary-general of the Radical party in 1969 and president two years later. His career gained momentum in April 1970 when he won a by-election in Nancy, but it suffered a setback when he challenged the Gaullist prime minister, Jacques Chaban-Delmas, in a Bordeaux by-election the following September and received less than 16 percent of the vote. Despite this setback, he sought cooperation with moderate elements through an alliance with Jean Lecanuet's Democratic Center party in November 1971. This move caused left radicals under Robert Fabre to break away and forge an alliance with the socialists and communists in what the left radicals hoped would be a new Popular Front. The traditional center proved to be far from unified and was in fact experiencing its death throes as French politics became divided between left- and right-of-center tendencies.

This division became apparent in the parliamentary elections of March 1973. When the left alliance won 45 percent of the vote, Lecanuet threw his support to the government of Pierre Messmer. The difficulties of forming a centrist concentration again appeared in the presidential elections of 1974, following the death of Georges Pompidou. After a close election the conservative but non-Gaullist candidate, Valéry Giscard d'Estaing, formed a diverse ministry headed by the Gaullist Jacques Chirac that included Servan-Schreiber as minister of reforms. Servan-Schreiber's moment as minister proved brief when he resigned a few days after his appointment in protest over the French government's decision to continue nuclear testing in the South Pacific.

In 1976 Servan-Schreiber led the radicals into formal union with the centrist parties headed by Jean Lecanuet and Jacques Duhamel, in effect ending the independent existence of the party that had dominated politics during the last half of the Third Republic. In 1978 this combination joined other centrist republicans to form the Union for French Democracy (UDF), which became the moderate conservative alternative to the Gaullists. In 1976–78 Servan-Schreiber served as president of the Regional Council in Lorraine. His attempt to win a seat in the European Parliament in 1979 foundered when his "Fifth List" obtained less than 2 percent of the vote. After this, Servan-Schreiber turned away from active politics. In 1985 he became president of the International Committee at Carnegie-Mellon University in Pittsburgh.

J.-J. Becker, *Histoire politique de la France depuis 1945* (Paris, 1988); M. Larkin, *France since the Popular Front* (Oxford, 1988); V. Wright, *The Government and Politics of France* (New York, 1983).

J. K. Munholland

Related entries: CHABAN-DELMAS, JACQUES; DECENTRALIZATION; GIROUD, FRANCOISE; GISCARD D'ESTAING, VALERY; LECANUET, JEAN; RADICAL PARTY; UNION FOR FRENCH DEMOCRACY.

SOCIALIST PARTY (PS), the party of François Mitterrand and today the dominant party of the French left. The old Socialist party (the *Section française de l'internationale ouvrière*, or SFIO), was transformed into the *Parti socialiste* (PS) in 1969. Its subsequent growth to become by 1981 the dominant political party was based on two factors. The first, fitfully undertaken in 1969 by First Secretary Alain Savary (elected in July 1969), was to seek an alliance with the

French Communist party (PCF). Since the previous socialists' attempt to create a centrist coalition had failed when faced with a Gaullist-led conservative majority, there was therefore no alternative other than to put together a left-wing coalition that included the communists, who polled 22 percent of the vote. Savary made some progress but was hobbled by a lack of authority, socialist hesitation, and a residual mistrust of the communists. The second factor was leadership, which Mitterrand supplied when he entered the PS at the June 1971 Epinay Congress to become its leader. Mitterrand had been the united left's candidate in the 1965 presidential contest and was the only figure of presidential stature on the left. Mitterrand, with a tactical flair close to genius, put together a deal with the communists that resulted in a joint manifesto, the Common Program, in June 1972. Mitterrand was able at the same time to appeal to floating (mainly centrist) voters, a task that had appeared impossible.

The 1973 legislative elections were the only elections fought on the joint platform, and although there was progress it was not spectacular. The breakthrough came in 1974 when Valéry Giscard d'Estaing won the presidency by a small margin (under half a million votes) from Mitterrand. By-elections in September of that year showed the PS to be ahead of the communists; in opinion polls the socialists took off (and hovered at 30%), and there was an influx of activists.

The irony was that a precondition of alliance success was that socialists dominate the communists and clearly appear to do so, but the communists had no intention of supporting an alliance that downgraded them to junior partner. Thus, the first signs of real socialist success were accompanied by attacks from the communists, which became increasingly aggressive; socialists, for the most part, kept a dignified silence. The socialists continued to make advances, particularly in cantonal and local elections: In 1977 they gained thirty-nine large towns.

Although the socialists appeared to be on the verge of government, the communists decided to end an alliance that profited them little, and the 1978 legislative elections were a defeat for the left even though the socialists (24.7%) outperformed the communists (20.5%). The growth of the PS in the mid–1970s had been continued against communist pressure and, although in 1975 (Pau Congress) the party's left had been evicted from the Secretariat, the leadership faced a more serious challenge from 1978 to 1981. In addition to communist hostility, an internal faction fight began between those who stayed loyal to Mitterrand's search for an accommodation with the PCF and those, around Michel Rocard, who wanted an alternative route. What made this serious was that Rocard was also challenging for the party's presidential nomination.

This bitter split became institutionalized at the party's 1979 Congress in Metz, when Rocard (along with Pierre Mauroy) was forced out of the party leadership and a poor showing in the European elections in June 1979 meant that the socialists' prospects for the presidentials in 1981 were widely written off. However, it was the Communist party, not the Socialist party, that disintegrated, and Mitterrand's refusal to turn his back on the PCF was vindicated when he won the 1981 elections. Most of the party's major figures and much of its administration moved into government; the party's new leader, Lionel Jospin, was a proxy for Mitterrand. From 1981 to 1988, under Jospin, the party held together rather than grew, and although it was briefly tempted by a role of outright opposition, it settled down fairly comfortably as a party of government. The party's input into government during this period was minimal, although it did have an influence (sometimes negative) on isolated issues.

When Mitterrand won the 1988 presidential and legislative elections, Jospin became minister of education and Mauroy became first secretary. The socialists now face the problem that the Communist party is negligible and votes have to be won from the center (the PS had only a relative majority in the 1988 elections), and that is a more difficult task than effecting the communist alliance of the 1970s. Mauroy wants to reshape the administration and increase membership, which have been refractory problems in the past.

From 1974 onward (when Rocard joined the party) the internal dynamics of the PS were relatively simple; there were four competing groups: Rocard, Mauroy, Mitterrand, and Jean-Pierre Chevènement (Center of Socialist Study and Research, CERES). These "tendencies" have had variable boundaries, have fluctuated in size, and there has been some crisscrossing of personalities. The tendencies were at their clearest at the Metz Conference in 1979 when they were as follows: The division at Metz was one of personalities (who would make the best presidential candidate, Rocard or Mitterrand), ideology (for and against the market), and strategy (what to do about the mounting aggressiveness of the Communist party). Mauroy and Rocard were pushed out of the party executive, and Mitterrand formed an alliance with Chevènement's group, CERES. Mitterrand's leadership was at no point under serious threat, but the Mitterrand/CERES search for an accommodation with the PCF and, failing that a program that would be radical enough to appeal to communist voters, was the one that prevailed. Rocard tried, prematurely, to establish a more moderate social democratic policy that would be reformist and hence appeal to communist voters, but also modernist and realist, and hence attract floating voters. Many in the party have not forgiven Rocard for his challenge to the leadership at the most difficult moment for the new party.

Since 1988 the factional position has been transformed because the prospect of the *après*-Mitterrand cannot be evaded (there are only two more congresses before the next presidential nominating convention) and because the Communist party has collapsed and it is irrelevant to electoral calculations. These two factors have given Rocard, who was prime minister from 1988 to 1991, a strong hand. Rocard is by far the most popular politician and the only socialist of presidential stature; his persistent advocacy of a social-democratic philosophy was designed to appeal to the center, which is now the party's task. However, the Mitterrand presidency was used to bar the route to Rocard, and his candidacy would risk uniting a "*cartel des non*" against him. The president can be assumed to be hostile to Rocard's inheriting the PS. But Mitterrand's supporters have themselves split three ways between Fabius, Jospin, and Louis Mermaz. Mermaz, forming a sort of left, has the least support, and Fabius and Jospin are quarreling essentially over who will inherit the Mitterrand support. Fabius should have been well placed but has never really recovered from his eclipse as prime minister, and Jospin, despite seven years at the head of the party, and since 1988 in the education portfolio, has been unable to make a mark.

As to Mauroy, who unexpectedly beat Fabius to become first secretary of the PS in 1988, he has ambition but reached his high point from 1981 to 1984 when he was prime minister, and his group has been steadily loosing ground (the Pas-de Calais, Mauroy's most important support after the Nord federation, declared for Fabius). Mauroy has placed a good deal of emphasis on the need for a deal with the PCF (which is not reciprocated), and he lacks impact. On the party's left, Chevènement's supporters (ex-CERES) are grouped in "Socialism and Republic," but with the disappearance of the need for alliance with the PCF have lost their way, although Chevènement is popular (ironically as a result of a notably conservative phase as education minister) and leads the most organized and self-publicizing group in the party. There are also small groups around Jean Poperen (probably 5% or so), Jacques Delors, and Michel Delebarre (a rising star), as well as a group called *Transcourants* that wants to end the perpetual squabbling.

In terms of party organization there has been much discussion of the inability of the PS to attract new members; subscriptions are high and the possibilities to contribute are said by some to be too limited. The party claims to have 202,000 members, but in all probability may count no more than 100,000 or so. The Socialist party has not recruited as strongly as might have been expected given its long period in government and its dominant position.

Despite an organizational weakness (which is not great compared to other French political parties), the Socialist party is in a strong position. The Communist party is in terminal decline and the right is hopelessly split; moreover, unless there is a real catastrophe the party will have a majority in the Assembly until 1993, and Mitterrand can retain the presidency until 1995.

G. Ayache, *L'Identité socialiste* (Paris, 1987); D. S. Bell, B. Criddle, *The French Socialist Party* (Oxford, 1984); J. F. Bizot, *Au Parti des socialistes* (Paris, 1976); R. W. Johnson, *The Long March of the French Left* (London, 1980); J. Kergoat, *Le Parti socialiste de la Commune à nos jours* (Paris, 1982); D. Lowe, N. Nugent, *The French Left* (London, 1979).

D. S. Bell

Related entries: COMMON PROGRAM; ELECTIONS; JOSPIN, LIONEL; MAUROY, PIERRE; MITTERRAND, FRANCOIS; POLITICAL TRENDS; SAVARY, ALAIN; SOCIALIST PARTY (SFIO); UNION OF THE LEFT.

SOCIALIST PARTY (SFIO, 1905–69), officially known as the *Section française de l'internationale ouvrière*, the forerunner of François Mitterrand's *Parti socialiste* (PS). In 1945 the end of the war and of the Occupation revealed a Socialist party deeply traumatized by the events of the previous decade. Prewar pacifists such as Paul Faure and those who had voted for Pétain in 1940 were expelled. Léon Blum returned from deportation, but to engage in governmental and diplomatic activities rather than to prioritize party renewal. Daniel Mayer, the founder of the wartime socialist Resistance movement, was defeated as general secretary of the party (during acrimonious debates at the national congress in August 1946) in favor of Guy Mollet, who represented a return to traditional socialist values. Thus the experience and ideals of the Resistance failed to achieve lasting impact on the postwar party.

The advent of bloc politics after 1947 put an end to the brief pragmatic experiment in tripartitism that had seen the SFIO sharing governmental responsibilities with the Communist party (PCF) and the Christian democratic *Mouvement républicain populaire* (MRP). Against the twin threats of communism and a resurgent Gaullism in the shape of the *Rassemblement du peuple français* (RPF), Mollet's party engaged in a doomed experiment with "third force" politics through a governmental alliance with a number of relatively feeble bourgeois parties such as the radicals, the MRP, the social republicans around Jacques Chaban-Delmas, and the tiny formation headed by François Mitterrand, the *Union démocratique et socialiste de la Résistance* (UDSR). Circumstances were hardly auspicious, and it was through an unnatural combination of traditional Marxist rhetoric and punctual opportunist pragmatism, assisted by France's new planning machinery as well as by the extension of the nationalized sector, that socialist ministers from 1947 to 1951 helped drag France back to its feet again. This artificial embrace of neocapitalism, together with a concomitant resistance to the promotion of structural social reform, was to cost the SFIO a high price in both membership and electoral loyalty. From 4.5 million votes in 1945, the SFIO slumped to 2.7 million in 1951, while the 300,000 party members fell to 140,000 over the same period. It was a time when the left was dominated hegemonically by the Communist party, and the SFIO's main concern was to ensure its very existence.

After a dismal showing in the 1951 elections, the party proceeded to tear itself apart over German rearmament and the European Defense Community (EDC). Guy Mollet, who in 1954 was to become president of the consultative assembly of the European Council, was a committed European. Unfortunately for him, his strongest support on this issue from inside the party came from men like André Philip, who were his bitterest critics on most other issues. On the other hand, leading socialists of governmental calibre such as Vincent Auriol, Jules Moch, Robert Lacoste, and Max Lejeune were all vigorously opposed to the rehabilitation of Germany. The vote on the EDC in 1954 saw a narrow majority of socialist deputies (53 to 50) defy party discipline by opposing the scheme. Pro-European socialists were nevertheless to get their "revenge" three years later when it fell to the government of Guy Mollet (prime minister since 1956) to sign the Treaty of Rome.

However, it is not for its European policy that the Mollet government will be remembered. On taking office in January 1956, the prime minister had inherited a wasps' nest in North Africa, with a major war brewing in Algeria, hotly contested independence pending in Tunisia and Morocco, and the future of the Suez canal threatened in Egypt. Throwing caution to the winds, Mollet engaged French conscript troops in the disastrous Algerian War, which was, within two years, to destroy the Fourth Republic. This decision to eschew dialogue with the national liberation movements went hand in hand with Mollet's equally disastrous participation in the Suez fiasco. Both courses of action were to widen the rift within the already divided party, but it was on financial policy that the inglorious socialist government was defeated in 1957. A year later, hardly surprisingly, the party split decisively over support for General Charles de Gaulle's plans for a radical revision of the constitution. Mollet's pro-Gaullist stance was given a temporary majority boost by the support of Gaston Defferre, but members of the old guard such as Edouard Depreux, revisionists such as Daniel Mayer, and admirers of Pierre Mendès-France like Alain Savary all left the SFIO to form the *Parti socialiste autonome* (PSA). The next ten years represented less a crossing of the desert, and more a futile treck in search of an oasis that never materialized.

On the surface the party remained much as it had always been, while beneath the surface of French life vast changes were taking place. The *trente glorieuses* were bringing economic comforts and industrial expansion, together with a rapidly evolving social structure. The new institutions of the Fifth Republic (the electoral shift to single-member constituencies and the downgrading of parliamentary power) inevitably pulled the rug away from the principal political functions of the SFIO as it had operated in the past. Renewal came slowly and painfully, and in large part through the political clubs and republican associations that proliferated in the vast center ground between the communists and the Gaullists (André Malraux was hardly exaggerating when he quipped that "between us and the Communists there is nothing"). By 1964, these many isolated discussion circles were intellectually prepared to attempt a synthesis, which came via the creation of the *Conventions des institutions républicaines* (CIR), founded by François Mitterrand and a number of his closest political friends, Louis Mermaz, Claude Estier, Charles Hernu, Roland Dumas, and Pierre Joxe. Mitterrand's preferred strategy for the reconquest of power was to form a tactical alliance with the communists, which he believed the noncommunist left would gradually come to dominate, thus neutralizing the PCF's capacity to obstruct. Others, however, such as Gaston Defferre, opted for the gradual forging of a center-left alliance of the old "third force" type. It was Defferre's spectacular failure to construct such a coalition in time for the presidential elections of 1965 that made the Mitterrand solution inevitable. Support for Mitterrand from both Mendès-France and Waldeck Rochet propelled him to the forefront of national politics.

Few on the left had foreseen the mobilizing and unifying potential of the new presidential regime. With the aid of the new audiovisual media, particularly television, François Mitterrand, who began his 1965 presidential campaign with opinion poll ratings of only 11 percent, emerged virtually triumphant after the first round with over 32 percent of the vote, forcing de Gaulle into a second round of voting. Hope began to resurface within the ranks of the left, which Mitterrand had taken one step closer to unity through the creation of the *Fédération de la gauche démocrate et socialiste* (FGDS), which embraced socialists, radicals, and members of the CIR. After the 1965 presidentials, the FGDS engaged in urgent discussions with the PCF with a view to offering a united opposition for the 1967 parliamentary elections. Mitterrand "appointed" from within his entourage a kind of shadow cabinet or "countergovernment" to give greater credence to the left's capacity to take the helm. The 1967 elections produced a fine harvest, with both the FGDS and the PCF making solid headway, the Gaullists hanging on to their overall majority by only one vote. But the most difficult task still remained: that of forging, from among the sectarian and multiple component parts of the old noncommunist left, something approaching a modern political party. From the 1967 elections to the 1968 "events," the SFIO spent most of its time in petty introspection, searching desperately for the elusive structural and doctrinal formula that would allow its fissiparous tendencies to hang together. Consequently, it failed utterly to see the depth of revolt against Gaullist society that was brewing quietly in many quarters, but especially among the young. May 1968 blew the whole artificial structure to pieces. The SFIO (and indeed the PCF) looked on like a bemused spectator as a new generation of political activists set a new agenda for the politics of the 1970s and 1980s. Mitterrand's ill-advised declaration, at the height of the turmoil, to the effect that he was ready to assume power, merely highlighted the extent to which the SFIO had become irrelevant. In the 1968 parliamentary elections, the FGDS lost fifty-eight seats, but worse was to come. In the presidential elections of 1969 (the only occasion under the Fifth Republic when Mitterrand was not a candidate), the hapless Gaston Defferre, running on the tired old "third force" ticket, could only muster 5 percent of the national vote. This disastrous score synchronized with the party's decision, at its Alfortville Congress in May 1969, to disband and seek a new fortune with a new name. The SFIO was quietly cremated and the new Socialist party (PS) emerged phoenixlike from the ashes—alas, with little more hope of success than its predecessor.

As was so often to be the case over the next twenty years, it was François Mitterrand, noting the forthcoming centenary of the Paris Commune, who quipped ironically that the new party "was born a hundred years old, and promptly died."

J. A. Faucher, *La Gauche française sous de Gaulle* (Paris, 1969); C. Hurtig, *De la SFIO au nouveau Parti socialiste* (Paris, 1970); D. Loschak, *La Convention des institutions républicaines* (Paris, 1971); R. Quilliot, *La SFIO et l'exercice du pouvoir, 1944–1958* (Paris, 1972); H. G. Simmons, *French Socialists in Search of a Role, 1956–1967* (Cornell, N.Y., 1970).

J. Howorth

Related entries: BLUM, LEON; CLUB MOVEMENT; ELECTIONS; FEDERATION OF THE DEMOCRATIC AND SOCIALIST LEFT; FRENCH

COMMUNIST PARTY; MITTERRAND, FRANCOIS; MOLLET, GUY; POLITICAL TRENDS; SOCIALIST PARTY (PS).

SOCIAL SECURITY, a nationally mandated social program, the foundation of the French welfare state, insuring for medical expenses and work injuries/disability, and providing family allowances, maternity, and retirement benefits. The landmark legislation of 1945–46 built upon the more limited programs of prewar years, and has undergone periodic expansion and reorganization.

Before the Revolution of 1789, care for the poor and the ill was undertaken by the Catholic church, promoting values of family and social solidarity. Proposals during the Revolution for national assumption of these responsibilities were never enacted. Slow industrialization in the nineteenth century dampened demand for state action, and private mutual aid societies provided some protection for skilled workers. Inspired by Otto von Bismarck's social legislation in Germany, the French government established free medical care for the indigent and an insurance fund for industrial injuries in the 1890s, followed by aid for indigent children, the invalid, and the elderly, and a mandatory pension fund for low-income workers and farmers.

Consequent to the ravages of World War I, public social expenditures increased dramatically. Moreover, the reintegration of Alsace-Lorraine sparked discussion of national legislation, and after much debate and delay a "Social Insurance" bill was adopted in 1928 and implemented in 1930. The law provided reimbursement for sickness expenses, work accidents, and maternity benefits, and created a fund for worker disability and retirement. Social insurance was nonetheless still seen as complementary to private individual or mutual insurance.

The wartime Resistance movement gave birth to the first overall vision of a universal Social Security program, largely inspired by the 1941 Beveridge Report in England. The Ordinance of October 4, 1945 had two objectives: covering all citizens, working or not, for all risks, and providing uniform benefits, regardless of income. The goal of a single, universal system was not achieved, however: Distinct agencies were set up for health insurance, family allowances, and pensions, and special funds for farmers, miners, railway workers, and so on. Also, merchants, artisans, and self-employed professionals lobbied successfully for their own pension funds. In addition, authority over the Social Security system was unclear: In principle, the beneficiaries were to manage the system, under state supervision; in practice, employers, mutual aid societies, labor unions, family associations, and several government ministries shared control.

Under the medical insurance scheme, the patient has free choice of doctors, and lays out costs for physician and hospital fees and charges for prescriptions and diagnostic tests. The local sickness fund later reimburses the patient, substantially but not entirely, to induce responsible consumption of services. In practice, private mutual insurance programs cover most of the patient copayment.

A family allowances program was created during the depression to help families in need, but was redirected in 1939 to stem demographic decline. The 1945 legislation greatly expanded the number of beneficiaries and the variety of aid categories. Today, the fund provides maternity and child-care benefits and monthly allowances to families with two or more children, independent of income, as well as special income-dependent aid for housing subsidies, back-to-school expenses, single-parent or low-income families, and families with adopted or handicapped children.

The pension fund program was initially based on the insurance principle, relating contributions to eventual benefits. More recently, special programs were introduced on the public assistance principle, to guarantee minimum pensions for the needy.

A number of financial problems have emerged in recent years, the most important and stubborn of which is the imbalance between revenues and mandated expenditures. This imbalance has several causes: the extension of Social Security to virtually the entire population; the demographic decline and consequent aging of the population; the advances in medical technology, which prolong life and increase the costs of care; the reduction of the retirement age; and the widespread industrial unemployment of the 1970s and 1980s, which dramatically reduced the system's wage-based revenues. Various remedies have been attempted: increasing either the rate of the payroll tax or the wage base on which the tax is imposed; creating a general income surtax or excise taxes on alcoholic beverages and tobacco products; borrowing surplus funds from one system (family allowances) to bail out another (sickness fund); and creating a variety of inducements (e.g., cost sharing, regulating medical fees, capping hospital budgets) to limit the growth of health-care expenditures.

Social Security expenditures today are greater than the entire state budget and account for nearly 30 percent of the gross domestic product. Despite the problems, Social Security remains a very popular institution, serving to reconcile traditional French values of individual responsibility and social solidarity.

D. Ashford, *The Emergence of Welfare States* (Oxford, 1986); A. Catrice-Lorey, *Dynamique interne de la sécurité sociale* (Paris, 1980); J.-J. Dupeyroux, *Droit de la sécurité sociale* (Paris, 1985).

P. J. Godt

Related entries: CATHOLICISM; COMMON PROGRAM: ECONOMIC POLICY; INCOME DISTRIBUTION; LABOR FORCE; POPULATION TRENDS; TAXATION; UNEMPLOYMENT.

SOCIAL STRATIFICATION, the distribution of French families throughout the social class system, can be derived by approximating the statistics for households whose heads are French and active, as given by the 1990 *Données sociales*.

The end of the peasantry. Farmers account for 6 percent of active French households, as opposed to a quarter of them just after World War II. The peasant style of life dominated the rural world: archaic methods, hard work, and much thrift on mostly small self-sufficient holdings; suspicion of the outside world and of one's neighbors; and a standard of living often inferior to that of the working class. Now, on much larger holdings, an estimated 10 percent of farmers enjoy a middle-middle- or upper-middle-class standard of living, and all have full access to urban culture, not only through the mass media, but also because half the farmers' families have at least one member who works outside the farm in the civil service, white-collar jobs, or in tourism.

The breakup of the proletariat. Approximately 32 percent (1989) of French households (including those involved in direct services to private parties) are working class, which used to be considered a segregated class without honor, manual labor being less valued than in the United States or Germany, and relatively homogeneous in its mores and clothing, and dominated by millenarian beliefs of a socialist or communist variety that promised it top status after the Revolution. Its standard of living has been multiplied three times during the "thirty glorious years" (1945–75). Its numbers have been declining since 1975. Foreigners and displaced peasants have been taking more and more of the low-skill jobs, and many native French workers have often become foremen or lower-white-collar workers. French workers have full access to car ownership, the standard household appliances, and five-week vacations with pay, items that used to be associated with bourgeois status. Roughly 12.5 percent of working-class children enter higher education; at least 34 percent of working-class sons leave the working class permanently. Moreover, 25 percent of working-class men have wives who are white-collar workers, allowing for some exposure to white-collar culture.

The lower-middle class (*petite bourgeoisie*). This class was composed, forty-five years ago, half by shopkeepers and artisans and half by salaried employees and lower-rung civil servants. The latter now make up three-quarters of this class, which today accounts for 44 percent of French households. Most salaried employees, especially office workers, have some secondary education and even the *baccalauréat*. Many have been promoted within the firm to white-collar positions (foremen and supervisors) after beginning as workers. Nevertheless, the movement up of the petty bourgeoisie through its own ranks seems greater in France (one-third) than in both England and Sweden (one-fifth). The distinction between skilled workers and petty bourgeois is often fuzzy in life-style because the former will often make more money than the latter and the workers are much more aware of middle-class consumption behavior.

The middle-middle class (*les classes moyennes*). This group is estimated to include 15 percent of French households. Its members have some higher education, which in France like everywhere else experienced enrollment increases—from 140,000 in 1950 to 956,000 in 1988. The diplomates of the second-rank *grandes écoles* belong here as well as all those called "engineers," the 20 percent most successful in the retail sector, 90 percent of the executives of the public and private sectors (*cadres d'entreprise*), and half of the employers of more than ten workers. It is a class that has sustained neo-Catholicism, the simplification of status rituals, partly because of a lack of means (whiskey tastes on a beer budget) and partly out of liberated convictions. It has also been the backbone of the expanding voluntary associations.

The upper-middle class and the social register (*la bonne bourgeoisie*). This category involves the "free professions"—although not the pharmacists, the bailiffs and the registrars (*huissiers* and *greffiers*)—the upper half of the employers of more than ten workers, and the upper 10 percent of the civil service and private sector executives. This group totals, according to French sources, about 2.6 percent of the active French households (320,000 families); however, this figure is probably exaggerated, given the fact that it takes about 600,000 francs of annual income to sustain an upper-middle-class life-style (apartment in a good section of a major city, a house in the country, private schooling for the children, two cars, a live-in maid or more frequently a daily cleaning woman, and an *au pair* for the children, club membership, vacations in summer and winter, and extensive entertaining). It takes more than 600,000 francs if one has to buy the houses and period furniture, and less if these are inherited.

The *Bottin mondain* lists the forty-five thousand families that make up the bulk of the French upper classes, from the top of the *bonne bourgeoisie* to the high aristocracy. Aristocratic-sounding names, with the particle *de* between first name and family name, make up about 40 percent of the *Bottin mondain*. About half the aristocratic names have been appropriated under the Third, Fourth, and Fifth Republics, but their holders are often compulsive conformists to aristocratic norms and standards.

The French *bonne bourgeoisie* is relatively closed. Only when second-generation members achieve prestigeful employment are they securely anchored in the class, which also has enough power to cushion the downward mobility of its inept offspring.

A phenomenon that is specific to France is the *Noblesse d'Etat*, made up of the elite of the first-rate *grandes écoles*, who at the end of their schooling enter the state high civil service in Estates (*Grands Corps*: *Inspection des finances, Conseil d'Etat*, *Cour des comptes*, *Corps des mines*, *Corps des ponts et chaussées*, etc.) and who are assured an upper-middle-class or even an upper-class placement. It is a meritocratic aristocracy, based on academic prowess that, although it affects only 300 students in a generational cohort of some 800,000, has enabled some great jumps in social mobility. Thanks to the *grandes écoles*, Georges Pompidou and Alain Peyrefitte, for example, whose fathers were grammar-school teachers, were propelled to the summit of the social class structure. Such successes have a mythical appeal and tend to legitimize a stratification system where diplomas play a great role.

Otherwise, upward social mobility in France is about average for Western Europe, less than Sweden or Britain, more than Italy or Spain. Differences, as found by research studies, are relatively small and the data is soft. There is a consensus that structural mobility increased and the resistance of status groups to the entry of outsiders declined between 1953 and 1970.

During the 1970s there was a common belief that France had greater inequality of income than other industrial democracies. There may have been some truth to that during the 1950s and 1960s, due to the scarcity of trained personnel for executive positions at all levels. Since 1973 the development of higher education has reduced the bargaining power of diplomates. The relation between the mean salary of workers and of higher executives (*cadres supérieurs*), which had reached a peak of 4.5 between 1959 and 1967, had fallen to 3.8 in 1985.

Finally there has been a transformation of the lower class, the poor, who twenty-five years ago could still work and whose low income was supplemented by products from their gardens and whose members included unskilled laborers and peasants eking a living from small plots. Today they have been replaced by the long-term unemployed, the handicapped persons, and unemployed single mothers with children in cities. They are helped by the state, but are essentially marginal to society.

R. Boudon, *L'Inégalité des chances* (Paris, 1979); P. Bourdieu, *La Noblesse d'Etat* (1989); R. Erikson, J. Goldthorpe, L. Portocarero, "Intergenerational Class Mobility in Three Western European Societies: England, France, and Sweden," *The British Journal of Sociology* 30, no. 4 (December 1979); J. Lautman, "Où sont les classes d'antan," in *La Sagesse et le désordre, France 1980* (Paris, 1980); C. Morrisson, *Les Inégalités de revenus* (Paris, 1986); C. Thelot, *Tel père, tel fils* (Paris, 1982).

J. R. Pitts

Related entries: AGRICULTURE; *GRANDES ECOLES*; INCOME DISTRIBUTION; LABOR FORCE; PEASANTRY; URBANIZATION.

SOCIAL TRENDS indicate that the postwar period has witnessed dramatic social change, especially with regard to birthrates, marriage, divorce, sexuality, immigration, and leisure. The end of World War II brought a radical departure from established birthrate trends. French Malthusianism, well established during the nineteenth century, had continued unabated during the interwar period. Only longer life expectancies and massive immigration prevented the depopulation of France in the 1930s. Depopulation occurred between 1940 and 1945 owing to higher mortality rates, deportations, and a reduced birthrate.

The downward trend was reversed in 1942, and by 1946 the birthrate had risen above the replacement level; French birthrates moved from the lowest to the highest among Western European nations in the postwar period. Whereas among the generation of women born around 1900 and coming to maturity during the 1920s and 1930s more than one in five did not bear a child, among the generation of women born in the 1930s only one in ten remained childless. As a result, and assisted by the resumption of high rates of immigration, French population growth was greater in the postwar period than during any other time in its history.

The abrupt change in attitudes can be traced to the prewar perception that relative to other European nations—especially Nazi Germany, where birthrates had revived well before the war—the French nation had lost its dynamism, a loss symbolized by a net rate of reproduction insufficient to assure the replacement of generations. This consensus helped to bring family subsidies (*allocations familiales*), which had been offered to some workers solely on the initiative of employers until 1932, into the realm of public policy in 1938. The shock of the defeat of 1940 helped to cement the change in attitudes. The new natalist mentality, encouraged by postwar optimism and monthly family subsidies equal to 20 percent of the average departmental wage for a second child and 30 percent for subsequent children, brought a kind of universalization of the child.

The baby boom turned abruptly to a baby bust in the 1970s. Between 1964 and 1975 the average number of children per woman of childbearing age fell from 2.9 to 1.9—Malthusianism had returned. The reasons were varied but had much to do with women's changing expectations of themselves and their lives. In 1965 one in three women received the *baccalauréat* as opposed to only one in four men. Higher levels of education for women induced a desire for fulfillment beyond—even instead of—marriage and family. During the 1960s a postwar decline in the proportion of women in the work force was reversed. Work became the norm not only for single women but also for mothers when, between 1962 and 1982, the percentage of mothers at work rose from 28 percent to 56 percent.

Not only women's attitudes changed. French society, traditionally centered around the family, became more individualistic in the 1960s and 1970s. Legalization of birth control (1967) and abortion (1975) effectively separated sexuality from reproduction. "Accidental" conceptions, which in the past had led to marriage for young couples, occurred with less frequency as the effectiveness of new birth control methods approached 100 percent. Men and women no longer thought of marriage as more or less obligatory in young adulthood. As young people began to attend university in record numbers in the postwar period, and as they left home in order to do so, they found they no longer needed to marry in order to escape parents and siblings. Young adults discovered a new sexual and personal independence outside of marriage. By the middle of the 1980s the number of marriages in France fell to its lowest peacetime level in twentieth-century France (265,000 marriages in 1986), even as the number of persons of marriageable age reached record levels. The number of unmarried women in the twenty-five to thirty-four age group rose from 15 percent in 1967 to 30 percent in 1987.

Those who did enter marriage were increasingly likely to leave it through divorce. French divorce law, little modified since 1884, was liberalized in 1975. Mutual consent replaced the requirements of the 1884 law, which stated that only specific offenses (adultery, violence) justified divorce. The new law, less a spur to divorce than a response to pent-up demand, made divorce easier and removed much of the stigma attached to it. The divorce rate had taken off before the 1975 liberalization; the annual number of divorces rose by 50 percent in the decade from 1965 to 1975, running from 34,877 to 55,612. The number of divorces nearly doubled from 1975 to 1985, by which time there were over 100,000 divorces per year. With the marriage rate falling off, the annual number of divorces exceeded 40 percent of the annual number of marriages for the first time in 1986. This trend suggests that French marriage/divorce proportions may soon match those for Sweden (44 percent).

"Marry late, divorce early" would provide a suitable motto for many French adults. The typical divorce in the 1980s occurred four to five years after marriage, instead of after seven or eight years as in the 1970s. In most cases, wives rather than husbands initiated divorce; in 1984, 73 percent of divorces were initiated by women. Once divorced, few remarried. Only two in five divorced persons remarried by the late 1980s. Cohabitation, both before and after marriage, thus became a common household norm. As marriages became more fragile in France, cohabitation and "monoparental" families emerged as major alternatives. The married couple with a family was still the dominant household type in France, but it was no longer the model of the majority of French households. In 1982, 39 percent of households consisted of married couples with children, down from 42 percent in 1978. Childless couples made up 24 percent of households in 1978. As marriage fell out of fashion, or as marriages were tried and failed, single-person households increased in importance. In 1982, 24 percent of households were single-person households, up from 21 percent in 1978. Where children were at stake in a divorce, the courts overwhelmingly awarded custody to mothers—the mother received exclusive custody in 85 percent of divorce cases in the early 1980s. Monoparental households increased in number; 5 percent of French households were monoparental in 1982. Currently, one in three infants in France is raised outside of the traditional two-parent family.

As divorce has become easier, French men and women seem to be less inclined to marry in the first place, even in order to have children. Indicative of new attitudes to marriage, divorce, and family are legitimacy rates in France. One in four babies born in France in 1990 was illegitimate, as opposed to one in twenty in the 1960s. Not even during World War I, when illegitimacy rates ran above 14 percent, were illegitimacy rates as high as they now are. Much of the stigma attached to illegitimacy has been removed—the designation "natural" has replaced "illegitimate" for children born out of wedlock, and such changes in designation and attitude have made it easier for parents to keep such children. Second, marriage is no longer seen as the inevitable consequence of unwanted pregnancy. Among teenage women in France in 1968, one in four births was illegitimate; in 1986, illegitimate births outnumbered legitimate ones by two to one. The increase in illegitimacy since the 1960s has spanned the age groups. Since 1980 most illegitimate births have occurred to women aged twenty-five or older. Part of the reason has to do with parental subsidies, which may actually be reduced if single parents elect to marry. For some, family life without benefit of marriage may simply be a matter of choice.

The decline of the working class and peasantry has been another outstanding social trend of the postwar era. Immediately after the Liberation, two-thirds of the active population worked in industry and agriculture. By 1987 nearly two-thirds were employed in services. The ethnic composition of the labor force has also changed, due to immigration. In 1946, 5.8 percent of the population of France was foreign-born. By 1982 the figure was over 11 percent and climbing. Such figures do not reflect the greater real impact of immigration concealed by naturalization: 1.8 million immigrants were naturalized between 1945 and 1986. In the postwar period, the origins of the immigrant population changed. In 1962 most immigrants were of European background, with Italians and Spaniards making up 49 percent. By 1982, 43 percent of immigrants were from Africa, mostly from Algeria and Morocco. Thus, as the size of the immigrant population grew so grew the cultural differences separating the native French from the world of the immigrants.

Postwar generations in France have enjoyed more leisure time. Thanks to longer life expectancy, more schooling, the lowering of the retirement age, the reduction of the workday and the workweek, and longer paid vacations, only about one-tenth of the typical French life span is devoted to work, as opposed to one-third during the industrial era. As the century closes, the progressive aging of the population and the inversion of the age pyramid have threatened the solvency of the retirement system and the vitality of the nation's economy.

Annuaire statistique (Paris, 1968–88); F. Dubet, *Immigrations: Qu'en savons-nous?* (Paris, 1989); J. Dupquier, *Histoire de la population française: De 1914 à nos jours* (Paris, 1988); C. Dyer, *Population and Society in 20th Century France* (London, 1978); H. Le Bras, *Les Trois France* (Paris, 1986).

R. A. Jonas

Related entries: ECONOMIC POLICY; ECONOMIC TRENDS; IMMIGRANTS; LABOR FORCE; LEISURE; NATIONALITY CODE; PEASANTRY; UNEMPLOYMENT; WOMEN, CONDITION OF.

SOS RACISME, an organization founded in 1984 under the leadership of Harlem Désir to combat racism and racial violence in France. The organization, begun in Paris, quickly spread, especially among students. It now has three hundred local committees and twenty-five thousand members and chapters in nine other countries.

The distinctive symbol of the organization is a hand raised in warning and inscribed: "*Touche pas à mon pote*" (Hands off my buddy). A series of huge benefit concerts, featuring several of the country's most popular musicians, has been especially effective in conveying the organization's message. The organization's primary aim of combating racism is pursued through efforts to change public opinion, to lobby for pertinent legislation, to provide legal assistance to victims of discrimination, and to improve public housing. Its chief target is the extreme-right National Front, headed by Jean-Marie Le Pen, which blames foreign workers for the economic ills of France and advocates the expulsion of immigrant workers, especially North Africans.

Désir, the highly regarded president of *SOS Racisme*, is himself of mixed racial background and was given the name Harlem because of his father's esteem for African-American culture. Désir acknowledges the influence of the American civil rights movement. He has thus far declined direct political involvement.

Désir seeks through persuasion to unite diverse elements within society to the common goal of justice for all.

H. Désir, *Touche pas à mon pote* (Paris, 1985), *SOS Désirs* (Paris, 1987).

F. J. Murphy

Related entries: IMMIGRANTS; LE PEN, JEAN-MARIE; MINORITIES, PROBLEMS OF.

SOUSTELLE, JACQUES (1912–1990), anthropologist, deputy, minister, member of the *Académie française*. Soustelle was born into a Protestant working-class family of Montpellier. He attended the *lycée* at Lyon and completed his studies at the *Ecole normale supérieure*. Study at the Trocadero Ethnography Museum, renamed the *Musée de l'homme* in 1937, sparked his interest in anthropology and the ancient peoples of central America. Beginning in 1932 he conducted fieldwork in Mexico among the Otomis and Lacandons, descendants of the great civilizations of pre-Colombian Central America. In 1937 he defended his thesis, and in 1938 he became deputy director of the *Musée de l'homme* and taught at the Collège de France.

Soustelle's earliest political allegiances were with the left. Open involvement in politics began during the Popular Front years when he wrote for the communist daily *L'Humanité*. He also wrote for *Vendredi*, a literary journal supported by intellectuals sympathetic to the Popular Front. Together with his mentor Paul Rivet, director of the *Musée de l'homme*, he organized the *Comité de vigilance des intellectuels antifascistes*. During the 1930s Soustelle was associated with efforts undertaken, in the spirit of the Popular Front, to bring culture to the people. He joined General Charles de Gaulle in London shortly after the armistice in 1940. In 1942 he became de Gaulle's minister of information.

After the war he was elected deputy in the department of Mayenne (1945) and served as minister of information, later as minister of colonies. He continued to serve de Gaulle after the general's withdrawal from politics. Between 1947 and 1951 he was general secretary of the new Gaullist political vehicle, the *Rassemblement du peuple français* (RPF). After 1951 he served as a Gaullist deputy (RPF, then *Républicain social*) from the Rhône.

Prime Minister Pierre Mendès-France named Soustelle governor-general of Algeria in January 1955, a position he held until February 1956. During his service as governor-general, Soustelle's commitment to the cause of French Algeria became a consuming passion, one that would remain with him well beyond the cessation of hostilities in Algeria. Soustelle's program for French Algeria included military pacification and investment for economic and social development, along with full legal equality of European and Moslem inhabitants and the integration of Algeria with France. In order to prevent an acceleration of Moslem defections to the Algerian National Liberation Front (FLN), Soustelle continually emphasized the permanence of the French presence and the mutual advantages to be derived from continued Franco-Algerian association.

After his year as governor-general, Soustelle resumed his responsibilities in the Assembly. In 1957 Guy Mollet appointed Soustelle to the French delegation at the United Nations. In this role Soustelle represented the French position on Algeria at the UN and before the American public. He remained in close contact with the partisans of *Algérie française*, and indeed served as one of their most effective leaders and spokespersons within the Assembly group known as the *Union pour le salut et le renouveau de l'Algérie française*. Along with many *pieds-noirs* and much of the French army in Algeria, Soustelle shared the conviction that the future of France was wrapped up in the struggle for Algeria and that success in the struggle for Algeria could only come about under the resolute leadership of General de Gaulle.

Soustelle helped to turn the revolt of May 13, 1958 toward a Gaullist outcome and worked with the press in Algiers to put the right twist on events. He also joined Generals Raoul Salan and Jacques Massu on the Committee of Public Safety created after the seizure of the government offices in Algiers. Soustelle's disaffection with de Gaulle began almost immediately after the general's accession to power; de Gaulle did not give Soustelle a cabinet post in the government he announced on June 1, 1958. On July 7 he was given a subministerial position attached to Prime Minister Michel Debré. After the events of Barricades Week (January 1960) in Algiers, Soustelle resigned his position in the government; in April he was driven from the Gaullist *Union pour la nouvelle République*. His break with de Gaulle and Gaullism was complete.

Soustelle created a new political vehicle, *Regroupement national*, and continued to appeal to public opinion through the bimonthly *Voici pourquoi*. He formed the *Comité de Vincennes*, through which he collaborated with such figures as Georges Bidault and Robert Lacoste on behalf of *Algérie française*. Soustelle went into exile after the launching of the abortive "generals' putsch" in April 1961, although there was no warrant for his arrest. Soustelle was charged subsequently with an "offense against the authority of the state."

Soustelle continued to publish both political and scholarly works during and after his exile, which lasted until October 1968. He refused the amnesty the National Assembly offered those charged with political crimes in connection with the cause of French Algeria, insisting instead that the charges against him were groundless—a point he made prevail and charges were dropped. In 1969 he became a *directeur d'études* at the *Ecole des hautes études en sciences sociales*. He resumed his political career on the municipal council of Lyon in 1971, and in the National Assembly in 1973. He was elected to the *Académie française* in 1983. Soustelle died in Paris on August 6, 1990.

J. Soustelle, *Aimée et souffrante Algérie* (Paris, 1956), *A New Road for France* (New York, 1965); J. Talbott, *The War Without a Name* (New York, 1980).

R. A. Jonas

Related entries: ALGERIA, RELATIONS WITH; DE GAULLE, CHARLES; GAULLIST PARTY; *ORGANISATION DE L'ARMEE SECRETE*; POUJADISTS; UNITED STATES, RELATIONS WITH.

SOVIET UNION, RELATIONS WITH. Franco-Soviet relations under the Fourth and Fifth Republics experienced two distinct phases: mutual hostility under the Fourth Republic, this being consistent with the Cold War mentality of that era, and uncertain rapprochement under the Fifth Republic, this being General Charles de Gaulle's ambiguous personal policy, leading in 1964 to détente. Since August 1944, de Gaulle had stated publicly the international role he envisioned for France: "the link between the two worlds." Thus, if France had ceased to be a great power, a result of its defeat in 1940, it could recover and play a mediating role between the two rival ideological systems supported by the two superpowers, the United States and the Soviet Union. The key for French success in this regard was Germany's reconstruction in terms favorable to France. But the French need for coal from the Saar and the Rhur was dismissed by the Soviet Union at the Moscow Conference of Foreign Ministers from March to April 1947. Finally the need for American economic assistance caused France to fall ever more surely under American influence. With the formation of the Organization for European Economic Cooperation (OEEC) in 1947 and massive infusions of American money into the French economy, France took its eventual, perhaps inevitable, side in the Cold War. De Gaulle's policy of mediation was then lost, assured, moreover, by his resignation as the head of the French government in January 1946. By April 1948 tension was so great that the French embassy in Moscow and the Russian embassy in Paris were without resident ambassadors.

The communist coup in Czechoslovakia in February 1948 strengthened the resolve of France and the Benelux countries to enter into a defensive military alliance, the Brussels Pact. This pact served as the nucleus for the North Atlantic Treaty Organization, which was formed in April 1949. The lifting of the Russian blockade of Berlin, which might have eased tensions, was accompanied by the establishment of NATO. This produced new communist agitation in France, associated with threats from the Soviet Union, warning France that by joining NATO it had violated the Franco-Soviet Treaty of 1944.

Thereafter, France, the United States, and Great Britain reorganized their three occupation zones in Germany without consulting the fourth occupying power, the Soviet Union. In response, the Soviet Union established the Council of the German People (government for Berlin) and converted its German zone into the German Democratic Republic (DDR).

The outbreak of the Korean War in June 1950 and the Soviet establishment of paramilitary forces in the DDR caused the United States to propose rearming the West German Republic. France, not wishing to see Germany rearmed, proposed instead the Pleven Plan. This called for an integrated European army to be called the European Defense Community (EDC). The Soviet Union, meanwhile (and China also), recognized Ho Chi Minh's government, which was in rebellion against French authority in Indochina.

The death of Stalin in March 1953 and an armistice concluded in Korea in July of the same year allowed for what was henceforth termed a "thaw" in

East-West relations. Prime Minister Winston Churchill's call for a summit conference to discuss international problems resulted in preliminary meetings at London. Although no progress could be made on the German question, a commercial agreement was signed between France and the Soviet Union on July 15, 1953.

The Pleven Plan for a European Defense Community languished up to the end of 1953, the French always hoping for a solution to the German question that would make the rearming of that nation unnecessary. A four-power conference, held at Berlin in late January 1954, registered no progress after three weeks of negotiations. The Soviet Union proposed a collective security treaty for Europe with the exclusion of the United States. The French rejected this. At this same time the Soviet Union recognized the sovereignty of the German Democratic Republic.

In 1954 the war in Indochina had reached a point where France could not continue the struggle. The defeat at Dien Bien Phu and the diplomatic intervention of the Soviets, benevolent toward France, resulted in a Five-Power meeting in Geneva in April 1954. In July, France acknowledged the independence of Indochina. Pierre Mendès-France then brought the EDC treaty before the National Assembly, which rejected it on August 30. In the months following, despite the constant resistance of the Soviet Union, the French government collaborated with the United States and Great Britain for an incorporation of West German military units into NATO. The French National Assembly ratified these changes on December 30, 1954. Mendès-France rejected the Soviet argument that the integration of a sovereign German country in NATO had annulled the Franco-Russian Treaty.

With the fall of the Mendès-France government and the advent of socialist Guy Mollet's government, a determined policy of détente with the Soviet Union was launched. As if to give a good augury for French policy, the Soviet Union disestablished the Cominform on April 17, 1956. But then abruptly the progress toward détente was halted by Soviet intervention in Hungary and Gamal Abdel Nasser's decision to close the Suez canal to international traffic. Israel declared war on Egypt, supported by France and Great Britain, on November 5. The day before the Soviet Union sent its forces into Hungary, it threatened to intervene in Egypt. The United States called for a cease-fire in the Middle East under the auspices of the United Nations. This terminated the conflict, but henceforth the Soviets used their influence against the establishment of the European Common Market (EEC). On May 18, 1956, Nikolai Bulganin called for the withdrawal of American forces from Europe (but connecting this demand with an offer for a nonaggression pact between NATO and Warsaw Pact countries and an end to nuclear testing). Finally Bulganin urged Mollet to terminate French involvement in Algeria, where civil war had erupted. The crisis in Algeria catapulted General de Gaulle back into office and resulted in the formation of the Fifth Republic.

Shortly after the formation of the new Republic, de Gaulle inaugurated an ambitious foreign policy. Retaining his hard line toward the East, typical of his public pronouncements during his long retirement from government, he maintained also a strong anti-American posture. In a secret letter to President Dwight D. Eisenhower on September 24, 1958 he revealed his ambitions by proposing a directorate of three Western powers. Eisenhower, in his own secret reply to de Gaulle, rejected the proposal. John F. Kennedy, succeeding Eisenhower, received similar secret proposals from de Gaulle. Kennedy rejected the French president's overtures also, but unlike Eisenhower, he offered something larger in return: an Atlantic Partnership, which implied an integration of the United States with what the Americans seemed to believe was a United States of Europe in gestation. De Gaulle, for whom European integration was anathema, seeing the Atlantic Partnership as implying permanent American involvement in Europe, countered with his own "vast plan." He wanted to see the Western European countries formed as "an organization that would be one of the three powers of the planet," not on an integrated basis, but rather "a Europe of the states."

In the next few years de Gaulle embarked upon a program of independence, destined to estrange the United States on the one hand, and on the other to create, perhaps inadvertently, the conditions necessary for a rapprochement with the Soviet Union. In quick succession he vetoed Britain's entry into the Common Market, suspended negotiations at Brussels for European political unity, rejected the proposal for a multilateral force, and refused to sign the atomic test ban lately negotiated by the United States and the Soviet Union. Thereafter, de Gaulle swept his broom worldwide. From Southeast Asia to the Caribbean, to South America, to Canada, to Africa, Franco-American frictions were plentiful. He traveled indefatigably, stirring up many disputes. His recognition of the People's Republic of China in 1964, a sensible step that the Americans would not consider for themselves for another decade, was received in the United States as a species treason. American horror for this act was confounded by a sense of treachery when de Gaulle pulled out of the Southeast Asia Treaty Organization (SEATO) the next year. France had ceased to participate in NATO for some years already.

In his contest with the United States, de Gaulle drew nearer to the Soviet Union. It was French "decolonization," initiated by Mendès-France and consummated by de Gaulle, that allowed for an eventual détente with the Soviet Union. The Paris-Bonn Treaty, signed in January 1963, signified a Franco-German entente putting a new pressure on the Soviet Union. On May 17, 1963 the Soviet government sent France a note that could be construed as a surrender to the fact of Europe as de Gaulle had envisaged it. Through cooperation of their two countries, said this note, "no force could arise to change the new map of Europe." There followed the five-year Franco-Russian commercial agreement of October 1964 that attested to the desire of both countries to normalize their relations. On June 29, 1966, de Gaulle visited the Soviet Union for ten days, "the visit of eternal France to eternal Russia," the general said on Soviet television.

De Gaulle returned to Paris on July 1, the day on which French withdrawal from NATO became official. In 1967 more agreements were signed between Russia and France. In June when the Six-Day War broke out between Israel and the Arab states, France joined Russia on the Arab side, de Gaulle in this case breaking a long-standing French precedent of supporting Israel. In July Georges Pompidou and Maurice Couve de Murville visited the Soviet Union for five days. In October a French and Russian space shot revealed another sign of rapprochement.

The year 1968 did not see the fulfillment of the promises seen in 1965. Russia exercised new repression in Czechoslovakia. Yet, however embarrassed, de Gaulle's government felt constrained to follow the path it had chosen. In its communiqué issued at the end of the Council of Ministers meeting on October 23, 1968, it said: "French policy must continue along the lines it has followed, which means détente."

After de Gaulle's resignation in 1969, successive French governments maintained détente with the Soviet Union, for it meant in general terms for France independence from either superpower, a superior position in Europe for France, and the prospect, however distant, that in de Gaulle's words, Europe "must establish herself from the Atlantic to the Urals through cooperation." In Eastern Europe the events of the winter of 1988–89 seemed to make de Gaulle's words prophetic, as one country after another experienced the same phenomenon: swift collapse of old and entrenched communist regimes.

During the decade before this sudden and unexpected denouement of the Cold War, François Mitterrand's socialist government had followed an essentially Gaullist line in the conduct of foreign policy, an effort to play a determining role in world affairs without the force or resources to be effective. On the question of placing Pershing and Cruise missiles in Europe, Mitterrand had supported the United States, necessitating a hard line toward the Soviet Union (besides worrying about a Soviet military buildup in Europe, Mitterrand at this time had four communist ministers in his government and had to show a certain vigilance toward the Soviets). But the infatuation of the Reagan administration with the chimera of SDI (Strategic Defense Initiative or "Star Wars"), alarmed Mitterrand and tended to drive French policy back toward an accommodation with the Soviet Union at a time when Mikhail Gorbachev's reforms—*perestroika* and *glasnost*—promised an end to the protracted struggle between the United States and the Soviet Union. The initiation of the Intermediate-Range Nuclear Forces (INF) negotiations between the United States and the Soviets again revealed that France faced a vital question of national security, but was powerless to influence the course or the outcome of these talks. Ambiguously, it seemed, Mitterrand, who had championed arms control in the 1970s when in the political opposition, now opposed it as president of France.

Mitterrand's evolving views on INF are thought to be found in France's changing posture in Europe in the 1980s. France was becoming a status quo power. Revisionist under de Gaulle and his successors, wanting the security that the United States' rivalry with the Soviet Union provided, France wanted independence at the same time. The Gaullist solution for a power that was inherently weak but aspiring to be a dominant power was to leave NATO but to cooperate with it. The INF treaties promised an end to the Cold War, thus a slow but inevitable withdrawal of American influence from Europe and Europe again confronted by its oldest and most dangerous condition—an association of sovereign and competitive states, free again from foreign influences, but insecure. Ironically, the Cold War—despite its terror—gave the French and their European neighbors security. The dismantling of the communist regimes and the reunification of Germany, and what appeared to be the first signs of the dissolution of the Soviet Union, left France without a coherent policy for the immediate future.

G. de Carmoy, *La Politique étrangère de la France 1944–1966* (Paris, 1967); J. W. Friend, *Seven Years in France: François Mitterrand and the Unintended Revolution, 1981–1988* (Boulder, Colo., 1989); A. Grosser, *French Foreign Policy under de Gaulle* (Boston 1967); W. Kulski, *De Gaulle and the World* (Syracuse, N.Y., 1966); B. Nygren, *Cooperation between the Soviet Union and Three Western Great Powers, 1950–1975* (Stockholm, 1981).

I. C. Scott

Related entries: DEFENSE POLICY; DE GAULLE, CHARLES; EUROPEAN DEFENSE COMMUNITY; FOREIGN POLICY; FRENCH COMMUNIST PARTY; MITTERRAND, FRANCOIS; PEACE MOVEMENT; UNITED STATES, RELATIONS WITH.

SPAIN, RELATIONS WITH. Influenced by the legacy of the civil war, the origins and nature of General Francisco Franco's regime, and Spanish behavior during World War II, postwar relations with Spain went through three phases: hostility between 1944 and 1956; steady yet hesitant rapprochement until the death of Franco in 1975; and after renewed tensions, an era of cooperation and development in the 1980s.

France first tried to isolate Franco and supported the republican opposition. Despite a commercial agreement signed in 1945, tensions increased in 1946 following the execution of republican opponents and Spanish fears of an invasion by a combined force of Spanish exiles and former French communist resistance members. Under heavy domestic pressure, the French government closed its border with Spain on March 1, two days after Spain. Four days later, France gained the reluctant support of the United Kingdom and of the United States in condemning that regime. Yet, France was unable to win international economic sanctions against Spain. Although the border reopened in 1948, relations remained tense until 1956. France opposed Spanish membership in the United Nations (UN) and NATO, while Franco criticized French Moroccan policy, courted Gamal Abdel Nasser, and let Spanish Morocco be used by Algerian rebels. After first moves toward a rapprochement were made in August 1956, foreign ministers met a year later. Spain (a member since 1955) supported France's Algerian policy at the UN, and for the first time in twenty-five years, a French parliamentary delegation (excluding the socialists and the communists) paid a visit of friendship in February 1958. Both colonial powers were concerned with growing Soviet influence in the Arab world and the increase in Third World nationalism, and were eager to develop economic ties.

In a shift from his first government policy, Charles de Gaulle gave a vigorous impetus to the rapprochement begun by the Fourth Republic. By 1959 France was ready to support Spain's membership in NATO. Cooperation widened, from a stop to anti-Franco broadcasts by Radio Paris, to a curb on the activities of Spanish exiles in France, and cooperation against Moroccan guerrillas. In June 1959 de Gaulle reiterated the proposal of a western Mediterranean alliance made by Félix Gaillard the previous year. Economic relations improved along with the importance of the European Economic Community (EEC) for the Spanish economy. By 1972 the EEC formed its largest single export market (48%), although France remained far behind Britain and Germany as a trade partner and source of investments. Spain accounted for 2.9 percent of its exports and 2.1 percent of its imports in 1973; in 1983 the figures were respectively 3.2 percent and 3.4 percent. While French tourists flocked to Spain, Spanish workers came to France.

The death of Franco in November 1975 removed a major obstacle to closer relations between the two countries. Both Presidents Valéry Giscard d'Estaing and François Mitterrand felt that new democracies had to be helped. Yet, the early 1980s were a period of difficult relations. Spain resented France's policy of granting asylum to Basque terrorists and its opposition to Spanish membership in the EEC out of concerns about its impact on French agricultural and fishing interests. Yet France also hoped that Spanish membership would displace the European center of gravity toward it, increase the influence of the Mediterranean region within the EEC, provide access to Spanish markets, and engineer Franco-Spanish reconciliation.

Relations came close to the breaking point in 1982, but the 1983 election of socialist and francophile Felipe González as Spanish premier helped defuse tensions. Economic, cultural, and political relations developed despite fishing disputes and anti-French press campaigns in 1984. French and Spanish police cooperated, and after hard negotiations Spain formally joined the EEC on January 1, 1986, under conditions that remained unchallenged by Jacques Chirac's *cohabitation* government. The two countries started annual summit meetings in 1987 and instituted regular high-level meetings in the civilian and military areas (a broad agreement on defense issues was signed in October 1983 following Spanish membership in NATO in 1982). Given the growing economic dominance of Germany, the uncertainties besetting NATO, and British hesitations about European economic integration, closer cooperation with Spain is becoming more important in helping France to maintain its position in Europe and to enhance its ability to help define the civilian and military future of the continent.

A. Fontaine, "L'Espagne, la France, et l'Europe," *La Revue de Paris* (March 1959); A. Grosser, *La IVe République et sa politique extérieure* (Paris, 1961); B. Pollack, G.

Hunter, *The Paradox of Spanish Foreign Policy* (London, 1987); A. Whitaker, *Spain and the Defense of the West* (New York, 1962).

P. Le Prestre

Related entries: COHABITATION; DEFENSE POLICY; EUROPEAN ECONOMIC COMMUNITY, RELATIONS WITH; GAILLARD, FELIX; MOROCCO, RELATIONS WITH.

SPORTS since 1945 have grown dramatically in a three-fold fashion: as an arena for government intervention, as a leisure activity, and as a commercial endeavor. In its sports organization France follows a middle path between the state-directed systems of Eastern Europe and the laissez-faire, commercialized pattern of the United States. As in so many other areas of French life, the impetus for postwar change in sports developed under the Vichy regime. The law of December 20, 1940 reorganized sport: Each federation was placed under the administration of a national committee of sports. This central direction was reaffirmed after 1945 in the spirit of national regeneration at the start of the Fourth Republic, and in 1958 in the mood of national reconciliation with which Charles de Gaulle inaugurated the Fifth Republic. Sport has been one of the few areas of agreement among the major political parties. Following the inspiration of Pierre de Coubertin, the Frenchman who founded the modern Olympic movement, politicians have been virtually unanimous in praise of sport as a means of promoting health, discipline, and fraternity. The events of May 1968, however, inspired a critical sociology of sport. Jean-Marie Brohm, Michel Caillat, and others associated with the journal *Quel corps?* argue that sport is one of the most important arms of repression, domination, and alienation in an advanced capitalist society. In 1980 during the presidential campaign, the socialists tried to forge a new sports policy equidistant from the traditionalists and the neo-Marxists, stressing a participatory, grass-roots view of sport-as-festival. However, French sport has not been radically altered under the Mitterrand presidency.

French sport is organized upon an associative network. Approximately 120,000 clubs and sporting associations are federated at the departmental, regional, and national level under the direction of the High Committee of Youth and Sport and a National Sports Council. Membership in sporting clubs has grown dramatically, soaring from 1,864,518 in 1949 to 12,022,170 in 1985. Nevertheless, despite impressive gains in popular participation, successive governments have been unable to make France a major competitor in international sport. France's best showing in the Olympics, for example, was in 1948 with ten gold medals. And aside from the likes of the skier Jean-Claude Killy, French athletes have seldom achieved international prominence. One reason for the persistent failure of the government sports program may be the lack of funding. Between 1960 and 1980 the sport budget has constantly declined. The socialist government, after its institution of a sports lottery in 1984, has increased the outlay for sports only marginally.

The great boom in participatory sports has been based upon the long prosperity of the 1950s through the early 1970s, and then the continued decline in the workweek under the socialists in the 1980s. Since 1960 sales of sporting goods have risen more than twentyfold. This trend did not abate during the economically turbulent eighties. In June 1984, as the total expenses of the French grew at an annual rate of 4.5 percent, sporting expenses rose by 6.5 percent. The French now spend roughly 5 percent of their clothing budget on sporting goods. Cities and communes have invested 8 percent of their gross fixed capital in sport, mostly in stadiums, playgrounds, and gyms. Sporting events also form a large part of entertainment outside of the home. One out of every five times that the French step out, they go to a sporting event. France has the number-one sporting daily in the world, *L'Equipe*, and television sports draw in excess of seventeen million viewers for soccer matches or the *Tour de France*. In sum, sport represents 1 percent of national consumption, and sport salaries compose virtually 1 percent of total salaries.

Although sport has been one of the most important ways in which the French have experienced prosperity in the postwar era, it has not been enjoyed equally among all sections of the society. Participation depends heavily upon age, gender, class, and region. Until recently, most adults stopped active sporting involvement by the age of forty. Although the percentage of women's participation is rising, men still compose 80 percent of all sports participants. Middle-age sport is essentially middle class; workers rapidly transform themselves from participants to spectators after the age of thirty. One reason for this is the lack of sports facilities in workers' housing projects. Finally, regional disparities abound. Bicycling is found especially in the coastal regions from Bordeaux to Lille. Equestrian sport dominates in the north. While rugby is almost exclusively played in the Midi, soccer is especially prevalent in the north. The Midi, in particular, has many distinctively regional games.

M. Caillat, *L'Idéologie du sport en France depuis 1880* (Paris, 1989); J. Toussaint, *Histoire du sport français de 1870 à nos jours* (Paris, 1984).

W. S. Haine

Related entries: LEISURE; SOCIAL TRENDS.

STALEMATE SOCIETY, a concept closely associated with the American political scientist Stanley Hoffmann and developed in the late 1950s and early 1960s to describe the socioeconomic structures of the Third Republic and its relation to the parliamentary regime; also a concept used to describe the Fourth and Fifth Republics. The concept emerged from a series of Harvard seminar papers published as *In Search of France* (1963). The American social scientists were considerably influenced by the French sociologist Michel Crozier, an expert on bureaucratic organizations and their dysfunctions in twentieth-century France.

In its initial formulation the stalemate society described French society and its economy between 1878 and 1934 as having reached an equilibrium between industrial capitalism and "feudal agriculture." A consensus existed between an aristocratically influenced bourgeoisie and the small property-owning peasantry to support the republican parliamentary regime. The political system maintained the status quo by limiting the power of the executive and relying on a highly centralized bureaucracy. Although the proletariat was excluded from this equilibrium, it posed no serious threat. Under the pressure of external economic and diplomatic developments from 1934 to 1960, this system broke down.

The consequence of this breakdown was the transformation of French society, its economy, and to some extent its values in the 1950s and 1960s. The peasant-agricultural sector declined and those remaining on the land supported modernization. The business elite exhibited a new dynamism and commitment to change. In general, expansion was valued over stability. The traditional bourgeoisie was transformed into a twentieth-century middle class with a high proportion of technocrats and managers. However, these changes did not extend to the political system.

A second meaning of the stalemate society, used more consistently by Crozier, is the failure of the Fourth or the Fifth Republics to adjust to the postwar transformations of France and the world. Hoffmann and especially Crozier stress that while some social values have changed, fundamental French attitudes toward authority have not altered significantly. French political systems and institutions remain trapped in an unproductive polarity between styles of limited authoritarianism and imminent individualistic insurrection. Neither can successfully cope with domestic and international realities, nor can either mobilize or direct newly released social energies. Both social scientists view the centralization of the state and the persistence of hierarchical bureaucratized institutions as the cause for this absence of political change. The values that support these styles of authority and maintain these outmoded systems are perpetuated by the French education system. Hoffmann points to both the Fourth and Fifth Republics as examples of the failure of the French political system to adapt. Crozier argues that May 1968 demonstrated the rigidities of the Fifth Republic, the persistence of archaic utopian insurrection, and a general despair with bureaucracies. Both Hoffmann and Crozier stress the need for decentralization of state functions, possible constitutional change, and especially educational reform as necessary to foster a new democratic style of authority.

M. Crozier, *Le Phénomène bureaucratique* (Paris, 1963), *La Société bloquée* (Paris, 1970); S. Hoffmann et al., *In Search of France* (Cambridge, Mass., 1963).

J. F. Stone

Related entries: EDUCATIONAL REFORM; ELECTIONS; GAULLISM; POLITICAL TRENDS.

STRIKES, legal in France since 1864, and a right enshrined in the constitutions of the Fourth and Fifth Republics, although for certain categories of state employees, notably the police, this right has been curtailed by law. The right to strike is not limited by collective bargaining agreements, and although there is a fairly sophisticated legal procedure for regulating strike activity (conciliation, mediation, and arbitration), it is seldom used. Strikes are defined in French labor law as work stoppages decided collectively in order to defend professional interests, and so political strikes are in theory illegal. However in practice, the line between political and industrial strikes has often been difficult to draw, and some of the most spectacular forms of industrial unrest in France have been manifestations of disaffection with government policy.

Contrary to some impressions, France is not particularly strike prone. In general terms the number of working days lost per one thousand employees during the postwar period is lower than in Australia, Canada, Finland, Iceland, Ireland, Italy, the United Kingdom, and the United States, although higher than in Austria, the Federal Republic of Germany, the Netherlands, Norway, Sweden, and Switzerland. Although there has been a general reduction in strike activity since World War II, it would be premature to talk of the "withering away of the strike," since French trade unions have generally been unenthusiastic about participating in institutions that regulate industrial conflict and encourage collective bargaining. As in other countries certain sectors of the economy tend to have proportionately more disputes, for example, the mining, transport, metalworking, and chemical industries. One specifically French characteristic is the short duration of strikes. In part this can be explained by interconfederal rivalry, which does not make for a coherent approach to industrial action; in addition, individual trade unions lack the financial resources to provide strike pay, and they can only exercise a limited level of discipline over their members and sympathizers.

During the late 1940s and early 1950s there was a high level of strike activity. The difficulties inherent in the immediate postwar economic situation engendered worker militancy. Moreover, at the onset of the Cold War the French Communist party used its dominant position within the largest trade union confederation, the *Confédération générale du travail*, to foment industrial unrest in protest against government policy.

The 1960s will be particularly remembered for the events of May–June 1968. This strike wave was so great that accurate statistics could not be provided by the Ministry of Employment, which estimated that 150 million days were lost due to strike activity involving ten million workers. What explanation can be given for this sudden outburst? Wages, as every survey of strike activity in France has shown, played an important role; at that time French wages were the lowest in the European Community (except for Italy), and they were also rising more slowly than in other countries. The workweek was the longest in the EC, and unemployment had just passed the half-million mark. Collective bargaining machinery was underdeveloped and was certainly too weak to institutionalize this level of unrest. In broader sociopolitical terms, the strike action undertaken by the students had shown that the authority of the French establishment could be challenged.

In the 1970s there were sporadic attempts to emulate the industrial unrest of the late 1960s. There was an increase in the number of factory occupations and, as the economic situation deteriorated, strikes were called in protest against redundancies. In addition, there were more strikes involving groups of employees (particularly women and immigrants) who had traditionally been poorly organized. In contrast, the 1980s was a time of reduced strike activity. The election of a socialist president in 1981, François Mitterrand, and the existence of a socialist government from 1981 to 1986 (with Communist party support from 1981 to 1984) and from 1988 onward, inhibited trade unions who were less willing to engage in strike activity for fear of playing into the hands of the political parties of the right. As the decade progressed and membership declined, trade unions were increasingly unable to mobilize the work force, and some of the major disputes in the 1980s (involving the hospitals in 1985, the railways in 1986–87, and the Paris metro in 1988) were not organized by trade unions but by extra-union ''coordination'' groups. While past experience has taught us to beware of any categorical predictions, there is nevertheless evidence to suggest that in the 1990s strike activity in France will decline further.

G. Caire, *La Grève ouvrière* (Paris, 1978); strike statistics can be obtained from Division conditions de travail et relations professionnelles, Services des études et de la statistique, Ministère des affaires sociales et de l'emploi, Paris.

J. Bridgford

Related entries: CONFEDERATION FRANCAISE DEMOCRATIQUE DU TRAVAIL; CONFEDERATION GENERALE DU TRAVAIL; ECONOMIC POLICY; ECONOMIC TRENDS; *FORCE OUVRIERE*; INDUSTRIAL POLICY; LABOR FORCE; TRADE UNION MOVEMENT.

STRUCTURALISM, the predominant intellectual current of the 1960s. Structuralism was less a school or a movement than a diverse set of intellectual positions in the human sciences based on the structural linguistics of Ferdinand de Saussure (1858–1913) and the science of signs, or semiology, developed by Roland Barthes (1915–1980) and others working within the tradition of Saussure.

Saussure's *Cours de linguistique générale* (1915) shifted the orientation of traditional linguistic study from a diachronic (temporal) to a synchronic (static, systemic) emphasis. Abandoning the tendency to produce ''biographies'' of individual words, Saussure argued that individual units of language have no inherent intelligibility. They only become intelligible through combination, especially for Saussure through binary opposition, that is, the very concept that was to become a cornerstone of the structural anthropology of Claude Lévi-Strauss (1908–). Saussure posited the ''sign'' as the fundamental source of meaning in human language. Any linguistic sign, he explained, is composed of its material component (syllable, letters, etc.) or ''signifier'' (*signifiant*) and that to which it refers, or its ''signified'' (*signifié*).

Meaning (''signification'') is thus produced through signs and combinations of signs. Not only can spoken and written language be understood in this way, but so can nonlinguistic cultural activities or practices. Semiology, or the science of signs—linguistic or not—to which Saussure's work pointed, was developed by Barthes and others to investigate clothing, cuisine, athletic contests, urban architecture, and a vast range of human cultural experience. By the early 1960s, the most prominent structuralist in France was Lévi-Strauss, who drew on the work of Saussure and later structural linguists such as Roman Jakobson (1896–1984), whose attention to Saussure's concept of binary opposition in language Lévi-Strauss elevated to a universal truism of human mental and cultural activity. Lévi-Strauss produced a long series of structural studies of kinship, cooking, and myths. His four-volume series, *Mythologiques*, was an attempt not merely to catalog myths but also, adopting Saussure's practice of looking not at individual items but at the structures of an entire system, to demonstrate larger claims about that irreducible aspect of human thinking that Lévi-Strauss called *la pensée sauvage*. In his book of the same name (1962), Lévi-Strauss ended with an attack on the historicism and humanism of Jean-Paul Sartre, whose *Critique de la raison dialectique* has been published to wide acclaim in 1960.

Lévi-Strauss was demonstrating more than a mere preference for synchrony or an anthropologist's disdain for the self-appointedly ''superior'' historical consciousness of the West. His rejection of ''humanism'' became one of the most characteristic stances of structuralism and, among other things, served as the bludgeon against the existentialist philosophy that had dominated French intellectual circles since World War II. This ''antihumanism'' grounded itself in a view of language as an all-determining network in which human beings are located, providing the circuitry through which the current of language pulses. Thus, language was not to be seen as a set of implements or devices whereby individual human beings accomplished carefully ordered linguistic objectives. With structuralism, it was more a case of language ''speaking'' and ''writing'' them.

This fascination with language and sign systems as vast seas in which human fish have no choice but to swim extended to each of the other most prominent intellectual figures who, often unwillingly, were branded with the label *structuralist*. In 1966 major publications appeared from two members of the structuralists. Jacques Lacan's massive volume *Ecrits* appeared, as did Michel Foucault's ambitious *Les Mots et les choses: Une Archéologie des sciences humaines* (The order of things, 1970). Their publication was viewed, however unfairly, as the zenith of the structuralist movement. Lacan's *Retour à Freud* was marked by the characteristically structuralist insistence on language (he had claimed that the unconscious was *structuré comme un langage* [structured like a language]). Foucault's archaeological investigation of modern systems of thought appeared in the intellectual context of its day to be a structuralist enterprise, but it was to become clear by the end of the decade that he was motivated by a far less totalizing Nietzschean genealogical perspective. As would be true of Barthes after 1970, Foucault was most uncomfortable with the structuralist label. Of the prominent French intellectuals of the 1960s, perhaps only Lévi-Strauss and Lacan (and to a lesser extent, Louis Althusser) exemplify the most ambitious explanatory confidence of full-blown structuralism. After 1968, when structuralism was tarred with the brush of the established university culture and rejected by the radical students, a much more skeptical and deliberately relativist intellectual mood replaced it. This so-called poststructuralism is not to be understood as a negation of structuralism, for such poststructuralists as Foucault and Jacques Derrida retained structuralism's concern with language and signification, even as they shunned its universalizing binary logic.

J. Sturrock, ''Structuralism,'' *Yale French Studies* (1966), ed., *Structuralism and Since* (Oxford, 1979), *Tel quel: Théorie d'ensemble* (1968); F. Wahl, *Qu'est-ce-que le structuralisme?* (Paris, 1968).

J. A. Winders

Related entries: ALTHUSSER, LOUIS; BARTHES, ROLAND; DERRIDA, JACQUES; FEMINISM; FOUCAULT, MICHEL; *GRANDES ECOLES*; INTELLECTUAL TRENDS; LACAN, JACQUES; LEVI-STRAUSS, CLAUDE.

STUDENT REVOLTS, two ''great'' student revolts under the Fifth Republic, revolts so vast that they induced political crises: the events of May–June 1968 and the demonstrations against the proposed Devaquet law in 1986. The student revolt of 1968 had among its origins the serious problems faced by French universities upon the arrival to college age of the baby-boom generation. These problems included overcrowding, frustrations with an overburdened and unresponsive university bureaucracy, dim employment prospects for students, and job insecurity for junior faculty.

The first incidents occurred at the Nanterre campus of the University of Paris. When François Missoffe, minister of youth and sports, appeared at Nanterre in January 1968 to inaugurate the campus swimming pool, a sociology student irreverently demanded to know the minister's plans to solve students' sexual problems. Missoffe suggested that the student, Daniel Cohn-Bendit, solve his sexual problems by cooling off in the pool.

On March 21 police arrested a group of Nanterre students on rue Scribe for smashing the windows of the American Express building in protest against the war in Vietnam. The following day Nanterre students, Cohn-Bendit among them, ran from classroom to classroom spreading the news of the students' arrest. Once mobilized, a group of students, about two hundred in all, occupied the administration building in protest. Nanterre administrators sought to defuse the situation by canceling classes. It was a victory for the March 22 Movement.

The students' revolt broadened into a general social and political crisis after a series of confrontations between students and police. The motto ''provocation, repression, solidarity'' expressed the student strategy to extend the movement; confrontations pitting students against armed and armored police would elicit the solidarity of other students and the population at large. On May 3, hundreds of students from Nanterre and Paris met at the Sorbonne. The dean and rector of the Sorbonne called on police to force the students out. Arrests followed, and the fate of the arrested students became yet another issue.

The ''night of the barricades'' followed the conviction, on May 5, of thirteen of those arrested at the Sorbonne. The UNEF (*Union nationale des étudiants de France*) called for a demonstration on May 6. By dusk, street fights had broken out. When the riot ended there were over three hundred injured and nearly two hundred vehicles damaged or burned. The unions, among them the *Fédération de l'éducation nationale* (FEN), called a general strike for May 13.

Here, properly speaking, the student revolt ended—a social and political crisis took the relay. By May 24, nine million were on strike, three times as many as during the Popular Front in 1936. On May 28, François Mitterrand announced his candidacy to succeed Charles de Gaulle and proposed a provisional government under Pierre Mendès-France. By then public opinion had turned against the strikes and political turmoil, given the prospect of civil war. Although discontent with Gaullism had fed the crisis (*''Dix ans, c'est assez!''*), the general persuaded the voters, as he had ten years earlier, that he alone stood between France and chaos. A month later he savored Gaullism's greatest electoral triumph.

French universities continued to suffer from high enrollments and inadequate facilities. Although Faure's Law of Orientation of Higher Education recommended that seminars contain no more than twenty-five students and that lecture courses close at two hundred, these goals proved difficult to realize in practice. Faure's goal of autonomy—allowing universities to set their own standards, to compete with one another for the better students, and to shape distinct identities—remained a desirable but largely unfulfilled goal. In October 1986 Alain Devaquet, *ministre délégué* for research and higher education, put before the Senate legislation that aimed to strengthen higher education in France through greater university autonomy and selectivity. Among the more controversial provisions of the plan were those calling for independent admissions standards and university-specific diplomas. Students sensed that the legislation's emphasis on selection threatened their right of access to the universities, traditionally assured simply by passing the baccalaureate.

On November 22 FEN, the teachers' union, called on students throughout France to strike on November 27, when the Devaquet legislation was to reach the floor of the National Assembly. About 200,000 university and *lycée* students marched from the Sorbonne to the Palais Bourbon on that day; 400,000 participated in demonstrations in fifty provincial centers. On December 5 thousands of students occupied the courtyard of the Sorbonne. That night student/demonstrator Malek Oussekine died after a beating at the hands of police. Leaders of the movement called a general strike for December 10, a decision endorsed by the General Confederation of Labor (CGT). Devaquet resigned on December 8; Prime Minister Jacques Chirac withdrew the legislation.

''L'Amère Victoire de la jeunesse,'' *Le Monde*, December 10, 1986; R. Aron, *La Révolution introuvable* (Paris, 1968); A. Touraine, *Le Mouvement de mai ou le communisme utopique* (Paris, 1968); M. Winock, *La Fièvre hexagonale; les grandes crises politiques, 1871–1968* (Paris, 1986); L. Wylie et al., *France, The Events of May-June 1968: A Critical Bibliography* (Pittsburgh, Pa., 1973).

R. A. Jonas

Related entries: COHN-BENDIT, DANIEL; DE GAULLE, CHARLES; EDUCATIONAL REFORM; FAURE, EDGAR; FRENCH COMMUNIST PARTY; JULY, SERGE; MENDES-FRANCE, PIERRE; MITTERRAND, FRANCOIS; POMPIDOU, GEORGES; TRADE UNION MOVEMENT.

SUEZ CRISIS, the military expedition that France and Great Britain, in collaboration with the Israelis, launched to regain control of the Suez canal, which Egypt's President Gamal Abdel Nasser had nationalized on July 26, 1956 following the withdrawal of American support for the construction of the Aswan dam. Whereas for the Israelis the issue was security, for Premier Guy Mollet and Prime Minister Anthony Eden much more than fair compensation to shareholders or the protection of oil shipments was at stake: One should not capitulate before a dictatorship. The French were also eager to weaken the Algerian rebels by disposing of their main external supporter.

In preparation since July, formally decided on October 16, the expedition was finalized at a joint meeting of the three countries on October 22. On October 29 the Israelis invaded Egypt, supported by the French air force. Having presented both armies with a fictitious ultimatum, France and Britain started bombing Egyptian positions on October 31. Ignoring an American-sponsored United Nations resolution calling for a cease-fire (November 1), they sent in paratroops on November 5 and landed the next day. Franco-British forces were marching toward Cairo when a cease-fire was called on November 6. Eden had succumbed to strong domestic and foreign political opposition (including a Soviet nuclear threat addressed to both countries) and to intense American financial pressure, thus forcing the French to withdraw, and denying Israel a complete victory. The last troops left on December 22.

Though the expedition remained popular in France, the Suez crisis left a disastrous legacy: oil shortages for months afterwards, a stronger Nasser, higher Soviet prestige, and a deeper French distrust of the United States and of the United Nations. Above all, it had revealed the changed character of the international situation.

M. Ferro, *Suez* (Brussels, 1982); A. Grosser, *The Western Alliance* (New York, 1982); H. Thomas, *The Suez Affair*, 2d. ed. (London, 1970).

P. Le Prestre

Related entries: GREAT BRITAIN, RELATIONS WITH; MIDDLE EAST, RELATIONS WITH; MOLLET, GUY; PINEAU, CHRISTIAN; THIRD WORLD, RELATIONS WITH; UNITED STATES, RELATIONS WITH.

SULLEROT, EVELYNE (HAMMEL) (1924–   ), writer, historian, sociologist, and journalist. Daughter of neuropsychiatrist and pastor André Hammel, Sullerot was born at Montrouge in 1924. She received the *licence* in letters and then a diploma from the French Press Institute of the University of Paris. She passed the *bac* in jail where she was serving a term for refusing to participate in a school ceremony required by the Vichy government. Part of her career has been spent teaching: professor at the French Press Institute (1963–68); professor at the Free University of Brussels (1966–68) and Paris X (Nanterre, 1967). She was a researcher in mass communication at the *Ecole pratique des hautes études* from 1960 to 1963. Since 1970 she has been a consultant affiliated with the European Economic Community and other organizations such as the International Bureau of Work, the Economic and Social Council, the High Council for Population and the Family, and the French Commission for UNESCO. Sullerot was a cofounder of the French Family Planning movement in 1955 and served as its general secretary from 1955 to 1958, then as honorary president. She founded and serves as president of the *Retravailler* centers. These centers offer small groups of women of all ages and backgrounds short seminars to help them enter or reenter the work force. Highly successful, they have been introduced in other countries. The majority of her publications—books, reports, and novels—relate to her internationally acknowledged expertise in women's issues. About half have been translated into English and other languages. Among her major publications are: *La Presse féminine* (Paris, 1963, her thesis); *Demain les femmes* (Paris, 1965, translated into a dozen languages); *La Vie des femmes* (Paris, 1965); *Histoire de la presse féminine en France des origines à 1848* (Paris, 1966); *Histoire et sociologie du travail féminin* (Paris, 1968, ten translations); *La Femme dans le monde moderne* (Paris, 1970); *Les Françaises au travail* (Paris, 1973); *Histoire et mythologie de l'amour* (Paris, 1974); *Le Fait féminin* (Paris, 1978); *Le Statut matrimonial et ses conséquences juridiques, fiscales, et sociales* (Paris, 1984); *Pour le meilleur et sans le pire* (Paris, 1984); *L'Age de travailler* (Paris, 1986); and the novels *Aman* (Paris, 1981) and *L'Enveloppe* (Paris, 1987), in addition to various official reports.

E. Sullerot, *Demain les femmes* (Paris, 1965), *L'Age de travailler* (Paris, 1986); *Who's Who in France, 1990–1991* (Paris, 1990).

M. C. Weitz

Related entries: FEMINISM; LABOR FORCE; SOCIAL TRENDS; WOMEN, CONDITION OF.

T

TAXATION, a system inherited from the Third Republic that the Fourth and Fifth Republics have done little to improve. The massive cost of government in the early twentieth century led to the supplementing of traditional indirect taxes by the direct taxation of incomes. When direct taxation failed to generate the needed revenues, the simple, highly effective turnover tax became a mainstay of government revenue. The intense dislike of direct taxation shared by the peasantry and middle classes has made republican governments prefer indirect taxation. While regressive in impact, indirect taxation has the benefit of raising large amounts of money without the taxpayer being conscious of how much he or she is paying. Fragile political consensus also militated against the use of taxation to redistribute incomes. Postwar governments have preferred to achieve this goal by channeling the benefits of growth toward the working classes through high wages.

The standard method for establishing income taxes for much of the middle class was the *forfait*. Taxpayers were allowed to estimate their incomes, bargaining between tax official and taxpayers followed, the outraged citizen appealed to his or her deputy for justice against the "fiscal inquisition," and both parties settled for less than they hoped.

The huge burdens of World War II required new taxes. Vichy heavily taxed excess industrial profits and renewed the effective taxation of farmers, a practice that had fallen into desuetude during the depression. The post-Liberation provisional government ordered the confiscation of all "illicit" wartime profits and levied an *impôt de solidarité nationale*, targeting both the total worth of the individual and the increase in wealth during the Occupation. These measures seem to have been subject to the usual evasion. Taxes were adjusted to encourage larger families. During 1948 a special anti-inflation tax sought to shift resources from consumption toward economic reconstruction. The turnover tax became payable on an accelerated basis to a government desperate to fill its coffers.

There is a constant struggle—driven by the need to raise additional revenues for new needs through the imposition of new taxes—between the proliferation of special taxes and the drive to simplify and rationalize taxation. Simplification in the mid-1950s saw the two parts of the income tax combined into a single tax, and a value-added tax replaced the turnover and production taxes. A host of smaller taxes were subsumed within the value-added tax in January 1966, and the tax was extended to distributional and artisanal enterprises. Reformers sought to standardize tax rates for various kinds of incomes in 1974. The renewal of serious inflation in the mid-1970s brought a return to the use of taxation to reduce demand and stimulate productive investment.

The resistance of the French middle classes and farmers to taxation has victimized the employees of large concerns who find it impossible to evade the *fisc*. One estimate held that a full quarter of the tax bill went unpaid under the Fourth Republic. Efforts in the early 1950s to tighten collection of existing taxes touched off bitter resentment among shopkeepers struggling to survive in tougher economic circumstances. These resentments were mobilized by Pierre Poujade in 1953. Faced with the success of Poujade's movement in the 1956 elections and fearing that any effort at reform would only diminish already inadequate revenues, French politicians preferred not to change the tax system significantly. The newborn Fifth Republic used decrees to raise corporate, excise, and personal income taxes, coupled with an effort at stricter enforcement. Critics predictably complained that the new tax structure favored industry at the expense of agriculture.

Despite these measures, the Fifth Republic has not had much better success mastering the French reluctance to be taxed than had the Third or Fourth Republics. In 1952 the French government drew scarcely one-fourth of its revenue from taxes on wealth and income, while deriving two-thirds from customs revenues and indirect taxes. This lumped France with Peru, Iraq, and Ceylon, all of whom had comparable rates. Moreover, French income taxes were much less progressive than those in Britain or the United States. By 1980 indirect taxes remained the chief source of government income, providing more than twice the revenue of income taxes and five times as much as corporate taxation.

M. Larkin, *France since the Popular Front* (Oxford, 1988); A. Neurisse, *Histoire de l'impôt* (Paris, 1978); M. Norr, P. Kerlan, *Taxation in France* (Chicago, 1965).

J. S. Hill

Related entries: ECONOMIC POLICY; INCOME DISTRIBUTION; POUJADISTS; STALEMATE SOCIETY.

TECHNOLOGY saw spectacular growth and competent management, particularly in the years 1945–70, and France moved from a position of relative technical backwardness to a place of occasional leadership in the industrial world. The strong and positive role taken by the state, the emergence of a highly skilled technocracy, first in the state and later in the private sector, and a broad, transpolitical consensus on the ostensibly inevitable character of positive technological change account for much of France's success. The nationalized industries, the planning apparatus, the Ministry of Industry, the *Commissariat à l'énergie atomique*, and later, the Ministry of Finance and some of the private sector industrial trade associations worked well together to direct France's new trajectory.

Study circles within the Resistance conceptualized many of the postwar institutional reforms. Participants agreed that France's defeat in 1940 was not merely a military matter, but also a reflection of France's failure to mobilize its human, natural, educational, and financial resources sufficiently to compete as a major power in the technology-driven twentieth century. Well before Liberation, a consensus ranging from communists, through Gaullists, and to the Christian democrats emerged, and it was determined (at least in the short term) to take most technological decision making away from the private sector and allow it to reside in statist and parastatist bodies.

Within weeks after the bombing of Hiroshima, General Charles de Gaulle decreed the creation of the *Commissariat à l'énergie atomique*, and a few months later Jean Monnet was appointed to head the indicative planning apparatus. During the same period, coal, rail, oil exploration, insurance, electrical energy, airplane construction, deposit banking, and Renault were nationalized and placed under technocratic management structures. The combination of planning and nationalized industries gave the state the key levers over technological development, particularly in terms of the infrastructural industries (energy, transportation, etc.) and financial structures and resources needed for later private industrial expansion. Coordination among sectors and industries was the work of the planning apparatus and, less publicly, the internal directories of the Ministry of Industry, which also set allocations of capital to specific projects and fought the Ministry of Finance for the needed funds.

By the mid-1950s the coal industry had been fully modernized (only to be phased out several years later), electrical energy output had more than doubled, much of the rail system was electrified, new natural gas fields in the southwest were opened, and France's first nuclear power plant was on line. The state sector's stunning successes of the first postwar decade—many of them emblematic, such as the massive hydroelectric projects, arching power transmission lines, and nuclear plants—performed two important tasks. They provided the material basis upon which private industry could develop (using cheap electricity, transportation services, and the like) and they helped to raise investor confidence that France was indeed on a sound trajectory to a bright technological future. The latter perception helped to reverse the traditional financial conservatism of French capital holders.

Politically, the strategy of building the technological infrastructure first meant that there had to be a long period of minimal improvements in popular living standards while the fruits of larger industrial output were rolled back into industry. This task was in large part facilitated by the weakness of organized labor through much of the Fourth Republic due to divisions within the trade-union movement and the political isolation of the communists. As a result, national income shares could be shifted away from consumption and toward investment. This approach was not changed until the planning apparatus programmed better living standards in the early 1960s.

The process of rapid development between 1946 and 1970 was not without considerable tension away from public view. At the outset, technocrats within the Ministry of Industry, many of whom were *Ecole polytechnique* alumni, battled for aggressive technological strategies against their more parsimonious *Ecole libre* counterparts in the Finance Ministry. A period of fifteen years was essential so that the older generation of conservative inspectors of finance could retire and be replaced by a more dynamic generation of *Ecole nationale d'administration* (ENA) graduates. Similarly, there were considerable battles among agencies and enterprises over specific strategies for development (rail versus road for freight transportation, coal versus oil versus hydropower for electricity production, contention over pricing of public services, American versus French nuclear plant designs, etc.), but few of the conflicts were openly aired. This helped to maintain the public image of a rapid, conflict-free path for technological progress.

Many of France's technological successes in the postwar era reflected the particular expertise of the French education system. Elegant, a priori designed systems functioned smoothly, from the national power transmission grid to the dense rail network. Nonetheless, at the level of detail, French impatience and lack of expertise showed: Most of France's heavy electrical equipment was based on foreign patents, as were many of its turbines and jet engines, and the computing and telecommunications industries lagged far behind their international counterparts. While France did not have firms on the scale of AT&T or IBM to design and develop communications and computing equipment, it did have Thompson-Brandt-TSF and Bull. Managers were never able to develop the necessary momentum at the micro level to give France the ability for self-sustained development in these fields. Large, elegant systems were well developed, yet detail-level design suffered.

By the mid-1960s France's task of technological catching-up was largely complete. The popular standard of living approached that of other industrialized nations, and the tedious tabled tasks of the previous years were attacked: rewiring all housing units for higher power and telecommunications capacity, updating the quality of transportation equipment, and raising the overall quality of the housing stock. None of these tasks had the compelling technological glimmer of the earlier projects, but by that time, the political identity of the technostructure had been built on monumentalism and technological audacity. Hence, the state began development on a number of largely symbolic technological ventures including the Concorde supersonic passenger jet, the plutonium breeder reactor at Creys-Malville, the high-speed train (TGV), and the Pompidou and La Villette museums. While the economics of some of these projects were often chancy, their political and cultural importance remained paramount. Each gave France the air of a technology leader, thereby facilitating internal investment and national prominence. Significantly, few of the later monumental projects were particularly contested politically. The technocracy had managed to gain a large measure of political autonomy from the traditional operation of political parties and parliament.

France's successes speak well for a positive strategy of bold, technocratic management. The aggressive nuclear program framed by Pierre Messmer in 1975 was started just as the worldwide trend toward nuclear power began to decline. Nonetheless, the relevant actors doggedly continued so that by the late 1980s France used nuclear energy to generate about 70 percent of its electricity, and its power was (on a factor-cost basis) some of the cheapest in the world—all without a major accident. The nuclear program's success can well be the symbol of France's postwar technological experience, one of massive material gains and stunning achievements, almost all of which were framed and pursued far away from democratic political inputs. A discourse on the necessity and benefits of technological progress loaded in advance the language needed to discuss the politics of technological change, but the nondebate could proceed in a warm, well-lit, and comfortable setting.

E. Chadeau, ''Etat, industrie, nation: La Formation des technologies aéronautiques en France (1900–1950),'' *Histoire, économie et société* 4 (1985); H. Chapman, *State Capitalism and Working-Class Radicalism in Twentieth-Century France* (Berkeley, Calif., 1990); R. Frost, *Alternating Currents: Nationalized Power in France (1946–1970)* (Ithaca, N.Y., 1990); P. Simonnot, *Les Nucléocrates* (Grenoble, Fr., 1978).

R. L. Frost

Related entries: DE GAULLE, CHARLES; ECOLOGY PARTY; ECONOMIC POLICY; ECONOMIC TRENDS; FABIUS, LAURENT; INDUSTRIAL POLICY; MARSHALL PLAN; MESSMER, PIERRE; MOCH, JULES; MONNET, JEAN; NATIONALATIONS; PLAN; TRANSPORTATION; TRIPARTITISM.

TERRORISM represents a symbolic act designed to influence political behavior by extra-normal means entailing the use or threat of violence. Terror and terrorism are rooted in French history, the word dating from the post–1789 epoch. Moreover, after the Revolution, France established itself as a ''*terre d'asile*,'' granting political asylum to many. Spared much of the international terrorism that plagued Europe in the 1960s and 1970s, examples of transnational terrorism have been by-products of its position as an asylum, exacerbated perhaps by France's position at the crossroads of Europe. The problem, however, is growing. While between 1972 and 1977 only eleven people died in France in terrorist incidents, between May and August 1982 fifteen were killed, and more died in the wave of Paris bombings in 1986.

Occasionally, the French state itself has been implicated. It is clear that part of French decolonization counterinsurgency tactics encompassed the use of irregular troops, hostage taking, and torture. Similarly, many have argued that the July 1985 *Rainbow Warrior* incident constituted an act of state terrorism.

One of France's first terrorist groupings, the *Organisation de l'armée secrète* (OAS), was a product of the Algerian conflict. Led by General Raoul Salan, the reactionary OAS plotted to assassinate Charles de Gaulle—the most spectacular attempt being in March 1962 when it gunned his car at Petit Chamart. The OAS was quashed in 1963 by the arrest or flight of its leaders.

During the 1970s Paris became a safe haven for several international groups.

The Japanese Red Army Faction, the Palestine Liberation Organization (PLO), the German Red Army Faction, the Italian Red Brigades terrorists who assassinated Premier Aldo Moro in 1978, and the Basque separatist group ETA all operated on or from French soil. It was a decade when France also faced another form of indigenous terrorism, militant Breton nationalism led by Lionel Chenevière and Patrick Montauzier. First active as a terrorist movement in 1966 and seeking regional autonomy for Brittany, the Bretons detonated over three hundred symbolically targeted bombs between 1966 and 1980. Valéry Giscard d'Estaing outlawed the *Armée révolutionnaire bretonne* (ARB) in 1974, and the police crackdown after the June 1978 Versailles bombing, coupled with cultural and economic concessions, brought this period to a close.

In the 1980s international opinion criticized France for being "soft" on terrorism. The August 1981 abolition of the State Security Court, the September 1981 amnesty for some prisoners, and a continuing refusal to extradite were hallmarks of François Mitterrand's early tenure as president that provoked bitter comment and a bitter harvest.

In August 1979 the best-known French group, *Action directe*, became operational. Led by Jean-Marc Rouillan (a beneficiary of the amnesty) and Nathalie Menignon, this extreme-left ideological group has similar roots to the Italian Red Brigades. No one emphatic political objective has animated all *Action directe* activities, but couched in Marxist-Leninist jargon, communiqués show the group to be first anti-American and anti-Jewish (indicated by 1982 attacks on the Goldenberg restaurant and the April 1982 assassination of American diplomat Ray Charles). Second, it is anti-"imperialist" (indicated by the March 1980 attack on the Paris Ministry of Overseas Cooperation and the April 1985 bombing of the International Monetary Fund [IMF] headquarters). Third, it is antibusiness (witness the November 1986 assassination of Renault tycoon Georges Besse). Fourth, it is antimilitary or against NATO. Numerous incidents after 1984 illustrate this, together with *Action directe*'s central role in the so-called Euroterror network (comprising the German RAF, the Red Brigades, and a Belgian group among others). By 1986, *Action directe* was working with Arab extremists; the demand for the release of FARL (*Factions armées révolutionnaires libanaises*) leader Georges Ibrahim Abdullah lay behind the 1986 wave of Paris bombings.

French responses to terrorism changed in the 1980s, as evidenced by moves in 1982 (the banning of *Action directe*, the creation of a secretary of state for public security, the announcement of stricter immigration controls) and 1986, when Prime Minister Jacques Chirac and Interior Minister Charles Pasqua increased police powers and unveiled a nonjury court for terrorist crimes. In 1984, the extradition of ETA terrorists began. The February 1987 arrest of leading *Action directe* members curtailed the group's activities.

The same cannot be said for the Corsican separatist group, the *Front de libération nationale de la Corse* (FLNC). Instigators of over forty-two hundred incidents since 1974, the FLNC has continued its violence (some 402 reported incidents in 1987), despite the March 1982 granting of a regional council and special status to the island.

J. Lodge, *Terrorism* (Oxford, 1981), *The Threat of Terrorism* (Brighton, Eng., 1981); E. Morris, A. Hoe, *Terrorism* (Basingstoke, Eng., 1987).

J. Bryant

Related entries: BASQUE QUESTION; CHIRAC, JACQUES; CORSICA; DECOLONIZATION; GREENPEACE AFFAIR; *ORGANISATION DE L'ARMEE SECRETE*; PASQUA, CHARLES.

THIRD WORLD, RELATIONS WITH, passed through two phases: Before 1962 relations were dominated by decolonization; after 1962 they were concerned with the maintenance of French influence in former colonies and export markets (largely for arms) in both former colonies and other states. Decolonization was bloody because the process was almost uniformly resisted by the governments of the Fourth Republic, their policies frequently manipulated by minorities of colonial officials or French colonists. They battled with reformist politicians, by refusing either to loosen French ties in time (Indochina), to provide political equality in either a federal or a unitary relationship (Algeria, sub-Saharan Africa), or forgo advantages incommensurate with their status as foreigners in a protectorate (Tunisia and Morocco).

Syria and Lebanon, promised independence during World War II, were granted it after further agitation in 1945. The constitution of the Fourth Republic created a French Union, but France resisted creating either the local autonomy of federalism or the equality of integration. A revolt in Madagascar in 1947 was brutally repressed.

The end of World War II left a power vacuum in Indochina, swiftly filled in the north by Ho Chi Minh's communist and nationalist Vietminh. As negotiations dragged on, a series of military attacks led swiftly to a war that lasted from 1947 to 1954. During the course of the conflict (underwritten economically after 1950 by the United States), French governments gradually gave political concessions to ''associated'' (puppet) governments that it had continually refused to Ho. The defeat at Dien Bien Phu (1954) and the subsequent Geneva conference consecrated French withdrawal from the peninsula, with Vietnam divided between a communist government in the north and a noncommunist one in the south, effectively under U.S. protection.

In the protectorates of Tunisia and Morocco, nationalist activity, though met with repression and occasionally counterterrorism, eventually led (in the case of Morocco after the deposition and recall of the Sultan) to independence in 1956.

Withdrawal from Algeria was not as simple, because it was legally French territory and had almost a million colonists. The failure to implement serious reforms and the brutal repression that followed the uprising in Sétif (1945) led to armed revolt in 1954. An exceptionally savage war (1954–62), accompanied by terrorism, counterterrorism, and torture, transformed the National Liberation Front (FLN) from a tiny minority to the leading group in Algeria and brought France to the edge of civil war. The Gaullist government that emerged was obliged to grant independence with few lasting concessions and to accept the repatriation of the French Algerian minority. The commitment to Algeria reinforced France's close ties to Israel and was the chief reason for French participation in the tripartite attack on Nasser's Egypt (seen as an FLN backer) during the Suez crisis of 1956.

The 1958 referendum for the constitution of the Fifth Republic became for the remaining overseas territories (largely African) a plebiscite on the new French Community. Only Guinea voted no, and it received immediate independence, but without any financial aid. By 1960, however, all the other territories chose independence, and the Community was officially abolished in 1961.

The end of the Algerian War permitted de Gaulle's reversal of Middle East policy, condemning Israel in 1967, and cutting arms sales to the Jewish state while nevertheless permitting them to non–front line Arab states like Libya, Saudi Arabia, and Iraq. France led the European acceptance of the Palestine Liberation Organization (PLO) and has criticized American support for Israel. In return, it has received assured oil supplies and lucrative regional contracts. During the protracted Iran–Iraq war in the 1980s, France lent support to Iraq, support that contributed to Iranian-inspired terrorist campaigns in France. With regard to Lebanon, French governments have not been able to prevent the gradual destruction of the Christian-dominated Lebanon that France had done so much to create.

In Africa, former colonies have been supported by financial and technical aid (reinforcing francophone education) and repeated military interventions to support existing governments (Gabon 1964, Zaire 1977, and even repeatedly in Chad while selling weapons to the Libyans it was helping to defeat in that country).

The desire to use a Third World focus as an alternative to international bipolarity also motivated rapprochements with the People's Republic of China and criticism of U.S. actions during the Vietnam War. Similarly, France condemned U.S. intervention in Santo Domingo in 1965 and in Nicaragua in the 1980s. Scarcity of resources (largely committed to francophone Africa) prevented any major penetration in Latin America. France has also continously supported calls for North-South dialogue and a more just international order. The Gulf crisis of 1990–91 pitted French willingness to work with the United States and concern over the security of oil supplies against its close relations with Iraq and its "Arab vocation."

A. Grosser, *Affaires extérieures, la politique de la France 1944–1989* (Paris, 1989), *De Gaulle et le tiers monde* (Paris, 1984).

A. Douglas

Related entries: ALGERIA, RELATIONS WITH; ARMS SALES; DIEN BIEN PHU; FOREIGN POLICY; IMMIGRANTS; INDOCHINA, RELATIONS WITH; MIDDLE EAST, RELATIONS WITH; MOROCCO, RELATIONS WITH; TUNISIA, RELATIONS WITH.

THOREZ, MAURICE (1900–1964), dominant figure in and general secretary of the French Communist party (PCF) from 1932 through his death in 1964, who exemplified the party's emphasis on working-class leadership. He was born to a coal-mining family in the Nord, quickly showed an aptitude for trade-union work, became a founding member of the PCF in 1920, and advanced rapidly in the party, apparently promoted by the Russians. He played an important role in the adoption of the Popular Front policy in 1934, which enabled him to combine his political radicalism and Soviet loyalty with a deep-seated and sincerely felt French patriotism. Yet, he accepted the Nazi-Soviet pact in 1939, left his army post, and spent the war years in Moscow; he was amnestied and allowed to return to France in November 1944. Thorez quickly reestablished control over the PCF, resuming an active role in promotion of a personality cult around himself modeled on that of Stalin, which began in 1936 with publication of a fictionalized autobiography entitled *Fils du peuple*. Thorez was very likely not even its author; yet it became required reading for all communists in France and for many of them the major source of their ideological sophistication. The PCF became known as "the party of Maurice Thorez."

Thorez shone as minister of state in the postwar tripartite governments of France, serving until the communists were ousted by socialist Paul Ramadier in May 1947. Thorez took particular responsibility for elaborating a statute for public employees, much of which is still in effect today; he enjoyed cabinet rank and met expulsion from the government with genuine regret, steering the party on a continued course as a government party until a rude shock and awakening administered at the founding conference of the Cominform in September 1947, during which he was attacked, in his absence, as the victim of legalist and parliamentary illusions. Thorez did his mea culpa and adapted well to the new sectarian line; he championed the Peace Movement, the major goal of Soviet foreign policy, and declared in 1949 that the French people would never make war against the Soviet Union and would greet an invading Soviet army as liberators. Yet, Thorez always aspired to resurrect the Popular Front and integrate the PCF, although internally authoritarian and Stalinist, into French politics.

In December 1950 Thorez suffered a stroke and was removed to the Soviet Union for treatment. However, he felt very much a prisoner there, and Stalin would not permit his return to France, which occurred only upon the dictator's death in March 1953. In the meantime Thorez appears to have intrigued by means of intermediaries to regain control of the party from second-in-command Jacques Duclos and the ambitious Auguste Lecoeur. Thorez's personal role in the purges of wartime resisters, culminating in the celebrated Marty-Tillon trials of 1952, remains cloudy. On the other hand, following his return to France he rid the party of Lecoeur and set it firmly on an integrationist course, supporting Pierre Mendès-France in 1954 and Guy Mollet in 1956. Thorez would not accept the consequences of Khruschev's reformism in the Soviet Union begun in 1956, and complained to Palmiro Togliatti, with whom he subsequently broke relations, that the Soviet leader had dragged through the mud a glorious past. Thorez's efforts to block knowledge of the de-Stalinization campaign in France were unavailing, and he was forced to repudiate aspects of his own personality cult, pretending that the PCF had always been run by collective leadership. He intrigued with Vyacheslav Molotov and the Chinese in the international movement, however, while making a kind of pitiful effort to stake out a claim as an original Marxist theorist by restating the theory of pauperization of the working class under capitalism in 1955, when the first fruits of consumerist prosperity were being felt in France.

Thorez followed a cautious line during the Algerian rebellion, supporting liberal efforts at reform but declining to endorse independence until very late and condemning *Front de libération nationale* (FLN) terrorism. This put him on a collision course with the emerging French new left, which was supported in the party by the Khrushchevian faction of Marcel Servin and Laurent Casanova. Thorez succeeded in purging them in 1961 (and his control remained unshaken to his death in 1964, which occurred, symbolically, during a vacation at the Black Sea). He continued to pursue entente with the socialists and advocated unity with them in opposition to Charles de Gaulle, properly claiming paternity of the pattern of left unity under the Fifth Republic. For this he has recently been criticized by the current PCF leadership, along with his historic "lateness" in assimilating the meaning of the changes in the Soviet Union consequent upon the twentieth Congress of the Communist Party of the Soviet Union in February 1956. On the other hand Thorez was something of a liberal by party standards with regard to culture and intellectual life; he put an end to Lecoeur's efforts to enforce ideological purity in 1953, reinstating Picasso, and he sponsored the heterodox Marxism of Roger Garaudy through the early 1960s. His legacy to the PCF remains ambiguous: ideological sectarianism in the international communist movement, internal Stalinist practices in the PCF, yet a social-democratic politics of elections and reformism.

J. Mer, *Le Parti de Maurice Thorez ou le bonheur communiste français* (Paris, 1977); P. Robrieux, *Maurice Thorez, vie secrète et vie politique* (Paris, 1975); M. Thorez, *Fils du peuple* (Paris, 1970); I. Wall, *French Communism in the Era of Stalin* (Westport, Conn., 1983).

I. M. Wall

Related entries: FRENCH COMMUNIST PARTY; GARAUDY, ROGER; TRIPARTITISM; SOVIET UNION, RELATIONS WITH.

TRADE UNION MOVEMENT, since 1947 has been divided along ideological lines among five major interindustrial confederations or centrals. The oldest and largest one was the *Confédération générale du travail* (CGT), founded in 1895, which has been under communist domination since the Popular Front (1936–38). The second oldest and most important was the *Confédération française des travailleurs chrétiens* (CFTC), formed in 1919 under the inspiration of Catholic social doctrine. In 1964 a majority of the confederation approved the formation of the secularized *Confédération française démocratique du travail* (CFDT), leaving behind a rump CFTC. The fourth central was the *Confédération générale du travail-Force ouvrière* (FO), an anticommunist reformist group that broke away from the CGT in 1947. The fifth one was the *Confédération générale des* *cadres* (CGC), which was formed in 1944 to represent the interests of supervisors and managerial personnel. Finally, one must mention the *Fédération de l'éducation nationale* (FEN), which left the CGT in 1948 to form an independent teachers' union.

The basic unit was the local trade union or *syndicat,* which originally organized workers according to trade in each locality. These unions were then grouped nationally into federations of trades and locally around municipal labor exchanges or *bourses du travail*. Craft unions and federations as well as *bourses du travail* were later amalgamated into industrial and departmental federations. In 1970 the CGT had forty industrial federations, The FO thirty-four, and the CFDT twenty-nine. Local unions fought for recognition within firms against employer resistance. Company-based union *sections* or branches achieved legal protection as a result of the general strike of May–June 1968 and bargaining rights under the Auroux laws of 1982.

Power within the confederations was shared between local unions, represented at biennial congresses, and departmental and industrial federations, which constituted interim national committees. The *bureau confédéral* or national leadership was selected either by these committees or in the case of the CFDT by a national body elected by the congress. While local unions and national federations enjoyed administrative autonomy, they usually followed the general policy orientation set by the confederal congress and leadership, not only in the CGT where factions were banned but also in the CFDT and FO, where in opposition to the CGT Edmond Maire and André Bergeron were able to quell dissent and maintain unity. Trade unions acted as much as political and social movements as economic interest groups. Ideological aims were reflected in union behavior and policy. The CGT derived its Marxist ideology from members of the French Communist party (PCF), who controlled virtually all industrial and departmental federations. It treated relations between workers and employers in terms of class exploitation and struggle. Its purpose—at least until 1978—was to limit the effects of exploitation and to raise the level of class consciousness and struggle for the essentially political battle for socialism. It attempted to represent and unite the material interests of all grades and categories and to raise industrial action to the national level. More concerned with mobilization than with negotiation, the CGT was maximalist in the formulation and negotiation of demands, voluntaristic in its conduct of strikes, and intransigent in its refusal of binding contracts. Through a process of competitive bidding with the other unions, it was able to prevent the formation of stable contractual relationships and to give French industrial relations its peculiarly adversarial edge.

In breaking with the communist-dominated CGT, the FO abandoned practices of agitational and political strikes and hard-line bargaining for a more modest bread-and-butter unionism. Since it lacked a militant presence in industrial plants, it became the main contractual partner for employers, signing conventions that allowed for minimal wage increases along with clauses for the mediation of disputes. Because of its strength among public servants and political neutrality, the FO obtained significant results in the 1970s by lobbying the government of Valéry Giscard d'Estaing, which used it to check the progress of the more radical CGT and CFDT.

The CFTC, whose ideology after World War II was a blend of Catholic corporatism, personalism, and American reformism, alternated between the maximalism of the CGT and minimalism of the FO. The CFTC was always sensitive to qualitative issues like wage equality, working hours, and democratic planning and control. Under the growing influence of its industrial federations, the CFDT practiced unity of action with the CGT, especially after its conversion to *socialisme autogestionnaire,* worker-managed socialism, in 1970. Following the split in the French left in 1977, it returned to a more conciliatory—and even concessionary—bargaining position, replacing the FO as the most accommodating central in France.

Because of the ideological nature and divisions of French unions, they were—with the exception of public utility and transport workers, miners, and printers—notoriously weak in membership and resources. France had perhaps the lowest rate of unionization among industrial nations—a maximum of 25 percent in the early 1970s and 15 percent in 1985. Dues were low and strike funds rare. A bare-bones bureaucracy of paid officials relied upon the ideological devotion of activists to carry out functions in the plants and sympathetic intellectuals to provide technical assistance. While only a minority of employees joined unions in private industry, a majority demonstrated their support in periodic elections for *délégués du personnel* or plant stewards, enterprise committees, and for the *prud'hommes* or wage courts. As the electorate expanded in the 1970s to include more workers from rural and Catholic areas, small firms, and white-collar employees, support for the CGT declined from 50 to under 30 percent to the benefit of the CFDT, the FO, and the nonunionized.

French unions possessed greater bargaining power and influence than numbers might indicate. They were represented in the Economic and Social Council, the Higher Commission on Collective Agreements, and committees of the Plan. After 1968 they were regularly consulted by governments on economic and social policy. Demands of the CGT and CFDT were relayed by the Communist and Socialist parties respectively, while the threat of mobilization and radical political change was enough to secure significant wage increases and social benefits from employers and conservative governments in the aftermath of 1968. Through its political connections and resonance, the trade-union movement made up in militancy and ideological commitment what it lacked in numbers and resources.

G. Caire, *Les Syndicats ouvriers* (Paris, 1971); V. Lorwin, *The French Labor Movement* (Cambridge, Mass., 1954); B. Moss, "Ideology and Industrial Practice: Federations CGT, CFDT, and FO," in *The French Workers' Movement, 1968–1982*, ed. M. Kesselman (London, 1984); R. Mouriaux, *Les Syndicats dans la société française* (Paris, 1983); J.-D. Reynaud, *Les Syndicats en France* (Paris, 1975).

B. H. Moss

Related entries: AUROUX LAWS; *AUTOGESTION*; BERGERON, ANDRE; *CONFEDERATION FRANCAISE DEMOCRATIQUE DU TRAVAIL*; *CONFED-*

ERATION FRANCAISE DES TRAVAILLEURS CHRETIENS; *CONFEDERATION GENERALE DU TRAVAIL*; *FORCE OUVRIERE*; FRACHON, BENOIT; FRENCH COMMUNIST PARTY; KRASUCKI, HENRI; LABOR FORCE; MAIRE, EDMOND; NATIONAL COUNCIL OF FRENCH EMPLOYERS; SEGUY, GEORGES; STRIKES.

TRANSPORTATION, modernized and transformed during the Fourth and Fifth Republics. During the nineteenth century the transportation network played a significant role in the geographical and cultural unification of France. Yet, by the end of World War II the French transportation network needed to be overhauled.

French roads, whether local, regional, or national, still formed a dense array and, with the exception of destroyed bridges, were still usable after the war. This network could easily withstand the presence of limited traffic (680,000 vehicles in 1944). However, the steep increase in the number of private vehicles during the 1950s and 1960s (4,950,000 in 1960; 11,860,000 by 1970) and the development of trucking led to an overload of the national network. Traffic jams became the norm on the eve of vacations, and the number of accidents increased significantly. The French government, which had undertaken a limited program of highway construction (only twenty-two kilometers of four-lane highway had been built by 1946 and seventy-seven by 1954), launched the construction of an extended network of four-lane highways throughout the country. The government chose various types of associations with private companies that built these turnpikes (174 km by 1960; 1,599 km by 1970; 5,251 km by 1980; 6,530 by 1988). At the outset of the 1990s France has a well-managed and extensive road network (802,218 km in 1986) with approximately 7,000 kilometers of turnpikes that ensure easy travel throughout the country both for individual vehicles as well as for a growing number of trucks transporting goods within the country or within the European Economic Community (EEC).

Urban transportation has often been hampered by the fact that the downtown areas of most French cities were built several centuries ago. Traffic in medium-sized and large cities is often hectic, and traffic jams are a common occurrence. Many cities developed public transportation systems in order to alleviate urban traffic. The *Régie autonome des transports parisiens* (RATP) was created in 1948; it has the monopoly of surface and underground public transportation in Paris. The Parisian subway network was modernized and slowly extended (167 km in 1947; 190 km in 1980); new lines were opened to serve the outskirts of the French capital. The 1970s and 1980s saw the construction of underground transportation systems in Lyon and Marseille. The public bus systems also played their role in and around most French cities and replaced local rail lines discarded by the French railroads. Taxis also form a significant link in urban transportation; there were 3,000 taxi cabs in Paris in 1946 and 14,305 in 1988. The end of the 1980s was marked by efforts against atmospheric pollution and traffic gridlock in urban centers, the encouragement of car pooling, and improved local bus service. Moreover, ''water buses'' now operate on the Seine River in Paris, and tramway lines are being built around the French capital.

The French railroad network, which had helped break the isolation of small provincial cities in the nineteenth century, withstood the conflagration of World War II and could be utilized again. Improvements in power and comfort characterized the postwar decades: Fuel-powered locomotives appeared in 1946, lines were progressively converted to electric power (Paris-Lyon by 1952 and Paris-Marseille by 1962), and pneumatic suspension was installed on cars as early as 1952. These transformations caused a steep increase in the deficit of the *Société nationale des chemins de fer français* (SNCF), which had been created in 1937. It was thus decided to discard the less profitable lines and focus on improving the major lines. The 1970s were marked by the concretization of the SNCF's efforts: more electric locomotives, more comfortable and faster trains. In 1972 the first *train à grande vitesse* (TGV) was tested, and in 1978 the first regular line was opened between Paris and Lyon. The success of the TGV (270 km per hour on average between Paris and Lyon) led to the extension of its network between Paris and Switzerland and the Mediterranean coast. TGV lines were also built between Paris and the western and southwestern regions of France, and new lines were opened in 1989 between Paris and Nantes; the TGV now also serves Bordeaux as well as Germany to the east. TGV lines are also planned between France and Spain (1992). The modernization of the network and its machines as well as better utilization led to a progressive diminution of the SNCF's deficit in the 1970s and 1980s; the SNCF is now breaking even and should realize a profit by the early 1990s.

Air France was created in 1933 but began regular transatlantic flights between Paris and New York City only in 1946. Domestic air traffic is limited in France because of the small size of the country, because of the reliability, increasing speed, and comfort of the French trains, and also because of the more extensive network of four-lane turnpikes allowing rapid travel by car. French airlines, in addition to Air France, include Air Inter (founded in 1954, originally for domestic service), UTA (created in 1963), as well as several other companies that rent their planes to charter or private companies (Corse-Air, Minerve, etc.). France's aeronautic industries have played a significant role in the construction of famous planes like the Concorde (built in the 1960s with Great Britain) or the Airbus (built in association with European companies). France's air traffic is ranked fifth worldwide (behind the United States, the Soviet Union, Great Britain, and Japan). French air carriers can be advantageously compared with other international carriers, but domestic air traffic remains limited owing to the existence of older, reliable, and more affordable means of transportation.

Other transportation systems include river transportation and sea-going vessels. By 1890 there were 11,000 kilometers of navigable canals in France, but barge traffic suffered from the competition of railroads in the early twentieth century. Efforts in favor of barge traffic (primarily between the Mediterranean and the North Sea) led to a small increase in river and canal transportation during the

1950s and 1960s. It appears that problems still lie ahead for barge owners since traffic diminished significantly between 1974 and 1987. France's merchant marine lost in importance worldwide (seventh in 1939, twenty-third in 1988) during the postwar decades: Marseille remains the first French commercial port, while Calais is the first French passenger port (the anticipated opening of the Channel tunnel in the 1990s may threaten Calais's success). France's prestigious cruise ships, *Normandie* and *France*, have not been replaced. As for particular transportation networks such as electric and telephone cables or gas and chemical products pipelines, their presence often goes unnoticed or unseen (underground wires in cities or in historically significant areas).

France's transportation networks of all kinds have been significantly influenced by the demographic, industrial, and administrative importance of its provinces and cities. It is well known that Paris is still the hub of all French transportation networks and that the development of these networks has been more important north and east of the famous Le Havre-Geneva line (where industrial development was more important). France's transportation networks are at least as good as those of the other Western European countries; in 1993, they will be easily integrated within the larger networks of the EEC.

J. Ardagh, *Ces drôles de Français* (Paris, 1989); D. Frémy, M. Frémy, *Quid 1990* (Paris, 1989); P. Pinchemel, *France: A Geographical, Social, and Economic Survey* (Paris and Cambridge, 1987); J.-Y. Potel, *L'Etat de la France et de ses habitants* (Paris, 1985); M. Verdié, *L'Etat de la France et de ses habitants* (Paris, 1987).

A. J. M. Prévos

Related entries: ECONOMIC TRENDS; REGIONS; SOCIAL TRENDS; URBANIZATION.

TRIPARTITISM, term used to describe the wide-spectrum political coalition that governed France from the Liberation in 1944 to the ouster of the communists in May of 1947. The three dominant parties consisted of the communists (*Parti communiste français*, PCF), the socialists (*Section française de l'internationale ouvrière*, SFIO), and the Christian democrats (*Mouvement républicain populaire*, MRP). General Charles de Gaulle presided over the regime from its beginning until January 1946. The prime ministers who followed included Félix Gouin, Léon Blum, and Paul Ramadier. The tripartite arrangement spanned three parliaments: the *Assemblée constituente provisoire* (ACP), from Liberation until October 1945; the *Assemblée nationale constituente* (ANC), until June 1946; and the regular Fourth Republic. The tripartite regime had to write a constitution for the Fourth Republic; yet the new document reimplanted the parliamentary ascendency of the Third Republic. On this issue, General de Gaulle resigned.

The PCF attained its zenith of political support during the tripartite era, gaining 27 percent of the vote in the elections of October 1945, followed closely by the socialists and the MRP. The PCF gained key cabinet posts, including the ministries of industry and labor, but was excluded from key financial-economic posts and military-police posts. In this period the PCF disavowed all attempts at revolution and committed itself to coalition partnership. As the center party of the coalition, the SFIO was the pivot of tripartite politics.

Major accomplishments of the regime include nationalizing electricity, gas, deposit banking, coal, insurance, Renault, and mass transit, as well as laying the foundations for indicative national economic planning.

P. Dujardin, *1946: Le Droit mis en scène* (Grenoble, Fr., 1979); B. D. Graham, *The French Socialists and Tripartisme* (Toronto, 1965); J.-P. Rioux, *La France de la Quatrième République,* vol. 1, 1944–52 (Paris, 1980); P. Robrieux, *Histoire intérieure du Parti communiste,* vol. 2 (Paris, 1981).

R. L. Frost

Related entries: CHRISTIAN DEMOCRATS; CONSTITUTION OF THE FOURTH REPUBLIC; DE GAULLE, CHARLES; FRENCH COMMUNIST PARTY; GOUIN, FELIX; MONNET, JEAN; NATIONALIZATIONS; PLAN; SOCIALIST PARTY (SFIO); THOREZ, MAURICE.

TUNISIA, RELATIONS WITH. After a long battle for independence won in 1956, Tunisia has maintained generally good relations with France. The protectorate instituted by the treaties of the Bardo (1881) and La Marsa (1883) left Tunisia a virtual colony under the nominal rule of its *Beys* (rulers) and a considerable number of Frenchmen and other Europeans settled the country.

Tunisian nationalism became personified, by the 1930s, by the French-educated, secularist Habib Bourguiba, founder of the Neo-Destour (Constitutional) party and frequently jailed for his activities. The deposition of Moncef Bey in 1943 for alleged pro-Axis activities (in reality he had pressured Vichy for reforms) only facilitated Bourguiba's rising legitimacy.

After the war a pattern developed similar to that in Morocco and tended toward a kind of cosovereignty in violation of the Treaty of the Bardo. French settlers in Tunisia, legally foreigners in the country, sought direct participation in political affairs, a right they were not willing to extend in practice to the Tunisians. The Residents (French officials in colonial regions), though appointed from Paris, were often controlled by the French settler community when the latter, through its influence in the Radical party, was not able to get its way directly in Paris.

The relatively liberal policies associated with Jean Mons were reversed in 1951 when Robert Schuman formally rejected the Tunisian government's request for movement toward autonomy and insisted on the participation of French colonists in Tunisian political institutions. In early 1952 a new Resident, Jean de Hautecloque, arrived to enforce the new policy. The government of the Bey appealed to the United Nations (which eventually called on France to move toward true self-government). The Residence responded with massive arrests, which in turn provoked a general strike. In the course of the crisis a guerilla war developed accompanied by heavy-handed repressions; there were numerous incidents, and the leading Tunisian syndicalist was assassinated, apparently by French counterterrorists.

Pierre Mendès-France reversed the policy of force upon his accession in 1954.

In a spectacular visit to the Bey in Tunis he announced a policy of internal autonomy, leaving France with control over external affairs. With Bourguiba's cooperation, agreement on internal self-rule was reached in 1955 with the Edgar Faure government. The independence of Morocco in March 1956 made the acceptance of mere internal autonomy politically unacceptable, and upon Bourguiba's demand, new negotiations led to the recognition of the full independence of Tunisia in November.

Independence did not end the conflict, however, because of the war raging in Algeria since late 1954. Bourguiba tried to mediate between the French government and the Algerian National Liberation Front (FLN) for a time, with the goal of securing access to Sahara oil. At the same time thousands of FLN troops used Tunisia as a sanctuary and base for cross-border raids into Algeria, creating a potential security problem for the Tunisian government itself. A first effort at mediation, involving Bourguiba and the Sultan of Morocco, was dashed when the French skyjacked the Moroccan plane carrying top FLN leaders to a conference in Tunis in October 1956.

In early 1958 another offer of Tunisian and Moroccan good offices also dissolved in crisis. In response to yet another cross-border raid, French planes bombarded the Tunisian border town of Sakhiet, missing the FLN camp but causing numerous civilian casualties and an international uproar that helped to bring down the Fourth Republic. President Charles de Gaulle liquidated the crisis by agreeing to remove all French military installations from Tunisia save those at Bizerta in the south. In July 1961, however, Bourguiba demanded the elimination of the remaining presence, and when de Gaulle refused, attacked the base in Bizerta. The French president reacted massively, killing over a thousand Tunisians, though he was obliged to agree to the evacuations in 1963, albeit after Algerian independence in 1962. Later relations between Tunisia and France, both diplomatic and commercial, have been smooth.

A. Grosser, *Affaires extérieures, la politique de la France 1944–1989* (Paris, 1989).

A. Douglas

Related entries: DECOLONIZATION; FOREIGN POLICY; THIRD WORLD, RELATIONS WITH.

U

UNEMPLOYMENT, relatively stable until the early 1960s, with roughly 200,000 out of work, compared to the 2,600,000 (9 percent) without work in France in 1991. One of the functions of the family firm, which dominated the French economy until the 1960s, was to protect its workers from unemployment. In recessions, instead of laying off workers, it preferred to put them on short time. For those living in company housing it would suspend or reduce rent collection. It would encourage the workers to use their idle time to cultivate gardens or tend the rabbit hutches and chicken coops that adjoined company housing, or simply work the small plots of land that many workers had inherited from their peasant fathers. Labor mobility was low, especially after marriage.

This pattern was basically able to respond to the shrinkage of the market that occurred during the world depression (700,000 full-time unemployed in France) and during the German occupation. There was hardship but it could not be compared with the fall in the standard of living experienced by German and American workers.

During the "glorious thirty years" (1945–75), France's economy lost some of its family-firm orientation, and management became more separated from ownership. Salaried employment replaced much self-employment in farms and shops. The state replaced family management in guaranteeing unemployment benefits for the unemployed. The fact that France experienced a labor shortage during that period made the transition easier. Until 1962 unemployment fluctuated around 200,000. From 1962 to the summer of 1974 unemployment increased to about 450,000 (2.2% of the labor force).

After that, the oil shocks had their effects on the French economy and unemployment, mainly conjunctural, rose to 6.7 percent in 1980 and stabilized at around 2,500,000 in 1985, representing approximately 10.2 percent of the labor force. The average time it took an unemployed worker to find a job stretched from eight to seventeen months. The unemployed in France register with the *Agence nationale pour l'emploi* (ANPE), which operates theoretically as a natural clearinghouse for job requests but more effectively as an agency where one must report every month to show that one is still unemployed.

Another agency important to the unemployed is the *Association pour l'emploi dans l'industrie et le commerce* (ASSEDIC), which administers unemployment insurance through a payroll tax (4.43% for employers and 2.47% for the employee). During the late 1970s, as unemployment grew, the French government was very concerned whether the country would tolerate high levels of unemployment, which were not part of its historical experience. It placed unemployment compensation at 90 percent of the last twelve months' salary, which encouraged fraud. Eventually compensation was reduced to 57 percent of the daily salary for a maximum of twelve to nineteen months, after which the *chômeur* became entitled to an *allocation de solidarité* of 2,105 francs (in 1989). (For comparison, the minimum monthly wage, SMIC, equaled 4,035 francs.) A youth (sixteen to twenty-five years of age) who has never worked is entitled to 1,242 francs per month for a year; since many youths live at home, this is a substantial amount.

Unemployment strikes the young (30%) twice as hard as others, and the young female unemployment rate is 68 percent higher than for young males, except when women have the *baccalauréat*. Foreign workers have a higher rate of unemployment than most of their French counterparts. For males it was double the native rate (12% versus 6% in 1982), but the incidence of undocumented workers is probably higher for the foreigners than for French workers.

Those who have the highest unemployment are the youths who end their schooling without any marketable skills (25% of a cohort) and the adults who are laid off in their fifties. In the large housing projects (*Les Minguettes* on the southeastern fringe of Lyon is an example) unemployed youth, especially those whose ethnicity affects their employability, such as the North Africans (*Beurs*), easily comprise 50 percent of the adolescents. They develop a culture of unemployment "*la galère*," expressed in hostility to adults and the police, "hanging out," petty theft, black market dealings (*magouille*), drugs, occasional paid employment usually undocumented (*les petits boulots*), and unemployment compensation. There is no real physical deprivation, but rather a growing marginalization from the world of work, which will have long-term effects for 5 percent of a birth cohort.

The French government until 1975 had often fought unemployment by subsidizing marginal firms in steel, textiles, ship building, and so on in order to preclude or postpone laying off the work force. Since 1975 it has preferred to cope with unemployment through social policies rather than economic ones especially after 1981 with the arrival of the socialists to power. They quickly discovered that massive state spending had a negative impact on the economy.

These policies are aimed at reducing the labor force in two ways. First, they do so by accelerating and subsidizing the retirement of people laid off in their fifties. The general age of retirement was lowered to sixty, the age at which both men and women can retire and still get 50 percent of their last year's salary. Second, by extending schooling, labor force rates for youth aged fifteen to nineteen have fallen by half between 1975 and 1988, with approximately 15 percent of boys and 10.5 percent of girls now working. Another policy is to subsidize job training, especially for youth, either in regular apprenticeships or in internships, mostly part-time in public services (*Travaux d'utilité collective*, TUC). The total costs of these policies, including unemployment compensation, is 250 billion francs, or about 3.5 percent of the GNP. It has been calculated that three people assisted remove one unemployed person from the rolls.

Since 1985 unemployment has stabilized: Unemployment was 9.3 percent in March of 1991, placing France ahead of Italy (9.7%) and Spain (15.2%), but behind Germany (6.2%) and Great Britain (7.4%).

G. Cornilleau, P. Mariani, B. Roguet, ''Quinze ans de politique de l'emploi,'' *Revue de l'OFCE: Observations et diagnostics économiques* 31 (April 1990); *Données sociales 1990*; F. Dubet, *La Galère: Jeunes en survie* (Paris, 1987); A. Sauvy, *Histoire économique de la France entre les deux guerres 1931–1939*, vol. 2 (Paris, 1967); D. Schnapper, *L'Epreuve du chômage* (Paris, 1987).

J. R. Pitts

Related entries: ECONOMIC TRENDS; IMMIGRANTS; LABOR FORCE; WOMEN, CONDITION OF.

UNIFIED SOCIALIST PARTY (PSU), the most influential of the many tiny parties that have emerged on the French left since 1945. Throughout its history, the PSU has never won more than 4 percent of the vote or four seats in the National Assembly. Nonetheless, it has been the source of some of the most important ideas and politicians for the left during its thirty years.

The PSU (*Parti socialiste unifié*) was formed in 1958, when three tiny splinter groups came together primarily to protest French policy in Algeria and to revitalize the noncommunist left. In its first years the PSU's leaders included former prime minister Pierre Mendès-France, former socialist deputy Edouard Depreux, and a number of prominent left-wing Catholics.

During the late 1950s and early 1960s, the PSU was in the forefront of opposition to the Algerian War. Afterward, the party turned its attention primarily to two larger questions confronting the left. First, it tried to get the Socialist party (SFIO) and the Communist party (PCF), its larger competitors on the left, to join together in a coalition, seeing the unification of the left as the only way to defeat the Gaullists. Second, more than the rest of the left, the PSU tried to bring new issues (e.g., the effects of urbanization, the role of white-collar workers in the ''new working class'') onto the left's agenda.

The high point in the PSU's history came in 1968. It was the only party to support fully the demands of the students from the beginning of the May revolt. Moreover, PSU *militants* played a major role in organizing the students' protest and beginning the factory occupations that brought the country to a virtual standstill for almost three weeks. Finally, the PSU was the one established party that was receptive to the humanistic and participatory ideals that rose to the surface that year, most notably *autogestion*, a decentralized and participatory form of socialism.

In the years after 1968 the PSU championed *autogestion*, women's rights, the environment, and the other issues that grew out of the 1968 protest. Polls often showed that its leader, Michel Rocard, was France's most popular politician.

By 1972, however, it was clear that another 1968 was not on the horizon. Meanwhile, the new Socialist party (PS) led by François Mitterrand had concluded a Common Program of government with the communists, thereby making a shift toward the right more appealing to the party's moderates. Other groups spawned by 1968 were undercutting the PSU's support on its left.

In 1974 the party went through the most serious of its many factional schisms when Rocard led much of the party into the PS. Its fortunes ebbed thereafter and it lost even more supporters when another group, led by Huguette Bouchardeau, decided to support Mitterrand's presidential candidacy in 1981. In the 1988 legislative elections, the PSU's support had dropped to barely 1 percent of the total vote.

Although the PSU never itself has had much influence, its former members include both intellectuals (e.g., Gilles Martinet, Claude Bourdet, Serge Mallet) and members of Mitterrand's governments after 1981 (Rocard, Bouchardeau, Alain Savary, Jack Lang, Jacques Delors).

C. Hauss, *The New Left in France*: *The Unified Socialist Party* (Westport, Conn., 1978); D. Singer, *Is Socialism Doomed? The Meaning of Mitterrand* (New York, 1987).

C. Hauss

Related entries: BOUCHARDEAU, HUGUETTE; CLUB MOVEMENT; COMMON PROGRAM; DELORS, JACQUES; DEMONSTRATIONS; ECOLOGY PARTY; ELECTIONS; FEDERATION OF THE DEMOCRATIC AND SOCIALIST LEFT; JUQUIN, PIERRE; MAIRE, EDMOND; MARXISM; MENDES-FRANCE, PIERRE; MITTERRAND, FRANCOIS; MOLLET, GUY; ROCARD, MICHEL; SAVARY, ALAIN; SOCIALIST PARTY (PS, SFIO); STUDENT REVOLTS; UNION OF THE LEFT.

UNION FOR FRENCH DEMOCRACY (UDF), an umbrella political party. It consists of three separate political parties that each maintain a separate identity, organization, and leadership. These parties are as follows: the Republican party (PR), the Radical party, and the Center of Social Democrats (CDS).

The Republican party originated in the breaking up of another party, the National Center of Independents and Peasants (CNIP). It represents that flank of the CNIP that did not go into opposition in 1962 over the issue of direct election of the president. Originally named the Independent Republicans by founder Valéry Giscard d'Estaing, the party took the name of *Parti républicain* in 1974 under the leadership of Michel Poniatowski. What strength it has is owing to the importance of its leaders, at both the national and local levels; the party has little organization and few active members. It characterizes itself as the party of "progress, dynamism, youth, technological innovation, and economic liberalism." Although it attracts a heterogeneous electorate, it is disproportionately strong among white-collar workers.

The Radical party was one of the strongest parties in the Third Republic and consistently produced some of France's greatest leaders, among them Pierre Mendès-France. However, sullied by its part in the defeat of France in 1940 and the opportunistic careerism of many of its deputies throughout the life of the Fourth Republic, it found itself unable to play a significant role after the crisis of 1958. In 1971 the party briefly joined in coalition with the CDS (see below) in opposition to the Georges Pompidou government, but shortly thereafter a splinter group broke away to form the Movement of Left Radicals (MRG), which now routinely forms electoral coalitions with the Socialist party. In 1971 Jean-Jacques Servan-Schreiber, a well-known editor and writer, became secretary-general of the remaining radicals. The present leader is Yves Galland.

The Center of Social Democrats has been led throughout much of its history by Jean Lecanuet, and more recently by Pierre Méhaignerie. Most of this group's original members had been members of France's Christian democratic party (MRP, Popular Republican Movement), which largely disbanded in 1958 and ceased to exist altogether in 1967. Originally supportive of Gaullist governments (under the name of Democratic Center), the party began to waver in 1968 and to divide. Under the leadership of Jacques Duhamel, and under the label Center for Progress and Modern Democracy (CPDM), its victorious candidates remained supportive of government policy, but by 1969 the followers of both Lecanuet and Duhamel agreed in opposing the referendum of April 1969, thereby helping force Charles de Gaulle from power. In the subsequent presidential election the two groups split again, with the Duhamel forces supporting Georges Pompidou, the followers of Lecanuet being more favorable to the candidacy of Alain Poher. Once Pompidou was in office, the Duhamel faction of the PDM took the name Center of Democracy and Progress (CDP) and gave its support to the new president. The Lecanuet faction remained in opposition and in 1971 joined the radical-socialists in the short-lived Reformers' Movement (*les réformateurs*). The CDP and PDM factions came back together in 1976 as the Center of Social Democrats (CDS). This complex history of shifting alliances and factions is owing in large part to the fact that this party has always been less a party than a collection of notables, having almost no organization at the grass roots.

The idea for the Union for French Democracy came as centrist politicians prepared for the parliamentary elections of 1978. The name of the new federation played on French Democracy, the title of a book written by Giscard d'Estaing, and Giscard was indeed the chief architect of the movement, convincing both the radicals and the democratic centrists, both of which had supported him in 1974, to band together in a more formal electoral alliance just two months before the election. In combination its various candidates took 21.4 percent of the vote and 119 seats in the legislature, making it second only to the Gaullists and giving it the motivation to function as a single parliamentary group. The UDF lost the presidency in 1981, and its share of the vote in the subsequent legislative election that year fell to 19.2 percent of the vote and sixty-three of the seats. Since then the movement has often entered into electoral alliance with the Gaullists, a tactic that gave it 15.6 percent of the vote in the 1986 legislative elections and 18.5 percent in those of 1988. In 1990 the UDF and the RPR (*Rassemblement pour la République*) announced the formation of a confederation known as the *Union pour la France*. For the first time in French political history the two parties will use primaries to choose a single candidate to represent them in the presidential elections scheduled for 1995.

Ideologically, the UDF has, following Giscard, been strongly committed to economic liberalism, modernization, and what it calls classical Gaullism but others often call neo-Gaullism (the term usually includes as well the Rally for the Republic, RPR, under Jacques Chirac). Although the movement normally seeks to situate itself to the left of the RPR, it attracts a considerably less popular following, having little working-class support, and a number of its local notables have entered into electoral bargains with the National Front on the local level that have seriously compromised the movement's claim not to be on the political right.

A key liability of the UDF has been the weakness and internal rivalries of its leadership corps, particularly since Giscard lost the presidency in 1981. Since then the movement has placed its hopes for regaining the presidency in Raymond Barre, the economist who was appointed by Giscard to the prime ministership in 1976. But Barre, although very much admired by some for his apparent personal probity and independent conservatism (especially in fiscal policies), has never joined any political party and has persisted in treating the UDF very much as de Gaulle and Pompidou treated their own loyal supporters, the Gaullists: They may follow him if they will, but it is of their own doing; he does not need them. This posture has, however, proved self-defeating in recent years, and Barre's extremely poor showing in the presidential election of 1988 (less than 17% on the first vote, making him ineligible for the runoff) made clear that his failure to rally the movement cost him more in votes than it gained him in popular respect.

Aside from Barre, the leadership corps includes the current leaders of the three component parties. However, neither François Léotard of the Republican party, nor Yves Galland of the radicals, nor Pierre Méhaignerie of the CDS is likely to accede to the wishes of either of the others to move to the role of *primus inter pares*. Giscard, whose fund of influence and respect among voters and politicians alike remains impressively strong, but whose age, combined with his defeat in 1981, suggest that his role henceforward is also that of respected senior statesman, became president of the UDF following the 1988 presidential elections.

P. Avril, *Essais sur les partis* (Paris, 1986); F.-G. Dreyfus, *Histoire de la démocratie-chrétienne en France* (Paris, 1988); P. Habert, C. Ysmal, *Elections législatives 1988, Le Figaro/Etudes politiques* (Paris, 1988); Y. Meny, "France: The Construction and

Reconstruction of the Centre, 1945–86,'' *West European Politics* 10, no. 4 (October 1987); C. Ysmal, *Les Partis politiques sous la Vᵉ République* (Paris, 1989).

K. L. Lawson

Related entries: BARRE, RAYMOND; CENTRIST PARTIES; ELECTIONS; GAULLIST PARTY; GISCARD D'ESTAING, VALERY; LECANUET, JEAN; LEOTARD, FRANCOIS; MEHAIGNERIE, PIERRE; POLITICAL TRENDS; RADICAL PARTY.

UNION OF THE LEFT, the alliance between the Socialist (PS) and Communist (PCF) parties signed on June 27, 1972, joined on July 12 by the small Left Radicals (MRG). They agreed on second-round support in elections, and on a Common Program stipulating measures to take when a left government won power.

In the 1973 elections the left made small gains, but Mitterrand's narrow loss in the 1974 presidential race encouraged hopes for 1978. In late 1974 by-elections favoring the PS incited a nervous PCF to quarrel bitterly with the socialists. Patching the rift in late 1975, both parties did well in 1977 municipal elections. Polls favored the left to win the 1978 parliamentary elections. Hoping to strengthen its position in any future government, the PCF demanded revisions in the Common Program. Mitterrand refused major changes, the PCF broke off negotiations in September 1977, and the right won in 1978.

The communists opposed Mitterrand in the 1981 presidential election. When he won, also gaining a PS parliamentary majority, he invited the communists into government—as a junior partner. The alliance was definitively broken when the PCF refused to enter Laurent Fabius's government in July 1984, systematically criticizing the socialists.

Both parties had hoped to exploit the other and dominate the left. The contest was won by the PS, while the PCF sank to half its 1972 level.

R. W. Johnson, *The Long March of the French Left* (New York, 1981); G. Ross, S. Hoffmann, S. Malzacher, eds., *The Mitterrand Experiment* (New York, 1987).

J. W. Friend

Related entries: COMMON PROGRAM; FRENCH COMMUNIST PARTY; LEFT RADICALS; MITTERRAND, FRANCOIS; SOCIALIST PARTY (PS).

UNITED STATES, RELATIONS WITH. Franco-American relations have gone through several phases since 1945: dependence, independence, and co-operation. During World War II the relations between the United States government and the French government-in-exile of General Charles de Gaulle, located first in London and then in Algiers, were exceedingly frosty. After the fall of France and the occupation of the northern two-thirds of the country by the German army, Washington had extended formal diplomatic recognition to the collaborationist Vichy regime of Marshal Henri-Philippe Pétain in the unoccupied zone. American officials justified this policy on the grounds that it would enable the United States to use its influence at Vichy to ensure that the French fleet and that portion of the French colonial empire under Vichy control would not be turned over to the Germans.

In the meantime, President Franklin Roosevelt, who detested de Gaulle as a would-be dictator, refused to recognize the general's authority over the French Resistance movement and promoted the candidacies of rivals such as General Henri Giraud and Admiral François Darlan. At the time of the Liberation of France, the United States had developed plans for the military occupation of the country (in effect treating it as a defeated enemy rather than a victorious ally) and did not include de Gaulle's Free French movement in the planning for or execution of the amphibious Allied landing at Normandy. It was only through his own shrewdness and determination that de Gaulle was able to prevail over his American-backed rivals and obtain Washington's belated recognition of his Committee of National Liberation in July 1944 as the de facto civil government of liberated France. Though the resignation of de Gaulle in January 1946 removed from the scene a major obstacle to Franco-American friendship, the wartime conflicts between the Free French movement and the United States government were to leave a legacy of ill will that was to have a negative effect on relations between Washington and Paris when de Gaulle later returned to power.

Under the Fourth Republic (1946–58) Franco-American relations were characterized by an unprecedented degree of French dependence on the United States in all areas. The French economy required a massive infusion of American economic aid under the Marshall Plan (1948–51) to recover from the devastation wrought by four years of war and occupation. French defense policy depended heavily on American assistance: By the end of the French-Indochina War in 1954, the United States was financing 80 percent of the costs of that doomed effort to retain control of the French Empire in Southeast Asia. In Western Europe American military forces were stationed in France as part of NATO's conventional defense effort, while France (along with the other European members of the Atlantic Alliance) benefited from the American pledge of extended nuclear deterrence. In return, the successive governments of the Fourth Republic loyally supported the United States in the Cold War. France joined the American-dominated international economic system of the noncommunist industrialized world, which was based on a modified gold standard, the free convertibility of currencies, and a commitment to free trade. In the meantime, American multinational corporations dramatically increased their direct investments in the French market, American cultural influence reached its apex through the medium of films, television, music, and consumer goods, and even the French language submitted to an invasion by the powerful forces of ''*franglais,*'' a combination of French and English.

It was against this backdrop of national subservience, and the inevitable resentments that it generated, that de Gaulle sought to restore France's independence from its transatlantic banker, supplier, and protector during his tenure as head of the Fifth Republic (1958–69). In the realm of national defense, de Gaulle armed France with an independent nuclear deterrent, withdrew French ground and air forces from NATO's integrated command, and expelled all American military bases from French territory. On the diplomatic level, de Gaulle strove to improve relations with the Soviet Union and communist China, attempted to woo West Germany away from the United States by means of a bilateral treaty in 1963, and severely criticized American military interventions in Indochina and the Dominican Republic. At the same time, France denounced the postwar international monetary system on the grounds that it conferred an unfair advantage on the United States by virtue of the privileged role of the dollar in the gold exchange standard. All of these actions reflected de Gaulle's conviction that a sovereign state such as France cannot depend on a foreign power, particularly one across a three-thousand-mile ocean, for its national security and economic well-being.

This sentiment clashed directly with the policy of the Kennedy and Johnson administrations in Washington, which sought to increase economic interdependence between both sides of the Atlantic and centralize American control of NATO. Kennedy's ''Grand Design,'' unveiled in a speech in Philadelphia on July 4, 1962, comprised United States support for European unity (including England) and economic cooperation with the emerging Common Market (EEC). De Gaulle's veto of the British application for membership in the EEC in January 1963 made a shambles of the Kennedy initiative. President Johnson's subsequent effort to obtain European support for the so-called Multilateral Nuclear Force (MLF), a mix-manned fleet of surface ships armed with Polaris missiles under the joint control of NATO states, was rejected by de Gaulle as incompatible with French independence. Widespread resentment in the United States at what was widely regarded as de Gaulle's high-handed tactics produced a chill in Franco-American relations that was to last for the remainder of the 1960s.

The acrimony that characterized Franco-American relations in the de Gaulle era dissipated considerably during the presidential administration of Valéry Giscard d'Estaing (1974–81). France tightened its links with NATO in a number of ways and began to cooperate with the United States in the management of the international monetary system following the end of the Bretton Woods system of fixed exchanged rates tied to the gold standard. French military assistance and interventions in sub-Saharan Africa on behalf of conservative, anticommunist governing elites won the approval of Washington, as did France's increasingly cordial relationship with Great Britain after President Georges Pompidou lifted de Gaulle's veto against British membership in the European Economic Community in 1972.

During his first seven-year term (1981–88), President François Mitterrand surprised American observers, concerned about the accession of a French chief of state who had run on a common electoral program with the French Communist party and brought four of its members into his first government, when he assumed a resolutely pro-Atlanticist, anti-Soviet position on a number of important international issues. He antagonized the Kremlin with his vociferous advocacy of human rights behind the Iron Curtain. He vigorously supported NATO's decision to deploy Pershing II and ground-launched cruise missiles in Western Europe to offset the Soviet SS–20 mobile, multiple-warhead missile force. He took the lead in promoting a greater degree of European defense cooperation, both multilaterally through a refurbished Western European Union and bilaterally with the Federal Republic of Germany through a number of joint Franco-German security projects. A former critic of the Gaullist *force de frappe*, he presided over a full-scale modernization of France's independent nuclear force that will be completed in the mid–1990s. He accelerated the trend begun under Giscard toward a greater degree of French cooperation with NATO. By the advent of Mitterrand's second term in 1988, France had become America's most reliable ally on the European continent, as West Germany began to demonstrate its independence within the Atlantic Alliance in such matters as nuclear policy and arms control. Moreover, in the early years of his second mandate, Mitterrand attempted to anchor a reunited Germany in the western camp following the fall of the Berlin Wall in 1989, and he even placed French forces under U.S. command in the war against Iraq (1991).

J.-B. Duroselle, *La France et les Etats-Unis des origines à nos jours* (Paris, 1976); J. Newhouse, *De Gaulle and the Anglo-Saxons* (London, 1970); M. R. Zahniser, *Uncertain Friendship: American-French Relations Through the Cold War* (New York, 1975).

W. R. Keylor

Related entries: DEFENSE POLICY; DE GAULLE, CHARLES; FOREIGN POLICY; *FRANGLAIS*; GISCARD D'ESTAING, VALERY; MARSHALL PLAN; MITTERRAND, FRANCOIS; POMPIDOU, GEORGES.

URBANIZATION, the expansion of cities into rural surroundings, which has been spectacular in France in the last forty years. Three main factors explain this trend: a continuous rural-population flight toward industrial areas, an unforeseen 40 percent increase in the population, and the rapid development of industry. In 1945, 47 percent of France's population lived in townships counting fewer than two thousand people. The traditional migration of workers from economically depressed rural areas to industrial regions increased sharply after 1950. Over 1.77 million people settled in the largest industrial cities and Paris suburbs from 1954 to 1975. Since 1968, however, this type of migration has favored medium-size regional centers and small towns and villages located in the vicinity of developing industrial areas. Today, of the 26 percent of the French who live in rural settings, 70 percent lead an urban-style life, participating in the suburbanization of the French countryside.

Meanwhile, the population, which was under forty million in 1945, reached fifty-six million in 1989. The high birthrate of the 1950s and early 1960s, the rise in life expectancy, the return of French nationals from the decolonized countries in the early 1960s, and a large contingent of foreign workers and their families account for this demographic jump. The population increase in urban areas had a catastrophic impact on housing and service facilities in a country plagued by a city housing shortage since 1919 and the destruction due to World War II.

Industrial recovery and development played the most significant role in the urbanization of France. Thanks to the Marshall Plan, reconstruction started in 1947 was quickly achieved when the 1949–50 industrial output topped prewar production. As new types of industries developed (electronics, chemicals, aerospace, etc.), so did the building industry. This beelike activity favored the already highly industrialized regions, accentuating the long-standing economic imbalance between the north, east, and southeast of France, and the center, west, and southwest regions. To remedy this problem, the French government offered financial incentives to the heads of industry to help relocate their activities to the depressed regions, as outlined in the Monnet Plan (*Plan de modernisation et d'équipement*). This policy had a notable effect on the industrialization of regional capitals such as Toulouse, Grenoble, or Rennes, but not as much as was hoped on the smaller cities and towns, at least until the late 1980s. By then, dramatic changes in industry, population, and transportation had led to an uncontrollable expansion of bursting urban centers and the irreversible transformation of the French landscape.

France's urban development went through several phases, but one can see roughly three major periods in forty years: a frantic building period from 1950 to 1965, which affected the largest cities, under government management but with little room for statewide planning; then, and until 1980, a period of grandiose, over-planned state projects coupled with a new trend toward detached suburban housing; and finally, for the last decade, a period of careful consideration for restoration of existing structures and limited new construction, thanks to true interaction and dialogue between government and local constituencies.

These three periods correspond to the changing part the French government played in urban renewal. In 1943 the central government's Office of Urbanism and Habitat took charge of delivering building permits. Renamed the Ministry of Reconstruction and Urbanism in 1945, this office was soon more involved in planning and financing individual projects than in holding the general direction of urban reconstruction it had spelled out in its *Plan national d'aménagement du territoire*, presented in 1950. At that time, France was just starting to rebuild its housing stock, but regardless of the Ministry's intentions the housing shortage was addressed only in the largest cities—Paris, Rouen, Lyon, Marseille—and with little overall planning. High-rise apartment buildings sprang up in the low-income areas of these cities and in their immediate suburbs. The concentration of these often unattractive, low-quality buildings produced the infamous *grands ensembles* made up largely of rent-controlled public housing known as HLM (*habitation à loyer modéré*), such as in Sarcelles near Paris, or Les Minguettes near Lyon. Nonetheless, built to relocate families living in overcrowded inner-city apartments, those housing projects offered modern comfort and conveniences, which were indeed not the norm in France at the time (in 1954, 60% of all dwellings had running water and only 8.2% had a bathtub or a shower;

the respective figures for 1988 were 99.8% and 92%). Badly needed hospitals and schools were also built in a hurry, again with no attempt at fitting the new construction into the predominant local architectural style. Industrial construction companies, in the hands of engineers who were not inspired architects, had to build quickly and cheaply. Within ten years housing projects were plagued with fast decay of the site, depressed dwellers, uninspired and even troubled youth.

Within the cities, state and local officials began to see the need for concerted urban planning while, in 1958, the central government moved to take full control of this unrestrained, almost feverish building activity. It gave little autonomy to the *circonscriptions régionales d'action économique* and allowed even less input into decision making from the *Groupes d'action municipales* (GAM). However, one more step was taken toward municipal autonomy in 1963 when the central administration created the famous DATAR (*Délégation à l'aménagement du territoire*) to study the various needs of the French regions and how to address them. This led to the regrouping of municipalities into consortia, which were better able to manage their affairs and in particular their development. It led also to the administrative consolidation of the eight largest urban centers (called *métropoles d'équilibre*): Lyon–Grenoble–Saint-Etienne, Marseille–Aix-en-Provence, Toulouse, Bordeaux, Nantes–Saint-Nazaire, Lille–Roubaix-Turcoing, Nancy-Metz-Thionville, and Strasbourg. Their role consists of leading the economic and social development of their region without the excessive interference of the capital when in need of government financial support and expertise in project planning. But decentralization took time, so this second phase of French urbanization is clearly marked by the heavy-handedness of centralized power during the presidency of Georges Pompidou, who wanted to give France a modern look. Strongly influenced by the work of Le Corbusier, ambitious projects were launched in Paris, Marseille, Dijon, and so on, favoring again the development of the large urban areas in need of office space rather than the medium-size cities in need of attractive condominiums.

Around 1965, faced with growing community problems and popular discontent, developers started to address the problems of bedroom communities. They paid more attention to district services, civic centers, local schools, playgrounds, and stadiums to bring people together. Smaller, better-quality apartment complexes were built in middle- and upper-class neighborhoods. Nine new cities were drawn and built: four in the Paris region and five near Marseille, Rouen, Lille, and Lyon. These *villes nouvelles* were designed to foster a real sense of community, but architects and urban planners did not consult with those most likely to inhabit the new cities. It will take ten years for each of them to develop its own identity and achieve, to varying degrees, the planners' goal: a true community enjoying modern comfort.

Parallel to this state-run urbanization, one witnessed the growing number of detached houses grouped in small districts at the outskirts of medium-size towns surrounding the large urban centers. The new village (*le village pavillonnaire*) was born and prospered: Individual homes accounted for 48.5 percent of all construction in 1962, increasing to 68 percent in 1984. Millions of French were fulfilling their dream of owning their own little house and garden: In 1954 one out of three households owned their own home, while close to one in two did in early 1980, 22.5 percent owning a condominium. This was the period when local zoning laws tried to curb unwise land development. The way was paved for the 1972 and 1982 regional reforms that gave an even greater autonomy to cities and towns regarding their renewal, housing, and transportation.

With the sprawl of building lots reaching into agricultural lands and the overwhelming style of government projects, local authorities searched for ways to control and limit new development, applying new zoning laws and responding eagerly to decentralized decision making. The municipalities finally were able to examine and protect the fabric of their cities without hampering acceptable growth. In the last ten years, restoration of old buildings, rehabilitation or destruction of early HLMs, and refurbishing of old markets and industrial buildings or sites have insured the revival and even gentrification of whole sections of the inner cities, which had experienced a steady decrease in population. But it has also facilitated a clear segregation of people with different income levels and ethnic groups (mostly made up of foreign workers and their families). For the first time since 1945 medium- and small-size cities are expanding; yet, the wealth imbalance of the two sides of France remains only slightly altered.

Clearly the urbanization of France has been too fast to be free from expensive errors. However, strict legislation regarding comprehensive plans for urban development (*Plan d'occupation des sols*) and better understanding of city life came out of these errors. Now that industrial and population growth have tapered off, the need for construction is slowing down. Moreover, a new trend toward city dwelling is checking the increase of individual homes. Considering that France is now anxious to maintain the picturesque charm of its towns and the beauty of its landscapes so praised by tourists, it may be able to stop the *sur-urbanisation* of its countryside and protect the architectural originality of its urban centers.

G. Bauer, J. M. Roux, *La Rurbanisation ou la ville éparpillée* (Paris, 1976); J. Chapuisat, *Le Droit de l'urbanisme* (Paris, 1983); G. Duby, *Histoire de la France urbaine* (Paris, 1985); M. Fromont, *Les Compétences des collectivités territoriales en matière d'urbanisme et d'équipement* (Brussels, 1987); J. F. Gravier, *L'Espace vital* (Paris, 1984); J. E. Havel, *Habitat et logement* (Paris, 1985).

L. J. Haenlin

Related entries: DECENTRALIZATION; ECOLOGY PARTY; ECONOMIC TRENDS; INDUSTRIAL POLICY; LYON; MARSEILLE; MARSHALL PLAN; MONNET, JEAN; PARIS REGION; PLAN; POMPIDOU, GEORGES; POPULATION TRENDS; REGIONS; TRANSPORTATION.

V

VEIL, SIMONE (1927–), minister of health from 1974 to 1979 under French president Valéry Giscard d'Estaing, and president of the European Parliament from 1979 to 1982. Veil's responsibilities during her tenure as minister of health were broadened in 1977 to include the areas of both health and social security. In 1978 President Giscard again extended her duties to include health and family affairs.

During the occupation of France by Nazi forces during World War II, Veil and her family, French Jews from Nice, were taken prisoner and sent to death camps in Auschwitz and later Bergen-Belsen. Veil's mother died of typhus during the internment, and she was never to see her father and brother again. She studied law and political science at the *Institut des sciences politiques*, but instead of pursuing a career as a trial lawyer she joined the staff of the Ministry of Justice (1956) as an attaché, taking on a number of controversial social issues and playing a key role in what were later to be regarded as ground-breaking decisions concerning adoption, the care of children born out of wedlock, and the treatment of prisoners and mental patients.

Simone Veil's name is often associated with matters that involve women and their efforts to advance in society. In particular, she is recognized as a staunch proponent of women's reproductive rights and as the author of France's first abortion legislation. Her advocacy of expanded access to and information about birth control led to the Law of December 4, 1974, which legalized a woman's right to procure contraceptives. Veil's efforts are also largely responsible for the passage of the Law of January 17, 1975, commonly known as the *loi Veil*, which legalized abortion, overturning the Law of 1920, an act of legislation that had made abortion illegal in France for fifty-five years.

She is also widely recognized for her advocacy of the rights of the underrepresented and the underprivileged. In addition, she has often taken controversial and unpopular stands on a range of issues. During her tenure as minister of health, for example, Veil campaigned relentlessly for strong antismoking legislation despite the powerful opposition of the French tobacco industry.

Seeking greater challenges and a wider constituency to serve, Veil mounted a campaign in 1979 to become one of the first popularly elected members of the

European Parliament. Her campaign focused on the need for greater unification among the member nations and a more powerful role for France. She also sought to include women's issues in her campaign, broadening them to cover the concerns of women in all nations of the European Parliament. On June 10, 1979 Veil won a seat in the European Parliament, and only days later its 410 members voted her their president. She remained president until January 1982. She was reelected to the European Parliament in 1984 and 1989. She served as the president of the *Groupe libéral, démocratique, and réformateur* of the European Parliament from 1984 to 1989. She is known as a pro-European centrist who has advanced the cause of women.

S. Veil, *L'Adoption: Données médicales, psychologiques, et sociales* (Paris, 1969); *Who's Who in France, 1990–1991* (Paris, 1990).

J. J. Flaitz

Related entries: EUROPEAN ECONOMIC COMMUNITY, RELATIONS WITH; FEMINISM; UNION FOR FRENCH DEMOCRACY; WOMEN, CONDITION OF.

VILAR, JEAN (1912–1971), actor, stage director, creator of the Avignon theater festival and the postwar *Théâtre national populaire* (TNP). Born in Sète, he trained under Charles Dullin and was influenced by Jacques Copeau. After the Armistice, he joined *La Roulotte*, a traveling theater company touring the provinces. In 1943 he formed *La compagnie des sept,* staging several foreign works in Paris. Dissatisfied with Parisian theater, he launched the Avignon festival in 1947, held during the summer in the historic *Cour d'honneur* of the *Palais des papes*. Here, experience of outdoor productions, with the imposing courtyard as backdrop, helped him evolve a distinctive manner combining simplicity of means with color, epic grandeur, and festive atmosphere. Appointed in 1951 to revive the TNP (created in 1920), he adapted this successful style to the vast auditorium of Paris's Chaillot Palace.

Vilar saw theater as a public service like gas or electricity, responding to a profound if hidden need. His aim at the TNP was to "assemble and unite," restoring theater's civic dimension and bringing social categories together in an ecumenical spirit of celebration. To achieve this, it was imperative to replace the divisive conventions that made theater an elite activity. He removed the proscenium arch, reduced prices and other expenses, made group-subscription and travel arrangements with workers' organizations, and took TNP performances out into the community. However, rejecting lowbrow or deliberately proletarian drama, he uncompromisingly believed in the universal value of the classics, which belonged to all regardless of class. Although TNP productions—of Molière, Shakespeare, Corneille—were consistently successful, Vilar encountered persistent opposition, provoked largely by the ambivalence of the term *popular*. The right detected political bias from an early stage. This intensified when, under Gaullism, Vilar explicitly chose plays that commented unfavorably on the regime. On the left, as Brechtian Marxism spread in the 1950s and 1960s, he was impugned for an idealist approach to production and an ideology of social harmony. Frustrated by his contract with the state, he left the TNP in 1963, though he remained in charge of Avignon. Here, ideological attacks recurred at the 1968 festival, when he was aggressively accused of managing a repressive "cultural supermarket." By his sudden death at age fifty-nine, he had become a somewhat isolated, unfashionable figure. In 1981, however, the new socialist government hailed him as an inspiration for its cultural policy, and François Mitterrand symbolically attended that year's festival. Vilar's recommendations in the mid-1960s for a popular opera house also prefigured the *Opéra-Bastille*.

Vilar's ambition as both artist and cultural engineer was to demonstrate theater's relevance to the nation. Unlike many contemporaries, he saw the director not as creator but artisan, subservient to the text. He was not a convinced decentralist, but his innovations in democratizing theater made him a leading figure in the early postwar popular movement. While he did not attract vast numbers of specifically working-class spectators, he did introduce a new, more socially diversified audience to serious drama, decisively assisting in the regeneration of French theater.

G. Leclerc, *Le TNP de Jean Vilar* (Paris, 1971); A. Simon, *Jean Vilar, qui êtes-vous?* (Lyon, 1987); J. Vilar, *De la tradition théâtrale* (Paris, 1955), *Le Théâtre, service public* (Paris, 1986).

D. L. Looseley

Related entries: CULTURAL POLICY; POPULAR CULTURE.

W

WESTERN EUROPEAN UNION (WEU), a regional security system created on May 6, 1955 to provide for the collective defense of Western Europe and to assist in the management of West German rearmament. It consists of a Council of Foreign Ministers, which may be summoned by any member state to discuss threats to regional security, an Assembly that meets in Strasbourg and is composed of the members' delegates to the parliamentary assembly of the Council of Europe, and a Secretariat that serves these two bodies. The headquarters of the WEU is in London.

The WEU was an expansion of the Brussels Treaty Organization (BTO), a regional security system that had been established on March 17, 1948 by Great Britain and France, Belgium, the Netherlands, and Luxembourg (Benelux). Originally intended as a demonstration to the United States that the countries of Western Europe were willing to contribute to their own defense, the BTO became the nucleus for, and was largely superseded by, the North Atlantic Treaty Organization (NATO) that was created in April 1949. But when the French Parliament rejected the project for a European Defense Community (which the United States supported as a means of permitting West Germany to rearm as part of a Western European army) in 1954, British prime minister Anthony Eden resurrected the moribund Brussels Treaty Organization, which was renamed the Western European Union. The former enemy states of Italy and West Germany were permitted to join, and West Germany was allowed to rearm and become a member of NATO.

The Western European Union remained an unimportant adjunct of NATO for thirty years, until French president François Mitterrand attempted to revive it in 1984 as a mechanism for promoting a greater degree of European defense cooperation. As European observers expressed concern about the declining credibility of the American nuclear guarantee and the increasing likelihood of a reduction of American conventional forces on the continent, Mitterrand hoped that the WEU could develop into a "European pillar" of the Atlantic Alliance that would effectively deter Soviet aggression. But French attempts to strengthen the WEU as a multilateral security system met with a lack of enthusiasm in

Great Britain and were less successful than simultaneous efforts to establish a privileged bilateral security relationship with Germany.

E. Kolodziej, *French International Policy under de Gaulle and Pompidou* (Ithaca, N.Y., 1984); D. Lerner, R. Aron, *France Defeats EDC* (New York, 1957); W. Wallace, "European Defence Cooperation," *Survival* 26 (November/December 1984); S. F. Wells, Jr., "The United States and European Defense Cooperation," *Survival* 27 (July/August 1985).

W. R. Keylor

Related entries: DEFENSE POLICY; EUROPEAN DEFENSE COMMUNITY; FEDERAL REPUBLIC OF GERMANY, RELATIONS WITH; FOREIGN POLICY; GREAT BRITAIN, RELATIONS WITH.

WINE PRODUCTION AND CONSUMPTION, have undergone nothing short of a revolution in the Fourth and Fifth Republics. France remains one of the world's great wine producers (like Italy it produces about 20% of the world's wine) but has also been able to produce an ever-higher percentage of quality wine. For the first time in French history alcohol and antialcohol forces are working together, rather than at cross-purposes as during the Third Republic. Consequently, the nature and treatment of alcoholism in France has also been altered.

The central government has played a vital role in all aspects of this transformation. As part of its commitment to economic planning, in 1953 Parliament passed a new wine code to limit production and improve quality. Government direction and subsidies have helped French grape growers replant their vineyards, mechanize, and form cooperatives. The replanting of vineyards has entailed uprooting the hybrid vines, planted after the phylloxera aphid had ravaged French vines during the 1870s and 1880s, and replacing them with high-quality vines of the merlot, cabernet-sauvignon, pinot, and gamy grapes. Hybrids have fallen from 25 percent of the vines in 1945 to less than 5 percent in 1988. The arrival of the tractor after the war helped keep a dynamic young generation of wine growers on the land by making their work both more efficient and less backbreaking. Tractors in the vineyards have been used primarily for spraying and pruning rather than plowing. Various tractor attachments allow the eradication of weeds with chemicals rather than through plowing. Approximately one-half of French grape growers now practice this *nonculture* (*nontillage*).

The cooperative movement has been as important as the new vines and technology. By pooling their talents, using state subsidies, taking instruction, and utilizing the services of trained experts in wine production (enologists), small grape growers have been able to improve both the quality and quantity of their vineyards. Without the rise of the cooperative, the small grower, beset by the rising costs of land and mechanization, would have been forced out of the winemaking business. Even so, by the late 1980s there were 60 percent fewer growers than in 1950. Of the remaining small farmers, 40 percent are in cooperatives. Their share of French wine production has steadily increased from 30 percent during the 1950s to 55 percent by the late 1980s. Especially significant is that they now produce 40 percent of the French wine that carries a special label (an *appelation*), stating the specific grape, the particular region, and the special process by which it was made.

As a result of these changes, French wine making is much more productive and of higher quality. Since 1945 the area devoted to the grape has declined by more than 30 percent—from 1,400,000 to 1,000,000 hectares—but wine production has increased from sixty million hectoliters in 1950 to seventy million in 1988. Unlike in previous eras, quality has also been improved. In 1950 only 10 percent of French wine carried an *appelation*, while today the figure is over 30 percent. Conversely, the percentage of mass production table wine has fallen to just a little over 50 percent. In between stand the intermediate classifications, country wine (*vin de pays*) and specified wine of a superior quality (*vin délimité de qualité supérieure*). According to Leo Loubere, an authority on the history of French vineyards, the wine "revolution" has accomplished a "leveling comparable to that accomplished by republican revolutions of the past." Just as postwar France has seen an increase in the middle strata of society, so has it also seen an increase in the middling strata of wine.

These changes in production have been mirrored by shifts in consumption. As living standards rose during the 1950s, 1960s, and 1970s, the French drank less but higher quality wine. Overall the average yearly intake of wine between 1950 and 1988 has fallen from 140 liters per year to only 80 liters. The maturing of the postwar baby boom has merely reinforced this trend. This generation, which grew up on fruit juices, carbonated sodas, and mineral water, does not buy the vast quantities of red table wine that their parents did. The consumption of mass-produced red table wine has fallen by two-thirds over the past thirty years. When the French drink today they are much more likely to drink an *appelation* wine. Whereas in 1950 only 10 percent of the wine consumed in France had an *appelation*, in 1990 the figure was over 40 percent (including all three types of classification listed above).

This decline is not merely the product of fashion. It was also the fruit of a renewed antialcoholic temperance; yet, this is an inaccurate term since the movement has seldom condemned wine as offensive. Since 1945 a struggle has been waged by three forces: government, medicine, and private antialcohol groups. The rise of a planned economy and the assumption by the state of health care produced a new concern about alcoholism. Pierre Mendès-France, during his brief 1954–55 government, provided the most dramatic example of state activism. His most enduring legacy was to found the *Haut comité d'étude et d'information sur l'alcoolisme*. This agency has promoted the study of alcoholism, drafted new antialcoholic measures, promoted public education on drink, and facilitated cooperation between governmental and private antialcohol efforts. The renewal of private initiative sprang from new theories on alcoholism that shifted emphasis from the older pessimist French theories, which stressed heredity and degeneration, to theories that emphasized social factors and rehabilitation. France was greatly influenced by the American theorist of alcoholic problems, E. M. Jellinek, and by Alcoholics Anonymous. Yet, even before AA's arrival in France in 1960, an association of reformed alcoholics, *Vie libre*, had already formed. Subsequently, a French doctor, Pierre Fouquet, has broadened the study of alcoholism with his concept of *alcoologie*, which situates the alcoholic within his or her physiological, psychological, cultural, and social matrix. The French antialcohol movement was rejuvenated in 1950 when the main prewar temperance association, the *Ligue nationale contre l'alcoolisme*, transformed itself into the *Comité national de défense contre d'alcoolisme* (CNDCA) under the direction of André Monnier, a high government official and former Resistance fighter. Monnier dropped the old fatalistic theory of degeneration but preserved the older movement's positive points: the stress on accurate information, moderation, and flexibility. The CNDCA has established close ties to the Ministries of Health and Education in government, helped various groups in industry, such as the railway workers, combat alcoholism, and created a network of departmental committees. It has also found common ground with alcohol interests, particularly with wine producers, in promoting production and consumption of quality wines. Its slogan—drink better, drink less, drink longer—is well suited to France's changing drinking habits.

Despite the renewed struggle against excessive drinking, France still ranks at the top in terms of annual alcohol consumption per inhabitant (at 13.5 liters in 1985). Nevertheless, consumption trends indicate that alcoholism will probably decline. Since the 1970s France is the only country that has experienced a continuous fall in the consumption of alcohol.

M. Lachiver, *Vins, vignes, et vignerons* (Paris, 1988); L. Loubere, *The Wine Revolution in France* (Princeton, 1990); P. Prestwich, *Drink and the Politics of Social Reform* (Palo Alto, Calif., 1988).

W. S. Haine

Related entries: CAFES; SOCIAL TRENDS.

WOMEN, CONDITION OF. Women in France, like their cohorts throughout Western Europe, have experienced substantive changes in their social, economic, and political well-being in the years since the founding of the Fourth Republic. Due to reforms in legislation (including the institutionalization of feminism), increased politicization, female infiltration of the work force, a decrease in religiosity, the birth of a strong feminist movement, and the rise of numerous astute and articulate women leaders, French women have emerged from the war years better positioned for equal participation in the life of their society than had previously been the case. Though they may still be said largely to occupy the margins of French society, their access to the organs of power has increased markedly and with it their status.

The most significant social, economic, and political changes affecting and involving women occurred not during the immediate postwar years but later, during the late 1960s, 1970s, and early 1980s. Up until this time traditional trends, behaviors, and attitudes that had earlier been characteristic of French women underwent little transformation as France attempted to regain its stability following the devastation of the war. A dramatic rise in the birthrate constituted one of the few noteworthy trends with regard to change in the social life of women during this period. This phenomenon, while predictable for nations in the aftermath of war, was also enhanced by the incentive of generous government subsidies for families with two or more children.

Starting in the late 1960s, however, the status of women in France became part of a larger movement in which many social conventions were challenged and alternatives considered. It was at this time that the birthrate in France began to drop, as did female religiosity; in the mid–1950s, 47 percent of women were active members of the Catholic church, but within twenty years the rate had dropped to only 21 percent, and it has continued to fall. The divorce rate, on the other hand, increased precipitously to the extent that today nearly half of all marriages in France end in divorce, and fewer women are marrying or remarrying.

Employment data also reveal changing realities for French women. Whereas in 1954 women constituted 34.7 percent of the work force, they now make up 44 percent, and though more women are occupying positions of authority, most women are still ghettoized in low-paying, low-status, low-mobility jobs. The situation is further aggravated by the fact that some 84 percent of all part-time workers in France are women, most of whom earn only the minimum wage; moreover, as of 1981 only 28 percent of French women were receiving any kind of professional training. In addition, unemployment hits French women especially hard. More women than men find themselves out of work, their numbers increasing by 12 percent per year compared to 9 percent per year for men.

The women's movement in France helped to articulate the changing needs and demands of women on all levels—social, economic, and political—and to provide leadership in breaking down gender barriers. Women such as Gisèle Halimi, Yvette Roudy, and Simone Veil each emerged during this era to play key roles in obtaining greater freedoms for French women. Halimi, for example, during the presidential election campaign of 1981 encouraged public, televised debate of women's issues. Yvette Roudy, France's first minister of women's rights (1981–86), initiated a steady stream of ground-breaking and often controversial legislation, including policy that addressed the issues of equality in the labor force, sexism in the media, and dissemination of information on birth control. Simone Veil, perhaps France's best-known female politician, while serving as minister of health under President Valéry Giscard d'Estaing, in 1979 successfully lobbied for reform of the abortion law despite opposition from 99 of the 291 majority deputies in the National Assembly.

The popularity of feminism, the advocacy it offered to women in France, and, to some extent, its effectiveness may be seen in the proliferation of organizations it spawned; by 1981 there were approximately 150 different feminist groups in France, the most prominent of which was the MLF (*Mouvement de libération des femmes*) led by Antoinette Fouque. Certainly the feminist movement contributed, at least in part, to the recognition of women occupying traditionally male roles as well. It was not until the 1970s that women were first elected to the academies of the esteemed *Institut de France* (Suzanne Bastid, *Académies des sciences morales et politiques*, 1971; Jacqueline de Romilly, *Académie des belles lettres*, 1975; Marguerite Yourcenar, *Académie française*, 1980; and Yvonne Choquet-Bruhat, *Académie des sciences*, 1980).

In the realm of political change there are two trends that are particularly salient. The first is the defection of a substantial portion of French women away from the ranks of conservative voters toward the left and, more recently, toward the center. The second is the passage of legislation guaranteeing greater equality for women in France. Increasingly over the years, from the time General Charles de Gaulle moved to enfranchise women in 1944 to the present, women have demonstrated greater political interest, diminished levels of voter absenteeism, and a greater willingness to identify with a political party; until 1968, their political preferences were characterized as conservative, and their tendency to embrace the platforms and candidates of the left was virtually negligible. In 1958, for example, only 24.7 percent of French women showed evidence of leftist partisanship, whereas in 1978, 56 percent identified themselves with a party of the left. Some 52 percent of women voters supported François Mitterrand in his successful bid for the presidency of France in 1981, the first time in the history of France that a majority of women voters had voted for the left.

This trend toward more liberal partisanship had less to do with the integrity and message of the candidates than with the realities that faced French women after enfranchisement. For many years women were heavily influenced by the Church, which traditionally supported the right and advocated conservative policies. Moreover, women had little experience with the levers of political power and saw little reason to become politically engaged. However, the effects of postwar urbanization, industrialization, secularization, the student-worker revolt of 1968, growing access to higher education, greater employment opportunities, rising inflation and reduced spending power, and the mobilization efforts of the left all contributed to the politicization of French women, who saw the possibilities for change inherent in the platforms of less conservative parties.

However, as France entered a period of economic austerity, enthusiasm for the left diminished and disillusionment set in. Women, however, did not return to conservatism, but began to align themselves, like their male counterparts, with more centrist positions. This trend is demonstrated in France's recent presidential and legislative elections, as well as in partisanship data emanating from the European Parliament elections in the 1980s.

Political change in the form of institutional reform transformed the lives of French women as well, especially in the mid-1970s. Birth control was legalized in France in 1967. In 1975 under Giscard, abortion was made legal, though the passage of the legislation is credited to the leftist deputies in the National Assembly. The abortion law, one of the most conservative in Western Europe, underwent reform in 1979, again under Giscard. The divorce law was also liberalized in 1975, making it possible to terminate a marriage based on mutual consent rather than cause. Other laws concerning nondiscrimination in education, training and hiring, salary equity, and maternity leave were passed in the late 1970s. Minister of Women's Rights Yvette Roudy took advantage of the momentum created by the passage of this legislation to push through additional legal measures designed to protect and promote women. While these laws have not been rescinded, it should be noted that the high-level positions created by the Giscard and Mitterrand administrations to advance the cause of women were dismantled for the most part with the return of a conservative government in 1986. The socialist government of Michel Rocard (1988–91), however, did include a secretary of state for women's rights, a post headed by Michèle André. Following Rocard's tenure, Edith Cresson was appointed as the first woman prime minister in May 1991 by President Mitterrand.

Thus, while the condition of women in France has improved markedly since 1946, gender gaps and inequities still persist into the 1990s.

W. Northcutt, J. Flaitz, "Women and Politics in Contemporary France: The Electoral Shift to the Left in the 1981 Presidential and Legislative Elections," *Contemporary French Civilization* 7, no. 2 (1983), "Women, Politics and the French Socialist Government," in *Women and Politics in Western Europe*, ed. S. Bashevkin (Bristol, Eng., 1985).

J. J. Flaitz

Related entries: AHRWEILER, HELENE; BARZACH, MICHELE; BEAUVOIR, SIMONE DE; CRESSON, EDITH; ELECTIONS; FEMINISM; GIROUD, FRANCOISE; LABOR FORCE; PIAF, EDITH; POLITICAL TRENDS; ROMILLY, JACQUELINE DE; ROUDY, YVETTE; SOCIAL TRENDS; SULLEROT, EVELYNE; UNEMPLOYMENT; VEIL, SIMONE; YOURCENAR, MARGUERITE.

Y

YOURCENAR, MARGUERITE (1903–1988), novelist, essayist, poet, playwright, and translator. She was born in Brussels in 1903, the daughter of upper-class and aristocratic parents who traveled extensively. When she started writing she chose as a pen name Yourcenar, a partial anagram of the family name, de Crayencour. While still a young woman her father died (her Belgian mother died shortly after her birth). This brought freedom unusual at the time, which permitted her to travel and live in foreign lands such as Greece, where she spent two years. The love and admiration she developed for the Mediterranean world is one of the major themes of her work. The outbreak of the war while she was on a lecture tour in the United States in 1939 prevented her from returning to Europe. Consequently, she undertook part-time college teaching and eventually decided to remain in the States, becoming an American citizen in 1947. The latter part of her life was spent on Mount Desert Island in Maine, where she died in 1988.

Yourcenar published several collections of poems while still an adolescent. She continued to write poetry throughout her life, along with plays, essays, and reflections on art. However, she is best known for her prose fiction, which brought literary fame. She also did some important translations: Virginia Woolf; Henry James; and Negro spirituals, which she collected and which were published in *Fleuve profond, sombre rivière* (1964); Constantin Cavafy; and Yukio Mishima. She was herself translated into many languages. In 1980 she became the first woman named to the French Academy. Other distinctions include: Commander of the Legion of Honor, Officer of the National Order of Merit, membership in the American Academy of Arts and Letters and the Royal Belgian Academy, and honorary degrees and literary prizes, particularly the grand literary prize of the French Academy for the ensemble of her work (1977). Her publications include: *Alexis ou le traité du vain combat* (Paris, 1929); *La Nouvelle Eurydice* (Paris, 1931); *Pindar*, (Paris, 1932); *La Mort conduit l'attelage* (Paris, 1934); *Denier du rêve* (Paris, 1934); *Nouvelles orientales* (Paris, 1938); *Les Songes et les sorts* (Paris, 1938); *Le Coup de grâce* (Paris, 1939); *Mémoires d'Hadrien* (Paris, 1951); *Sous bénéfice d'inventaire* (Paris, 1962); *L'Oeuvre au noir* (Paris, 1968); *Théâtre I, Théâtre II* (Paris, 1971); *Souvenirs pieux* (Paris,

1973); *Archives du Nord* (Paris, 1977). Her best-known character, the emperor Hadrian, meditates on one of her concerns, the empathetic participation in other lives. Yourcenar's expressive writings reveal an acute sensibility and concern for others, an awareness of the importance of history, and a deep love of the lands she chose to live in.

J. Blot, *Marguerite Yourcenar* (Paris, 1971); P. Rosbo, *Entretiens radiophoniques avec Marguerite Yourcenar* (Paris, 1972); M. Yourcenar, *With Open Eyes* (Boston, 1984).

M. C. Weitz

Related entry: LITERATURE.

APPENDIX I: Chronology of the French Fourth and Fifth Republics

1946

October 13, constitution of the Fourth Republic approved in a referendum
November 27, adoption of the Monnet Plan
December 4, official birth of the Fourth Republic
December 16, Léon Blum becomes prime minister

1947

January 16, Vincent Auriol elected first president of the Fourth Republic
January 28, Paul Ramadier becomes prime minister
April 7, founding of the *Rassemblement du peuple français* (RPF)
May, suppression of revolts in Madagascar
May 4, dismissal of communist ministers from government
November 13, Nobel Prize for literature awarded to André Gide
November 22, Robert Schuman becomes prime minister

1948

January 26, devaluation of the franc
July 24, André Marie becomes prime minister
August 31, Robert Schuman becomes prime minister
September 11, Henri Queuille becomes prime minister

1949

April 4, signing of the North Atlantic Treaty Organization
May, Council of Europe founded
October 27, Georges Bidault becomes prime minister

1950

May 9, Robert Schuman announces European Coal and Steel Community
June 30, Henri Queuille becomes prime minister

July 13, René Pleven becomes prime minister
October 26, Pleven Plan on the European army

1951

March 9, Henri Queuille becomes prime minister
April 18, official birth of the European Coal and Steel Community
June 17, legislative elections
August 8, René Pleven becomes prime minister
December 13, Schuman Plan ratified

1952

January 17, Edgar Faure becomes prime minister
March 6, Antoine Pinay becomes prime minister

1953

January 7, René Mayer becomes prime minister
June 26, Joseph Laniel becomes prime minister
July 22, beginning of the Poujade movement
August 7, general strike in public services
December 23, René Coty elected President of the Republic

1954

May 7, fall of Dien Bien Phu
June 18, Pierre Mendès-France becomes prime minister
July 22, Geneva settlement ratified by the National Assembly
August 30, National Assembly rejects European Defense Community treaty
November 1, beginning of the Algerian insurrection
November 10, Pierre Mendès-France begins antialcoholism campaign

1955

February 25, Edgar Faure becomes prime minister
June 3, agreement signed giving internal autonomy to Tunisia
December 8, formation of the *Front républicain*

1956

January 2, legislative elections
February 5, Guy Mollet becomes prime minister
February 29, three weeks of paid vacation granted by law
March 7, independence granted to Morocco
March 20, independence granted to Tunisia
July 26, beginning of the Suez crisis

1957

March 25, Treaty of Rome signed
June 12, Maurice Bourgès-Maunoury becomes prime minister
October 7, Nobel Prize for literature awarded to Albert Camus
November 5, Félix Gaillard becomes prime minister

1958

January 1, opening of the European Economic Community (EEC)
May 13, insurrection in Algiers; Pierre Pflimlin becomes prime minister
June 1, National Assembly approves General Charles de Gaulle's return to power as prime minister
September 28, constitution of the Fifth Republic approved in a referendum
November 23 and 30, legislative elections produce a large Gaullist victory
December 21, Charles de Gaulle elected first president of the Fifth Republic

1959

January 8, Michel Debré becomes prime minister
September 16, Charles de Gaulle offers self-determination to Algeria

1960

January 1, the New franc is introduced
February 13, France explodes its first atomic bomb

1961

January 8, Charles de Gaulle wins victory in referendum in France on self-determination for Algeria

1962

March 18, signing of the Evian agreement ending the Algerian war
April 14, Georges Pompidou becomes prime minister
October 28, referendum approves election of the president by popular vote
November 18 and 25, legislative elections produce another Gaullist victory

1963

January 14, Charles de Gaulle announces his opposition to British entry into the European Economic Community
January 22, Franco-German treaty of reconciliation
July 29, Charles de Gaulle announces France will not sign the limited nuclear test ban treaty

1964

January 27, France recognizes the People's Republic of China
February 6, Franco-British agreement on building a Channel tunnel
April 16, Charles de Gaulle announces that France will develop its own nuclear strike force
April 18, André Malraux inaugurates the *Maison de la Culture*
October 22, Nobel Prize for literature awarded to Jean-Paul Sartre, who refuses it.

1965

March 14 and 21, municipal elections
October 14, France wins its first Nobel Prize for science since World War II

December 5 and 19, presidential elections in which Charles de Gaulle defeats François Mitterrand in the second round with 55 percent of the vote
December 23, fourth week of paid vacation becomes law

1966

February 24, Christian Fouchet announces university reforms
March 10, France announces its decision to withdraw from NATO

1967

March 5 and 12, legislative elections; Gaullist majority reduced to three seats
July 24, in Montreal Charles de Gaulle proclaims, "*Vive le Québec libre!*"
November 27, Charles de Gaulle rejects another attempt by Great Britain to join the European Economic Community

1968

May–June, student-worker revolt threatens the Gaullist regime
June 23 and 30, legislative elections lead to a Gaullist victory
July 10, Maurice Couve de Murville becomes prime minister

1969

April 28, Charles de Gaulle resigns after losing a referendum
May 31 and June 15, presidential elections, won by Georges Pompidou
June 20, Jacques Chaban-Delmas becomes prime minister

1970

May 20, expulsion of Roger Garaudy from the French Communist Party (PCF)
November 9, death of Charles de Gaulle

1971

January 7, creation of a ministry of the environment
June, François Mitterrand assumes leadership of a new Socialist Party (PS) following the Epinay congress

1972

April 23, referendum approves enlargement of the European Economic Community
June 9, Georges Pompidou inaugurates an international research center for cancer in Lyon
June 27, French Socialist and Communist parties establish a Common Program of government
July 5, Pierre Messmer becomes prime minister

1973

March 4 and 11, legislative elections won by the majority (leftist opposition captures 176 seats)
April 8, death of Pablo Picasso
September 13–17, official visit of Georges Pompidou to the People's Republic of China
September 23 and 30, left makes advances in cantonal elections

1974

March 14, opening of the Charles de Gaulle airport outside of Paris
April 2, death of Georges Pompidou
May 5 and 19, Valéry Giscard d'Estaing defeats François Mitterrand by approximately 1.5 percent of the vote in the second round of the presidential elections
May 27, Jacques Chirac becomes prime minister
July 16, creation of a Secretary of State for the Condition of Women
November 29 and December 15, National Assembly and Senate approve abortion law

1975

April 10, official visit of Valéry Giscard d'Estaing to Algeria (first French president to visit Algeria since independence)
September 30, Nobel Prize for literature awarded to Saint-John Perse

1976

January 21, first commercial flight of the supersonic Concorde airplane
February 4 and 8, French Communist Party at its XXII congress renounces the notion of the ''dictatorship of the proletariat''
March 7–14, leftist opposition advances in cantonal elections
August 25, Raymond Barre becomes prime minister
September 22, Prime Minister Raymond Barre announces a plan to fight inflation
December 5, creation of the *Rassemblement pour la République* (RPR) by Jacques Chirac

1977

March 13 and 20, left wins municipal elections
March 25, the Gaullist Jacques Chirac elected mayor of Paris
July 15, violence in Corsica sponsored by pro-independence forces (violence spreads in coming months)
July 31, anti-nuclear demonstrations in Isère
September 23, rupture of the union of the left between the socialists and communists

1978

March 12 and 19, legislative elections won by the majority
March 16, *Amoco Cadiz* oil spill disaster off the coast of Brittany
July 16–17, fourth summit of the seven leading industrialized nations of the Western world

1979

March 14, adoption of the European Monetary System
March 18 and 25, leftist victory in the cantonal elections
April 6–8, Michel Rocard challenges the leadership of François Mitterrand at the Metz congress of the Socialist Party
June 7 and 10, universal suffrage used for the first time in the European Parliament elections
July 7, France launches its first nuclear attack submarine
July 17, election of Simone Veil as president of the European Parliament

1980

March 6, election of the first woman, Marguerite Yourcenar, to the *Académie française*
April 15, death of Jean-Paul Sartre
October 3, bombing at a synagogue on Rue Copernic in Paris

1981

April 26 and May 10, François Mitterrand wins the presidential elections by a small margin in the second round against Valéry Giscard d'Estaing
May 11, panic at the stock exchange; trading suspended for forty-eight hours
May 21, installation of François Mitterrand as president of the Republic
May 21, Pierre Mauroy becomes prime minister
June 14 and 21, François Mitterrand's Socialist Party wins an absolute majority of seats in the legislative elections
June 23, four communist ministers appointed to government
October 4, first devaluation of the franc by the socialist government
October 26 and December 18, National Assembly approves law on nationalizations
November 29, Jacques Delors, minister of the economy and finances, calls for a "pause" in the reforms of the socialist government

1982

February 1, fifth week of paid vacations and a thirty-nine hour work week established
March 14 and 21, success of the opposition in cantonal elections
June 4–6, Versailles summit of the leading industrialized nations of the Western world
June 12, second devaluation of the franc by the socialist government
August 8, anti-Semitic terrorist attack on Rue des Rosiers in Paris
September 15, France receives a $4 billion international loan
October 18, death of Pierre Mendès-France

1983

March 6 and 13, success of the opposition in the municipal elections
March 23, third devaluation of the franc by the socialist government
March 25, second austerity plan announced
April 5, forty-seven Soviets accused of spying expelled from France
August 9–November 10, 1984, operation *Manta* in Chad
October 15–December 3, demonstrations against racism by the youth of France
October 23, 58 French soldiers and 239 American soldiers killed in a terrorist attack in Beirut

1984

March 28, government publishes its plan for the steel industry that includes the loss of 20,000 jobs over three years
June 17, European Parliament elections won by the opposition
June 24, more than 1 million demonstrate in Paris against the reform of private schools (*écoles libres*)
July 12, President François Mitterrand announces the withdrawal of the Savary law for private schools

July 16 and 17, resignation of minister of education Alain Savary and prime minister Pierre Mauroy
July 17, Laurent Fabius becomes prime minister
September 23, former President Valéry Giscard d'Estaing elected to the National Assembly from Puy-de-Dôme
November 15, meeting on Crete between President François Mitterrand and Colonel Muammar Qaddafi
November 22–May 21, 1985, clashes in New Caledonia between separatists and antisepartist forces

1985

January 1, Jacques Delors assumes the presidency of the Commission of the European Community
March 10 and 17, success of the opposition in the cantonal elections
April 4, resignation of the minister of agriculture, Michel Rocard, to protest the socialist plan for proportional representation for the 1986 legislative elections
July 10, sabotage of the *Rainbow-Warrior* in the port of Auckland; beginning of the Greenpeace affair
September 20, resignation of Defense Minister Charles Hernu as a result of the Greenpeace affair
October 11–13, Socialist Party congress at Toulouse, the Bad Godesberg of the PS
October 18, electoral accord announced by the opposition (RPR–UDF)

1986

January 20, Franco-British accord on a Channel tunnel linking the two nations
February 16, beginning of operation *Epervier* in Chad
February 19, nomination of Robert Badinter to the presidency of the Constitutional Council
March 16, victory of the opposition in the legislative elections
March 20, Jacques Chirac becomes prime minister and *cohabitation* begins
March 21, terrorist attack on the Champs-Elysées
April 9, prime minister Jacques Chirac presents his government's program, including a privatization plan
April 14 and 15, deaths of Simone de Beauvoir and Jean Genet
May 4–6, both François Mitterrand and Jacques Chirac represent France in Tokyo at the twelfth summit of the seven leading industrialized nations of the Western world
September, a wave of terrorist attacks in Paris linked to French policy in the Middle East
November 17, assassination of Renault chief Georges Besse by *Action directe*
November 17–December 10, student demonstration against the University reform of Alain Devaquet, deputy minister of research and teaching
December 6, resignation of Alain Devaquet

1987

March 11–12, Franco-Spanish summit in Madrid
May 11–July 4, trial of SS officer Klaus Barbie in Lyon
June 29–November 29, Franco-Iranian crisis
July 19, agreement between François Mitterrand and Margaret Thatcher to construct a Channel tunnel linking the two nations

September 2–4, François Mitterrand and Jacques Chirac attend Francophone summit in Québec
October 19, stock market crash in New York, Paris, and elsewhere

1988

January 7–9, East German leader Erich Honecker makes official visit to Paris
January 22, West German Chancellor Helmut Kohl visits Paris to celebrate the 25th anniversary of the Franco-German friendship treaty; defense and security council and an economic and finance council established between France and West Germany
April 24 and May 8, François Mitterrand wins an unprecedented second term in the presidential elections with a landslide victory over Jacques Chirac
May 9, Michel Rocard becomes prime minister
June 5 and 12, legislative elections fail to give left or right a clear majority
September 28–29, François Mitterrand visits the United States and addresses the United Nations
October 2, regional council elections, socialists poll more than 37 percent of the vote
November 6, referendum in France supports the agreement between the government and opposing factions in New Caledonia
November 9, François Mitterrand and European leaders attend ceremonies at the Panthéon where the ashes of Jean Monnet are transferred on the hundredth anniversary of his birth
November 25–26, François Mitterrand visits the Soviet Union and signs financial and commercial agreements and watches launching of a Soviet–French space mission
December 1, French government lifts ban on Iranian oil imports
December 15–16, fifteenth Franco-African summit in Casablanca

1989

March 12 and 19, socialists and ecologists make gains in the municipal elections
May 2–3, PLO leader Yassar Arafat visits Paris at François Mitterrand's invitation and declares that the twenty-five-year-old Palestinian National Charter is ''obsolete''
June 4, Chinese army suppresses protest in Tianamen Square; François Mitterrand issues a strong condemnation
June 18, European Parliament elections in which UDF–RPR list headed by Valéry Giscard d'Estaing wins twenty-six seats compared to twenty-two for the socialists
July 14, a memorable Bastille Day celebration in France culminates a year-long celebration of the Bicentennial of the French Revolution; François Mitterrand hosts in Paris the fifteenth summit of the seven leading industrialized nations of the Western world
October, beginning of the debate in France over the wearing of Islamic veils by students while in class
November 18, François Mitterrand convenes a special meeting of the European Economic Community's heads of state and government to discuss the upheaval in Eastern Europe
December 8–9, European Council meeting in Strasbourg agrees to establish a European Bank for Reconstruction and Development to aid Eastern Europe
December 21–22, European-Arab conference in Paris
December 31, François Mitterrand in his New Year's Eve address calls for a European Confederation, reminding some of Charles de Gaulle's earlier call for a united Europe from the Atlantic to the Urals

1990

March 15–18, Socialist Party congress at Rennes witnesses intense rivalry between Laurent Fabius and Lionel Jospin, presidential hopefuls in the post-Mitterrand era

April 19, François Mitterrand and U.S. President George Bush meet in Key Largo, Florida, and stress that a united Germany should be a full member of NATO

April 25–26, Franco-German summit focuses on German unification

May 13–14, tens of thousands demonstrate in Paris and other cities to protest the desecration of a Jewish cemetery at Carpentras

May 25, François Mitterrand holds summit in Moscow with Mikhail Gorbachev to discuss situation in Europe and Soviet Union

July 1, free exchange zone goes into effect in eight out of twelve EEC nations, the first phase of the EEC's plan for economic and monetary unity

September 24, François Mitterrand addresses the UN General Assembly and proposes a four-point plan, including an international conference on the Middle East, to resolve the Gulf crisis

November 19, special summit in Paris of the Conference on Security and Cooperation in Europe to respond to the historic changes in Eastern Europe and the Soviet Union; Charter of Paris for a New Europe signed

December 5, François Mitterrand and German Chancellor Helmut Kohl call for a strengthening of the European Council and a common security policy for the EEC

December 13–14, European Council takes steps toward a political federation by supporting a common foreign and security policy and a single currency

1991

January 3–5, French peace initiative to Baghdad fails, followed by war against Iraq

January 29, Pierre Joxe appointed Defense Minister after the resignation of Jean-Pierre Chevènement who protested allied policy in the war against Iraq

February 7, François Mitterrand tells the nation in a television interview that a ground war against Iraq will require sacrifices

May 15, Edith Cresson becomes the first woman prime minister of France

October 16, France and Germany call for a genuine European identity in defense and security based on the Western European Union

November 10, François Mitterrand, anticipating the 1993 legislative elections, announces plans to reform the constitution, including reducing the presidential term from seven to five years, strengthening the powers of Parliament, and enhancing the authority of the judiciary

December 9–10, Maastricht summit of European Community leaders, who take significant steps to forge an economic, monetary, and political union (including a common currency and a central bank by 1999) and to work toward a common foreign and defense policy

December 17, France and the world learn that Boris Yeltsin and Mikhail Gorbachev agree to dissolve the Soviet Union by the end of the year, as a Commonwealth of Independent States emerges (a Commonwealth officially proclaimed on December 21)

APPENDIX II: Entries Classified by Categories

Politics

Anti-Semitism
Attali, Jacques
Auriol, Vincent
Badinter, Robert
Balladur, Edouard
Barbie, Klaus
Barre, Raymond
Barzach, Michèle
Basque Question
Baudis, Dominique
Bérégovoy, Pierre
Bergeron, André
Bicentennial Celebration
Bidault, Georges
Blum, Léon
Bokassa Affair
Bouchardeau, Huguette
Bourgès-Maunoury, Maurice
Capitant, René
Carrefour du développement Affair
Centrist Parties
Chaban-Delmas, Jacques
Chalandon, Albin
Chevènement, Jean-Pierre
Chirac, Jacques
Christian Democrats
Club Movement
Cohabitation
Cohn-Bendit, Daniel
Common Program
Compagnies républicaines de sécurité
Constitutional Council
Constitution of the Fourth Republic
Constitution of the Fifth Republic
Corsica
Cot, Pierre
Coty, René
Couve de Murville, Maurice
Cresson, Edith
Debray, Régis
Debré, Michel
Decentralization
Decolonization
Defferre, Gaston
de Gaulle, Charles
Delors, Jacques
Democratic and Socialist Union of the Resistance
Demonstrations
Dreyfus, Pierre
Duclos, Jacques
Dumas, Roland
Ecology Party
Elections (Presidential and Legislative)
Electoral System
Elleinstein, Jean
Fabius, Laurent
Faure, Edgar
Federation of the Democratic and Socialist Left
Foccart, Jacques
Frachon, Benoît
French Communist Party
Gaillard, Félix
Gallo, Max
Garaudy, Roger
Gaullism
Gaullist Party

Foreign and Defense Policy

Economics

Society/Culture

Paris Region
Piaf, Edith
Picasso, Pablo
Popular Culture
Population Trends
Press
Regions
Romilly, Jacqueline de
Sartre, Jean-Paul
Social Stratification
Social Trends
SOS Racisme
Sports
Structuralism
Sullerot, Evelyne
Transportation
Urbanization
Vilar, Jean
Wine Production and Consumption
Women, Condition of
Yourcenar, Marguerite

APPENDIX III: Presidents of the French Fourth and Fifth Republics

Fourth Republic

Vincent Auriol, 1947–53
René Coty, 1953–59

Fifth Republic

Charles de Gaulle, 1959–69
Georges Pompidou, 1969–74
Valéry Giscard d'Estaing, 1974–81
François Mitterrand, 1981–

APPENDIX IV: Prime Ministers of the French Fourth and Fifth Republics

Fourth Republic

Paul Ramadier (January 28, 1947)
Robert Schuman (November 22, 1947)
André Marie (July 24, 1948)
Robert Schuman (August 31, 1948)
Henri Queuille (September 11, 1948)
Georges Bidault (October 27, 1949)
Henri Queuille (June 30, 1950)
René Pleven (July 13, 1950)
Henri Queuille (March 9, 1951)
René Pleven (August 8, 1951)
Edgar Faure (January 17, 1952)
Antoine Pinay (March 6, 1952)
René Mayer (January 7, 1953)
Joseph Laniel (June 26, 1953)
Pierre Mendès-France (June 18, 1954)
Edgar Faure (February 25, 1955)
Guy Mollet (February 5, 1956)
Maurice Bourgès-Maunoury (June 12, 1957)
Félix Gaillard (November 5, 1957)
Pierre Pflimlin (May 13, 1958)
Charles de Gaulle (June 1, 1958)

Fifth Republic

Michel Debré (January 8, 1959)
Georges Pompidou (April 14, 1962)
Georges Pompidou (January 8, 1966)
Georges Pompidou (April 7, 1967)
Maurice Couve de Murville (July 10, 1968)
Jacques Chaban-Delmas (June 20, 1969)
Pierre Messmer (July 5, 1972)
Jacques Chirac (May 27, 1974)
Raymond Barre (August 25, 1976)
Pierre Mauroy (May 21, 1981)
Laurent Fabius (July 17, 1984)
Jacques Chirac (March 20, 1986)
Michel Rocard (May 9, 1988)
Edith Cresson (May 15, 1991)

Index

Pages in italics represent main entries

About the Editor

WAYNE NORTHCUTT is professor of history and coordinator of the International Studies Program at Niagara University. He is the author of *The French Socialist and Communist Party Under the Fifth Republic, 1958–1981* (1985); *Mitterrand: A Political Biography* (1992); and has published a number of articles in scholarly journals on political, social, and intellectual trends in postwar France.